Showcasing the Great Experiment

Showcasing the Great Experiment

Cultural Diplomacy and Western Visitors to the Soviet Union, 1921–1941

MICHAEL DAVID-FOX

OXFORD
UNIVERSITY PRESS

OXFORD
UNIVERSITY PRESS

Oxford University Press, Inc., publishes works that further
Oxford University's objective of excellence
in research, scholarship, and education.

Oxford   New York
Auckland   Cape Town   Dar es Salaam   Hong Kong   Karachi
Kuala Lumpur   Madrid   Melbourne   Mexico City   Nairobi
New Delhi   Shanghai   Taipei   Toronto

With offices in
Argentina   Austria   Brazil   Chile   Czech Republic   France   Greece
Guatemala   Hungary   Italy   Japan   Poland   Portugal   Singapore
South Korea   Switzerland   Thailand   Turkey   Ukraine   Vietnam

Library of Congress Cataloging-in-Publication Data
David-Fox, Michael, 1965–
Showcasing the great experiment : cultural diplomacy and western
visitors to Soviet Russia, 1921–1941 / Michael David-Fox.
p. cm.
Includes bibliographical references and index.
ISBN 978-0-19-979457-7 (hardcover: alk. paper)
1. Soviet Union—Relations—Western Countries.   2. Western Countries—Relations—Soviet
Union.   3. Intellectuals—Travel—Soviet Union—History.   4. Visitors, Foreign—Soviet Union—
History.   5. Propaganda—Soviet Union.   6. Soviet Union—Cultural policy.
7. Soviet Union—Foreign public opinion, American.   8. Soviet Union—Foreign public
opinion, European.   9. Soviet Union—History—1917-1936.   I. Title.
DK268.5.D38 2011
303.48'2470182109041—dc22

2011006702

1 3 5 7 9 8 6 4 2

Printed in the United States of America
on acid-free paper

For Katja, Jacob, and Nico

CONTENTS

PREFACE

As I made my first visits to the Soviet Union starting in the late 1980s, it was impossible not to become aware of the extraordinary stature foreigners, especially visitors from the West, were accorded by almost everyone from the most humble to the most powerful. My own reception there, particularly as a participant in certain foreign "delegations" that still bore the imprint of earlier eras, gave me some personal insight, even if only on a small scale, into what foreign travelers experienced when the Soviet experiment was still young: lavish yet formulaic hospitality, evaluations on both sides, and, yet, also intense unofficial exchange meaningful to visitors and hosts alike. The most recent turn—from the effusive post-Soviet opening to the outside world, to a frequently anti-Western, Putin-era reaction against humiliating treatment as inferiors—fits with almost perfect logic into the long-term patterns of the Russian historical process. So did the initial post-Soviet influx of Western travelers, experts, and advisors. The idea for this book was born as I became increasingly aware of the need to analyze continuities in the long history of European and American interactions with Russia and the USSR that stretched across radical changes of regime. Looking back, I can see how my personal experiences as a frequent visitor and foreign resident in Russia contributed, in their own way, to the original interpretive framework I have developed: to approach the reception of foreign visitors through the prism of expressions of superiority and inferiority on both sides.

In researching and writing this study, I received an extraordinary amount of support, which allowed me to make eight research trips to former Soviet archives lasting a total of about two years. Early on, a National Council for Eurasian and East European Research (NCEEER) grant gave me two semesters for research. American Councils for International Education (ACTR/ACCELS) provided unparalleled logistical support during several research trips. I would like to express special appreciation to the Humboldt Foundation in Germany for its support for more than a year when I was a Humboldt Research Fellow in Berlin. In the final year of writing, I was a visiting professor at the École des hautes études en sciences sociales (EHESS) in Paris and a fellow at the Davis Center for Historical Studies at Princeton. The Department of History at the University of Maryland, and its successive chairs John Lampe, Gary Gerstle, and Richard Price, provided unflagging support for my research. Of the new colleagues who have welcomed me at the School of Foreign Service and the Department of History at Georgetown University, I would especially like to acknowledge David Edelstein, Catherine Evtuhov, David Goldfrank, Aviel Roshwald, and Angela Stent.

I feel fortunate for the generosity shown by numerous friends and colleagues who offered constructive criticism. In particular, members of the Princeton Russian Studies faculty and graduate student *kruzhok* met to discuss a draft of the entire manuscript in April 2010, and for their comments I am grateful to Michael Gordin, Ekaterina Pravilova, Mischa Gabowitsch, Michael Reynolds, Mayhill Fowler, Kyrill Kunakhovich, and Jeffrey S. Hardy. At Princeton as well, Stephen Kotkin gave a stimulating response to my Davis Center presentation on Potemkin villages, and Mary Nolan shared her forthcoming work on cultural diplomacy in Europe during the Cold War. The tireless director of the Davis Center, Daniel Rodgers, in the end recalled the pre-history of this project: some two decades earlier, under his direction, I wrote my Princeton senior thesis on American perceptions of the Soviet Union in the 1930s. At the University of Pennsylvania, the Russian History and Slavic Circle read and commented on a first draft of the introduction, and for their valuable suggestions I am particularly grateful to Benjamin Nathans and Peter Holquist. To Peter I owe a special debt. His unwavering friendship and his pioneering commitment to setting modern Russia into its European and international context were a direct encouragement to me as I undertook this project. Indeed, our joint goal since we helped launch *Kritika: Explorations in Russian and Eurasian History* in 2000—shared with our co-editor Alexander Martin and the entire editorial collective—was to help internationalize the Russian and Soviet field. This was a constant presence as I formulated my own plans for this book.

In Moscow, at the outset of my research, A. V. Golubev and V. A. Nevezhin greeted me with valuable tips and encouragement, while later, Elena Zubkova and Vladimir Pechatnov offered aid at crucial moments. Sergei Kapterev, my old *soratnik*, not only gave me crucial help in the archives but was a constant sounding board for ideas. In Paris, Sophie Coeuré and Sabine Dullin arranged a series of opportunities for me to test my arguments. Even more, they responded to them as expert commentators at my presentations at CERCEC, the Sorbonne, and the École normale supérieure, while Yves Cohen afforded his fascinating take on transnational entanglements. In Germany, Anne Hartmann and Reinhard Müller generously shared their research on Lion Feuchtwanger and German exiles in the USSR. Jörg Baberowski, Susanne Schattenberg, Jan Behrends, David Feest, Christoph Gumb, Malte Rolf, Alexandra Oberländer, and many others from two successive cohorts of researchers and graduate students at the Lehrstuhl Geschichte Osteuropas of the Humboldt University in Berlin created a collegial, scholarly environment for me to present and conduct my work during my 2006–07 and 2010 stays. In Berlin, Moscow, and elsewhere it was a pleasure frequently to meet Sheila Fitzpatrick, whose work on so many topics relevant to this book has been a measuring stick for my own interpretations from the moment I entered the field. I vividly recall many conversations with Alfred J. Rieber as we drove to and from College Park during his semester as a visiting professor at Maryland in 2008, for they sharpened my understanding of persistent factors in Russian history. The European Reading Room at the Library of Congress was probably the best place in the world to do much of the research and writing, and the presence there of my former student Erika Spencer was particularly valuable throughout. Lengthy conversations with Zdeněk V. David over the years have enriched my work. For their help on specific parts of the manuscript, I am grateful to Daniel Beer, Katherine David-Fox, Mikhail Dolbilov, Steve Grant, Eric Lohr, Addis Mason, Elizabeth Papazian, Jan Plamper, and Irina Zhdanova. I thank Tisse Takagi, formerly of the New York office of Oxford University Press and now at Basic Books, for her sharp eye and deft editorial hand. I am fortunate that Susan Ferber of OUP-New York, with her incredible organizational skill, supported and oversaw the project throughout the publication process.

It is a great pleasure, finally, to acknowledge some of my most longstanding debts. György Péteri's reading of a first draft of the manuscript encouraged, or better to say forced, me to undertake a reorganization of the entire work. Susan Solomon not only gave sound suggestions about the entire manuscript but has been an inspirational font of ideas during the entire time this book was in preparation. I have been influenced by Katerina Clark during all the years I was working on this book. I fear our exchange of manuscripts was an unequal trade, for her forthcoming work on the international dimensions of Stalinist culture—not to mention her comments on my chapters and interventions at panels and conferences almost too numerous to recall—enriched my approach in several ways.

My family members Vivian, Greg, and Diana have helped in more ways than they may know. The memory of my father, Sanford J. Fox, who did not live to see this publication, has been with me in the years I have worked to complete it. To Katja, my wife, and to Jacob and Nico, my sons, this book is dedicated.

I am thankful for permission to draw upon and include in revised and updated form material from earlier publications: "From Illusory 'Society' to

Intellectual 'Public': VOKS, International Travel, and Party-Intelligentsia Relations in the Interwar Period," *Contemporary European History* 11, no. 1 (February 2002): 7–32; "Leftists versus Nationalists in Soviet-Weimar Cultural Diplomacy: Showcases, Fronts, and Boomerangs," in Susan Gross Solomon, ed., *Doing Medicine Together: Germany and Russia between the Wars* (Toronto: University of Toronto Press, 2006), 103–158; and "Troinaia dvusmyslennost'. Teodor Draizer v sovetskoi Rossii (1927–28): Palomnichestvo, pokhozhee na obvinitel'nuiu rech'," in Alexander Etkind and Pavel Lysakov, eds. *Kul'tural'nye issledovaniia* (St. Petersburg and Moscow: European University and Letnii sad, 2006), 290–319. The book incorporates some reworked, expanded, or significantly altered material from other articles: "The Fellow-Travelers Revisited: The 'Cultured West' Through Soviet Eyes," *Journal of Modern History,* 75, no. 2 (June 2003): 300–335; "Stalinist Westernizer? Aleksandr Arosev's Literary and Political Depictions of Europe," *Slavic Review,* 62, no. 4 (Winter 2003): 733–759; "The 'Heroic Life' of a Friend of Stalinism: Romain Rolland and Soviet Culture," *Slavonica,* 11, no. 1 (April 2005): 3–29; and "Annäherung der Extreme: Die UdSSR und rechtsradikalen Intellektuellen," *Osteuropa* 59, 7–8 (2009): 115–124.

I have used the Library of Congress Russian-language transliteration system, with the exception of names standard in English: Trotsky, Gorky, Ehrenburg, and so forth. In the interests of promoting source criticism, I have devoted much precious space in the notes to giving the Russian-language headings or titles for the most important documents cited. In writing the transliterations of these titles I have preserved the language as given in the original documents, including capitalization practices and acronyms, rather than altering anything to conform to contemporary Russian usage. While it is my hope that this book will be accessible to many readers, I also believe the benefits of this citation method in the notes will be readily apparent to scholars in the field.

—Washington, D.C., August 2011

Showcasing the Great Experiment

Introduction

"Russia and the West" in a Soviet Key

The interwar "pilgrimage to Russia" is one of the most notorious events in the political and intellectual history of the twentieth century.[1] During the 1920s and 1930s, approximately 100,000 foreigners visited the Soviet Union, including tens of thousands of European and American writers, professionals, scientists, artists, and intellectuals who came to record their impressions of the Soviet experiment.[2] Their numbers increased steadily after 1922, jumped dramatically in the years of the first Five-Year Plan and the Popular Front, and then declined as the xenophobic terror of the Purges and the shock of the Nazi-Soviet Pact cut their number to a trickle in the late 1930s. These interwar visits marked a period of intensive Soviet-Western cultural and intellectual interactions and were a crucial factor in the rise of Soviet cultural diplomacy in this, its most successful era.

This book is a history of the Soviet reception of Central and Western European and, to a lesser extent, American visitors in the interwar period. It provides a new account of one of the most consequential encounters of the twentieth century, the Soviet reception of prominent foreign visitors and intellectuals, through the prism of evaluations of superiority and inferiority on both sides. It aims to open up a neglected international dimension to the formation of the Soviet system, for the way foreigners, and above all, representatives of the "advanced West," were perceived and treated deserves to be seen as central to early Soviet and Stalinist culture, ideology, and politics. Indeed, the journeys and accounts of European travelers are fundamental to the study of Muscovy; the topic of "Russia and the West" is at the heart of imperial Russian history starting with Peter the Great's Westernization. For several generations, however, the formation of the Soviet system has been examined as a domestic process, denuded of its substantial international and transnational interactions. Almost completely unexplored is the way internal and external initiatives of the Soviet party-state interacted and influenced one another. This study suggests how the "West"—in the guise of models to be emulated or repudiated, the opinion of an outside world that needed to be cultivated or altered,

1

the crucial differentiation of friends and enemies, and, last but not least, the far-reaching impact of the system devised to receive celebrated visitors—was ever-present during the two tumultuous decades in which the Soviet system took shape.

By the same token, the debate about Western views of communism, and particularly the simultaneous cresting of European and American intellectuals' hopes placed in the Soviet experiment and the murderous repressions of Stalinism, has long been central to the intellectual and political history of the twentieth century. This is also a topic that has long been cut off from its other half: until the opening of formerly classified Soviet archives, the Soviet side of this interaction remained something of a black box. Only now has it become possible to revisit Western observers of communism through the prism of their Soviet interactions while reconsidering Soviet history through the prism of its intense international preoccupations. Once the Soviet side of the relationship is better grasped, we can better understand the time spent inside the Soviet Union by even some of the best-known figures.

Profound and troubling questions are raised by the central fact that the height of Western admiration, including among some of the leading minds of the epoch, coincided with most repressive phase of Soviet communism—the Stalinist 1930s. This remains a durable and thorny problem without simple answers—whatever the importance of the Great Depression and the rise of fascism as factors pushing Western observers into pro-Soviet stances, whatever the importance of the gap between the presentation of Soviet socialism and what was known by some then and most now about the nature of the regime. Indeed, the topic of intellectuals and communism remains one of heated debate in many Western countries, to a certain extent a proxy for earlier debates about socialism and the Soviet model whose acrimony faded from scholarship after the collapse of communism.

Yet, there remains a decisive gap between these long standing debates about intellectuals, which date back to works such as Julien Benda's 1927 *Trahison des clercs,* or the 1950 *The God That Failed,* and what we now can learn from Soviet sources about them. Unlike the sophisticated works on scientific and cultural interactions across borders and leading biographical treatments of key figures (which this book draws on whenever possible) the most influential interventions on the fellow-travelers have been polemics attempting to expose the flaws of intellectuals in general (their utopian disposition, alienation, or naiveté in politics) or reduce their political blindness to one master explanation.[3] We can gain much by shifting focus: the center of this book's inquiry is the mutual interaction between Western observers and travelers with their Soviet hosts and the Soviet system. This was an inherently unequal relationship, to be sure, given that the hosts were officials of a powerful state. But that inequality itself is in certain ways advantageous, for it generated and preserved many sources, and not only Soviet ones, for Russian archives contain Western documents in many languages.

This lens of analysis dictates that much attention is paid to unraveling mutual observations that, from many visitors' point of view, combined appealing familiarity with radical novelty. For example, many features of the Soviet order that were most attractive to visitors—welfare measures, penal or juvenile-delinquency reform, pedagogy—altered or "sovietized" pre-revolutionary Russian reform or intelligentsia traditions that themselves had developed within a pan-European context. This history of circulations ensured that the presentation of the Soviet experiment would appeal beyond the circle of committed followers. More concretely, this study sets out to investigate specific transactions between visitors and Soviets, including patronage relations and the implicit rules structuring the relationship between Western sympathizers and the Soviets. On both sides, an evolving, yet surprisingly formal, code of "friendship" assumed importance, and the Soviet side ensured that its most fundamental precondition was public praise for the Soviet experiment.

The sources generated from within the Soviet Union thus offer a means of probing beneath the most scripted and politicized pronouncements, and also for examining the entire spectrum of visitors—not merely committed fellow-travelers. This perspective contributes to the conclusion that even at the height of Western praise for the Bolshevik Revolution, visitors' reactions, especially those expressed *in situ* (as opposed to the sought-after declarations from sympathizers or works heavily influenced by Soviet materials) were often complex amalgams that included more negative and critical reactions than previously supposed.[4] Comparing sources generated inside the Soviet Union during visits to published works reveals more reservations, doubts, and suppressed condemnations even among those who are today notorious as apologists for Stalinism, such as Beatrice Webb and Lion Feuchtwanger. This fact dictates that we pay more attention to self-censorship and its mechanics, as well as to the reasons behind it. Many prominent fellow-travelers nurtured dreams of influencing Stalin or the course of the revolution. Most visitors, moreover, were not in every instance projecting preconceived notions onto the USSR; as this book consistently shows, time spent inside the country was a crucial experience in the lives of key figures, and the actions of travelers and hosts alike could dramatically affect the results.

Let us begin to explore these problems with one striking example. In December 1927, the exhausted, cold, and irritable American literary celebrity Theodore Dreiser found himself in the snowy plains on the outskirts of Khar'kov, despising everything Russian and Soviet. At the end of a remarkable eleven-week journey that took him from Leningrad and Moscow across

Ukraine and the Caucasus, he railed against filth, cockroaches, and vile gulash that he declared would make Béla Kun start another revolution. Seemingly always ready to condemn the lazy Slavs or to mystify the exotic East, Dreiser also took a perverse delight in defending American rugged individualism to his collectivist hosts. But Dreiser's entire attitude changed quite suddenly when he saw a skyscraper "which looked as though it had been taken out of New York and set down here in the snow plains." This made on him "a most tremendous psychological impression," because "it seemed to symbolise the industrialisation of Russia." Setting aside all his prejudices and accusatory belligerence, he went on to predict not only that a "Ukrainian Chicago" would emerge in Khar'kov in ten years but that America would become sovietized.[5] Dreiser's 1927–28 journey was directly related to his transformation into one of the most prominent fellow-travelers of the 1930s. His works were translated by the Soviets in millions of copies.

Although the curmudgeonly progressive was hardly typical, Dreiser's extraordinary journey epitomizes the way images of Russia, political views of the Soviet Union, and experiences inside the country were intricately intertwined. Why, though, did the Khar'kov skyscraper so win him over? Was it because it meant the Soviet Union would become more like the United States, because a new Soviet modernity would raise up the backward Russians, or because the Bolsheviks were building a system worth emulating even in the land that had invented the skyscraper?

In many ways, it was all three. The allure of the Khar'kov skyscraper, set in a broader context, is emblematic of how Soviet communism offered vastly different focal points of attraction to foreign observers, from modernization to a radically different path of development, from the gentle allure of the welfare state, world peace, and disarmament to the ruthless logic of regimented mass mobilization. Almost every Soviet sympathizer kept a key hope or concern especially close to his or her heart: from labor to cooperation to women's emancipation, from sexual revolution to the national question, from the strong leader to the vanguard party. In the land of the militant godless, even the Archbishop of Canterbury was a fellow-traveler. Ultimately, the sheer breadth and diversity of this attraction, while tempered by many condemnations and negative reactions, is what made Soviet communism one of the most potent and expansive touchstones of twentieth-century political and intellectual history. Soviet cultural diplomacy, already inclined to distinguish audience by class and political affiliation, was endowed with tremendous advantages solely by virtue of the broad-based nature of the Soviet myth. By explicitly attempting to tailor its message to many different audiences and individual visitors, Soviet outreach to the "cultured West," while its history was marked by many failures and misunderstandings, took advantage of this great historical opportunity.[6]

At the core of this study is the voluminous archive of the All-Union Society for Cultural Ties Abroad, known by its Russian acronym VOKS, and its precursor institutions from the early 1920s. VOKS was the key institution of Soviet cultural diplomacy. It defined its mission as cultivating the "bourgeois intelligentsia" and focusing on "culture" in Soviet dealings with the outside world.[7] Its focus, especially in the early years, was first and foremost on the West, defined largely as the advanced capitalist countries of Europe plus the United States.[8] Concentrating on the VOKS material from Western and Central Europe (Germany, France, Great Britain, and, to a lesser extent, other European countries) and the United States, while episodically comparing it to material from non-Western countries, furthered the goal of an in-depth, and as far as possible systematic, look at those records and the institution from which they came.

The investigation, however, quickly became far broader than VOKS—always a mid-level and frequently embattled player in a much larger endeavor—even as it closely analyzes and interprets its fortunes. VOKS (and hence many of the documents in its archive) formed but one part of a much larger party-state and international communist system that crystallized in the early 1920s to handle cultural diplomacy, international propaganda, and attempts to influence Western public opinion.[9] This work also deploys archival material from, among other sources, the Trade Unions' Commission on External Relations, charged with handling workers' delegations and resident specialists; the Agitprop Department of the Comintern; Intourist, the Soviet foreign-tourist agency founded in 1929; and the Foreign Commission of the Union of Writers. Since in works on Soviet international behavior "Stalin" so often stands in as a cipher for the entire Soviet system, approaching that evolving system first and foremost from the middle, as it were, yields a richer and more complex texture in understanding other levels, from rank-and-file guides to the top leadership. At the same time as these institutional sources are quintessentially political documents, they also provide a rich vein of insights into Soviet practices and the cross-cultural assumptions, insights, and misconceptions of key observers and their European and American interlocutors.[10] The new archival riches are a window into political and institutional history, but in this book, they are also read culturally and thematically to shed light on the reception of foreigners and the effects of interaction on visitors and Soviets alike.

The list of visitors to the Soviet experiment is a virtual "who's who" of the international Left and intellectuals of the interwar era. This book develops its range of biographical case studies of visitors on a selective basis: only when new documentation was found and when a new avenue into understanding Soviet-Western interactions was offered by the visit and visitor involved. The parade of visitors included pedagogues, scientists, engineers, artists, and thinkers of many political hues, and a number of them make appearances in the pages that follow. But literary figures and writers played a special role, especially in the 1930s, reflecting the oversized role of the writer and the written word in Soviet culture. Just as literature and the Union of Soviet Writers dominated the elaboration of Stalinist culture, so the "friends of the Soviet Union," as the most prominent foreign fellow-travelers were called by the Soviets, were dominated by literary figures. Because the many dimensions of "friendship" (and its far more frequently investigated yet closely related inversion, enmity) are key to the entire relationship between foreign visitors and the Soviets, this book pays special attention to the select club of "friends." Those featured here include Theodore Dreiser, Romain Rolland, Bernard Shaw, Sidney and Beatrice Webb, André Gide, and Lion Feuchtwanger. Literary organizations also played a major role in anti-fascist culture, a key arena during the Popular Front for a Soviet quest for predominance and hegemony (and, hence, ultimately superiority) in the realm of culture.

Most of the important Western figures examined here are thus non-Communists, although the lives or activities of intellectual party members like Henri Barbusse and György Lukàcs figure at key moments. Some scholars or scientists, such as the prominent German historian and Russian expert Otto Hoetzsch, become windows into the history of VOKS and its partner organizations abroad, while the German "National Bolsheviks" are explored in the context of the little-known history of Soviet cultural outreach to the fascist Right. Other characters are brought in to illustrate special themes; for example, the African-American singer Paul Robeson is discussed in the context of his emotional identification with the "socialist homeland" as a solution to racial and national problems. While many important visitors are inevitably excluded, their overall number is so great that a number of famous figures make cameo appearances, from Walter Benjamin to John Maynard Keynes to the future Czechoslovak Minister of Culture Zdeněk Nejedlý.

On the Soviet side, the cast of characters includes a group of prominent Bolshevik intellectuals and shapers of Soviet cultural diplomacy, whom despite their diversity I have united under the rubric of Stalinist Westernizers. These were figures who knew European languages, had spent considerable time abroad, and were connoisseurs of European or American culture and politics, often through their experiences as émigrés. All of them were immersed in, and often in one way or another admired, the Western world on the basis of first-hand knowledge.[11] The term does not imply that they, like some of the classical Westernizers of the nineteenth century, advocated that Russia should follow a European path of development, which even in the previous century was far from always the case. Nor does the label fit a number of the leading lights of Soviet cultural diplomacy in the NEP period, such as Ol'ga Kameneva—the first head of VOKS, the wife of Politburo member Lev Kamenev, and the sister of Lev Trotsky—who was not in any sense a Stalinist, even as many of the practices she innovated survived her demise. By contrast, her successor during the Popular Front, Alexandr Arosev, was from the outset an adherent to the Stalinist wing of the Party. But even he was always a tormented, if ambitious, figure in culture and politics. As this suggests, the term is not intended to characterize these figures politically in a narrowly homogenous way. What it should convey, rather, is that starting in the late 1920s the leading officials and intellectuals involved in the reception of Western visitors adapted to the Stalin era, and many contributed directly to the configuration of the Stalinist order in the 1930s. Maxim Gorky must be considered perhaps the most prominent architect of Stalinism in culture, although he is by no means a simple or undisputed figure. Others featured here include two who miraculously survived the Terror and Stalin himself in order to emerge as key figures in the Soviet re-opening to the outside world in the Thaw: Ilya Ehrenburg and the diplomat and ambassador to London Ivan Maiskii. Most of the rest, including the head of the Union of Writers' Foreign Commission, Mikhail Kol'tsov, did not survive the Purges of the late 1930s. The key players in Soviet cultural diplomacy are joined by a host of more minor guides, translators, diplomats, and analysts who often had strong views even as they operated within the bounds of official orthodoxy and the political pressure cooker of the Soviet cultural revolution.

Persistent Russian Patterns and Soviet Innovations

How new and how modern was the Soviet approach to foreign visitors? Descriptions drawn not from the annals of communism but from the Orthodox civilization of Muscovy in the sixteenth and seventeenth centuries discuss restrictions on the movements of foreign visitors. They were surrounded by state minders who spoke in a scripted fashion even in private conversations; elaborate spectacles were staged with the goal of overawing influential visitors. The state made every effort to control travel across its borders in both directions, and locals who feared interacting with foreigners and the threat of invasion from abroad frequently made the outside world appear hostile. All these measures were accompanied by attempts to isolate foreigners in Moscow's successive "German quarters" or foreign settlements.[12]

While Muscovite attitudes toward foreigners are only rarely recalled in discussions of the twentieth century, to this day Potemkin villages—the hollow façades Prince Grigorii Potemkin purportedly erected to pull the wool over the eyes of Catherine the Great and an array of foreign dignitaries—appear as the single best-known label for the Soviets' methods of showcasing their great experiment. As discussed below, however, research on the eighteenth century suggests that the notion of Potemkin villages was a myth. Born out of diplomatic strife and entrenched across a political and cultural gulf, the legend served to distort and conceal what occurred in "New Russia" in 1787. This work argues that to view Soviet model sites of socialism as Potemkin villages built solely to dupe foreigners is to misunderstand their importance for the push to transform the Soviet population and the origins of Stalinism.

Was there a Russian component in the Soviet approach to that long and illustrious list of European and American intellectuals, writers, scientists, and artists who lined up to see the Soviet experiment in its early years? While works on communism too rarely situate their topics in the broader sweep of the Russian or pre-revolutionary past, it was impossible to write this book without being acutely aware of the broader and enduring significance of that set of historical problems that go under the rubric of "Russia and the West," issues that have also been central to post-Soviet Russia since 1991. The book begins by raising the question of what communism inherited from the Russian tradition. To ask what was Russian about the Soviet approach is also to ask what was distinctive, even unique, about the Soviet reception of foreign visitors and, more broadly, practices and attitudes toward the outside world after 1917.

There are good reasons why Catherinian Potemkin villages represent one of the world's most enduring myths: they described an elaborate, top-down political stagecraft that was very convincing to foreign and domestic observers alike, for it was, in fact, lavishly enacted on a regular basis. The legend about the duplicitous façades of Prince Potemkin's villages is important for another reason. In exposing deceptive claims of great achievement, it directly engaged in and perpetuated a dialogue about superiority and inferiority between "Russia and the West" that for three centuries was buffeted by powerful and intricate geopolitical, cultural, and, later, ideological cross-currents.

Despite this continuity, a number of seemingly obvious similarities between the Soviet treatment of foreigners and earlier periods of Russian history crumble under close scrutiny. Ceremonies, surveillance, and attempts to control movement across borders were common features of numerous states, pre-modern and modern. That they were prevalent in old Russia does not constitute evidence of direct bequeathals. To trace continuities across the centuries also becomes difficult when we are dealing with attitudes and policies that were divided or contradictory. Synthesizing a broad literature, Eric Lohr suggests that Muscovy consistently encouraged immigration for service to the tsar but restricted emigration and foreign travel. This "keep and hold" strategy was far from uniformly xenophobic. The widely known establishment of Muscovy's "foreign settlement" can be seen as something of an anomaly, given the crucial role a constant influx of foreigners played in Muscovy's military and economic modernization; in this context, the segregation of foreign residents represented Church-sponsored reactions to the rapidly growing interaction between Muscovy and Europe in the seventeenth century.[13]

The most celebrated continuity theories straddling the 1917 divide, including some bold attempts to draw direct lines from Muscovite to modern institutions and practices, also find themselves unable to establish direct pedigrees. They are forced to bore down deep into the historical substrata in order to reveal hidden and ultimately speculative connections: underlying mentalities, fundamental dynamics of political culture, or the structural common denominators of reoccurring socio-political patterns.[14]

More compelling than theories of either directly transmitted legacies or Soviet reversions to Russian tradition is Alfred J. Rieber's concept of persistent factors conditioning similar responses toward the outside world over time, a key aim of which is to dispel myths about fixed or single roots of Russian and Soviet behavior.[15] As this book will show, the formation of the Soviet system of receiving foreign visitors and the interwar attempt to shape the Soviet Union's image internationally proceeded with a heavy focus on the West, meaning, in this period, Western and Central Europe and, as a separate and differently perceived subcategory, the United States. The most salient "persistent factor" that Bolshevik Russia's new rulers took over from their autocratic predecessors was a perennial imperative to overcome backwardness vis-à-vis the Western powers against which they measured themselves—except that, in the Soviet case, this imperative became vastly more ambitious. The Bolshevik Revolution aspired not to catch up but to overtake, to leap over the industrially advanced countries into a new, alternative modernity.[16] Yet even to pass through and leap beyond the bourgeois stage meant to assimilate, accept, or reject the experience of the "advanced" countries. This dictated a continuing obsession with the West.

The West, of course, meant a great many things. Each major country and culture had its own longstanding traditions of interactions and associations with Russia that formed a legacy for the Soviet Union. From early modern times on, Russia's road to Europe often led through Germany, and the importance of Central Europe assumed meaning in light of major divisions in the continent that held special significance for Russia: between the different role of the state in continental Europe, Britain, and the United States; between the post-1789 liberal democracies and the monarchies and empires of Central Europe; and between those countries that presented the most compelling models in science and culture, Germany and France. In the interwar period, there were key distinctions among the Western countries that directly affected political and cultural relations. For example, the British Empire was still widely seen by the

Soviets as a chief geopolitical rival; the United States exerted its own powerful and particular pull through conceptions of efficient *amerikanizm* and industrial modernity. But Soviet perceptions of the United States as young, uncouth, and beneath Europe in the level of its culture put America into a distinctly separate category within the West. The Soviet relationship with visitors from Western and Central Europe engages most directly the rise of Soviet cultural diplomacy and the communist interwar crusade to invert the old discourse of Russian backwardness, and this explains their emphasis in this book. At the same time, the large number of visitors from the United States and America's stature as an alternative to Europe on modernity's Western flank are important parts of the story. One of the advantages of a multi-polar, as opposed to a bilateral, study is that it can probe these kinds of contrasts.

After all, Russia, and then the USSR, had its own longstanding history of images and interactions with each European country. In the wake of Peter the Great's Westernization, moreover, Russia in many ways became European, just as in the Soviet period it was in many ways modern—to what extent, and on what continuum, and with what qualifications is the Sphinx's Riddle of Russian and Soviet history. The very notion of the West rested on large doses of mythologizing, oversimplification, and sheer distance. It remained, however, one of the most fundamental concepts in Soviet, as well as imperial Russian, history.

In physics, the act of observation is known to influence the phenomenon observed. Far more potent than any observer effect was the idea of Russian and Soviet difference, which deeply shaped relations, and therefore historical realities, for all involved. The idea of the West as a single aggregate, powerfully potent in Russia in the eighteenth and nineteenth centuries, was only reinforced by the communist tendency to lump together "bourgeois" capitalist countries, using the West as a synonym for them.[17] As the autocracy had for more than two centuries before it, the early Soviet Union consulted and employed foreign experts, attached even in rejection crucial importance to Western judgments, and constantly reinforced the concept of the West as a single entity. In this sense, the system that the revolutionary regime quickly built up after 1917 to receive foreign visitors did not derive its specific practices, goals, or ethos from an established tradition but, rather, was conditioned by this post-revolutionary extension of the fateful dyad "Russia and the West."

At the same time, the new regime, with greater resolve than even the most reactionary tsars of old, followed a countervailing imperative to block out pernicious influences from abroad. Here was another persistent dilemma that the Soviet Union inherited: how to protect itself from perceived threats while interacting, borrowing, and modernizing. Much of Muscovite and imperial Russian history was marked by suspicion and curtailment of elite travel abroad.

For the tsars, subversive political ideas, the "moral climate" monitored by the Foreign Ministry and Third Section in reports on European countries, and revolutionary movements near and far prompted isolationist moves.[18] For the Soviets, of course, the threats from abroad were labeled counter-revolutionary. The Bolsheviks, with their universalistic revolutionary mission fueling greater international ambitions than even the most far-reaching Westernizing tsars, at the same time oversaw an unprecedented intensification of security measures, isolationism, and, ultimately, autarky.

The Bolshevik Revolution thus produced a dual radicalization, intensifying a dialectic of rejection and imitation, hostility and engagement, that had arisen even before the "Petrine revolution" of Westernization.[19] This study traces how the two countervailing tendencies of engaging and distancing the outside world crystallized and clashed in concrete circumstances, providing one key to understanding the course of the new regime as it hurtled toward xenophobic terror under Stalin.

It was a result of this dialectic that periods of openness, often associated with international weakness, military defeat, or crises that appeared to necessitate internal reform, were followed by periods of reaction, counter-reform, and greater isolationism. The Russian historical process incorporated alternations between defensive repudiation of perceived external threats and radical internal restructuring based on European models (and, under communism, between popular frontism versus "socialism in one country" and crackdown versus thaw). Of course, these oppositions are only points upon a continuum: although heights of anti-Western isolationism were reached circa 1848 and 1948, and peaks of "cosmopolitanism" achieved after 1855 and 1987, even the extreme periods contained countervailing trends, and each historic reversal held its own formidable particularities. Insofar as the pattern was shaped by intense pressures to borrow and restructure that combined with countervailing imperatives to quarantine outside ideas and influences, the top-heavy state was crucial, for it was the force that simultaneously imported and banned, reversing the emphasis in successive periods of openings and closings. All the great domestic reversals of both imperial Russian and Soviet history were intimately connected to explicit shifts in policies and attitudes toward the outside world.

This book is centrally concerned with one of the most crucial alternations in all of Russian and Soviet history: the turn from the 1920s order to the 1930s and Stalinism. In one sense, the Stalin Revolution, with its reversal of many 1920s forms of engagement with the outside world, represents one of those great turning points in Russian and Soviet history during which the internal order and the relationship with the West simultaneously were transformed. In another sense, however, it appears as one of multiple shifts within a single historical period: the new Soviet system for receiving foreigners and influencing public opinion abroad was entrenched in the 1920s and only modified thereafter. The dual nature of Stalinism in this sense explains the intensive scrutiny given in this work to countervailing tendencies and shifting balances of engagement and hostility within discrete phases of the 1920s and the 1930s. It also accounts for the close analysis of the political and cultural dynamics of periods and years in which the balance suddenly shifted, such as 1928–29, 1932–34, and 1936–37.

In talking about persistent factors, however, it is not enough to consider only the strategies of the rulers or the state. For one thing, the Bolsheviks were not only the political masters of the new regime but also heirs of the radical intelligentsia; for another, far from everyone involved in Soviet cultural relations was a Bolshevik. The rise of the intelligentsia and the emergence of nationalism made the formative period for Russian national identity in the nineteenth century a time when the multifaceted articulation of Russia's relationship to Europe was far less exclusively a matter of monarch, court, state, or nobility. As Catriona Kelly has observed, the large-scale import of "foreign" values and standards of behavior into post-Petrine Russia meant that "three quite separate concepts—civilization, modernization, and Westernization—became entangled, both among foreigners, and among Russians themselves."[20] More and more, Russian *imaginaires* of the Western countries were shaped by the educated public, high and popular culture, and "society"—something that would already be a longstanding given by the time the Soviets pursued their program of radical etatization in relations with the outside world. No modern Russian thinker or movement could avoid this question; the "idea of Europe" became the main referent by which the "idea of Russia" was defined.[21] Some of the paradoxes of this nineteenth-century legacy provide clues for digging underneath the surface of the ideological pronouncements of the twentieth.

Looking West

Chief among these paradoxes was the fact that imported ideas were used to construct notions of Russian uniqueness, on the one hand, and that the most ardent Westernizers contributed mightily to notions of Russia's special path, on the other. Among the most cosmopolitan Russians of the eighteenth century were the Freemasons, who were steeped in Enlightenment universalism but nonetheless proved pivotal in the initial articulation of theories of Russian spiritual uniqueness.[22] Alexander Herzen famously likened the Slavophiles and Westernizers to the two-headed Russian eagle: the heart that beat within them was one. The classic nineteenth-century split between Slavophiles and

Westernizers defies easy classification. The Slavophiles, who wished to return to a pre-Petrine conservative utopia, or rather to combine it with European elements to create a new Russian synthesis, tilted against Westernization by importing the German Romantic nationalism and the French culture of the Restoration period.[23] By the same token, the most famous Westernizer, Herzen, was a "Russian European" especially in the sense that he yearned for a "new Europe." After 1848, he stood in opposition to the flaws of the bourgeois West and became the first exponent of a specifically Russian socialism based on the peasant commune.[24]

Much of the great nineteenth-century discussion in Russian thought on the Russian soul and national character was defensive in nature, in that it countered European notions of Russian backwardness. It also, however, attempted to affirm elements of Russian national uniqueness, and by the late nineteenth century an array of political, philosophical, and aesthetic movements openly embraced the non-Western, "Asian" nature of Russian identity, effectively turning what for Europeans was the touchstone of the trope of backwardness into an advantage. Even the Westernizing trend of Social Democracy was also in certain ways the heir of populism, and ultimately it became Lenin and Trotsky's innovation to skip the bourgeois stage and build a new and unprecedented "proletarian dictatorship."[25] Against this historical backdrop, the simultaneously Westernizing and anti-bourgeois dimensions of Bolshevik ideology appear as an unstable amalgam.

Liah Greenfeld has famously interpreted the formation of Russian national identity in the imperial period as a product of the competitive desire to escape the curse of inferiority. *Ressentiment*, existential envy of the West, in Greenfeld's thesis, was the "most important factor" in the crystallization of Russian national consciousness: "Russians looked at themselves through glasses fashioned in the West—they thought through the eyes of the West—and its approbation was a *sine qua non* for their national self-esteem. The West was superior; they thought it looked down upon them. How could Russians overcome this obstacle...?"[26] In one sense, this argument can be extended: evaluation and comparison with the West became central not only for the articulation of national identity, but also for all the movements spawned by the intelligentsia—including those, like Social Democracy, that defined themselves as internationalist and analyzed the world in terms of class rather than nation.[27] Even further, the Soviet elevation of culture and "culturedness" into a virtual secular religion—and the material this book presents on how foreign visitors, routinely portrayed as prisoners to bourgeois luxury, were ranked not only by political but also cultural level—suggests a secular analogue of the Russian soul, a Soviet replacement of Orthodox or Russian spirituality with a combination of socialist ideological and cultural values. The commitments of the New Soviet Man were far weightier than what Maxim Gorky, on the cusp of the Stalin Revolution, termed the "external glitter" of the West, the superficiality of its prosperity and technological advance.[28]

Were continuities enacted across the revolutionary divide by just such perpetuations or reconfigurations of ideas? Empire, Orthodoxy, and autocracy could leave subtle as well as overt imprints on the Russian intelligentsia, including ardent foes of those institutions. Certainly, a similar thesis about resemblances between pursuers and pursued born in the struggle between the tsarist police and Bolshevism has long been present in the history of Russian Social Democracy.[29] More recently, a new generation of historians has investigated not only ideas but state practices and social institutions on both sides of 1905, 1914, and 1917, positing, in place of simple continuity, novel, postrevolutionary directions for previously established techniques and patterns.[30]

There were, however, enormous differences between tsarist and Soviet Russia. Despite the centuries-old tradition of importing skilled foreigners, the travel of foreign visitors was vastly more decentralized in the imperial period than it became shortly after 1917. While European national diasporas were well established in the empire, each cut its own "deal" with the state—so that "one can hardly speak of the 'foreigner' in the Russian Empire as a single generic category."[31] The first guidebooks aimed in part at foreign travelers date to the late eighteenth century, but tsarist Russia lacked the myriad state agencies dealing with foreign visitors and the first steps toward the development of a foreign tourist industry that were taken by the new regime in the mid- to late 1920s.[32] With the rise of the mass press in the late nineteenth century, Minister of Finance Sergei Witte—the pioneer in so many other parts of Russia's telescoped push to modernize—innovated ways of manipulating Russia's most influential daily newspapers for political goals. His targets were not just domestic audiences but also foreign public opinion. Publications in European languages, and even special ministry funds allocated for bribing French editors, aimed at creating an image of Russia as an attractive environment for foreign investment.[33] Even so, in terms of the role and capabilities of the state, the big picture is largely one of discontinuity between the old regime and the new.

By the same token, despite heavy borrowing in the international system and constant circulation of practices across borders, there were also major differences between that unique new formation, the Soviet party-state, and its leading industrialized rivals in the West. Cultural diplomacy—if defined as the systematic inclusion of a cultural dimension to foreign relations, or the formal allocation of attention and resources to culture within foreign policy—was largely a twentieth-century phenomenon. European state and diplomatic efforts to manipulate public opinion in foreign countries and to deploy new methods of propaganda outward across borders began to take shape in the late nineteenth century, however, as the discrete, gentleman's game of diplomacy "began to change dramatically with the extension of voting rights, the advancement of compulsory education, and the emergence of the mass circulation newspaper."[34] The major turning point came with the onslaught of World War I, when the turn to total mobilization of extra-military forces and the vastly expanded use of propaganda aimed abroad led to diplomatic attempts to use those most capable of influencing public opinion. Russia participated in the wave of international propaganda but not yet in developing a specifically cultural dimension to it. Here, France was the leader, and the Quai d'Orsay "began to utilize teachers, authors, missionaries, artists, film directors and athletic champions among others—all 'representatives of the French spirit and culture.' "[35] A novel force in international relations in this same period was what Akira Iriye has called cultural internationalism—movements to promote cultural and scientific cooperation among countries—and, inevitably, states tried to bend this force to their own purposes.[36]

Well before these developments, however, the Bolsheviks had cut their teeth as revolutionary mass mobilizers with their own theories and experiences of agitation and propaganda. Although some in the party leadership were well aware of how other countries participated in the diplomatic and propaganda revolutions, to them it was self-evident that in this realm they needed no tutelage from the bourgeoisie. There were exceptions, such as the proposal of Ol'ga Kameneva, the leading figure behind Soviet cultural diplomacy in the 1920s and a significant presence in this book, to create a Soviet version of the *Alliance française*, the institutional vehicle by which France had innovated modern cultural diplomacy, to spread knowledge of the Russian language abroad. This was turned down by the Commissariat of Foreign Affairs for lack of funds and on the grounds that Soviet citizens abroad were greeted with too much suspicion.[37]

Indeed, in cultural diplomacy, as in propaganda, in numerous respects the Soviet regime became an innovator different or ahead of its Western counterparts.[38] Many countries, including Britain, Czechoslovakia, and Japan, did not establish official cultural diplomacy programs until the 1930s. The United States had long had a universalistic mission in foreign policy, but (aside from precedents set by the propaganda activities of George Creel's Committee on Public Information for two years during World War I) it did not try to centrally manage information or cultural exports until the creation of the State Department's Division of Cultural Affairs in 1938.[39] There was always a great deal of overlap between propaganda and cultural diplomacy, however. In the wake of World War I, Britain and the United States reacted to revelations of wartime manipulation of information and the press, helping to turn propaganda into a bad word in the West, but its application was nonetheless stretched in many countries to included activities later designated as cultural diplomacy. For example, the Third Section of the Czechoslovak Ministry of Foreign Affairs published foreign-language magazines, entertained foreign visitors, ran a semi-private publishing house, and crafted an image of the country directed above all at Western elites.[40]

The period following World War I was also a caesura in the sense that states had far more levers of influence on media and communications, including cultural industries. Thus, the interwar United States loosely linked political decisionmakers with the "private" activities of foundations and internationally ascendant film, radio, and other media and communications corporations.[41] By contrast, even after the Soviet revolutionary regime reconstituted conventional diplomacy, by 1920 the attempt to influence minds and transform culture was such a fundamental part of its ethos that shaping public opinion and the Soviet image abroad was not subordinated to the foreign-policy apparatus. Instead, it was pursued by an entire network of state, party, and Comintern efforts.

What specifically, then, was new about Soviet cultural diplomacy? It is possible to exaggerate the uniqueness of the conspiratorial or Machiavellian nature of communism. For example, the secret war-propaganda bureau the British set up at Wellington House to secure U.S. entry into World War I, like many Soviet initiatives, concealed the origin of printed materials and targeted influential, sympathetic figures who would then themselves direct the press and public opinion.[42] The Soviets aspired, however, to alter not merely the views but also the world views of visitors. Their international aspirations of influence were not localized in the foreign-policy establishment or to wartime aims but were built into the very fabric of the drive to build socialism. International initiatives, therefore, included a uniquely large and important domestic component involving the reception of foreign visitors, the presentation of model sites, and the inculcation of proper responses to the outside world. At the same time, the entire early Soviet period was marked by an ongoing cultural revolution involving wrenching pressures and upheavals; the "cultural front" abroad became an only partially insulated extension of intense battles at home. All these features of the Bolshevik Revolution, however novel, in their initial focus served to preserve and expand the pre-revolutionary Russian obsession with the West.

What is crucial is the whole into which the pieces are put. This work argues that the Soviet Union developed an unprecedented system for receiving foreign visitors and influencing the image of the Soviet Union abroad that crystallized in the specific conditions of the early 1920s. The totalizing thrust of the Soviet party-state ensured that there was a constant interaction between external and internal missions and tasks. The new regime was not motivated only by ideological universalism; the isolated and diplomatically weak international position of the revolutionary state made the sympathy of Western cultural and intellectual elites into one of the only trump cards the Bolsheviks possessed, and, thus, the development of new means to reach them became a matter of relatively high priority. The early split between conventional diplomacy and the pursuit of world revolution, moreover, ensured that international cultural initiatives and operations were never exclusively, or even mainly, the province of the Commissariat of Foreign Affairs.

Soviet cultural diplomacy, as a result, can be defined as a phenomenon with several distinctive features. Cultural relations (*kul'turnye sviazi*) were, as befits the Marxist-Leninist regime from which they sprang, understood in class terms as interactions with the foreign intelligentsia, which included scientific and technical specialists. The realm of culture was closely associated with the intelligentsia, or the "Western intelligentsia" as it was often called. By the same token, relations with foreign Communists and visits by workers' delegations were put in separate categories. At the same time, the regime's innovative and overlapping initiatives to engage international audiences went well beyond cultural and scientific exchanges, exhibitions, and the like, for they were closely connected with propaganda and novel attempts to influence public opinion in other countries. They were also far greater than the sphere of diplomacy, for the oversized importance of foreign visitors and tours inside the land of socialism gave it a large domestic component. In this sense, Soviet cultural diplomacy was both broader than culture and broader than diplomacy. In this work, the term "cultural diplomacy" designates the entire complex of missions the Soviet Union directed at the foreigners classified as members of the intelligentsia, both inside and outside the USSR.[43]

In other ways, however, the Soviet Union fits well into a broader comparative frame. In other settings, cultural diplomacy was also channeled according to the priorities of political systems and societies and the international agendas of the policymakers. The French emphasis on language and high culture, the German preoccupation with academic scholarship and ethnic Germans outside Germany, and the importance of private philanthropies and corporations working in the "national interest" of the United States all reflected the ways international behavior meshed with domestic orders. So did the intensive Soviet concern with propaganda, political-ideological leverage, and scientific-technological development.

To return to Greenfeld's theory of ressentiment against the backdrop of this broader panorama of the nineteenth and twentieth centuries: if it is but a partial explanation of pre-revolutionary Russian stances toward the West, it is even more limited in the Soviet case. For one thing, it does not explain

Russian self-confidence in the superiority of its own political and social system, which before the revolution waxed above all during the period ushered
in by the victory in 1812. Ressentiment loses some of its salience, moreover,
with the cultural effects of Russia's far greater integration into Europe in the
late nineteenth century.[44] The phenomenon of tsarist-era self-confidence can
be compared to convictions about present and future superiority fostered by
Soviet ideology. In particular, the Great Depression lent a certain plausibility
to propaganda about the demise of capitalism. More importantly, the depth
and complexity of Russian relationships with Western countries cannot be
reduced to a single social-psychological reflex.[45]

The theory of ressentiment, in sum, captures the long trajectory and defensive pervasiveness of the Russian attempt to overcome inferiority vis-à-vis
Europe but avoids probing a long history of interactions that were conditioned by practices and institutions. By contrast, Rieber has called attention to
Russia's ongoing cultural distinctiveness from the surrounding world and the
internal debates over orientation that arose even in times of relative integration. The drive to overcome this persistent "cultural marginality" was made
more urgent and complicated by the canon of foreign commentary, established
in early modern Europe, that portrayed Russia as fundamentally non-European, a "rude and barbarous kingdom."[46]

Looking East

At first glance, the deeply ingrained Western discourse of Russian barbarism
and despotism provides precisely the opposite backdrop for the Soviet-Western
interactions in the interwar period, so marked by the effusions of Sovietophilia.
But here as well, the picture is one of certain continuities amidst decisive historical change. Narratives of barbarism and backwardness were perpetuated
across vast stretches of time in part through the tradition of re-reading and
imitating the most prominent early modern travelers' accounts, thus multiply-
ing and disseminating notions that only in the nineteenth century were caught
up with the East-West divide.[47] There was also, from the time of the earliest
European writings on Russia, a counter-strain of praise for Muscovy, through
which foreign observers used Russia to criticize their own societies.[48] Russia in
the wake of Westernization was both radically different and noticeably familiar, both Europe yet not Europe. For this reason, "Inventing Eastern Europe
was inseparably dependent upon the reciprocal process of inventing Western
Europe." Russia, whether portrayed as redeemable or barbaric, was therefore
centrally in view during the birth of the modern concept of civilization in eighteenth-century France.[49] In the age of imperialism and European industrial

dominance, that minority of Western accounts holding up non-Western societies as instructive examples for imitation shrunk still further.[50]

Set against this longstanding backdrop of disparaging judgment, the interwar period and Western enthusiasm for the Soviet experiment can in fact be appreciated as a great historical novelty. It was one of the first times a non-Western, or partially non-Western, country was held up on such a scale as a model for the future, with the power of politics and ideology leading the way. In the view of Furet, never had there been such a reversal in the stature and image of a country before the revolution suddenly transformed Russia from "backward" to "a guiding light."[51]

In the *longue durée* of European views of Russia, however, the post-revolutionary reversal that Furet perceived is significant but not quite as dramatic as it might appear. As Martin Malia has suggested, European views of Russia evolved within their own series of "fluctuations." First was the shift from the Enlightenment enthusiasm for Russia, particularly under Catherine the Great, as apt pupil, guided by reason on the road to civilization, to the condemnation of Nicolaevan Russia as Oriental despotism, followed in the other direction toward fin-de-siècle fascination with the exotic East. After the old pre-revolutionary tropes of backwardness were subsumed by the panegyrics of interwar Sovietophilia, these were revised yet again with Cold War theories about red-brown totalitarianism.[52]

There is clearly a direct relationship between these Western alternations and the equally broad cycles of Russian postures toward the outside world. For example, the height of Enlightenment enthusiasm for Russia matched the height of Russian imitative embrace of Europe in the eighteenth century; the prevalence of European notions of the "Huns of our time" coincided with heavy-handed Nicolaevan measures against censored European ideas. The twentieth-century repetition of this reversal came in the form of the shift in Western opinion from widespread Sovietophilia to the anti-totalitarianism of the Cold War. This coincided with the Soviet transformation this book will chart: from an ambiguous, yet sustained and influential, engagement with the outside world lasting into the Popular Front to the ideological xenophobia of the Great Terror that drastically curtailed the high point of success in showcasing the Soviet experiment. Western stances toward Soviet Russia and Soviet approaches to the West have profoundly affected one another in a centuries-old embrace.

As Western fluctuations moved roughly in tandem with Russia's own cycles of openness and hostility, these shifts were intimately connected to the import and presence of foreign visitors and their accounts. The stakes, moreover, were high for both tsarist and Soviet Russia. Western accounts were closely linked to great power rivalries and international relations, which, in the modern period, were increasingly affected by popular opinion. Western visitors, in turn, could not fail to become aware of the extraordinary importance their opinions held and the exertions made to impress them.

It was in this competitive context that the "cultural myth" of Potemkin villages was born. Aleksandr Panchenko has examined how hostile rumors of false façades erected by Catherine II's favorite, Potemkin, actually emerged several months before Catherine made her 1787 visit to Crimea with influential foreign diplomats and dignitaries in tow. While elaborate entertainments staged for this glittering entourage were undoubtedly spectacles designed to project the extent Russian power and civilization, "Here is what is important: Potemkin did in fact decorate the city and settlements, but never hid the fact that they were decorations. Dozens of descriptions of the journey to New Russia and Tauride have been preserved. In none of these descriptions made in the actual course of events is there a trace of 'Potemkin villages,' although the decorativity is recalled constantly."[53] In other words, Potemkin's impressive choreography of *divertissement* was countered and undercut by a narrative of duplicitous stagecraft so enduring it has persisted to the present day. The notion of Potemkin villages, in the sense of fake sites for fooling foreigners, would reappear with a vengeance as international debate raged about Soviet communism in the 1920s.

It was precisely the prospect of tearing down an even greater façade—the deceptive veneer of civilization—that was key to the long-lasting influence of the aristocratic French travel writer Astolphe Louis Léonard, the Marquis de Custine. With his landmark exposé of Russia's Asiatic soul in his *La Russie en 1839*, Custine created perhaps the most influential travel account ever written about Russia. To him, the vast empire was nothing but a gigantic "theater," on whose stage Russians were less interested in being civilized than making Europeans believe they were so.[54]

Custine's mode of penetrating the façade to condemn Russian tyranny, which during the Cold War came to be seen as prophetic, succeeded in deepening the Potemkin village myth because it too appeared plausible. After all, an extreme centralization of power, oppressively cumbersome bureaucracy, heavy-handed censorship, the top-down political culture of the unreconstructed autocracy, and a range of less obvious factors— such as the powerful state-service traditions of the nobility—all too obviously fostered a chilling atmosphere of group uniformity in Nicolaevan Russia. More subtly, the Westernized façade behind which Russian patterns persisted is indeed crucial to the history of Russian Europeanization—quite literally, if one takes its urban and architectural dimensions.[55]

The point is, however, that by uncovering the "Tatar" essence behind the civilized façade, Custine was amplifying a *tout court* condemnation of barbaric

Russian culture and society that was fueled by (and itself ignited) political condemnation and great power rivalry. Custine may have trotted out all the clichés "brought forward by anti-Russian French publicists ever since the Revolution," but the particular resonance and mass printings of his work derived from his ability "to reach beyond the strategic discourse and latch the image of the barbarian at the gate onto the wider issue of a *Kulturkampf* between Russia and Europe."[56] The intricate links between views of Russian society and geopolitical interests and antagonisms remained as salient after 1917 as they did in the age of Custine. What appears genuinely new was the way aspects of the communist belief system and Soviet culture could influence, and even be internalized by, significant numbers of Western observers in the twentieth-century age of ideologies.

For the Russian state, the diplomatic and geopolitical stakes involved in countering cultural prejudice and political criticism alike (and, *mutatis mutandis*, for the Soviets in countering "alien" ideologies) were high. In moving to counter Custine's stinging 1843 bestseller, the autocracy took measures that anticipated the later, more systematic practices of cultural diplomacy. The tsarist government, in what the Soviets would later call a counter-campaign, apparently sponsored anonymous essays that condemned Custine's work. Also in direct response to Custine, Nicholas and his ministers, subsequently backed by a coalition of interested Russian groups and individuals, seized the chance for the first time to craft a positive image of Russia for a broad European public by participating in London's Great Exhibition at the Crystal Palace in 1851.[57]

In the wake of Custine's bombshell, the tsarist government commissioned Baron von Haxthausen's four-month, 4,000-mile jaunt across Russia in 1843–44. Tsarist largesse included an interpreter (von Haxthausen knew no Russian), a government minder who was surreptitiously to observe him, and others to censor or withhold information he requested. In a precursor to precisely the kind of influential boomerangs and East-West entanglements this book attempts to uncover in the early Soviet period, the Romantic German's theory of the egalitarian, propertyless Russian land commune proved so influential that it did more than just undergird generations of debates about Russia and the West among the intelligentsia. Haxthausen appears to have actually influenced the reality he purported to describe by helping to enshrine the commune in the 1861 emancipation of the serfs.[58]

As the case of Haxthausen suggests, the intellectual and cultural history of "Russia and the West" developed a hall-of-mirrors quality that holds implications for how it is studied in this book. "Russia's image and self-image," notes Daniel L. Schlafly, Jr., "perhaps more than any other country's, has been shaped from abroad." Not only did an extraordinary panoply of resident foreigners play a prominent role from Muscovy on, but "accounts by foreigners have had a far greater impact on Russia than foreigners' accounts on other nations."[59] After the "Golden Age" of Russian culture and the explosive growth of professionals and experts after the Great Reforms, the oversized role of imported foreign specialists diminished. But there was still ample precedent for Soviet-era examples of privileging Western views even in rejection, the influx of resident foreigners and workers that peaked during the first Five-Year Plan, and the very special place reserved in early Soviet and Stalinist culture for "friends of the Soviet Union."

Long before the fellow-travelers, there was also a complex and tangled correlation between views of Russia and the political divisions between Left and Right. After the French Revolution, despite exceptions, most anyone in Europe "who considered himself liberal, revolutionary, or socialist was anti-Russian"; the dynamic was by and large reversed with the Revolutions of 1905 and 1917.[60] During the late imperial period, however, even as some of the hoariest tropes of anti-Russian discourse from earlier eras survived and evolved (and were transplanted to the United States by way of France),[61] a growing strain of cultural Russophilia took flight internationally. Russia and the Russian soul as a symbol of a non-Western, anti-bourgeois, and non-liberal path of development proved attractive, among others, to the extreme Right. After the fin-de-siècle, cultural Russophilia in Germany conditioned, via such figures as Moeller van den Bruck and Oswald Spengler, the new nationalist and "conservative revolutionary" fascination with Soviet Russia as an alternative to Western modernity.[62] This phenomenon plays an important role in this book. Many works on early Soviet outreach to Western intellectuals focus only on left-wing sympathizers, just as they forget to recognize that fellow-travelers of fascism were also a significant interwar phenomenon.[63] This book pays close attention to the fascinating episodes in which Soviet cultural diplomacy came into contact with the opposite side of the political spectrum, partly in Fascist Italy, but above all with the German "revolutionaries of the Right."

The broad, international interest in the Soviet claim to be leaping forward into a non-capitalist future went beyond the allegiances of politics and ranged across the ideological spectrum because of a profound interwar crisis that seemed to place a sword of Damocles over the liberal tradition. In the trenches of total war starting in 1914, the nineteenth-century belief in progress and the stability of the *belle époque* met its demise. The interwar conjuncture can be viewed as general crisis of the restricted incarnations of modernity developed in the nineteenth century. The new era of mass mobilization and collective politics was marked by a "protracted struggle over societal reorganization" in which many proposals aimed at a "greater degree of social organization than any liberal political or economic theory prescribed."[64] Strong state interventionism, rather than the old individualism, animated the entire spectrum of communist, fascist, and social-democratic projects—not to mention the New Deal in the United States. Despite the radical differences among them, many of these projects shared certain common ideological lineages, based themselves on internationally circulated practices, or were influenced by experts who could migrate or convert from one to the other.[65] The history of the entire range of foreign visitors' interactions with the Soviets opens a window onto these kinds of exchanges and reactions to the Soviet alternative modernity-in-the-making.

The wave of international Sovietophilia after the Russian Revolution was, thus, a genuine historical novelty. Crucially, it could still be blended with earlier currents of Russophilia and Russophobia in complicated ways.[66] As many of the visitors examined here suggest, longstanding prejudices about Asia, Russians, and the Slavs could coexist with favorable views of the Bolsheviks, who, after all, were bent on modernizing backward Russia. Many Western visitors, even the most abjectly pro-Soviet, brought with them notions of cultural superiority over the "Russian" national character; for many others during the interwar crisis of liberalism, it was precisely the association of the Soviet order with non-Western or non-European difference that was fascinating and attractive.

The Soviet revolutionary experiment thus enjoyed large amounts of what is now commonly called soft power, but it was also handicapped by the legacy of past prejudices. Some pro-Soviet observers confronted this new amalgam of backwards Russia and the advanced Soviet Union by deliberately attempting to disaggregate politics and ideology, in which Soviet Russia was now seen as advanced, from economics and culture. Liberals and socialists, unsurprisingly given that despotism had been central to European conceptions of Russia since the early modern period, frequently found it possible to justify repression that they deemed unacceptable in their own countries in the backward, perennially autocratic land of the Bolsheviks.[67] At the same time, even as the Soviet question loomed large, the great experiment faced stiff competition on many levels. As Mary Nolan has noted, in interwar Europe, Bolshevism appeared as but one of two major "models for economic and social modernity": the other was "Americanism."[68] Culturally, moreover, there were multiple poles of attraction with which the Soviets competed.

The Bolshevik Revolution thus created a situation in which both the new regime and its Western interlocutors were deeply divided. The new regime oscillated between new forms of engagement and heightened ideological and security measures to limit contagion, between assimilating advanced modernity and repudiating the bourgeois West. In Central and Western Europe and the United States, older views of Russians as inferior and deeply hostile reactions to the revolution went side by side with an unprecedented embrace—itself, however, as we shall see, often internally divided or contradictory. Even as they negotiated these divisions, a number of the figures who will appear in this book, visitors and Soviets alike, could be shrewd and direct observers whose judgments were based on experience in direct apprehension of the other side.

The Bolshevik intellectuals who shaped early Soviet politics and culture were deeply invested in interpreting and altering foreign views of their country, and they believed and hoped the transition to socialism would make the dichotomy of Russia and the West wither away. "The proletariat is Europe"—such was the striking, almost defiant attempt by Anatolii Lunacharskii, the first Soviet Commissar of Enlightenment, to equate the proletarian revolution with the legacy of Western progress. Lunacharskii penned that sentence in a short-lived periodical, *West and East,* sponsored by VOKS. His explicit goal was to untangle the Soviet construction of socialism from what he called "the Euro-Asiatic problem." In European countries, he observed, anti-Bolshevism was portrayed as a defense of the Western civilization from revolutionary barbarians even as cultural trends in Berlin and Paris flirting with *aziatchina* (Assianness) and the "end of the West" were drawn to Bolshevism. The Old Bolshevik intellectual, of course, entirely rejected those categories. The Bolsheviks were "Asiatics" only insofar as communism wished "to attract non-European peoples into universal civilization." Although he found it worrisome that even young Communists, and not just foreigners, mistakenly thought in terms of East and West rather than through the prism of class, he ended with a characteristic note of optimism. The Bolshevik Revolution would remain true to the principles of European civilization; it merely needed to "cleanse Europe" of capitalism.[69]

The communist cleansing operation, directed above all internally, proved more challenging and far bloodier than Lunacharskii ever dreamed. Little did he know that the latter-day communist Westernizers had launched a trajectory that would ultimately take his country further away from Europe than it had been in more than two centuries. The time has come to examine the interwar pilgrimage to the Soviet experiment as a crucial window into Soviet history and a singular Soviet-era encore to the dance between "Russia and the West" begun in the time of Muscovy.

The master theme of this book, which connects the early Soviet era to the great pre-revolutionary topic of "Russia and the West," concerns expressions of superiority and inferiority. As students of national identity have long observed, these are always close to the surface in historical articulations of the self and the other. In the words of Michael Geyer, "national imaginaries" are "never innocent," for a "sense of superiority is deeply invested in these imaginaries—and so too is a sense of inferiority."[70] For several specific reasons, the advent of communism marked a qualitatively new peak in competitive evaluations, a phenomenon that structured and informed the Soviet interactions with the Western world. Political tourists on the road to Russia reported their balance sheets on the "new Russia" to the world often before they had even left the train station. This was the era of countless evaluations of Soviet claims, which were invested with a burning new political significance. Now, left-leaning bourgeois intellectuals faced their own curse of inferiority before an idealized proletariat. In an extraordinary inversion of the Orientalist trope of the Slavic East as mysterious, exotic, feminine, and, therefore, inferior, now a number of fellow-travelers admired Bolsheviks, and in the 1930s Stalin in particular, as marking the advent of a new breed of intellectual men of action. The Soviet case thus formed a fundamental part of the interwar era's debate over the role of intellectuals. Even further, Marxism-Leninism, as it faced outward, developed and cultivated a remarkably hierarchical view of the world. The new Soviet methodologies of receiving foreign visitors were all about ranking and evaluating; the Holy Grail of Soviet cultural diplomacy was to secure a formal foreign recognition of superiority.[71] In sum, Western observers and Soviets alike thus developed new ways to respond to, and not infrequently deflect, others' evaluations.

For these reasons, as this book ranges across many topics and figures in the history of Western visitors to the Soviet experiment, its approach throughout has been to detect, trace, and interrogate the expressions of superiority and inferiority that were at the heart of the interwar pilgrimage. These were rarely straightforward and were invariably responsive to the stances of the opposite side. This approach of analyzing cross-cultural encounters and transnational interactions through the prism of assertions of superiority and inferiority emerged out their prominence in the longue durée of Russian history and their intensification after 1917 in this mutual culture of evaluation. Yet, it can also be applied to other times and places.

The story of the Soviet reception of foreigners during the interwar period's intense scrutiny and exchange, as this suggests, offers much more than the familiar conclusions about Soviet control that have hamstrung the interpretative reach of first Cold War and then post-Soviet discussions of this book's subject.[72] Let me be clear: the Soviets presented forced labor in the Gulag as enlightened rehabilitation, staged images of plenty in the midst of horrific famine, and systematically lied about terror, torture, and repression. What Western visitors knew or suspected, and why so many were nonetheless attracted to the great experiment, is an integral part of the analysis. But this book also shows that more than deceptive machinations was involved:

this was one of the most intensive and consequential cross-cultural and political-ideological encounters between Western countries and another part of the world in the twentieth century. It is interesting in many ways because Soviet Russia was not distant and remote but in many aspects very familiar, a proximate "other." The Soviet engagement with the West was central to the shape the Soviet order took, while contacts with Western intellectuals were vital to a remarkably talented and often cosmopolitan generation of Bolshevik and Soviet cultural and political elites. By the same token, Western visitors, who included a virtual encyclopedia of European and American intellectuals and scholars, were actors in their own rights. Some were willing partners and some were filled with naïve illusions, but they were all more than mere dupes. This is why I prefer to differentiate among figures examined in depth rather than extend the long tradition of either demonizing or heroicizing the intellectuals.

The Soviet quest for influence and control itself becomes revealing when it is historicized. Bolshevik proclivities to measure individuals as part of class and political collectivities, the way Leninism was codified around political maneuvering, and party-state practices of mobilizing and pressuring the intelligentsia ensured that an instrumental approach to foreign visitors was given high value in internal deliberations and thus taken to an extreme. The conspiratorial and instrumental language favored within Bolshevik political culture, however, could conceal the avenues in which the huge investment in influencing the West ended up shaping the Soviets themselves.

For example, many early guides, with their methods of "cultural show," were involved in an effort not merely to pull the wool over foreigners' eyes, but to change or convert them. They tried to inculcate a mode of looking at the heritage of the past and the promise of the future that became relevant, even decisive, for Communists and Soviet citizens too. Or, alternately, they assumed that foreigners could not overcome their bourgeois or intelligentsia natures—itself the tortured goal of many Soviet citizens and Communists.[73] The assumptions of Marxist-Leninist class analysis and political utilitarianism on the ground, moreover, need to be interpreted against a broader, and sometimes tension-ridden, set of Soviet aspirations toward the representatives of Western Europe and the United States—which, on the individual level, included doses of sometimes covert admiration.

The superiority-inferiority calculus ultimately holds direct implications for understanding Stalinism and foreigners' reactions to it. In the 1920s, Lenin's dictum that the Soviet Union had much to learn from the advanced West was widely disseminated even as the revolution's "achievements" were touted, but it is impossible to understand the 1930s without examining the new Stalin-era declarations of across-the-board Soviet superiority. As this became the new orthodoxy, Western visitors confronted its widespread effects. This book establishes and probes an entire superiority-inferiority complex, constructed by Soviet hosts looking West and Western visitors to the East, that bore the imprint of the specific transactions involved in showcasing the great experiment.

1

Cultural Diplomacy of a New Type

While the first years after the October Revolution were foundational in myriad ways for the Soviet system, the fledgling state was still quite insular. The number of travelers from abroad was severely limited before the early 1920s, and cultural relations and international contacts were broken, for all intents and purposes, as the Civil War extended and deepened the period of total war.[1] Yet, in another sense, the period of war communism in 1918–1920 created the Janus face of the Soviet approach to foreigners and representatives of the West: it was marked simultaneously by internationalist euphoria and hostile suspiciousness toward outsiders.

The first phases of Bolshevik rule undoubtedly mark the most "internationalist" phase of Soviet power as Russia's new rulers imagined world revolution to be right around the corner. But the new regime's stance in relationship to foreigners was inconsistent. On the one hand, foreign radicals like John Reed and Victor Serge were welcomed as comrades when they arrived as observers or to join the cause; sympathetic former prisoners of war were allowed to stay. Class, not nationality, was supposed to determine Soviet citizenship, and in 1918 the government declared its intention to allow foreign laborers to become naturalized citizens of the proletarian homeland. Foreign citizens also played a significant role in various Civil War fronts. On the other hand, foreign intervention on all sides of the red zone bolstered a mentality of implacable antagonism and determination to overcome "capitalist encirclement." A firm ideological link, reinforced by political violence, was forged between the bourgeois enemy without and social and political opponents within. Both were "alien elements," and in general, "the Soviet government remained suspicious of foreigners."[2]

With the belief that October would spark the outbreak of world revolution further west, interest in the proletariat and the nascent international communist movement overshadowed systematic concern with other segments of "bourgeois" society. Major initiatives to showcase socialism triumphant were initially made for foreign Communists and domestic audiences. For example, the arrival of delegates to the Second Congress of the Comintern was timed to coincide with perhaps the greatest Soviet festival ever staged, the November 1920 reenactment of the storming of the Winter Palace in 1917, involving thousands of actors and a viewership of one-quarter of the population of Petrograd.[3] May Day and Revolution Day became two times of year especially reserved for foreign delegations and honored guests.

During the Civil War, there were a number of abortive attempts by state agencies to set up foreign bureaus that would channel information and equipment to the Soviet Republic, and the Commissariat of Enlightenment had an International Section from the end of 1918, headed by F. N. Petrov (future head of VOKS, the All-Union Society for Cultural Ties Abroad, in the early 1930s), that was concerned with establishing ties with revolutionary artists. Only by the early 1920s, however, did several state commissariats, including the commissariats of health and enlightenment, have permanent representatives abroad, while others invited and received specialists. This set up a situation in which virtually each commissariat maintained its own international operations, inviting guests and arranging travel for its own officials.[4] For example, the Berlin-based Bureau of Foreign Science and Technology of Vesenkha, the Supreme Council of the National Economy, whose activities were interrupted in 1918 but restarted again in late 1920, bought up foreign publications and equipment, attempted to establish ties with sympathetic scientists in European countries, and organized a group of German and Russian artists to make production posters for Vesenkha's Section on Economic Propaganda.[5] The avant-garde, one of the few intelligentsia groups to embrace the Bolshevik Revolution, was particularly active in forging international contacts.

As soon as the military situation stabilized, the Old Bolshevik engineer Leonid Borisovich Krasin, with his trade and financial operations in London, showed an early interest in importing foreign specialists and workers. His archive contains a 1922 English-language declaration to be signed by American trade unionists recruited to work in the Kuzbass, promising that they would endure a "number of privations...in a country rather backward and unprecedentedly destroyed." The foreign workers should pledge to maintain "productivity of labor and discipline surpassing the standards of capitalism, for else we will not be able to surpass or even to reach the level of capitalism."[6] The language of hierarchical competition with the industrialized West—to overtake and exceed—was firmly embedded in this early document.

After the Revolution, a number of leading Bolshevik figures, the Old Bolshevik writer Maxim Gorky included, made uncoordinated efforts to influence Western views of the new regime and establish Soviet international contacts. In an era of non-recognition of the new state, intellectuals were often seen as alternative channels to conventional diplomacy. At the same time, precedents were established for the restricted import and hierarchical distribution of foreign information and literature. This was made accessible to Bolshevik leaders and reflected great concern not only with countering the criticisms of the Russian emigration but also "bourgeois" commentary on the fledgling Soviet experiment. "Books for comrade Lenin" collected by Foreign Affairs in 1920 included *La Russie bolcheviste* by the French economist and jurist Étienne Antonelli, *The Practice and Theory of Bolshevism* by Bertrand Russell, and 43 other works in English.[7]

Foreigners and Famine

The greater numbers of foreign visitors in the early 1920s corresponded with the gradually increasing Bolshevik recognition that Western states and non-proletarian, non-communist segments of those societies would have to be approached in a sustained way. The massive famine of 1921—the combined result of disastrous Bolshevik policies of grain requisitioning, the disruptions of world war, revolution, and drought—made for a public relations crisis. Because it prompted both an influx of foreigners and a more serious attempt to influence Western public opinion, the crisis of the famine proved one of the most important contexts out of which the international operations of the Soviet system emerged.

Gorky, increasingly at odds with Lenin and the Soviet leadership over the persecution of the intelligentsia, was still the figure designated to address the outside world. In July 1921, the writer spoke out not in the name of revolutionary socialism, but of the Russian cultural and scientific heritage most familiar to Western intellectuals, calling for "all honest European and American people" to save the "country of Tolstoy, Dostoevsky, Mendeleev, Pavlov, Mussorgsky, Glinka, etc."[8] To the new regime, international famine relief presented opportunity and danger, along with a particular blend of "internal" and "external" tasks. After much negotiation, the Soviet government allowed Western relief organizations unprecedented leeway to operate inside the country and in famine areas. At the same time, more foreigners were able to enter and visit Soviet Russia, and guiding their visits became a concern for the first time. The visible appeal to Western public opinion for famine relief raised the possibility of influencing the image of the new regime among visiting non-partisan opinion makers, something that might bring dividends of the most concrete kind—recognition by Western powers, a top diplomatic priority. In this fashion, the domestic function of receiving foreign visitors became integrally linked with international goals of molding Western views and public opinion.

An August 1921 policy paper sent from a Soviet representative in Paris to Krasin, then an influential representative of the Soviet Republic in Great Britain, promoted awareness of new opportunities presented by the crisis. Written after Gorky's appeal, in the midst of negotiations leading to the Riga Agreement hammered out between Herbert Hoover's American Relief Administration (ARA) and the Soviets, it argued that the sympathy evoked within the Russian emigration could affect Western public opinion, generating greater cooperation with the Soviet government. At the same time, however, the famine raised the prospect of Western recognition of Soviet "weaknesses" that could lead to attempts to extract concessions. The dangers could fall away if foreign groups most supportive of Soviet power were organized and bolstered. In sum, Soviet power could bypass conventional diplomacy and appeal directly to public opinion (*obshchestvennost'*) in Western countries.[9]

Cooperation with civic forces at home in order to produce a favorable reaction abroad, however, proved difficult for leading Bolsheviks to swallow. For a time, prominent members of the Russian intelligentsia with international reputations were put in charge of an All-Russian Committee for Aid to the Starving (the so-called "Prokukish" committee, an acronym created out of the names of its politically moderate leaders). Lenin, Kamenev, and the Bolshevik leadership were making a calculated trade: in return for giving a committee of prominent organizers freedom to operate in the old traditions of *zemstvo* and professional civic activism, they hoped to receive increased Western aid for the crisis. Shortly after it began operations in July 1921, this early attempt to utilize the prestige of the intelligentsia abroad began to stoke Bolshevik fears. First, foreign officials such as the British trade representative became interested in dealing with the committee directly, outside of party control. Second, wild rumors about Bolshevik weakness and the prospect of the Prokukish committee forming a shadow government circulated among the Russian emigration and the Western press. Even some underground Mensheviks in Moscow, reporting on the anxieties of their erstwhile Bolshevik cousins, talked about the impending end of one-party dictatorship. The immediate pretext for the committee's dissolution was the imminent arrival of foreign aid workers who might link up with the non-party activists. On August 27, 1921, revolver-toting Chekists burst into the committee's meeting, arresting its members and detaining the foreign journalists present.[10]

The Party had from the first created an official Soviet famine-relief organization, Pomgol, which was ready to step into the breach. Top Foreign Affairs officials remained intensely concerned with perceptions of Soviet weakness and loss of face. A letter from Litvinov to Chicherin on August 30, 1921, made clear that Foreign Affairs' press strategy revolved around combating the widespread Western press reports that famine had led to a "weakening of Soviet power."[11]

The ARA, Hoover's quasi-private organization with close ties to the U.S. government, launched a two-year relief expedition that, at its height in the summer of 1922, was feeding nearly eleven million Soviet citizens a day. The influx of foreign relief personnel and "bourgeois" operations deep inside the Russian interior, by far the most important of which was ARA, coincided with the "retreat" of the New Economic Policy (NEP), which ushered in a crisis of revolutionary purity and profound anxiety within the Party about the fate of the socialist revolution. The sheer extent of the famine-relief operation, which after hard-fought negotiations gave the Americans an extraordinary degree of autonomy, elicited a potent Bolshevik brew of intense suspiciousness of and admiration for advanced American efficiency.

As David Engerman has shown, the ARA's strict policy of channeling aid only to relieve famine conditions, consistently avoiding the economic recon-struction projects the Soviet leadership craved, was a major source of tension between the two sides in the period between 1921–23. Hoover vetoed any non-relief projects that might aid the Bolshevik cause, while many of his own mid-level staff disagreed, believing that economic progress would hasten the end of the regime.[12]

Lenin, for his part, initially displayed deep suspicion, pushing for Cheka sur-veillance to "shadow Hooverites," but he also saw the ARA presence as a golden opportunity for the Soviets to "master trade" by emulating the Americans.[13] A hard-line opposition to ARA relief emerged immediately and was exemplified by Aleksandr Eiduk, who in October 1921 was appointed RSFSR Plenipotentiary for All Foreign Famine Relief Organizations. A leather-jacketed member of the Cheka Collegium who had fought with the Latvian troops in the Civil War as a machine gunner, Eiduk shadowed the Americans with a team heavily drawn from the secret police.[14] In a March 21, 1921, letter to Lenin and other top lead-ers, Eiduk bitterly denounced the ARA for being neither apolitical nor "loyal." Formally, the ARA observed the text of the Riga Agreement, but its real goals were to generate anti-Soviet publicity and self-enrichment: it attempted to use any opportunity "to expose deficiencies in our Soviet apparatus."[15]

Soviet hostility in the localities was ignited as the ARA employed and sup-ported 6,000 Russian citizens, comprising large numbers of the old intel-ligentsia and nobility. At the same time, the famine-relief operation led to ARA celebrity in towns and villages across the country, where, as one Russian co-worker noted, everything "American" holds "fascination and weight in all classes of the population."[16] The aid operation had a deep impact on the Soviet concept of *amerikanizm,* with all its positive connotations of modern, industrial-age efficiency. An article in the journal *Kommunist,* summing up the "results" of ARA activity, called famine relief with the presence of foreigners "the first significant business operation for us."[17]

On the American side, the equation of Russian national character with backwardness, "Oriental fatalism," ignorance, and other defects ran like a red thread throughout the ARA's internal discussions. Despite the power and celebrity enjoyed by young American relief personnel in 1921–23, and despite the horror of what they saw in the famine regions, in certain respects the young ARA men (for "no women, no Jews" were the two unwritten rules of recruitment for Hoover's mission) displayed attitudes comparable to later European and American visitors.[18] Many talked about Russians and Bolsheviks using racial and anti-Semitic slurs. One letter intercepted by Kamenev called Russians a "filthy race" and Bolsheviks a "filthy sneaking ignorant crowd of...revengeful Jews."[19] As among later visitors, the flip side of such naked prejudice was a fascination with Russian exoticism.

The famine of the early 1920s turned the need to boost Soviet status in the eyes of the world and the need to manage foreigners on Soviet soil into urgent issues. It also provoked Foreign Affairs commissar Boris Chicherin to express deep concern to Politburo member Lev Kamenev, the point man in the leadership on famine relief, about discrepancies in Soviet reports on conditions in the famine regions reaching the outside world. The conclusion was that the regime urgently needed to improve the image of Soviet Russia internationally.[20] The concerns about foreign perceptions and contacts heightened by the famine contributed directly to their institutionalization in the new organs of cultural diplomacy.

Such was the case with the Committee on Foreign Aid (*Komitet zagranichnoi pomoshchi,* or KZP) of the Presidium of the Central Executive Committee (*pri Prezidiume TsIK SSSR*). In the fall of 1923, it succeeded the Central Commission for Relief for the Starving (*Pomgol*), chaired by Lev Kamenev, and its successor, the Central Commission for the Consequences of the Famine (*TsK Posledgol*). Both these Soviet organizations had many dealings, often hostile, with the foreign philanthropic organizations active inside the country. Posledgol also had representatives abroad, and the Commission on Foreign Aid was intended to continue this practice, aiding "the organizations of the progressive intelligentsia" to contact relevant Soviet institutions.[21] At least some of the two famine committees' personnel later went into cultural diplomacy with Ol'ga Kameneva, Kamenev's wife, who initially launched KZP to attract aid and donations from "friends" of Soviet Russia abroad. KZP and Kameneva were in contact with U.S. and French Communists and labor groups organizing aid in relief organizations. KZP also facilitated visas for relief workers among "friends" and philanthropic groups with the Foreign Affairs and the foreign section of the secret police (INO GPU).[22] Kameneva's committee quickly broadened its activities from favorably impressing visitors to improving the image of the country. It began to monitor foreign press coverage, launched a successful international book exchange and the photographic agency Russ-Foto, and began arranging international exhibitions and artistic tours.[23]

Much later, Kameneva made a startling revelation about the origins of Soviet cultural diplomacy and intelligentsia visitors. Under political fire from subordinates who smelled blood because of her associations with condemned oppositionists—her brother, Trotsky, and her husband, Kamenev—she wrote about how much she had personally achieved without much initial support from the Party, saying, "In essence the material side of the cause was founded with bourgeois money: from the leftovers (*ostatkov*) from bourgeois organizations giving aid to the starving."[24] This was corroborated by a letter from Kameneva to Chicherin dated December 1924: all "informational" work with foreigners had been carried out "with the funds coming for 'food supply aid' (the State for all this work for 15 months has not given a single penny)."[25] Kameneva cited this fact to demand regular funding, not to express compunction about diverting international donations sent to starving peasants.

The first "propagandist of the achievements of Soviet construction abroad" after the October Revolution was the Commissariat of Foreign Affairs, the Press Section of which was headed in the early 1920s by high official and member of the commissariat's collegium, Fedor Rotshtein. The Press Section worked with Posledgol in its time on presenting information on the famine to the world, and Rotshtein subsequently became Foreign Affairs' closest contact with the nascent Soviet organs of cultural diplomacy and propaganda.[26] The latter were initially formed in response to increasing opportunities for travel in 1922–23, as well as heightened interest in early Soviet culture in Europe. Among the first Soviet art exhibitions, for example, were those held in 1922 in Berlin, Florence, and Prague, and the interest they sparked highlighted the need for a more specific focus on the foreign "intelligentsia."

Thus did the immediate precursor to VOKS take shape. In December 1923, KZP formed a United Information Bureau (*Ob"edinennoe Biuro Informatsii*) to coordinate information, as it was put to other Soviet agencies, for "all foreigners arriving here to acquaint themselves with the scientific and cultural life of the USSR." The tasks of OBI, which at its founding had only seventeen employees, were defined as "propaganda among the foreign intelligentsia through acquainting them with the cultural gains (*zavoevaniia*) and work of the Soviet Republic." In an initial attempt to convince foreigners of the neutrality of a Soviet international cultural initiative, the existence of OBI was announced abroad as an "unofficial" informational center with no links to the Kremlin. OBI published a bulletin on Soviet cultural life, started the attempt to place articles in the non-communist press abroad, and worked with Soviet diplomats stationed in foreign countries, who were asked to steer foreign travelers to the new outfit.[27]

The contours of OBI's work that emerged from the particular circumstances of the famine period were, in embryo, the set of functions that would later be formalized and expanded with the creation of VOKS in 1925, which at that time became the primary agency involved in showcasing Soviet culture for foreigners and arranging the visits of members of the intelligentsia (generally, but not always, excluding such groups as foreign Communists, diplomats, trade union delegates, and journalists). All of OBI's activities would continue to be pursued in similar or expanded form; among the only things new about VOKS were its officially non-governmental status as a "society" and, connected to that, its deeper involvement with Soviet intellectuals and public groups (*obshchestvennost'*). Moreover, KZP's negotiations with foreign philanthropic missions and involvement with visa and travel permission for their representatives, such as the Vatican-funded Catholic Mission, brought Kameneva into close working contact with secret police leaders such as Genrikh Iagoda and Viacheslav Menzhinskii.[28]

The early-1920s conjuncture from which Soviet cultural diplomacy emerged linked heavy state involvement in international cultural exchange to attempts to influence foreign (above all, Western) public opinion and target all those classified as part of the Western "intelligentsia." The reception of foreign visitors became squarely embedded in this constellation of tasks. Through this set of missions, OBI and then VOKS became involved in "external" operations abroad and domestic functions involving visitors and the Soviet non-party intelligentsia, creating a powerful, live link between foreign and domestic agendas and pressures that was exemplified more broadly in the history of party-state engagement with the outside world.

The driving force behind OBI (and later VOKS) was Ol'ga Davydovna Kameneva (née Bronstein). She and her brother, Lev Trotsky, were born in rural Kherson province to a father who had the distinction of being one of the few substantial Jewish landowners in the empire. Like her more famous brother, Ol'ga was an early adherent to Social Democracy, following him into the party in 1902. As the wife of Lenin's lieutenant, Kamenev, the young Ol'ga helped the Bolshevik leader with the editing of party publications. Educated in Bern and a "graduate" of the Bolshevik leadership's long European emigration before 1917, Kameneva had the ability to make herself appear the imperious commissar or energetic patron to non-party Russian intellectuals and the polished "Madame Kameneva" to visiting foreign dignitaries. Like a number of wives of the top Old Bolshevik leaders, Kameneva took up a cultural post after the Revolution, heading the Theater Administration of Narkompros in 1918–19. This apparently did not satisfy her ambitions, for the Politburo noted in 1919 the "constant requests from comrade O.D. Kameneva to leave for political work."[29]

In creating OBI and later, VOKS, Kameneva's main project in the 1920s, she remained in "cultural" work but with a heightened political significance. Kameneva threw herself into the bureaucratic politics of state building with the revolutionary energy typical of the Bolshevik intelligentsia in the 1920s: OBI, centrally located in Moscow at the Metropol Hotel, was known as the "Kameneva Institute" to foreign visitors.[30] Facilitating Kameneva's efforts was her place in the top echelon of the Bolshevik elite, but in many respects she faced quite an uphill battle—funding was scarce in conditions of early NEP and only a small group of party members had the foreign-language skills to work in this area.

Kameneva's whole career in state building during NEP was caught up with a certain paradox. Much of what was "modern" about the Soviet project related to the strong commitment to mold minds and alter psyches; much of what was new and even unique about the totalizing Soviet project was the extent of its concern with creating and managing the new culture. In conditions of fiscal constraint, however, Bolshevik statism and Marxist economic determinism contributed to a situation in which party-state initiatives had greater clout if they were connected with such areas as industry, technology, trade, and interstate relations—or even agitation and propaganda on a mass scale. Much later, when she faced political attacks in the late 1920s, Kameneva reminded the Central Committee that she had created a very successful venture "from scratch" without "even much moral support from the Party."

> I'll risk saying it even more sharply: there was even an open disdain for this work...From the TsK [Central Committee] all directives were limited to the laconic pronouncement: 'Do not object' (*Ne vozrazhat'*).

Kameneva's personal initiative thus proved fundamental for shaping one key part of Soviet reception of foreigners and cultural ties with the outside world. What approaches and proclivities did she bring to the table as she molded this nascent enterprise? Unlike the most visible and vocal Bolshevik intellectuals, such as Lunacharskii, Kameneva deliberately stayed behind the scenes and hardly even published. She left some intriguing clues in one of her only books, an obscure 1926 edited volume on workers' canteens, however. There, she wrote about "culturedness" (*kul'turnost'*) a key concept throughout all the twists and turns of cultural revolution in the 1920s and 1930s. There was much debate in the 1920s over what *culturedness* meant, but most definitions juggled three component parts: literacy and knowledge, hygiene and behavior, and social-political activism. Kameneva herself was concerned in this context to emphasize the last two: *kul'turnost'* was not just a function of literacy and bookishness but also included "manners, tidiness, cleanliness, discipline, respect, recognition of rights of others, interest toward societal life." Kameneva's involvement in this debate demonstrates how the concept was intimately linked, whether one liked it or not, with understandings of Europeanness. Kameneva's civilizing mission included many party members themselves—who lacked these qualities, she sharply noted. The organization of model institutions such as clean, well-serviced "show canteens" (*pokazatel'nye stolovye*) was one way to raise the cultural level.[31]

There was nothing unique in this formulation of the civilizing mission inherent in the cultural revolution of the 1920s, nor was Kameneva's belief in the edifying power of showcases unusual. Kameneva's understanding of *kul'turnost'*, however, sheds light on two fundamental principles informing her international activity. On the one hand, the "victories" (*zavoevaniia*) achieved by Soviet power needed to be propagated as widely as possible. Kameneva relentlessly focused on the political dimensions of her international work and, above all, on securing sympathy for the regime. On the other hand, she consistently expressed the belief that Soviets badly needed a clearer picture of the outside world and especially of the advanced countries of the West.

In other words, with her simultaneous preoccupation with Soviet achievements and Western advancement, Kameneva embroidered a Bolshevik variation on the old tapestry of superiority and inferiority vis-à-vis Europe. Her admiration for aspects of the West extended not merely to countries of "highly developed technology and economy" but also to those that had achieved a high cultural level.[32] For Kameneva, the political, ideological, and propagandistic dimensions of her work with foreigners were intertwined with the notion that cultural contacts with the West and general knowledge of the outside world were of intrinsic importance for the young Soviet society. An article of faith she was forced repeatedly to defend was her conviction that in international work, a focus on the bourgeois "intelligentsia" was critical, because it "created" public opinion through the press: "The intelligentsia in bourgeois countries plays a dominant role."[33]

Kameneva managed to survive politically after Trotsky and Kamenev were condemned as deviationists in 1924 and 1927, respectively. The most salient fact behind her survival was that she avoided oppositional activity, and also that she was estranged from Kamenev by the late 1920s. But it is also the case that in political terms in those years her work with bourgeois foreigners was considered a slightly unsavory assignment. Thus, for example, the party leadership considered it acceptable to send condemned oppositionists abroad as diplomats. By the time Kameneva was swept out of her post, in July 1929, at a time of widespread ouster of the NEP-era cultural establishment in the Party, Kameneva had thoroughly shaped the rise and early history of VOKS and a large part of the Soviet approach to foreign visitors.[34]

The opportunity to mobilize Western public opinion created by the famine of 1921–22 launched not only Kameneva's trajectory but also the most prominent Comintern-based initiative in propaganda and front organizations for left-leaning intellectual sympathizers. The organs of the Comintern, founded in 1919, were primarily concerned with communist parties and labor movements. International communism, however, inevitably became heavily invested in the image of Soviet socialism and the opinions of left-leaning intellectuals. Attention to the radical segment of Western public opinion and "cultural propaganda" was pursued not only by organs of the Comintern (itself subordinated to the Soviet Politburo, and the Comintern's Agitprop division to the Central Committee's Agitprop), but by the Profintern and the Communist Youth International.

At the same moment that Lenin and the Soviet leadership were negotiating with ARA and "bourgeois" philanthropy, in August 1921, Lenin charged trusted communist operatives Willi Münzenberg and Karl Radek with creating a "foreign committee" for workers' famine relief in action. This led to the emergence of what would, like VOKS, also surface in the mid-1920s as the crown jewel of Münzenberg's publishing and front-organization empire, the Internationale Arbeiter Hilfe (IAH, also known by its Russian acronym *Mezhrabpom*). While Münzenberg's Berlin-based initiative was formally under the aegis of the Comintern, and Kameneva's Moscow-based outfit was under the party-state, both figures had close personal ties to the Kremlin leadership. Münzenberg had met Lenin in April 1915 and was part of his inner circle in Zurich after February 1916. Close to Radek, another member of the Zimmerwald Left, Münzenberg did not accompany Lenin on the famous "sealed train" only because of Münzenberg's German citizenship. His pedigree in the same circles ensured he ultimately answered not to the Comintern but the Kremlin.[35] This independence gave him leeway to devote considerable attention to inclusive campaigns attractive to left-leaning intellectuals.

If one considers the peculiar combination of threat and opportunity that the famine conjuncture presented to Soviet communism in the early 1920s, the simultaneous rise of Münzenberg and Kameneva becomes comprehensible. Like Kameneva's Soviet base, Münzenberg's Comintern operations gained traction as a counterweight to the perceived dangers of bourgeois philanthropy and its new foothold inside Soviet Russia.[36] But the heightened sense of danger was soon matched by sudden visions of success.

For example, the U.S.-based Friends of Soviet Russia, affiliated with Münzenberg, soon raised unexpectedly large amounts of money among sympathetic Americans for famine relief. Münzenberg freely borrowed attention-grabbing ideas, such as the use of stamps and buttons to jazz up the fundraising campaign, from the Americans.[37] At the same time, the innovative use of photography in his flagship mass publications, such as *Die Welt am Abend* and *Arbeiter Illustrierte Zeitung*, and his later investment in film and film clubs were in close dialogue with the Soviet "propaganda state." They were also very much in interaction with the politically committed Russian avant-garde.[38] Münzenberg's IAH was a prime mover behind the 1922 Berlin exhibition of Soviet art on Unter den Linden that featured many avant-garde works and had an electrifying effect on the German public. The Soviet Foreign Affairs press analyst was ecstatic: the exhibit's success strengthened Soviet prestige abroad and refuted the charge that the Soviet order could not produce significant works of art.[39] Much as in the case of Kameneva's outfit, the initial famine-related concept behind IAH soon expanded to a much broader set of image-shaping projects.

There were, however, differences and rivalries between Kameneva's and Münzenberg's initiatives. Kameneva, in Moscow, placed great emphasis on the reception of foreign visitors, and settled on cultural and scientific exchange as the main vehicle for her activities; Münzenberg's activities among intellectuals, while a personal forté, were nonetheless a sideshow for mass political propaganda. Coming out of the early 1920s conjuncture, however, the two functioned together as part of the network of new communist institutions dealing with the image of the Soviet Union abroad.[40] Like Kameneva, who started her work by taking the "left-overs" from bourgeois philanthropy, Münzenberg always put propaganda and the operations of his organization ahead of any actual famine relief.[41]

In a movement that initially scorned or feared bourgeois intellectuals, both Münzenberg and Kameneva, in their own ways strong and independent operators, cleared the way for cementing Soviet and Comintern backing for intensive, patient, and artful work among groups that many communist militants would have preferred simply to attack. Münzenberg had seemingly endless energy and a rare talent for drawing people in; Kameneva had the skills and polish to forge working relations with Western scientific and cultural elites. Certainly, Münzenberg's claim on resources in the 1920s was greater than that of Kameneva's, but by the 1930s the Soviet state was allocating vast sums to receiving the most famous foreign intellectual dignitaries. Kameneva pursued a deliberate strategy of keeping a focus on cultural and scientific activities and a low-key and ostensibly neutral tone in publications; Münzenberg, while using fronts to avoid the stigma of Comintern sponsorship, was more inclined to a staccato burst of high-profile campaigns—against fascism, foreign intervention in the USSR, and so on.[42] Both Kameneva and Münzenberg were creators of institutions that required a degree of organizational independence and ideological flexibility.[43]

VOKS as a Front Organization in Moscow

By 1924, a consensus had emerged in Moscow that a larger commitment to cultural diplomacy was needed. Given suspicions about Soviet and Comintern activities in many countries, several schemes emerged to disengage the new effort from the Soviet state. First, Foreign Affairs proposed a "private society" (*chastnoe obshchestvo*) to succeed OBI for "Cultural Ties with the West" (*Obshchestvo kul'turnoi sviazi s Zapadom*). Kameneva canvassed the opinion of prominent Bolshevik intellectuals, explaining that it had become "politically inconvenient" to continue to run cultural ties through the Soviet state. "Do you think it advisable to create a 'social organization'? Foreign Affairs is coming out in favor of this latter solution, but also considers government funding necessary for the work of such a 'Society for Cultural Ties Abroad.'"[44] A special commission headed by N. N. Narimanov was created to found this new society, VOKS, which began functioning in April 1925. Given state funding and party control, the question marks Kameneva and others ironically placed around the words "society" and "social organization" signified that its independent status was a fiction for outsiders, especially bourgeois foreigners. VOKS was created as a front organization in the heart of Moscow. As Commissar of Health Nikolai Semashko advised Kameneva, using reasoning she herself was fully to adopt:

> It seems to me that given the importance of ties with the cultured West (*s kul'turnym Zapadom*) and those achievements you in part have managed to make, these relations abroad should be made not by a [state] agency or interagency organ but by a special Society, following the example of those existing abroad (the Societies of the Friends of Russia), which in fact might be able to capture broad cultural circles.[45]

VOKS's charter (*Ustav*), ratified in the Kremlin on August 8, 1925 and published in *Pravda* on August 14, codified the blend of tasks at home and abroad that had emerged in the early 1920s. Abroad, its tasks included cultivating relations with foreign organizations, the press, and individuals and running the new international network of cultural friendship societies. Organizing exhibitions, arranging travel by Soviet figures, and publishing bulletins and guidebooks were also part of the mission. More broadly, VOKS was to cultivate the image of Soviet culture and society by providing the press and others with "information" about the USSR. At home, its tasks included receiving and guiding foreign visitors, providing materials published abroad to relevant Soviet organizations, and hosting foreign scholars and cultural figures. VOKS's status as a "society" came into play with the formation of a galaxy of "sections" that involved leading non-party figures in various fields, initially including film, science and technology, law, museums, ethnography, and pedagogy. The list of the society's "founders" included high officials like Lunacharskii, Foreign Affairs Press Section Deputy Shubin, science administrator and Sovnarkom executive manager (Upravdelami) N. P. Gorbunov, and representatives of the Comintern and Central Committee, along with a range of figures such as the cooperative non-party permanent secretary of the Academy of Sciences, the orientologist S. F. Ol'denburg, the pedagogue A. P. Pinkevich, and academician V. N. Ipat'ev, a leading chemist.[46]

Kameneva initially thought of these sections as useful camouflage: "These scientific, literary etc. sections will endow to the work an externally civil (*obshchestvennyi*) character."[47] She soon realized, however, that they offered greater possibilities: the various VOKS sections would draw in leading figures from their respective fields, facilitate the establishment of ties with foreign scholars and cultural figures, and expand the clout of the organization beyond the capabilities of its permanent staff. What was not made public was that the VOKS administration (*praveleniia*), in a fashion typical of Soviet state institutions in the 1920s, also had a communist "fraction," in addition to the five VOKS "responsible workers" who were Communists.

The institution Kameneva created was at best a modest, mid-level force in power-political terms within the party-state, but, at the same time, it was a major player among agencies dealing with shaping public opinion abroad. In terms of scientific and cultural travel and exchanges, it became crucial. Its Moscow center and leadership was relatively small (a staff of 60 in 1929), but it was a sprawling operation; VOKS representatives abroad held primary posts elsewhere, mostly at embassies, and their number was increasing around the globe. Bureaus within VOKS included those for the reception of foreigners, press, book exchange, film exchange, banquets, exhibitions, translations, and the photographic agency Russ-Foto. These were important priorities, but "the basic operative unit" of VOKS, something that became the main counterpart to the public sections, was its geographically based *referentura,* or analysis unit. *Referenty* would follow the cultural life of their assigned countries and locate foreigners who could become "conveyors of our cultural influence."[48] The VOKS *referentura* mirrored the structure of Foreign Affairs, except that the first four VOKS sectors all dealt with Europe and the United States; at the end of 1926 the "Eastern" section was still not set up.[49]

The Soviet intelligentsia was thus accorded a prominent yet subordinate role in VOKS, and VOKS participated in what might be called the Sovietization of civic life. Mobilizing Soviet intellectuals to work with foreigners for the goals of the state, and sponsoring their travel abroad, marked the advent of a new kind of Soviet *obshchestvennost'*, an untranslatable term connoting the public sphere, civil society, the educated public, socially and politically engaged groups, and even the intelligentsia. A sharp reduction of non-governmental ("social") organizations came in the late 1920s, after which the number of all-Russian or all-union institutions dropped precipitously, to fewer than twenty in 1934–38. In the early 1930s, the VOKS sections lost importance, and the *referentura* became dominant in its activities.[50] By that time, however, the sections were deemed less necessary. Expectations for non-party intellectuals to play proscribed "civic" roles in "international" activities—such as signing petitions and meeting visitors—became much stricter toward the end of the 1920s. The history of VOKS reveals how prominent members of the Soviet intelligentsia were involved and mobilized, becoming one of Soviet cultural diplomacy's greatest assets.

VOKS's status as a society was not merely a fiction for external consumption, then, but part of a broader project to involve and mobilize the Soviet intelligentsia, in this case in international cultural relations. This status carried with it unexpected political ramifications, however. It meant that VOKS, deprived of a single oversight agency, became something of an orphan within the Soviet bureaucratic hierarchy. Initially, it had seemed that this role, at least for VOKS's precursor OBI, might be at least partly filled by Foreign Affairs, which would have fit the model of cultural diplomacy in European countries.[51] While the new agency continued to maintain close contacts with Foreign Affairs and foreign policy goals, VOKS developed according to a unique political paradigm. The secret police had a strong presence in VOKS's work, particularly in terms of invitations to foreigners, their presence inside the USSR, and information-gathering activities about them. High-level strategic decisions involved the Central Committee and party leadership. All the same, VOKS was not the special province of any one supervisor. As Kameneva told the Central Committee in 1928, VOKS made sure to "agree in advance with all interested organizations (Foreign Affairs, the Executive Committee of the Comintern, the Commissariat of Enlightenment, the OGPU, etc.)." The "society's" anomalous position within the party-state left it open to bureaucratic attack, even as the scale and importance of its activities increased dramatically after 1925. In 1929, Kameneva noted that each commissariat had its own set of international activities, but "each year the existence of our organization was put into question."[52]

One bureaucratic victory Kameneva did score for VOKS was to keep its international work "centralized,"—that is, it fended off attempts to involve the union republics as independent actors in cultural diplomacy. Proposals to involve the union republics more substantially were present during the debates about the creation of VOKS in 1924, but Kameneva used all her efforts to ensure that the new organ would be "authoritative" and therefore "all-union." A Central Executive Committee official she enlisted in this cause wrote that any new organization that involved the union republics as separate players on the international stage would "undoubtedly lower its authority abroad."[53] VOKS moved quickly to establish offices in the union republics.[54] To be sure, there were a number of challenges to this centralization in the 1920s and VOKS could not simply monopolize all international contacts by decree. But after 1925, VOKS was in a position to gather material from the union republics and present it in its foreign-language materials distributed abroad within its own framework. For example, Kameneva turned to the Transcaucasian party organization to provide materials for a special VOKS bulletin. The explicit goals were to counter Georgian and Menshevik émigrés active in Europe and to shape French interest in Armenia, to present a positive image of the Baku oil industry to "capitalist" and intellectual circles, and to show the "real successes" of Soviet power in developing national culture and the liberation of women.[55] The twin emphasis on achievements and counter-campaigns was also the cornerstone of VOKS press and public opinion work in other areas.

The divergences between the organs of the Comintern and of the Soviet state formed the context for a more serious political challenge to VOKS from the Agitprop Department of the Comintern. Headed by exiled Hungarian communist leader Béla Kun and the German writer Alfred Kurella, the Comintern's Agitprop maintained one of its primary levers in communist party publications abroad. A combination of the need for covert action in Western states and the period of United Front tactics with other parties, however, led to a new emphasis on broadening the scope of operations to include "masked" or front organizations (not only IAH, but also International Red Aid, the Pacifist League, and others). Ludmila Stern has recently argued that the Comintern forged the prototype for international cultural propaganda and the engagement of foreign intellectuals by VOKS and other Soviet state organs.[56] Yet the multi-agency system that included both organizations first emerged out of the conjuncture of the early 1920s and matured in tandem in the period 1923–26. Not only were there overlapping memberships and common subordination to the Soviet party leadership, but interagency commissions attempted to systematize work precisely in this period—for example, coordinating "placing information abroad" between the Comintern, Foreign Affairs, ROSTA, the telegraph agency Inprekorr, and VOKS (which was given the task of propagating "cultural information").[57] What Stern portrays as the Comintern's innovative methods—placing "counter-material" (*kontrmaterial*) in its organs to parry without explicitly replying to "anti-Soviet" publications in European countries, and the organization of "campaigns" around specific themes—were pursued in the early 1920s in the Soviet response to the Russian emigration, in the former case, and developed as a component part of the Central Committee Agitprop's modus operandi, in the latter.

What can be said is that within the new, interrelated system that emerged in 1923–26, Comintern organs developed distinguishable emphases and goals. For example, if a cornerstone of VOKS "information" work was to highlight Soviet "achievements" (*dostizheniia*), the Comintern's Agitprop considered its focus the "achievements" specifically of the Communist Party. Its counter-material was aimed at other political parties, countering the "slanderous campaigns" of Social Democracy and anarchism, and the intended audience was concentrated in communist and labor movements.[58] Just as the Central Committee's Agitprop was a hard-line agency within the organs of Soviet cultural policy at home, disdaining "cultural-enlightenment" work as insufficiently political, so the Comintern's Agitprop looked down on VOKS's missions of targeting the "bourgeois" intelligentsia, which included non-communist leftists and establishment elites.

In a mid-1926 power play, the Comintern's Agitprop called for a reorientation of VOKS's work abroad to encompass "proletarian organs" and the communist press. VOKS's orientation around the "bourgeois intelligentsia" should be coordinated with communist parties in order to create more "ideological unity" with communist propaganda work, and the Comintern itself would exercise a "certain control" (*eine gewisse Kontrolle*) over VOKS. To the Comintern's Agitprop, Kameneva replied vigorously in German that "the whole work of VOKS is based on communist ground and is present in the propaganda of Soviet culture. How can one make it into an opposite of communist propaganda?" With justification, she insisted here and elsewhere that if VOKS were to become an appendage of the Comintern, it would lose the chance to cultivate many of the "big names" among European intellectuals.[59] Similar skirmishes followed in the years to come.[60]

Münzenberg went ahead with his separate, labor-oriented organization close to the communist parties, confusingly called the Bund der Freunde der Sowjetunion (League of Friends of the Soviet Union). He enraged Kameneva and VOKS officials by enlisting some of the very same intellectuals who were members of the VOKS-run cultural friendship societies.[61]

Attacks on VOKS for making intellectuals and not the "working masses" into its main priority did not subside until the mid-1930s, after the end of the militant "proletarianization" policies of the Great Break.[62] The critique of Kameneva's orientation toward the intelligentsia gained traction especially in the period starting in the late 1920s, when workerism and "proletarianization" policies held the cachet of ideological orthodoxy and the appeal of potentially influential "mass" work.

Kameneva, repeatedly forced to counter such sentiments from within and without, wielded a pragmatic argument: VOKS had more than enough difficulty consolidating relations with "scholars and the intelligentsia" in foreign countries.[63] To militants, her definition of VOKS's international work in terms of culture and the bourgeois intelligentsia smacked of "conciliationism" and potentially rendered the cadres of cultural diplomacy politically vulnerable, because they were open to bourgeois contagion. This represented one of the most important live links between external missions and domestic politics and culture.

In the end, Kameneva successfully fended off all attempts to reorient VOKS. By 1927, an intertwined multi-agency communist system that combined a rough functional division of labor with a typology of foreigners defined by class and political affiliation had matured. As a 1927 report signed by Kameneva put it:

> In the system created by the party for foreign relations, VOKS is assigned tasks that are completely precise in definition. If the Comintern and Profintern concern themselves with the workers movement, then VOKS, aiding these organizations, influences (*obrabatyvaet*) an intermediary stratum—the intelligentsia "public" (*obshchestvennost'*) not entering [the other organizations'] field of vision, using the flag of a "neutral" society for penetrating these circles.[64]

In 1927, Kameneva won a Central Committee resolution that ratified this division of labor among organizations conducting international work. On another occasion that year, she ventured another take on defining VOKS's mission by referring to "uniting the Left intelligentsia around the idea of Soviet culture."[65]

Yet any such division between science or culture and politics was dubious in Bolshevik thought and ideology, especially in those years. Ironically for someone for whom the political dimensions of cultural exchange were so important, Kameneva's drive to focus on the Western "intelligentsia" forced her into the position that cultural affairs could be considered a separate realm: "We deal with culture in its pure form, insofar as general culture is outside of politics and economics."[66] This was an unfortunate formulation for such a savvy administrator, appearing to clash with Bolshevik class analysis and Leninist politics.

Kameneva defined this division of labor and asked for political confirmation so often precisely because it was vulnerable. In practice, moreover, none of the propositions she made about it was strictly true. The Comintern, as we have seen, was also involved with non-communist intellectuals. In its work with visiting foreigners and in its publications, VOKS could hardly limit itself to presenting Soviet "culture," because foreigners were interested in the entire Soviet system. VOKS never engaged solely with leftists or the intelligentsia, however defined. Nationalists and right-wing figures fascinated by the Soviet example, as well as non-leftist scholars, were constituencies, and in practice, a wide array of tourists and other visitors used VOKS's services, especially before the rise of Intourist in 1929.[67] Kameneva had fought tenaciously to carve out and defend a roughly defined sphere for her brainchild. The intense politicization of culture during the Great Break at the end of the 1920s, during the first phase of Stalinism, would jolt, but not destroy, the definition of roles and the approaches taken within the party-state system of international work set up under NEP.

Yet Kameneva was aware of the bigger picture: the unprecedented scope of Soviet ambitions to choreograph foreign visits and manage the external cultural relations of the entire country, even if those ambitions were far from realized. She had reason to boast to an audience of VOKS guides in 1927 that no comparable institution existed elsewhere, given that cultural diplomacy in other countries was largely a subdivision of ministries of foreign affairs.[68] VOKS had built on the historically novel aspirations of the party, state, and secret police to control travel and information to and from the Soviet Union. The most unusual aspects of Soviet cultural diplomacy lay elsewhere, however, for they grew out of the intensely didactic thrust of Soviet political culture itself. Foreigners would be not merely influenced, but won over and converted, and if that were not possible, they could at least be taught to see the Soviet system through different eyes.

Guide, Rank, Teach

The approximately 100,000 foreign visitors and tens of thousands of foreign residents of the interwar years were a diverse population in many ways: country of origin, occupation and class, motivation for travel, and political outlook. While favorable interest in the Soviet experiment was at its height, even many non-committed travelers would not have made the journey without the political factor. Those with the greatest stake in singing the praises of Soviet socialism were not representative of travelers as a whole.[69] In other words, despite the prominence of Sovietophilia, it was far from hegemonic. What did unite large numbers of travelers was their preoccupation with personally evaluating the Soviet experiment. Even for those professionals, tourists, or other travelers not explicitly planning to report back in the press or in books on their impressions, the very nature of the trip to the land of socialism made instant appraisal into a priority.

The Soviets wanted very much not merely to shape those outside impressions but to recruit sympathizers and identify enemies, and they set themselves the task of evaluating the foreigners. Soviet scrutiny of these visiting personifications of the "West" was intense. The height of intellectual sympathy for Soviet socialism in this period hardly prompted the international wing of the party-state to let down its apprehensive guard, nor were the Soviets complacent about how easy it was to manipulate naive foreigners. If anything, the opposite was the case; the Party was highly suspicious of even the most ardent friends.

Along with the new institutions of cultural diplomacy, a new Soviet culture of evaluation emerged in the early 1920s that attempted to measure and predict foreign visitors' judgments and to gather useful information. Soviet evaluators had to find ways to counter the most common criticisms; they inevitably grappled with the issue of explaining, and often deflecting, outsiders' assertions of Western superiority. For these reasons, the nascent Soviet system of receiving foreigners, lashed as it was from the outset to the complementary external task of influencing the Soviet image abroad, became a site of innovation for ways to teach foreigners to focus on Soviet achievements and the bright future rather than on grim poverty, backwardness, or repression.

If political and ideological evaluations were so important to both foreigners and Soviets, why did the Soviets so persistently try to assess visitors' cultural level? In the context of the great concern with "culturedness" already present in the Bolshevik project in the 1920s, it is clear that by judging Western visitors' cultural level, often harshly and derisively, Soviet evaluators implicitly showed they stood above the stereotypical association of Europeanness with cultural superiority.

This strategy was combined with highly practical motivations, as well. One of the earliest significant Soviet reflections on the new methods for receiving foreigners, written by OBI around August 1924, demonstrates that many features of what became standard VOKS practices were already in place. First, "record-keeping" (*otchetnost'*) had turned into an important part of the operation, even though at that point only fifty-three foreigners had been welcomed over the previous twelve months.[70] Second, visitors were sorted by importance and connections: Kameneva personally received only those visitors who came with recommendations from Münzenberg's IAH or were known to her own staff. Finally, an embryonic mode of guiding foreigners proceeded in "three directions." The first was to effectively respond to foreigners' questions. The second was to interest them in questions they did not ask but that had significance in illuminating the progress of socialist construction. This was to be done with great care, so that foreigners would not, as it was put, believe they were being shown a "Potemkin village." The third, which became VOKS's trademark approach, was to flexibly tailor individual visits through meetings and visits with key figures and institutions. In each field, from medicine to pedagogy to theater, "The foreigner above all will be shown in general terms the distinguishing feature of the given issue in the USSR...Familiarizing foreigners with the issues that interest them is not done mechanically, [but] by showing the source where they might receive an answer." This methodology necessitated classifying the foreigner from the start: it was crucial to know whether the visitor was an uncultured "dilettante, seeking only impressions," or a qualified and knowledgeable "specialist" who needed to be steered into contact with "responsible" (otvetstvennye), that is high-level, Soviet cultural figures and officials. Most interesting of all, the anonymous OBI analyst felt it important to conclude with a sweeping assertion of revolutionary superiority over all non-Soviets. "Experience...has shown the following: foreigners, getting to know the life of the USSR, approach the question they are studying with that narrowness of vision characteristic of foreigners; they do not have that broad view of the question that was created by the revolution."[71] Only Soviets possessed that.

As enterprises' "self-financing" deepened after the introduction of NEP in the early-mid 1920s, there was a movement to restrict perks, such as free housing, for all foreign sympathizers who appeared impecunious, even as they remained widespread for privileged visitors. A tension appeared between political and economic goals in hosting foreigners, which was heightened by the inadequacy of Soviet facilities, especially lodging. As a result, restrictions were put in place for those not vetted or approved—yet another function of evaluation. In November 1923, Foreign Affairs second-in-command M. M. Litvinov went as far as to imply that extending non-monetary privileges to foreign visitors in conditions of NEP would be flouting the standards of civilized behavior. The habit of supporting "guests of the Government" was begun in the "pre-NEP period," before there were "private stores," restaurants, and hotels, he explained, but now "guests in the USSR, as in every civilized state, must support themselves." His prescriptive tone, however, was prompted by the fact that all sorts of expensive benefits were still being distributed to favored guests upon invitation or arrival.[72] The evaluation of foreigners' cultural level along with political outlook, so prominent in the often acerbic Soviet reports on foreigners, served a practical purpose here, too, in establishing their stature.

Guides, despite considerable variation in their reports, produced a distinct genre of evaluations that centered on the subject's attitude toward the Soviet system and included an assessment of cultural level. One convention was to establish a factual, scientific tone through the detailed elaboration of times, places visited, and other basic information. Usually the report would proceed to a description of conversations and events, and toward the end it would summarize the *kharakteristika*—a term that literally meant character-ization and was also applied to the way party members, workers, and employ-ees were described in domestic documents ranging from biographical referrals to purge results. By 1929, these three components of the report had become formalized.[73] Typical evaluations from the late 1920s and 1930s included descriptions such as: "a serious, intelligent, and curious person"; "narrowly specialized"; and "something of a sympathizer, but not very well oriented and in general not well developed" (*razvityi*).[74] In the first case, the guide was prais-ing the pro-Soviet musicologist Zdeněk Nejedlý, the head of the Czechoslovak Society of Friends.

VOKS guides needed a working knowledge of foreign languages, so before the late 1920s, many came from privileged class backgrounds, which may explain why they were frequently not party members. Even so, many had pro-Soviet credentials. Biographical information in the archives shows that a good number were Jewish; VOKS, in fact, had a reputation for employing Jews, many of whom had seized the chance for assimilation and rapid promo-tion into the ranks of the party-state after 1917.[75] After all, in the 1920s even the rank-and-file cadres of the secret police's Foreign Section reorganized by Feliks Dzerzhinskii at the end of 1920 (Inostrannyi Otdel VChK, or INO), the major organ of international espionage and reportage on international poli-tics for the Soviet leadership, were non-party and non-proletarian figures who often worked simultaneously for other Soviet international agencies or media.[76] Throughout the 1930s, VOKS staff boasted large contingents of females as well as Jews. Many VOKS employees continued to be cultivated members of the intelligentsia, which provided another reason why their reports intertwined culture and politics.[77]

One guide who produced some of the most scathing, yet penetrating, eval-uations was a non-party Jew, an English teacher named Aleksandr Lobovich Trakhterov. Born in 1900 to a merchant family in the Donbass, Trakhterov had served in the combat troops of the Cheka until 1922, and had never lived abroad. One can only imagine his interactions with Edward C. Finch, a Republican state senator and respectable founding father of the city of Aberdeen in Washington State, a man with a background in real estate, rail-roads, and finance. Finch arrived with his niece and spent his time (as did quite a few wealthier visitors) buying up palace antiques. Trakhterov blasted him for his arrogance, his "bone-headed (*tupoi*) undeveloped taste," his "greediness for titles and insignia," and everything else "typical of his class." The overall evaluation: "a type of provincial financial big-wig (*tuza*)...in Mr. Finch there is beautifully manifested the interesting combination of financial might and internal spiritual emptiness of America." This recalls the pre-revolutionary insistence on a Western lack of "spirituality" as a means of transcending

superiority in other realms, except that in Soviet guides' reports this is frequently recast as a bourgeois—and in this case specifically non-European—
lack of culturedness.

All the same, neither the shadow sparring of the VOKS guides with the
Westerners' arrogance nor the ideological exposé of their flaws negated psychological insight about individual personalities. Trakhterov, in 1928, painted
the following portrait of the American coal engineer Sidney W. Farnham, an
unusually energetic yet "typical American engineer": "Completely at home
in the technical details of his profession...Mr. Farnham builds his theory of
economic prosperity according to an all-American 'standard stamp': the basis
of welfare is 'personal efficiency,' that is, the individual productivity of labor,
which in his opinion is bound to stimulate personal competition based on private capital – and not at all on the principles of socialist construction, which
appear to him as very weak stimulus for productivity."[78] Reducing visitors to
typical examples of their class or occupation, Trakhterov still felt compelled to
explain and polemicize against the key weaknesses of their worldviews.

Guides reported extensively on the merest hint from any foreigner about
Soviet insufficiency, including in the realm of culture or everyday life, in part
because to do so was a form of political insurance—they needed to suggest
how they had corrected the criticism. The exception proves the rule: when the
American director Herbert Biberman (who during the McCarthy era was one
of the "Hollywood Ten" jailed and blacklisted in 1947 for refusing to answer
questions from the House Committee on Un-American Activities) visited in
October 1927, he toured Soviet theaters and met with artists and directors.
There he happened to express the view that Soviet poster art "had not achieved
the level it could." The "guide-translator Gal'perin"—born in 1905, Jewish, a
non-party student at the Second Moscow University who nonetheless had good
political credentials as a member of the editorial board of the journal *Krasnyi
student* [Red Student]—neglected to report if or how he countered this innoc-
uous, yet negative, judgment. This provoked a big blue question mark (and presumably an inquiry) from the VOKS administrative reader.[79] More typically,
guides took enormous care to show how they corrected "wrong" ideas. In addition, the contents of political conversations were recorded in depth, such as
an American journalist's discussion with Lunacharskii, who assured him that
Soviet censorship was not nearly as great as believed abroad and mostly suppressed pornography.[80] When a father and son from Cincinnati by the name
of Kenig were led by M. Geiman on a tour of the Lenin Museum and a china
factory in September 1927, they were surprised not only by the "great number
of beggars and homeless children in Moscow" but also by the guide's description of the great measures the state was taking to fight child homelessness. The
guide's evaluations suggested how positive impressions of political sympathy

and evaluations of culturedness could be linked: "I must note the extremely sympathetic attitude of Mr. Kenig to Soviet Russia... In general Mr. Kenig and his father produce an impression of highly cultured people... The questions they posed show a serious interest in [socialist] Construction in the USSR."[81]

The guides' reports were a form of surveillance, reporting on the activities and utterances of their foreign charges. But they were also part of a broader information-gathering project, the creation of dossiers on visitors and foreigners of interest. Guides' reports (*otchety*) were numbered and could be accessed by name of the guide and the foreigner involved; the "diaries" of VOKS's Department for the Reception of Foreigners (*Otdel po priemu inostrantev*) were cross-referenced with the guide reports. A card catalogue (*kartoteka*) of foreigners was arranged alphabetically. In 1929, the catalogue was portrayed as a working record of what foreigners had seen, their interests and conversations, and how they had been evaluated during their visits.[82] As we shall see, a major effort of VOKS officials and *referenty* (as well as the broader party-state system involved in Western public opinion) was devoted to tracking how favorable or negative visitors' publications in the press and elsewhere were after their return home.

The VOKS reports served other uses, too. In conversations, sometimes with guides but frequently with higher-level officials, foreign visitors were routinely pumped for information about figures of interest. To give just one example, in 1928, French communist intellectual Henri Barbusse provided an "evaluation" of Romain Rolland—then a pacifist but steadily moving closer to the status of friend of the Soviet Union—as a person "who always leaves a path for retreat behind him." This was registered, along with Barbusse's reservations about organizing a trip for Rolland to the USSR. Guides were also in a position to gather information about foreigners' professional activities and business dealings; for example, details of the American writer Sinclair Lewis' negotiations with the State Publishing House (Gosizdat) in 1927 were recorded and filed, along with the guide's speculations about his sincerity and motivations.[83] One should not exaggerate VOKS's efficiency, but it is likely that the secret police had access to VOKS records.

The party-state thus gathered surveillance and registered information on foreign visitors in a fashion that corresponded with its efforts to keep tabs on the domestic population. The literary historian Leonid Maksimenkov, referring not only to VOKS but also to later organizations, such as the Union of Writers Foreign Section, speaks of "a process of sorting" that turned into an "accountant's totalizing count and recount."[84] This constant updating of files on foreigners was a form of assessing individuals, not entire categories of human beings. Thus, foreign guests, with their elevated importance, corresponded with the keeping of individual records on personnel and political figures within the Soviet Union far more than it did with the blunt aggregates of social engineering, which "reduced the population from a complicated mass of individuals to a range of simplified types."[85] By recording sympathetic and critical actions and comments, the VOKS system of information gathering permitted officials to track levels of friendliness over time and to prioritize resources for inviting and hosting in an advantageous way.

The VOKS information-gathering system that emerged in the 1920s serves as a reminder that the secret police's activities in surveillance and classification were but one part of a broader effort that involved an entire archipelago of party-state organizations. A main goal of information–gathering on foreigners in the new cultural diplomacy was to win them over and convert them into friends, bearing out those historians who have emphasized how the Soviet state ideologically measured outlooks in order to transform them.[86] On the other hand, data gathering on foreigners can also be considered a form of classification that established undesirables by recording their dubious activities and thoughts, fixing the stigma of enmity. It thus conforms with the views of historians who have argued for the key importance of Soviet registration (*uchet*) of compromising information in marking enemies.[87] Ultimately, in the case of foreigners, as elsewhere, the branding of individuals and the urge to use information as a form of influence appear as intertwined functions within Soviet surveillance.[88] The difference between the system directed inward at Soviet citizens and that directed outward toward visitors was that strategically important foreigners were routinely given far more leeway about their pasts and ideological outlooks than Soviets, whose paper trails could turn deadly long before the cataclysm of the Great Terror.

As in so many other areas, VOKS's aspirations (and, by extension, those of the entire multi-agency apparatus for receiving foreigners and influencing foreign opinion) greatly exceeded its capabilities. The VOKS archives are filled with constant and sometimes comical problems with fluency in foreign languages and political acumen, as well as basic lack of familiarity with cultural context in dealing with visitors. Materials were sent abroad sporadically or with a large degree of randomness. These human failings were combined with poor facilities, long delays, disappearing transports, lost baggage, and so on, which hurt or spoiled relations with many guests. Bureaucratic bumbling and gross inefficiency, well-known features of the Soviet bureaucracy writ large, permeated contacts with foreigners. In 1925, Leonid Krasin, then at the Commissariat of Foreign Trade and an old hand at foreign relations, lectured his colleagues on how properly to conduct affairs with French scientists:

> Abroad they have their own habits and customs. If some scholar or litterateur writes to you with one or another question and does not

receive from you a written reply in the next few days, then this rudeness, extremely common here, will spoil relations with the given person, in all probability forever. It is not hard to see what kind of disappointment is produced in foreigners as a result of that chaotic and inefficient approach that we often take in establishing cultural ties.[89]

In preparing for the arrival of a high-level German parliamentarian in 1927, Chicherin, in a fit of pique, called VOKS an incompetent institution and told Foreign Affairs official Vladimir Lorents that "one should never rely on VOKS too much." He had done so in the recent past for an important French visitor, and the result had been a "harmful" (*zlovrednaia*) book produced in response to VOKS's "poor fulfillment of its obligations."[90] VOKS's height in terms of its effectiveness and stature came during two periods, its rise under Kameneva in 1925–29 and the Popular Front years of 1934–36. The periods when the organization was purged and rocked by waves of ideological vigilance, first in 1930–32 and to a far greater extent in 1937–39, hampered operations and foreshadowed the giant but bumbling and relatively low-level epigone of the post-war years.

Inexorably, the harsh spotlight of evaluation that the guides trained on foreigners was turned on the guides themselves. As the political demands on guides increased, and cadres from non-party elite backgrounds increasingly came under fire in the late 1920s, VOKS officials deprecated their political skills. On January 2, 1927, Kameneva presided over the opening of VOKS's new training courses for guides. In the new system of guide education, thirty-two subjects were studied, many of them (political economy, Lenin and Leninism, and other "political literacy" subjects) staples of party schools and the Marxist social sciences. What was unusual was the focus on learning about the outside world: instruction was given in the "constitution and state structures of the most important countries of the world," the rights of foreigners in the USSR, the Comintern, and world geography. Guides already were required to be versed in one cultural field, but here they would also concentrate on areas of "socialist construction" routinely important in work with foreign guests, such as labor legislation, Soviet education, the national question, and women in the USSR. Finally, the courses taught translation and the preparation of "reports, theses and resolutions."[91]

The work of the guide-translators, Kameneva told the group, would be utterly different from that of other countries' tour guides, who mechanically repeated the information in tourist books, "looking at views and ancient castles and the like." VOKS guides should be highly qualified not merely in terms of language; they needed to be "highly literate in civic affairs," a phrase that might be meaningfully rendered as adept Soviet political animals. Guides should study each group for its specifics in advance; they should know how to address and explain the thorniest questions (*bol'nye voprosy*) in a comprehensible manner. They should be skilled enough to independently "verify the methods and manner of acting on the foreigner."[92] One tool, given that so few visitors were fluent in Russian, was creative, partial, or openly mendacious translation. This was an admitted focus of VOKS's Translators Department, which that year had 300 translators on its lists. The VOKS translator had to be "politically literate" and "he himself must choose" what to say—in addition, of course, to translating "exactly."[93]

Far-reaching implications flowed from the innovations VOKS, and by extension the entire multi-agency system that emerged in 1923–26, developed to present Soviet socialism to foreigners. For new guides, Kameneva brilliantly encapsulated the approach of blaming the past and pointing toward the bright future. As she put it, foreigners must know of the terrible heritage of tsarism and the international blockade during the Civil War. "You know, for example, that our most vulnerable issue (*samoe bol'noe mesto*) is child homelessness... You need to know how to relate that this is our heritage... from the past." If the problems of the present were to be blamed on the past, the present would also appear much more promising if presented as the kernel of the bright future around the corner. "We cannot 'impress' foreigners with our economic wealth, although in science we are not backward," Kameneva continued. "We can only impress foreigners... from the point of view of speed [in which things are changing] and from the point of view of development."[94] Soviet reality needed to be presented not as it was, but as it was becoming.

An identical focus on heritage and achievements, the one shunting present problems into the past and the other magnifying present strengths by predicting the future, found its origins in the broader effort in 1923–26 to craft the Soviet image abroad. The Comintern's Agitprop may have placed special emphasis on the Soviet Communist Party so as to provide a model for foreign Communists, but the underlying stress on highlighting achievements was also present. The Comintern also placed emphasis on what might be called managed authenticity: whenever possible, the oppression of the tsarist past or the success of such social measures as workers' sanatoria should be expressed through the voices of ordinary workers and Soviet citizens.[95]

In keeping with the twin focus on receiving visitors at home and shaping public opinion abroad, the strategies developed for VOKS guides meeting foreigners on the ground were roughly similar to those reflected in VOKS publications. In keeping with Kameneva's expressed desire, the twelve issues of the VOKS bulletin in 1925–26, translated into major European languages, strove to keep a low-key approach that listed a range of Soviet publications and events. The red thread that ran through the articles on contemporary Soviet science, art, literature, exhibitions, music, and national cultures was that they were framed, often explicitly, in terms of "achievements." Here, though, the past was not solely invoked as the source of contemporary problems; efforts were made to prove that the Soviet Union preserved the best cultural and scientific legacies of the past, a theme that emerged as refutation of the post-1917 émigré charge that the Bolsheviks were destroying culture. The 200th jubilee of the Soviet Academy of Sciences in 1925, which happily combined preservation of high culture, the scientific achievements of the present, and the promise of the future, was featured in no fewer than three successive issues.[96]

There is evidence that the Soviets had more than a little success in "teaching" sympathetic foreigners to read Soviet reality simultaneously in light of yesterday and tomorrow, both in the 1920s and during the heyday of Socialist Realism.[97] Both temporal perspectives were strongly present in efforts to convince representatives of the "advanced West," who needed not only to hear about the future but also to appreciate the oppressive weight of the past. The fundamental approach of reorienting the observers' sense of the present was therefore at hand simultaneously in "information" aimed abroad and the efforts of VOKS guides enjoined to impress foreigners from the "point of view of development."

The Soviet culture of evaluation of individuals emerged in tandem with a highly hierarchical mental map of the globe implicit in the international cultural apparatus' orientation and writings. If the Soviet Union was leaping ahead, other countries and nations were ranked according to their place on the scale of development—industrial, technological, economic, and also cultural.

In 1926, for example, VOKS sponsored a short-lived journal, *West and East.* With a circulation of 5,000, it was designed, according to Kameneva, to inform Soviet readers about the outside world so that one could know the capitalist enemy better. The journal, as its title suggested, was to try to look in both directions, but Kameneva's introduction was mostly concerned with "bourgeois" countries, and when she spoke of knowledge of the world abroad, it was focused on "the countries with highly developed technology and economics." The eminent non-party orientologist Ol'denburg deliberately reversed the title of the journal in his own article, "East and West," lambasting ignorance of the East. Instead, he claimed, "We are free from European prejudices about the superiority of the West over the East, and in this is our great strength." Well before 1917, Ol'denburg and a number of prominent colleagues built Russian Oriental studies by propounding the notion that Russia could know the East better than could Europeans, a position that was radicalized along with anti-German sentiment in World War I and presaged anti-bourgeois positions after 1917.[98] In Kameneva's introduction to Ol'denburg, those "European" prejudices were well on display: when it came to the East, knowledge was important not to advance socialist construction but because it would be useful for Soviet nationalities' policies. The peoples of the East needed "help" in development, "help" in the reconstruction of their national cultures, and, because the intelligentsia there was small, "help" in "developing culture" (*v kul'turno-sozidatel'noi rabote*). The journal *West-East* itself had, aside from Ol'denburg's article, only a lone piece on Chinese language reform; it was heavily oriented toward European cultural events and, to a lesser extent, science and technology. Kameneva made her stance even more explicit when opening the courses for guides in 1927: the greatest goals (*maksimal'naia programma*) in international work were to share Soviet experience and "to study that technology, that science, that degree of achievement in scholarship that Europe and America have achieved."[99]

The teleological view of the world reflected in the hierarchical ranking of individuals and countries was not simple or inflexible, for cultural and political factors were inserted into it along with industrial and scientific levels of advancement. Soviet class analysis, proletarian internationalism, and revolutionary universalism could at least potentially invert some of the hierarchies born in nineteenth-century ideologies of progress, which purported to rank humanity by objective criteria ranging from levels of industrialization and national character to race. Someone like Ol'denburg, although himself highly concerned with European scientific literature and contacts, was an important exception to the crude exclusivity of Kameneva's "Western" orientation. But despite the exceptions, the ubiquitous practice of ranking foreigners' importance and orientation reinforced hierarchical assumptions.

The preoccupation with the West, moreover, went far beyond rhetoric. Even as European contacts and initiatives had been growing rapidly since the early 1920s, Kameneva reported to Chicherin in August 1925 that VOKS had "practically no ties" with China and had managed just a small exchange of scientific literature through the embassy in Japan. The disproportion was of course heightened by the practical factors of relative European proximity and difficulties of operating elsewhere, but it also reflected the priorities of the Old Bolshevik emigration with its European contacts and experiences. In fact, VOKS contacts with scholars in China and Japan were furthered only on the initiative of professors in the Far Eastern University in Vladivostok in 1925.[100] A friendship society in China was not founded until a full decade later, in October 1935, by which time the rise of authoritarian nationalism in Japan had necessitated the closing of the Japanese-Soviet Cultural Society. The most important exception to the rule was the Mexican Revolution, which made Mexico the first country in the Western hemisphere to establish diplomatic relations with the Soviets, facilitating visas and cultural exchange. Many visitors from the other revolutionary state were searching for way of jump-starting their own stalled revolution under relatively conservative Mexican presidencies.[101]

Certainly, Soviet cultural relations expanded steadily and became far more global in scope, especially in the 1930s; starting in the late 1920s, conditions were far more favorable for the Soviet cultivation of more extensive contacts in some non-Western countries. For example, "The solidity of friendly relations between the USSR and Turkey and the general internal direction of Kemalist policies has created broad opportunities for the development of cultural relations," as one country report put it in 1935. Yet, even in the most favorable Kemalist case, the VOKS analyst still depicted Soviet priorities in a fashion strikingly similar to Kameneva's conception of Soviet "help" in the East a decade earlier. Cultural relations were conceived as a one-way street, namely the "transfer to the Turks of the experience of our cultural construction in various areas, something that the Turks themselves view with great interest and attention."[102] The stance toward the "West" taken by the international wing of the party-state in the 1920s, VOKS included, was ambiguous in that propagation of Soviet "achievements" was tempered by a powerful craving to assimilate and import Western advances and even enlighten the Soviet population about them. When the agency that claimed as its own the realm of culture and the intelligentsia turned elsewhere, however, even when it came to some of the world's ancient civilizations and richest cultural traditions, there reigned an unselfconsciously superior, tutelary air.

" 'They' Were Everywhere"

No account of foreigners inside the Soviet Union can be complete without considering the several roles played by the organs of state security. The challenge in attempting to integrate one of the most powerful players among the agencies dealing with foreigners is that, unlike the records of the East German Stasi, Soviet documentation has remained mostly inaccessible. Despite some notable exceptions, most documents that have seen the light of day concern a handful of topics, such as the structure of the "organs," the administration of the Gulag, or reports on the "moods" of the population—not the involvement of the secret police with foreign visitors or international cultural initiatives. Yet, there is no doubt that a heavy secret police presence shaped the reception of foreigners by VOKS and other host organizations as well as the experiences of foreigners within the Soviet Union—often in ways about which the visitors themselves knew little or nothing. Piecing together what is available with fragments from the declassified archival records of VOKS and the extant memoir literature clarify some of the levels on which the Cheka/GPU/OGPU/NKVD had an impact on cultural diplomacy.

One key fact about the organizational structure of the secret police is that internal dissent and foreign contagion were institutionally connected. The primary secret police agency charged with operations abroad and foreigners within the USSR was the Foreign Department (*Inostrannyi otdel*, or INO), which, when founded in 1921, included a chancellery, a section of agents (*agenturnoe otdelenie*), and an office for visas (*biuro viz*). From 1923–29, INO was headed by Meier Abramovich Trilisser—born in 1883 in Astrakhan, party member since 1901, and Cheka member since 1918—who also became deputy director of the entire OGPU. Trilisser was the secret police official most heavily involved in VOKS affairs in the 1920s judging by the frequency with which his name appears on documents.[103]

Like other Soviet agencies involved in international operations, the Foreign Department had one foot in international operations and the other in domestic activities involving foreigners inside the USSR. Starting in 1921, it maintained an informer section (*osvedomitel'naia chast'*), and contacts between foreigners and Soviet citizens fell within its purview. INO itself was a subdivision of the Secret-Operative Administration (*Sekretno-Operativnoe Upravlenie*). During the famous "philosopher's steamboat" affair in 1922 that deported dozens of the country's most prominent scholars and thinkers deemed a threat to the new order, the Secret-Operative Administration began much more actively to maintain agents, informers, and an investigative *apparat* to uncover "anti-Soviet" movements among the Russian intelligentsia. At the same time, informers drawn from the network of secret associates (*sekretnye sotrudniki*, or *seksoty*) were, in addition to their role in surveillance throughout Soviet society, attached to foreign visitors or attended gatherings of foreigners. *Seksoty* generated the material for agent reports sent to the leadership of the secret police and the party.[104]

One set of documents from 1932 shows how VOKS facilitated secret police tracking of the movements of foreign visitors, including their visits to the sites of communism, by furnishing planned arrivals and excursions of individual foreigners for the upcoming months.[105] In addition, some VOKS representatives abroad, like other figures in Soviet international cultural institutions that were used to conceal espionage activity, were NKVD *rezidenty*. In terms of secret police recruitment of foreigners as agents, the young Soviet Union enjoyed the almost unique advantage that many potential spies were willing to cooperate out of ideological sympathy as opposed to material incentives. Anthony Blunt, the art historian and senior member of the famous Trinity College, Cambridge, spy ring that included Kim Philby, was recruited after he published a favorable account of an Intourist trip to the Soviet Union in 1935, during which he was observed by the agency's personnel.[106]

All VOKS work of significance, Kameneva assured the Central Committee in 1928, was coordinated in advance with the Party and the OGPU.[107] Secret police involvement had a range of environmental effects on the visits and interactions of foreigners inside the Soviet space, especially in the 1930s. "'They' were all dressed alike and looked the same," recalled the future dissident Raisa Orlova, who was a true believer of the 1930s generation and budding party literary intellectual when she began seven years of work in the VOKS Anglo-American Section. She was, of course, speaking of the *Chekisty*. Orlova and her co-workers had "become quite adept at distinguishing 'them' as a generic and typological concept." As she put it, "'They' were everywhere foreigners were...We knew that every recorded conversation we had with foreigners was forwarded to the NKVD." Orlova's recollections came after the Great Terror, but it has to be considered that long before that, VOKS employees, as well as various Soviet officials, intellectuals, and ordinary citizens coming into contact with foreigners, adjusted their behavior because of cognizance of secret police activity surrounding them.

Foreign visitors, on the other hand, especially sympathetic ones, were unlikely to grasp the extent of the secret police effort to monitor their activities. The American writer Theodore Dreiser, visiting in late 1927, took a strong dislike to a VOKS official he called in his diary a "diplomat who is also a spy or watch dog of some sorts." In Leningrad Dreiser complained that he was entirely surrounded by "VOX-men" who ushered him around, and it would be easy for a "fool" to get a false sense of his own importance.[108] The grand old man of the Popular Front, Romain Rolland, had access to information about Soviet life from his son-in-law, Sergei Kudashev, who remained a student at Moscow University after Mariia Kudasheva married Rolland. Even after Kudashev told Rolland about his discontent with the constant presence of policemen following his movements around Maxim Gorky's villa, Rolland remained unsure whether this represented surveillance designed to track them or a service to protect them.[109] Because the role of the secret police was much disputed among foreign observers, Sidney and Beatrice Webb promoted the idea that the NKVD's "constructive work" at its showcase secret-police commune for reforming juvenile delinquents at Bolshevo overshadowed lamentable, yet necessary, repression.[110] At the other end of the spectrum, the American engineer Zara Witkin, who did have dealings with the secret police during his employment by the Soviets in the early 1930s, became so obsessed with its influence that he attributed his failure in love with the Russian actress Emma Tsesarskaia to its long hand, something she much later credited to completely different reasons.[111]

The most profound area of secret police influence was at once the most hidden from view and the most mundane: the compilation of information on foreigners and those who met them. VOKS checked with INO before inviting foreigners, to see if there was any "compromising evidence" on figures who had previous Soviet contacts—such as work in the American Relief Administration in the early 1920s.[112] Sometimes the organs checked with VOKS on individual foreigners to see if it would vouch for them.[113] As suggested earlier, there is evidence that the catalogue of information VOKS compiled on foreigners— guide reports and evaluations, summaries of discussions and meetings, classifications as friends and enemies—was put at the disposal of various other institutions, including the secret police. These materials ranged widely, from the record of a long conversation between Kameneva and a visiting American agricultural expert whose contacts had relevance for the highly sought U.S. diplomatic recognition of the USSR to chance tidbits and remarks made by foreign guests. In the latter category, in 1936, VOKS dutifully sent the NKVD materials on conversations with foreigners that had a bearing, however slight, on security and espionage—including a French psychologist who mentioned Trotsky's brief sojourn in Paris and a Czech pedagogue who asked where Stalin lived in the Kremlin.[114]

The secret police itself was the most powerful player in developing Soviet practices of evaluation and recordkeeping, which preserved political and psychological "characterizations" of Soviets and foreigners alike. As it developed its own system for classifying foreigners, VOKS became an auxiliary player in the secret police's effort. For example, VOKS's portrait of one visitor—"a person in theory highly sympathetic to the Soviet system, but in practice more than anything else interested in his own personal career"—was received by the NKVD.[115] How the NKVD reacted, we do not know. But by summing up foreigners' profiles, such subjective interpretations, culled from conversations of guides and staff with visitors, held direct implications for operational practice.

All these activities were facilitated by their domestic setting, in which the party-state reigned supreme. Assembling information and exerting power would present many more challenges to the newly established initiatives of Soviet cultural diplomacy when it came to acting abroad.

2

Going West: Soviet "Cultural" Operations Abroad

In the fall of 1926, engraved invitations to an Arbat venue were sent to high party officials, diplomats, and intelligentsia luminaries. Dubbed an "evening of rapprochement" (*vecher sblizheniia*), the VOKS event was devoted to Soviet-German relations. The honored guest was the Berlin historian Otto Hoetzsch—a leading figure in German *Ostforschung*, a foreign policy expert with close ties to the German Foreign Office, and a center-right nationalist proponent of Germany's "Eastern orientation" that sought a post-Versailles alliance against the Western powers. Hoetzsch was also the spiritus rector of one of VOKS's most important partner organizations in Germany, the German Society for the Study of Eastern Europe (Deutsche Gesellschaft zum Studium Osteuropas).[1]

The diplomatic significance of the event was suggested by the attendance of Soviet Foreign Affairs deputy director Maksim Litvinov. In his speech, tailored for German ears, he emphasized the importance of the Rapallo treaty, signed by the two international pariahs in 1922, as well as the Soviet Union's anti-Versailles credentials. Also present were high Soviet foreign trade officials and a delegation of twelve industrialists from East Prussia, underscoring the economic importance of the reception, and the role cultural diplomacy could play in fostering international trade. VOKS was eager to cultivate a Russian-German Club in Königsberg, founded earlier in 1926, in which representatives of Soviet economic organs mixed with high East Prussian officials, industrial figures, and social scientists "primarily from right-wing circles." Introducing Hoetzsch, Kameneva frankly acknowledged that he was far from being "our ideological sympathizer." She announced that it was precisely for that reason that "he was trusted" when reporting positively on the USSR in his home country.[2] In doing so, Kameneva highlighted a major reason Soviet cultural diplomacy was interested in non-sympathizers such as Hoetzsch, a strategy that would come under increasing stress with the great clash brewing in Germany and Europe between extremes of Left and Right.

Hoetzsch, who had first visited Russia in 1904, made Kameneva's remarks about his intellectual distance from the Bolsheviks seem like a tactful understatement. Quoting Alesha from *The Brothers Karamazov*, he spoke of the "Russian land" with its birch trees as the basis for the "Russian soul." Playing on the Russian émigré slogan, *"Rossiia byla i Rossiia budet"* ("Russia was and Russia will be"), he summed up his geopolitical credo: *"Rossiia sushchestvuet"* ("Russia exists"). Telegrams and press releases emanating from Moscow left out the Russian soul but underlined the hopeful expressions of various speakers about Soviet-Weimar relations.[3]

The cultivation of ties with key individuals and partner organizations was perhaps the largest part of the VOKS's external operations, although this emerged in tandem with a broad repertoire of "informational" work connected to publications, photographs, exhibitions, and analysis of cultural and political developments abroad. The emergence of two classes of partners—ideological sympathizers and influential yet ideologically distant figures interested in Soviet connections for diplomatic, economic, or scholarly reasons—dates to the arrival of the first wave of foreign visitors in the early 1920s. More specifically, it was linked to two types of German visitors in the fall of 1923.

The first was Hoetzsch himself, the earliest "bourgeois" German scholar to visit the Soviets, during a month-long stay in Moscow that began on September 20, 1923. Earlier that year, Hoetzsch had played a leading role in setting up the Westphal Committee, a group of forty-four leading German professors and scientists, including Max Planck and twelve members of the Gesellschaft, who were interested in furthering scientific relations. Preparing for his visit, Hoetzsch wrote to the German ambassador in Moscow, Graf Ulrich von Brockdorff-Rantzau, an ardent proponent of the Eastern orientation, playing up the importance of cultural exchange for economic and political relations. In the midst of visits to museums and scholarly institutions, Hoetzsch met with Chicherin and consulted with Kameneva. On his return, in published statements well known to Kameneva and recalled by her during his 1926 visit, Hoetzsch's impressions were largely positive, although he compared the Communist Party to a religious order and lamented the disappearance of the old, cultivated classes. His visit paved the way for a longstanding partnership with VOKS.[4]

Before the illustrious bourgeois scholar had even departed, Kameneva welcomed a very different group of Germans: the pro-Soviet founding members of the newly created Society of Friends of the New Russia (*Gesellschaft der Freunde des neuen Russlands*), the prototype for VOKS's cultural friendship societies around Europe and, later, the world. Among the visitors were the radio engineer Georg Graf von Arco, the art critic Max Osborn, and the women's rights activist and pacifist Helene Stöcker. All three had attended the founding meeting of the Society of Friends in Berlin on June 1, 1923, and became core members of the society's presidium. Kameneva found that the visit cemented their outlook as actively "sympathizing" journalists and litterateurs.[5]

Germany deserves special attention because the Weimar Republic was at once a paradigmatic and an exceptional site for the nascent Soviet cultural diplomacy to confront this division between sympathizers and convenient bedfellows. At first the chief repository for hopes for a Soviet-type revolution, which waned considerably only after the failure of the "German October" in 1923, Germany became the crown jewel in Chicherin's foreign policy of "peaceful coexistence" after the Rapallo pact. Germany, of course, had occupied a position of exceptional importance in Russian scientific, scholarly, and cultural life in the two centuries preceding the revolution, and the particular international conjuncture, leading to favorable diplomatic and military cooperation of a kind decidedly absent in relations with all the other major powers (despite the counter-force of Gustav Stresemann's Westward tilt after 1923), served to perpetuate the special significance of German-Soviet connection in other realms. Despite all German and subsequent invocations of the "special relationship," however, this did not mean the Soviets were not actively seeking influence and partners elsewhere or that they consistently valued German connections more.[6] There were numerous rivalries among foreign scientists, experts, and organizations jockeying for access or scrambling for position within the great new Soviet "laboratory," which seemed to offer new vistas for experimentation. That said, Berlin was the epicenter of Soviet European-centered activities of all kinds in the 1920s, including VOKS's international cultural policy. For these reasons, innovations first applied in the German context—such as, most obviously, the friendship society—served as models for Soviet activities elsewhere.

Yet German-Soviet relations, despite their influence as precedents for the Soviets, proved exceptional in crucial ways. In the wake of Versailles, there were far more nationalist and right-wing partners with an "Eastern orientation" hoping to engage the Soviets; philo-Bolshevism was uniquely strong on both sides of the German political spectrum. To be sure, geopolitical factors and "enemy-of-my-enemy" thinking were hardly unique among the factors pushing many other Europeans toward the Soviet Union. For example, anti-German and anti-British sentiment played an important role among pro-Soviet circles gathered around the Soviet embassy in interwar Paris; in the mid-1930s in Britain, during the years of the Popular Front and collective security, Soviet ambassador Ivan Maiskii launched initiatives to foster ties with British Conservatives, whom he viewed as increasingly ready to engage the Soviets, essentially because of the foreign policy conjuncture.[7] Soviet analysts dealing with foreign intellectuals, moreover, routinely formulated plans to alter their message depending on varying national and international passions of the target group. Examples of this in a 1929 strategy document were countries defeated in World War I, which would have "moods" that VOKS could "utilize"; "semi-colonial" countries, in which resentments against great powers would prompt intelligentsia to "proceed parallel with the foreign-policy interests of the [Soviet] Union"; and the discontent of "national minorities" in Poland and Czechoslovakia, which should be taken into account in recruiting, along with extra propaganda about the Soviet "solution" to the national question.[8]

In no other country, however, were geopolitical factors across the non-leftist political spectrum comparable to the allure a non-Western alliance exercised on Germany in the 1920s. A strain of fascination with Bolshevism ran through the new nationalism of Germany's "conservative revolution." As a result, the Soviet dilemma of choosing between leftist sympathizers and non-leftist people of influence became uniquely stark in the Weimar context. As a result, the broader problem of choosing partners reverberated from the specificities of the German-Soviet relationship to influence VOKS's own approaches and aspirations.

By the time VOKS's foreign activities commenced in the mid-1920s, Soviet communism had already passed through at least two major phases in its relations with the outside world. The first, from 1917–21, was defined by the expectation of immediate revolution abroad; the second was marked by a simultaneous pursuit of regular interstate relations and revolutionary agendas. The turn to NEP in 1921 was not fully coordinated with the articulation of the concept of "peaceful coexistence," as Lenin and Chicherin started to use the term in 1920–21, but a series of treaties and policies moved conventional diplomatic relations and commerce (as opposed to revolutionary offensive) to the fore. From this point on, and especially after the Genoa conference and Rapallo, the Soviets pursued revolution and diplomacy simultaneously on the world stage. The failure to export revolution to Germany in 1923, in particular, extended peaceful coexistence from a breathing-space tactic to a more long-term strategy. The Western powers responded with a "predictable mixture of fear and pragmatism," in the words of Carole Fink, as "large segments of the Western world were frightened of bolshevism." Genoa and its aftermath exposed a range of responses from strict non-recognition (the United States), willingness to do business (Britain), and a policy of extracting concessions and demanding full repayment of the tsarist debt (France). The Soviets' twin pursuit of world revolution and interstate relations was thus met by what Jacobson has called a Western "dialectic of detente and intransigence."[9]

Historians of Soviet foreign relations have referred to the two modes of Soviet international activity as the "dual policy," and how to conceptualize its contours and consequences has been one of the most important interpretive issues in Soviet international history.[10] Since the dual policy has been studied primarily by historians of foreign relations, studies have focused almost exclusively on the division and clashes between Foreign Affairs and the Comintern, the one representing conventional diplomacy, the other the pursuit of revolution. This discussion goes beyond the rigid dichotomy between ideology and Realpolitik, or world revolution and socialism in one country—the first associated with the Comintern and the second with the Soviet state—that have structured the debate over Soviet foreign behavior. The material here suggests that the dual policy created criss-crossing missions and deep-seated inconsistencies among Soviet actors on the international scene within institutions, not to mention individual minds.

Soviet cultural diplomacy had to confront its own version of the dual policy and decide whether to focus on ideological sympathizers or influential yet politically distant—sometimes diametrically opposed—groups and individuals. The first two sections of this chapter elucidate the origins of this dilemma in Soviet-Weimar cultural relations; the rest of the discussion examines the limits of the Soviets' "German model" in other parts of Europe and in the United States. The chapter concludes with an examination of VOKS patron-client relations with foreign and Soviet intellectuals alike, suggesting that they served both ideological and institutional goals.

There were two major features of Soviet international operations that worked against communist aspirations of influence. First, there was a persistent dilemma of control: VOKS, for example, while often bureaucratic and inflexible, hoped to manipulate the levers of initiative from Moscow, relying on its motley group of representatives stationed abroad, while at the same time fostering independent initiative and concealing the front-like nature of its friendship societies. Second, Bolshevik intellectuals and Soviet *apparatchiki* alike faced intense pressure to justify their successes abroad to the political leadership at home in misleading ways. To its political masters, VOKS showcased its foreign operations as increasingly successful and constantly expanding—so much so that it could obscure their nature to the party leadership and sometimes to itself. In this way, even as model Soviet institutions presented a rose-colored picture for viewers at home, rhetorical showcases were constructed for internal political purposes out of VOKS's partner organizations abroad.

Willing Partners: The Eastern Orientation in Germany

The German search for an alliance in the East was both a policy and an ideological issue, and both elements prompted Hoetzsch himself, like so many others, to seek out the Soviets. Hoetzsch exemplifies several of the longstanding motivations that lay behind the Gesellschaft's cooperation with the Soviets in the 1920s. He insisted that scholarship should be politically relevant but non-partisan, and his own academic work was marked by a lifelong concern with Great Power politics, German imperial might, and the "primacy of foreign policy." In Hoetzsch's view, German national interests were best served by an alliance of strong German and Russian states; the Soviet internal order concerned him far less than the international arena. Underlying this thinking was a deeply ingrained anti-Polonism and the widely shared nationalist desire to revise the Versailles settlement, which locked in his "Eastern orientation" for the duration of the Weimar period.[11]

Hoetzsch made Berlin the greatest center of Russian studies of the day. British diplomat and historian E. H. Carr spoke of the "Hoetzsch School," and a newly hired State Department official, George F. Kennan, was selected to attend his lectures as "training for Russia." In post-Nazi Germany, therefore, he has come to stand for, in the words of the most sophisticated incarnation of this nostalgic version of his biography, the "tragedy of a German scholar and his field."[12] Instead of reading Hoetzsch's life backwards through the prism of his later vilification and internal exile under the Nazis, we might ask how such a respectable, nationalist member of the Wilhelmine and Weimar establishments developed such close ties with the Soviets. Much of the answer has to do with Hoetzsch's distinctive way of linking scholarship to politics and foreign policy. His main goal was to make his Gesellschaft into the leading forum for commentary on contemporary Soviet politics and history. For access to the raw materials of scholarship, Hoetzsch needed the Soviets and particularly VOKS; for the finished product, he needed close ties with the German state.

Within the spectrum of post-war politics, Hoetzsch staked out a center-nationalist and foreign-policy-oriented position. A monarchist early on, he belonged to the "moderate" wing of the rightist Deutschnationale Volkspartei (DNVP) and became a *Vernunftrepublikaner* (republican on rational grounds) propounding a "Tory democracy" that would maintain a degree of elite hegemony in the democratic age. He opposed anti-Semitism within the DNVP but, as the party's foreign policy expert in the Reichstag until 1930, agreed wholeheartedly with the anti-Versailles and strong-Reich planks in the party program.[13] While the German Foreign Office hoped that investing in the Gesellschaft's scholarly and cultural initiatives might moderate Soviet international behavior in a crisis, Hoetzsch dreamed of far more: a historically destined geopolitical partnership.[14] Hoetzsch was attracted by the dynamism of late imperial Russia, with its upward movement of self-made men like himself, and this positively colored his views of Soviet Russia's "will to live."[15]

Hoetzsch, then, happily married scholarship to politics, and it worked brilliantly—as long as the politics were those of the Weimar Republic. In this sense, he was an ideal personification of the Gesellschaft, which in the decade between its pre-war founding and its emergence as a leading center of Eastern European studies deliberately linked scholarly, state, diplomatic, and economic interests. One might expect that the Gesellschaft's close ties with the German government would have aroused the suspicions and hostility of the Bolsheviks, but these connections were in fact responsible for much of its allure. In the 1920s, the Gesellschaft became the most important German organization devoted to Russian studies. At its height, it included about 300 members, most of them in Berlin, from within and without the academic world.Even as it found in VOKS a reliable partner for ensuring access to travel and publications, the Gesellschaft continued to maintain the tight linkage between the worlds of academia and policy that had characterized its existence since its founding in 1913.[16]

The various interests represented within the Gesellschaft's membership constitute a virtual encyclopedia of non-leftist motivations behind the "Eastern orientation" favoring positive relations with the USSR. Hoetzsch's main partner, and president of the Gesellschaft, was the science organizer Friedrich Schmidt-Ott, a longtime higher education official in the Prussian Kultusministerium who rose to the rank of minister in 1917. In 1920, Schmidt-Ott assumed the leadership of the *Notgemeinschaft der deutschen Wissenschaft* (Emergency Association for German Science), which became the leading German force behind Soviet-German scientific cooperation. Schmidt-Ott thus boasted close ties to the German cultural and foreign policy establishments and great administrative experience in science. Like Hoetzsch, he assumed that scientific and cultural connections with Russia were "above all political"—a phase that could have come from any Bolshevik—in that cultural initiatives would serve the goals of German foreign policy. Indeed, the Gesellschaft was directly supported by funding from the Cultural Division (Kulturabteilung) of the Foreign Office, VOKS's counterpart as the main German vehicle of cultural diplomacy.[17] As a scholarly center promoting "modern" research agendas with contemporary relevance for German-Soviet relations, the Gesellschaft actively sought out financial, industrial, and trade interests. Leading figures from Deutsche Bank, Siemens-Werke, AEG, and other firms interested in promoting exports or economic relations with the USSR were represented in the organization's leadership.[18]

Soviet relations with Hoetzsch's Gesellschaft developed with most intensity in 1923–25, the period leading up to the foundation and emergence of VOKS, ensuring a continuing and ubiquitous comparison with the left-leaning Society of Friends. The first issue of the Gesellschaft's organ *Ost-Europa* appeared in August 1925. In the month before its appearance, the general secretary of the Gesellschaft, Hans Jonas, who had learned Russian as a POW during World War I, formally requested VOKS "support" for the journal, by which he meant that VOKS would supply articles from Soviet authors. *Ost-Europa* became the first German scholarly publication devoted solely to contemporary Soviet and Eastern European affairs. The range of its articles, relatively high level of coverage, and regular commentators made it valuable to the German Foreign Office, and most embassies in Moscow subscribed. Hoetzsch's own prolific output "registered German-Soviet relations like a seismograph."[19]

For its part, VOKS greatly valued the opportunity to publish prominent Soviet authors—including such figures as Commissar of Education Lunacharskii, the pedagogue Pinkevich, the sociologist Reisner, and many others of a more "specialist" bent, such as jurists and statisticians—in a non-leftist venue.[20] Kameneva agreed to send contributions on the condition that *Ost-Europa* would ban Russian émigré authors, make no changes to Soviet articles, and provide a larger honorarium. Hoetzsch proved willing to break his ties with members of the Russian emigration.[21]

Despite a number of moments of friction over publications in *Ost-Europa* that VOKS considered unflattering or anti-Soviet, the relationship proved attractive to both sides. Indeed, Hoetzsch jealously guarded his VOKS connections. There was a distinct element of rivalry and competition between the Gesellschaft and the Society of Friends as the society of sympathizing "friends" arose under the aegis of the very Soviet institution with which the Gesellschaft was most closely involved. Symbolically, in her trips to Germany, Kameneva visited both organizations. On one occasion, in 1928, when Kameneva was in Cologne for the Pressa exhibition, she urged the mayor, the future German chancellor Konrad Adenauer, to create a local branch of the Society of Friends. The Gesellschaft reportedly responded by warning Adenauer about the "political character" of its Soviet-sponsored rival and tried to persuade him to open a chapter of the Gesellschaft instead.[22]

By 1925, the allure of potential influence over prominent German policymakers had so turned the heads of Soviet embassy personnel in Berlin that some began to favor a complete reorientation of VOKS's cultural efforts toward the Gesellschaft. Significantly, the most optimistic assessment of the Gesellschaft's potential came from the Soviet embassy in Berlin, where the VOKS representative and Berlin diplomat Nikolai Nikolaevich Shtange became the point man for the publication of Soviet authors in *Ost-Europa*. Precisely because the Gesellschaft was conservative and nationalist in orientation, Shtange maintained, it would not be suspected of Soviet manipulation and might thus better serve as a cover for Soviet interests. On August 24, 1925, he wrote to Kameneva that the Gesellschaft held "more and more significance for us." It had great resources, visible names, and a "purely German character"—a phrase that could have come from any German nationalist—that endowed it with advantages over the Society of Friends. Because *Ost-Europa* maintained a "national political physiognomy," it would be authoritative to those wide circles of the educated public that the leftist *Das neue Russland,* the VOKS-sponsored organ of the Society of Friends, "is completely incapable of penetrating." In contrast, Shtange avowed, "very many" people harbored "doubts and mistrust about the information in *Das neue Russland.*"[23] In general, Soviet cultural officials and diplomats placed exaggerated faith in the results that would accrue merely from placing materials of Soviet origin in foreign publications.

To Shtange, the Gesellschaft's "direct ties between government and scholars" were not liabilities, but assets. He insisted that "we have influence over it" and the situation is "profitable."

> Of course, we must not close our eyes to the fact that bourgeois figures and scholars who are "well-disposed" toward us will hardly defend our interests in the case of a serious crisis between Germany and the USSR. But they will all the same not speak out openly, even if we were not connected to them by other means. During the conflict [in Soviet-German relations] last year many of the members of the "Society of Friends of the New Russia" distanced themselves from the society and even left it. In normal circumstances we have in the Gesellschaft a highly powerful apparatus, which we can use for the propaganda of the idea of rapprochement among bourgeois circles in Germany.[24]

Kameneva agreed with Shtange that the Gesellschaft deserved "broad support," and she agreed to provide articles for its journal, set up a book exchange, and arrange lectures, securing the approval of Litvinov for all of the above. Significantly, Shtange also favored ceding the Society of Friends to Comintern control, in this case not out of militancy but out of his overwhelming interest in the non-leftists. Yet Kameneva, who did so much to fend off Comintern incursions into VOKS affairs, was adamant about maintaining oversight over the Society of Friends and insisted on cultivating the German leftists and nationalists simultaneously. Her sharp retorts to Shtange on these questions, it seems, prompted the latter to proffer his resignation as VOKS representative in September 1925.[25]

Relations between VOKS and the Gesellschaft continued to progress, and reached their high point after the 200th jubilee of the Russian Academy of Sciences in 1925. Gesellschaft cooperation with VOKS did play a role in helping to bring to fruition a series of high-profile scientific and cultural events, including, among several others, the week of Soviet natural science and history, held in 1927 and 1928 in Berlin, and the week of German technology in Moscow in 1929.[26] By claiming some of the credit associated with the peak in German-Soviet scientific initiatives in this period, Kameneva defended VOKS's success and indispensability. These claims rested squarely on VOKS's work with influential non-leftists.[27]

Like the Society of Friends, however, the Gesellschaft was not immune to stinging critiques from Soviet analysts and officials. Indeed, its intimacy with the German state and foreign policymakers rendered the notion that the organization could easily be used for Soviet purposes open to easy rebuttal. Moreover, in the years after 1927, the Gesellschaft's organ *Ost-Europa*, in the words of one historian, underwent a "slow transformation" as the result of "pressure from without … and compromise within," which made it increasingly risky to "say anything positive about the Soviet Union."[28] The Gesellschaft was blocked from attempts to establish independent ties with cultural officials in Ukraine and Georgia, as VOKS jealously guarded its all-union monopoly, and for good measure, "influential circles" of the Gesellschaft were accused of maintaining connections with the Ukrainian "white emigration" in Germany.[29] In 1929, VOKS Central European analyst Levit-Livent emphasized that the Gesellschaft "cannot be viewed as our ally" and that "it will always remain a weapon of German policy, of the German Ministry of Foreign Affairs."[30]

By the end of the 1920s, in the eyes of closely involved Soviet observers, the Gesellschaft was, if not discredited, then at least not living up to expectations. Yet, it is telling that Levit, severe critic of the Gesellschaft though he was, did not reject the kinds of goals the Soviets harbored all along vis-à-vis German nationalists—he only criticized the Gesellschaft as an adequate vehicle for them. "We must have influence in Germany over the left-wing and middle bourgeoisie, embracing the laboring intelligentsia, and also over a part of that right-wing bourgeoisie that is the opponent of the policy of agreement with the Western allies," he stated, qualifying class with political categories. "Through this influence we will get into the ranks of bourgeois circles themselves, neutralizing hostile attitudes toward us."[31] Once a parallel disillusionment with the Society of Friends started a search for new levers of influence in the early 1930s, the door was open to a courting of potentially influential figures in the extreme nationalist German Right.

Given these internal VOKS discussions, it is startling to see the extent to which the organization touted the Gesellschaft as a major asset to the political leadership. It was almost a point of pride that the Gesellschaft had resources and got results, and in 1930, it was even portrayed as nothing less than VOKS's instrument for acting on the "national conservative bourgeoisie."[32] The Gesellschaft, like the Society of Friends, had become a showcase in VOKS summary reports to higher authorities. By the same token, to his own domestic audiences, Hoetzsch played up the Gesellschaft's service to German foreign policy—indeed, he ensured that the Gesellschaft took no major step without consulting the Foreign Office—as increasingly powerful right-wing forces attacked the Gesellschaft for being pro-Soviet or as manipulated by, in the words of one such denunciation, "comrade Kameneff Bronstein" [Kameneva] and the GPU.[33] In 1933, Hoetzsch inserted phrases like *Ostraum* (Eastern space) into an article and signaled that the Gesellschaft's journal might be "harmonized" with the Nazi regime, but he withdrew when Nazi Party members were appointed to the editorial board. Under attack for his close Soviet ties, Hoetzsch approved the dissertations of two Jewish students, in 1934 and 1935, and he lost his post at the University of Berlin on May 14, 1935. Hoetzsch's Gesellschaft was condemned as a clique of "Jewish-freemason-liberal Soviet friends and salon Bolsheviks" (*Sowjetfreunde und Salonbolschewisten*).[34] The insults of the Nazi campaign were patently false. Hoetzsch and his colleagues may have been good partners for the Soviets, but they were never "friends": at the height of his success in the 1920s, what sustained VOKS's relationship with the Gesellschaft was each side's hope that it was successfully manipulating the other.

First Friends of the New Russia

As the Gesellschaft offered visions of influence over hard-to-reach bourgeois and government circles, the Society of Friends, a new institution created by Comintern and Soviet initiatives, held out an equally elusive prospect: direct Soviet control over sympathizers. The Society's debut in the years after 1923 was impressive, and here a degree of influence was assured. Its lectures, cultural events, meetings, and visitors from the Soviet Union, as well as its influential journal, *Das neue Russland*, were all partially able to fill a hunger on the part of German intellectuals for greater contact with the new socialist society to the east. Indeed, to many, the Society's attraction lay not only in the badge of sympathetic identification it offered but also in the opportunities it presented for contact with visiting Soviet figures and pursuing interests in Soviet culture, science, and society.[35] For example, the sex reformer Helene Stöcker was a founding member of the society and frequent traveler to the Soviet Union. Her many-leveled interests in the Soviet order were shaped not only by her socialism, feminism, and pacifism, but also by a fervent commitment to eugenics. Her social-radical brand of eugenics was collectivist and conditioned by the concept of the "new person" even before the Soviet Union existed, but it also meshed with central tropes of human perfectibility in Soviet culture and ideology.[36] In 1925, Kameneva characterized Stöcker to the Leningrad OGPU as a pacifist journalist who was known for writings and speeches that worked "to the advantage of Soviet Russia."[37]

Yet, a diffuse influence was hardly the same as calling the shots from Moscow. Although the Society of Friends' membership was sprawling, size was always considered an asset by the Soviets. Equally important was that it included a number of cultural and scholarly luminaries. While a number of famous figures joined at the outset—including Albert Einstein, the writers Thomas and Heinrich Mann, the sociologist and political economist Franz Oppenheimer, and the first director of the Frankfurt School for Social Research, (karl Grünberg—they rarely took part in the Society's activities. In the late 1920s, VOKS analysts boasted about the membership of other cultural figures who were deeply involved in Soviet affairs, including theatrical director Erwin Piscator and the architect and urban planner Bruno Taut. In 1925, the Society of Friends was reported to have 700 to 800 official members, who "more or less" paid official dues; this number was supplemented by a large group of KPD members who also took part in its activities (these comprised the approximately 200 "unofficial members" who were not registered, clearly because they would have altered the Society's claims to neutrality). The German Society was also unique in its proximity to the Soviet colony in Berlin, and from the outset, Kameneva's personal emissary worked to add twenty to twenty-five high-level Soviets who knew German well to "liven up" the organization. In 1930, the Society, including its several new regional affiliates, was reported to have 1,300 members.[38]

The ethos of the Society was consistently pro-Soviet: Kameneva herself vetted the core group of active members of the Society for their sympathy to the Soviet experiment.[39] The activists were a motley group of radical democrats, social reformers, pacifists, and others united by the pull of the first socialist society. The membership over the years also included teachers, doctors, jurists, and artists interested in Soviet activities in their disciplines; scientists and scholars primarily interested in broadening German-Soviet scholarly relations; parliamentarians and public figures, including a small group of Social Democrats; and politicians and even some non-leftist or nationalist intellectuals whose primary interest lay in the "Eastern orientation."[40] The communist head of the Society, the publicist Erich Baron, underlined to Kameneva in 1928 that a number of high German officials attended the Society's talks and evenings depending on the Soviet topic presented; for example, when Soviet law was discussed, officials from the Justice Ministry attended. When well-known Soviet figures such as Lunacharskii or Semashko spoke, "all of intellectual Berlin" showed up. The number of non-leftist visitors also included parliamentarians and officials, professors of varied political persuasions, and, on many occasions, the German ambassador to the USSR, Brockdorff-Rantzau. All these figures and more would be lost, according to Baron, if Soviet connections behind the Society of Friends were revealed.[41]

Some members of the Society of Friends were the same kind of non-leftist men of influence who prompted such marked Soviet enthusiasm for the Gesellschaft. Despite the Society's leftist profile and orientation, there was a degree of overlap between the Society and the Soviets' nonleftist German interlocutors of the era.

Some intellectuals who considered themselves deeply interested in Soviet politics and culture, such as Walter Benjamin, found tensions between the official neutrality of cultural exchange and the society's role as a space for a Soviet-German intellectual cross-fertilization problematic. Freshly back from his Moscow journey in 1927 and reflecting on the news of the founding of the new Franco-Soviet friendship society, Benjamin hoped the organizers would go beyond what he disparagingly called the "harmless treadmill of international cultural relations." This he contrasted with the "eminently political fact of an acquaintance with the intellectual agendas of Russia." All the same, he praised the Berlin society as "a very useful informational institution."[42] Benjamin craved access to the latest Soviet cultural trends, themselves obviously political, rather than any quasi-official, outward segregation of culture and politics.

The openly pro-Soviet nature of the Society of Friends did significantly affect the kinds of goals VOKS articulated for it, as opposed to those it formulated for more politically and ideologically distant figures. One constantly reiterated task was to propagate a favorable view of Soviet "achievements" in culture and science specifically, as well as in the construction of Soviet socialism as a whole. The possibilities opened up by the Society of Friends, therefore, revolved around influencing the attitudes of cultural elites, the outlook of the "intelligentsia," and, as it was often termed, "mobilizing public opinion" in Europe. By contrast, Soviet aspirations with the non-leftists and nationalists revolved less around openly disseminated cultural propaganda and more around influencing foreign policy, neutralizing hostility on the part of politically influential figures in the event of a crisis, gathering information and covert contacts, and penetrating otherwise closed groups and milieus.

Unlike Hoetzsch's Gesellschaft, the Society of Friends was a cultural front organization that offered the Soviets the prospect of behind-the-scenes direction. Soviet cultural diplomacy produced skilled practitioners of the art of directing front organizations by establishing a covert chain of command, either with a selected local leader or a pliable presidium. This remained VOKS's preferred *modus operandi* with the friendship societies for decades. In the German case, matters were initially made easier by the fact that Baron was a KPD member close to Lunacharskii. He served as the main contact with VOKS until 1933, and a succession of VOKS representatives in the German embassy served as liaisons between Baron and the VOKS leadership. The record shows that in

1924, Kameneva was in frequent touch with Baron, sometimes objecting to German authors in his journal, recommending German contacts of her own, and offering advice on setting up the society's specialized sections.[43] During the heyday of the Society of Friends, Kameneva maintained direct ties with certain core members and key figures as well.

VOKS's contribution to the Society was organizational and financial. From Moscow, VOKS arranged lectures, cultural events, and tours for Soviet cultural and political figures and was heavily involved in supplying *Das neue Russland* with reports by well-known Soviet authors on Soviet culture and "socialist construction." Neither the journal nor the Society, moreover, would have survived without VOKS's direct financial subsidies. In mid-1924, to cite just one example in a lengthy parade of financial crises, Kameneva was told by Gol'dshtein, the VOKS representative at this point: "As I have already written you constantly, such a society cannot survive on its own resources."[44]

Despite all its dirigiste urges, VOKS was constantly forced to conceal and to limit those levers it did have in order to maintain the appearance of the Society's vaunted "neutrality." Frustrations were built into the enterprise of covert oversight from a distance and the attendant reliance on local emissaries. The initial close cooperation of Baron with VOKS petered out after the Society entered a period of stasis after 1925. In late 1925, Kameneva complained to Nikolai Krestinskii, the Soviet ambassador in Germany, that despite VOKS's hard-currency subsidies, Baron had not yet bothered—or, perhaps, had resisted the obligation—to submit a single substantive report (*otchet*) on the Society's activities.[45] Even worse, it turned out that a very large portion of those who had signed up as "friends" of the USSR were completely inactive in the Society, so that—just as in many Soviet "social" organizations—there were massive numbers of "paper" members. In the late 1920s and early 1930s, fourteen regional affiliates were founded in other German cities, but, as a 1933 letter by the VOKS deputy director charged, "a large portion of them in reality remain on paper." In Munich, the local branch was allegedly used to recruit tourists for Intourist trips by a Bavarian entrepreneur, and Baron was accused of not even knowing the number of members in Berlin and elsewhere.[46] Baron, who had a background in publishing, reportedly devoted the bulk of his time to producing the Society's *Das neue Russland*.[47]

Levit-Livent, an energetic and perceptive VOKS Central European *referent* who took his post in March 1929, wrote of a plan to simultaneously rejuvenate and take charge of the Society: replace the old stalwarts on the presidium with figures such as Taut, Piscator, and Heinrich Mann; to commercialize the distribution of the journal so Moscow subsidies would not be necessary; and to replace Baron. Baron resisted, however, refusing to replace or alter the Society's presidium between 1925–33, and without "reliable executors" on the ground, all such plans remained "fantasies." As Germany moved rightward in the late 1920s and early 1930s, there were mounting criticisms of Baron and the Society's original core figures as unsuitable for influencing German public opinion.[48] Indeed, until 1933 there were repeated Soviet discussions about the need to replace Baron, but this never happened.

In light of the mounting problems with creating an organization that would be both vibrant in its German milieu and controlled by Moscow, VOKS's optimistic proclamations to Soviet party and state organs about the upward climb of the Society seem like fantasies indeed. Typically, one early document baldly asserted that "we" guarantee the "leading influence" of Communists in the Society, either through Society members or the VOKS representative.[49] For all the rhetoric, however, Kameneva, apparently realizing how fragile the Society of Friends really was, did not press matters with Baron. Kameneva wanted to have her cake and eat it too: to project the image of effective VOKS control while championing the Society's autonomy when she wished to fend off Comintern and KPD proposals to enlist the Society for short-term political goals. The German Communist Party, for its part, did not claim the society as its own but viewed it as belonging only to the "outermost periphery of our circle of influence."[50]

The dilemma of control VOKS faced was compounded by the fact that diplomats in the Soviet embassy in Berlin, whose number included those also working as VOKS's representatives in Germany, tended to be far more keen on pursuing influential non-leftists rather than the sympathetic "friends." In late 1924, Roman Veller, Kameneva's executive assistant, reported to Moscow that VOKS's representative Nikolai Shtange and other embassy officials devoted almost no energy to the Society of Friends, speaking of it "sourly" and depriving it of their support: "Shtange has an extremely cold attitude towards the Society of Friends. This is explained by the fact that the Society, which has many prominent names, in fact has shown no influence in affecting German public opinion."[51] As we saw, in 1925, Shtange articulated a strong position favoring the Gesellschaft over the Society of Friends. That position involved a critique of the Society of Friends as a sponsor of purely "decorative" activities, with the majority of "friends" joining merely as a token of "more or less friendly relations with the Soviet Union."[52]

Kameneva firmly rejected Shtange's position in favor of pursuing both kinds of partners—and simultaneously. In high-level 1928 discussions with the Central Committee, she revealingly asserted that "leftist tendencies" in Europe were more advanced than those of philistine Soviets who aped European bourgeois and commercial mass culture. The European intellectual Left, she asserted, would import the best features of the new proletarian culture from the Soviet Union and in the process give them valuable reinforcement inside the socialist homeland.[53] This was an extraordinary declaration: European intellectuals would save Soviet culture from its worst instincts, in effect forming a *Kulturträger* alliance with its most advanced elements. Small wonder that Kameneva was so unwilling to downplay the significance of the fellow-traveling German "friends." VOKS's own "dual policy" of pursuing both leftists and nationalists as partners in Germany remained the mainstream VOKS position even during the controversial outreach to the German far Right after Kameneva's removal in late 1929. The obvious need for direct Soviet sponsorship in propping up even the German "front" organization, the strongest cultural friendship society in Europe, offers one ready explanation for why VOKS consistently preferred not to stray far from its few selected partner organizations.

Cultural Friendship Societies in Comparative Perspective

There are intriguing clues that, before the Fascist March on Rome, a number of Italian intellectuals associated with Futurism, which in the early 1920s experienced acrimonious splits into pro-Fascist, pro-communist, and independent factions, were the first to start a society of "Friends of Russia."[54] The Fascist consolidation of power made Italy into an exceptional case, however, with severely restricted cultural contacts and no friendship society. The German Society of Friends, which appeared so successful at its founding in 1923, became the model for similar societies in Europe and then around the world. The Berlin model was first applied to six more societies or affiliated branches in new cities founded in 1924. In the case of Austria and Czechoslovakia, there was a direct link with the German example, as Willi Münzenberg, among others, traveled to Vienna and Prague in early 1924 to help export the model from Berlin.[55] By 1931, there were societies in 17 countries, with a total of 42 branches in major cities and a combined (paper) membership of 7,231.[56] The societies of friends became VOKS's primary institutional partners and its chief instrument for long-term cultivation of individuals outside the Soviet Union. They loomed large in cultural diplomacy in several ways, both as targets for VOKS publications and Soviet lecturers abroad and as prime recruiting grounds for travel invitations to the Soviet Union.

But VOKS representatives stationed in European countries soon informed Moscow of several ways in which the German situation was distinctive above and beyond the "Eastern orientation." Variations among the societies give insight into a range of broad national differences in politics, culture, and intellectual orientation affecting Soviet attempts to influence public opinion abroad. While there were noteworthy variations in the particular mix of factors pushing intellectuals toward sustained "friendly" contact, key individual figures and personal relationships could have a major impact on the success of each national venture.

Red Vienna

Each country's internal political configuration, particularly the relations between the communist and social-democratic parties, was decisive for the membership of the new friendship societies. In Germany, where both the far Right and the far Left were substantial, polarized, and extreme, KPD relations with the SPD were hostile—not only on ideological grounds but also due to intensive political competition.[57] The German Society of Friends was able and willing to attract and retain only a tiny handful of Social Democrats. In "red Vienna," by contrast, where the Social Democrats after 1918 launched their own experiment in municipal model building, VOKS encountered great interest on the part of sympathetic Social Democrats. Austrian Social Democrats and academic figures formed two large blocks within the initial membership, and they reportedly did not see the need for attracting different groups, be it among the political elite, industry, or "nonpolitical" figures. On the other hand, the Social Democrats in the Austrian society were wary of appearing too pro-Soviet. Inevitably, they provoked Soviet suspicions that the society could fall under the influence of their party organization. The VOKS representative announced efforts to reduce the Social Democratic contingent and recruit non-party members supposedly immune to its leadership. As late as 1932 half of all present and former members in the Viennese "citadel of social-democracy" were either "left" Social Democrats or party members who were not politically prominent.[58]

In another departure from the Berlin "model" (*skhema*) that the VOKS representatives in Vienna were supposed to replicate, a significant group of Austrian friends favored including the improvement of Austro-Soviet trade relations as one of the society's major functions. Asked by her deputy in Vienna if that should be sanctioned, Kameneva admonished that "the main task is to attract cultural and scientific workers of the West into closer relations." The Commissariat of Foreign Trade welcomed the foundation of a friendship society but vetoed any "operational functions of a commercial character" as completely impermissible.[59] In the decade after its founding, however, hopes for an economic dimension to cultural friendship apparently remained a notable current in the Austrian membership; its failure to materialize was the reason given in 1931 for an overall drop in society activities. In the period leading up to and following outbreak of Civil War, in February 1934, and the establishment of "Austrofascism" (the term favored by the clerico-authoritarian *Ständestaat* that ruled between 1934 and the 1938 *Anschluss* into Nazi Germany), society members kept their activity secret for fear of losing their positions.[60]

Arosev in Prague

Recruiting friendly intellectuals in the friendship society in Prague, also organized on the German model in 1924, was shaped by a factor not present elsewhere in Western Europe: Slavic solidarity. Russophilic sentiment was a widespread feature of Czech intellectual life since the national revival in the nineteenth century. Numerous VOKS reports on the First Czechoslovak Republic note a Slavic or "Slavophile" interest in Soviet art and science, a factor also noted as creating fertile soil for "our influence" in Bulgaria and Yugoslavia. One 1931 analyst judged the level of knowledge about Russian culture and the Soviet Union in Czechoslovakia to be greater than in any other Western European country.[61]

The unusual strength of the political and cultural Left in Prague was also key. In 1924, Baron, writing from Berlin, informed Kameneva of the "large number of friends" in Czechoslovak "intellectual and economic circles." Baron was in close contact with his counterpart in Prague, the musicologist Zdeněk Nejedlý (1878–1962), as the latter assumed the leading role in founding the Czechoslovak society.[62] As a student of history and aesthetics at Charles University in 1896, Nejedlý had traveled to the Caucasus and met Lev Tolstoy. As a professor ordinarius at the same university after 1919, he became an active publicist close to the Communist Party in the 1920s. We will meet Nejedlý again as one of the most enthusiastic visitors to the USSR in the 1930s. His fellow-traveling days prepared the ground for Moscow exile in 1939 in the wake of Munich. After teaching at Moscow State University, he returned to post-war Czechoslovakia as minister of education and culture during the late Stalin period. In this case, committed "friendship" led to great prominence in the Czechoslovak Communist Party.

The Czechoslovak Left was stronger, freer to act, and hence more legitimate than in any other country of Eastern or Central Europe, and the Communist Party operated above ground throughout the twenty years of the First Republic's existence. Left-wing politics exerted a strong hold among interwar Czech intellectuals, in particular among the literary elite.[63] Calculating strategy, Soviet analysts also highlighted the potential uses of national tensions as a recruiting tool—in this case, Slovak resentments of Czech dominance in the new republic. Furthermore, the Czechoslovak society, unlike, for example, those in New York or Chicago but in this case very much like in Berlin, could draw on a large and influential Soviet colony to further its activities. When Vladimir Maiakovskii visited Prague in April 1927, he gave poetry readings once to an invited audience of 150 at the Soviet embassy and then to a crowd of 1,000 Czechs, Soviets, and Russian émigrés at the friendship society, providing "incalculably valuable propaganda beneficial for the USSR."[64]

The Soviet ambassador to Czechoslovakia from 1929–32 was Aleksandr Iakovlevich Arosev, who, from 1934–37, during the height of the Soviet Union's outreach to Western intellectuals during the Popular Front, became the most important director of VOKS after Kameneva. Born in 1890 in Kazan into the family of a merchant of the first guild, he was a third-generation radical. October 1917 found him a member of the Military Revolutionary Committee of the Bolshevik Party of Moscow and Moscow Region, where he was prominent in the Bolsheviks' armed uprising.[65] Arosev's close ties to Viacheslav Molotov, later Stalin's right-hand man, almost certainly prompted his early adherence to the Stalinist wing of the Party. With two other middle school students, Molotov and Arosev formed the first Social-Democratic fraction in Kazan, and in 1909, the two friends were imprisoned together. Arosev also had personal connections with Nikolai Ezhov, head of the NKVD during the Terror, with whom he served during the Civil War.[66]

Arosev was thus a seasoned Old Bolshevik with high-level political connections, but he was also a minor celebrity from the early years of Soviet literature in his own right. As ambassador, he was inclined to pay significant attention to Czechoslovak intellectuals and cultural affairs (Litvinov once called him more a writer than a politician).[67] This points to an important factor on the Soviet side affecting the success of cultural diplomacy: the attitude of the Soviet embassy and the energy and interests (and, not infrequently, the basic competence) of the VOKS representatives in them.

Despite his natural affinity for Stalin and Molotov during the inner-party struggles, Arosev's cosmopolitanism led him to disdain the masses of untraveled, uncultured apparatchiki whom the rulers promoted rapidly in the Party, starting in the late 1920s. His identity as an Old Bolshevik Europhile made Arosev into a great asset for VOKS in Prague, however. In the salon-like atmosphere of the villa Tereza, the ambassador's residence in Prague, Arosev declaimed Silver Age poetry and made his presence felt among Czechoslovak intellectuals. An example of a mediator between the Soviet Union and European culture as the borders became increasingly difficult to cross, Arosev traveled around the continent from Prague so that his daughters would "succeed in knowing and loving Europe." He married a Czechoslovak ballerina of Jewish origin, Gertrude Freund, who was remembered by Arosev's daughter from his first marriage as very non-Russian, a "European woman" highly organized and "reserved." Unable to remain ambassador while married to a Czechoslovak citizen, he returned home to comrades who could not comprehend how he could marry a foreign *burzhuazka*.[68]

In Arosev, we can get a glimpse into how much international cultural engagement could mean to Bolsheviks propagating a positive view of the Soviet system. Arosev, proud of the success of Soviet cultural diplomacy in Europe in part because he himself wished so much to participate in European culture, cherished his contacts with European intellectuals. Throughout the 1920s and 1930s, however, he recorded a series of internal conflicts between his ambitions in Soviet politics and diplomacy and his identity as a man of culture. His diary records internal doubts as to whether his administrative positions contributed to his failure as a writer, and he urged his children to pursue the success in art that he had never achieved.[69]

As a diplomat in several countries in the 1920s and as Soviet ambassador to Prague, Arosev was continuing an extensive European experience that served at once as a source of authority and vulnerability at home in the USSR. When Arosev met Stalin on a return trip to Moscow in 1929, the general secretary mused in his half-jocular, half-deadly manner that the diplomat had become "as polite as a bourgeois." In one of his many letters to the dictator, Arosev tried to prove him wrong with a combination of revolutionary bravado and flattery: "Our diplomats until now have stayed in the role of old women and are glad if everyone is quiet.... During my three exiles and three flights I most often heard your name."[70] In another letter to Stalin, Arosev called for a reorientation of Soviet diplomacy: it should serve the propaganda of the idea of communism and "proceed from the assumption that a clash between us and capitalism is inevitable." Stalin's speeches had "frightened Europe (and undoubtedly America)."[71]

Around the very same time as he paraded this crudely competitive stance with Europe as a badge of political loyalty, Arosev, in his diplomatic practice, socialized and befriended figures of many political orientations. For this, he was denounced to the Central Control Commission (TsKK) by a secret police official for his non-communist "way of life" abroad. His friend since 1917, Emel'ian Iaroslavskii, who as head of the TsKK was chief watchdog on "communist ethics," wrote to Sergo Ordzhonikidze that further "separation from the USSR" would be "dangerous for him as a party member," since Arosev was beginning to act like a *barin* (aristocrat).[72] The liabilities from his European connections would trail Arosev into the 1930s, even as he continued simultaneously to pursue his political ambitions in front of the top Stalin leadership and his cultural admiration for left-leaning European men of letters.

Arosev's tenure in Prague corresponded exactly with the Great Depression and the first Five-Year Plan; here, as elsewhere, the Soviet Union was the beneficiary of a great upsurge in sympathy. For a time, the toleration of the Czechoslovak Communist Party allowed for a uniquely open penetration of the friendship society with Communists. In 1931, Arosev personally led a change of the administration (*pravlenie*) of the Czechoslovak friendship society, reporting to VOKS that the communist fraction had become the institution's leading group. Nejedlý remained president, but the society's communist fraction now convened separately. In addition to these behind-the-scenes activities in the society, Arosev as ambassador participated in many VOKS events in Prague.

In part because of Arosev's unusual contribution, VOKS had numerous highly placed contacts in Czechslovakia. Files included lists of up to nine "very important" names in the categories of science and technology, pedagogy, music, theater and film, and literature and journalism. In the friendship society, the new leadership boasted not only Communists but figures close to Czechoslovak president, Tomáš Garrigue Masaryk, despite the generally anti-Soviet disposition of the Czechoslovak leadership. By the mid-1930s, VOKS analysts expressed preference for members of the mainstream National Socialist Party over the Communists in the society's leadership because of their greater ability to attract the "highly-qualified intelligentsia." In sum, in the Czechoslovak case, VOKS had achieved the doubly rare feat of attracting politically influential, mainstream non-Communists and a large group of openly active party members. Far from a cause for celebration, however, this success typically only fueled dark fears in VOKS and the Soviet embassy that the Communists were not sufficiently obedient, that non-Communists retained contacts with the Russian emigration, and that influential bourgeois and Social Democratic groups would "use" the society for their own purposes.[73]

London, Labour, and the Arcos Raid

The British society for cultural relations, in turn, vividly demonstrates the impact that foreign policy conjunctures could have on the organization of intellectual sympathy. The foundation of a friendship society in London intended to be "analogous" to the Berlin organization started in late 1923 and continued into early 1924, when Ramsay MacDonald became the first Labour Prime Minister. This timing was extremely propitious. On February 1, 1924, the Labour government, first among the Allied powers, extended de jure recognition to the USSR, and improved relations continued even after Labour's loss of power at the end of the year. A British trade union delegation, the first of its kind, was elaborately hosted by the Soviets in November and December. Khristian Rakovskii, the fiery Bulgarian-born ally of Trotsky who was sent to

London in July 1923 to negotiate recognition, directly supervised the VOKS representative, Varvara Polovtsevaia, in organizing intellectuals for the society; furthering the improvement of diplomatic as well as cultural relations was one of the initial missions of its members. VOKS analysts themselves noted, however, that the initiative for founding the society came not from the British but from the Soviet *aktiv* in London.[74]

The new British society declared "closer contact" and the "intellectual progress of both peoples" as its goals in 1924, when the society initially included fifteen Soviets either living in England or traveling there. Favorable relations with the Labour government initially allowed for open advertisement of Soviet members. Academician A. N. Krylov, the applied mathematician, and writer Alexei Tolstoi were included along with the British names advertised in the society's 1924 organizing brochure alongside Bertrand Russell, H. N. Brailsford, Julian Huxley, John Maynard Keynes, E. M. Forster, and Virginia Woolf. As in Berlin, however, most of the big names participated rarely, if at all, either at the time of founding or in the 1930s. The organizers emphasized the strong pre-revolutionary intellectual bonds between England and Russia, going back to Byron's influences on Pushkin and the importance of Darwin, Owen, and Mill in Russia. Closer contact would inform British observers of Soviet innovations, notably in literature (Blok, Maiakovskii, Esenin, Gastev, Gorky, and Aleksei Tolstoi), pedagogy ("the application of Professor Dewey's principles"), and science (Pavlov, Rozhdestvenskii, and Ioffe).[75] Not advertised was the fact that the executive committee included Polovtsevaia herself and the son of Foreign Affairs press official Fedor Rotshtein, Andrew, as well as a Soviet secretary.[76]

The favorable diplomatic and political conjuncture at the time of the London society's founding led, as in the German case, to an initial flush of success, as figures such as H. G. Wells, Bertrand Russell, and Keynes attended events or gave talks under its aegis. VOKS was also fortunate to have as the society's president a prominent and seasoned organizer, the socialist and feminist Margaret Llewelyn Davies (1861–1943). A longtime suffrage activist, she led the Women's Cooperative Guild from the beginning of the century through its interwar heyday, when it boasted tens of thousands of members, and she viewed the cooperative movement as a peaceful and evolutionary start to a "great revolution."[77] Polovtsevaia greatly admired Llewelyn Davies as "one of our most true friends and one of the figures most deserving of respect that I know in England."[78] There was a price for having such an asset, however; in return for her energy and sympathy, Llewelyn Davies demanded organizational and intellectual independence. In 1925, in a letter to Polovtsevaia, Llewelyn Davies made it clear that Soviet attempts to stage-manage the society through communists with direct ties to the embassy endangered the "cooperation of

English intellectuals." She wrote: "As you know, from the beginning I have said that we must choose between a Communist cultural Society, and a Society, which, while being on friendly terms with the Soviet Government, must not be in any way dominated by it...I would not remain Chairman if the Society became an official Communist one." Strong resistance to Soviet political meddling, as opposed to activities considered cultural, reappeared in the early 1930s. By then, however, VOKS had to conduct a "struggle on two fronts" against both independent-minded members and radicals on the Left who wished to put the society in the service of the English Revolution.[79]

VOKS's delicate balance of attempting to direct behind the scenes while allowing the societies to trumpet their independence foundered in the country with the weakest Communist Party in Europe and a prickly insistence on rights. Perhaps this was what Kameneva intriguingly referred to as "the specificities of English conditions." Forced to take a hands-off approach, Kameneva confessed in London to Soviet diplomat A. P. Rozengol'ts that the society "is developing its work rather freely and independently."[80] In this context, the rhetoric of manipulative control that VOKS served up to the party leadership was itself a front.

British-Soviet relations became strained in the wake of the May 1926 General Strike, since Soviet support channeled to the strike movement stoked fears of the "red menace." Most British Conservatives, unlike the German nationalists under Weimar, saw in the Soviet Union an implacable and unreformable opponent. For their part, most Bolshevik international analysts viewed the British Empire as the Soviet Union's primary enemy, and the 1927 crisis in relations with Britain formed a key part of the war scare of the same year. On May 12, a large group of British police raided the extraterritorial premises of Arcos, Ltd., the Soviet trade delegation in central London, seizing documents in an effort to confirm Soviet espionage activities. In the resulting uproar, the Baldwin government nullified the Anglo-Soviet Trade Agreement of 1921 and ended up severing diplomatic relations until the summer of 1929, while the Soviets conducted an operation of rounding up and executing citizens accused of being British spies.[81] The departure of a large number of Soviets in the wake of the Arcos raid was only the most direct effect of the crisis on the friendship society. Helen Crawford, who belonged both to the society and to the Central Committee of the British Communist Party, was charged with reporting on its internal state, and she briefed Kameneva three times in Moscow in 1927. Crawford reported that it was "financially" in a "very poor way" after Arcos, since it had been financed largely by the Soviets in London. While it enjoyed just a "sprinkling of support" from "cultural elements in London," it had no roots elsewhere and "is of practically no value whatever."[82]

In 1928, Kameneva confessed that she "absolutely [could not] imagine" how VOKS's subsidy to the British society of 300 pounds sterling per year, more than any other country's friendship society received, was being spent. In a plaintive refrain of inveterate and frustrated mobilization that runs through all the friendship-society documents of the period, she hoped yet again to make the society more active. After the Arcos affair, VOKS became far more circumspect in protecting the society from accusations of communist influence, and by the early 1930s even the society's printed letterhead declared it was "non-political—non-sectarian—non-propagandist." But the British Society never overcame its financial problems through membership dues, even during the rising tide of Sovietophilia during the Depression and Popular Front. On paper, its membership did reach a height of 1,700 members, more than 1,000 of whom were in newly formed affiliates throughout the country, including a gallery of prominent new adherents such as Beatrice Webb and the "red" Dean of Canterbury, the Very Reverend Hewlett Johnson.[83]

Even as the Popular Front made conditions favorable for attracting non-communist sympathizers to the friendship society, however, the foreign-policy conjuncture made courting Conservatives in the diplomatic establishment a more rewarding proposition for ambassador Ivan Maiskii, who had been a trusted and committed collaborator of Kameneva and VOKS in the 1920s. In the hundreds of pages of his diary entries between 1934–39, Maiskii fixated on the foreign-policy establishment and wrote about the Society of Cultural Relations only once. On this occasion, moreover, he thought of it only as part of plans to attract "more respectable and politically less radical representatives of the English intelligentsia" into the Soviet orbit. Thus were friendship societies a victim of the dual policy: involving quintessentially ideological work, they had to be separated from the Comintern and local communist parties while diplomats often had distinctly different concerns.

Infighting in Paris

In Paris, diplomatic and political relations were less favorable in the early-to-mid 1920s than in Berlin or even London, and there were fewer Soviet organizational outposts than in the other two capitals. Soviet cultural diplomacy in France also faced a more challenging atmosphere in the press and among intellectuals than in, for example, Germany or Czechoslovakia. The late rise of a stable friendship society in France also demonstrates how VOKS's search for heterodox "bourgeois" partners, ranging from influential non-leftists to ardent sympathizers, led to a degree of incoherence compounded by French factionalism and Soviet organizational failures.

As in the United States, the general political climate for Soviet work in France was tough: non-recognition before 1933 in the case of the United States, the most intractable set of foreign relations among Western powers even after recognition in 1924 in the case of France, and a history of virulent "red peril" coverage in the press in both countries.[84] No fewer than three attempts were made to found a friendship society in France: the short-lived *Nouvelles amités franco-russes* in 1924, a scientific committee for rapprochement in 1925 that was primarily linked to the Soviet Academy of Sciences and tied to the French Ministry of Public Education, and, finally, the society *Russie neuve*, created only in January 1928 after false starts and delays.[85] The first contained the kind of political elites with influence that the Soviets cherished in Germany, but it quickly fell apart; the second was made up of scientists brought into contact by the preparations for the 200th jubilee of the Soviet Academy, which largely bypassed VOKS and was suspected for its ties to a French state institution.[86] In the case of Russie neuve, some of the eminent intellectuals involved in 1927, in particular the writer Georges Duhamel but also the prominent Slavist André Mazon, proved too independent minded and insufficiently motivated.

In late 1927, the VOKS analyst for France, Tsetsiliia Rabinovich, advised that leftist sympathizers rather than "representatives of the intelligentsia who were too eminent" would be more reliable partners. One historian presents this remark and early organizational failures in France as proof of a Soviet requirement for pliant, ideologically committed partners. True, VOKS's often inadequate formula for influencing the friendship societies from afar rested heavily on close contact with a friendly leadership and covert links with selected proxies. It is also true that the number of Communists active in the French society was higher in the 1930s than in the 1920s. Typically, although the membership at times exceeded 1,000, at most 50 figures in any given period were considered "active," and a VOKS analyst revealingly referred to the "decorative" part of the organization.[87] The search for influential opinion makers of various political orientations, and not just pliant tools, carried on in France as elsewhere, however. Moreover, the earlier failures in France, such as the demise of the abortive society in 1924, had little to do with Soviet disillusionment with insufficiently subservient members, since these included members a VOKS representative enthusiastically called "the most visible Fr[ench] politicians and scholars." The problem in France was constant internal splits among diverse groups of French scholars, publicists, and intellectuals. Kameneva was fully exasperated by her laconic representative in Paris at the time, who was preoccupied as the embassy's main legal advisor and admitted "I just can't find out" why the society broke up.[88]

Ultimately, Soviet emissaries, in France as elsewhere, found fault with all the many varieties of bourgeois intellectuals they dealt with. The wide net cast by Soviet cultural diplomacy from the outset ensured they would always be looking for what they did not have. In 1931, reflecting on the Depression-era

upsurge in interest in all things Soviet, Foreign Affairs and VOKS French analysts were once again dreaming of attracting larger and more prominent circles
of French scholars, some of whom were repelled by Russie neuve as overly propagandistic.[89] The same year, however, the sympathizers in Russie neuve were
disparagingly evaluated for not being quite sympathetic enough: they "are not
distinguished by great courage in political questions, especially when it comes
to political actions directed against generally accepted views or government
policy." Taking into account "French psychology" and French "individualism," a Soviet diplomat ventured to say, it would be difficult to imagine one big
society successfully uniting "industrialists, financiers, journalists, scholars,
the petty-bourgeois intellectual and the pacifist."[90] The increasingly leftist profile of the French society from the 1920s to the 1930s reflected the possibilities
created by the political polarization in the final decade of the Third Republic
and one hoped-for solution to longstanding organizational dilemmas particularly apparent in France.

America's "Idealistic Liberalism"

The friendship society in the United States got off the ground not in the early
wave in Europe, in 1923–24, but only in 1927, something that, as in France,
reflected organizational difficulties, an unfavorable climate in politics and
the press, and, in this case, difficulties arising from non-recognition. VOKS's
Anglo-American Sector focused mainly on Britain, and Kameneva's plans for
an American tour in 1927 were dashed when, as in many other cases of Soviet
political figures, the State Department denied her a visa.[91] Initially, Kameneva's
executive assistant (otvetstvennyi sekretar´)—the future head of VOKS's book
exchange Roman Veller, who had worked with Kameneva in the famine-relief
days after returning from emigration in the United States to Soviet Russia
after the revolution—was sent on a scouting expedition to Washington and
New York from December 29, 1924, to January 28, 1925. He found a total
lack of coordination among the myriad Soviet agencies with representation
in the United States, including the Commissariats of Health and Land; the
Amtorg Trading Corporation, founded in New York in 1924; the state publishing house, Gosizdat; and Boris Svirskii, who ran the Russian Information
Bureau in Washington that began operations in September 1923. Svirskii soon
became a kind of unofficial ambassador to the United States and a key player
in the Soviet battle for recognition, so he was especially preoccupied by other
matters after he became the VOKS representative.

During his U.S. tour on behalf of Kameneva, Veller attended conferences
of political scientists and the American Association for the Advancement of

Science, ate breakfast with the editors of *The Nation*, and found much time for research on a brochure about American folklore. In between, he held talks on a friendship society during his visits to New York and Washington. In his perceptive remarks, Veller reported that "the picture of the USSR among a huge number of Americans cannot even be called false; it simply does not exist." He also discoursed on the distinctiveness of American "idealistic liberalism," which sought in the Soviet experiment that which was unrealized in the contemporary United States; at the same time, he explained, private rather than state solutions were the norm, which would make potential sympathizers especially suspicious of Soviet state institutions. The main goal Veller foresaw in a friendship society, in keeping with the prime objective in many Soviet calculations at the time, was to influence public opinion in order to further U.S. recognition of the Soviet Union. He concentrated most of his energy on the VOKS book exchange, which, unusually in the case of the Library of Congress, held out the possibility of securing hard currency for VOKS.[92] Veller, who had shown energy and initiative during his time at VOKS, later disappeared from its affairs. He had used his ARA contacts from the famine-relief days to find a job at Macy's department store.[93]

When the American Russian Society for Cultural Relations with Russia was founded in 1926 and met for the first time in April 1927, it was through the initiative of the "local intelligentsia"—a New York group including Lucy Branham and Graham Taylor. This, according to VOKS's own analysis, stood in contrast to Britain, where emissaries from the Soviet colony took the lead in setting up the friendship society. VOKS reports from the late 1920s and early 1930s—partly in keeping with "proletarianization" campaign radicalized during militant turmoil of the Great Break, which pointed to a preference whenever possible for the "laboring" and "democratic" intelligentsia abroad—were dissatisfied with the prominence within it of the intelligentsia's "elite layers" and wealthy left-leaning socialites. Like the London group, the New York society reportedly had a closed character and too many "respectable gentlemen."[94] VOKS's evaluation was, in fact, accurate. The American society kept a low profile to avoid conflicts whenever possible. With headquarters on East 55th St. in New York—and music, arts, and book committees formed by 1928 and rather less active affiliates to follow in Chicago, Philadelphia, and San Francisco—the new institution, in the words of one historian, was populated by "affluent and generally respected" figures engaged with "the liberal social causes of mainstream America."[95]

Notable in the U.S. society was the preponderance of liberals, mainstream academics, and social reformers who predominated over a sprinkling of socialists. In 1928, the society's president was William Allan Neilson, a professor of English and the president of Smith College from 1917 to 1939. The group of vice presidents included educational philosopher John Dewey, whose visit to the USSR in 1927 coincided with the height of his favorable views of the Soviet experiment and his impression that the country had widely implemented his pedagogical theories; Stephen P. Duggan, a foreign-policy expert and founder of the Institute of International Education; social reformer and public-health-nursing pioneer Lillian D. Wald, the peace and women's suffrage activist who founded the Henry Street Settlement House on the Lower East Side; and the radical journalist Floyd Dell, onetime editor of the socialist magazine *The Masses*.[96] In 1930, George S. Counts, whose progressive and child-centered pedagogy was influenced by Dewey, returned from his seven-month, 6,000-mile automobile journey across the USSR to assume the post of secretary. Counts kept in touch with VOKS, sending clippings and reports about his sparring with the conservative press and his calls for the end of the USSR's international isolation.[97] During his 1924 trip, Veller had discussed the friendship society with Franz Boas, the Columbia University cultural anthropologist whose writings played a major role in shifting explanations of cultural differences from racial to historical-environmental factors. The advisory council eventually did incorporate Boas and a number of other luminaries, including the economist and planning advocate Stuart Chase, Stanford University historian and famine relief alumnus Frank Golder, and renowned social reformer and peace activist Jane Addams.[98]

In the case of the friendship society in the United States, with its characteristically prominent liberals, a combination that VOKS seemingly craved had come into being: a gathering of influential and mainstream figures who despite their political distance from communism were sympathetic to the Soviet cause. Once again, however, both before and after the era after U.S. recognition of the Soviet Union in 1933, Soviet handlers were congenitally unprepared to approve of their American friends. Svirskii told Kameneva in 1927 that "as you know, liberals here are uneven, cautious, and tempering." Later, the VOKS representative in the Soviet embassy in Washington, Umanskii, disparaged those types of friends who were attracted to the Soviet Union for "philosophical-political" considerations. In prose dripping with scorn, he claimed that they sought through the friendship society to "purge their capitalist property and redeem themselves from their bourgeois sins," that they were astoundingly passive in practical work and, worse, that they took an intransigently "liberal" attitude toward Trotskyists and Trotsky sympathizers.[99]

As this suggests, VOKS analysts could be harsh as well as pessimistic about foreign friends and the organizational and political setbacks that Soviet cultural diplomacy faced in Europe and the United States. Such condemnations protected them ideologically and also justified less-than-spectacular results. The difference remained startling, however, when VOKS officials directed general assessments of its activities abroad to the party-state leadership (and when they touted the organization's foreign contacts to domestic intelligentsia audiences). Now, erstwhile critics played up the strength, depth, and reliability of their associations abroad. Like tons of pig iron in the Plan, the numbers of societies and affiliates were always presented as rising inexorably upward; famous names, even if they were not active members, were dropped with pride. VOKS did not merely showcase Soviet socialism for foreigners; it showcased its connections abroad for Soviet audiences.

Motivations for exaggerating the significance of the friendship societies are not hard to discern. VOKS was always hard pressed for scarce hard-currency resources and faced a good deal of indifference and even hostility to its work on the part of the party-state leadership.[100] In her Central Committee correspondence in the late 1920s Kameneva was particularly concerned with combating a political mentality that counted only "mass" work rather than small groups of intellectuals. A picture of constant growth and the wide influence of friendship society intellectuals was a good antidote: "VOKS in this sense represents a rather serious threat for the bourgeoisie." Still, Kameneva was careful not to exaggerate too much. In her August 1928 missive to the Central Committee secretariat, Kameneva could justifiably claim that VOKS had achieved much given its heavy reliance on unpaid representatives abroad. The organization's official reports, however, especially after Kameneva's removal during the Five-Year-Plan era, made far more grandiose claims. Political and organizational challenges went unmentioned as VOKS claimed the ability to "organize public opinion abroad by means of attraction into the orbit of our influence social elements friendly to us."[101]

Because of the difficulties of managing friendship societies from afar, VOKS proved conservative in deviating from the model first developed in Berlin in 1923. It stuck to its established partners in part because of the showcase mentality pervading VOKS's bureaucratic self-evaluations for the political leadership. In this sense, ironically, the friendship societies in these types of presentations had become a kind of distant Potemkin village erected on foreign shores.

International Travel and Transnational Patronage

The friendship societies were building blocks of a broader phenomenon: the rise of outposts of Soviet culture and politics abroad. In cities with significant Soviet colonies, including pre-1933 Berlin, Prague, Paris, and London, a kind of "Soviet Union abroad" arose around the embassy communities that provided a red counterpart to the larger and more diffuse "Russia abroad" of the Russian emigration. The friendship societies were places where VOKS supplied its bulletin and a library of materials on Soviet politics and culture; where Soviet scientists, scholars, writers, and poets regularly gave lectures and recitals; and where Soviet diplomats and Communists mixed with interested local figures.

But the cultural friendship societies were also places where the Soviet presence was, by political necessity and design, kept relatively unobtrusive and where the foreign sympathizers and experts predominated with their own reports and activities. The German society took the lead in forming specialized sections by field, and critical, independent views were also solicited by the societies themselves. For example, on November 2, 1925, John Maynard Keynes spoke at the London society. The economist had visited the USSR for two weeks that year after marrying the ballerina Lydia Lopokova, but he bluntly criticized Marxist economics as an anachronism and described Marxism-Leninism as a political religion.[103] In other words, the friendship societies created not just a piece of the Soviet Union abroad but a syncretic mix of Soviet exports and largely sympathetic yet distinctly non-Soviet approaches. A comparable phenomenon on a larger scale, in which Soviet and foreign pro-Soviet contributions combined to create a new admixture, occurred in the 1930s with the rise of anti-fascist culture. Also a hybrid, the European culture of anti-fascism was sponsored and spread through various front organizations and cultural interaction.

Travel to and from the Soviet Union and the regime of Soviet patronage attached to it played a distinct role in the rise of this syncretism. From the first, Kameneva made it a priority to "provide service to" (*obsluzhivat'*) the friendship societies—in the same sense that visiting foreigners, as it was put, were "provided service" when their visits and tours to the USSR were arranged. This meant publications, exhibitions, and visits from traveling representatives of the Soviet intelligentsia and political elite, from stars like Lunacharskii and Maiakovskii, to Soviet academicians, to a galaxy of lesser-known figures.[102] In 1925, Kameneva asked the head of the Foreign Section of the secret police (INO OGPU) to provide VOKS with information on all Soviet scholars, artists, pedagogues, engineers, and cultural figures traveling abroad when they were issued foreign passports, so that VOKS could attempt to secure their participation in its program of "cultural rapprochement." In the other direction, the practice began of sponsoring leading foreign liaisons in the friendship societies to visit the socialist homeland as a reward for friendship but also to cement their relationships with VOKS. "Through experience with Germany we know that such trips can bring great results" Kameneva wrote in 1925 to the VOKS representative in Paris.[104] Foreign friends willingly became enmeshed in patron-client relations across the boundary of the Soviet border.

It was an attractive proposition to have an institutional sponsor to navigate the difficulties of travel to the USSR. Foreign friends even acquired some influence on the opaque bureaucratic system involving Soviet travel westward. For example, in 1923, Otto Hoetzsch wrote to the Soviet embassy in Berlin to support an extension of the Berlin visit of the Moscow State University ethnographer Bruno Fridrikhovich Adler. Partnership had its benefits; the Soviet embassy in Berlin assured Litvinov of how important it was to "accommodate the intervention (*khodataistvo*) of Prof. Hoetzsch."[105] Throughout the interwar years, friendship society officials from various countries angled for favorable conditions and financial support for their own recommended travelers to the Soviet Union. As VOKS's reputation increased abroad in the late 1920s, requests for invitations and other kinds of aid poured in from well beyond the friendship societies. In 1928, American businessman Armand Hammer, whose import-export business with the Soviets in the 1920s began a long history of intimate dealings, turned to VOKS when he wished to have the son of a U.S. friend admitted to the Moscow Conservatory.[106] Some foreigners, especially those working or living inside the USSR or with longstanding Soviet connections, attempted to make themselves useful by providing information and contacts on their own initiative.[107]

By the end of the 1920s, it was regular practice to invite "active workers" of the friendship societies to Moscow, especially for the annual Revolution Day and May Day festivities favored as a time to impress foreigners, in order "to deepen their work by means of energetic giving of instructions."[108] Foreign friends came to expect such invitations as their due. In 1936, shortly before the first Moscow trial, VOKS's system of coordinating invitations with the embassies was disrupted by a series of Central Committee instructions that strengthened the prerogatives of the "directing organs." The barrister Denis Nowell Pritt, author of a number of pro-Soviet foreign policy pamphlets (he was later expelled from the Labour Party after supporting the Soviet invasion of Finland), was not approved for travel by the higher authorities. Nor was the secretary of the London society, M. E. Pheysey. In the wake of these unexpected rebuffs, Maiskii and the VOKS representative in England, Vinogradov, both reported the appearance of a "defeatist mood" among the British friends. Rumors circulated that if VOKS no longer had the wherewithal to invite society leaders, as in the past, then it signified that VOKS itself had either ceased to be important or was about to be "liquidated."[109] Insofar as Western intellectuals came to expect invitations for travel and other benefits to accrue from their contacts with the Soviets, their status as "friends of the Soviet Union" assumed concrete significance.

The designation "friend" became crucial for Soviet officials as well. To give just one example, when VOKS second-in-command Cherniavskii wrote to the

Central Committee's Angarov in 1936 about the Danish "proletarian" writer Martin Andersen Nexø, a staunch supporter of Soviet socialism since his first visit in 1922, his biographical record as one of the first European writers to defend the Soviet Union was rehearsed in detail. Nexø was active on the presidium of the Danish society of friends and published actively against fascism. He was both influential and in need; despite the great resonance of his works in Scandinavia, he was blacklisted and impoverished. "Inviting him to the USSR," Cherniavskii pleaded on his behalf, "would be for him both material and moral support."[110]

International aspirations, in this fashion, quickly led VOKS and other Soviet agencies to create clientelistic relations across borders and extend patronage to foreigners. At the same time, given increasing restrictions on outgoing travel and the more complex bureaucratic channels that needed to be navigated to leave the Soviet Union, access to the outside world became an increasingly valuable commodity sought and cherished by Soviet intellectual and cultural elites. Agencies like VOKS forged a form of patronage that furthered their institutional goals and thus contained a strong ideological component. To foreign friends, VOKS proffered aid and services in return, hopefully, for favorable publicity and a willingness to mobilize during various campaigns; to the Soviet intelligentsia, VOKS offered foreign contacts and aid with international travel in order to secure authoritative and orthodox speakers, above all at the friendship societies. Needless to say, members of the Soviet intelligentsia were subject to a much greater degree of coercion, especially starting at the end of the 1920s, when prominent Soviet intellectuals were pressured to do things such as sign international petitions and receive foreign visitors in the proper way.

What, then, did VOKS offer to the Soviet intelligentsia in concrete terms? In 1925, VOKS requested 3,000 rubles from the Gold Section of the Commissariat of Finance to be used for payment to scholars making appearances at the friendship societies. Its overall hard-currency allocation from the Soviet state in 1927 was 50,000 rubles, to which it could add 20,000 in foreign revenue. Perhaps more important and feasible than direct financial support was political aid for selected figures in gaining hard-currency allocations, including those beyond the standard amount (vne limita), from Finance's Hard-Currency Directorate (Valiutnoe Upravlenie). Maiakovskii, traveling to Warsaw, Prague, and Paris in 1927 on VOKS work, was afforded such support, given the "serious political significance" of his appearances abroad. The writer Vsevolod Ivanov received such support in 1927 as well, for travel to Europe and the United States.[111]

But these were privileged cases. More prosaically, VOKS circulated a form letter to scientists it knew were being sent abroad to study foreign "achievements," offering to share its international contacts and soliciting meetings with the prospective travelers. VOKS functioned as a kind of courier for the intelligentsia in an increasingly closed society, transferring and receiving materials from outside the Soviet Union for its intelligentsia clients. This became especially important after the late 1920s as a legitimized way of contacting the outside world and as a channel abroad for those in the provinces whose connections were limited. During a short period in 1929, for example, VOKS transferred photographs and correspondence between a scholar at the Nizhnii Novgorod Archeo-Ethnographic Commission and H. F. Osborn, a leading eugenicist in the United States ("I will always be glad to be useful to Osborn and VOKS," the grateful scholar wrote); located the address of Max Planck for a Soviet physicist; and, among many other similar services, exchanged correspondence between the Bodleian Library in Oxford and the Leningrad State Public Library.[112] For the cultural elite, VOKS could even arrange publications abroad. In June 1929, to cite only one example, VOKS actively sought out Parisian publishing houses that it hoped would publish a work on the Meyerhold Theater.[113] Many Soviet intellectuals jumped at the chance to pursue their own professional, personal, and intellectual agendas.

Far from everyone was entirely clear about what VOKS could do for them. An engineer from Ufa who wanted VOKS's help in obtaining a foreign passport in 1929, for example, was told his offer to work for VOKS could take the form of a small article about cultural construction in his region to be published in the VOKS bulletin.[114] A more pointed and savvy inquiry about how VOKS might deploy its services, in light of the increasing dangers of foreign connections in the late 1920s, came from academician Marr, the linguist whose theories and stature were on the rise even as the still-independent Academy of Sciences was under siege.[115] "We speak [about this] at home," he told Kameneva at the late 1928 meeting of the scholars' union, "so we should therefore speak about it openly. How can I be guaranteed that I will not only be published abroad, but that I can do so in a way, in a publication, that will not result in a whole mass of unpleasantnesses for me later on?"[116] There was, of course, no guarantee. Rather, there were demands and expectations: not just to meet with visitors or make favorable reports on the USSR abroad, but to make statements, sign petitions, and take part in various campaigns.

Starting in the mid-1920s, party organs began to mobilize the intelligentsia for various campaigns demanding signatures to pre-prepared manifestos. For example, in 1925, the Comintern planned to circulate "open letters from various circles of Russian scientists and cultural workers" in defense of the USSR, and such practices increased by the end of the decade. In 1930, for example, VOKS published 700 signatures in its Bulletin as part of its campaign to denounce the wreckers in the "Industrial Party" trial of 1930, and a

November 23 meeting in the House of Scholars provided grist for radio and press reports.[117] Soviet intellectuals who traveled abroad inevitably had to give something back to their party-state patrons—first and foremost, evidence of ideological loyalty that took increasingly concrete form.

The upsurge in demands altered the tenor of patron-client relations and made foreign "bourgeois" contacts distinctly more dangerous. If the great concern of the early 1920s was that intelligentsia travelers would not return from abroad or talk to the émigré press, the fear after travel controls tightened over the course of the 1920s was that those with marketable skills might defect. This was expressed in a denunciation to Kameneva of ballet dancers whose international travel she was warned against.[118]

Because making foreign contacts through VOKS seemed to offer political protection, the intelligentsia desire to approach VOKS appeared noticeably greater after the anti-specialist assault of the Great Break. Professor A. A. Sidorov of the Academy of Arts (GAKhN) wrote a handwritten appeal to Kameneva regarding his Berlin-published album about the city of Moscow, which VOKS had recommended to German intellectuals. By April 1929, the album and Sidorov were attacked in the Soviet press because the work displayed an incriminatingly high number of churches. Using the emotional language of the supplicant, Sidorov turned to Kameneva "in great personal pain." He then got down to business. Citing "concrete services rendered in cultural relations with the West," he insisted that this gave "VOKS every reason to rehabilitate my book from exclusively hostile attacks."[119] The avant-gardist Sergei Tret'iakov, who traveled to Berlin in 1930 under VOKS auspices, fulfilled his assignment of promoting the collective farm system and justifying the death sentences of the Industrial Party trial. But he also made lasting intellectual connections in a series of mutually influential interactions with Brecht, Benjamin, Piscator, and other Berlin avant-garde figures as he pursued his own mission—which did not contradict that of VOKS—of promoting Moscow as the center for an avant-garde international.[120]

VOKS developed into a mid-level patron of members of the Soviet intelligentsia within the byzantine system that became entrenched in the 1920s for allocating travel permissions out of the USSR. Its role was augmented by a simple fact: travel requests from scholars and artists were rejected with far greater frequency than those of technical and trade specialists, diplomats, and other state officials traveling abroad. In 1921, Cheka chairman Feliks Dzerzhinskii protested to the Central Committee about Commissar of Enlightenment Lunacharskii's "systematic" endorsements for foreign travel for figures in the theater and art worlds. "Iron Feliks" charged darkly that some were linked to foreign intelligence. The need for recuperations and cures were hardly convincing justifications for foreign travel, he remarked caustically; let them travel to the provinces for their holidays. As this suggests, genuinely "private" travel after the early 1920s became largely a thing of the past. Travel had to be arranged, even if at one's own expense (*za svoi schet*), through a sponsoring state institution. Approval and paperwork from several layers of bureaucracy and its special committees became more daunting. These included, most frequently, endorsements from place of work (and from the party hierarchy for Communists), organizations sponsoring travel abroad to conferences or for exhibits or events, commissariat to which one's institution belonged (i.e., the commissariats of enlightenment, health, national economy, etc.), and, after 1924, the Central Committee's cumbersomely named Commission for Verification of Foreign Travel for State Institutions and Social and Economic Organizations. Each of these layers of approval, of course, increased the chances of delays and rejections. Each traveler had to be checked by the secret police, representatives of which sat on the Central Committee's commission. The primary destination for cultural and scholarly travel before 1933 (trips sponsored by Narkompros), as for technical and economic specialists, was Germany, with other European countries and the United States a distant second.[121]

VOKS participated in the politics of foreign travel in many ways. It was itself a clearing house for invitations from abroad and thus could serve as a primary sponsor for international travel. Starting in 1924, KZP and then VOKS played a role in determining, often in conjunction with the relevant Soviet embassy, the desirability of travel for artists, musicians, and performers on tour. It also routinely supported the travel requests from people traveling through other institutions, and this co-sponsorship (*sodeistvie*) was actively sought by a wide array of scientists, scholars, students, and other members of the intelligentsia. VOKS provided "interventions" (*khodataistva*) and formal expressions of support within the bureaucracy. Figures with ties to VOKS initiatives, such as the linguist and phoneticist S. K. Boianus in 1928, who hoped to travel to London, were granted aid. He was helping VOKS's new program of promoting "foreign languages for the masses," and his work was thus endorsed as having positive "civic benefit." When a Lappologist, Professor Griuner, who had made a good impression on the VOKS representative in Sweden for his reports on the conditions of Soviet scholars, was found "literally starving" in that country in 1927, VOKS attempted to obtain 500 rubles for him from the Special Hard Currency Directorate (*Osoboe Valiutnoe Upravlenie*) to pay his debts, given his past services and the blow to Soviet prestige created by his condition. Professor V. Bunak, director of the Anthropological Institute of the first MGU in 1930, also was traveling to London for the Conference of the International Federation of Eugenic Institutions. VOKS's Anglo-American sector fully supported his application because he was prepared to give a paper at the Society of Cultural Relations on the position of Soviet scholars, repudiating reports in the *Times* and elsewhere that Soviet "non-party scholars are supposedly not given the opportunity to conduct scientific work, etc."[122]

As this suggests, the record of services rendered by the intellectual in question and the political-ideological and foreign-policy justifications for his travel were prime considerations in the messages of evaluation that Soviet officials sent through the system. Such categories were also routinely involved in VOKS's participation in higher-level commissions involving group travel, exhibitions, and policy matters regarding travel. Considerations of technical expertise could replace the political justification, as when Kameneva participated in a special Orgburo commission approving travel for a Soviet delegation to an international cinematography exhibition in Holland. The clinching argument was that eleven Soviet directors would be able to familiarize themselves with the latest developments in the "film production of the West."[123]

When the same figures who dispensed or withheld the coveted *komandirovki* (business trips) for others themselves wished to travel, they suddenly turned to the same combination of wheedling and political grandstanding that their clients also displayed. Kameneva reported to the Central Committee secretariat that a two-week vacation in Turkey was ordered by her doctors and received "full support" from Chicherin and Mikoian. It would also be important for VOKS, not to mention the non-Western world: "Eastern ambassadors have jokingly told me on many occasions that I show special sympathy for Europe and do not give them attention." Permission for international travel was a constant concern at the highest levels of the Party and the state. Radek, once the peripatetic chief strategist of the Comintern in the early 1920s, reported to Stalin that he had not been allowed out of the country after the time he fell into disfavor as a member of the Trotskyist Opposition. Now a top advisor to Stalin, he wished to become oriented again by traveling as an *Izvestiia* correspondent to the Geneva disarmament conference; there he could also, he implied, play a role in securing U.S. recognition of the USSR by talking to American representatives in the wake of Franklin Roosevelt's election to the presidency. The Politburo approved his request.[124]

The patron-client relations endemic to the functioning of the Soviet system in general have often been taken to prove that in the Soviet case personalistic ties trumped institutions. Patron-client networks were supposedly pre-modern, what Sheila Fitzpatrick has called an "archaizing" feature of Stalinism. In Soviet-style patronage, Fitzpatrick has noted, "the ultimate allocational decisions were made by bureaucrats—but on personalistic, not bureaucratic-legal reasons."[125] The case of VOKS and Soviet intellectuals traveling abroad, however, illustrates a longstanding relationship between party-state patrons and intelligentsia clients defined in terms of the organization's particular need for international services to the party-state. Even as the intelligentsia rendered its thanks in the personalistic language typical of Soviet patronage relation-ships—deep respect, gratitude, attention, and friendship—the strategies and priorities governing this system of patronage were bureaucratically defined and ideologically directed. The Soviet patronage system could be at one and the same time personalistic and anchored in the formal institutional divisions of the highly bureaucratic party-state.[126] In his study of patronage and the Stalin cult, for example, Jan Plamper establishes how, unlike, for example, in Nazi Germany, "a newly won client had to 'want' to be a client and had to show signs of 'belief.'"[127] This Soviet brand of ideological personalism was also present in the remarkable way that this patronage system extended across borders to foreign clients. Soviet patronage was integrated into institutional structures, extended across borders to international networks, and overtly reflected the prominence of ideology in the communist order.

VOKS, with its powerful interest in the nexus of propaganda, influence, and cultural relations, was at the forefront of the new regime's concerted and often adroit use of patronage in the service of cultural diplomacy. At the same time, repetitive routine was from the outset a big feature of the Soviets' bureaucratic international machine. A standard repertoire of VOKS activities abroad became entrenched, revolving around the friendship societies, written materials aimed abroad and attempts to influence the press, and harnessing the Soviet intelligentsia through travel, publications, and exhibitions. Adept as Kameneva, Arosev, and others could often be, permanent features of VOKS international activities included delays, bumbling, execrable translations, lack of qualified cadres, and cultural misunderstandings of the outside world. In this sense, the external operations of VOKS were truly the product and reflec-tion of the social and political system that created them.

3

The Potemkin Village Dilemma

The arrival of significant numbers of travelers in the years after 1923 quickly spurred the development of novel methods and modes of presenting the Soviet experiment. The mid-to-late 1920s marked the emergence of a set of ways of guiding foreign visitors that became known to its adepts as *kul´tpokaz*—one of those newspeak Soviet acronyms that can be translated as the presentation of culture, or cultural show. Fundamental to this practice were visits to model institutions, the display of which became recognized as "the very best method of propaganda of our ideas."[1] Even the relatively small number of the most famous and well-visited sites played a historical role not only for visiting outsiders but also internally within the Soviet system. Far from all the places visited by foreigners were either showcases or model institutions, however. A larger number of sites were simply in good enough condition that they made it onto the long list of places approved for foreign visits.

There were good reasons that arranging visits to selected sites became the linchpin of presenting the Soviet system to outsiders. Prima facie conditions—what visitors could see, smell, and feel—were hardly favorable for the kind of awed public praise that the Soviets craved and, in this era, so often received. To Western eyes, even those of the many sympathizers during the few relatively stable periods in the mid-1920s and mid-1930s, the cities appeared drab, the store shelves bare, and the population thin and poor. The scale of child homelessness was shocking, and the system's inefficiency, even for honored guests and those paying a premium in hard currency, was at once frustrating and comical. Overcoming outsiders' often negative first impressions and reshaping the perception of general conditions became a crucial task.

The term "cultural show" itself has a great deal of resonance. The noun *pokaz*, which means "display" or "presentation," also contains the root of the adjective *pokazatel´nyi*, or "demonstration," used in the term "show trial" to denote a staged political lesson. Demonstrative political lessons were at the heart of Soviet political culture, and so were models; the adjective "show" was widely used to designate selected model or experimental factories, prisons, labor communes, collective farms, and so on.

Later, Soviet citizens often used the slang word *pokazukha*, which transformed that root word for show, *pokaz*, into a derogatory term signifying the wool pulled over someone's eyes. When French Radical Party leader and three-time prime minister Édouard Herriot visited Ukraine from August 26–September 9, 1933, denying accounts of massive famine and likening the country to a garden in full bloom, the young A. G. Man'kov, a future prominent pre-Petrine historian but then a young student from a rural background, recorded in his diary: "Ekh, Herriot, Herriot! Now you too are in the USSR! Here they receive you joyfully, they lead you down the showcase road (*po pokaznoi doro-zhke*) of Russian reality... But narrow, narrow is that little path!"[2]

It is useful to make a distinction between "showcases," a relatively small group of places that were substantially influenced by the fact that they became the most prominent destinations for foreign visitors, and a broader number of working institutions designated as "models" (*obraztsovyi*) within various Soviet hierarchies. Many models were also sites that came to be considered desirable for foreign eyes. Both labels are an ideal type, for not all showcases were created as such, certain parts of institutions could evolve into showcases for foreigners, and even those places groomed most deliberately for foreign eyes played roles for Soviet actors and audiences as well.

"Cultural show" arose as the increasingly codified practice of presenting these sites to foreigners. They were intended to be microcosms from which foreigners could make positive generalizations about the new Soviet society as a whole. Other states have tried to show their most attractive sides; it is the extent of the Soviet effort to shape foreigners' outlooks, first and foremost through the presentation of such a large array of models, that was distinctive.

The display of models was a brilliant way of "arming" foreign friends with the evidence of their own eyes. If visitors encountered bands of homeless children as they swarmed the streets, so also would they be shown a solution to the problem in a well-appointed children's commune; if there were widespread reports of forced labor and political prisoners, so the new penitentiaries "reforging" inmates into new people would prove the progressive humanism of socialism. Even as showcases and models carried with them a sense of pathbreaking exceptionalism inside the Soviet system, through them one was encouraged to generalize about the current state of, say, kindergartens or maternity wards throughout the land. Quality would be transformed into quantity. At the same time, perhaps even to the most hard-headed and ruthless Bolsheviks, model sites appeared to hold out the possibility of mapping the future landscape of socialism. The best examples would become universal, heralding what socialism could be once the heritage of the past was overcome. This was not necessarily staged exclusively for foreigners. Designing models became a quintessential practice for a group of revolutionary modernizers with scarce resources in a sea of "backwardness."

Model institutions were hardly unique to Soviet socialism. They were, for example, widespread in interwar Romania, where post-World War I agrarian reform led to "model" and "demonstrative" farms, villages, and even sanitary districts. Just as the Soviet models influenced much larger projects, these Romanian microcosms provided conceptual precedents for the murderous project of ethnically pure model provinces in wartime Bessarabia and Bukovina.[3] Like their Soviet counterparts, Romanian models were supposed to be beacons of conquered backwardness; they, too, were facilitated by a strong state, a *Kulturträger* tradition, and activist intelligentsia involvement. If, however, the focus on agricultural models emerged in a country in which the peasantry was seen as the backbone of the nation, Soviet "socialist construction" aimed at transforming virtually everything—here the scope and extent of models turned out to be unprecedented. Unique as well was the extent to which Soviet model institutions became part and parcel of an elaborate system of impressing and converting foreign visitors, as the world-historical, universalistic thrust of Soviet communism was layered on top of the ingrained comparative sensitivities of "Russia and the West."

Model-based methods of cultural show held a deep and many-faceted ideological resonance. Model communities, such as those rehabilitating prisoners or forging new people, harked back to utopian community-based blueprints for socialism and the religious, political, and experimental communes with which socialist utopianism was historically intertwined, in both Russia and the Western countries. Building on pre-revolutionary intelligentsia and reformist traditions embedded in a European context, and sometimes constituted in the early Soviet period with the participation of foreign experts, many model institutions highlighted commitments to science and culture, industry and the proletariat, and, not least, the social-welfare measures through which Soviet socialism made one of its most important appeals to non-socialists in an age of embattled liberalism.

Precisely because they were so central, the ideological significance of model institutions spanned the divide between displays aimed specifically at outsiders and the simultaneously emerging Soviet and Stalinist domestic order, centrally concerned with altering the psyche of its own citizens. The practices and strategies that emerged to convince foreigners and that became embedded in cultural show in the 1920s arose at the same time that the Soviet state and Soviet culture designed unprecedentedly widespread methods of molding the outlooks and psyches of the domestic population.

Foreign Delegations and Potemkin Villages

A remarkable resurgence of accusations about Potemkin villages occurred in the 1920s, as the old European tradition of depicting Russian deceptiveness was combined with the controversial political nature of Soviet claims. Foreigners who remained unconvinced frequently labeled these places Potemkin villages, implying that there was something primordially Russian about Soviet practices. Foreign rumors and accusations surrounding Potemkin villages starting in the 1920s were so widespread that they were quite familiar to Soviet officials involved in the reception of visitors and even played a distinct role in the development of *kul'tpokaz*.

Discussion of Potemkin villages, either to dispel or further the accusation, was a staple of the voluminous travel literature written by Europeans and Americans—the very publications most frequently tracked by the Soviets. Some former guests even wrote hostile letters to tell their hosts that they had not been fooled. A trade unionist from Berlin who had been in Moscow for famine relief in early 1922 charged: "They could not show me Potemkin villages, but these workers' delegations will be shown only such, I am sure of this from personal experience." As a result, declarations signed by labor and other delegations, the templates for which were provided by Soviet or foreign Communists, routinely declared that visitors roamed free and could examine whatever they pleased: "We walked with complete freedom," an English delegation of cooperators insisted in 1926. As an analyst for the Comintern's Agitprop section reported in 1927, even sympathetic delegates to the 1927 Congress of Friends "arrived in the USSR with great prejudices (a result of indoctrination in their own countries) that they would be shown spectacles specially prepared in advance, something like 'Potemkin villages.'" A conclusion this analyst drew was that arranging teas for visitors in the homes of workers and citizens with an "everyday" atmosphere in supposedly typical surroundings was the most effective means of thwarting those expectations. Visits to model workers' homes were innovated that year, and they became a staple of cultural show during the Five-Year Plan.[4]

Many Soviet guides and officials thus realized that the greatest Soviet successes could be scored when they dispelled expectations about Potemkin villages. The term was increasingly used by foreign visitors in the mid- to late 1920s, not in the original sense of false façades but referring to all unrepresentative, propagandistic models. For example, a VOKS guide in 1932 reported that one German visitor suspicious of all pre-planned visits was overwhelmed when she unexpectedly followed children's cries to a kindergarten found "in model order and cleanliness." She reportedly told the guide: "In Germany it is frequently reported that foreigners can see only what Intourist and VOKS show, and they will of course show only that which is allowed to be seen. Now I see that this is untrue."[5]

The Soviet architects of cultural show did not jettison their vocabularies or world views when they talked about foreigners in closed meetings among themselves. Even top-secret documents repeat the mantra of "telling the truth" about the Soviet Union. To penetrate practices and attitudes, one needs to decipher and find clues in documents of several provenances. For example, it was easy to deny the existence of Potemkin villages (and the Comintern analyst wrote of foreign expectations of "something like" them), because the term historically signified something erected specially to hoodwink visiting notables, whereas genuine yet unrepresentative model institutions were ubiquitous in the Soviet system. In one sense, understandings of the Potemkin label were academic: the circle that needed to be squared in Soviet cultural show was to isolate foreigners from unpleasant discoveries and to shuttle them from one favorable model to another, yet at the same time attempt to allay the widespread fears that they were being isolated and manipulated.

When the American engineering prodigy Zara Witkin crossed the Soviet border from Finland in April 1932, he was fired up with sympathy for the Soviet experiment and ready to donate his considerable talents and energies to the cause. In one of the most perceptive memoirs ever written of a Soviet sojourn by a technical "specialist," he recalled the shock of his first glimpse of the promised land:

> Suddenly the border! The train stops…About the little station clusters a group of people, clad as I have never seen people clad before, in rags and tatters of furs. They move slowly. They are slovenly. Neglect and disorder all about. The station house is broken down. Pieces of equipment lie scattered in the snow.

The vast train station in Leningrad and his hotel room, both "unbelievably dirty," did nothing to improve his first impressions.[6] Travelogues and other literature suggest such initial negative reactions as well as critical judgments about conditions and standards of living were common among Western visitors but peaked in periods of the most acute hardship and social dislocation, notably the early 1920s and the early 1930s.[7]

Pro-Soviet travelers often recorded euphoria at the border and experiencing the crossing into the "new world" as a significant moment; for the Soviets, the potent combination of security concerns and a two-camp ideology made the border a powerful symbol of Soviet patriotism, replete by the 1930s with a cult of border guards. The border-station greetings for delegations and the most honored guests originated simultaneously out of pragmatic concerns for creating good first impressions and the heightened ideological significance imparted to the gateway to the proletarian homeland. At the arrival of the British trade-union delegation of November-December 1924, the first of a large-scale influx of workers' delegations in the mid-1920s, the Presidium of the Central Council of Trade Unions (VTsSPS) placed "extraordinary" political importance on the mobilization of local workers by nearby affiliates to meet the train at the border crossing.[8] Orchestras playing the *Internationale*, banners, speeches, preparatory cleaning of train stations, and removal of unsightly passers-by became routine.

By the end of 1925, Profintern general secretary Solomon Lozovskii, speaking at a session of the Soviet trade unions' Commission on External Relations (the organization charged with organizing workers' visits), declared: "We have moved to the mass production of delegations." Indeed, in the two years after the English workers' delegation, twenty-four others followed, all from European countries, with the exception of one Australian group.[9] In 1929, Finnish delegates found 1,000 people gathered to greet them at the train station in Voronezh. The border crossing and the hospitality ceremonies at arrival, like the participation of delegations at the November 7 and May 1 parades, the visit to the Lenin Mausoleum—where foreigners were let in ahead of Soviet citizens waiting in line—and the "fact-finding" visits to factories, soviets, resorts, and other "objects of show" (*ob"ekty pokaza*) became principal and well-worn rituals of this "mass production." It is hardly a surprise to find, however, that among the delegation arrivals of 1927 were "highly unsuccessful meetings at the train station" when only a few greeters showed up, delegates' luggage was lost, and, worst of all, "delegates mixed with the ordinary public." Some foreigners were not met at all.[10]

The phenomenon of visiting delegations, which from the mid-1920s were sometimes elaborately prepared in the delegates' home countries and certainly on arrival, became highly formulaic. It was, thus, one early laboratory for the Soviet mission of transforming negative perceptions into positive testimonials. The delegations commanded significant attention and resources, and consequently had an effect on "providing service" (*obsluzhivanie*) for all important visitors, including intellectuals.

The Commission of External Relations and other interagency discussions of workers' delegations from the mid-1920s reveal a range of differing Soviet priorities for delegation visits, but all of them resurfaced consistently over time. Foreign policy considerations, "connecting [delegations] to the current political tasks of the moment," influenced decisions about countries chosen from which to solicit delegations. In 1927, for example, "special political significance" was attached to England, the United States, Mexico, and India.[11] Second, specific industries and large factories in the country of origin were targeted as recruiting grounds for delegates, with a view toward aiding the strategies and recruiting policies of the foreign communist parties. Third, the goal was not merely to solicit positive public declarations but also to promote targeted counter-propaganda. Examples ranged from delegations that were urged specifically to refute individual articles on Soviet workers' unrest in the Social Democratic press to directing a delegation in the winter of 1933 to Ukraine in order to repudiate reports circulating abroad about the man-made famine of the collectivization era that left millions dead of starvation and hunger-related diseases. This deadly bit of counter-propaganda thus formed part of a concerted international cover-up campaign that enlisted foreigners to deny the famine. Why did a delegation such as the one to Soviet Ukraine play its part? A major part of the explanation comes from Rachel Mazuy's research on French delegations. Mazuy revealed elaborate preparations made for the selection of delegates, who were designated by local Communists according to specific procedures in advance of their "elections." Delegations were seeded with a proportion of communist delegates, and special attention was paid to oral preparation before the trip and on the train, where the delegation head led sessions on how travelers should pose questions to Soviet workers. The Soviet journey was thus both a rite of passage and a part of cadre politics, since it could—providing positive testimonials were given—boost careers in the trade unions and the French Communist Party.[12]

British communist Albert Inkpin, head of Willi Münzenberg's working-class League of Friends organization (not to be confused with VOKS's friend-ship societies), wanted a fixed percentage of non-communist workers who were "capable of being convinced" in "accordance with a prepared informa-tional plan." Delegates' motivations for visiting the USSR often diverged from Soviet plans, however. During the Great Depression, Soviet trade union files were jammed with requests from delegates who attempted to stay and find work.[13] Some Soviet strategizing was specific to workers' delegations, but the principles of planning travel based on elaborately ambitious political scenar-ios, the practice of advance preparation of the travelers, and the crucial role of post-departure measurements of sympathizers' loyalty were principal features of the reception of intellectual visitors as well.

The visits of foreign delegations prompted unusually explicit discussions of measures devised to affect the psychology, political loyalty, and memory of the time spent in the Soviet Union. On the eve of departure, delegates were presented with bound leather albums with photographs, posters, and "photo series," which in 1932 included eighteen items, among them portraits of Lenin and Stalin.[14] Delegates thus returned home with visual "evidence" that might help shape their memories. Delegations always went through a ritual of ham-mering out signed parting resolutions. Tamara Solonevich's *Notes of a Soviet*

Translator—published in Sofia eleven years after she served on the forty-day visit by a 1926 English workers' delegation—is especially vivid on this point. One rationale behind the negotiations over parting declarations, Solonevich wrote, was that the signatures of delegates on the documents meant something to the signers, who would thus be less likely to contradict them later. Templates were given to the delegation leaders in advance, and the goal of the political sessions with the delegates was to have as little as possible crossed out and as little criticism as possible added. However, because of the Soviet disorganization that typically accompanied these elaborate preparations, a novice translator like Solonevich herself ended up with a big role in this potentially delicate political work without any advance preparation.[15]

The basic "techniques of hospitality" employed during travel by important delegations and other dignitaries—chief among them wining and dining, attempts to isolate foreigners from ordinary citizens, travel on special trains, pre-approved and often standard itineraries avoiding troublesome areas—have long been known.[16] Solonevich wrote that four *Chekisty*, two of whom knew English, were present at the English delegation's encounters with Donbass workers, and that the chaperones on the delegation's train were armed party members, usually former Red Army men, one of whom shot a particularly persistent homeless child in front of the author. Long after her flight from the Soviet Union across the Finnish border into emigration in 1934, Solonevich vividly recalled the complexity of her own attitudes when Western visitors were concerned: "I very often caught myself realizing that I had a split consciousness," she wrote. "On the one hand I wanted to be able to tell the English the truth about the present condition of things, on the other I felt a kind of irresponsible Russian pride rising up and burning when they talked ecstatically about our spaces, our far-off Caucasian nature, our hospitality."[17]

Given what is known about official hospitality and the more recent evidence about preparatory and follow-up operations, it is noteworthy that transcripts of worker delegations' conversations with Soviet and factory officials show recurrences of pointed and combative skepticism. In 1927, French delegates asked why the official press did not publish data on supplementary hours workers labored (they were told these were not long), about large numbers of strikes (they were told that only 0.5 percent of workers participated), and nonpayment of social insurance and pensions. Others mentioned safety conditions, unemployment, late payment of wages, party control of trade unions, and rising industrial accidents. To be sure, many such incidents were prompted by the regular inclusion in the delegations of small numbers of social democrats, anarchists, and anarcho-syndicalists: an effort to win over converts. Some questions were doctrinaire or naive: "Does the factory committee defend narrow craft interests of workers when they contradict the interests of the working class as a whole?"[18] Guide reports of positive impressions were commonplace. In one case in 1929, an "oppositionist" who fell in among a group of Scandinavian workers to tell them how they had been deceived was delivered to the OGPU by the delegates themselves.[19]

There are some direct analogies that can be drawn between worker delegates and sympathetic intellectuals, as there are analogies between the reception of worker delegations and the practices developed for other types of visitors. The public reports of both delegates and intellectual "friends," whether in the form of press statements or travelogues, were partisan political documents considered crucially important by the Soviets, something made amply clear to guests. Often these proclamations said more about their authors' political and personal sympathies than their impressions and views. Mazuy has referred to the Soviet voyage as a "test of identity" in which any apostasy risked a rupture with the "communist counter-society in which one was dependent politically." Her distinction between the "exterior" voyage (in which most delegates faithfully played the role of propagandist as arranged) and the "interior" voyage (often masked by the orthodox discourse) is comparable to the self-censorship of leading fellow-travelers.[20] In both cases, the Soviets innovated and refined a wide range of often sophisticated practices surrounding foreign visits while ingraining their own orthodoxy that only the lavish praise they wished to hear was the "truth."

Translators, guides, and officials commonly referred to foreign enthusiasm for the Soviet experiment as recognition of the "entire truth" about the Soviet system, and equally ubiquitous were expressions of satisfaction that "slander" propagated abroad had been dispelled. Solonevich later wrote, "This leitmotif about 'the entire truth' was repeated during the whole time of our trip."[21] However poorly it sometimes functioned, the Soviets developed an intricate and elaborate system for managing foreign visits at the very time that their manner of discussing their practices was reduced to a crude, inflexible orthodoxy equating belief with truth. In this lay the self-censorship of the Soviet hosts.

Sites of Communism

In October 1930, the head of VOKS's Department for the Reception of Foreigners (*Otdel po priemu inostrantsev*) wrote of the intolerable nervous stress his organization faced. Foreign visitors wanted to see everything connected to the Five-Year Plan, including industrial enterprises, factories, and planning organizations. But in most cases, Soviet economic institutions wished only to avoid foreign visitors, and even for eminent guests his office was forced to call

10-15 times in advance and "virtually beg" for a visit to be scheduled.[22] In 1936, the Central Committee passed a resolution declaring the work of Intourist was unsatisfactory, in part because too many museums and other "old" places of traditional tourism were being shown—partly because of difficulties in persuading economic commissariats to agree to open up factories and industrial sites.[23] As this suggests, the "showing of sites" (*pokaz ob"ektov*) was based on the principle of pre-approved selectivity, but visitors were not taken to a small number of displays specially designed for foreigners. Of the hundreds of locations routinely visited, relatively few might be called showcases: institutions, like the Lefortovo prison or the secret police's Bolshevo children's commune, where conditions were carefully groomed for regular group visits. A second group comprised institutions that were not standard destinations for foreign inspections, although those sometimes did occur, but that were designated as "model" (*obraztsovye*) or "model-experimental" (*obraztsovo-opytnye*) within various Soviet hierarchies. The great construction projects and industrial "giants" of the Five-Year Plan were by nature showcases, because their monumentalism was, from the first, politically motivated. The largest number of locations for political tourism—including educational and research institutions, medical and hygiene institutions such as prophylactoria for reforming prostitutes, social-welfare institutions such as sanatoria, collective farms, museums, theaters, and many others—were simply prominent and presentable enough to be approved for organized foreign access.

Master lists of approved sites, which could differ among host organizations depending on their connections to the commissariats in charge of each, were far larger than those planned for specific groups' schedules, and they were, moreover, continually shifting. In 1930–31, for example, VOKS listed more than 300 "objects of show." In 1935, it founded a special "protocol" department to keep track of the list and the selection of sites thereon. Since VOKS and other agencies that hosted foreigners had to obtain permission from reluctant commissariats to gain entry to the sites they controlled, VOKS's reception department turned to higher party organs in 1931 for "pressure" (*nazhim*) to force them to permit visits.[24]

"Programs," or schedules of places to visit, were treated as important political decisions, and ratified in advance for important guests and delegations. Much like the itineraries for foreign travel through the country, there was not only the possibility but the expectation that the plan would vary depending on the interests and professions of the visitors. As with all important international matters, these had to be approved at the highest levels of the Party. In 1925, for example, the size and itinerary of the German workers' delegation, proposed by the trade unions and the Comintern, was approved by the Politburo. The Commission on External Relations' list of fourteen Moscow factories for this delegation included only one (a newspaper factory) labeled a "model"; another, the top chocolate factory *Krasnyi oktiabr'* (Red October) was a regularly featured treat for foreign guests. Lists of factories in Moscow *oblast'* set for delegation visits in 1932 included five metal works, two textile factories, four chemical plants, and four railroad enterprises. Whereas, during the same year, foreigners celebrating the fifteenth anniversary of the October Revolution were directed to three factories and twelve "cultural institutions," including a school, a hospital, a *sovkhoz*, and the Dzerzhinskii commune for reforming juvenile delinquents, which the leading pedagogue of the Stalin era, Anton Makarenko, headed from 1927–32.[25] Busy schedules kept foreigners occupied with presentable places, while some foreigners' suspicions about Potemkin villages were allayed simply by the sheer quantity of institutions.

The Soviet reception of foreign visitors was always focused on certain designated parts of the country, because visitors' "programs" of travel (most frequently arranged by the institutions inviting them) were concentrated in certain standard routes. In 1931, Intourist had developed only twelve standard itineraries from which tourists could choose; by 1933, there were thirty-six. Each had a special role to play in the presentation of the country. Sunny Crimea, for example, would demonstrate the successes of Soviet nationalities policy.[26]

Given jumps in the number of visitors first during the Great Depression and again in the period of the Popular Front, shortages of suitable locations were still being felt in the mid-1930s, when Intourist's Service Bureau (*Biuro obsluzhivaniia*), like VOKS before it, reported serious opposition to regular visits by foreigners on the part of those in charge of industrial and agricultural sites. The reasons are not hard to discern: the presence of foreigners demanded preparation, disrupted work schedules, and made local conditions into a matter of high political importance. In the peak tourist year of 1936, the Commissariat of Heavy Industry attempted to curtail the number of visits per month to each factory. As this dispute made clear, Intourist turned to the Politburo both when sparring with the commissariats over sites and when compiling the "general list of objects of show."[27] The work of the censorship agency Glavlit revolved around a constantly updated master list of items that could not be mentioned, popularly known to officials as the Talmud; similarly, agencies receiving foreigners continually revised the master list of those places that could be shown.

In his widely known work on Western intellectuals and communism, Paul Hollander emphasized first and foremost the power of utopian-seeking predispositions among leftist intellectuals, more so than Soviet techniques of hospitality, to generate the naive and uncritical enthusiasm they expressed about their visits to the "good society." It is indeed striking how the most ecstatically Sovietophilic travel memoirs invested momentous significance into "inherently ordinary" places like construction sites. Hollander, however, deliberately selected out the most ardently pro-Soviet travelogues and treated them as "excellent sources," not only to establish intellectuals' alienation writ large but also as a historical record of foreigners' experiences within the Soviet Union.[28]

Hollander gave little intimation that the published works of the most fervently fellow-traveling writers constituted a genre of political text par excellence, with all the literary strategies and formulas that went along with it. Many sympathizers decided explicitly to use their accounts of the Soviet experiment to counter negative public and press images. Furthermore, writers whose views on documentary genres were developing in tandem with the trajectory of Soviet culture promoted theories of harnessing the authenticity of travel writing and its political potential simultaneously. For example, Egon Erwin Kisch, the Prague-born journalist and travel writer active in Czechoslovakia, Austria, and Germany, advanced a theory of reportage as a combination of art and a militant (*kämpferisch*) political weapon.[29] Political commitment, not just among Communists but also among "friends of the Soviet Union" or fellow travelers, was the most important factor determining overall assessments of the Soviet Union that a new study finds among French and German leftist intellectuals.[30] This is one reason that the archives, with their transcripts of foreigners' questions and guides' reports, show reactions distinctly less uniformly naive and uncritical than the travelogue literature.

It is interesting to compare the impression created by Hollander of the virtual absence of critical reactions among visitors with the almost diametrically opposed perspective of Natal'ia Semper, a VOKS guide in the 1930s. Semper did not read the pro-Soviet travelogues, but was keenly sensitive to the reactions of the Western guests she was charged with impressing. As a well-educated and cultivated young Russian intellectual, she also inherited a complex of sentiments toward the West to the point that she herself viewed the objects around her through the eyes of her "civilized" guests, as opposed to those of the uncouth party hacks who rose up rapidly in the bureaucracy in the 1930s: "The higher authorities, selecting various construction sites and enterprises as exhibit-worthy sites for foreigners, probably never spent time at them, believing in successes on paper; all these mediocre, gray, socially promoted directors suddenly going from rags to riches (*iz griazi da v kniazi*), could not imagine what kind of impression filth can make on civilized people." One English tourist, in a visit to a reform house (*profilaktoriia*) for former prostitutes, was told by the director that the Soviet Union had liquidated prostitution, only to prove that very statement wrong the same night after a visit to a Moscow train station. Semper vividly describes the visit by the American scholar Owen Lattimore, who published prolifically on China and Mongolia, when he led a group of U.S. economists and businessmen interested in Soviet agriculture to a recommended collective farm in 1935. Hit with impressive facts and figures—"How many hectares! How many tractors!"—the Americans took notes with their big golden ballpoint pens. Their disgust visibly increased, however, in the course of a lengthy visit to a run-down, muddy farm at which they could not find a single person at work—despite a rich variety of contradictory explanations and excuses. As Semper recalled, "I did not know where to hide from shame."[31]

In fact, the ecstatic credulity described by Hollander and the exasperation stemming from botched exposure to unfavorable conditions described by Semper are both reactions commonly reflected in Soviet archival sources. The very system of identifying suitable places for foreign presence—above and beyond the general crisis of the post-collectivization countryside—is partly responsible for some of the mishaps. Lists of *kolkhozy* and *sovkhozy* suitable for display, with directions on how to get there included, were sent to VOKS by collective farm authorities, who listed as many as ten of each in Moscow *oblast'* with laconic notations, such as "a new livestock pen of the American type" and "the mood of the collective farm workers is healthy, optimistic." In May 1931, VOKS's reception department maintained a more limited set: "Right now we have three kolkhozy selected by Kolkhoz Center available for visits." The Soviet countryside was devastated by the massive dislocation of collectivization in the late 1920s and early 1930s. Given the nature of Soviet bureaucracy, the number of institutions needed to keep foreign programs full, and the levels through which recommendations had to pass—from those who inspected or knew the farms, to the Kolkhoz Center, to VOKS or Intourist, to the guides—it is not surprising that far from favorable conditions could be revealed. At the same time, "show" farms certainly were maintained, and were referred to as such, as in a 1934 trip of Austrians to "southern plantations, show (*pokazatel'nye*) kolkhozy and show sovkhozy and other agricultural and agronomical institutions."[32] As this suggests, a small number of special showcases were maintained within a larger group of farms approved for foreign eyes— exactly the same situation prevalent for the other sites of communism. One guide-translator who took Americans into the hungry countryside around Kiev around 1934 recalled receiving a list of three kolkhozy suitable for foreigners' visits, and in each case, he had to take up to a day to contact the farm director through poor telephone connections before arrival.[33]

Among the thousands of foreign technical experts inside the USSR during the era of industrialization was a smaller group of foreign agricultural specialists advising the Soviets on modern mechanized farming. Most of the American agriculturalists were advisors on the mammoth State Experimental

Farm Verbliud (Camel), the second largest Soviet sovkhoz, located forty miles southeast of Khar'kov. Its massive 375,000 acres, which dwarfed the largest American farm at the time almost fourfold, stunned the foreign experts and led them, Deborah Fitzgerald has argued, to view the "giant Soviet farms as huge experiment stations on which the Americans could test their most radical ideas for increasing agricultural production." Not only the image of Soviet agriculture but also the experience of these experts' supremely confident, large-scale experiments inside the USSR played a role in the industrialization of American agriculture.[34] Interestingly, "Verbliud" also figures in VOKS documents and memoirs as one of the model collective farms shown to VOKS and Intourist visitors; its condition on the eve of the Ukrainian terror-famine of 1932–33 was monitored by the secret police.[35] In an unforgettable description of his 1932 Intourist visit to Verbliud, Zara Witkin found absent administrators, "paralysis" in the fields, and "indescribable" waste and disrepair in the machine shop.[36] In a triple irony, the Soviets took an American-influenced experiment and showed it as a model of collectivized agriculture to foreigners; at the same location, American experts downplayed differences between Soviet and U.S. agriculture in order to promote dubious theories for their own country. Even so, the farm created a terrible impression on Witkin, the American tourist.

The embarrassing failure of "cultural show" described in Semper's memoirs was, thus, hardly an isolated event. One English economist complained to VOKS about a lengthy Intourist trip to a collective farm in 1936, after which "it turned out there was nothing to see—everything was in deplorable condition and we had difficulty finding one cow." Not everyone was predisposed to swallow Soviet boasting about achievements. Much like the foreign workers' delegations in the factories, some visitors seized the chance to pose pointed and challenging questions—about agricultural output levels lower than in tsarist times, attacks on kolkhoz officials by peasants, the fate of kulaks, and industrialization financed by the "exploitation" of the peasantry. These visitors were told that the kulak was alien to the masses of the peasantry, which on its own initiative had demanded the liquidation of kulaks as a class.[37]

At the same time, Soviet files were also filled with foreign praise for collectivization based on what foreigners were shown even in the midst of a virtual civil war in the countryside, massive dislocation, and famine. As the improbably successful international Soviet cover-up of mass famine in 1932–33 Ukraine demonstrates, the most elaborate measures to stage conditions of prosperity for foreign visitors were deployed for the most important visitors and the highest priority counter-campaigns. A number of contemporary foreign and postwar émigré memoir accounts converge on the scale of preparations made for such visits in the early 1930s, which paved the way for mid-1930s receptions of prominent European fellow-travelers as state visits of the highest order. These accounts mention clean-up mobilizations, stocking stores and restaurants with goods and food, and importing personnel to act as bystanders, and point to the organizing role of the NKVD. In the absence of secret-police archives, one can hypothesize that the great downturn in conditions and great upturn in mass repressions during Stalin's Great Break provided an impetus for wider applica-tion of such staging methods. Accounts mention them during Bernard Shaw's visit of 1931 and Herriot's tour of a spruced-up, bustling downtown created in starving Kiev in 1933.[38]

However elaborate such staging became for high-priority visits, willing or eager suspension of disbelief on the part of many visitors also remained cru-cial to the success of Soviet displays of sites both large and small. Herriot, for example, had a long history of making positive statements about the Soviet order in order to pursue diplomatic priorities revolving around his "*idée fixe* on Franco-Soviet relations" from the early 1920s on: the need for French rap-prochement with the USSR to counter a resurgent Germany. His Soviet visit of 1922 was a prelude to his co-chairmanship of the short-lived society *Nouvelles amitiés franco-russes* in 1924, and he was accurately viewed by VOKS as instru-mental in using the society in order to make French recognition of the USSR into a successful campaign issue. Herriot played the leading role in securing French diplomatic recognition of the USSR the same year. By the same token, the main purpose of his 1933 visit was to pursue a rapprochement that led into the Franco-Soviet Pact of 1935.[39] Often mentioned as a naïve dupe, Herriot was a politician who had a compelling interest in not finding evidence of fam-ine during his quick tour of Ukraine.

But even without such compelling interest, foreign visitors later in the 1930s often displayed a predisposition to look favorably upon collectivized agricul-ture. The American professor Charles Taylor, identified as an aviation special-ist who lived in a large farmhouse in the United States, mused to his guide about the dilemmas of giving up his material privileges for the sake of the communist movement. Having visited the "Pioneer" kolkhoz on the Riazan' highway in 1937, he not only praised its condition but also insisted that the collective-farm system should be adopted in the United States regardless of the system of government. He displayed embarrassment only when forced to admit that the collective-farm workers knew the works of Theodore Dreiser better than he did. At the same time, it was also common for foreigners to try to use their favorable attitudes as leverage to make themselves important to the Soviets. One of many such visitors was a Lithuanian professor interested in Michurinist biology who visited the "Il'ich" kolkhoz in 1935 and offered to raise yields ten times over. Unperturbed, the chairman of the collective farm shot back that he already planned to lift them twenty-fold.[40]

On the basis of a quantitative analysis of the places VOKS visitors went in 1935, Sheila Fitzpatrick has suggested that it was not only ideological or political sympathy that conditioned enthusiastic responses. The kinds of sites foreigners were shown and the figures they met at receptions, she argues, remained conspicuously "avant-garde," both in the aesthetic and in a social sense (that would include even collective farms).[41] Fitzpatrick makes an important point: the continuing prominent participation of avant-garde giants like Vsevolod Meyerhold in welcoming foreign figures, and the cutting-edge feel of a range of social-welfare and medical institutions shown to visitors, played a significant role in generating positive reactions. State support for science was not the only feature of the Soviet order that appealed to the many scientists who were sympathizers in the interwar period; the coincidence of a revolution in "big science" after World War I and the Bolshevik statist-revolutionary drive to create new institutions led to the founding of a number of specialized research institutes in the 1920s that were the "the world's first" in new fields.[42]

More open to question is how avant-garde were such new creations tightly connected to Marxist-Leninist ideology, such as the Museum of the Revolution and the Marx-Engels Institute, which many foreigners visited. In addition to showcasing modernism, moreover, Soviets throughout this period also routinely claimed credit for the preservation of Russian high culture (on display in outings to such places as the academic theater and the Bolshoi). At the same time, the sites of socialism were expected to appeal to a wide range of foreigners, and singling out the social and cultural from their political dimensions is difficult when they were thoroughly intertwined. Perhaps the only common feature of all the places foreigners were shown was that they were all Soviet and all exceptional, or intended to be so.

Precisely how they were exceptional, then, becomes a topic of some importance, and the nature of exceptionality varied. For example, institutions that carried that label "model" within the Soviet system were often designated as model or "model-experimental" within the wave of institution-building that started after 1917, not because they were later connected to cultural show. The one elementary school visited by a high Turkish education ministry official in 1932 was School No. 25 in Moscow, a destination for many other pedagogues and visitors.[43] Even other institutions designated as "model" (*obraztsovye*) schools after 1931 did not have the financial resources or the reputation of School No. 25, which was probably the most famous school in the USSR— attended by many children of the top party elite, including Stalin's son and daughter, as well as the children of fellow-traveler Paul Robeson and foreign Communists Klement Gottwald and Palmiro Togliatti.

As Larry Holmes has suggested, the policy shifts that led to the creation of model schools were connected to the rising emphasis on larger-than-life individual heroes that was emerging within Stalinist ideology of the time. The Central Committee's August 5, 1931, resolution requiring the Commissariat of Enlightenment to create "model" elementary schools was more specifically connected to the broader repudiation of attacks on established institutions and "leveling" tendencies during the 1928–31 period. School No. 25 became a leading actor in the 1930s repudiation of the educational experimentalism of the 1920s. Clearly, foreigners were shown an exceptional place. It was representative, however, in that it exemplified the stress on discipline, orderliness, and drill that came to dominate Stalinist education. Its model status was meaningful to Soviet pedagogy, influencing the twists and turns of Soviet educational practice throughout the country. It was not created for foreign eyes, but the presence of foreign observers was a major factor, in this case and elsewhere, in the affirmation of its model status.[44]

The Soviet Union turned to models on such a scale in no small part because Soviet development, mating a war on backwardness with scarce resources and a vanguard ideology, was predicated to a significant extent on singling out high-priority sectors. The designating of models fit in with a deep Soviet political logic of instruction through signals and official approbation; models provided the real-life material for a future-oriented culture, anticipating the centralizing and sacralizing features of Stalin-era Socialist Realism. The need to present images of progress to the world became one more factor spurring the designation of unrepresentative models; lavish and prestigious foreign praise, in turn, served to increase the authority of those already designated as special institutions.

Models were so ubiquitous in the early Soviet Union that there was no uniformity of model status. Whereas schools were formally designated as models in the turn away from Great Break "leveling" in 1931, another common way of designating models was to give them the label *opytno-pokazatel'no*, or "experimental-show." Makarenko's first labor colony for rehabilitating "morally defective" waifs, the Gorky agricultural colony near Poltava, became one of two model-show institutions of the Ukrainian Commissariat of Education in 1923 at a time when Makarenko was not hosting foreign visitors but was instead engaged in a tough struggle for food and resources. The status merely meant that it was a prototype of something that did not exist on a broader scale. Juvenile labor colonies were promoted as an alternative to what was by far the dominant institution for homeless children, the *detdom*, or orphanage. The methods based on discipline and competition that Makarenko first elaborated at the Poltava colony went against the dominant pedagogical trends of the 1920s. Makarenko's move to the Dzerzhinskii commune, a far better-equipped industrial commune run by the OGPU, put him in a place that was a prime destination for foreigners and on the road to an all-union fame that made him into the dominant pedagogue of the Stalin era.[45]

The Lefortovskii Isolator might be considered more a showcase than a model; a standard stop on foreign tours, it was clearly maintained for foreign eyes in order to demonstrate humane penal conditions and the principle of rehabilitation. The translator Tamara Solonevich recalls taking two Australians to this "show" prison, where, followed by two *Chekisty*, they were warmly welcomed and told that the USSR had no prisons, only correctional houses with workshops, clubs, libraries, and lectures. There were even model prisoners. One, whom Solonevich considered to be acting out the role of prisoner, just happened to speak very convincingly in French to a group of French visitors. Indeed, one guide reported that a French socialist lawyer who was at first "reserved" and skeptical became enthusiastic about prisons as places of learning after meeting some French-speaking prisoners.[46] But prisoners speaking foreign languages were not always plants—in 1927, political prisoners speaking German and French complained to the foreigners that they were being held without charge.[47]

Even in the case of Lefortovskii prison, there is evidence that it acted as a positive symbol for those Bolsheviks who continued to believe in the original promise of rehabilitation. With no connection to foreigners, for example, a member of a commission sent to investigate the status of "political enlightenment" in Moscow correctional institutions in 1925 demanded reform of sanitary conditions and facilities of certain prisons, which were so atrocious that all political-enlightenment work was out of the question. By contrast, Lefortovskii and the Sokol'nicheskii correctional institution (Ispravdom), both showcases for foreigners, were praised for their good sanitation and educational initiatives. In these prisons, the report concluded, the principle of turning tsarist prisons into genuine correctional institutions was gradually coming to life. In the mid-1920s, it was still possible for someone acting within the penal system to believe that Lefortovskii was a kind of prototype.[48] In the 1930s, Moscow prisons, which were under the aegis of the Commissariat of Justice, were shown less frequently, and the secret police's colony at Bolshevo came into its own as a prime destination for foreign guests.

Western visitors' praise for Soviet prison and labor-colony conditions— featuring enthusiastic reports about the prisoners' humane rehabilitation, freedom of movement, and well-being to the point that punitive relations had practically withered away—has rightly been termed by Hollander as "one of the most fascinating...thought-provoking and disturbing" features of Western political pilgrimages. It is striking that Heeke's recent study of more than 100 German travelogues, which highlighted far more critical and even hostile stances among visitors than Hollander's study, found that "all travelers" who were shown Lefortovo and other prisons by VOKS left with a "positive impression" of Soviet penal practice. Heeke's survey of the published record misses some of the more critical stances recorded in the archival paper trail on what foreigners did and said inside the Soviet Union, however. For example, VOKS and Mezhrabpom delegations in 1927 were sent to Batumskaia prison because "local comrades'" made "assurances" to the sponsoring organizations about its good conditions, but the foreigners reported overcrowded cells, and this time conversations with German- and French-speaking prisoners produced complaints. Solonevich, like some of the foreigners, reported overcrowding of cells even in Lefortovo and claimed that she had many conversations with critical English and German Communists who saw conditions even at this showcase institution as worse than ordinary prisons in their own countries.[49] Communists, of course, were far more likely than many others to have seen the inside of prisons, and it was a general phenomenon that many foreign intellectuals publicly praised factories, prisons, and industrial sites that they had rarely, if ever, seen elsewhere.

Even so, some intrepid foreigners unsuccessfully pushed for entry to the secret police prison, the Lubianka, while the generally pro-Soviet Congress of Friends delegates in 1927 created "tense situations" by demanding to see prisons that were not on the planned itinerary. In the same year, Lavrentii Beriia, then chief of the Georgian GPU, met with such delegates after they had toured a Tbilisi correctional institution. The transcript shows how he responded to questioning that was far from gullible or deferential. Beriia was asked about prisoners who had told the guests they were being held for long periods without being charged; one delegate asked whether Mensheviks would be arrested if they spoke out at a meeting, while others inquired about the "bad hygienic conditions" and rooms of ten square meters that held three to five prisoners. Beriia flatly denied that there were any prisoners held without charges, but when specific names were supplied, he promised to check into it. Any remaining bad conditions, of course, were the "heritage" of tsarism.[50]

Despite the exceptions, the case of prisons brings across just how successful the approach at the heart of "cultural show"—to prompt foreigners to generalize from unrepresentative samples—could be. Ultimately, both the ambitions behind political tourism and, even more, the generic features of intellectuals' reports on the Soviet experiment that developed with the burst of publications starting in the 1920s, meshed deeply with the Soviet methodology of presenting models. Western Europeans and Americans wanted, and were expected, to report on the progress of the Soviet experiment; returning travelers tended to crave grand and authoritative conclusions in order to heighten the importance of their findings. To make the modest, positivistic confession that one did not have the evidence to generalize would have undercut the whole enterprise in which they were invested. It is not surprising, then, that Uhlig's study of Swiss travelogues, like Hollander before her, found numerous examples of foreigners talking about Soviet social and political practice writ large based on one or two sites they had visited.[51] In his *Moscow Diary* of his two-month visit in 1926–27, Walter Benjamin decried the "facile theorizing" and "abstractions" that came so effortlessly to European visitors. Alternately tormented by his inability to communicate in Russian and break out of his psychological and cultural marginality, on the one hand, and congratulating himself with the illusion of having penetrated "more deeply into the Russian situation," on the other, Benjamin's frustrated and often myopic musings represent a chronicle of ambivalence very different from the canon of published pro-Soviet reportage—despite the fact that he was toying with joining the Communist Party at the time.[52]

The internal-external nexus in Soviet development was a phenomenon far broader than VOKS or Intourist. The most successful model sites intertwined features of particular importance to Bolshevism and the Soviet order with "achievements" that had the potential to appeal well beyond party-political lines. Perhaps the weightiest example of this was Moscow itself, the model socialist city. While plans for a "new Moscow" were launched shortly after the Revolution, and the metro was originally a pre-war project, large-scale planning and intensive debates over the future "socialist city" began with the first Five-Year Plan—several years after Moscow had become the epicenter for foreign travel, visited by the overwhelming majority of foreign visitors. The first phase of the creation of model cities, including the start of Moscow's reconstruction, lasted from 1929 to 1931 and was in many ways an international project involving scores of foreign architects, firms, and city-planning debates in which modernism dominated.[53] Even in these years, when construction was only just under way, foreigners were already being treated to a classic exercise in futurology: tours of the "new socialist city."[54]

Even the 1931–32 shift away from modernism and the foreign planners was made with international considerations and foreign visitors in mind. For example, when the idea was raised for a massive new Moscow University building, as early as 1931–32, Commissar of Education Andrei Bubnov remarked upon how it would impress foreign dignitaries who would use it to judge the state of all Soviet universities.[55] The leading political figure in charge of Moscow's reconstruction, Lazar' Kaganovich, spoke about the drive as a means of catching up with the "technically advanced cities of Europe." The long-awaited 1935 "Master Plan" for the city's reconstruction underscored the monumental dimensions of the project. It railed against Moscow's "barbarous past" and hailed the city's supreme status—in front of Athens, Rome, and Paris. Diagrams and statistics for the reconstruction themselves became a form of propaganda. As Schlögel has pointed out, however, most foreigners would not see the "other Moscow," the sprawling conglomeration of settlements outside the city center. The two Moscows were the reality; the new socialist city was the dream. As Bukharin put it, Moscow would become the "new Mecca" for pilgrims "from all ends of the earth."[56]

Investing Moscow with international significance as capital of the world proletariat was key to the history of the capitol city's symbolic and physical reconstruction. At the same time, the number of big urban and industrial areas given so-called regime status, with privileged supplies and policing, shot up from the early to the mid-1930s (from three—Moscow, Leningrad, and Khar'kov,—to seventeen), prompting secret-police chief Genrikh Iagoda, in 1935, to speak of cleansing these key locations of undesirable elements in order to produce "models of socialism."[57] The new Moscow-in-the-making—or, rather, its showcase center rather than its undergoverned periphery—quickly became the primary socialist city on many levels. Better provisioned by far with goods than anywhere else in the planned economy, digging deep for its renowned metro and high for its skyscrapers, it was a model not only for foreigners, but first and foremost for Soviet citizens. In the cultural geography of Stalinism, the city itself served as a microcosm for the Soviet state, and by the late Stalin period, Moscow was firmly enthroned as destination No. 1 for domestic Soviet tourism, also serving as the model for republican cities and socialist imperial core for all non-Russians in the multiethnic state.[58] If "cultural show" set the stage as a model-based methodology for illustrating the initial achievements of Soviet power to outsiders, Stalinism made centralized showcases into a dominant motor of "socialist construction" itself.

Important is not only what foreigners were shown, but, in the words of one high Intourist official in 1936, "how we show our sites (*ob"ekty*)."[59] "Providing service" (*obsluzhivanie*) was the standard term for organizing visits and living conditions, guiding daily itineraries, and in general handling foreign guests. This was the space in which the attempt to influence foreigners' apprehension of the Soviet system met cross-cultural encounters often far different from the aims of an evolving Soviet "methodology of cultural show." In practice, much depended on the individual guides and translators and those in charge of receiving foreigners at individual sites. If in the 1920s these often young and well-educated personnel were frequently non-Communists, and even later came from intelligentsia families, in the tense economic and ideological conditions of the 1930s they still needed to be specially groomed to be presentable for foreign eyes—or, in Semper's sardonic words, to "completely change one's habits, to change from a wild beast into a European." As she remembered it:

> Orally they warned me: VOKS translators are not Intourist guides,
> everyday services do not enter into their responsibilities, one has to

conduct oneself with dignity, to dress attractively; do not get to know foreigners, do not meet on the side and do not accept any gifts, except for books, which must be shown to the censor.

Semper joined a "prestigious circle" transformed by its constant interaction with foreigners, even at a time when mass purges revolved around charges of foreign espionage.[60]

While guide reports on meetings with foreigners were closely monitored, for many years there were few effective attempts from host organizations such as VOKS fully to standardize the actual manner in which sites were shown. Attention focused, as we saw earlier, on conveying the guiding principles of teaching foreigners to see achievements. Although guidebooks for guides were compiled on specific sites—the so-called *metodichki*—in practice, much was delegated to tour guides and those assigned to meet visitors at the sites themselves. Thus, VOKS's "guide-translator Rabinovich" in 1927 only laconically reported that he had conveyed the main principle elaborated for each site: "Visit to the Radishchev show-model school on Voznesenskii St. Explanation of the system of labor upbringing...Visit to the Sokol'nicheskii Correctional Institution. The system of imprisonment; the reeducation of criminals etc."[61]

During the first phases of the Stalin era, further efforts were made to systematize the way model institutions were presented and to train personnel to reply to foreigners' questions. For example, in 1932, VOKS organized consultations for its own cadres and "responsible workers" in commissariats, presumably those involved in receiving foreign visitors, on how to answer "the most varied questions...of interest to foreigners." The same year, 136 "responsible" comrades vetted by the Moscow Committee of the Party attended seminars on the political and practical tasks involved in "providing service to" foreigners. A major push toward centralization and "verification" at Intourist came only in 1936, when the leadership resolved as a result of Central Committee criticism to found twelve "methodological offices" in various cities and to revise the *metodichki*. Since the Intourist central offices had previously circulated these with little or no central or local investigation into how they were actually applied, they resolved to carry out check-ups in the provinces on the methods and terminology used on the ground. The goal was to "explain objects of show in a Soviet way." Despite these measures, it was still recognized at the top how much depended on the guides and, therefore, on authorities' evaluation of them.[62]

If elaborate preparations were made for the most honored guests, on the lower end of the hierarchy were the "rank-and-file" political tourists. Here, much regularly went wrong. Witkin drily conveyed his 1932 experience with Intourist: "We visited schools, factories, nurseries, apartment houses, and theatres. Our guides were none too intelligent. The tourists were frequently misdirected with humorously wasteful results." In keeping with the paranoid practices of internal Soviet censorship in the 1930s, the Intourist leadership became obsessed with any and all mistakes in the political information fed to foreigners, however absurd, such as the Sevastopol guide who slipped up by calling French interventionist forces in 1918 "heroic" rather than "counter-revolutionary."[63]

The attempt to shield foreigners from informal contacts with Soviet guides and personnel and to minimize spontaneous contacts with Soviet citizens was a goal emphasized especially after the late 1920s. It was also built into the structure of foreign visits. The "massive" daily schedules that "worked over" delegates in 1927 were noted as a "defect" and attributed to the eager officiousness of multiple bureaucracies.[64] But over-scheduling and the difficulties of exploring off the beaten track remained a ubiquitous complaint among foreign delegations and all other kinds of visitors. Additionally, punitive exchange rates and lack of transportation, along with the language barrier, served as relatively effective brakes on independent wandering for many.

Intentions and execution, theory and practice were very different beasts in the land of the Soviets. While some guides and other handlers were cautious and politically correct to a fault, bombarding foreigners with rote regurgitation of facts and figures, others—perhaps, under some circumstances, the very same people—sought and welcomed unofficial contacts and pursued what increasingly, in the 1930s, became illicit relationships. There was reason for caution, for those who met with foreigners in official capacities such as consultations and meetings were most often not alone. In 1935, for example, a guide denounced a Narkompros official for discussing the Soviet system of rationing and the closed distribution of goods at length with a Hungarian visitor, something "idiotic to such an extent that it became uncomfortable for him." On the other hand, Witkin, who in 1932 had been well advised to bring a gift of the latest fashion periodicals for his Intourist guide in Leningrad, was invited to visit her apartment, and she later came to Moscow to see him on two other occasions. Contacts with ordinary citizens and those outside the circle of handlers may have been discouraged, but they happened all the time. In 1927, "friends of the Soviet Union" were reported to be wandering around the city without guides, visiting acquaintances in their homes, and shuttling around to "private parties, etc." Even visitors touring the Kremlin the same year were reportedly approached with whispered complaints in foreign languages.[65]

At the same time as the allure of semi-illicit contact increased, vigorous currents of popular xenophobia were fortified by Soviet political and security "vigilance" and the well-worn habits of the Soviet bureaucratic-economic system. The close association of foreigners with security concerns and espionage runs through the documents well before the "war scare" of 1927 and the spy mania of the 1930s. At the same time, Soviet files are filled with incidents in which Soviets—including service personnel, hotel managers, and translators—coming into contact with foreigners, especially those with complaints or requests, rebuffed them rudely or treated them with hostility. Some Western travelogues noted the cautiousness of Soviet citizens in meeting foreigners outside official capacities, especially in the 1930s; but others, perhaps especially those traveling off the beaten path, reported the great eagerness of locals to converse.[66] Both extremes were possible and indeed reinforced by the very special position foreigners occupied.

Both the security and ideological concerns associated with foreign contact and the allure of access to the outside world intensified in the shift from the 1920s to the 1930s. The oral instructions the VOKS guide Semper reported in the mid-1930s forbidding informal friendships with foreigners were in place because relationships did form. Semper's own foreign-language training in the late 1920s is a notable example. Her English teacher at the higher courses in modern languages at the second Moscow University, one of several places where guide-translators learned languages, was Elsie Millman—a writer and ethnographer who had previously worked and traveled in central Africa, China, and Malaysia and who was one of those bohemian adventurers who not infrequently found their way to the USSR in those years. Millman talked frankly about such topics as Western sociology and Soviet problems, and this unusual woman—independent, physically active, and unafraid—exerted a life-altering influence on the young Semper. For her, Millman was the very model of the "new woman": "I became very interested in this free, unique personality and everything that she carried within herself." It was her admiration for Millman that motivated Semper to devote her career to work with foreigners.[67]

The ways that foreigners were to be impressed and that Soviet subjects were to be inspired were different, of course. There was, however, a distinct overlap in the development of approaches designed for each. One example is the promotion of model sites for traveling Soviet citizens, which came to the fore with the rise of the proletarian-tourism movement in the late 1920s. With the creation of the Society of Proletarian Tourism (OPT) as a mass organization in 1929, activists tried to promote travel around the Soviet Union as an edifying and politicizing venture, as opposed to mere relaxation or adventure, which "always left the scent of a poorly masked imperialism." The point was that travelers should observe, or better yet aid, socialist construction, rather than see "remnants of the olden days."[68] Guide books credited with stimulating the development of tourism within the USSR for Soviet citizens included such titles as *Travel in Winter (To Industrial Centers, Sovkhozy, and Kolkhozy Near Moscow)*.[69]

In similar fashion, a primary aim of VOKS's *All over the USSR* (*Ves'
SSSR*)—a Soviet version of the "Baedeker" guide for travelers, published in
10,000 copies in German, English, and French as well as Russian starting in
the Five-Year Plan period—was to pay special attention to the landmarks of
the "new socialist economy."[70] There were different rationales at play in the
promotion of the sites of socialism to Soviet workers and to foreign dignitaries,
however. The goal of proletarian tourism was not merely to generate sympathy but also to enable full conversion into activists for the "general line" of the
Party. In theory, its practitioners would be fully mobilized to campaign for collectivization, conduct literacy campaigns and collect loan pledges, and further
military preparedness. They were encouraged to assault the class enemy: in
1931, tourist-workers from Elektrozavod were recorded as boasting that they
had unmasked eight kulaks in *Kosinskii raion*. Perhaps most consistently, the
organizers of the proletarian-tourism movement hoped that showcasing the
great construction sites of the Five-Year Plan would improve work habits and
raise the cultural and political level of the masses—the old war on backwardness in yet another guise.[71] But even at the height of this Great Break fervor,
journals mixed in grainy photographs of industrial landscapes with mountain
panoramas and the costumes and physiognomies of native Soviet peoples identified in the captions—presumably in order to signify the friendship of peoples
rather than a poorly masked imperialism, but exotic all the same. By the end
of the 1930s, along with the rehabilitation of recreational tourism, domestic
tourism guidebooks served the Stalin cult and Russian patriotism by opening
with places associated with the leader's life and battlefields of the fatherland
war of 1812.[72]

The very fact that the proletarian tourism movement during its heyday
turned to some of the same methods already in place for presenting Soviet
socialism to foreign visitors suggests how Soviet political culture generated
model sites as a prime way of shoehorning the projected transformation of
the entire society into present-day examples that could generate enthusiasm.
There was a distinct interaction or interpenetration—rather than a simple or
direct progression—between the means the architects of Soviet culture and
propaganda discovered to address visitors from the outside world and to reach
their own population.

A Congress of Friends

If the Soviet reception of foreign visitors was evolving throughout the decade
in reaction to the experience of handling larger numbers of visitors, in 1927 the
tenth anniversary celebrations of the October Revolution marked a milestone

in the process. The sheer scale of the event, which involved hosting 1,000 foreign delegates for visits punctuated by a "Congress of Friends," was a test for the methods of cultural show and prompted sustained Soviet reflection on what did and did not work.

The Comintern's Agitprop and Willi Münzenberg, VOKS, and the foreign commission of the trade unions (VTsSPS) were the major players in the 1927 visits. In keeping with standard strategy, Communists were mixed into the composition of delegations in order to steer them and shape their resolutions, but most of the guests were to be sympathetic outsiders whose commitment would be strengthened by the experience. Thus, even the Comintern's Agitprop later criticized the inclusion of fifteen communist writers in MORP's twenty-two-person delegation as an exceptional blunder. By contrast, it crowed about major success in the case of a French anarchist intellectual who supposedly arrived full of anti-Soviet prejudices and left believing that the Red Army defended the workers of the world.[73]

Undertaken as a major opportunity to win international alliances, the Congress marked one peak in the party-state's optimistic strategy of engagement. The types of foreigners included reveals much about the priorities and strategies behind the event. A full 500 of the delegates were foreign workers invited through the trade unions: 100 places were reserved for "peasants," 50 for cooperators, 100 for delegates from "Eastern" countries, 200 for European invitees of IAH, and 30 for, as it was put, leaders of national revolutions in oppressed countries and colonies. VOKS was charged with inviting the "politically sympathetic intelligentsia from Europe and America" (eighty places) and scholars "sympathetic to the societies of 'friends of the New Russia'" (sixty places). Among the workers, significant numbers of Social Democrats and non-communist socialists were included (thirty-six of the seventy-eight German workers were SDs), but no such non-Communist Party affiliations were permitted for those who already had attained political "consciousness," i.e., the intellectuals.[74]

When the event was over, Comintern and Soviet analysts proceeded to examine the foreigners' public evaluations. It is striking how foreigners' written words, perhaps intended as polite or encouraging, were taken by the Soviets at face value as a sign of the outsiders' political growth and enlightenment. In this additional layer of gauging political-cultural level, there are distinct hints that the class, gender, and nationality of visitors could affect the Soviet response and their frequent assumption of superiority. For example, one report discussed the demanding personalities of foreign cultural and scientific celebrities (respectfully referred to as those with "European-wide reputations") complaining how they were not treated delicately enough or accorded enough personal attention.[75] Yet an entire women's delegation—identified in the document only as such, not by country of origin—was indicted for "jealousy" of other delegations. A female German tobacconist arrived in the USSR "surprising everyone with her apolitical nature," since "she was located at that level of development where she was only interested in issues of the economic struggle of the working class." A month in the land of socialism "produced significant leaps forward in her consciousness."[76] One guide came to the remarkable insight that not everyone from the capitalist West was alike: "Germans have different traits than the English and look on things differently than, for example, the French. The French will not sign anything that a German has proposed, and the other way around."[77] It proved practical to segregate visitors by class and nationality.

In his speech to the assembled Congress, head of state Aleksei Rykov, whose post had no direct connection to cultural diplomacy, demonstrated that he was fully conversant with the core conventions of "cultural show." The Soviet Union should be judged not by present differences, for example, between the Soviet and American states and standards of living; rather, the achievements of Soviet power, in which he included the trajectory of the upcoming industrialization drive, should be placed alongside tsarism. Rykov next anticipated potential concern among the sympathizers by raising the issue of Soviet political violence. "We are forced to employ repression for the defense of the dictatorship of the working class," Rykov said, claiming the mantle of restraint while denying that terror was a principle of state rule. Finally, Rykov could not miss the opportunity to hammer home for the foreign guests the reversal of Russia's place in the world hierarchy of advanced countries: with unprecedented speed, the new society had emerged from one of the most backward states of Europe.[78]

Several foreign speakers at the Congress demonstrated in their own words and languages that they were apt pupils of the lessons of cultural show, reiterating Rykov's point. This trope was combined with the traditional European stress on Russia's non-European nature. As the German delegate Schopmann put it at the second session of the Congress, "It is above all things noteworthy that we should not view Russian construction through West European glasses," since that would omit the great contrast between tsarism in Old Russia and the direction of the new.[79] Soviet efforts to teach foreigners to see, or rather to see beyond what was in front of their eyes, had demonstrable effects.

At the same time, delegates' recorded statements can also be read in terms of what the Soviets could not control: Western assumptions of superiority crept through even among the most ardent admirers. A number of European delegates could not help noticing antiquated factory equipment and technology. One Belgian delegate commented that "the methods of work used in Russia are not superior to those in western countries."[80] The American radical Scott

Nearing chided the Soviets for assuming he and his comrades needed bourgeois comfort: "too much food and too soft!"[81]

When Lenin's widow Krupskaia opened the Congress of Friends on November 10, 1927, she lavished praise on the 947 delegates present as the "best flower of everything progressive, everything revolutionary...the best flower of the future civilization." If anything more flattering was the remark in German by Aleksandra Kollontai, then ambassador to Sweden, at a VOKS reception: she hoped the delegates would learn something from their Moscow visits, but "we see many friends from whom we ourselves have learned something."[82] The evocative label of "friends of the Soviet Union" in 1927 further entrenched an important category that had meaning for the Soviets as well as for foreign guests. On the other hand, when their guests were not present, the hosts of the foreign sympathizers made remarks that differed greatly from the public praise. They were the objects of condescension, distancing, or ideological condemnation. In each case, the implication was one of inferiority, because of delegates' status as members of the intelligentsia, or on certain occasions their Eastern provenance, or even their status as simple workers. In perhaps the earliest proposal for the anniversary events, Willi Münzenberg made a routine reference to Krupskaia's flower of the new civilization as "petty-bourgeois intellectual circles."[83]

More fully articulated were the confidential opinions of keynote speaker Rykov, who wrote a "highly conspiratorial" strategy paper on how to approach the congress of friends' final resolution. There was no need, Rykov argued, for them to ratify an essentially Bolshevik platform. That could not serve to unite those diverse circles "in Western Europe" (he simply ignored the delegates from the rest of the world) that the congress had brought together. Because most delegates did not belong to any party, "It is useless to conceal the fact that these circles represent in a political sense the most passive elements of the Western European working class, and together with Social Democrats, anarchists, and in general members of the intelligentsia (*intelligenty*) who have a range of preconceptions about the USSR, they represent the majority of the entire conference." The goal was to turn them into "our defenders in the capitalist world," but for this purpose, full "rebirth" into Bolsheviks was not necessary.[84] Friends needed to be supporters, not comrades.

When the guests had gone home, the reports generated by the 1927 jubilee proved so voluminous that the interagency commission, in a major self-evaluation of the "insufficiencies" in the system, announced the goal of creating an archive for them in order to study them statistically. Many of the problems noted were endemic to foreign visits throughout the interwar period: disorganization, missed meetings, vanishing luggage, poor service in the hotels, and badly prepared guides. Some VOKS minders requisitioned the best theater tickets for themselves. In a number of delicate situations, tactlessness reigned over diplomacy: intellectuals requesting to meet with some Mensheviks in the Transcaucasus were told they could visit all the Mensheviks they liked in their own countries. Female delegates among the so-called mental laborers noted harsh work conditions in a fur-and-textile factory.[85] The problems were all typical issues and almost impossible to fix; they resulted from general conditions and human failings.

But the most intractable problem was the Potemkin village dilemma that came to the fore in 1927. Widespread expectations about Potemkin villages prompted even the pro-Soviet delegates to try suddenly to change their schedules in order to foil pre-arranged plans. The hosts were so aware of this that the commission report recommended allowing visitors to suddenly alter their schedules—if that could be planned in! Even with this knowledge, the entire system for receiving foreigners worked against permitting more freedom of movement given the overwhelming political need to avoid anything that might spoil a favorable evaluation. The most that could be explicitly allowed was planned spontaneity: home meetings and teas with selected workers. By the same token, the 1927 commission was perfectly aware that it was a "significant defect" that honored visitors were overloaded from morning to night with official meetings, ceremonies, banquets, and demonstrations—yet this common phenomenon served precisely to minimize unexpected exploring, for Soviets with knowledge of foreign languages might complain about harsh conditions. As the commission's report warned, "A situation in which any 'bystander' might approach or infiltrate their company is, of course, undesirable."[86] The dilemma raised by the label "Potemkin villages" was real: it exposed the Soviet urge to plan, limit, and control what visitors did and saw.

While the Soviet and Comintern agencies working together generally cooperated, behind the scenes the 1927 celebrations were not devoid of conflict, and remarkably, some foreign delegates entered the fray. In particular, VOKS and the Comintern continued the sparring that had begun years before with Comintern criticism over VOKS's orientation toward the intelligentsia. Since then, Kameneva had successfully defended that mission, keeping its societies of friends oriented around scholars and other intellectuals. In this effort, she enlisted a number of the European friendship society members present in Moscow in 1927, and prevailed when they passed a formal resolution favoring the continued "apolitical and non-party" character of the societies.[87] The head of VOKS and her invited foreign friends had engaged in alliance-building to deliver a rebuff to the Comintern.

The 1927 festivities and the self-analysis they prompted marked the maturation of the Soviet system for receiving foreign visitors, marking the debut of certain developments that would grow in importance in the coming years. First, the invitation of intellectuals in tandem with the other delegations ensured that VOKS and "cultural" considerations would be increasingly caught up with an approach originating in the campaigns of mass propaganda: to "connect" invitations and the content of the visits, as one planning report put it, "to the current political tasks of the moment."[88] If the incipient campaign mode dictated a concern for linking visits to current preoccupations, such as the war scare of 1927, the disgust for "useless" foreigners ensured that VOKS would pay greater attention to influential foreigners who could potentially influence public opinion. The stresses on short-term political goals and foreign figures of influence were in tension with one another, because the most influential intellectuals were often not the most amenable to propagandistic campaigns. This conflict between mobilization and flexibility would continue to play itself out for years to come.

The tenth anniversary of the 1917 October Revolution marked the first time an audience with Stalin would be a feature of the visits of the most honored foreign visitors. Eighty delegates from eleven countries met with Stalin for six hours on November 5, 1927, and it was in keeping with Stalin's later meetings with Western visitors that a carefully edited text of selected questions and answers was prepared afterward for possible dissemination. "Why is there no freedom of press in the USSR?" read one query submitted on a slip of paper, as was the custom. Stalin answered "For which class—the bourgeoisie or the proletariat?" To one question—"Is Ruth Fischer's and [Arkadij] Maslow's contention, now circulated in Germany, that the present leaders of the Comintern and the Russian Party are betraying the workers to the counter-revolution correct?"—Stalin joked that the Bolsheviks had also decided to become cannibals and nationalize all women. The document recorded voices from the crowd: "Who could have asked such a question?"[89] As the delegates joined Stalin in the "general laughter," their very presence as part of the mass influx of foreign guests in 1927 marked the maturation of the system for engaging foreigners.

Theodore Dreiser's Accusatory Pilgrimage

The remarkable 1927–28 journey of American realist writer Theodore Dreiser, who was in the process of becoming a literary icon in Soviet culture and who later became one of the most widely translated American authors in Soviet history, can be viewed as an unexpected product of the Potemkin village dilemma. Dreiser, along with the Mexican artist Diego Rivera, was one of the only Western intellectual celebrities to accept VOKS's invitation to the Congress of Friends. While there was a strong positive response from active members of the cultural friendship societies, these figures were already established sympathizers and not necessarily of the stature the Soviets craved. Many of the most prominent figures could not make it: Upton Sinclair, Jane Addams, John Dewey, and eleven other Americans declined, as did Albert Einstein and Frankfurt School director Carl Grünberg in Germany, and H.G. Wells, John Maynard Keynes, and George Bernard Shaw in Britain (Dewey, Wells, Keynes, and Shaw all did visit at different times). Dreiser's knowledge of the Soviet Union was virtually nil, but one thing he had heard about was Potemkin villages. He aggressively used the leverage he had to extract promises that he would not be shown "a pageant." Instead, he demanded an extended journey to "see the real, unofficial Russia—the famine district in the Volga, say."[90] He seems to have never attended the Congress of Friends except for an appearance at a VOKS reception for the delegates.

Instead, Dreiser embarked on a remarkable eleven-week journey that took him not only to Moscow and Leningrad but Nizhnii Novgorod, Kiev, Khar'kov, Rostov and South Russia, Transcaucasia, and the Crimea between November 4, 1927, and January 13, 1928. After he arrived in Moscow, when Kameneva and VOKS took over the arrangements for the writer's stay, he still had to threaten a public relations fiasco in order to gain a degree of independence while traveling. Kameneva was not at all pleased that Dreiser had chosen not to rely solely on VOKS guides but had instead hired a personal secretary.

This was Ruth Epperson Kennell, a thirty-four-year-old American woman who had been living in Moscow for five years working on literary affairs ranging from the Gosizdat translations of Dreiser's fiction to the library of the Comintern. Kennell, although not a Communist, was a lifelong leftist who at that point was far closer to orthodox communist positions than Dreiser. Culturally, she was enamored of Russians far more unambiguously than Dreiser; during the Cold War, she devoted her career to writing children's stories crafted to dispel cultural stereotypes about Russians.[91] Kennell knew the Russian language and Soviet life in a way few Americans did at the time, and she began, in part under the corrosive influence of Dreiser's skepticism, to experience a crisis of belief that brought her out of the Soviet Union for good soon after Dreiser's own departure.

Kennell later described how Dreiser, in a "belligerent mood," arrived by sleigh at VOKS's headquarters to argue with Kameneva. Their dispute centered on Dreiser's plans to hire Kennell as his secretary for the long trip:

> The [VOKS] director, Madame Kameneva, Leon Trotsky's sister, at once expressed disapproval of his hiring a secretary without consulting them. Understandably, she objected to a private secretary who was not responsible to VOKS...Squinting at me out of

nearsighted eyes, she declared in Russian: *"Ona nye sovsyem soviets-kaya zhenschena."*

What's she saying in that blasted language? [Dreiser] demanded.

Before I could respond, Trevis [Trivas], a VOKS guide who was favored by Kameneva, eagerly translated for him: "She is not at all a Soviet woman."

"What do you mean by 'Soviet woman'?"

"That is," Trevis responded insinuatingly, "not entirely reliable."

Madame Kameneva, who could speak English when she wished, hastened to explain, "I meant she is a non-party technical worker..."

"Splendid!" interrupted Dreiser. "A perfect recommendation."

"But," she protested, "you will need a guide and interpreter, and *Tovarish* Trevis [sic] is fully qualified to serve as both."

The American delegate began to shout. "You promised me a private secretary and a private tour. If I can't have what I want, by God, I'll leave and you can all go to hell!"[92]

Dreiser got his way, but Kameneva, taking advantage of Dreiser's age and hypochondria, found a way to monitor his tour by commissioning Sofiia Davidovskaia, a physician and trained nurse, to accompany him when he left Moscow. Kennell knew her as the politically trusted house doctor at the Hotel Lux, famous as the Comintern residence, where Kennell also lived. "Davi," as Dreiser called her, incurred the writer's wrath for so conscientiously monitoring him but was judged a "kindly, dependable woman" by Kennell; at the end of the journey, "She agreed to report nothing derogatory about me, and I promised to speak no ill of her."[93] In the long run, Kameneva's gamble of conciliation paid off handsomely as the renowned American traveler was transformed into a leading fellow-traveler in the years after his Soviet visit.

Dreiser, both in his published writings and even more in his self-confident—indeed, arrogant—defense of American superiority inside the USSR, appears very far from the duped and sycophantic political pilgrim who merely projected his alienation from American society onto everything he saw. A self-professed individualist who frequently berated his Soviet handlers and tartly held up the United States as an example, Dreiser held views of Russians and Slavs that were shaped by longstanding stereotypes about national character. Even so, his views of what he saw could be penetrating and highly critical. It is remarkable, then, that Dreiser, who despised so much of the hard times he spent in the squalid, conformist land of collectivism, emerged to censor himself and generate a windfall of favorable publicity for the Soviets.

The roads to Sovietophilia were many, including even Dreiser's cantankerous individualism. Dreiser was already fifty-eight years old when he embarked for Moscow, and he was at the height of his critical and public acclaim as a writer. His 1925 *American Tragedy* was a major popular and critical success. Several features of his biography are particularly relevant for understanding his encounter with the Soviets. Unlike many other intellectual friends of the Soviet Union, Dreiser was not at all self-analytical, and he had a weak grasp of philosophy (his only formal higher education was a year at Indiana University). In fact, these qualities are what make his views on the Soviet Union so potentially revealing: "Dreiser held 'views' that reflected his deepest prejudices, many of which were not altogether conscious."[94] The son of German immigrants who grew up in dire poverty, he remained a lifelong champion of the poor and disadvantaged, which is of course a major factor in what attracted Soviet publishers and critics to his writing. In the early years of the twentieth century, he broke with the rigid Catholic upbringing of his youth and adamantly rejected organized religion, something that affected both his sympathy with official Soviet atheism as well as his many comparisons of communism with Catholic dogma.

Dreiser's intellectual formation dates to the period 1890–1914. As a journalist in the 1890s, he imbibed the entrepreneurial creed of the self-made man and was heavily influenced by the ubiquitous Social Darwinism of the period. Later, when in his fiction he turned to grand cosmic (and in the 1920s, social) forces to explain the human condition, he rejected the survival of the fittest as a mythical explanation for wealth and success, but he reiterated the theme of the "big mind"—the financier or industrialist or, later, great artist dominating the herd. In the 1910s, he lived in Greenwich Village as part of New York's growing bohemian milieu, and his rejection of American bourgeois morality also became an influential part of his writings. His rejection of marriage and his constant affairs were important in this respect.

Thus, in the 1910s and 1920s, there emerged what Mookerjee has called the two Dreisers: one the champion of the poor and the oppressed, the other the Darwinian admirer of the cult of success, the great individual, and the superior artist not bound by convention. In fact, Dreiser's peculiar mix of Social Darwinism and progressive social conscience, determinism and rugged individualism formed a layered melange that, as is often the case, was neither fully "Left" or "Right" politically. When Soviet publishers began printing translations of his works in the 1920s, they tended to see only the "progressive" side of the two Dreisers. When the earnest young Marxist literary critic Sergei Dinamov, the Institute of Red Professors graduate who later befriended Dreiser when he was in Moscow, entered into correspondence with the American writer on December 10, 1926, Dinamov predictably asked Dreiser whether he stood for socialism and what he thought of Soviet communism, given the anti-capitalism of his works. Dreiser replied with his typical folksy *épatage*, shocking his interlocutor: he had "no theories of life" or solutions to political and economic problems, and, "We can do nothing in the final analysis."[95]

In a letter to Stalin, Kameneva blamed Kennell for exerting "a bad influence" on "the great American writer-realist," thus attributing Dreiser's criticisms to a bourgeois source. It is not clear whether Kameneva knew or suspected that Kennell had become Dreiser's lover soon after they met. Certainly, the two Americans often worked to evade or ignore their official VOKS guides. One of these, the "flashily dressed" and "rather clever" Trivas, who accompanied them on the Leningrad trip, had approached Kennell with a conspiratorial wink: "Between us we ought to be able to manage the old man—right?"[96] The American suspected Trivas of making advances to Kennell, and his attitude was tinged with anti-Semitism: Dreiser later called Trivas an opportunistic Jew and a "grafter" who was no more a Communist than Dreiser himself.[97]

The world knew of Dreiser's trip mainly through his 1928 book, *Dreiser Looks at Russia*, a work Kennell helped to edit. This was for the most part a hastily written, poorly organized account, based partly on VOKS materials and highlighting political and social aspects of the Soviet system on which the writer was poorly equipped to comment. Having returned to the United States before he wrote this work, Dreiser pulled his punches and muted his criticisms considerably for public consumption.

The diary, by contrast, is a remarkable text both in its provenance and in its content. The bulk of it was, in fact, written in the evenings over the course of their travels by Kennell herself; she was instructed by Dreiser to use the first person and write as him. Dreiser, upon his return to the United States, then made some corrections to this text but mainly added and interspersed his own notes throughout. Kennell, then, was writing in Dreiser's voice, knowing it would later be read by the much older man whose magnetic power, as she later acknowledged in several love letters to the writer, she was feeling most intensely. Although the voices and views of the two traveling companions are intertwined in elaborate ways, Dreiser's later additions at many points have the function of "correcting" or modifying impressions left by Kennell. Yet another complication is that Kennell, in an act of loyalty to the Soviet authorities she was soon thereafter to abandon, transferred parts of the diary (including those about Dreiser's meeting with oppositionist Karl Radek in his hotel room) to VOKS as she wrote them, without Dreiser's knowledge.[98] In the quotations that follow, Dreiser's later additions appear in italics and Kennell's writing in roman script.

Throughout their two-and-a-half month period of intimacy during the Soviet tour, Dreiser and Kennell engaged in an extended and heated argument over the drawbacks and benefits of the American and Soviet systems. In

Figure 3.1 Sergei Dinamov circa 1931. A graduate of the Institute of Red Professors and an expert on American literature, Dinamov was one of Theodore Dreiser's main interlocutors in 1927–28 and later an official in the Foreign Commission of the Union of Soviet Writers. He was arrested during the Great Terror in September 1938 and died on November 20, 1939. Source: Theodore Dreiser Papers, Rare Book and Manuscript Library, University of Pennsylvania.

the Hotel Grand, on November 24, the two met with Dinamov, and Kennell recorded: "I got into an argument with Dinamov about individualism, or rather, intellectual aristocracy, as opposed to mass rule." Dreiser added: "*The little brain & the big brain came in for their customary share in the argument...As opposed to Communism and its enforced equality I offered international, benevolent capitalism as very likely to achieve the same results.*"[99]

Dinamov, who played a major role in the translation of Dreiser's works and who in the 1930s became an important official in the Union of Writers Foreign Commission, appears to be one of those Soviet mediators pulled at times painfully between his personal admiration for his foreign charge and his defense of Soviet ideological orthodoxies.

In Kennell's words, Dinamov expected to derive great "pleasure" from his interactions with the American writer he had studied so much from afar, but Dreiser constantly made him struggle to find the English to defend ideological orthodoxies. "Under communism would Rockefeller or Gary be paid the same as a swineherd? You want to bring every human being down to the same level," Dreiser accused. Kennell recorded their confrontation in her own secretly kept diary that she later quoted in her book: "The poor fellow was completely exhausted by the ordeal, but he (Sergey) staggered up time after time with a fresh onslaught." This time, Dinamov retorted: "You are advocate for intellectual aristocracy versus mass rule. All you hear and see in Soviet Union teach you nothing. I am ashamed for you, Drayzer."[100] Dinamov's personal admiration for the great writer was overwhelmed by the certainty that just seeing the Soviet world would "teach" the foreigner.

Many of Dreiser's observations were astute and critical. He discerned the persistence of social and cultural hierarchies in Soviet society and state. He doggedly compared Soviet education and ideology to the religious dogma he knew, Catholicism, and deplored the nascent gray uniformity all around that he attributed to Soviet "enforced equality." Pointedly, he advised a Soviet journalist that the USSR should get the homeless waifs (*besprizorniki*) off the streets before sending Soviet money for revolution abroad. "*I figure the Lenin Statue Population of Russia to be at least 80,000,000,*" he added to Kennell's laconic note about Lenin Corners. To Bukharin, as well as many other major and minor Soviet officials with whom Kameneva and VOKS arranged audiences, Dreiser was defensive about the United States and confrontational in style. He argued with Bukharin over how many millions of Soviet citizens actually agreed with, or even understood, the ideological aims of the Soviet state and whether in imposing communist ideology it was therefore different from any other "intellectual despotism."[101] Dreiser modified Kennell's entry on his meeting with the director of the rubber factory "Red Triangle": "*[S]ince he proceeded to attack America* I answered at length about the unselfish work of scientists in America and the achievements of American financiers in building up industry... [and] gifts of rich men to [the] country... 'And perhaps the next step' *I added* 'will be the Soviet system, and I believe if this system were put to the masses in America, they would accept it.' "[102] As these unexpected leaps of logic suggest, Dreiser was able to envisage a kind of pro-Soviet "convergence theory" based on a belief in the advanced nature of Soviet modernization blueprints, yet, in the next breath, he could lambaste the Russian national character and Soviet society as Asian, backward, and hopelessly different.

Even as she began to look at the Soviet Union through Dreiser's more disparaging eyes, Kennell exerted much influence over her older friend and employer, supplying Dreiser with many of the positive arguments about communism that he later used in his 1928 book and even more so in the 1930s.[103] At the same time, even in the midst of his journey, Dreiser laced his defenses of his homeland with panegyrics to the social equality of the Soviet system. Here, as opposed to America, there was no graft; party leaders gave themselves selflessly for little pay, as opposed to *"sly religionists"* or corrupt police officials preying on commoners; and *"true station"* was fixed not by wealth but by *"mind or skill."* Later, Kennell recalled of their ongoing disputes, "I had the feeling he was arguing with himself, not me."[104]

Dreiser's visit underscores more general features in the history of the inter-war influx of foreign intellectuals to the Soviet Union that have remained less explored than political sycophancy. These relate, first and foremost, to the overwhelming preponderance of the theme of national character and "Asiatic" backwardness. While the Soviet state was taken as a potentially advanced social experiment, "Russia" was backward, primitive, Asian, Eastern, dirty, inherently collectivist, yet also, in many ways, exciting and exotic.

Dreiser's own reasoning through the categories of national character and race was an integral, if loosely linked, part of his pattern of arguments about the strong individual and economic modernity. Still, en route in Germany, he declared to an acquaintance, contra the notion that humanity can be molded, *"I have sometimes thought that some nations or races might have (as in the case of the Jews & the Slavs) a giant capacity for misery."*[105] Upon his border crossing into the USSR, he gave way to one cliché after another about the feminine East: *"One senses a change at once. Something softer—more emotional, less iron."*[106]

Dreiser's associations with Asiatic Russia can be clustered into three separate categories. The first was the exotic: upon arrival in Moscow, he referred *to* "quaint oriental droshky" and "exotic looking" priests in "strange caps."[107] This sense of fascination, in part, allowed him to disassociate the Soviet Union with aspects of American modernity he disliked; there is no better illustration of this than the issue of marriage and sexuality. In *Dreiser Looks at Russia*, he wrote approvingly about Russian attitudes toward sex, deducing his conclusions half from Soviet policymaking and half from assumptions about the authenticity of noble savages: "They just do not see sex the way we do. It is normal and natural...If there is no rape or murder [as opposed to adultery] there is no real crime...it is the only sane treatment of the sex question I have ever encountered."[108]

The second cluster of Asiatic imagery concerns the consideration of economic backwardness, both in terms of his defense of American superiority and the need for Soviet modernization. Viewing the "wretched collection of autos" in front of the Moscow train station, he noted "the shabbiest Georgia or Wyoming town would outclass them. And the people! This mixture of Europeans & Asiatics!...One gets a sense of strangeness and dilapidation."[109] Insofar as the Soviet state was altering the "herd instinct" and primitive poverty of old Russia, then, Dreiser could approve wholeheartedly. The commissar of trade, Anastas Mikoian, apparently impressed Dreiser so much "as a coldly practical, implacable Communist public servant," Kennell later wrote, that "for the first time, and perhaps the last, in his interviews with Soviet officials, he did not display his American sense of superiority, his assumption of the right to say what he pleased and do what he pleased when a guest in a foreign land."[110]

Asianness and Slavic sloth was connected in Dreiser's mind with economic and industrial backwardness. Dreiser explicitly and implicitly compared everything he saw to the advanced industrial civilization of America, which he tended to defend abroad but condemn at home. Indeed, it was because Soviet communism appeared to be modernizing this age-old backwardness that Dreiser was able to blend much praise into his pointed complaints about Soviet conditions. In this admiration for the perceived benefits of Soviet moderniza-tion, as distinct to communist ideology, Dreiser followed in a long line of non-communist and sometimes well-informed American observers who shared a "fervent belief" in what the young diplomat George F. Kennan a few years later called the "romance of economic development," or the Soviet Union's rapid, if ruthless, push to "starve itself great."[111] This was one key strand of Dreiser's Sovietophilia that emerged and, indeed, overwhelmed all his derisive and hard-hitting criticisms of 1927–28.

The third kind of association Dreiser made between Russia and the East was a nationalist and even racist condemnation of the Slavic or Russian "tem-perament." He compared the "less developed state" of Russians to that of "Negroes," since "instead of having to accumulate & organize and execute in a constructive way they prefer to dream & play & talk like children." He clearly connected this primitive childishness in his mind with Soviet utopian dreams of creating an earthly paradise.[112]

Dreiser unselfconsciously linked the theme of the inferior Russian national character to his ubiquitous discussion of everyday life and hygiene, a subject that proved crucial in his encounter with the Soviets. He did not necessarily see temperament as eternal: because Soviet leaders were intro-ducing "modern equipment" into "slow, backward ... resigned" Russia, he implicitly held out the hope that Sovietization would in "15–25–35" years transform the Russian character. In terms of the everyday conditions he so deplored, it was Asiatic sloth that explained such things as the hous-ing and the toilets, which he viewed with "honest American horror and astonishment."[113]

As in the case of so many visitors, poor cleanliness and sanitation, the execrable quality of food and lodging, and the miserable appearance of Soviet humanity are extraordinarily predominant themes in Dreiser's diary. As the conditions of his journey worsened outside the two capitals, Dreiser expressed more and more antipathy for the masses he so often defended. Kennell even wrote for him: "The huddled masses gave me a sense of nausea. Russia is per-manently spoiled for me by the cold and dirt."[114] After his childhood poverty and many years of struggling, the publication of *American Tragedy* had finally made Dreiser financially well off; by 1927–28 he resented the notion that what he considered necessary comforts were to the Soviets unheard-of, bourgeois luxuries. Kennell noted a distinct correlation between his mood swings and the quality of the food and lodging.[115] It was not implausible to relate those moods to his equally fluctuating degree of optimism about the Soviet experiment and his evaluations of communism. However, even a highly observant foreigner such as the British liberal James Farson, who realized other visitors' judgments could be clouded by poor material conditions, was led to ruminate about dirt and civilization:

> [Visitors have been] unable to clear their judgment from their own personal discomfort. They attach, think the Communists, too much importance to such material things. On the other hand, what is civilization? It was strange, I reflected, trying to wash and dry my hands and face at the communal tap—without letting my cake of soap touch the appalling sink—that after eleven years of absolute freedom the proletarian washing place behind me was infinitely more filthy than any cage in a zoo.[116]

Everyday squalor dehumanized the Soviet masses for both observers, but Farson deployed class rather than national terms.

The intimate linkage between Dreiser's view of Soviet communism and his experience of Russian "dirt" was thus not at all unique. It was brought across to VOKS in several ways. His guide in the south, Davidovskaia, bore the brunt of his often resentful pickiness. By the bitter end of his journey, when he declared "I'd rather die in the United States than live here," he had irritably broken off all relations with her.[117]

Yet, the most important way in which VOKS gained sustained insight into Dreiser's outlook was through his lengthy pronouncement on his impressions that he dictated to Kennell on the eve of his departure, and which was conveyed to VOKS by Dinamov.[118] For Soviet cultural officials, whose main tasks revolved around influencing Western views of the Soviet Union and intellectuals' understanding of Soviet "achievements," this could not but be taken as a document of the highest significance.

All of the attitudes that have been unpacked at length above were compressed into this one pronouncement, which was punctuated by Dreiser's trademark alternation between praise and deliberately crusty criticism. He was fulsome in his "immense delight" over Soviet anti-religious policies, selfless and talented Soviet leaders, and the housing projects, new schools, and scientific institutions dotting the land. Yet, he declared all this to be the achievements

Figure 3.2 Theodore Dreiser (center) with Dr. Sofiia Davidovskaia (second from left), Ruth Epperson Kennell, a Latvian agronomist, and a local guide, Donetsk Basin, in 1928. Kennell, the American writer's secretary and lover during his Soviet sojourn, recorded most of his remarkable *Russian Diary*; Davidovskaia, the house physician at the Comintern's Hotel Lux, provoked Dreiser's wrath for monitoring him on behalf of VOKS. Source: Theodore Dreiser Papers, Rare Book and Manuscript Library, University of Pennsylvania.

of a "superior group of idealists" (i.e., the Bolshevik leadership) rather than the rule of the "laborer," and he took the opportunity to declare himself a lifelong "individualist" who subscribed to the "individual dream of self-advancement." He then lectured his hosts on cleanliness, adding that "there are certain obvious defects in either the Russian temperament or the fulfillment of [the Soviet] program, or both." Repeating the adjective "Russian" over and over almost as a pejorative, he called hygiene not a matter of state imposition or prosperity but of "the very essence of the individual himself."

> The Russian house, the Russian yard, the Russian street, the Russian toilet, the Russian hotel, the individual Russian's attitude toward his personal appearance, are items which convey to the Westerner (and particularly to a traveler from America), a sense of something which is neither creditable nor wholesome and which cannot possibly be excused on the ground of poverty... Your hotels, trains, railway stations and restaurants are too dirty and too poorly equipped. You do not wash

your windows often enough…You live too many in one room and are
even lunatic enough to identify it with a communistic spirit.[119]

It was a sign of the importance Kameneva attributed to Dreiser's visit that
on November 25, 1927, she wrote two letters to the top two party leaders at the
time, Stalin and Bukharin. Despite his behavior, Dreiser had been received by
such intelligentsia greats as the theater director Konstantin Stanislavskii, the
poet Vladimir Maiakovskii, and the filmmaker Sergei Eisenstein. Kameneva
herself had already met with Dreiser on two occasions. She now asked the
duumvirate to receive Dreiser as part of her effort to dispel the "unhealthy
atmosphere" that had arisen from Dreiser's angry outbursts. In other words,
arranging attention from top intelligentsia figures and Bolshevik leaders was
assumed to be a significant means of generating positive sentiments. It is also
revealing that, in this context as well, Kameneva developed her own evaluation of the foreign visitor as a matter of course. "He [Dreiser] gave me the
impression of an informal, if not to say rude person. His questions gave evidence of a complete incomprehension of all that is occurring in our country. Unquestionably, this is a person who is inclined toward skepticism and
irony and this, side by side with his clear talent, could produce unpleasant
results." Like the most lowly of guides, she labeled her remarks a *kharakteristika*, an evaluative assessment.[120] Her report was clearly designed to assess
what Dreiser might say to the world.

A more extensive, yet anonymous, VOKS evaluation of the American writer
may have been written by Trivas, the smooth-talking interpreter Kameneva
favored, or by an official from the VOKS Anglo-American sector. Unlike many
others, this report was, in its overall thrust, neither preponderantly positive
nor overwhelmingly negative. The reason for this was that it built directly
on Dreiser's own farewell pronouncement to produce the mirror image of
the writer's own mixed and ambivalent assessment about the Soviet Union.
Whereas Dreiser had begun with praise and ended with criticism, the VOKS
report reversed the order. Unsurprisingly, it accepted the American writer's
self-description as an individualist: he was "a typical bourgeois writer, with
a specific petty-bourgeois individualist ideology." Too old and sick to subject
phenomena around him to "deep analysis," he "understands absolutely nothing
in economics and very little about politics." Yet the second half of the report,
in a neat reversal of Dreiser's own composition, moved from harsh criticism to
growing praise. Singled out for approval was the writer's understanding that
the Soviet order helped the working class, his praise for Soviet anti-religious
policies, and his appreciation of the selflessness of Soviet leaders. Now Dreiser
was said to represent a group of "radical litterateurs" who were driven more
and more to the Left because of the situation in capitalist countries.[121]

Just as the Western visitors commented extensively on cleanliness and everyday life, the vast corpus of guides' reports in the interwar period paid close attention to visitors' attitudes toward comfort and material conditions. On the one hand, foreigners' attitudes, so important for the hosts, were influenced by often intractable issues of infrastructure; on the other, the rejection of bourgeois comfort and the acceptance of hardship, especially in the more ascetic 1920s, was one important component of Bolshevik identity. Further, a major component of the Bolsheviks' "cultural revolution" launched in the early 1920s was the transformation of everyday life, or *byt*, comprising the civilizing missions of hygiene, efficiency, and manners.[122] These battles on the cultural front drew heavily on the assumptions of the Europeanized, intelligentsia leadership of the Old Bolsheviks like Kameneva, so it was especially galling to be criticized as backward barbarians by high-handed Western visitors. In the logic of many guides' reports, higher standards of living further west could be inverted as addiction to "bourgeois comfort," explaining outsiders' negative judgments about the USSR in terms of materialistic prejudice.[123]

In the case of Dreiser, a key aspect of the dualistic evaluation was the manner in which it linked Dreiser's attitude toward his own material comforts and his reactions to Russian backwardness. His "mood" was said to "waver" in "relation to the degree of comfort in which he finds himself." Also, having arrived "from a country which has achieved a high degree of technological development, his petty-bourgeois spirit could not adjust to a country in which technology, of course, stands at a lower level of development... at every step his nature, used to standard comforts, experienced shocks." If Dreiser, like many other visitors, tended to generalize about the entire Soviet order based on the conditions he observed in his hotel chamber, the VOKS report reduced his barrage of opinions back down to their material base, namely his own dependence on luxury. Thus, in an entirely typical linkage, was Soviet technological inferiority to the West offset by Western inability to see beyond the comforts of bourgeois *byt*.[124]

After his return to the United States in 1927, Dreiser made public only inconsistent fragments of the criticisms of the Soviet Union and the Russian "race" so amply in evidence in his diary. Even so, it is important to note that *Dreiser Looks at Russia* contained some hard-hitting political criticisms that reflected the conditions he observed. He deplored the "inescapable atmosphere of espionage," the ubiquitous presence of the secret police, and the "nightmare" of "endless outpour and downpour of propaganda." The regime, he concluded, "fears and mistrusts most of its visitors and a very large number of its native Russians—really trusts no one." All of Dreiser's published criticisms, however, were bracketed within expressions of praise of Soviet "political and general achievements."[125]

Dreiser's public stance—exemplary of so many intellectual visitors—was to a significant degree the result of self-censorship. Indeed, as Kennell observed as she carefully preserved the press clippings he sent her, Dreiser in America lavished praise on the Soviet Union he had been so glad to leave behind. To the crowd of reporters waiting as he stepped off the Hamburg-American cruise line on January 22, 1928, he proclaimed (as quoted in *The New York Times*): "I cannot understand why there should be bread lines in a nation as rich as America...Nowhere in Russia will you find men without overcoats standing in breadlines waiting for a handout." In the first of his eleven-part series on the USSR in the *Morning Oregonian,* Dreiser predicted: "I think our own country will eventually be sovietized."[126] The balance of praise and blame had visibly shifted once he left the Soviet Union behind. His first letter to Kennell after his arrival in New York, dated February 24, 1928, establishes that this was initially deliberate. "I felt that I should not confuse my personal discomforts and temperamental reactions to a changed world with the actual Russian approach. Most of all I decided that, however little I might, I should not seriously try to injure an idealistic effort."[127] Dreiser's decision to censor himself was the most effective rebuttal of the Marxist thesis that Kennell, and then VOKS, advanced about the relationship between the bourgeois "discomforts" and political conclusions: that being determined consciousness and not the other way around.

The 1927 journey marked a moment of political and literary transition for Dreiser. His Soviet encounter accelerated his shift, begun in the 1920s and especially with the publication of *American Tragedy,* toward a new appreciation of social rather than cosmic or biological forces. Dreiser, who went on to become one of the most consistently pro-Soviet fellow-travelers of the 1930s, years later even recalled that he had been "delighted" with the food in 1927–28. He finally was allowed to enroll in the Communist Party a halfyear before his death in 1945.[128]

The case of Dreiser illuminates a number of the pressures and dilemmas that were embedded in the Soviet system for receiving foreign visitors. Dreiser showed how influential foreigners, even those ultimately well-disposed toward the Soviet Union, could be demanding and less pliable than lesser-known friends. If luxury and confinement were administered to the bourgeois visitors in excessive doses, they could be accused of bribery and building Potemkin villages; if the Soviets refrained from improving the visitor's own level of comfort, then poor Soviet standards of living and "backwardness" might seriously influence the visitor's all-important public statements on the USSR. The instrumental and utilitarian lessons VOKS drew from the Dreiser visit, as well as the increasing Soviet proclivity to choose the safer option, can be judged by the opening sentences of the VOKS report on Dreiser. The crucial fact for understanding this visit, it asserted, was that when Dreiser was invited, he was promised "material conditions" that were beyond the organization's ability to provide.[129] Dreiser's freewheeling trip was an effort to counter the rumors of staged pageants and Potemkin villages he had imbibed; although Kameneva's gamble was richly rewarded, the Soviets after 1927 would attempt to script the visits, above all of the most renowned foreigners, much more tightly.

During the height of Western intellectual enthusiasm for the "new Russia" in the interwar period, the Potemkin village legend began a new life. This latter-day Western discourse of Potemkin villages implicitly linked old Russia to a system of receiving foreigners that was in many ways distinctively Soviet. Presentation of the Soviet system to foreigners, revolving around model sites, involved more than highlighting a few showcases. Through the manner hundreds of model sites of socialism were displayed, it attempted to facilitate a mode of thinking, an intellectual leap from the exemplary to the systemic that would furnish sympathizers with an optics of enthusiasm.

But there was also hardly a single model shown to outsiders that did not have its own important role for insiders. It was as if Potemkin's decorated villages had been *divertissements* not for diplomatic elites but instead had been promulgated on a mass scale to inspire Russian peasants throughout the land. In the original myth, however, Potemkin villages were not merely façades for foreign visitors, but first and foremost the means to dupe Catherine the Great; they can thus be interpreted as a form of self-deception. There were Soviet practices that did recall that sense of the term. The "Potemkin methods" that at least one Western journalist and other eyewitnesses recorded of elaborate preparations for particularly important visitors—cleaning up buildings and evacuating the unsightly sick and homeless—are strikingly similar to the preparations made for the visits of top Soviet leaders in the regions, most famously later in Soviet history.

As the nature of Soviet model-building shifted and model sites became less the blueprints of expectant hope and more like canonical proofs of the superiority of the Soviet system, models acquired the status not merely of experimental or specially designated institutions but of a central means for shaping the world view of the new Soviet person. As such, they became a primary vehicle of the Soviet Union's trumpeting of its own superiority to itself, internally. In this sense, the model sites of socialism came full circle back to that original connotation of Potemkin villages as a form of self-delusion—this time, not as farce but as tragedy, involving not a handful of notables but an entire civilization.

4

Gorky's Gulag

Maxim Gorky, a longtime proponent of Bolshevism who left Soviet Russia in 1921 after a falling out with Lenin, came back in 1928 to throw in his lot with the Stalin Revolution. Upon his return, he took a tour around the country that in striking ways resembled a visit by an eminent foreign guest. He toured many industrial monuments of the Five-Year Plan and visited the secret police commune for juvenile delinquents at Bolshevo and other model sites. He chronicled his journey in his famous 1929 travelogue *Around the Union of Soviets*, a work filled with references to foreigners and the West. Because of his hero's welcome, Gorky, half ironically, referred to himself at this time as a "foreign notable" (*znatnyi inostranets*). At this fateful moment in the writer's transformation into an architect of Stalinist culture and Socialist Realism, he acted out the role of an outsider. By constantly criticizing the blindness of most Western observers, Gorky implied the superiority of his own version of the Soviet tour. "Why do so few foreigners visit us on the Volga?" a politically enlightened sailor cried out to Gorky at one moment in the travelogue.[1] Gorky himself replaced those absent foreign eyes unable to interpret the true meaning of Soviet achievements, providing his own paradigm for viewing the sites of socialism.

Gorky's tour upon his return from exile in Europe provides the most concrete and deliberate linkage between the model-based methods of guiding foreign visitors developed in the 1920s and modes of pointing mass Soviet audiences toward the bright future. Cultural show and Socialist Realism both emerged from the same cultural and political system, and there were bound to be many points of intersection and overlap between the two. Gorky's return was a milestone in the direct transfer of methods first developed for foreign visitors to domestic Soviet audiences.

Gorky, however, was allowed to visit a very different kind of model institution, a place where no foreigners were allowed—the OGPU's prototype concentration camp for forced labor in the nascent Gulag, located in the far-north prison monastery of Solovki. There, at a site carefully prepared for his visit,

he repudiated international accusations of forced labor and secret police bru-
talities. Gorky's international reputation and presence at the most notorious
Soviet labor camp thrust him into the middle of a Soviet counter-propaganda
effort that had been going on since 1925. That was the year when a volume of
Letters from Russian Prisons, which included Solovki, appeared in New York;
in late spring of that year, S. A. Mal'sagov escaped from the far-north archipelago and quickly published *An Island Hell*. These were quickly followed by
the writings of other escaped prisoners in other languages, mostly Russian,
German, and French. Despite their very different political orientations and
tones, these first Soviet camp memoirs published abroad conveyed a similar
picture of Solovki as a place where most prisoners were forced into hard physical labor in brutal conditions with little food and frequently sadistic guards.
By the time of Gorky's visit, international competitors had accused the Soviet
Union of exploiting forced labor to lower the price of lumber, and by 1930,
the United States, France, and other countries had imposed restrictions on or
entirely banned Soviet imports. Soviet responses to the international outcry
starting in the early to mid-1920s—including the reports of a parade of special
commissions on Solovki and excerpts from Gorky's Solovki essay published in
the central Soviet press in 1929—focused on the successful rehabilitation and
re-education of prisoners.[2] Gorky's widely trumpeted public praise of Solovki
was, therefore, an integral part of the ongoing Soviet counter-campaign that
brazenly denied all evidence of forced labor. However, Gorky also had his own
agenda—or, better to say, aesthetico-political mission. Gorky's visit to the far
north became the first test case for his project of presenting a future-oriented,
yet ostensibly factual, picture of Soviet superiority to the Soviets themselves.

The debate about Gorky has revolved around two diametrically opposed
poles. One, following Aleksandr Solzhenitsyn's famous charge in *The Gulag
Archipelago*, has indicted the writer as the cynical tool of emerging Stalinism
whose main goal was to whitewash the regime in front of international public
opinion. The defense, mostly mounted in Russia in recent years, has claimed
the old critic of the Red Terror during the Civil War and protector of the intelligentsia was himself the dupe of "Potemkin villages" or, at the very least,
hopeful of softening Stalinist political violence.[3] In her recent book, Elizabeth
Papazian addresses the riddle of Gorky by referring to his "duality" or "split
identity"—his legacy as humanist critic who objected strenuously to Leninist
violence after 1917 and the Stalinist cultural bureaucrat who sang the praises
of *Chekisty* as creators of culture and "engineers of souls."[4] In certain respects,
however, the concept of the "two Gorkys" is more useful for understanding
subsequent debates than Gorky himself. His role as defender and patron
of the intelligentsia and his deep-seated ideological approval of key aspects
of Stalinism, his shrewd political calculations, and the tight, yet gilded, cage

of systemic constraints in which he found himself operating were not always contradictory. What is crucial to understand is the nature of Gorky's return— how he parlayed his resentment against the West and his role as returning "foreigner" into a decisive impact on the course of Soviet culture.

Maxim Gorky as Famous Foreigner

Gorky, then, was neither cynic nor dupe. His return from abroad, so crucial to the direction taken by emerging Stalinism, can be seen as the political act of a cultural and ideological agent who successfully designed his ascent. Many of the seemingly stark disjunctures in the debate over the "two Gorkys" can be better understood in terms of an axis between outsider and insider that he repeatedly negotiated at key moments in his career. His pre-revolutionary persona of *bosiak*, the rebellious hobo who was a social outcast from the depths of society, which he had played with the "skill and savoir-faire of an experienced actor," obscured his activities as an ambitious and disciplined intelligentsia patron, charismatic circle (*kruzhok*) leader, and successful publisher.[5] After 1917, the old ally of Bolshevism then turned into a kind of internal critic, insider as outsider, who parlayed his close friendship with Lenin and access to the top leadership into a license for increasingly unwelcome interventions protecting the intelligentsia and condemning political violence. The result was failure and exile.[6] As Evgeny Dobrenko has perceptively noted, "In 1917 and 1918, the era of *Untimely Thoughts*, Gorky for the first time not only lost the mass reader but was also rejected by him. At that time he realized that he had ended up on the side of the losers. Gorky did not know how to lose."[7] Gorky returned to the USSR in 1928 as an outsider rising to defend the Soviet system, even as he reached for the crown of creator of the new culture. It was his own self-transformation that thoroughly informed his endorsement of forging "new people" through labor.

Gorky's vehicle of choice for this new role was the travelogue, a genre suggesting a "revealing distance between the visitor (traveler-outsider) and the object of his description," through which Gorky skillfully played on his identity as "a great Russian writer and an outsider in Russia, all at once."[8] Yet Gorky deployed these documentary methods not merely to heighten the appearance of objectivity but "in the pursuit of a higher truth"—not a photographic or "naturalist" representation of the present, but a deeper truth of the future.[9]

Like a giant, Gorky straddles Soviet culture as it developed in the 1930s. The Gorky-Stalin correspondence establishes how, between 1929 and 1936, virtually all of his influential initiatives—a complex of publishing houses, journals, publication series, institutes, and seminal collective projects—were approved and often personally furthered by Stalin.[10] Initially cautious toward the dictator, Gorky reached the height of his influence and personal interaction with Stalin in 1931–32. Although it is impossible to establish a direct link between the writer's failure to write a biographical ode to Stalin and his falling out with the leadership that followed, by 1933 he was restricted from foreign travel, and in his last years he was living under virtual house arrest. By that time, however, Gorky had made his mark not only as a broker and shaper of policy, but as the single most important figure behind the emergence of Socialist Realism. In the words of Spiridonova, "Of course Stalin often used Gorky in his interests, but he succeeded only when those interests did not contradict the convictions of the writer himself."[11]

In the 1920s, it was in his Italian villa in Sorrento, his personal "window on Europe," that Gorky became familiar with the Soviet conventions for conveying present-future "achievements" in comparison with an oppressive past. The epistolary relationship that Gorky struck up with the pacifist and high-minded man of letters Romain Rolland (whom he did not meet in person until 1935, when the Russian writer helped bring Rolland to Moscow) illustrates how Gorky himself became involved in the presentation of the Soviet system to European intellectuals. In the aftermath of his departure from Soviet Russia in 1921, Gorky felt free to express exasperation with the Soviet regime over the persecution of the intelligentsia to the Frenchman. He even enlisted Anatole France to support his protest over the 1922 show trial of the Socialist Revolutionaries, a step that infuriated the Bolshevik leadership. After the clashes of the early 1920s, the party leadership's relations with both the intelligentsia at home and Gorky in emigration stabilized. By 1925, the dynamic of Gorky's correspondence with Rolland had shifted. Gorky was moving back into the good graces of the regime, and Rolland was moving with him, from his 1920s admiration of Gandhi, to his 1930s fascination with Stalin. During this shift, the fastidious *grand écrivain* would worriedly write with one or another doubt or the latest charges about Soviet repudiations of human rights in European debates; Gorky would hasten to explain them away.[12]

When Rolland's letters turned on specific questions and complaints, such as those regarding Francesco Ghezzi, an Italian anarchist arrested in the Soviet Union in 1929, Gorky forwarded Rolland's correspondence to someone who might take action—NKVD chief Genrikh Iagoda, a regular at Gorky's mansions in Malaia Nikitskaia in Moscow and in the town of Gor'kii between 1931–36. To Iagoda, Gorky assumed a tone of utilitarian disdain when speaking about his warm, respectful missives to his longtime literary colleague: the French writer's sympathy for the USSR was filled with philistinism (*obyvatel'shchina*), but he might prove useful in influencing European public opinion.[13]

Gorky's deep involvement with the "worker-peasant correspondent" (*rabsel'kor*) movement, which became a prime outlet of the new Soviet mass journalism and proletarian literature of the 1920s, was marked by a strenuous attempt to persuade the local writers to praise "achievements" rather than expose indignities and flaws. The world was watching, he assured the correspondents in 1927: every "little word" (*slovtso*) of the Soviet press would be picked up by hostile Russian émigrés and then spread to the Western bourgeois press.[14] The "enlightenment" function of Soviet activist journalism and its ability to intervene as a "weapon" in socialist construction was the focus of the "Pressa" exhibition in Cologne in 1928, which Gorky visited as part of his return to the Soviet Union. The Soviet pavilion was a high-priority project for VOKS and was visited by Kameneva, who helped put together the blueprint for a team of sixty artists headed by El Lissitzky. The forward-looking dynamism of the exhibition, depicting the direction in which Soviet achievements were heading, deeply impressed Gorky and prefigured the aesthetic ideology of Socialist Realism.[15] Gorky's reaction to the exhibition is a "smoking gun" showing that he was positively influenced by the codified methods of presenting the Soviet system to foreign eyes.

Ultimately, the far-flung, seemingly contradictory passions of Gorky's intellectual make-up—his "romanticism" and mythopoesis on the one hand and his rationalism and scientism on the other, his Marxism and his Nietzscheanism, his preservationist efforts on behalf of Russian and European high culture and his promotion of the new Soviet culture as superior—became those of the emergent Stalinist culture writ large. The old critic of Red Terror cultivated Iagoda and his entourage of *Chekisty*. But it was only with such high-level connections that he could act as an effective patron and protector of the intelligentsia. In similar fashion, Gorky reconciled his many faces into a single whole. Another opposition, not nearly as well known, was the key to his fateful return by way of an all-union pilgrimage to the sites of Soviet socialism: Gorky as European and cosmopolitan, the internationally famous face of the regime facing West (a position he assumed through his appeal for international aid during the 1921 famine), and Gorky the sharp-tongued purveyor of *ressentiment* and Soviet/Russian superiority over bourgeois European barbarism. In other words, the old love-hate relationship with the West and its concomitant complexes of inferiority and superiority were an integral part of the proletarian writer's worldview, later canonized as he became a cultural icon in the 1930s. It has not provoked much mention, but this was very much on display during the entire period of his reconciliation with Soviet reality.

While Gorky was full of admiration for Europe when he began his second European exile in 1921, this stance was reversed as he drew closer to his return to the USSR in the second half of the decade.[16] For example, writing from abroad in *Pravda*, Gorky took an openly hostile position toward foreign visitors in his celebratory paean to the tenth anniversary of the October Revolution. At the very moment when several thousand foreign sympathizers were being fêted in Moscow with the goal of producing a wave of Western adulation, Gorky found European visitors not only ignorant but anti-Soviet. To be sure, some of his complaints were justified: "Having lived among Russians two or three weeks, they return home and tell about what they saw," he charged, observing that Europeans still reflexively emphasized Russian cultural backwardness (*nekul'turnost'*). Far more tendentious was his accusation that European travel reports noted only the "insufficiencies" of Soviet power. Gorky's analysis of this, attributing it to bourgeois intellectuals' "class psyche," appeared as something of an afterthought. The primary explanation he offered was that "outmoded disease of the Europeans—a grotesquely exaggerated and laughably pompous consciousness of their superiority over Russians."[17]

If Gorky saw European assertions of superiority as "outmoded," it was because Soviet achievements had rendered them obsolete. The successes Gorky listed on this celebratory occasion—state support for science, electrification, and the growth of culture—are clues to his thinking but are ultimately less important than the notion of achievement itself. To him, the concept connoted feats, even miracles, carried out by heroes in order to bring an organic unity of will and belief. Twenty years after the fact, he unabashedly recalled his adherence to the condemned "godbuilding" heresy of leading Left Bolsheviks after 1907. What he had earlier called the godbuilder, he said, was nothing other than the new hero—the "superior, honest, this-worldly worker" (*prevoskhodnyi, chestnyi rabotnik mira sego*)—who, "within himself and on this earth is creating and carrying out the ability to work miracles," unified and organized by the state.[18]

Literary scholars and cultural historians have invested much energy into the search for the origins of Socialist Realism, and in almost all accounts, the Soviet Union's most powerful writer has figured prominently. The "international" factor, the display of positive models of the future to foreigners, figures in none of these discussions, however. This missing international link does not preclude other explanations, but it calls attention to the enormous significance foreign eyes held for the evolution of Soviet culture and reinforces the notion that Socialist Realism needs to be conceived as, even more than an aesthetic doctrine, a cultural-ideological mode for showing the Soviet system. Gorky took the internationally propagated notion of Soviet "achievements" and invested it with a powerful formula of his own: they would become the fruit of the heroism of the new man in order to create the new culture and unity of purpose of a secular religion. The interlocking place of heroes, the "reforging" of man, and mythopoesis were at the crux of his contribution to Soviet culture.

Through his idea of the "Soviet hero," as Hans Günther has discussed, Gorky became instrumental in rehabilitating myth within the ostensibly materialist Soviet ideology and aesthetics.[19] By the 1930s, when he worked to add the element of "revolutionary romanticism" to literary doctrine, he held that "true realism" required adding "wishes and possibilities" to reality. Myth was thus freed from the burden of reality and, under Stalinism, fact and fiction became virtually indistinguishable.[20]

In a sense, Gorky was not so different from any famous foreigner: his decision to throw his support behind the Stalin Revolution, while of a different order from that of foreign writers and intellectuals, was not based on ideological or political calculations alone. Like some of the most prominent Western fellow-travelers, it emerged out of an intricate web of convictions as well as professional, aesthetic, and personal motivations. Gorky, who had from an early age loathed peasant ignorance, heartily approved of the forced collectivization drive; he reviled the conservative, religious, and anarchic nature of peasant Russia. In a 1930 letter to Stalin, Gorky conveyed his hatred of the peasantry along with a sense of awe at the Party's "almost geological" transformation of the countryside: "a way of life that has existed for a thousand years is being destroyed, an order that has created an incredibly ugly creature capable of horrifying with its bestial conservatism... There are twenty million of such people. The task of reeducating them in the shortest possible time is incredibly difficult. But, however, it is practically being solved."[21] For Gorky, the Stalin Revolution would not only transform those millions of less than fully human philistines, but by doing so it would also decisively change the calculus between Russia and the West.[22] On this he was in substantial accord with Stalin's own views. "Things here are not going badly," Stalin wrote him at the end of 1930, having taken the time throughout this period to court and consult the writer with unusually long and substantive notes. "Both in the realm of industry and agriculture there are indisputable successes. Let them whine over there, in Europe... about the 'collapse' of the USSR. With this they will not change our plans or our affairs by one iota... Holy Russia will be no more. Of course! There will be a powerful and advanced Russia."[23]

Like other great intelligentsia patrons, Gorky surrounded himself with a large household, at once a literary circle and an entourage of intimates, guests, and lovers; "he did not want to moderate his appetites."[24] To return to the USSR meant not only stupendous acclaim as the greatest proletarian writer—after all, his literary stature in Europe was on the wane—but the chance to build a new culture with an entrée into the inner circle of the top political leadership. The courtship began in the mid-1920s and intensified in 1928, when Ivan Skvortsov-Stepanov, an Old Bolshevik, was put in charge of a Politburo special commission to handle questions related to Gorky's return. His "celebratory reception" was a hero's welcome attended by at least as many high-level dignitaries as the most important foreign delegations. In late 1929, Stalin arranged a Politburo resolution defending Gorky from attacks on him from the camp of the *enragée* "proletarian" militants on the literary front, making it clear to all that Gorky, like the top party leaders, was off limits during the Great Break frenzy of aesthetico-ideological infighting. Gorky's proposals in the realm of literature, "cultural construction," and patronage were handled with what Kaganovich called "special care" by Stalin and his lieutenants—at least until the fall of 1933, when Gorky was refused permission to make his regular trips to Italy and started falling out with the inner circle.[25]

Then, there was the money. Gorky was above handling financial details, which were arranged by his personal secretary (and secret-police minder) Petr Kriuchkov, who communicated by telegram to the head of Stalin's personal chancellery, Aleksandr Poskrebyshev.[26] Until 1932, a special fund at the State Publishing House was kept for Gorky, facilitating rapid transfers abroad; when this was ended and he began being paid from the hard-currency accounts earmarked for authors' honoraria, it triggered a crisis. According to the head of the press in that year, the amount Gorky was slated to receive equaled 40,000 hard-currency rubles. The funds allotted to all the presses of the USSR for honoraria in hard currency—the primary purpose of which was to pay foreign authors, among them some of the most prominent fellow-travelers from the literary world—was 100,000.[27] H. G. Wells, mounting the grand marble staircase in Gorky's house during his visit in 1934, turned around to his old friend to say, "Tell me, is it good to be a great proletarian writer?" Gorky reportedly blushed and replied, "My people gave me this house."[28]

Solovki and Socialist Realism

The far-north island fortress of Solovki that Gorky visited and wrote about in 1929 was also an experimental microcosm, but of a kind very different from those conventionally shown to foreigners. Built as a monastery in the fifteenth century, its long and tumultuous history made it symbolic in several respects: as a major achievement in the art of fortification, as a center of religiosity and religious dissent in the Russian North, and as one of the strictest tsarist prisons for Orthodox clergy and enemies of the tsars. Much later, in 1920, it became a concentration camp for Civil War POWs, and in 1923 was designated the Solovetskii Lager' Osobogo Naznacheniia (SLON), the Solovetskii Camp of Special Designation.

In internal documents, however, SLON continued to be designated a "concentration camp," just as in the early years of Soviet power the term "forced

Figure 4.1 The far-north island fortress at Solovki in a shot from Marina
Goldovskaia's documentary film *Vlast' Solovetskaia*. The fifteenth-century monastery,
used by the Orthodox Church to imprison heretics, was designated the Solovetskii
Camp of Special Designation (SLON) in 1923. In the late 1920s, it became the
prototype for the nascent Gulag. Source: RIA Novosti Photo Library.

labor" (*prinuditel'nyi trud*) was current. In 1930, all clandestine secret-police
camps were renamed "correctional-labor" institutions— the very designation used for the showcase models of rehabilitation shown to foreigners such
as the well-appointed facilities for juvenile delinquents at Bolshevo—well
after the early 1920s heyday of rehabilitationism in the Soviet penitentiary
system.[29]

Iurii Brodskii has called Solovki, or more precisely, the system of camps
run from the fortress in the Solovetskii archipelago, a miniature state-within-
a-state: it had its own Kremlin, political elite, and stratified classes of inhabit-
ants, and even its own currency. It became a laboratory—a model institution,
if you will—for the secret police, which from 1922–28 lost the battle for control over camps to its rivals (the Commissariats of Justice and Interior) and
was limited to SLON and a few other possessions. New techniques aimed at

making forced labor economically profitable proceeded along with the organization of internment with few guards and the use of favored classes of prisoners to keep discipline. After the secret police emerged as the institutional
master of the explosively expanding camp system at the outset of the Stalin
period, Solovki's "graduates" staffed camps throughout the nascent Gulag
archipelago. In 1929, which Stalin called the year of the Great Break, Solovki
was explicitly mentioned in decrees as the prototype for new concentration
camps that would place economic profit and settlement of new areas at the
top of the agenda.[30]

Solovki was therefore a path breaker in the shift from "isolating" political
prisoners to the search for profit and colonization of the far north. In 1924,
OGPU chief Feliks Dzerzhinskii expressly mentioned Solovki as a model for
the expansion of forced labor and exploitation of uninhabited areas, functions
he expressly distinguished from the rehabilitation of criminals so prominent
in early Soviet judicial theory.[31] One account attributes the plan for the first
concerted secret police attempts to derive economic profits from forced labor
to an entrepreneurial former NEPman who served time in Solovki.[32] In 1926,
the camp was given a contract to export timber for hard currency.

But at the very moment that the Solovki model was being replicated in the
Gulag and the number of camps and prisoners in the Solovki archipelago and
elsewhere shot up, its profitability had declined, after several years of intensive
logging. Typhus ran rampant and food rations dwindled; guards became even
more brutal and punishments and humiliations more intense. The result was
mass death from overwork and an epidemic of self-inflicted injuries as prisoners sought to avoid it. A Moscow commission sent to the Solovetskii camp in
1930 uncovered "chilling facts of mass violence against prisoners," including
murder, beatings with sticks hardened by fire, and multiple forms of torture,
including leaving recalcitrant prisoners out to mosquitoes in summer and
frostbite in winter.[33] Gorky's visit coincided with this crisis and downturn in
camp conditions.

One sign of the international importance the secret police and the Party
invested into Gorky's visit to Solovki was the almost contemporaneous filming of the widely distributed film *Solovki*, a feature-length documentary commissioned by the OGPU.[34] Contrasting the harsh tsarist internment system
with the humane Soviet rehabilitation of prisoners, the film was shot after a
sanitizing of conditions and staged presentation of prisoners similar to those
reserved for Gorky's visit. "God, what an impudent and underhanded staging
of all views and scenes," wrote one prisoner present during the filming, when
prisoners were filmed playing chess and reading newspapers. For Gorky's visit,
an alley of trees was set up in front of the barracks, the grounds were land-
scaped, and buildings were painted and washed. On September 21, 1929, a

few months after Gorky's visit in June of the same year, an item in *Izvestiia* appeared about the secret-police film, screened widely throughout the USSR: "The film wonderfully explains the methods of correction and destroys all the idiotic things made up about the 'horrors of the GPU'... It needs to be shown abroad." Or, as a worker identified as a political emigre from Latvia declared in the Dzerzhinskii Club for foreign technical specialists, "There exist two terrible words abroad: 'GPU' and 'Solovki.' This picture 'Solovki' dispels the legends about the Bolshevik inquisition, it is unlikely to be permitted abroad." Gorky, of course, had the power to reach an international audience, however. After the moment when the honored guest, on the conclusion of his visit, signed his name to the camp's "control journal" in an entry that endorsed camp conditions as "excellent," camp officials fired off a special telegram directly to Stalin to announce the news.[35]

Playing the role of the famous foreigner, Gorky forged his pact with the Stalin Revolution. But he did it his way, highlighting his particular cultural-ideological concerns and viewing himself as a builder of the new culture rather than as a servile toady. What Gorky emphasized was human transformation: refuting Lombroso and the theory of the born criminal, he declared that "The Solovetskii Camp of Special Detention is not Dostoevsky's 'house of the dead,' because there one is being taught life, literacy, and labor."[36] The re-education of criminals showed the success of the entire project of transforming people into communists. The *Chekisty* could, thus, be accredited with a cultural achievement, a pedagogical miracle that, if properly understood by the Soviet masses, would create unity of purpose. In sum, Gorky was not describing Solovki as it was, but as it should be. His "around the union" cycle can be considered an early prototype of Socialist Realism.[37]

Gorky's Solovki and the "union" cycle more broadly replicated the principal features current in writing about Soviet achievements for foreigners developed in the 1920s, redirecting them toward a mass Soviet audience. The first feature was the constant contrast between the tsarist past and the Soviet present (Dostoevsky's "house of the dead"). The device for achieving this contrast in the "around the union" cycle was Gorky's personal recollections as a witness to the transformation. His visit to Baku's oil industry, for example, began with his memories of the nightmarish hell he had seen in 1892 and 1897, then fast-forwarded to the workers' sense of collective unity and pride, the "fantastic miracles" (*fantastiki*) he witnessed today.[38] A second feature of writing for foreigners was the concern for reading the present in light of the future, to value present achievement more highly for what it was about to become. Thus, he peppered the cycle with such phrases as "the will and reason of the laboring people is transforming the figure and face of the earth"—focusing heavily on children and youth as the new people of the future.[39]

Finally, there was the mission of cataloguing and showcasing revolutionary "achievements." In the mid-1920s, a series of coordinating strategy meetings among the agencies involved in crafting the Soviet image abroad—including VOKS, the Comintern, Profintern, the telegraph agency ROSTA, and IAH—came to their most far-reaching agreement by settling on Soviet "achievements" (*dostizheniia*) as a unifying theme.[40] Gorky himself used the word constantly, and also interchanged it with the "miracles" that needed to be apprehended by the Soviet people rather than by foreigners. If any of the "cultured" governments of Europe had created the pedagogical achievements of reforming juvenile offenders that had been achieved at Solovki and Bolshevo, he wrote, they would be propagandized "like a drumbeat," but "we do not know how to write about our achievements."[41]

Gorky received approval for his new journal *Our Achievements* in 1928, around the time when he visited the forward-looking VOKS press exhibit in Cologne. When the new journal began publication in 1929, the country was wracked by the self-criticism campaign, a controlled paroxysm deeply linked to the overthrow of the political and cultural order of the New Economic Policy (NEP). To Gorky, however, with his cherished project of promoting affirmative and unifying myths of heroism, self-criticism had channeled far too much attention toward mistakes. Literature aimed at foreigners was already organized around the principle of teaching outsiders to recognize Soviet achievements; as Gorky himself wrote in a *Pravda* piece addressed "To Foreign Workers," foreign visitors had to learn to see not only beyond the "external glitter" of their own comfortable, bourgeois West but also beyond the outward "unculturedness" of undisciplined Russian work habits and ramshackle conditions. Only then could they grasp the unbelievable successes achieved through collective unity of consciousness.[42] The goal set by Gorky's journal was to re-educate the Soviet masses along the same lines: to register, supposedly with the accuracy of a cinematographer's footage, what, in an oblique reference to backwardness, he revealingly called "our victories over ourselves." Gorky's own "achievement" was to take the combined stress on scientifically measured fact and future-oriented fiction implicit in the presentation of Soviet achievements to foreigners and elevate it to the level of a doctrine aimed, as the opening editorial of the journal put it, at the re-education of tens of millions of "little" Soviet people.[43]

This reorientation becomes even more striking when we consider the pervasive, almost obsessive concern with Russian superiority and overtaking the West woven into the fabric of Gorky's "around the union" cycle. As Tolczyk has noted, the diachronic opposition between pre- and post-revolutionary Russia in Gorky's travelogue was complemented by the synchronic opposition between the USSR and the "rotting West." Referring again and again in quotation marks to "cultured" Europe and the United States, an expression of bitter irony and resentment, Gorky noted with satisfaction that juvenile delinquency was sharply on the rise abroad, while here it "should"—a careful expression of the present becoming the future—"fall and fall."[44] The head of the leather factory at Solovki, a former prisoner who was freed and who thus serves as an example of successful re-education through labor, speaks about how in "leatherwork we lag behind Europe but in semi-finished material we are more advanced."[45] It was not hard to guess what the future would bring. Reflecting on the miracles he had witnessed in Dneprostroi, Moscow, and Baku, Gorky pictured the Soviet example teaching Europe in a reversal of the old position of Russian inferiority: "The time is not far off when the working class of Europe will also...start to work on itself in the same way, as we have begun this work in the Union of Soviets."[46]

The connection between "our achievements" and the shape of Gorky's grand strategy for Soviet culture was clear. Unifying the simple masses around inspiring feats would help channel their instinctive striving for change and teach them to transform themselves and "reality." Only then would the old and infuriating position of inferiority toward Western literature—and the West—wither away.

Gorky's actual visit to Solovki was extraordinary for the hopes it raised among the rank-and-file prisoners, something first written about by Solzhenitsyn in his composite account.[47] Numerous recollections of the visit by prisoners from various walks of life who survived have been discussed and reproduced by recent Russian scholars.[48] M. Z. Nikonov, arrested as leader of a peasant rising in Nizhnii Novgorod province, wrote that the inmates' excitement was spurred by Gorky's reputation as the friend of the oppressed and his ability to reach the outside world. Nikonov and other memoirists recalled how prisoners found occasions to whisper to the famous writer about hard labor, sadistic punishments, or the cruelty of the camp regime. Chernukhina is able to suggest that at least some of these examples were rumors rather than eyewitness accounts, but the fact that such rumors spread like wildfire testifies to the hopes raised by the famous writer's visit. Other incidents, some written about in multiple sources, are hard to dismiss: prisoners among those shown reading newspapers turned their copies upside down in protest, and Gorky silently righted one of them; when the honored guest moved away from his secret-police minders during an intermission smoke during a theater visit, he was besieged with handwritten notes, which shortly thereafter disappeared when one of his suitcases was stolen.[49]

Gorky, however, decided to use his position as returning hero from abroad not to expose prisoner suffering but to convey an exemplary, model version of the Soviet tour itself. In describing the Solovki camp as it should be, not as it was, he was shelving the rebellious persona of the *bosiak* and assuming the mantle of a creator of the great proletarian writer, which virtually became his honorific in the years to come.

When Gorky described Solovki as a place of re-education, he was ignoring or not investigating many things: mass deaths from overwork, attempts to extract maximum profit from forced labor, hard-labor punishments like carrying water up and down stairs until some started to look like living corpses. One former prisoner present at the time charged in his memoirs that Gorky had "morally justified the extermination of millions of people in the camps." By deceiving world public opinion, Gorky lost the chance to become a Voltaire, Zola, or Chekhov and became that which he despised most, the most ordinary of philistines.[50] This moral condemnation concentrates on replacing truth with lies. But Gorky did more than deceive; he created a system for self-deception on a mass scale. Gorky did not invent re-education and "cultural-enlightenment" work at Solovki: he magnified an unrepresentative sample that actually existed into a redefinition of reality that recalled the way foreigners were supposed to read the sites of communism.

"Far from everything was limited to suffering, humiliation, and fear," wrote one of the camp's most famous prisoners, the future academician Dmitrii Likhachev, who was arrested as a young philologist and linguist. Likhachev observed the camp from his own office, where he was charged by the authorities with compiling a dictionary of criminal slang. "In the terrible conditions of camps and prisons to a certain measure the life of the mind was preserved." Prisoners took full advantage of the opening offered by officially sanctioned "cultural-enlightenment work"; the resulting contrast between the camp's punishing standard of living and Solovki's thriving intellectual life was extraordinary. The camp had a museum, a lecture hall, and a theater that was considered one of the best in the country outside the capital cities; these were run by the "labor-enlightenment department" of the secret-police camp administration. One inmate counted the camp journal and newspaper among the freest publications in the USSR. Likhachev himself survived through a sinecure in the criminological laboratory headed by a former tsarist procurator in which some prisoner-scholars, one with a doctorate from the Sorbonne, conducted sociological research.

One former prisoner speculated that these activities were first launched not to parade in front of international public opinion but because they were noted by the upper levels of the Party. In other words, this prisoner believed they allowed Old Bolsheviks to believe humanistic rehabilitation was actually taking place. Perhaps. It comes as no surprise, however, as one camp official openly complained in the camp journal, that most prisoners returned

Figure 4.2 Pages from the Gulag album of academician Dmitrii Likhachev, from a stand at a 1989 exhibition on the Solovki Camp. The captions for the photographs are made in his own hand and commemorate his imprisonment from 1926 to 1930.
Source: RIA Novosti Photo Library.

from the day's work so exhausted that cultural activities were out of the question.[51]

From the earliest years of the revolution, the notion that crime was environmentally determined and could be corrected through re-education and labor was offset by classification of unredeemable enemies. Numerous historians have seen a hardening of essentialism in social, political, and, by the 1930s, ethnic categories that decisively weakened the rehabilitative strand in early Soviet penal policy. Even so, through the early 1930s, according to Khlevniuk, the Gulag had not yet "acquired the extreme brutality" of the late 1930s and a certain "punitive idealism" of the revolutionary period remained.[52] In some cases, "cultural-enlightenment" institutions in the camps remained extensive in the 1930s, such as in the Dmitlag camp zone north of Moscow where the forced-labor project of the White Sea Canal was directed. The ferocious hurricane of violence during the Great Purges marked another great downturn in camp conditions, and advocates of the idea of rehabilitation such as Dmitlag's director Semen Firin were shot for "sympathy for criminals and recidivists."[53] Even later, however, it was still possible for some to transform themselves from inmates to free loyalists of the regime through "cultural-enlightenment work." As Stephen Barnes has argued, the different kinds of penitentiaries within the Gulag tended to replicate practices and institutions from the Soviet system writ large, as in certain ways "the Soviet authorities sought to replicate Soviet society behind the barbed wire."[54]

The shifting balance between rehabilitation and stigmatization was only one part of the relationship between utopianism and terror, for the history of Soviet political violence is marked by a dialectical tension between utopian plans and disastrous human catastrophe.[55] Significantly, model institutions were a key part of this internal logic. The vision of the withering away of the prison endorsed by Gorky was shared by his friend, secret-police deputy Iagoda, in his fantastic internal memorandum of April 1930 that furthered the new project of "special settlements"—justified as an "experimental-show" institution that would colonize the far north. Iagoda, in turn, built on the January 1930 report of Fedor Eikhmans, the militaristic director of the Solovetskii camp complex from 1924–28, who boasted how the labor camp was a pioneering model that had helped colonize the frontier and now could play a decisive role in the industrialization drive. Iagoda fantasized about what were already shaping up to be nightmarishly destructive experiments in special settlements of deportees to the far north by predicting that labor and prison camps would become a vestige of the bourgeois past; with no need to guard those who would have no desire to run away, the landscape would become dotted by new proletarian mining towns. In the same vein, Likhachev recalled the "maniacal" Solovki camp leaders and the "phantasmagorical atmosphere" they created by shunning small-scale, prosaic projects in favor of outlandish plans.[56] As with the models presented to foreigners, putatively universal ideal types masked, even justified, horrendous realities.

Prominent in the model-based logic Eikhmans and Iagoda applied—not to places seen by foreigners but to the sites of forced labor and resettlement—is the link between re-education and political enlightenment (reflecting Bolshevism's powerful didactic and propagandizing urge) and industrialization and proletarianization (with all the physical and economic exploitation it brought). They were all connected in the notion of labor itself as redemptive, to which Gorky also subscribed, as we shall see, in order to equate Solovki with

Bolshevo. The big red banners plastered around Solovki, which at first riveted prisoners' eyes but soon became an unnoticed part of the landscape, embodied the conflation between physical labor and human transformation. *"Chtoby drugim ty snova stal, tebia trudlag perekoval!"* (In order to change, you need to be reforged by the labor camp!), announced one slogan on the former monastery. A banner far more common throughout the Gulag system represented what could be read as a cruder exhortation to work harder: *"Cherez trud—k osvobozhedeniiu"* (Through labor—to emancipation!).[57] The Nazis, hanging "Arbeit macht frei" on the entrance to Auschwitz, came by a different route to almost the same exact slogan. It is precisely the lack of planned, systematic extermination—the possibility of redemption—that remained a key difference between the Gulag and Auschwitz.

In its way, Gorky's cultural-ideological program was as phantasmagorical as the violent fantasies of Eikhmans and Iagoda. Understanding Gorky's role as whitewashing or fabrication is to minimize his innovation. Gorky sought nothing less than a redefinition of truth, made explicit in his contemporaneous theory of "two truths"—one belonging to the past, the other to the society-in-the-making. At Solovki, he took an increasingly abortive part of what went on in the labor colony and called it a truth representative of the future society, recapitulating the move inherent in the presentation of model institutions to foreigners. As Dariusz Tolczyk has shown, Gorky's writing on Solovki became the widely imitated, seminal Soviet text marking the shift from a 1920s "revolutionary discourse of terror, vengeance, and class-cleansing" to a "pedagogical discourse of re-education and resocialization through compulsory labor." The camps that became the Gulag were no longer justified; they were redefined, or, like terror, no longer openly discussed.[58] In fact, Gorky's innovation went beyond the camps. He helped elevate a strategy for universalizing models for the future to the level of doctrine. The writer's opportunity to do so, conferred by his reconciliation with the regime, made it into perhaps his chief contribution to Stalinist culture.

The Bolshevo Commune's "Road to Life"

The secretive, far-north concentration camp Gorky visited as the "famous foreigner" was, in a twisted way, tied to one of the most famous sites of socialism displayed to foreign visitors, the commune for reforming juvenile delinquents at Bolshevo. Both were run by the secret police; Gorky played a key role in the history of both places. Yet, there exist more hidden connections, as well.

The ability of models and showcases to transport a bit of the future into the present was important not only to Gorky, but to leading Bolsheviks. In the early years of the revolution, harsh measures one day were justified in terms of the bright future. What, however, were the reasons prompting "Iron Feliks" Dzerzhinskii, founder and first head of the Cheka, to attach himself to the cause of homeless children? Why did Dzerzhinskii, Iagoda, and other *Chekisty* play such a big role in founding the OGPU's Bolshevo children's colony near Moscow, which became a world-famous institution several years after it was launched in August 1924? In 1921, Dzerhzhinskii was the primary figure behind the Central Executive Committee (TsIK) Commission for the Improvement of Children's Life, which was primarily concerned with addressing the catastrophic growth in the early 1920s of up to seven million homeless waifs (*besprizorniki*). This cause addressed not merely a pressing domestic problem but an international public relations disaster. No other issue so shocked visitors from Europe and the United States as child homelessness. Juvenile crime in the early 1920s became a major problem in Moscow, where almost all foreigners were concentrated.

It is not hard to come up with self-serving explanations: the commune served to humanize the dreaded secret police, garnering large amounts of good publicity; and it did so internationally, as the colony, conveniently located in the countryside twenty-seven kilometers outside Moscow, became a showcase for propagating the virtues of rehabilitation in the Soviet penal system. There are also ideological reasons: in Bolshevo, an intense revolutionary focus on youth as the future of the new order was wedded to the principle of the environment shaping the new man. The commune was a successful form of socialism writ small, the miniature obverse of gargantuan, grandiose monuments to the new order. It is clear, however, that Bolshevo was dear to Dzerzhinskii's heart well before the institution became a showcase, which in fact occurred after his death in 1926. It was one of his "few diversions" to visit the commune; he once told the commissar of justice that "these dirty faces are my best friends. Among them I can find rest. How much talent would have been lost if we had not picked them up!"[59] While Dzerzhinskii has been known for his steely fanaticism, he has more recently been depicted as a "growing force of moderation" within the secret police and party leadership between 1921 and 1926, as he moved uneasily toward reassessing the "balance between terror and consent."[60] Could it be that his role as savior of the street children of Bolshevo allowed him on some level to justify the role he played in repressing the unredeemable enemies of the revolution?

According to some secret-police defectors, graduates of OGPU labor communes provided substantial cadres for the secret police.[61] Perhaps more important, the secret police had lost the battle for control over camps and prisons during the turn to NEP in 1921–22, when its chief rivals, the Commissariats of Justice and the Interior, had promoted themselves as champions of re-education and economic self-sufficiency, respectively.[62] Bolshevo and the two other high-profile children's communes, in Liubertsy and Khar'kov, gave the secret police credentials in both these areas. Gorky and high-profile foreign visitors alike helped call attention to the secret police's "achievements."

The secret-police founder of the Bolshevo commune was Matvei Samoilovich Pogrebinskii, born in 1895 in a Poltava shtetl to a family of nine. He fought in World War I and joined the Red Army in 1919, joining the OGPU only months before he opened the commune in 1924. Without any pedagogical experience, studying literature on child homelessness "day and night," Pogrebinskii also launched a successful career as a secret-police administrator and NKVD chief of the Gor'kii *oblast'*. Not mentioned in official versions of the commune's history, however, was that the Bolshevo commune was formed out of the Rosa Luxemburg Children's Labor Commune, founded in February 1924 by the energetic and experienced pedagogue Fedor Melikhov, whose successes had attracted Pogrebinskii's interest. A central feature of waifdom in this period was the roving bands of homeless children, led by so-called *vozhaki*, group leaders who established often brutal command over the others. Melikhov had developed a successful set of methods to curtail the influence of the *vozhak* and the temptations of the street by giving the children a sense of belonging through self-governance and employment in a boot workshop. Pogrebinskii selected the Luxemburg Commune to transfer to the secret police's sovkhoz in Bolshevo, and on August 18, 1924, in an order signed by Iagoda, Melikhov was subordinated to Pogrebinskii "in all respects." The pedagogue Melikhov continued to labor in obscurity; the Chekist Pogrebinskii became famous as Bolshevo's founding father.[63]

An extraordinary fact about Bolshevo was that its path to fame was cleared not by the OGPU, not by VOKS, and not even by the Soviet press—but by the left-liberal U.S. magazine *The Nation*, which carried a wide-eyed article by William Reswick in the November 11, 1925 issue. Boris Svirskii, the VOKS representative in Washington, started receiving inquiries from curious Americans about the "Russian farm colony for boy criminals." Svirskii sent a request to Moscow for more information, rightly sensing the triple appeal of social rehabilitation, penal reform, and humanism. In response to Svirskii's inquiry, though, VOKS official Tsetsiliia Rabinovich mistakenly directed an inquiry to a collective farm in "Bolyshevo," not Bolshevo, suggesting at very least that she did not know where it was located.[64] Thus did *The Nation* bring the news about Bolshevo to VOKS. Only after foreign interest began stirring in 1925 did the Soviet central press start to publicize the Bolshevo commune in a growing number of articles in 1926.[65] The conclusion is inescapable: Bolshevo was not founded as a showcase for foreigners; rather, the process by which it became a showcase was launched only in response to international acclaim.

Reswick became the first person ever to sign the Bolshevo visitors' book, which soon filled up with scrawls of praise from luminaries from around the world.[66] Foreign interest bolstered its status within the Soviet Union. The commune thus rose to fame abroad and at home simultaneously, and its rise and fall was determined by a remarkable interplay of international and domestic developments. Throughout, Gorky's role runs like a red thread. As it became one of the prime destinations for the most important foreign guests and delegations starting in the late 1920s, Bolshevo was far more than just a showcase for foreigners. Its "graduates" left a mark in Soviet society; in Soviet culture, its celebration as a locus for the rehabilitation of criminals took off just as that principle was increasingly subsumed in practice by counter-principles of irredeemable guilt and exploitation of the labor of those arrested.

Productive labor and the making of new proletarians, the most specifically Bolshevik and Soviet features of Bolshevo, were not what first impressed *The Nation*'s Reswick and other Western guests. They were interested in the place's relevance for progressive penal and social reform as they affected juvenile delinquents and the criminal poor. Quite typically, Bolshevik and Soviet principles combined with a broader appeal to progressive foreigners of many political hues. Also typical was the fact that programs furthered by the revolution had emerged out of social reform movements of late imperial Russia.[67] Reswick highlighted features of Dzerzhinskii's "experiment in penal reform" that later continually impressed other foreigners: freedom of movement for the communards, lack of fences and guards, and the seemingly astounding ability of a "change of environment" to transform even the most hardened criminals. The goal was to turn "some of the worst juvenile criminals in Russia into decent human beings... Most of them appeared well fed, ruddy, and broad-chested, their eyes sparkled with health and vigor. It was difficult to believe that only a year or two ago these boys were murderers and ruffians." The article, as no doubt hoped when the American journalist was given access to Bolshevo, represented a windfall of favorable publicity for Dzerzhinskii, depicted not as the "living terror of the Revolution" but as the humanitarian patron of his "'baby' farm."[68]

In terms of conditions and resources, Bolshevo and the other OGPU communes were virtually unique even among those orphanages and penal colonies designated as models or well-run institutions. There existed vast variations among children's homes, as in other Soviet welfare institutions, but the norm for juveniles under state care was frequently harsh punishments and material conditions ranging from poor to horrific.[69] Even so, Bolshevo's "achievements" were genuine and deserve scrutiny, for foreigners were not impressed without reason. Part of what struck visitors, of course, was what made it exceptional: excellent facilities in an idyllic location on a former estate, with a fine chef and courts for tennis, an expensive and elite sport in the West. Yet, none of this would have mattered without a remarkable transformation of street children, drug addicts, and criminals that Bolshevo took in increasingly large numbers—32 in 1925, 96 in 1927, 197 in 1929, 655 in 1930, and after a mass influx, 1,200 in 1931 and 2,200 in 1933—who were rapidly "brought to order" (to use Gorky's expression about Solovki), educated, and turned into highly skilled craftsmen. They shared in the profits of a highly successful sporting goods equipment and clothing enterprise. In 1932, the Dzerzhinskii Commune in Khar'kov produced the first FED cameras, the exceptionally successful Soviet version of the Leica named with Dzerzhinskii's initials. Many former communards continued to work in the enterprises after they "graduated" from the commune; many other former delinquents went on to become talented athletes, actors, and musicians. Certain opportunities afforded to them, moreover, were undoubtedly greater than those of even the most elite boarding schools of the West. In part because its fame had spread abroad starting in the late 1920s, well-known scholars, writers, and party intellectuals regularly made appearances at the commune; the satirists Il'f and Petrov wandered the grounds, and Bukharin gave a lecture in 1935. The music program, which boasted a talented choir and orchestra, was headed by the conservatory pianist A. G. Dreirin.[70]

It was the children who impressed visitors the most. One of Bolshevo's sister institutions, the Dzerzhinskii commune near Khar'kov, was visited by the no-nonsense American engineer Zara Witkin in 1932, who found "the best modern machinery" and premises "noticeably in better condition than many of the adult factories we had already seen." But it was spirit of the children, playing Russian martial songs in their band, that really "thrilled us. With flushed, happy faces, after the impromptu program, the boys and girls crowded around us, asking innumerable questions."[71] One of the most lasting successes was not even apparent while the commune still existed: a striking number of "graduates" went on to occupy prominent positions as educators, chief engineers, factory directors, and writers, and as this suggests, some went on to higher education. There were, as the foreigners' guides never tired of repeating, no fences or guards. Among the wide array of Soviet orphanages and "new model nurseries" in the 1920s there were, Catriona Kelly has found, those that promoted "genuine self-governance."[72] Was it really the freedom and trust granted by the secret police that produced what Gorky called a miracle?

Only recently has it become possible to compare the publicized version of Bolshevo's success to its internal history. A treasure trove of archival documents and recollections was gathered by museum officials and local historians, who in turn collaborated with a handful of former communards who strove for decades to preserve materials on the institution's history in the late Soviet years.[73] The materials make clear that the commune's directors worked out a distinct program that did effectively prove the strength of environment—only it was not the entirely non-coercive environment the commune projected but a potent, illiberal form of group socialization.

The Bolshevo narrative presented to foreign visitors and, as we shall see, simultaneously represented in Soviet culture, centered on humanistic socialization through the environment: unexpected trust shown the communards, the voluntary nature of commune membership (as in some showcase prisons shown to foreigners), complete self-government by the children themselves, and the uplifting role of labor. This version of the commune's story was not entirely false, but it was incomplete. The commune was developing, like many party cells and organs of party discipline in the 1920s, effective techniques of self-discipline and horizontal, mutual surveillance. This was ironic, given that the sponsor of Bolshevo, the secret police, was also the most prominent locus of vertical surveillance and punishment in Soviet society. But this second form of discipline was developing on the grassroots level of the collective, or *kollektiv*, which in the wake of Makarenko's canonical writings of the late 1930s came to be considered "the basic unit of Soviet society."[74] In the public narrative, key elements of hierarchical discipline were suppressed (as was the role of income from the communes' commercial enterprises in helping to socialize the children, which was attributed to labor itself). Through Makarenko's writings, the secret police children's labor communes of the 1920s in a certain sense lived on in the theory of the collective, the fabric of Soviet society's self-definition.

In practice, it was Bolshevo's exceptionalism and the ways it combined vertical and horizontal forms of discipline, both hidden from public scrutiny, that formed the backbone of its indubitable success. Only with some detective work can Bolshevo's methods of discipline be pieced together. The commune's rules were few but firm; the bigger the carrot offered with commune membership, the bigger the stick involved in taking it away. One former communard, M. F. Sokolov-Ovchinnikov, recalled in his autobiography how Pogrebinskii interviewed him in a GPU prison on the eve of his first "isolation" in a "concentration camp" (*konts-lager'*). He was told of five "commandments" to which he would need to adhere if he came to Bolshevo: no theft, no drinking, no snorting (a number of street children used cocaine), no gambling, and subordination to the general assembly. If he did this, his criminal record would be lifted, and he would gain full citizenship rights on "graduation." As Götz Hillig has noted, the effective practices of enforcing a complete break with contacts from communards' former life and participation in work and study were not invented by Pogrebinskii but were already present in 1924 in the Rosa Luxemburg Commune directed by Melikhov. Violators of the rules were sometimes "isolated" and sometimes sent back to Moscow prisons or their previous place of incarceration temporarily or permanently.[75] Expulsion from the commune's marvelous facilities was perhaps the greatest behavior-changing inducement for the children.

Even so, the rules would not have been effective if they were not woven into a broader, effective system of socialization (or "re-education"). The commune immediately set about establishing another, horizontally based hierarchy that broke the authority of the band leaders, or *vozhaki*. From the "first days," an *aktiv* or leadership group of children who worked best with the commune director and staff established, in the words of Pogrebinskii "a critical mass around which the whole life of the commune revolved and which worked over the kids and attracted new activist forces." With the great expansion of the commune in the early 1930s, the *aktiv*, which encompassed Komsomol and party members, became even more important, and former communards were appointed below the adults in positions of authority. The transformation was impressive, but hardly miraculous. The early years were filled with unpublicized problems of recidivism. Issues of crime and punishment dominated the communards' general assembly, which was held collectively responsible for thefts and other violations of the rules, making "self-governance" decisive in a way the foreigners never learned. With the onset of "one-man management" in Soviet industry, however, the authority of the director was strengthened in all the secret-police communes in 1931, as pedagogues running daily operations were replaced by *Chekisty*.[76] The rapid, Great Break expansion of the commune in the early 1930s was typical of the era's promotion of quantity over quality, and led to flight risks, food shortages, reports of new communards' bad attitudes and shirking of work, and internal clashes between activists and others.[77]

If Solovki had innovated the practices of delegating the enforcement of discipline in the concentration camp to privileged classes of prisoners, Bolshevo in a very different way also came to function through enforcement "from below." No wonder Pogrebinskii, in an unguarded moment, referred to *krugovaia poruka*, the ancient Russian principle of collective responsibility—which in the era of serfdom allowed thinly spread officials to hold peasants collectively responsible for finding and delivering violators of order.[78] But while Bolshevo's discipline may have centered on group accountability, it was particularly Soviet in its dependence on an *aktiv* and a severe division between the benefits available to those who participated in the transformation and those who were left outside. Even so, in their most general contours the combination of group solidarity, horizontal self-monitoring, and effective incentives for self-transformation could be replicated in settings that had no trace of Bolshevism—such as Father Edward Joseph Flanagan's Boy's Town, founded on a Christian-democratic philosophy of love in the revolutionary year 1917.[79]

This similarity of methods within radically divergent educational philoso-
phies and historical contexts only affirms the extraordinary power of group
belonging to influence the behavior of the communards, who could link victory in their personal struggles in the past to a shared pride in the successful commune. The many autobiographies written by communards in the late
1920s and later about their "rebirth" were filled not with ideological jargon,
but rather with pride about how they had lifted themselves from their former
lives and acquired skills and careers. At the same time, the theme of a "second
birth" in the commune consistently runs through them. Born-again communards were well suited to support the notion of a Soviet revolutionary break
with an oppressive past, and they were encouraged to record their transformations.[80] At first, not all the youth communes uniformly encouraged the further
step of attributing the personal transformation to the Party—for example,
outside political controls and even the establishment of a Komsomol organization were blocked at Makarenko's Gorky colony until 1925—but, certainly
by the late 1920s, linkages between personal and revolutionary breaks with
the past were being promoted and articulated at the communes in numerous
ways.[81]

Far from everyone was deemed capable of transformation, however. The
selection of new communards was carried out "strictly and meticulously." A
sympathetic German journalist who wrote extensively about Soviet penal
reform, Lenka von Körber, rightly became quite interested in the issue. She
discovered that a precondition of the entire enterprise's success was that
each new member was carefully chosen in prison visits to assure that only
"honest thieves" who upheld their word were picked—in other words, children who could likely be socialized into the commune's system of collective
responsibility.[82]

In sum, the commune's brilliant success was to a large extent predicated
on its uniqueness—precisely the opposite of the general solution to child
homelessness that was proclaimed. Representative was only the sharp Soviet
division between those who successfully adapted and those outside the fold.
Even the commune's patrons did not seem to recognize the unique nature of
their creation, however, for they saw it as a potentially replicable model. In
a striking precursor to his utopian statements about deportations and special settlements in 1930, Iagoda had five years earlier tried to convince Avel'
Enukidze that Bolshevo had changed from a "small experiment" to a general
"method" that could radically reduce criminality while bringing in economic
profits. In 1935, on the tenth anniversary of Bolshevo, Iagoda repeated the
idea that in the re-education of criminals, the commune would be a "model"
for other labor colonies as child homelessness was entirely eliminated in the
near future.[83]

Gorky's involvement with the Bolshevo commune was, like his intervention at Solovki, decisive. It influenced the course of Soviet pedagogy, marking another shift from the 1920s to the 1930s—the demise of the experimental NEP-era enthusiasm for domesticating American progressive pedagogy and the rise of an overtly discipline-centered orthodoxy centered on the teachings of Anton Makarenko. It was with Gorky's close involvement that Makarenko began his upward rise from the obscure founder of the "Children's Home for Morally Defective Children No. 7" in Poltava in 1920—the next year renamed the Gorky Commune and in 1926 moved to a location near Khar'kov. The commune's early years were later immortalized in Makarenko's 1933 *Pedagogical Poem*, published in Gorky's journal with the writer's aid, encouragement, and financial assistance. This patronage was crucial as Makarenko pursued his trajectory from obscure outsider to the dominant pedagogue of the Stalin period. A correspondence began between Gorky and Makarenko's child colonists in 1925, and Gorky eagerly assumed the role of Makarenko's patron. Returning to the USSR with a wave of triumphal publicity, the great proletarian writer toured the colony named after him with Makarenko in July 1928.

Figure 4.3 Maxim Gorky (first row, seated) and Anton Makarenko (standing) at the Gorky Commune for homeless children. The July 1928 visit, part of Gorky's highly publicized Soviet tour marking his return from abroad to support the Stalin Revolution, was a key moment in the writer's patronage of the rising pedagogue.
Source: RIA Novosti Photo Library.

They also traveled to the Dzerzhinskii Youth Commune of the Ukrainian secret police, also located near Khar'kov, which Makarenko began to direct in October 1927 after clashing with the Ukrainian educational establishment over his methods.[84]

Like Gorky, Makarenko had close ties with the secret police; in both the 1920s and 1930s he was "under the special protection of the highest-ranking Chekists of Ukraine." Despite these connections, Makarenko never joined the Party. He portrayed himself as a "non-party Bolshevik" in the 1930s, and his previously inaccessible notebooks and other evidence reveal that he made often biting anti-Bolshevik, anti-Soviet, and (unlike Gorky) anti-intelligentsia comments not only in the early 1920s but into the next decade.[85] Even so, both Gorky and Makarenko were outsiders in the early 1920s who moved into the center of cultural construction under Stalinism. As a former child of the urban depths himself, Gorky was strongly attracted to the cause of rehabilitating children, and he clearly admired Makarenko's energy and ability to get things done.[86] Gorky was attracted to potential vanguards of success: the ethos of group solidarity Makarenko was able to achieve in his communes meshed with Gorky's belief in inspirational models for the creation of new people.

Makarenko attentively studied the Bolshevo model, and his pedagogy also featured key elements of the Bolshevo narrative, such as self-governance and trust. But he combined Bolshevo's stress on self-discipline and group solidarity with a finely tuned system of military-like games, uniforms, drills, "socialist competition" based on rivalry, and firm punishment. These last elements provoked stiff opposition and high-profile attacks on the part of the NEP educational establishment. Opponents included Lenin's wife Krupskaia, who in the central press dubbed Makarenko's Gorky colony a "school for slaves." In July 1928, Makarenko and his communards visited Bolshevo, the "older brother" of the Dzerzhinskii commune in Khar'kov, and were especially impressed by its economic enterprises. At the same time, Makarenko noticed how different certain practices were from those prevalent in his own communes. Makarenko preferred to keep greater distance between the adult pedagogues and their charges than in Bolshevo, where Pogrebinskii was dubbed "Uncle Serezha." Ironically, while Bolshevo became internationally famous in the 1930s, its influence on Makarenko was forgotten after Bolshevo became a taboo topic following the Great Terror, even as Makarenko's methods became dominant in pedagogy and related fields. Makarenko's *Pedagogical Poem*, his greatest and later canonical work, received crucial support from Gorky as it was written between 1929 and 1933.[87]

The transformation of Bolshevo and Khar'kov secret-police communes into prime destinations for privileged foreign groups was also connected to Gorky's patronage of Makarenko, for Gorky depicted the pedagogue in glowing light as he popularized the labor communes at Bolshevo and Khar′kov (and the second oldest OGPU labor commune, founded in a former monastery outside Moscow in Liubertsy). Gorky then endorsed two books by Pogrebinskii: *The OGPU's Labor Colony* (*Trudovaia kommuna OGPU*, 1928) and *Factory of People* (*Fabrika liudei*, 1929). These works, written for a Soviet audience and linking the commune to the great early Soviet theme of the "new man," were influential in cementing a narrative of the commune's origins and achievements that substantially corresponded to the version told to visiting foreigners. Details of Chekist organizers' trust in the children, such as the absence of a "convoy" from prison and entrusting the band leader (*vozhak*) with money for the group's food, illustrated the principles of self-governance and, as Pogrebinskii put it, "not the slightest hint of compulsion." Pogrebinskii echoed Gorky in calling this re-education one of the "miraculous achievements" of the Soviet republic. He also made the foreign response into a kind of litmus test for international visitors: "enemies are embittered, but the good-hearted look with delight and love on this factory for the remaking of people."[88]

Once the founders and patrons had codified the commune's publicly presented principles, Nikolai Ekk's cinematic masterpiece *Road to Life* (*Putevka v zhizn′*), a Mezhrabpom film first shown on June 1, 1931, popularized secret-police communes to mass audiences at home and abroad. The blockbuster film, the first full-length Soviet sound feature, was gripping in its depiction of the transformation of wild, abused, and thieving street urchins into proud and conscious laborers—highlighting the emotional bond of trust but omitting complicated contextualizations of communal self-governance and child homelessness. Many of the details of the cinematic commune's origins correspond to Pogrebinskii's writings in 1928 and 1929. Moreover, the consultant to the film was the Chekist M. G. Tipograf, who was involved in the real-life communes. Nikolai Batalov, who played the role of the wise and easygoing commune director, met Pogrebinskii in his several visits to Bolshevo. Iyvan Kyrlya, the actor who played Mustafa, the reformed ethnic Mari *vozhak* who is killed in the end by the commune's criminal enemy, visited Bolshevo many times to study the gestures of communards for the role. The film enjoyed phenomenal success at home and abroad. In the new sound theaters of Moscow, Leningrad, and other cities, the film played for over a year; it won high honors at the Venice film festival, and a German version played in twenty-five theaters in Berlin. By November 1932, it had been shown in twenty-seven countries. Sympathetic foreign intellectuals, including Egon Erwin Kisch, Martin Andersen Nexø, and Romain Rolland, all praised the film for its social and political message. It was precisely the "epic" quality that pleased Rolland but angered militant Soviet "proletarianizers," who attacked its "sentimental-humanist" sweetness.[89] The entertaining qualities of the film and its mastery of new technologies in one sense only served to reinforce the message of its didactic prologue, dramatically read by actor Vasilii Ivanovich Kachalov: the humane and trusting methods of the labor commune were the Soviet solution to child homelessness and the re-education of juvenile delinquents in general. This, of course, followed precisely the same principle by which the sites of socialism were presented to foreign guests.

Bolshevo proved a great asset for the Soviets, but not all visitors were uniformly impressed. Foreign visitors' reactions to Bolshevo follow the patterns of other sites of communism. As guide reports indicate, fulsome praise and readiness to generalize were common. George Bernard Shaw, writing in 1932, had also been taken to Soviet children on a collective farm; he found them "so appallingly civilized that my first impulse was to denounce them as a parcel of insufferable little Marxian prigs." Yet, he expressed no doubts that Bolshevo proved the problem of Russia's "famous wild children" had been solved and, with remarkable credulity, claimed that all Soviet penal institutions had become virtually indistinguishable from farms and factories. As elsewhere, however, a number of visitors were skeptical or hostile. In the first category, Gabrielle Duchêne, an anti-fascist member of the French society of friends, had her suspicions aroused when she "accidentally" met a French-speaking young communard in exactly the kind of incident reported in showcase prisons. André Gide, after being regaled by communards about their former crimes, conversions, and the "excellence of the new regime," was "oddly" reminded of the crude and psychologically unsatisfying public testimonials of religious converts: "I was a sinner; I was unhappy; I did evil; but now I understand; I am saved; I am happy."[90] Just as preconceptions facilitated pro-Soviet conclusions, pre-existing suspicions fueled skepticism. One American visitor produced a "highly unpleasant impression" on his guide when he expressed doubts that an English-speaking boy was really a member of the commune and that eight-hour workdays were the norm. Two Australian journalists were described as "reserved" in their conduct, a sure sign of doubts when compared to the enthusiasm expressed by more pro-Soviet visitors.[91]

Between the early and the mid-1930s, as Bolshevo reached the height of its international fame for humane rehabilitationism, the flood of favorable foreign commentary was mobilized for internal Soviet audiences as proof positive of great, even miraculous leaps forward. Interested questions about Bolshevo from a high U.S. prison official, forwarded to Soviet Procuror Vyshinskii by the American Embassy in 1935, suggest just how far Bolshevo's favorable reputation had spread.[92] Yet, this was precisely the time when a hardening of attitudes toward juvenile delinquency transformed the relatively lenient Soviet justice system of the 1920s. Repressive measures against juveniles deemed difficult to rehabilitate were implemented after the era of forced collectivization and famine between 1930–33 produced waves of child homelessness and urban crime. This change in attitude toward juveniles and orphans began with the police and secret police, but the link between recidivism and socially harmful elements was part of a broader phenomenon, the "martial-law socialism" of the 1930s that made repression of marginalized populations, much of it carried out on Iagoda's orders, into an engine of mass incarceration and political prophy-laxis.[93] Ironically, the apogee of Bolshevo's international reputation in Popular Front years corresponded with another milestone, the "most repressive set of campaigns against juvenile lawbreakers in the entire Stalin era." This culmi-nated in the decree of April 7, 1935, lowering the age of criminal responsibility from sixteen to twelve, and coincided with mass sweeps of cities to remove homeless children. Iagoda, the patron of Bolshevo, was once again at the fore-front of measures based on the increasingly widespread Soviet assumption that "hardened," "malicious," and "corrupted" criminal elements must be removed from protected, socialist urban spaces and isolated in closed labor camps. The mid-1930s attack on "child crime" was made in terms that evoked the punish-ment of enemies rather than the rehabilitationism showcased at Bolshevo.[94]

Simultaneously, foreign acclaim for Bolshevo assumed a special place in the internal propaganda about Stalin's new order. Foreign delegations were enlisted to buttress the Gorkian theme of miracles coming true. French com-munist intellectual Henri Barbusse, who had visited the commune, gained the most acclaim, because his remark hit the nail on the head: Bolshevo was a metaphor for the entire social system, a "little republic inside a big one." At hundreds of other places around the USSR, a 1930 article in Gorky's journal noted proudly, criminals were being re-educated by labor. Indeed, it was the "special designation" camp Gorky visited at Solovki, not Bolshevo, which was the prototype for those hundreds of places, which came to be known as the Gulag archipelago. As in Ekk's *Road to Life*, some of whose most stunning shots captured children mastering tools and doing the rhythmic heavy lift-ing involved in building a railroad track, the skilled and specialized craftwork that took place at Bolshevo was conflated with hard manual work of the camps under the single rubric "labor."[95]

Gorky's writings on Solovki repeatedly referred to the far-north island of Solovki as a "preparatory school" for the Bolshevo commune, once again link-ing the secret police's concentration camp with the successes of the secret police's showcase children's commune. Incredibly, Gorky was able to make the connection because the Solovki forced-labor camp had in fact launched its own well-appointed children's labor colony. During his time at the Solovki criminological laboratory, one of the tasks of future academician Likhachev was to help select former homeless children and delinquents for the Solovki *Detkoloniia* (Children's Colony), "soon renamed the *Trudkoloniia* (Labor

Colony) and sadly known in connection with Maxim Gorky's visit to Solovki."
Likhachev recalled this as a place where children were "saved" in clean, privileged, and highly anomalous conditions.[96] In fact, it was during Gorky's first
visit to Bolshevo, in the company of Iagoda on June 8, 1928, that the idea of the
returning writer's trip to Solovki appears to have been born. Pogrebinskii, who
became close to Gorky, was one of the *Chekisty* in Gorky's entourage when he
traveled to the far north, and one of the purposes of the trip was to select 300
youngsters (and at least one prisoner) for transfer from Solovki to Bolshevo in
1929.[97] Thus did Bolshevo sanitize Solovki.

Gorky's writings on Bolshevo, like his essay on Solovki, hinged on trump-
ing the civilizational norms of the advanced West. In a 1928 newspaper article
on the commune, he wrote that the much-vaunted humanism of the advanced
West had led to such barbarisms as the castration of criminals in the United
States; Lombroso's theory of the born criminal denied humanity and ultimately justified a kind of class-based genocide by concluding that criminals
needed to be destroyed. By contrast, true humanism (*podlinnyi gumanizm*) was
to be found in the USSR, in places like Bolshevo. As Daniel Beer has shown,
however, the early Soviet emphasis on criminology and other human sciences
of rehabilitation and the primacy of environment concealed a conflation of
sociological and biological categories. In 1928 and again in Gorky's notorious
1934 celebration of the marvels of rehabilitation at the forced labor project of
the Belomor Canal, "Gor'kii's language betrayed the tendency, consolidated
over the previous half century, to read social experience through a biological lens. Although they could, and did, repudiate the existence of Lombroso's
born criminal, early Soviet criminologists in effect saw class consciousness
and class instincts as something that could be ... transmitted from parents to
offspring."[98] This explains why Gorky turned so readily to a dehumanizing
physical description of the Bolshevo communards, replete with the same language of eugenics that he condemned in the U.S. context: the children there
were healthy, well-formed (*khorosho postroennye*), with very few sickly, degenerate (*degenrativnye*) or imbecilic (*tupye*) faces. By the time of his introduction
to the 1936 *Bolshevtsy*, a collectively authored, 549-page fictionalized account
of the history of "reforging" of children at the commune, Gorky had turned his
anti-Western sentiment into a total dehumanization of "bourgeois Europe,"
claiming that it was becoming "animalized" and losing even "the remnants of
human nature."[99]

It was in the context of children's labor colonies in his "Around the
Union" cycle that Gorky explicitly justified the practice of building showcases. Significantly, he did so as he signaled to his readers that he was
indeed no "famous foreigner" and understood very well that such places
were hardly representative: the Dzerzhinskii commune, sparkling with

cleanliness and fitted with the newest machinery, was "done like a model" (*obraztsovo*), "for show" (*na pokaz*), and its children, brimming with health, were selected "as if for show" (*kak budto na pokaz*). Gorky, however, went on to explain why showcasing was useful, even obligatory: "At this colony builders of such institutions can learn much." More than that, "it clearly was founded in order to show the ideal of what a children's labor colony for 'criminals' and the 'socially dangerous' should be."[100] In other words, the showcase would play the very same instructive role, bringing life as it should be closer to reality, that Gorky came to invest in literature and Soviet cultural production.

In writing his screenplay *Criminals*, Gorky solicited comments on the text both from former homeless waifs and from Iagoda. On September 13, 1932, *Izvestiia* published a notice that the prominent director Abram Room would make the film. It was never made.[101] However, a different and more obscure historical trace did result from Gorky's unrealized script. During preparatory work for the film, Room visited Bolshevo for three days in September 1931, and his team of assistants stayed for seven days. One of Room's young assistants—sixteen-year-old Iurii Solonevich, who in 1934 escaped across the Soviet-Finnish border and published a 1938 memoir in Sofia—talked with Bolshevo youths and understood their slang.[102]

Warned by Room to be careful because Bolshevo was "little a piece of the GPU," Solonevich found a theater in which some of the best groups in the USSR went on tour, food that was like "heavenly manna," and goods purchased by the youthful laborers that were only available elsewhere in hard-currency Torgsin stores frequented by foreigners. Occasionally, Solonevich wrote with sarcasm, groups with Kodak cameras and binoculars would appear, observing everything as if they were in a zoo: these were the foreign notables (*znatnye inostrantsy*). Solonevich, then only a youth himself, recalled his conversations with a group of boy communards late at night. In guarded, Aesopian slang they let him know they had come from a Kostroma isolator for delinquents where conditions and beatings were harsh. The Bolshevo authorities held the threat of return to those places over their heads: "They told us: become honest laborers—and you will stay." Another reforged communard chimed in with his ultimate explanation for his good behavior, also the ultimate of ironies: "Here we have a kind of Europe" (*U nas tut takaia Evropa*).[103]

Gorky's death in 1936 and canonization as the most prominent Soviet cultural icon coincided roughly with the demise of Bolshevo and the decline of the once-experimental concentration camp of Solovki. If the model of the rehabilitative children's labor commune was initially used in propaganda to justify the hard-labor concentration camp, the vast new upsurge in child homelessness and criminality in the era of collectivization increasingly led to a merger of the two forms in the mid-1930s. As a result of a high-level meeting on child waifdom in the Kremlin on June 3, 1934, at which Iagoda presided, the Gulag OGPU and the Main Administration of the Militia was given a prominent role in fighting child homelessness. In 1935, in an ironic twist on Iagoda's dream a decade earlier that secret-police communes would end juvenile crime—and the same year that Iagoda trumpeted Bolshevo-style rehabilitationism as an all-union model during Bolshevo's tenth-anniversary jubilee—the secret policeman lobbied Stalin to expand the network of "closed NKVD institutions for sentenced juvenile delinquents." He was successful: all juvenile labor colonies and temporary detention centers were transferred to the NKVD in that year, putting it in charge of a large population of juvenile offenders—85,000, in Iagoda's estimate of June 1935. On Iagoda's orders, in an action reminiscent of the human catastrophes that came out of the deportation of kulaks as special settlers, 5,000 homeless children from Moscow and other cities were transported to Western Siberia outside Tomsk and left at an empty spot, with only tents for housing, from where, as in the special settlements, they engaged in "mass flight." Gladysh has discussed how the two types of institutions, children's labor commune and forced-labor camp, became "mixed up" by 1934–35, years before the camp principle triumphed during the Great Purges. It was emblematic of this conflation that one solution to stabilize the Tomsk catastrophe was to send in graduates of Bolshevo.[104] In a move also symbolic of this conflation, in 1935, Makarenko, now decked out in the uniform of an NKVD division chief, took the post of senior inspector for education and upbringing in the NKVD department of labor colonies.[105] In a stroke of supreme irony, or cynicism, Bolshevo's international fame reached its apogee in the mid-1930s by propagating the notion that virtually any child could be rehabilitated at the very moment when Soviet policy became most firmly anchored on the assumption that anti-socialist criminality was driven by those impervious to rehabilitation.

By the time Bolshevo's secret-police personnel themselves fell victim to the Great Terror of 1937–38, it became impossible to show any leniency to child criminals by sending them to the secret-police children's communes, particularly Bolshevo, which had been named after Iagoda in 1935 and was widely seen as the creation of Iagoda's associate Pogrebinskii. With Pogrebinskii's suicide following the arrest of Iagoda, Bolshevo's fate was sealed. In a mere three days in 1937, more than 400 people were arrested in the commune, many of whom were shot. In the course of 1937–38, all the secret-police labor communes for children were liquidated as educational institutions; the

Bolshevo Commune was turned into a "Plant for the Production of Sporting Goods Inventory."[106] Around the same time, the Solovki camp lost its status as a special kind of innovative model. In the late 1930s, the weak and infirm were removed from Solovki to other sites of forced labor, many dying in transit, and Solovki was folded into a vast network of other camps.[107] Gorky's most lasting contributions turned out to be not institutional, but ideological.

5

Hard-Currency Foreigners and the Campaign Mode

The years of Stalin's Great Break (*velikii perelom*), 1928–31, were denoted by the height of two all-out drives that deeply marked the enterprise of cultural diplomacy. Industrialization required a coercive-utopian mobilization to overfulfill the plan; a frenzy of ideological infighting that went under the watchwords of "Bolshevization" and "proletarianization" turned the most radical and militant fringes of the cultural revolution of the 1920s into the new mainstream. The two upheavals were sometimes in tension, and affected the reception of foreigners in different ways. The new prominence of economic considerations in the service of state building led to the rise of Intourist, which became the dominant foreign-tourism organization privileging foreigners as a source of hard currency. At the same time, VOKS struggled to escape from the stigmas of focusing on bourgeois intellectuals and the realm of culture, finding partial refuge in a campaign mode of militant, sloganeering cultural propaganda defined around short-term political goals. VOKS and Intourist became bitter rivals. But in their differing Great Break approaches, they both displayed a novel urgency and utilitarianism: the former now emphasized mobilizing the intelligentsia at home and abroad, the latter extracting resources for the state's drive to build socialism.

This imperative to harness contacts with foreigners to immediate, short-term goals was often ineffective, but it reached its height during the Great Break because of the intense political pressures of the age. The opening phase of the Stalin era is thus one of the clearest examples of how the crucible of internal upheaval, and by extension any period of internal, militant turmoil, directly altered international practices—the reversal of the previous chapter's boomerangs from abroad into domestic settings. The insistent need to show results was closely connected to a shift in the levels of hostility and competition with the outside world, especially with the bourgeois West, that went hand in hand with the Stalin leadership's new restrictions on travel abroad.[1] The battle over priorities played itself out not only in the VOKS-Intourist conflict, a revealing yet contained clash, but across the workplaces and construction sites around the country as tens of thousands of foreign technical specialists and workers entered Soviet industry during the Five-Year Plan.

At the same time, internal turmoil shaped external agendas only in part. The Great Break sharpened a new dissonance: the gap drastically widened in the regime's continuing courtship of the "Western" intelligentsia, as it was sometimes called, and the persecution of the domestic non-party intelligentsia within the USSR.[2] As an open assault on the class enemy and political opponents was the order of the day at home, organizations like VOKS continued to woo foreigners far more "bourgeois" than surrogate domestic "aliens"—persecuted non-party scholars and professionals. Privileging and honoring foreign "bourgeois" and intellectual sympathizers remained a protected Soviet mission.

The Rise of Intourist

At the same historical conjuncture when Gorky was touring the country, the foreign-tourist agency Intourist began to exert a far-reaching impact on the Soviet reception of visitors from abroad. The records remaining in the Intourist archive for its early years are sparse.[3] Enough material has survived, however—especially when combined with documents about the hitherto obscure origins of Intourist's founding in 1929—to illuminate the role economic profitability came to play in the Soviet reception of foreigners.

At the height of NEP, in 1926, two groups vied for control of the nascent Soviet tourism trade. The ambitious Kameneva correctly saw that if VOKS could capitalize on the rising number of tourists with their potential for hard-currency earnings, it could significantly increase the standing of her organization. Kameneva's ally, the Soviet diplomat Ivan Maiskii, was the first to urge her to position VOKS to take advantage of the "source of income for our country" presented by foreign "excursions of the non-proletarian type." While Kameneva agreed with Maiskii on the political importance of all foreign visitors, her lobbying efforts for VOKS emphasized the earning potential of a subset of visitors she termed "hard-currency foreigners" (*valiutnye inostrantsy*). Ironically, her relegation of some foreigners to the category of cash cows was predicated on the consolidation of Soviet practices of classifying and ranking foreigners, which led to the conclusion that some presented first and foremost financial, rather than political or cultural, gain. Kameneva, uncharacteristically using a commercial term, argued that foreigners already recognized the VOKS *marka*, or brand. Her bid for supremacy on the tourism front involved a proposed expansion of VOKS's Bureau for the Reception of Foreigners that would operate on the NEP-era practice of "self-financing" (*khozraschet*), i.e., covering costs from revenue.[4] Had it been successful, Kameneva's efforts would have changed the history of both VOKS and Intourist.

But Kameneva's proposal represented a failed response to a rival initiative spearheaded by N. M. Epshtein, a top official in the Commissariat of Foreign Trade. Epshtein was bolder than Kameneva in playing up the economic potential of foreign tourism, and he discussed the eminently political phenomena of foreign workers' delegations and "social tourism" (that is, travel motivated by interest in the Soviet experiment) mostly to illustrate the selling power of the USSR. To party leaders, Epshtein dangled the image of Americans spending $226 million the previous year in France alone.[5] A new joint-stock company (*aktsionernoe obshchestvo*), he promised with fantastic exaggeration, would bring in hundreds of thousands of tourists with enormous profitability. Centralizing foreign tourism within one institution turned out to be important for the secret police's foreign department, because it wished to maintain "at least minimal control" over determining who could enter the country on visas that by necessity had to be issued quickly.[6] In March 1927, the party leadership (*vysshie instantsii*) decided to go the route of a joint-stock company. By the time the new State Joint-Stock Company for Foreign Tourism, Intourist, began operations on April 1, 1929, the big economic commissariats, such as Anastas Mikoian's Commissariat of Trade, had taken a leading role. The Travel Agency (*Biuro Puteshestvii*) of the Soviet trading fleet, Sovtorgflot, which for years had carried foreign tourists with some profitability and had earlier allied itself with VOKS, was transferred in its entirety to Intourist.[7]

From the first, "Intourist was deemed (and its leaders referred to it) as a 'commercial' institution with tasks tied closely to the financial needs of the state." Intourist's first chairman, the Georgian Bolshevik Aleksandr Svanidze, was the brother of Stalin's first wife and "a personal friend" of the dictator.[8] For all its high-level connections, Intourist got off to a rocky start: it lost money. Instead of a projected 4,000 tourists in 1929, only 2,542 came, and in its first year, the inexperienced enterprise blew 52,000 rubles on the reception of the American Trade Union Delegation alone. As this suggests, the old tendency to firmly place politics over the economic bottom line, born in the years of war communism, remained an ingrained habit. The early 1930s, despite harsh and chaotic conditions, witnessed an ambitious program of hotel construction—twenty-two new hotels were built to be ready by 1932–33. Early failures only spurred Intourist further to prioritize hard-currency concerns. A 1930 commission investigating the first-year losses called for cuts in unnecessary expenditures on "providing service" (*obsluzhivanie*) for foreign tourists. Intourist documents prioritized the "acquisition" of greater numbers of foreigners who commanded larger amounts of *valiuta*.[9]

With this agenda, Intourist and foreign tourism expanded rapidly in the 1930s. The number of Intourist employees expanded from 1,222 in 1932 to more than 7,000 in 1934–36, and, at the height of pre-war foreign tourism in 1936, the number of tourists hosted reached 13,437. Although these numbers were paltry compared with those countries with well-developed tourist industries, the scale of Intourist's activities immediately dwarfed those of VOKS and other agencies involved with the reception of foreigners. Intourist's monopoly on foreign tourism was strengthened by party decrees in 1936.[10] The rise of Intourist sparked intense emotions of rivalry and disdain among VOKS employees that lasted straight into the Purge era, when both VOKS and Intourist were decimated for their connections with foreigners.

VOKS officials viewed their methods as superior to the new touristic behemoth in many ways. They spoke of Intourist, not only to party leaders but also among themselves, as more commercial than cultivated, incapable of tailoring programs to important foreigners' needs (although Intourist did provide special services to travelers deemed valuable), and known for "superficial displays" of model sites. Early attempts at cooperation—trading Intourist's hotel facilities for VOKS's pool of experienced guides and cultural programmers— quickly fell apart. Intourist was unwilling and unable to reliably make hotel rooms available and quickly hired its own guides and translators. In the end, VOKS was rendered dependent on its rival's infrastructure, however shoddy and inaccessible. As a new VOKS director in Leningrad was told in 1932 by a Moscow colleague, "Intourist, as a commercial organization, has a deeply commercial approach...Providing cultural service, such as showing of historical treasures and new factories, etc. will be carried out strictly for payment in foreign currency or gold...Yes, [relations with Intourist] are a sore point in our work."[11]

In fact, Intourist included one morning excursion in the price of its tours, expecting that tourists would pay for an afternoon activity. Despite their disdain, VOKS officials could only envy Intourist's size and support from the top leadership. In his efforts to boost the stature of VOKS in the mid-1930s, the ambitious VOKS chief Aleksandr Arosev launched several attempts to get his representatives appointed to the Intourist administration and to merge VOKS with its larger rival.[12]

Of course, Intourist could not function within the Stalinist order without heavy-handed propaganda in guides' interactions with foreigners, loading visitors down with notoriously long schedules that also served to prevent wandering around. Within the Soviet system, however, it represented an unprecedented stress on the bottom line, defined in terms of hard currency, and this

Figure 5.1 "See USSR," an undated Intourist poster from circa 1930. The poster juxtaposes images suggesting Soviet power, the red flag over the Kremlin and the rising sun, alongside those evoking expanse and exoticism: a reindeer-pulled sled with a fur-clad driver, along with two camels led by a figure in Central Asian dress, a Muslim prayer tower, and a palm tree. Source: Hoover Institution Archives, Stanford University.

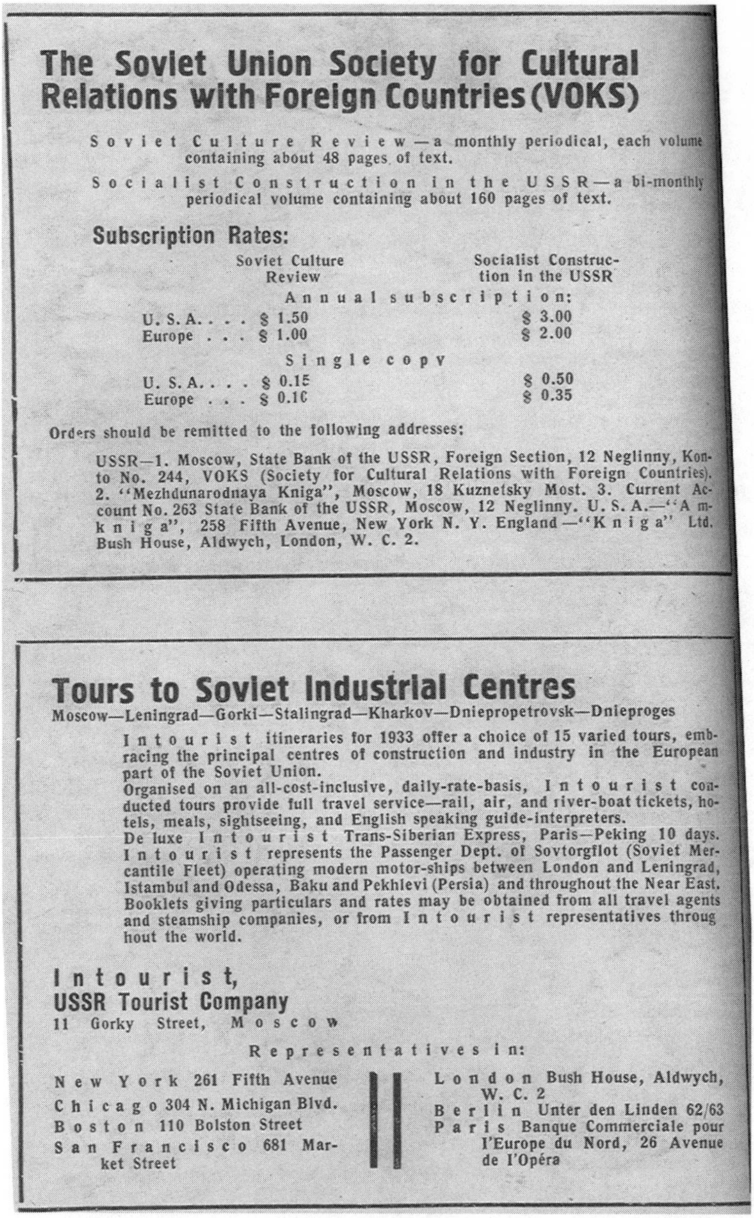

The Soviet Union Society for Cultural Relations with Foreign Countries (VOKS)

Soviet Culture Review—a monthly periodical, each volume containing about 48 pages of text.

Socialist Construction in the USSR—a bi-monthly periodical volume containing about 160 pages of text.

Subscription Rates:

	Soviet Culture Review	Socialist Construction in the USSR
	Annual subscription:	
U.S.A.	$ 1.50	$ 3.00
Europe	$ 1.00	$ 2.00
	Single copy	
U.S.A.	$ 0.15	$ 0.50
Europe	$ 0.10	$ 0.35

Orders should be remitted to the following addresses:

USSR—1. Moscow, State Bank of the USSR, Foreign Section, 12 Neglinny, Konto No. 244, VOKS (Society for Cultural Relations with Foreign Countries). 2. "Mezhdunarodnaya Kniga", Moscow, 18 Kuznetsky Most. 3. Current Account No. 263 State Bank of the USSR, Moscow, 12 Neglinny. U. S. A.—"A m k n i g a", 258 Fifth Avenue, New York N. Y. England—"K n i g a" Ltd. Bush House, Aldwych, London, W. C. 2.

Tours to Soviet Industrial Centres
Moscow—Leningrad—Gorki—Stalingrad—Kharkov—Dniepropetrovsk—Dnieproges

Intourist itineraries for 1933 offer a choice of 15 varied tours, embracing the principal centres of construction and industry in the European part of the Soviet Union.

Organised on an all-cost-inclusive, daily-rate-basis, Intourist conducted tours provide full travel service—rail, air, and river-boat tickets, hotels, meals, sightseeing, and English speaking guide-interpreters.

De luxe Intourist Trans-Siberian Express, Paris—Peking 10 days. Intourist represents the Passenger Dept. of Sovtorgflot (Soviet Mercantile Fleet) operating modern motor-ships between London and Leningrad, Istambul and Odessa, Baku and Pekhlevi (Persia) and throughout the Near East. Booklets giving particulars and rates may be obtained from all travel agents and steamship companies, or from Intourist representatives throughout the world.

Intourist,
USSR Tourist Company
11 Gorky Street, Moscow

Representatives in:

New York 261 Fifth Avenue
Chicago 304 N. Michigan Blvd.
Boston 110 Bolston Street
San Francisco 681 Market Street

London Bush House, Aldwych, W. C. 2
Berlin Unter den Linden 62/63
Paris Banque Commerciale pour l'Europe du Nord, 26 Avenue de l'Opéra

Figure 5.2 The back cover of the English-language edition of the VOKS Bulletin in 1933, advertising subscriptions to the VOKS publication and Intourist "Tours to Soviet Industrial Centres." Source: *VOKS*, no. 3 (1933).

only increased in the post-Stalin period. Rather than regarding economic concerns as dichotomous from ideological ones, the early history of Intourist suggests that the two were viewed as intertwined.

Reflecting the Western yardsticks inherent in the Stalinist push for modernization, the Intourist leadership immersed itself "in the vocabulary of tourism as it evolved out of London, Brussels, Copenhagen, Berlin, and Paris." By 1932, it had opened three travel bureaus: in Berlin, London, and New York.[13] In the hoary tradition of Russian state servitors sent to study abroad, Intourist in the era of industrialization sent young employees West to learn the tourist trade. In 1931, Intourist deputy chairman Marshevskii delivered a series of lectures on the "tourist market" to prepare these new Soviet servitors for departure. These suggest how Intourist's commercial priorities did not efface political ones in the new organization's mission. Rather, they formed a new and durable mix. Quite rightly, Marshevskii underscored that hard-currency foreigners were attracted to the USSR in the first place by the building of socialism; ignoring politics out of economic consideration was not an option. He was also versed in the history of U.S. and European tourism and fully cognizant of problems that would plague the Soviet tourist industry for decades: the lack of inexpensive options in visiting the country and the deficit of trained personnel. In his last lecture, he gave a rousing injunction to his charges to go out into the "foreign market" to master "cultured tourism work." The phrase echoed the terminology of "cultured trade" that justified the commerce of the retail sector—often viewed as ideologically dubious and, therefore, often low-prestige—in terms of cultural improvement, implicitly in comparison to Western countries. In Marshevskii's view, tourism had to catch up and overtake the West in order to prove the advantages of the socialist organization of labor; Soviet tourism would show enemies strength and turn neutral visitors into friends.[14] It is clear that for this high Intourist official, earning hard currency was quite simply the best means of serving the Soviet state and building socialism. In a revealing addendum, he felt it necessary to cite contemporary French writings on the spread of cultural influence to prove that Western countries also highly rated the political uses of tourism. Apparently, his young charges would better grasp the need to serve political and financial missions simultaneously if West European precedents were invoked.

Given the magnitude of the challenges Marshevskii outlined for the Soviet service sector, it is fascinating to observe how Intourist's "internal informational bulletin," distributed to its own employees, dismissed virtually all foreign criticisms about service and conditions—on political grounds. The bulletin translated pro-Soviet praise from returning foreign tourists in the European and American press in order to triumphantly proclaim: "Intourist has met the challenge of the cultural-political show of the Soviet land."

While criticisms were also translated, among them complaints about high costs, poor facilities, and restrictions on the movements of tourists, they were summarily dismissed with the comment: "There are also evaluations by a different category of tourist, which in their content and criticisms represent only hostile attacks against the USSR. These indictments are so unfounded and often so rude and false that tourists who have been in the USSR find it necessary to refute them in foreign newspapers."[15] Intourist employees were thus encouraged to attribute foreign clients' complaints to ideological enmity. Only criticism from on high, notably the 1936 Central Committee resolution on the organization's poor standards of service, could prompt a scramble to engage in "Bolshevik self-criticism."[16]

All the more poignant, then, were the missives of those sympathetic foreign tourists who wrote Soviet leaders and Intourist's top brass with constructive criticisms and helpful hints in order to prevent seemingly minor matters of living conditions from interfering with international appreciation of the Soviet experiment. The American Hermann H. Field, an organizer of a short-lived summer school for American students in Moscow, wrote in 1934 from "violently reactionary" Switzerland about issues raised by countless visitors of all stripes—the effects of the much-despised official exchange rate in preventing tourists from making the most simple purchases outside of Intourist and hard-currency Torgsin stores. "Likewise [the tourist] can't use street cars...He is bound to Intourist and organized group sight seeing...Obviously one can't get a convincing and accurate idea of a country and people from the seat of a sight-seeing bus or even from going through factories and museums." Another friendly American, in 1934, explained how the "isolation" and "endless irritation" of visitors was due not to Soviet secrecy but to the prohibitively high cost of rubles and the inability to find cheap transportation. "One and all foreigners feel a certain...sterility in the language used...It isn't sufficient for guides to dwell upon the 'Lenin-Marxist ideology,' words which mean little or nothing to the average foreign visitor." On Savoy Hotel stationery, another tourist, identified only as B. Jenkins, wrote to the chairman of Intourist about how his desire to inspect workers' living conditions remained unfulfilled: "Most of the things I desired most to see and acquire information upon have been barred to me. I wanted to know how the worker was living—did he get enough to eat, was he adequately clothed." Jenkins' concern for the Soviet working class was matched only by his obsession with Soviet filth. He called for a "cleanliness campaign at once" and helpfully shared his expertise in lavatory fittings: "It would be better to use a pan in which the faeces dropped straight into fair deep water, thus being hidden and all effluvium being trapped." The biting conclusion to his fourteen-page letter read, "Intourist...exhibits the usual features of capitalist trading systems."[17] All these letterwriters professed hope that their criticisms would help the Soviets win friends abroad; the thrust of each was to deny the rumors of Potemkin villages current in the West. If tourists were limited in what they could see, it was due to the system set up by an acquisitive Intourist, not to political concerns. They failed to grasp how, in the history of Intourist, the economic and the political were less incompatible than intertwined.

Economic Miracles and Western Experts

The presence of foreign specialists and workers during the industrialization drive and the Great Depression touched Soviet development in different ways than tourism or cultural diplomacy, for a significant presence of resident foreigners at enterprises and high-priority industrial "giants" was far more directly buffeted by social and economic relations at the workplace as well as popular attitudes towards foreigners and the West. Two milestones on the road to the Great Break—the war scare of 1927 and the anti-wrecking campaign against "bourgeois specialists," greatly accelerated by the 1928 show trial of engineers connected to the coal-mining region of Shakhtii—implicated the domestic class enemy directly with foreign threats. The war scare flared up after a series of foreign policy setbacks linked to the rise of Józef Piłsudski in Poland, the Kuomintang break with the Chinese Communists, and the British raid on the Soviet trading company Arcos in London, which led to a break in Anglo-Soviet diplomatic relations. The threat of imminent military attack trumpeted throughout the land was a far-reaching development with resonance in the party-state and in the population. Analyzing military and secret police reports that crossed Stalin's desk, James Harris concludes that Soviet intelligence gathering was "designed to find evidence of anti-Soviet coalitions" and therefore a steady stream of information, from the 1920s on, fueled Stalin's "misperceptions" that threat of military intervention against the USSR was never far away. On the other hand, a significant recent study lends credence to the notion that the war scare of 1927 was deployed as a weapon in the Stalin leadership's domestic struggle with Trotsky and the United Opposition, for the militarization of the Soviet economy had preceded the scare and the feverish rhetoric about capitalist encirclement did not lead to significant changes in defense policy.[18] However, overestimation of the imminent threats of "capitalist encirclement" and its use as political weapon were hardly incompatible.

The 1927 war scare had dramatic repercussions. The Shakhtii trial of 1928 (the first show trial since the trial of the Socialist Revolutionaries in 1922) breached the *cordon sanitaire* that so often separated domestic political

campaigns from privileged foreigners and international affairs. Swept up were
not only hitherto protected technical specialists but also foreign "saboteurs"
and "wreckers" in the guise of five German engineers from A.E.G. working
in the Shakhtii coal mines, a move that came at considerable cost to relations with the Soviet Union's only genuine international partner of the 1920s,
Germany. The engineers, among other accusations, were portrayed as pawns
of the Polish counter-espionage service.[19]

The Shakhtii trial furthered a drive to root out "wreckers" that connected the class struggle at home more tightly with the threats of "capitalist
encirclement" and espionage. The anti-wrecking campaign in fact preceded
the Shakhtii show trial, for it had roots in the workplace conflicts between
Communists and "bourgeois specialists" in industry. The publicity of the
show trial greatly ramped up the pressure, but, as Stone has shown, arrests
of wreckers in the case of the defense industries were largely kept out of the
press.[20] More generally, between 1926 and 1930, citizenship policies affecting
foreign contact—immigration, emigration, naturalization, and denaturaliza-
tion—were all severely restricted under the tightened supervision of the secret
police. According to one secret 1928 report, a re-registration of foreign residents showed a figure of 80,000 living in the USSR, one-twelfth of the number in the pre-war Russian empire. Foreign concessions were ended in 1930,
and the Five-Year Plan influx of foreign workers and experts occurred under
temporary and conditional contracts.[21] Even so, the end of the NEP era in the
late 1920s did not contain a uniform message about all foreigners, for even as
arrests threw key industries into disarray, the party-state financed and touted
the benefits of an unprecedented influx of foreign technical specialists, supposedly to repair the damage that the wreckers had done.

Resident foreign workers and specialists came from many countries,
although many were re-emigrants who had left in the tsarist period, and the
single largest contingent consisted of Germans arriving in the late 1920s
and early 1930s. Politically, they were a motley group, ranging from political émigrés, Communists, and foreign shock-workers (*inoudarniki*) to highly
paid, hard-currency "bourgeois" engineers; there was no centralized system
for recruiting them, and many agencies were involved in issuing invitations.
Foreigners arriving as tourists frequently tried to stay and find work. In the
context of the Soviet workplace, the number of foreign residents was relatively
small, as the total number who were concentrated in industrial enterprises in
this period ranged from 20,000–30,000.[22] Yet, the specialists—engineers,
architects, city planners, and others—were prominent beyond their numbers
due to the high-profile, privileged place they were accorded in terms of salaries, living conditions, and prestige. Intense, even utopian, hopes were invested
in their presence during the period of the first Five-Year Plan. Judging by the

number of invitations issued to foreign specialists, which jumped to approximately 10,000 in 1931, the height of the Great Break coincided with the peak of the turn to imported Western expertise for forced industrialization.

If Lenin, referring to the non-party experts at the outset of NEP, had talked about building socialism with bourgeois hands, it thus seemed at the outset of the Stalin period that the country would "catch up and overtake" the industrialized West in no small part with Western hands. Among the Soviets who came into contact with them, the foreign specialists brought out with special intensity high levels of hostility and suspicion on various levels and, at the same time, an often greatly exaggerated respect invested in the advanced countries of Europe and the United States. It is of special interest, then, to ask how Soviet authorities sought to influence the outlook of these types of foreigners. After all, foreign specialists living and working for extended periods in the country without doubt knew the Soviet Union better than other foreign visitors. Even though many lived in surprising isolation in their own linguistic communities and in specially designated housing, they were considerably freer in their movements than diplomats, journalists, and honored guests. They were also far less likely to accept model institutions as representative; large numbers of extant memoirs of engineers and other professionals tend to be consistently more skeptical about the Soviet order than politically engaged travel writings.

It would be misguided, however, to draw too sharp a distinction between short-and long-term visitors, associating the first solely with ideologically driven, fellow-traveling intellectuals and the latter with specialist professionals. Powerful political-ideological attractions were often intertwined with professional motivations in pulling short-term travelers and foreign residents alike to the Soviet Union. To give just one example, the section of foreign architects of the Union of Soviet Architects had between 800–1,100 members in the mid-1930s; in the words of Anatole Kopp, "Soviet Russia seemed to be the country where the ideas of modern architecture were becoming the guiding principles of architecture and town planning." Rather than the narrow, humiliating tasks that, for example, Le Corbusier saw Western architects fulfilling, here the architects' client would be the "people." The scale of possibilities appeared endless. In some cases, it took time for disillusionment to set in. Some, like the great Frankfurt city planner Ernst May, brought in to make Magnitogorsk into a model socialist city, became tangled in a web of bureaucracy and chaotic implementation, muting their enthusiasm. At the same time, the Soviet administrators and professionals saw the foreign experts as rivals to their own standing or resented their privileges, working against them behind the scenes.[23]

There was a kind of parallel between the Western sympathizers' view of the Soviet Union as the land of the future and the Soviets' own *amerikanizm*, the concept widespread in the 1920s that imparted an almost cult-like status to the modern efficiency and know-how of the far-off land of the machine.[24] The often exaggerated expectations surrounding the import of foreign experts in the late 1920s was caught up with *amerikanizm,* for it accompanied a shift from the German engineers brought into Soviet industry after the Treaty of Rapallo to an influx of high-profile American technical specialists after 1927–28. The intensity of the disappointment that followed these inflated hopes in turn conditioned a backlash against them, which in 1932 took shape in policy form with the end of systematic foreign recruitment and highly favorable pay scales.[25]

Strikingly, those charged with propagandizing foreign residents, such as the special "Group on Work Among Foreign Workers" of the trade unions (VTsSPS), were ardently committed to holding up foreign technical experts and workers as living models for Soviet citizens. They viewed their agency's mission of fostering positive views of the Soviet system among foreign residents as a necessary step in turning representatives of the West into conscious transmission belts of know-how and enlightenment. In other words, the so-called minders placed in charge of the political "re-education" of hired international employees were themselves carriers of an often exaggerated respect for the foreigners' expertise and cultural levels. Thus did an elitist and "Westernizing" promotion of constructive foreign influence lurk behind the Soviet attempt to catch up and overtake. Indeed, in this regard, the trade-union apparatchiki were only the most loyal foot soldiers of the Soviet political leadership that decided to hire the foreign specialists in the first place.

In keeping with the emphasis on the advanced efficiency of the Western specialists emanating from the top, on November 21, 1930, the Central Committee called for the organized "transfer of the [foreigners'] experience, habits and knowledge to Soviet workers."[26] Well before this, the trade-union group had positioned itself as the defender of the foreign specialists and, thus, was unsparing in its criticisms of the "mute enmity" toward them that it found widespread in its two-month investigation of six industrial regions of the country in 1931. Soviet engineering-technical personnel were lambasted as conservative and fearful of competition, while workers were described as xenophobic, rude, and resentful, calling the foreigners "lords" and other epithets. The flip side of the coin to this rampant hostility was an exaggerated respect for Western qualifications, which allowed some foreign residents to falsify their qualifications with ease. They included the draftsman from Amsterdam who posed as a famous Dutch architect and the highly qualified "specialists" in the Moscow Motor Truck Factory who had been bench workers at the Ford factory in Detroit.[27]

Although foreign technical specialists provoked such wildly contradictory attitudes, cultural and propaganda measures that targeted long-term residents were virtually identical to those arranged for valued short-term visitors. For example, foreign workers and specialists selected as shock workers for their contributions to industry in 1933–34 were rewarded with cost-free Volga steamboat tours. Three trips included a total of 613 foreigners and their families. Although the places they visited were confronting the aftermath of a severe famine, the cities along the way were prepared with a special "clean-up campaign," and the honored guests were greeted by orchestras. Top local trade-union officials and unnamed "special people" (likely secret-police cadres) were sent to prepare the soil in places such as the city of Engels, where the "class enemy" was the strongest and might affect interactions with the foreign shockworkers. Since the foreigners already worked in Soviet industry, they were to avoid factories and focus on "cultural-everyday achievements" such as kindergartens, schools, and pioneer camps. However, there were some important differences between this tour and the short-term foreign visits. The honored foreign residents were expected to have an impact on their local Soviet counterparts by raising the prestige of shock work and furthering the "international upbringing" of Soviet workers.[28]

By 1932, after the height of the influx of foreign specialists had passed, significant tensions were readily apparent in official stances toward the Western experts. On the one hand, the organization of political-enlightenment work among the foreigners became more efficient only after this point. In the first all-union conference of foreign specialists in 1932, convened by the External Relations Commission of the trade unions, an "honored place" was accorded "foreign comrades" in the construction of socialism. Officials went to great lengths to speak the language of pure internationalism: "We do not look on foreign workers and specialists as foreigners." On the other hand, in an ominous note, the gathered crowd was told that among them in the audience were foreigners who planned to discredit the Soviets and who had arrived "with the goal of becoming agents of the world bourgeoisie."[29]

At this 1932 conference, the work of the Office of Supply to Foreigners, Insnab, was cited as evidence of the special commitment to the specialists by the Party and the state. Indeed, a concerted effort was made to secure privileged living conditions for the foreign specialists, although in the catastrophic chaos of the time the foreigners also faced shortages. Despite Insnab's original intentions, however, the Torgsin ("trade with foreigners") stores stocking hard-to-get foodstuffs and luxury items until the end of rationing in 1936 spread on a large scale only after they were opened to Soviet citizens in 1931. In the midst of famine and acute shortages, citizens who sold valuables or spent hard currency sent from abroad created assets for the state on a scale so great, according to Osokina, that it offset the cost of importing foreign equipment for most of the industrial "giants" of the decade. A measure invented for foreigners quickly acquired large-scale domestic importance. At Torgsin stores, diplomats, tourists, and foreign residents brushed shoulders with Soviet elites buying luxuries and ordinary Soviets cashing in their valuables at huge losses in a hungry search for basic necessities.[30]

The investment in the foreign-specialist presence, and with it the dream that they would produce a great leap forward by re-educating the Soviet workforce, spiraled into decline after the end of the first Five-Year Plan. Significant numbers of foreign residents left the country after it became policy to restrict or eliminate pay in hard currency. This spontaneous, but hardly unexpected, outmigration was supplemented by the active deportation of "fascist elements, degenerate types, [and] suspicious persons." Not surprisingly, those who stayed behind in 1933—according to the report, a total population of foreign specialists and workers of more than 16,000, about 50 percent of whom were German and Austrian and 25 percent of whom had U.S. citizenship—contained a higher proportion of foreign Communists and sympathizers.[31] This group was, therefore, more open than others to Soviet cultural and ideological programs among the foreign-resident population. Yet even a number of committed foreign sympathizers and Communists had departed by the mid-1930s, when they were pressured to take Soviet citizenship, and some German leftists even preferred to face the risk of returning to Nazi Germany.[32] By then, the early wave of hope in an economic miracle assisted by the import of "advanced" people from the West had long since foundered on the shoals of difficulties and resentments associated with the expensive foreigners. The illusions of the Five-Year Plan were now replaced by a new set of international dreams that corresponded to the heyday of the Popular Front.

Capitalist Encirclement and the Campaign Mode

To many activists, it seemed quite possible in the midst of the Great Break maelstrom that international cultural initiatives would not continue to be insulated from the domestic campaigns for proletarianization and Bolshevization. In the aftermath of the Shakhtii trial, VOKS's mission of influencing non-communist and non-proletarian foreigners, established and defended so vigorously by Kameneva, was once again thrown into question. At the very least, it seemed awkward to defend solicitous courtship of the very same groups that were contagious at home. One 1929 VOKS mission statement settled on the formula of the "working intelligentsia," which would supposedly be targeted in mass rather than elite organizations that were "more radical and close to us in social composition."[33]

The stakes of these debates were heightened because in 1929, VOKS, like other state institutions, was racked by a purge. Seventeen members of the staff, including six party members, were removed. In addition, many of VOKS's most valued collaborators, both in the Party and the cooperative non-party intelligentsia, such as Anatolii Lunacharskii and Sergei Ol'denburg, lost their posts. Those qualified to work with foreign visitors frequently lacked proletarian and party credentials themselves, and this increased the vulnerability of the entire enterprise. A "verification" (*proverka*) of the eighty employees of VOKS's central apparatus in January 1931 revealed that 75 percent were not members of the Party and only 10 percent could claim proletarian status.[34]

In a 1929 conversation with his staff, Kameneva's successor, Fedor Petrov, admitted to being torn about the mission of the organization he now headed. He allowed that VOKS's "self-isolation" from foreign workers and Communists was "a bit odd" and admitted that it left him with a dubious "aftertaste." But he concluded that tactical maneuvering was now more necessary than ever. At a raucous general assembly of VOKS employees in 1930, the height of the Great Break furor, Petrov endorsed the notion that the main task "for our work inside the country" must be an "attack on bourgeois culture." As for international affairs, he lectured upstart critics with the reminder that "more competent organs"—a transparent reference to the party leadership—would decide what represented "opportunism" and when it was acceptable to "maneuver" ideologically.[35]

As this suggests, the frenzy of the Great Break never seems to have seriously jeopardized the priority placed on attracting "bourgeois" foreign sympathizers, especially given the opportunities opened up by the Great Depression and the Five-Year Plan. However, internal pressures and processes did leave a mark on external activities. In 1931, there was a move to formally amend the VOKS statement of purpose enshrined in the founding charter of 1925. Now, the organization's official goal would be to "exert influence through various channels on non-proletarian social strata abroad with the goal of combating interventionist and, in general, hostile attitudes toward the Soviet Union and socialist construction."[36] In other words, it became conceivable to reduce VOKS's entire mission to a struggle with anti-Soviet views and even to a specific campaign, the anti-interventionist propaganda drive of the early 1930s. A campaign mode born in the Great Break altered the ways foreigners were approached.

One feature of the campaign mode was the demise of the low-key, factual tone Kameneva had advocated for VOKS publications in the 1920s. The escalation to an increasingly strident tone followed the trajectory of Soviet press and propaganda in general, but was also due to an inability to set conceptual limits on the use of propaganda. A case in point was the VOKS bulletin, published in Russian, German, French, and English. While Kameneva repeatedly pressed for "relaying information in a calm way, not with agitation skits (*agitki*),"[37] this was difficult to maintain. The bulletin, like the materials generated for foreign publications, covered a wide range of topics within a basic formula of putting both Soviet cultural output and the social-political system in tandem favorable light. Precisely because the medium was not agitational in form, the temptation grew to exploit its greater potential to convince. The VOKS press section increasingly turned to the bulletin for purposes of counter-propaganda.[38] The stakes were raised as VOKS's external operations increased in size in the late 1920s—its bulletin, distributed in sixty-three countries in English, French, and German, had a circulation of more than 100,000 by 1929. Counter-propaganda was supplemented by an emphasis on shrill mobilization, reflecting just how severely the Great Break had destroyed boundaries across the realms of publishing and education between the conventions of agitprop and more rarified genres in which restricted or elite audiences could be targeted in less exhortative forms.[39] Now, the highest priority became attached to mobilizing international contacts for specific campaigns. Approaches and claims common to propagandistic genres now spread to those previously separated as elite and "high." The campaign mode went further than the 1920s counter-campaigns against émigré and foreign critics, because it barraged all foreign audiences with publications and letters repeating a limited number of high-priority themes.

Chief among these was the alarm about hostile capitalist encirclement and military intervention against the USSR. The 1930 "Industrial Party" show trial of leading engineers, in which the formerly protected "bourgeois specialists" were accused of "wrecking" with the goal of staging a coup d'etat, was a major inspiration for this anti-interventionist theme. Stalin, taking great interest in the transcripts of the forced confession of one of the defendants in the trial concerning a counter-revolutionary conspiracy to aid an invading Franco-Polish-Romanian army, ordered the material to be made available to Comintern and to mount a public campaign against military intervention.[40] At VOKS, the campaign assumed the highest priority and was extensively pursued through the VOKS bulletin, circular letters, and the societies of friends. Its goal was to "show foreign public opinion that the danger of intervention has turned into a direct threat to...the very existence of the USSR."[41] In 1931, this was prioritized as a "shock-work" (*udarnaia*) campaign, and a special tour of Moscow was even designed to show foreigners the losses that would accrue from the upcoming invasion. A tone of shrill exhortation, termed "militant and politically sharp," was explicitly advocated for all publications, while a "narrowly informational character" would be shunned.[42]

The campaign mode, which reached its height in 1930–31, achieved notable results—though not necessarily among the influential cultural and intellectual opinion makers abroad whom VOKS aspired to reach, as they were now asked to believe that their own countries were on the verge of declaring war on the Soviet Union. Indeed, the campaign involved an implicit trade-off: it rallied non-Communists abroad to spring into a full-throated defense of the socialist homeland in favor of the attempt to bring them gradually closer through the cultural or professional interests that so often propelled them toward Soviet contacts. Perhaps the greatest impact of the anti-interventionist campaign lay in its boomerang effect, for it set important precedents for the conduct of Soviet cultural diplomacy. First, an inextricable connection between internal wreckers and capitalist interventionists was being asserted, not only in the show trial itself, but in propaganda aimed around the world. This internationalization of the enemy altered the precarious balance between suspicion and opportunity already present in terms of the place foreigners occupied in Soviet political culture. Second, defense of the socialist homeland explicitly put the interests of the Soviet Union above all other considerations, for, as one of the campaign's talking points put it, intervention spelled "destruction not just for the USSR but the future of all humanity."[43]

In this supreme value placed on defense of the USSR, one can discern the direct roots of a Stalinist superiority complex, which had its analogue in the further reorientation of international communism around Soviet state interests. By necessity, mobilizing sympathetic foreigners for defense of the USSR implied recognition of Soviet precedence, but VOKS strategists inspired by the industrialization drive claimed more. As a 1930 report put it, "Every foreigner who visits, must inevitably...recognize" that economic crisis in Western Europe and the United States was leading to the imminent "collapse of bourgeois culture and civilization."[44] The desired effects of these campaigns as expressed internally in numerous documents at the time were thoroughly statist: to prompt a segment of public opinion in the West to oppose military action against the USSR and thus neutralize it in the event of a serious clash.

The coincidence of the "crisis of capitalism" and the drive to construct socialism emboldened such claims, but if there was still one area in which the Soviet Union could seemingly compete only in the future tense, it was living standards and infrastructure. Collectivization led to dire urban food shortages immediately noticeable to foreign residents and visitors, and to widespread rumors of rural famine. The end of the NEP's private trade and the chaotic early stages of centralized distribution of goods, combined with the priority given to defense and heavy industries, produced rationing and a severe decrease in real wages. The manifestations of this severe economic dislocation and radical drop in standards of living, even if minimized to outside eyes, simply could not be concealed.[45]

In this light, the denial of forced-labor charges made by the Trade Unions' Commission on External Relations in 1931 to foreigners who had visited the country as members of workers' delegations is extraordinary, and illustrates how the Great Break campaign mode was hardly limited to VOKS. The circular letter did not merely counter Western press reports of Soviet forced labor and "starvation" as "savage lies and sheer nonsense." It made the additional claim of comprehensive Soviet superiority in workers' welfare benefits and living conditions. The rhetorical competition with the capitalist world over living conditions is something different from the Soviet "dream world" of retail consumption created later in the 1930s, which began to develop a consumer sector with reference to Western department stores, advertising often unattainable consumer goods in line with Socialist Realism's depiction of "life as it should be." In the Great Break, by contrast, the claim made to foreign visitors—who in this era were shown model workers' homes as proof—was that housing and workplace conditions must be recognized as superior in the here and now.[46]

The practice of touring showcase working-class housing was paralleled by the 1931 publication of the photo essay "24 Hours in the Life of a Moscow Worker Family" in Willi Münzenberg's mass circulation *Arbeiter Illustrierte Zeitung* (*Workers' Illustrated Newspaper*). This was, in the words of Erika Wolf, a "positive fantasy image of conditions in the Soviet Union for distribution to workers in the West." As Wolf has shown, the German publication not only had a profound impact on the history of Soviet photography, but also provided a communist propaganda coup against the German Social Democrats, who had denounced the photo-essay as a fabrication. In a carefully planned move, the Moscow family, the Filippovs, was then revealed to visiting delegations, even as a domestically published selection of photographs with altered captions was geared toward a Soviet audience more familiar with Soviet life.[47] As always, tours on the ground were trickier to manipulate than publications, and a British Labour politician brought to view model workers' housing in 1934 concluded that the population was saddled with poor material conditions, exactly the opposite of what was intended.[48] Even so, the significance of the Soviet claim on superior living conditions in the midst of the catastrophes of the Great Break lies not only in the perceptions of viewers at the time but also in the long-term implications of the claim itself, which was reborn in altered form during the Cultural Cold War.[49] The campaign mode of the Great Break prompted the dissemination of such overreaching and overtly competitive claims.

At the same time, VOKS itself underwent a consequential restructuring, although in the midst of the momentous political upheavals of the day, its implications were hardly discussed, even behind the scenes. In the 1920s, participation by prominent members of the non-party intelligentsia in foreign cultural relations through VOKS's cultural and scientific "sections" may initially have been camouflage for its status as an independent society, but it quickly assumed a key role in the organization's activities and Kameneva's plans. Now that the intelligentsia and leading authorities of NEP were under assault, these disciplinary sections suddenly withered away, greatly changing the nature of the organization.[50] In their stead appeared a new willingness to aggressively mobilize Soviet scholars and cultural figures for constant international campaigns. Two days before the start of the Industrial Party show trial, on November 23, 1930, VOKS convened scientists, writers, and artists to pressure them to sign statements condemning the wreckers (whose guilt was a foregone conclusion) for use in publicity about the trial abroad. The organizers of this campaign made scarcely concealed threats to force non-party figures to sign: "[The Industrial Party trial] gives Soviet scholars and artists another opportunity to reveal their stance toward Soviet power, on the one hand, and its enemies, on the other."[51] With the decline of its intelligentsia "sections," VOKS was left without a fig leaf for its claim to the status of a non-governmental organization.

The loud words of the campaign mode concealed much internal disarray. Officials at VOKS still talked about achieving hegemony for their agency in the realm of foreign cultural relations, but the stature of the organization was in decline. While Kameneva had on a regular basis wielded her personal access to the top leadership, there were complaints that her successor, Petrov, was overburdened with work on the *Great Soviet Encyclopedia*. He worked at VOKS for only two to three hours a day, mostly receiving visiting foreign dignitaries. Important posts remained vacant. To the chagrin of VOKS representatives abroad, materials were sent from Moscow in an even more haphazard fashion than before, with little regard to the differences among the receiving countries. The rise of Intourist, as discussed earlier, undercut VOKS's importance and quickly put it in a dependent position in terms of translators, guides, and hotels, so much so that in 1931, the VOKS representative in Leningrad proposed a merger with its bitter rival in his city. To the alarm and outrage of the VOKS "shock workers" planning their Industrial Party campaign, their agency was denied tickets to attend the show trial, a rejection they rightly took as a sign of the institution's diminished authority.[52]

The combination of chaos and diminished stature for the cultural relations society in the new era made it an easier target for ominous accusations about security breaches as suspiciousness about ties with the outside world became a distinctly more prominent strand of the political culture. New measures attempted to limit interactions with foreign visitors. In 1931, the staff was charged with "uncritical, overtly friendly socializing" with foreigners and for lax handling of packages from abroad. Both behaviors were depicted as aiding hostile intelligence organs, charges that would resurface during the Great Terror. It was around this time, as well, that both official and less scripted statements began to advertise protection from pernicious capitalist intrusions (rather than import of the most useful parts of advanced countries' science and culture) as the main part of the organization's mission. VOKS would be an "organ filtering and controlling" all "alien cultural influences" emanating from abroad.[53] The Great Break heightened the dangers attached to work with foreigners—even if during this period the contagion was defined in class terms, as proximity not to foreigners per se but to the Western intelligentsia and the bourgeoisie.

At the same time, three momentous developments—the Great Depression, the rise of fascism, and the Five-Year Plan's drive to build socialism—ushered in a new age of Western fascination with the Soviet experiment. Leading fellow-travelers, such as Romain Rolland and André Gide, who had earlier remained aloof, now sealed their friendship with the Soviet Union, and the practice of lavishly receiving and celebrating foreign friends such as Bernard Shaw commenced. A constituent part of the post-iconoclastic phase of Soviet culture after 1931, as Katerina Clark's work suggests, was the party intellectuals' dream to make Moscow into the symbolic and organizational cultural center on an international scale. At a time when Soviet culture under the sign of Socialist Realism paradoxically sought to define itself as the culmination of a great global or European tradition, these figures were thus poised to make the shift from traveling to far-off construction sites and industrial giants during the Plan years to flitting around European capitals during the era of antifascist culture.[54] From the outset, Stalinism incorporated variations of two competing and well-entrenched ideological codes: one playing up the dangers and hostility of the West and, more broadly the outside world, and the other seeking out and seizing the opportunities raised by international perceptions of the revolution's success. The agenda set during the Great Break to "catch up and overtake" implied not only repudiation but also an embrace.

At the same time, the ubiquitous watchword of "catching up and overtaking" the capitalist West led directly to more crudely adversarial and competitive understandings of cultural exchange. The productionist mode of the Five-Year Plan deeply affected the language and practices of Soviet culture in this period. An applied and utilitarian calculus was applied to education, scholarship, and cultural fields; in addition to quotas and planning, brigades, shock-work, and the "intensification of class struggle" permeated the cultural front. The organs of international cultural relations, fully enmeshed in the pressure-cooker of the Soviet system, discussed and formulated their goals within the framework of Great Break culture. A scant two weeks after Kameneva left VOKS, on July 17, 1929, the new director, Fedor Petrov, revealed his balance-sheet approach to the "interaction of cultures." Time and again, he pushed a defensive Levit-Liven, his analyst (*referent*) on Central Europe, to admit not only weak Soviet influence but also scientific and cultural dependency on Germany:

Petrov: In your opinion, whose culture actually exerts more influence: ours, or theirs on us?

Levit: In the realm of technology they influence us.

Petrov: And in medicine?

Levit: In medicine too, but there are other areas, such as theater, where we have a colossal influence. One must say that [Erwin] Piscator, who founded three theaters in Berlin, is completely under our influence.

Petrov: And in musical relations it is the opposite?

Levit: That's completely right...But...in cinema we have exerted enormous influence. Our exhibitions have colossal success in Germany. We also have a certain influence in pedagogical relations...

Petrov: You said that film directors come to us to study, but, after all, not technology?

Levit: In all questions relating to technology, we of course study in Germany, but even despite weak technology our films are considered models (*obraztsovymi*).[55]

Striking here is not Levit's defensive listing of Soviet areas of strength but the way he accepted Petrov's premise that cultural exchange was a struggle for hegemony between "us" and "them" that could be quantified, like the balance of imports and exports and the possession of assets such as Piscator.[56] Despite the implication behind Petrov's leading line of questioning, it was unlikely that anything VOKS did could greatly alter the balance of cultural-scientific power he perceived. The strategy session at VOKS suggests the extent to which the Great Break drive to "overtake" capitalist competitors could be interpreted as no less a zero-sum cultural competition than a drive to overfulfill industrial outputs.

Even so, while Great Break wrecked one after another of the NEP era's fragile compromises, Lenin's old assumption that the advanced and cultured West had much to teach the land of socialism remained prominent. As Petrov's leading questions suggest, party leaders and intellectuals often still took Western superiority for granted in areas beyond the most easily acknowledged realms of technology, industrial efficiency, and (to a lesser degree) science. To give one example, a short-lived VOKS program to promote foreign-language study was described as part of a mission of "informing workers of the cultural achievements of the West." Other programmatic statements in the same era reiterated the Leninist nostrum of adopting everything "useful" from "West-European scientific-cultural thought."[57] The ideological relationship with the West remained profoundly contradictory. Soviet avant-gardists and party intellectuals in this period eagerly cooperated along transnational networks—or became trendsetters for Western writers and artists transfixed by Soviet culture in Berlin, Paris, Prague, and elsewhere—even as condemnations of cosmopolitans and "formalists" first appeared around 1930.[58]

Less than a decade before the Great Terror and two before the anti-cosmopolitanism of the Zhdanov period, the identification of foreignness with domestic counter-revolution remained far from complete. Nonetheless, the political logic that came to the fore during the Stalin era—to tie any and all opposition in the crusade to achieve socialism to a unified conspiracy of external and internal foes—was embedded in these landmark events of the Stalin period's incipient phase.

Strategic Myopia and Western Public Opinion

Exerting influence successfully requires not only means and strategy but, at least to some degree, an understanding of one's target audience. There were two modes in which VOKS and allied institutions could display that understanding: in materials sent to influence the press and public opinion in Western countries and in internal commentary on cultural and political life abroad. The first endeavor had crystallized in the mid-1920s, but was significantly altered by the upheaval at the end of the decade; at VOKS, at least, the second endeavor came into its own during the Great Break.

The productionism of the Great Break, in which greater quantity took precedence over quality, heavily influenced Soviet international-press operations. For example, a prime arena for attempted influence—and the object of great attention—was the supply of articles and photographs to foreign newspapers and periodicals. In practice, influence came to be equated with simply placing Soviet-generated materials in foreign publications or even producing greater quantity: at one point, 500 articles were reportedly sent abroad during the Industrial Party campaign of 1930. Actual publication rates were another matter: six articles were reported published in Czechoslovakia and thirteen in Germany during the period between July 1, 1929, and March 1, 1930, and similarly low figures were reported in other years. It was not specified where the VOKS-prepared pieces were published. In fact, major outlets were communist-managed organs such as *Das neue Russland* and Henri Barbusse's *Monde*.[59]

The Great Break's pressures prompted an even greater turn to the ostensible objectivity of evolving documentary genres to promote political goals. This was often accomplished in innovative ways, the best example of which is the use of the photograph. Here, agencies such as VOKS and IAH involved in propagating positive images of the USSR participated in a broader cultural field with the avant-garde and pro-Soviet intelligentsia. Intensive experimentation with the "workers' correspondent" movement—reportage, travelogues, and documentary film in Germany as well as in early Soviet culture—suggests how much the fascination with the political power of "the new objectivity" was internationally cross-fertilized. The urge was simultaneously to heighten objectivity through the medium and to manipulate it. As Bertolt Brecht, writing on the tenth anniversary of *Arbeiter Illustrierte Zeitung* in 1931, revealingly articulated: the task of the illustrated newspaper was to tell "the truth," but "the camera can lie just as well as the printing press."[60] Indeed, in this realm, the Soviets were decisively influenced by German initiatives. Willi Münzenberg's *Workers' Illustrated Newspaper*, which published VOKS and other Soviet photographs as well as the shots of worker-photographers, was a resounding financial success. The power of the photographic sequence to narrate the typicality of highly atypical and staged living conditions proved irresistible to a succession of avant-garde and Socialist Realist efforts to reach domestic Soviet viewers.[61]

If Münzenberg's Comintern-sponsored empire in Berlin was at the forefront of sequencing photographs, text, and graphic design in an extended narrative, VOKS also came to an early realization of photography's ability to convince, and therefore control, impressions about Soviet conditions. Photographs depicting "socialist construction" were sold to Western press outlets through the VOKS agency Russ-Foto (VOKS's involvement in film was far less substantial than IAH's influential import and screenings of Soviet film). VOKS officials saw not only that photography was viewed less suspiciously by international audiences than exported printed materials but that it was profitable commercially. True, the numbers were relatively large only in Germany and France (989 and 593 photographs placed in Germany in 1925–26 and 1926–27, 657 and 702 in France in the same period), whereas the number was under 100 in the United States, Britain, and other countries. Once again, however, international efforts had big domestic repercussions. In 1925–26, Russ-Foto distributed 19,833 photographs in Moscow and 1,916 elsewhere in the USSR, because it was easier to find domestic outlets.[62]

The twin allures of undetectable propaganda and hard-currency profit soon clashed. For even after supplying the friendship societies and Soviet embassies with photographs and using them in handsome albums for visiting foreigners, the venture almost never required a financial subsidy. In 1926, the head of Russ-Foto became eager to expand the commercial potential of the venture abroad, which purportedly meant putting the photographic "illumination of the achievements of the USSR" at the mercy of the international press market. Such an abdication of "ideological leadership" was attacked by VOKS officials and categorically forbidden by Kameneva. Characteristically, even as she assured the Press Section of the

Central Committee, in 1928, that the photographs were politically "very forcefully" controlled so that only favorable images would be distributed, she also insisted that the project would create a documentary "chronicle of our reality."[63]

Photographs and written materials were seen as an especially valuable means of penetrating countries with which the USSR did not have diplomatic relations or in which it was especially difficult to travel, for geographical or political reasons. The case of Fascist Italy is an especially interesting example. In 1928, the Soviet embassy in Rome requested guidebooks about Moscow and materials on artistic life, economic achievements, and sport. In 1930, the VOKS representative in the Soviet embassy in Rome wrote that he had stopped receiving even the bulletin, but, given the upturn in diplomatic and trade relations that year, there was "now the possibility of placing in local journals and newspapers a range of articles on the USSR." He requested material in French, especially on the Five-Year Plan with the latest figures, but also on education, literature, and art.[64]

Italy had recognized the Soviet Union diplomatically in 1924, and ideological fulminations on both sides did not prevent often cordial periods of anti-Versailles diplomacy and mutually beneficial trade relations. Indeed, anti-fascist campaigns in the Soviet press usually waxed and waned in tandem with the turns of Italo-Soviet relations. A blend of repulsion and attraction was present on the Fascist side as well. While Mussolini fulminated against the infection of socialism and masonry emanating from the Orient, and other Fascist thinkers linked Stalin and Ford in a "Bolshevik-American barbarism," historians have established a consistent strain of fascination for the Soviet experiment not only among Italian non-Fascist intellectuals but also among the regime's ideologists. The summit between Dino Grandi and Maksim Litvinov in Milan in 1930 signaled a new era in diplomatic and trade relations that continued through the 1933 Italo-Soviet friendship pact and noticeably affected cultural diplomacy.[65] The VOKS bulletin began being sent, Soviet presence in Italy through exhibitions and musicians picked up, and VOKS was asked to pay special attention to Italian scholarly visitors. The VOKS representative in Italy noted the possibility of inviting so-called liberal scholarly opponents of the *fashrezhim* and even those among the "fascist-leaning" (*fashistvuiushchaia*) public.

But VOKS during the Great Break was unprepared to take advantage of the Italo-Soviet thaw. In 1930, the Soviet embassy described how Italians, upon hearing the word "VOKS," would "wave their hands" frenetically in a sign of hopelessness, since all requests either went unanswered or were sent to other institutions—out of either bureaucratic bungling or political wariness. By 1933, VOKS was mechanically sending to Italy articles destined for the trash on Stalin's speeches or the anniversary of Marx's death, much to the scorn of the VOKS representative. Articles that might be publishable in English or French were odious to the Fascist regime of political terror, he instructed drily, advising that articles on city construction, medicine, and art would be put to better use.[66] Crude mistakes inspired by inertia and red tape have to be considered a large part of Soviet cultural diplomacy.

Other published materials sent abroad or provided to foreigners did hit their mark. American physician Ralph A. Reynolds, who was involved in setting up the American-Russian Institute in San Francisco, visited Moscow and received VOKS materials for articles and lectures in 1930–31 on Soviet medical institutions and prisons. His article in the *Journal of Social Hygiene* acknowledged his debt to VOKS for "a considerable part of the statistical data set forth in this paper." But he borrowed more than that: the whole framework of his piece followed the Soviet schema of contrasting the horrors of tsarism with the achievements of the Soviet years. The USSR is the only country in the world, he wrote, in which "the idea of retributive punishment of crime has been completely discarded. The prisons are now converted into vocational training schools."[67]

Photographs enjoyed another advantage: the effectiveness of written materials was hampered by poor translations and the broader difficulties of rendering the arcane terms of Soviet ideospeak in a form accessible or even comprehensible to outsiders. Over the years, even highly sympathetic foreign consumers of communist propaganda made it abundantly clear that Soviet publications in their native tongues left much to be desired. In 1932, the honorary secretary of the British Society of Cultural Relations made a concerted effort to persuade Isidor Amdur, himself a young Jewish Communist from London working as head of the VOKS Anglo-American sector, that the quality of the materials needed to be improved. Louis Anderson Fenn, a pro-Soviet writer who wrote several books in the early 1930s on poverty, wealth, and problems of the "socialist transition," offered to come to Moscow to lend Amdur the "purity" of his "English style." This sympathetic critic, who pointed out that he had contributed to *The Spectator*, reviewed an entire number of the *Soviet Culture Review* for the unreceptive Amdur. Readers are "misled and mystified by the unusual phrases and constructions" common in Soviet publications; the strange typeface repelled English sensibilities and was "terribly dull and unattractive in appearance." Amdur assured Fenn that the VOKS press section would take all necessary steps to fix the problem, but made sure to include the word "probably." Fenn's offer to serve in Moscow was ignored. Instead, in a bureaucratic twist, he was put on the list to receive the very VOKS publications he had offered to improve.[68]

As VOKS turned away from encouraging the participation of the non-party intelligentsia in its "sections" at the height of the Great Break, it began to focus

Figure 5.3 A 1932 cover from the English-language edition of the VOKS *Bulletin* showing Maxim Gorky arriving in Moscow. Note the error in the English caption. Source: *VOKS*, no. 3–4 (1932).

much more on providing analysis of cultural and intellectual life in key countries abroad. This newly important endeavor formed part of a new politics on international information that took shape in the 1920s and shifted significantly after the onset of the Stalin period. VOKS took part in a much larger system of secret information on international affairs that helped shape the worldview of the top Soviet elites and was different in form and content from the triumphal pomposity of the press. The shape and tone of the new system of information on the outside world were firmed up starting in the mid-1920s by Stalin's secret chancellery, the Central Committee's Information Bureau, and, after 1932, Karl Radek's Bureau of International Information. Secret reports and access to information on the outside world were rationed according to a hierarchical, need-to-know basis and surrounded by a special degree of conspiracy; this was tightly linked to operational practice, as special reports and channels of information were born amid the antagonisms of the "dual policy" separating the Comintern's world revolution and the conventional diplomacy of Foreign Affairs.[69]

However, in spite of all the secrecy and centralization that surrounded the conveyance of privileged information—or rather, in part because of it—the international reports gave a distorted picture of the outside world. VOKS took its place in the broader system with its brief to report on cultural developments abroad, expanding its *referentura*, or network of country analysts. The *referent*, or analyst, was defined in 1929 as a "responsible director" (*otvetstvennyi rukovoditel'*) charged with following the cultural life of an assigned country, searching for individuals and organizations to become "transmission belts" of Soviet cultural influence. In 1931, the number of analysts was increased from six to eight for the Central European sector, from four to seven for the Anglo-American sector, and from three to six in the Romance sector, for a total of twenty-one *referenty*.[70] The sectors produced reports, biweekly in 1933, with overviews of the foreign press. The rubrics are revealing of the way analysts meshed their surveys with VOKS's institutional goals: they usually summarized the overall position of the "intelligentsia" or "intelligentsia groups" for each country, tracked visitors or figures with Soviet ties for statements about the USSR in the press, monitored the friendship societies and their publications; and, most important, highlighted "campaigns for and against the USSR," as though the Western press was dominated, like the Soviet, by "campaigns."

Clearly, the purpose behind these practices was operational: to help sort friends from enemies and track those with whom VOKS and other Soviet institutions previously had or potentially would have dealings. One result, however, was to convey a black-and-white world in which all anti-Soviet statements were lies and all praise was the objective truth. At the height of starvation in rural parts of the country in late winter 1932, one summary referred to reports of famine as the favorite invention of right-wing intellectual circles.[71] Potentially even more important than the proliferation of taboo topics, however, was that intellectual and cultural life in the countries under examination was not explored for its own dynamics within a national context but picked over for the statements it produced for and against the Soviet system. Unwittingly, the narrowly utilitarian brief of the analysts helped create a mirage, a world focused solely on the question of whether to greet or condemn Soviet communism.

Diagrams at an Exhibition

Nothing demonstrates more clearly how plans for Soviet participation in cultural events abroad were tied up in an explicit calculation of political rewards than exhibitions and musical, theatrical, and other artistic tours. Because these demanded more planning and hard currency than other forms of travel, they generated concrete strategizing about the contents and results. Within the Soviet system, utilitarian political justification was king, even if the reasoning was sometimes far-fetched. When Soviet participation in an international musical exhibition in Frankfurt was pitched to Molotov in 1927, it was noted that the city was located not far from the zone that had experienced occupation by the Entente. Hence, a demonstration of peaceful Soviet cultural work would become a "vivid counterpoint to the forms of influence of the Entente." Only 14,000 rubles were needed. On many occasions, state economic and foreign-policy goals served as primary justifications, but for events with the potential to attract large audiences (such as exhibitions) the political benefits of touting the achievements of Soviet socialism were never far behind. When Leonid Krasin, commissar of foreign trade, and Kameneva advocated to the Politburo a significant outlay of at least 500,000 rubles for a Soviet pavilion in the Philadelphia World's Fair of 1926, it was called a way of putting on an exhibit "worthy of a 'great power,'" as well as a means of pursuing the "exceptional importance which we attribute to the development of our economic relations with the USA." Upstaging or countering the "White emigration," a major theme of the early 1920s, was still effective as late as 1936, when VOKS director Arosev argued for approving Soviet participation in a staging of *Eugene Onegin* at the National Theater in Prague in order to prevent émigré participation.[72]

Exhibitions presented Soviet organizers and artists with the dilemma of balancing exhibits with didactic texts and frequently mountainous statistics. At the Soviet press pavilion in Cologne in 1928, VOKS supplied the materials, and El Lissitzky headed a team of sixty artists in implementing the design. The results, which had so impressed Gorky, were strengthened by the decision to subordinate text to the visual components.[73] Yet even the Soviet pavilion at the World Fair in Paris in 1937, which had the benefit of lavish funding and a "dynamic unity" between the architectural design of Boris Iofan and the sculptures of Vera Mukhina, was nonetheless marked by the same didactic urge to barrage the viewer with texts, facts, and figures that dominated the far more common, low-cost exhibits sent abroad. "Too many diagrams, tables, and photographs," Soviet ambassador to London Ivan Maiskii recorded in his diary after visiting the Paris pavillion, "and too few striking and convincing objects."[74]

International fairs and competitions, which involved architectural components and major expenditures, were a rarity in comparison to the small-form Soviet exhibition that VOKS and others helped develop for export in the 1920s. Sometimes called the "portable" (*portativnyi*) exhibit, this was an inexpensive combination of objects, images, and texts with either a specific cultural-political focus or highlighting a combination of artifacts and features of the Soviet Union. Posters, models, arts, and crafts were frequently combined with a montage of written texts, photographs, statistics, and diagrams. In these portable presentations, which VOKS regularly sent to the friendship societies, exhibited objects (*eksponaty*) ran the gamut from china, textiles, Palekh boxes, and handsomely published books, to theatrical posters, children's drawings, and various kinds of art, but they were often few in number and overwhelmed by text.

After all, text was cheap—and could easily be altered to reflect current campaigns. The dual requirement of political and financial authorization wreaked havoc with advance preparation. For example, the extensive celebrations of the tenth anniversary of the October Revolution were marked by wide dissemination of exhibitions dominated by diagrams, posters, and photographs for consumption in four foreign languages. These were prepared with frenetic storming when funding was approved by the Central Committee only two months in advance. Hasty preparation and missed deadlines were the norm rather than the exception given the hierarchical system of political and financial control over international events. As in other areas, the levels of political approval became even more stringent and numerous in the 1930s, often seriously impeding preparations. In the 1920s, exhibitions followed the standard formula of contrasting the Soviet present with the "oppressive heritage of tsarist Russia," in the words of one exhibit of books for the blind that touted the advantages of being sightless in the USSR. In a significant shift, this orthodoxy was reversed in Pushkin jubilee exhibitions of 1936–37, which paired Russian and Soviet achievements together.[75]

Tilting the balance toward didactic texts, as opposed to exhibited objects, saved money and was easier to organize, but it was also an attempt to overdetermine audience response. The result, judging by reports, could be deadening and, even so, viewers' reactions were sometimes diametrically opposed to the intent. Polovtsevaia, the VOKS representative in London, reported in 1925 with obvious pride on the success of a Soviet poster exhibition at the Society for Cultural Relations: "Directly in front of the entrance, on a bright blue background, the red color of our symbols stood in sharp relief." She described the posters as focusing on Lenin, cooperatives, labor, and health, but the hostile review in the *Westminster Gazette* sent to Moscow with other clippings singled out the "pathetic" hygiene posters, which only proved that Russians were "often ignorant of the elementary laws of hygiene."[76] In 1928, a Soviet diplomat stationed in the United States wrote a pointed critique to VOKS on no less than thirty exhibits VOKS had sent to the United States involving achievements in various areas of industry, science, and art. His catalogue of grievances was a long one: items sent to be put on exhibit were often not the best examples available in the USSR, they were eclectically thrown together, and they played second fiddle to diagrams, statistics, maps, and other written materials. The texts were, as elsewhere, spoiled by poor translations into English; boxes stamped only with the Russian word *"ostorozhno"* (handle with care) had no translation at all and arrived with broken contents. Achievements were touted in the texts but not demonstrated in the objects, since top-quality Soviet editions of books and other Soviet cultural products capable of competing with the best of the West were in short supply. "Please do not get angry at me, comrades," the diplomat wrote back apologetically to VOKS after his criticisms, "for my evaluation of the items you have sent for exhibit."[77]

The most ambitious predictions about influencing audiences were reserved for large international events, because impressive results were a sine qua non in the game of securing high-level approval. In the case of Fascist Italy, major international competitions, such as the exhibitions in Venice and Monza (Milan) in 1930, were invested with even more significance since, as VOKS director Petrov in 1930 assured A.I. Ugarov at the OGPU, they were among the only possible demonstration of Soviet achievements VOKS could organize in that country. Explicit political themes were intertwined with cultural exhibitions in the four halls in Monza, later sent to Amsterdam, including one on the Five-Year Plan and collectivization of agriculture, one on cultural life, a *kino-gorod* devoted to film, and, winner of a *grand prix*, an exposition of graphic arts and the Soviet book. Soviet organizers tended to be more than optimistic about audience response. The Seventeenth Venice Exhibition of fine arts of the USSR, for which Petrov requested from the director of the Tret'iakov Gallery ten paintings of high quality that would demonstrate contemporary Soviet "reality," is a good example. Petrov expressed confidence that the intended messages would be received, for in keeping with all such events at which Soviet representatives were allowed to be present, great emphasis was placed on the possibility of directly explaining meaning to the viewing public to assure, as he put it, the correct political and cultural-enlightenment effect. In this case, the sole figure deemed suitable and available was the art historian Viktor Lazarev, a non-communist yet trusted museum official who knew Italian well. Soviet participation and Lazarev's travel were fully supported by all the relevant party-state authorities, Petrov reported, since the leadership believed this to be of "great political significance."[78]

Even this incautious optimism could not make the political goals predicted for exhibitions more coherent, however. Although top-level political approval for the Italian exhibitions of 1930 was eased by the upturn in Italo-Soviet relations of the same year, organizers continued to make sweeping and openly contradictory promises about their effects on Italian viewers. At one point, Petrov predicted that a walk through the Soviet hallways would do nothing less than immunize Italian public opinion (*obshchestvennost'*) from "many of the attacks of the fascists" on the Soviet Union. Simultaneously, a top-level VOKS planning document justifiably noted an "indubitable interest" on the part of Fascist leaders themselves for the Soviet system, "in spite of the deep and insurmountable contradictions [of Fascism] with the proletarian dictatorship." Furthermore, the VOKS representative in Italy noted that no less than half of the Italian intellectual world was opposed to Fascism (*nastroen antifashistski*), leading Petrov at another point to predict that the Soviets could stoke the fires of dissent.[79] In other words, the same exhibitions were at once intended to seduce Fascist ideologues attracted to the Soviet Union, stimulate intellectual opposition to Fascism, and convince the Italian public to reject Fascist criticisms of communism. All the while, specifics on how the presentation would target different foreign audiences were utterly lacking.

The Soviet conventions for justifying and planning exhibitions could never acknowledge that the messages foreign audiences took away could defy all expectations. Among the reviews translated into Russian and sent to Moscow was a favorable, even gushing assessment from *Il Popolo di Roma*. It is unlikely that this particular piece was intended as a diplomatic-political signal to the Soviets, since it expressed gratified surprise to discover the vast influence of "our" Fascist iconography on the Soviet system. This was evident in images of marching rows of youngsters with raised hands, Lenin amid a great crowd just like "our Duce," and pictures of leaders similar to Fascists in every respect except for the color red and the hammer and sickle. "One must marvel," it concluded, "at the wisdom with which the ideals and practical activity of the Red Republic are displayed."[80]

In exhibitions, as in printed material sent abroad, the articulation and pursuit of conspiratorial strategies and political results was matched by cultural misunderstandings, spotty knowledge of specific national contexts, and bureaucratic bungling that reached new heights in the midst of the Great Break. The "achievements" of a well-honed conspiratorial instrumentalism—the practice of judging everything in terms of a pro- or anti-Soviet bottom line—led to an acute myopia in analyzing and influencing Western public opinion.

In February 1931, Stalin made a famous and oft-quoted speech to industrial managers. "Everyone beat Russia because of her backwardness. Because of military backwardness, cultural backwardness, state backwardness, industrial backwardness, agricultural backwardness...We are 50–100 years behind the leading countries. We have to cover this distance in ten years. Either we do it, or they crush us."[81] In the words of the general secretary, on the one hand, the outside world took the guise of a perennial adversary waiting to prey on Russian, and hence Soviet, weakness. On the other, Stalin made it clear that there was no area in which the country did not still lag behind. This message differed significantly from the unambiguous new orthodoxy about Soviet superiority that took hold later in the 1930s. Yet the two were linked: Stalin's broad strategy of projecting strength and concealing weakness may have been first and foremost directed outward to a hostile capitalist world, but it could hardly be separated out from domestic ideology and culture.[82]

The Great Break, the most militant phase of the broader Soviet cultural revolution, was, thus, in many respects an intensification of earlier phases in the 1920s and a bridge to later ones in the 1930s. As it was in this sense a "transition period," it never made the leap from anti-bourgeois, anti-capitalist iconoclasm to a uniformly anti-Western or anti-foreign movement. A more contained, official Soviet "Occidentalism" developed only much later, with the post-war Zhdanov period and anti-cosmopolitanism campaign of late Stalinism, which came after the heyday of Western enthusiasm for the Soviet experiment.[83]

The newly intense determination of the Great Break to overtake and repudiate "the leading countries" of the West while maintaining an ambivalent respect for what they could offer Soviet socialism made this, in many ways, an exceptional period in Soviet attitudes toward the outside world. It was no less transitional and no less exceptional in the history of Soviet cultural diplomacy. The campaign mode reached its apogee, and the advent of Intourist marked a newfound interest in visiting foreigners as sources of hard currrency. Internal upheaval and intense political and ideological pressures interfered with the effectiveness of external operations, and what was later condemned as sectarianism detracted from at least some of the international gains the Soviets accrued from the Five-Year Plan and the Great Depression. When sectarian approaches were partially reversed in 1932–34, the stage was set for the more flexible and effective methods of the era of the Popular Front, the period of Soviet cultural diplomacy's greatest success. Although it was later modified, the urgent utilitarianism the Great Break brought to the fore in so many ways left a lasting mark on the subsequent evolution of Soviet cultural diplomacy.

6

Stalin and the Fellow-Travelers Revisited

By publicly embracing Stalinism as humanity's best hope, the leading fellow-travelers were defending, if sometimes with caveats, the basic superiority of the Soviet order. Underlying the assessment of the entire Soviet experiment was a personalized evaluation of Bolshevik intellectuals and, in the 1930s, especially Stalin, filtered through a longstanding European debate about thinkers versus men of action. In the Soviet mirror, many of the interwar period's most celebrated "friends of the Soviet Union" found a superior breed of intellectual, even a philosopher-king. Such views, however, would have meant little without a web of concrete ties binding them to their object of sympathy. Much remains to be learned about how the fellow-travelers' ideas were reinforced by these concrete practices, not least from the records of Soviet cultural institutions. Building on the perspective afforded by these hitherto missing pieces of the puzzle, this chapter seeks to recapture motivations behind intellectual panegyrics to Stalinism.

The interwar period launched the debates that continue to reverberate over the proper role of intellectuals vis-à-vis power and politics. Caute observed that "none of those prominent French and German humanists who embraced the Soviet Union late in life ever quite overcame the inbred apartheid of *Geist* and *Macht*," or *pensée* and *action*, the belief that "the true vocation of art and intelligence is incompatible with politics."[1] That division was built in before it was swamped in the deluge of the era of total war and revolution—hence, Julien Benda's challenge in his 1927 *Trahison des clercs* for intellectuals to remain true to the life of the mind. The allure of power may be common among intellectuals, but it is not somehow an essential quality of all professionals, scholars, and artists; it is marked by the historical conjuncture. The powerful new yearning for political action of the interwar period provoked a counter-movement, and intellectuals in Europe and the United States were torn. This chapter treats intellectuals not as an unchanging or unified stratum of modern society but as buffeted by their newfound politicization and these interwar debates over their proper role. Precisely because many fellow-travelers never completely overcame that inherent dichotomy, they were all the more fascinated by the Bolshevik revolutionary intelligentsia and Stalin as a kind of intellectual in power.

The term fellow-traveler was not what the Soviets called sympathetic foreign intellectuals, nor was it a term the intellectuals applied to themselves. It was a translation of the Russian *poputchik*, an old Russian Social Democratic term that Trotsky applied pejoratively in 1923 to non-proletarian, non-party literary figures who cooperated with the Soviet regime.[2] The term the Soviets used at the time for the leading foreign intellectual sympathizers was "friends of the Soviet Union," a label derived from the friendship societies and the 1927 Congress of Friends. This was a standard term applied in the Soviet press, in publications about foreign intellectuals, and in public receptions of sympathetic figures. Like Trotsky's *poputchiki*, almost all of the most celebrated foreign "friends" were literary figures, which can be attributed to their perceived influence as makers of public opinion—a view itself connected to the supremacy of the written word in Stalinist ideology and the paradigmatic nature of literature in Stalinist culture. It is significant that the same discourse of friendship used in public to trumpet foreign admiration was also standard fare in internal party-state discussions of foreign figures, especially when it came to allocation of resources and organized hospitality.[3]

The support provided to foreign "friends"—in return for loyalty—was simultaneously becoming part of the party-state's modus operandi for treating its own domestic intelligentsia, which, as Soviet history progressed, gained increasingly lavish material conditions. In a social-economic system in which patron-client relations were often put in personalistic language, arguments over providing Soviet funds and favors for foreign figures were made in terms of their status as friends. The status that foreign sympathizers assumed was, in this sense, an extension of the Soviet way of treating its own most valued intellectuals.

There is ample evidence, moreover, that foreign intellectuals internalized the concept of "friends of the Soviet Union" themselves. Fellow-travelers had to be willful or blind not to be aware of the increasingly formalized rules of the game that the Soviets set for friendship: public defense and praise of the Soviet Union. Some reservations and criticisms had to be allowed, because even the most pro-Soviet commentators would lack credibility otherwise. Perhaps the most distinguished European intellectual friend to consistently defend Stalinism in public—and remain silent during the Purges—was Romain Rolland. This frail, high-minded idealist displayed full understanding of the terms of friendship, pledging loyalty and public support in return for the status. In such cases, friendship was virtually a contractual relationship that both sides understood.

What, then, did fellow-travelers hope to gain from this kind of relationship? First, as case studies of the visits and Soviet connections of prominent foreign friends show, admiration for Bolshevik theoreticians as "men of action" was tied to many of the greatest friends' own illusory aspirations for influence over the Soviet experiment. Second, most developed crucial, personal relationships with those Soviet mediators—party intellectuals with significant international experience, who in this chapter are referred to by the deliberately paradoxical name Stalinist Westernizers—who courted, handled, pressured, and, yet, also frequently admired the Western intellectuals as cultural giants. Third, communism was a flexible myth, and cultural diplomacy pushed on many sides of it, so that no single feature attracted intellectual sympathizers uniformly or exclusively; at the same time, each figure often had a main or most cherished hope invested in the Soviet system. Finally, the ideas and beliefs that allowed admirers to justify odious features of the Stalin system assumed meaning in a context defined by a concrete, quasi-official friendship, proffered and accepted during visits and maintained by personal relationships. Many of the leading twentieth-century intellectuals who became fellow-travelers publicly heaped praise on Soviet socialism as a superior society in part because they harbored the fantasy that through those connections they could claim a measure of power over it.

Stalinist Fabians

Perhaps no test case is as illuminating for interpreting the multiplicity of attractions of Stalinism for Western intellectuals than the leading Fabian socialists in Britain. In the European country with the strongest liberal tradition and the weakest Communist Party, the Fabians had elaborated a version of socialism that was gradualist, eschewed violent revolution, and enshrined the virtues of civil liberties and parliamentary democracy. Its leaders were hardly alienated from their own society, *contra* theories of Sovietophilia as the outlet of alienated intellectuals; rationalist and pragmatic, rather than quasi-religious believers, they were all establishment figures who exerted great influence on the Labour Party. How was it then that the former "Fabian Triumvirate" of George Bernard Shaw and Sidney and Beatrice Webb, leading members of the Fabian Society since its founding in 1884, found their place among the most prominent intellectual supporters of Stalin and Stalinism in the 1930s?

The Great Depression, mixing the proximity of bread lines with the far-off images of Soviet success in the first Five-Year Plan, certainly made them more pro-Soviet; in this sense, the Depression was for them like the other two great "push" factors propelling intellectuals toward the Soviet Union in the 1930s, the rise of fascism and the Popular Front. Other prominent intellectuals who had exhibited little interest in the Soviet Union in the 1920s, such as Gide and Rolland, became "friends" of the Soviet Union during precisely this period. Shaw and the Webbs, who first visited the Soviet Union in 1931 and 1932, were also party to the "pull" factors of Soviet outreach, including the efforts of key intermediaries in recruiting each of them as eminent foreign visitors. They were, however, individually influenced by features of the Soviet system that appealed to their differing intellectual make-ups. Shaw, who also expressed sympathy for fascism, was particularly drawn by the cult of the leader; Sidney Webb, the consummate civil servant, lauded the interventionist machinery of the Soviet party-state; Beatrice Webb, the old cooperative-movement theorist, longed for equality and justice. The myth of communism was flexible indeed; among the Fabians alone, motivations drawing them toward friendship were multiple and varied. At the same time, there were commonalities: all were inclined toward elitism and social engineering, which helped Shaw and the Webbs to set aside other Fabian principles when they looked East. They were fascinated by Bolshevik men of action and strangely preoccupied with their imagined influence over the revolutionary in the Kremlin.

The Irish playwright George Bernard Shaw, the world-renowned contrarian with the rapier wit, was the propagandist and performer of Fabianism, while Beatrice Webb was the scholar and Sidney the draftsman of political programs. As Shaw himself put it in a tone of "comic mock-modesty," the Webbs were the brains, he was the megaphone. While it is often noted that he was enamored of fascism and eugenics and praised Stalin-era communism to the skies, Shaw has also been dismissed as being merely an exuberant provocateur, out to shock the bourgeoisie. Yet, shock was his preferred method of political discourse; after all, he was one of the most "famous and prolific" political intellectuals of the age.[4] Few would take the words spoken by characters in Shaw's plays literally as his own views, but they can certainly be interpreted to delineate his primary concerns; the same is true for his performative political pronouncements.

Before he was a Fabian, Shaw was a revolutionary Marxist; he read the first volume of *Kapital* in the British Museum in 1882, when it was available only in French, and, he recalled, had "a complete conversion." It was as a young socialist orator that he originated his trademark method of provocation through "shock tactics." The publicist of parliamentary socialism thus began a lifelong conversation with Marx that periodically "awakened in him un-Fabian revolutionary tendencies that persisted to the end of his life."[5] After 1917, these internal struggles and periodic flirtations with violent revolution were transposed from Marx to Lenin and then to the Stalinist "revolution from above." He reconciled his own political credo with the Soviet order in two basic ways. First, he periodically strayed from core tenets of his Fabian credo of parliamentary, non-violent change, especially in the 1930s; second, he portrayed the Soviet order, first under NEP and then in the 1930s under Stalin, as a gradualist repudiation of the utopianism of 1917.

"The few...will organize the many," Shaw wrote in his Fabian tract *Socialism and Superior Brains*. At the heart of Shaw's views of the Soviet Union lay a fundamentally elitist brand of social engineering that he shared with the Webbs but that in his case manifested itself in an obsession with strong leaders—fascist as well as communist—who knew how to organize society. Since his 1903 *Man and Superman*—a work influenced by Ibsen, Lamarck, Schopenhauer, and, to an extent, Nietzsche—Shaw had pictured these elites as a special order. In one of his un-Fabian moments he avowed that under socialism "social misfits" should be "made to do useful work or be put to death."[6] As Beatrice Webb observed about Shaw's publically expressed admiration for Mussolini, "This naive faith in a Superman before whose energy and genius all must bow down is not a new feature of the Shaw mentality." Shaw called Hitler a "very remarkable man, a very able man" in 1933, although his enthusiasm for Nazism was tempered by his view that racial extermination was an impractical distraction, as "stocks are hopelessly intertwined."[7]

Far from prostrating himself before Stalin as a strong leader, Shaw pictured himself as a prophet behind the throne. Virtually all the fellow-travelers tended to compare themselves in highly personal ways to Stalin or the Bolsheviks. For example, in 1933, Shaw referred to himself as a "professional talker" but avowed that "action" rather than "talk alone" was necessary to save the world.[8] The flamboyant Shaw assuaged his insecurities by loudly proclaiming his own decisive influence on the course of the revolution. "In typical Shavian fashion he began to consider himself the teacher of Lenin and Stalin and thus proceeded to equate Fabianism with Marxism." As he never tired of pointing out, his own Marxism had predated Lenin's by fourteen years. In the wake of his 1931 Soviet visit, Shaw increasingly referred to himself as a Fabian communist, or simply a communist. Even after the Great Purges, he continued to push his self-centered convergence theory, wittily boasting that the Soviets had become "sound Fabians and are on the way to become complete Shavians." In his later years, Shaw also dubbed Stalin a Fabian.[9] Yet, the more outrageous his (only partially tongue-in-cheek) assertions of influence became, the more he revealed the insecurities behind his addictive admiration for dictators in general and Stalin in particular. Shaw scholar H. M. Geduld hits the nail on the head: "GBS had triumphed as a jester and a man of letters, as a mahatma who seldom was taken seriously, but never as a politician and an influential 'world-betterer.'" In the end, behind his bold appropriation of Stalin's communism for Fabianism lay "a deep sense of personal failure."[10]

With the "human material" they had to work with, the Soviets could hardly go wrong; Shaw's ten-day visit to the Soviet Union in 1931 has to be considered one of the greatest of many success stories in the history of the Soviet reception of foreign intellectuals. Indeed, the triumph began before the trip even started, when the Soviets lured the world-famous writer to celebrate his seventy-fifth birthday in Moscow in the great hall of columns in the House of Trade Unions, the old nobles' club that was later the site of the show trials. One source credits Ivy Litvinov, the English wife of the commissar of foreign affairs, as a prime mover in persuading Shaw to visit, but members of VOKS's Society of Friends had also been pursuing Shaw as the centerpiece of their efforts to send sympathetic visitors for more than a year before the final arrangements were made.[11] While Shaw had expressed a preference for informal meetings rather than a guided tour, the carefully fixed itinerary—a visit to the Bolshevo commune led by Litvinov himself, a showing of Elektrozavod, appearances at a workers' literary circle and the theater, and audiences with Gorky, Stanislavskii, and Krupskaia, not to mention Stalin—went off without a hitch.[12]

It was a classic case of superficial experiences confirming a visitor's predispositions, themselves forged in direct anticipation of ideological battles to be fought back home.

Figure 6.1 George Bernard Shaw (second from left) at a luncheon in a garden at the Lenin Children's Commune, Kirsanovskii district, Tambov region, August 15, 1931. Making light of the notion that there was hunger or starvation in the Soviet Union, the world-renowned playwright started to refer to himself as a Fabian communist after his visit. Source: RIA Novosti Photo Library.

The most the Soviets had to fear was Shaw's acerbic wit, although his irreverent patter of jokes was sometimes incomprehensible to his audience. His choice of an aristocratic entourage, including his outspoken confidante, the Conservative Member of Parliament Lady Nancy Astor, can almost certainly be understood as one expression of this impishness, although Lady Astor's support for town planning, a massive housing program, and state health care, and Waldorf Astor's enthusiasm for social engineering, demonstrated that there were bridges across their political divide. "Never in my life have I enjoyed a journey so much," Shaw wrote on August 13, 1931, eleven days after his return, in a personal letter to a friend, Molly Tompkins. "You would have been disgusted at my reception as a Grand Old Man of Socialism, my smilings and wavings...but it made things very smooth for us all." Indeed, many of Shaw's letters about the USSR from the period of his visit were primarily concerned with creature comforts.[13]

One time that Shaw did appear genuinely moved was at the Lenin mausoleum, where he asked to be taken immediately after his arrival in Moscow. According to the account of a traveling companion, "Perhaps no foreigner ever lingered so long looking at the figure of the dead Lenin." An argument flared up between Lady Astor, who tried to discredit Lenin by calling him an "aristocrat," and Shaw, who insisted that he was a "pure intellectual type."[14] Shaw's most emotional episode of the visit was prompted by identification of the creator of the Soviet system as an intellectual like himself.

To his Soviet hosts, Shaw was concerned precisely with establishing himself as the grand old man of socialism who had always been a defender of the Bolshevik Revolution and who had known and corresponded with Lenin. The transcript of Shaw's speech on June 26, 1931, suggests a visitor eager to give his hosts more than they could have hoped. Shaw himself loudly asserted Soviet superiority: "The English people ought to be ashamed of themselves" for not having made a great revolution; "all the Western nations should feel that feeling of shame...[it is] imperative for the Western countries to follow your footsteps." In a time of impending famine and mass hardship, Shaw mocked his "weeping relatives" back home who "brought large baskets of food, imploring us not to risk our life, etc."[15]

The VOKS-sponsored birthday celebration at which Shaw made this speech was one of the first big Stalin-era public celebrations of a Western intellectual in the USSR, and, as such, had the function not merely of cementing Shaw's friendship but also of introducing Shaw to Soviet audiences. Featuring an extensive musical program ranging from a peasant choir to artists from the Bolshoi, the evening was punctuated by tributes to Shaw as "friend." Lunacharskii, the keynote speaker, accentuated Shaw's literary greatness with comparisons to Jonathan Swift and Saltykov-Shchedrin but took care to call "the great Irishman" to "our side of the barricades." At the same time, Lunacharskii had the delicate task of criticizing Shaw's Fabian socialism— "slow, comfortable . . . peaceful . . . very cultured and very subtle, but nonetheless petty-bourgeois." In an implicit assertion of superiority over the sympathetic foreigner, Lunacharskii called European writers to embark upon the proletarian trail forged by Soviet culture.[16]

Shaw accepted Lunacharskii's call with great fanfare, as indeed he had already decided to do. He was not one of those many visitors who said one thing inside the country and another at home; in his case, there was no need for self-censorship. Substantively, his remarks to Soviets during his visit were identical to the high-profile press and radio appearances upon his return: assertions of Western backwardness vis-à-vis the USSR, along with rebuttals to international charges of famine, forced labor, Potemkin villages, and lack of Soviet democracy, which were then publicized to Soviet audiences in *Pravda* on October 6, 1931. From Prague, Arosev wrote Stalin, "The visit to us by Bernard Shaw literally shook the minds of the miserable intelligentsia here. Their best . . . representative turned out to be the messenger of the USSR's

Figure 6.2 Gala ceremony to mark the seventy-fifth birthday of George Bernard Shaw at the Hall of Columns in the House of Unions in Moscow, July 26, 1931. The VOKS-sponsored gathering was one of the first big Stalin-era public celebrations of a Western "friend of the Soviet Union," an important component of Stalinist culture. Source: RIA Novosti Photo Library.

wishes."[17] The sense of triumph and mastery was clearly something Arosev thought Stalin wanted to hear.

Shaw had met and even exceeded the conditions for becoming a great Soviet "friend." His visit marked a "significant shift in Shaw's attitude toward the Russian Revolution," for in the early 1930s, the playwright pursued his theme of Fabian Stalinism and his most explicit justifications of Soviet political violence. For Soviet cultural diplomats, Shaw's visit served for years afterward as one of the best examples of how a visit to the land of socialist construction favorably worked on a famous Western intellectual. The literary critic Sergei Dinamov, writing in 1933, put Shaw in a pantheon including Dreiser and Rolland, repeating the dualistic script—great praise laced with muted criticism for not being completely communist—that Lunacharskii had already fashioned. Predictably, Dinamov emphasized that Shaw was still "attempting to understand" the USSR and "still has much to overcome." An official evaluation in a 1933 translation of Shaw's works referred to the "great break" in Shaw's consciousness after his visit, which allowed him to put aside his intelligentsia waverings and join the best—the most pro-Soviet—representatives of the Left intelligentsia of the West. Although he spoke with greater erudition than his successors, Lunacharskii, at the time of the visit, had articulated the basic ideological framework in which Shaw and other non-communist friends were presented in the Soviet Union for years to come.[18]

The two other most important figures in the Fabian Society, Sidney and Beatrice Webb, were joint authors of one of the most monumental and notoriously uncritical descriptions of Stalin's Soviet Union ever penned, their two-volume 1935 *Soviet Communism: A New Civilization*. These two intellectuals from the same country, the same political trend, and even the same family were motivated quite differently in their sympathies for the Stalinist USSR, and they thus reacted differently, if one judges from Beatrice Webb's remarkable diary, as they observed the tumultuous events of the 1930s. Sidney, the social engineer, was fascinated by the top-down machinery of state in the service of socialism; he was won over by the blueprints of the Soviet planned economy. As VOKS's file on Sidney noted in 1934, the draft of the Webbs' book was originally called "The Constitution of Soviet Communism"—a title that recalled their 1920 piece of imaginative social engineering, *A Constitution for the Socialist Commonwealth of Great Britain*. While Shaw loudly christened Stalin a Fabian, the Webbs, far more discreetly but in no less personal a fashion, portrayed the Soviet system as the fulfillment in practice of their own earlier conception of a democratic, cooperative society. Only this can explain their 1935 book's emphasis on Stalinism as the apogee of consumer cooperation and "community consumption." Even the term "civilization," which they finally settled on in the subtitle of *Soviet Communism: A New Civilization*, inverted the usage of their 1923 tract against inequality and poverty, *The Decay of Capitalist Civilization*.[19] Like Shaw, then, the Webbs came to see in Soviet communism the fulfillment of the causes they had championed their whole lives. Beatrice, who shared with Sidney the influences of positivism, utilitarianism, and evolutionary sociology (as the young Beatrice Potter, she had been personally mentored by Herbert Spencer), differed in her attraction to the Soviet order.[20] In her heart, she was pulled most of all by notions of justice, comradely collectivism, and equality.

Whereas Shaw redirected his failure as a politician toward a glorification of dictatorial men of action, Beatrice Webb held up the Fabian intellectuals to the Bolsheviks and found the Russians' daring dedication a reproach to her set's establishment privileges. The comparison made the Webbs' well-known frugality and ascetic rejection of aristocratic luxury seem tame indeed. "Starting to really work on Soviet Communism," she wrote in her diary on May 11, 1933, noting she had read Lenin's works and Krupskaia's biography:

> An amazing concentration and intensity of intellectual life and self-dedication under hard and dangerous conditions, in poverty and exile, spied upon by police agents, at risk of imprisonment, torture and death, surrounded by comrades in like circumstances. Comparing it with the comfort, ease, freedom, social esteem of the Shaws, Webbs, Wallaces, Oliviers and other labour and socialist leaders, how safe and enervating seems our own past existence.

On July 16, Beatrice reflected further on the Fabians as the quintessence of respectable, successful, establishment figures, "the ultra-essence of British bourgeois morality" and possessors of an "almost comical self-complacency." At the same time, she took distinct pride in the irony that this group had become the "most effective exponents and defenders" of Soviet communism; it made up for their earlier lack of revolutionary sacrifice. Beatrice's diary from the 1930s demonstrates how she internalized her status as "friend" of the Soviet Union. She observed how friendship with the Soviets dominated the Webbs' social life (which had always been an extension of their political preoccupations), since the "narrow circle of those who wish to see us" was "mostly friends of Russia."[21] While Shaw glorified the leader and Sidney Webb worshiped the system, Beatrice ruminated on the "vision of universal brotherhood" she found in a far-off community of revolutionary intellectuals.[22]

Both Webbs were in their early seventies when they began work on *Soviet Communism* in the early 1930s, and Beatrice confessed in her diary something inadmissible in public: as a research enterprise, the massive study was "an illegitimate venture—neither our equipment nor our opportunities suffice." All the same, it would be like a "preliminary survey of a new island by a knowl-edgeable geologist" and would "give zest to our declining years." Yet, the prob-lem of research became moot with their assumption that the Soviet system was the realization of blueprints drafted by fellow intellectuals, a real-life incarnation of the kind of imaginative constitution for British socialism the Webbs themselves had penned. The descriptions of its designers expressed in voluminous Soviet documentation thus became crucial evidence of how the system really worked. The published and statistical Soviet materials that the Webbs' work incorporated so unquestioningly were collected only in part dur-ing their Soviet visit of 1932 and Sidney's trip in 1934. For three years, Soviet ambassador to London Ivan Maiskii "systematically" arranged for "mountains of materials" to be delivered to the Webbs via diplomatic pouch.[23]

The Webbs may have been naive, but they were not completely gullible. They began their work in 1933, when reports of famine were rife. Beatrice's niece, Katherine Dobbs, was married to Malcolm Muggeridge, the initially pro-Soviet journalist from the *Manchester Guardian* who in 1932 traveled by train through to Ukraine and the Caucasus, smuggled out his notes through diplomatic pouch, and managed to publish some of the most forthright cov-erage of the great famine in the English-speaking world. There is *"some* fire behind this smoke of Malcolm's queerly malicious but sincerely felt denuncia-tion of Soviet Communism," Beatrice wrote on March 29, 1933. "What makes me uncomfortable is that we have no evidence to the contrary and that the violent purges of the C.P. and the passionate pleadings for greater and more sustained efforts on the agricultural front indicate a fear of catastrophe."[24] This was not an isolated concern. Throughout the 1930s, Beatrice, in the pri-vacy of her diary writing, expressed continual doubts about the Soviet Union, whose flaws she could only explain through its violent and backward "dark side."[25]

The Webbs traveled to the Soviet Union (together in 1932, Sidney alone in 1934) craving that "evidence to the contrary," wishing to be convinced by first-hand evidence to repudiate unsettling charges. For Sidney in particular, the visit was a chance to see how a new social system functioned in reality; each model institution visited therefore demonstrated that the blueprint worked. On September 19, 1934, Sidney Webb toured two collective farms designated for foreign visits, the Path of Il'ich and the Lenin Kolkhoz. These excursions dispelled his doubts in a resounding fashion. His VOKS guide reported his exclamation: "How vile appear the legends spread about famine and poverty in the USSR after this!"[26] Indeed, in their published works, the Webbs devoted a section to denying the famine. The work at once downplayed hunger's signifi-cance as a "partial failure of crops" and pointed to the handiwork of peasant "sabotage," necessitating the regrettable ruthlessness of kulak "liquidation."[27]

On September 17, Sidney Webb visited Arosev at VOKS and presented parts of *Soviet Communism* to him for corrections and commentary. He appeared to Arosev as "friendly and well disposed." Arosev deflected Webb's questions about Ukrainian separatism and particularly emphasized the "brilliant successes of our collectivization," reporting Webb's appreciative laughter when Arosev ridiculed reactionary views. Webb also asked his VOKS guide to read the book and not hesitate to make any corrections he deemed necessary. The draft chapters Webb presented were given to the Institute of Soviet Law for expert commentary as well.[28] Given all this evidence of Webb's friendship during his 1934 visit, it is remarkable how cautious the Soviet mediators were before the final publication of the Webbs' book. The 1934 VOKS file on Sidney Webb was reserved in tone, although it summed up his attitude toward the USSR as "positive" (*blagopriiatnoe*). Arosev was unsure of whether VOKS should give comments on Webb's manuscript because it did not have the entire text. Asking Kaganovich for instructions, Arosev was frankly worried: "It will be only part of his book, and the rest of his book could be to a certain measure and degree directed against us."[29] This underlines how suspicious Soviet authorities remained about even the most sympathetic friends and how final confirmation of the status of friend was reserved for those who had definitively proven support through publications and public statements.

In Soviet publications, the Webbs' *Soviet Communism* was criticized for its Fabian rejection of violent revolution and the depiction of the Party as a combination of "religious order" and corporate or professional body. In its more than 1,100 pages, there were more than enough awkward moments and divergences from Soviet orthodoxies—including, for example, references to the "persecution of the intelligentsia," the use of terror, and "elaborately staged" show trials—that the work, while quickly translated into Russian in 1936, was withheld from a wide Soviet readership.[30] The Politburo reviewed the Russian version of the Webbs' opus in May 1936 to discuss its Fabian deviations, deciding that it could be released only in a small run of 2,000–3,000 copies and distributed to a pre-approved list (and rejecting Radek's proposed trick of announcing publication in the press but displaying only a few copies for show in bookstore windows).[31]

The Webbs started their work in the aftermath of collectivization; they finished it on the eve of the great Moscow show trials and the subsequent news of the Nazi-Soviet Pact. Given her investment in the Stalin order as a fulfillment of comradely justice, Beatrice was devastated by the events of the late 1930s, and all her nagging doubts from previous years resurfaced with a vengeance. The Moscow trials were a "nasty shock," utterly bewildering and "absolutely incomprehensible," and could be explained only by the failure of Soviets to repudiate their medieval past. Any explanation dependent on Russian backwardness, she realized full well, was not exactly "consistent" with her book's glorification of Soviet communism as a new civilization. Even worse was the moment she received news of the Pact, a "day of holy horror": "Satan has won hands down. Stalin and Molotov have become the villains of the piece." She wished she could die: "Surely the aged and decrepit Webbs, having declared Soviet Communism as a new civilization in the hope of the human race, can sink out of life with a smile?" Throughout it all, Sidney remained unruffled. For him, it was not current events that were crucial but the historic transformation that had been set in motion by Soviet political and economic institutions. "To me [the Pact] seems the blackest tragedy in human history. Sidney observes that, within a century, it may be a forgotten episode. He refuses to be downcast."[32]

Stalinist Westernizers

Perhaps no less contradictory a phenomenon than Fabian Stalinists were their Soviet counterparts: the Stalinist Westernizers. These intellectuals and cultural figures were the Soviet mediators at the forefront of Soviet cultural diplomacy, and they were invested in interactions above all with European countries and cultivated meaningful relationships with foreign intellectuals. These figures influenced, even dominated, the fellow-travelers' points of contact with Soviet civilization in the 1930s. With the increasing restrictions on travel abroad and the import of foreign publications, Soviet intermediaries became increasingly privileged and increasingly important, for it was they who shaped Soviet coverage of the outside world. After the late 1920s, cosmopolitan Old Bolshevik intellectuals like Lunacharskii and Kameneva were swept aside. The new Stalinist leadership and the rapidly promoted "1930s generation" of cadres were mostly ignorant of foreign languages and in possession of, at best, limited international experience. While they faced many constraints and pressures, there remained a significant opening for those Westward-looking cosmopolitans who remained prominent. The Stalinist leadership, Soviet foreign policy, and the Comintern all remained focused to a large degree on Western Europe and the United States, and influencing Western opinion remained a potent aspiration.

Like the fellow-travelers themselves, the Westernizers were a motley group. They included some of the leading figures of the party-state with international pedigrees, such as Karl Radek, the ex-Trotskyist who became Stalin's top international advisor in the early 1930s; former "Right deviationist" Nikolai Bukharin, who launched a second career as international emissary and publicist though the mid-1930s; and Gorky, who personally knew and received high-priority foreign guests such as H.G. Wells. These Bolshevik giants, immersed in Soviet relations with the West, all had problematic pasts or unique arrangements with the Stalin leadership.

In a different category were prominent officials and ideologists, such as the influential journalist Mikhail Kol'tsov—head of the Foreign Commission of the Union of Writers, a member of the editorial board of *Pravda*, and a figure closely connected to the Comintern and secret police. Kol'tsov was one of the most authoritative Soviet commentators on international topics. He published more than 2,000 newspaper articles in his career, most notably as a correspondent, emissary, and combatant in the Spanish Civil War.[33] He covered Western political and cultural developments in his feuilletons and actively published and promoted foreign writers as effective head of a network of publishing houses employing more than a quarter of a million people. Kol'tsov, who had joined forces with the Stalin faction as early as 1924, was entrusted as a key organizer informing Moscow about the landmark meeting in Paris in 1935, the International Congress for the Defense of Culture. Among the French, Kol'tsov socialized comfortably with André Malraux, Antoine de Saint-Exupéry, and Louis Aragon; he was closely connected to the German intellectual diaspora in Paris and Moscow through his German common-law wife, Maria Osten.[34]

With the increasing mobilization of scientific and cultural figures, the line between Soviet cultural officials and Soviet intellectuals involved in the cultural-propaganda organs of the state became blurred. In 1936, for example, Kol'tsov's foreign commission of the Union of Writers included not only the polished former VOKS official Mikhail Apletin and the literary critic Sergei Dinamov, the old admirer of Dreiser in the 1920s, but two literary figures not often associated with the back rooms of the apparat: Boris Pasternak and Boris Pil'niak.[35] Many cultural officials were also cultural figures in their own right, such as Sergei Tret'iakov, a leading figure of the avant-garde and theorist of revolutionary culture. In the 1930s, Tret'iakov was flitting around Europe on behalf of Comintern and then Union of Writers international literary organizations, but he maintained his identity as a revolutionary artist working in theater, literature, and film until his arrest for espionage in July 1937.[36]

Moscow in the 1930s was the Comintern capital in which international émigrés mixed with Bolshevik re-immigrants, and, by virtue of nationality or biography, many members of the multinational communist elite were not only linguistic, but also cultural, amphibians. Perhaps the most remarkable case was that of Ilya Ehrenburg—who began a decades-long residence in Paris as a young Bolshevik Party member in the pre-war period and had a nasty falling out with Lenin but remained a close personal friend of Bukharin even as he evolved into a bohemian poet, political novelist, and café-frequenting intimate of Picasso and Diego Rivera. After 1921, Ehrenburg found a new modus vivendi, "to live in the West and publish in the USSR." In the 1920s, he was a fellow-traveler in the internal Soviet, literary sense of a non-party writer who remained in the good graces of the regime, although he was the constant target of proletarianizing militants. By the late 1920s, it was no longer possible to be a fellow-traveler in the former sense; Ehrenburg was hardly published in the Soviet Union, and the Depression-era crisis in book publishing deprived him of a living in Europe as well. In 1930–31 he came to his decision to adapt to the Stalin revolution.[37] He had to constantly declare his allegiance, as he did pointedly at the Union of Writers' conference: "One thing is for me incontestable: I am a rank-and-file Soviet writer. This is my joy, this is my pride. Of course, I have written and I write for foreigners too, but I do this as a Soviet writer."[38]

In fact, Ehrenburg was anything but. He quickly became a uniquely privileged, if embattled, Soviet cultural ambassador who was entrusted with sensitive international assignments, from organizing landmark Soviet-directed, anti-fascist cultural activities of the Popular Front to exerting pressure on French intellectuals at key moments. Boris Frezinskii has written that "Ehrenburg became a figure who for the repressive organs was counted as one of the leader's own, who could not be destroyed without his approval." Like other Stalinist Westernizers, such as Kol'tsov and Tret'iakov, Ehrenburg became a leading correspondent in republican Spain; like Tret'iakov, he was Jewish, and while his Jewish identity was exceedingly complex, it did give him a visceral commitment to anti-fascism. Just as anti-fascism played a major role in attracting Western intellectuals to the Soviet Union, in the case of Ehrenburg, it reinforced his decision to adhere to Stalin.

Foreign friends, of course, could be associated with and influenced by not just one but many mediators. Some were even married to them: Romain Rolland's wife was Mariia Kudasheva, who had worked as a translator and literary figure in the 1920s, including for VOKS, and who handled Rolland's voluminous Soviet correspondence in the 1930s. Elsa Triolet, sister of Maiakovskii's avant-garde muse, Lili Brik, was the wife of the surrealist Louis Aragon, who joined the French Communist Party and traveled with Elsa as his official interpreter to the Congress of Soviet Writers in 1934. As Sophie Coeuré has noted, Aragon, like many fellow-travelers, discovered Russia along with the USSR; for him the country was "incarnated by a woman, Elsa." Loves and friendships, fallings in and out, enmities and rivalries—such as those between Barbusse and Aragon, or Ehrenburg and Kol'tsov—all became intertwined with high politics on this international stage.[39]

Soviet diplomats were a special kind of mediator. Unlike the covert operations to recruit people of influence, such as the counter-espionage arm of the Red Army or the Comintern, diplomats functioned openly in the Soviet embassies in European capitals that were both outposts of Soviet life and a crossroads where politicians, journalists, and intellectuals met. Before 1933, by far the most important Soviet embassy on the continent was the one on Unter den Linden 7 in Berlin, which Karl Schlögel memorably described as a portal to the "USSR in miniature" and the center of the entire "German-Soviet scene."[40] The history of the Soviet embassy in Paris on the Rue de Grenelle as a landmark space in Soviet-European cultural relations remains to be written. But Sabine Dullin has tracked visitors to the embassy that, after 1933, turned into the primary "Sovietophilic milieu" in Europe and whose most habitual visitors were friendly journalists and radical intellectuals.[41] When Aleksandr Arosev was ambassador to Prague in 1929–32, he mixed with leftist intellectuals and cultural figures perhaps more than any other leading diplomat; his residence at Villa Tereza became a kind of cultural and political salon where the Soviet colony fraternized with Czechoslovak artists and intellectuals. In the evenings, Arosev recited the poetry of Blok and Briusov and declaimed the prose of Zoshchenko.[42]

The political and cultural landscape in Britain was less conducive to making the London embassy into a pro-Soviet intellectual and cultural center, but even so, among the prominent and talented Soviet diplomatic figures who became important for the intellectual friends of communism was the diplomat and former Menshevik, Ivan Maiskii. Like Arosev and other revolutionaries of his generation, Maiskii had had early and sustained experiences in Western Europe, learning English and French during his emigration after 1908. He forged close ties to Kameneva's cultural diplomacy in the 1920s and became ambassador to London from 1932–43.[43]

Maiskii's preoccupation with the world of the Foreign Office and the political establishment was accentuated by the weakness of the Communist Party and the radical Left in Britain. A protégé of commissar of foreign affairs M. M. Litvinov, Maiskii was sent to London in 1932—the same moment (as we shall see in the next chapter) as the Soviet pursuit of the extreme nationalist Right in Germany—with a mission to improve relations with British Conservatives.[44] The 1930s, however, were also the years when, arguably for the first time, a sizeable radical intelligentsia appeared in Britain, and with the efforts of figures like John Strachey, Harold J. Laski, and the Webbs, Soviet communism for the first time became "respectable." Among an elite in which "the bonds of family, school, university, profession and club" often trumped political divisions, Sidney and Beatrice Webb became Maiskii's most important bridge between the high politics of the Foreign Office and the public opinion of the intellectuals.[45] After one of his many weekends at Passfield Corner, the Webbs' country house, Maiskii wrote in his dairy about his love for the quiet intellectual enclave, where books and manuscripts took precedence over any display of luxury.[46]

The attraction mixed with reverence that Maiskii felt for the Webbs did not prevent him from using his visits shrewdly to shape their outlook on the USSR as they were preparing their two-volume work on Soviet communism. During the height of Beatrice Webb's doubts about famine and violence of collectivization in 1933, she wrote that Maiskii's weekend at Passfield "comforted us about the food shortage…Already in the spring sowing, good results were appearing." On the eve of publication of *Soviet Communism*, in March 1935, Maiskii spent another weekend with the couple, poring over the proofs, "he giving us corrections and additions to our statements or criticizing our conclusions." After publication, Maiskii hosted a celebratory lunch for forty admirers of the Webbs at the embassy.[47] In his well-known memoirs, Maiskii recorded with pride all the ways in which he had influenced the Webbs: their book represented a "great ideological victory."[48] Not only was it prestigious for mediators to rub shoulders with prominent foreign intellectuals, but winning them over as friends of the Soviet Union was a brilliant career boost.

What was absent in Maiskii's recollections, but not from his unpublished diary, despite the caution he took in his personal notes, was acknowledgement of what the Soviet diplomat received from his relationship with the Webbs. Sidney and Beatrice may have been in a state of learned ignorance when it came to the Soviet system, but they were acute observers of the personalities and trends of British politics and foreign relations. Over the course of their weekends together, Maiskii sought their advice and recorded their opinions in his diary at length. In particular, he found confirmation for his view that British "Conservatives can allow themselves the luxury of greater courage in relations with the USSR." After a weekend at Passfield in 1935, Maiskii recorded in his diary that the Webbs were the "cream of the world intelligentsia."[49]

Arosev, director of VOKS from 1932 to his death in the Great Purges, displayed of all the Stalinist Westernizers perhaps the most intense admiration of prominent intellectual friends of the Soviet Union. Internally tormented and pulled sharply between his political ambitions and a cultural orientation towards the West, Arosev in 1935 accompanied his Czechoslovak wife, Gertrude Freund, on one of her trips abroad as far as the Polish-Soviet border. There he penned a diary entry while stuck on the border station of Negoreloe on the westernmost fringe of the USSR, expressing a sentimental Westernism that might be considered shocking for a Stalin-era official: "For a long time I walked in the direction in which the train disappeared. Like a Scythian or a Mongol, I harbor inside me a great longing (*toska*) for the West and nothing acts on me like the evening sky or the setting sun…I adore the West and would like to follow the sun."[50] This emotional affinity colored his relations with European intellectuals, especially in the era of the Popular Front, and fostered hopes that the best of European and Soviet culture could be, if not ultimately merged, brought into a mutually supportive alliance.

It was not merely Arosev's European side that clashed with Soviet political realities; it was his identity as a writer, a man of culture, and a member of the intelligentsia. Indeed, Arosev was preoccupied with the same relationships between power and culture, intellectuals and politics that were central to the fellow-traveling of many of the Western intellectuals. He filtered this through a special preoccupation in the revolutionary movement—the raging debate about the relationship between workers and the intelligentsia.[51] Arosev pursued his political ambitions in voluminous letters to Stalin; he lamented his failure as a cultural creator to his diary. "Akh, my diary!" he wrote on March 6, 1935. "I write it as my terrible evaluation of myself and for nobody. I write in the evenings...I don't have time to write a diary...I need to write because I am a hard luck story, a failure, and lonely."[52]

The diary and the letters to Stalin converged on one topic: Russia and the West. In 1933, Arosev wrote in his diary about an economic crisis in Europe that coincided with a Soviet "crisis of culture," a heretical thought in light of official Soviet triumphalism. In an encounter in a Crimean sanatorium with Lev Mekhlis, the Institute of Red Professors graduate who was rising to great heights as editor of *Pravda* and one of Stalin's closest assistants, Arosev judged the ideologist severely as a representative of the new generation of cadres: "He displayed an ignorance that is characteristic of almost all our current cultural workers." Seeing events through the eyes of "European enthusiasts" such as Aragon, he was ashamed of the "lies and stupidities" of Soviet writers who met with the French in Paris in December 1935. He quoted the poet Esenin, "I am as a foreigner in my own land" (*V svoei zemle ia slovno inostranets*). On Stalin, he often exclaimed, "What an Asiatic!" (*Okh, aziat, aziat!*).[53]

Arosev's language and orientation appeared drastically different in his letters to Stalin. Pleading again and again for a more important diplomatic posting, he emphasized above all the danger of foreign enemies, rising Soviet strength and influence, and capitalist encirclement. In 1929, he openly used the imagery of masculine strength in an association with the *vozhd'*: goaded by Stalin's barbed comment to him that his time in Europe had made him as polite as a bourgeois, Arosev equated his own approach to the "complex psychology of *the leader of state and revolution*"—that is, to Stalin's own—while blasting abroad to the "bureaucratic" inclinations of cautious, diplomatic "old maids" (*starykh dev*). In 1931, writing from Prague, he talked as if he were on the front lines in a war, working from inside the "most important nests of the enemies of the USSR." In this formulation, not only the bourgeoisie, but the

West as a whole, was a despicable enemy: "Ah, if you could only see with what gigantic steps that old prostitute Europe is being destroyed."[54]

While it may be tempting to interpret Arosev's divergent depictions of Europe as simple hypocrisy, this is not the most convincing explanation. Although Arosev moved in differing directions in the midst of his tormented conflicts, he managed to reconcile Soviet loyalties and Western admirations. He wrote in his diary to explore his discontent; he wrote to Stalin to overcome it. Arosev also swelled with pride in describing Soviet achievements in his diary; his "testament" to his children, written over the course of six months in 1935, instructed them to "trust the collective" and "continue the revolutionary family line."[55] What Arosev admired most about the West were the cultural and intellectual figures who were friends of the Soviet Union, the great contributors to culture who also saw their future with the Soviets. They, too, wanted to link the best of Soviet and European culture; they, too, took risks in standing up against the Soviet Union's capitalist foes. If the old prostitute was destroyed, they would help create the new Europe.

For Arosev, then, the fellow-travelers were nothing less than a steadying factor in the longstanding balancing act between his Western orientation and his revolutionary and Stalinist commitments. In terms similar to Maiskii's praise of the Webbs, Arosev expressed a powerful sense of admiration for the Western intellectuals whom he met, especially during his multiple trips to Europe in 1934–36. The fellow-traveler to whom Arosev was closest, and whom he admired the most, was the French writer Romain Rolland. On January 7, 1935, he was inspired to the point of euphoria at Rolland's Swiss villa:

> In the villa the smell of books and the garden. I slept well. And the conversations with this great man moved me completely. Everything changed from its place. One wants to work as the bird sings, that is, as he does. Simple. No, I have never breathed in the atmosphere of the work of thought and literature as here, at his place.[56]

Arosev repeated, yet modified, his message about Western intellectuals in revealing ways when he was not confiding his insecurities to his diary but addressing other audiences. On May 4, 1935, he presented a talk to the Foreign Section of the Soviet Union of Writers entitled "Meetings and Conversations with the Most Prominent Representatives of the West European Intelligentsia." Arosev's descriptions of figures such as Gide and Rolland, and even specific phases, are at certain points similar or identical to those in his diary, unpublished records of public speeches, and widely disseminated published writings. In both the diary and his talk to the foreign section, Arosev maintained that not enough was being done to help the European friends of the Soviet Union.

The language of praise was less personal and effusive to the writers' organization, but there was still a large dose of hero worship. Arosev likened Gide's
apartment to a "laboratory of thought," the very phrase he used about his refuge from the bureaucracy, his own diary.[57]

The difference was that Arosev organized his public talk around the class
analysis of the intelligentsia—in Marxist-Leninist terms, a wavering stratum caught between the great poles of the bourgeoisie and the proletariat,
a nostrum that Arosev adapted and interpreted through the prism of his
observations about the differences between European and Soviet culture and
psychology. Thus, all Soviet writers, great and small (the latter presumably
including himself), were made significant by their participation in a unified
ideology and culture: "This is what distinguishes us from the West European
intelligentsia." In this light, even the greatest minds of Europe, including
Rolland and Gide, understood Soviet culture insufficiently: "[Gide] understands the character of the USSR rather well, but he is nonetheless French,
a person of West European culture, he is an individualist." While it is significant that Arosev altered the thrust of his messages about the West very
differently depending on his audience, there are hints in his diary that Arosev
was fundamentally sincere when he described the lack of a unifying ideology
as the great difference between Western and Soviet intellectuals.[58] Except, in
his diary, he added about the European intellectuals: "And they cannot not
see in all of us the mark of functionaries, a certain pallor and woodenness
in our faces." He regretted Stalin-era suspiciousness of even these outsiders:
"And we give little to them. We are even obliged, it seems, to be a little afraid
of them."[59] Arosev was fully capable of imagining himself and other Soviets
through foreign eyes.

To a mass Soviet audience, Arosev's depiction of the Western intellectuals
shifted yet again. In his pamphlet, *Conversations and Meetings with our Friends
in Europe*, published in a 1935 edition of 50,000 copies, Arosev popularized
his admiration for pro-Soviet European intellectuals. Rolland was the personification of the "entire past of European culture": "Both of them—Leonardo
da Vinci and Romain Rolland—share such strikingly identical eyes!" Here,
however, Western figures' positive traits consist almost entirely of their recognition of the great socialist homeland as a superior system to be emulated.
When he conveys his conversations, Arosev's Soviet views are contrasted with
the Europeans' lack of understanding. The analysis of intelligentsia wavering
is now split down a strict Western/Soviet divide, as European intellectuals
are guilty of "Hamletism."[60] In terms of its crude political message, Arosev's
propagandistic pamphlet for the Soviet masses most resembled the obvious
subtext of his confidential reports to Stalin: Western admiration for Soviet
socialism was proof of Soviet superiority and Stalin's own greatness.

For all the vast differences between the political and cultural contexts in which they operated, Western intellectual friends of communism and Soviet mediators had a number of traits in common. Sometimes, the Soviet Westernizers were motivated in their political service by considerations similar to those prompting Western intellectuals to assume the status of friends— most notably, anti-fascism. More frequently, a powerful cultural romance pulled them either to Soviet Russia or to the West. As intellectuals in politics, both groups eagerly mobilized themselves to crisscross the divide between culture and power. Above all, they had one other to admire. Surely it made a difference to the fellow-travelers that their Soviet "handlers" were among the most brilliant and accomplished figures in Soviet culture. Even as the Stalinist Westernizers carried out officially prescribed functions frequently requiring pressure and manipulation, they often harbored an intense respect and admiration for their European friends and the culture for which they stood.

Conversations with Stalin

The fascination of the fellow-travelers with power was fed by the remarkable circumstance of Stalin opening his Kremlin office to hours-long interviews with the foremost European intellectual visitors. Soviet mediators were also thrust into close contact with Stalin and the top leadership in preparing for and translating during these remarkable encounters, some of which were widely publicized. The conversations with visiting intellectual celebrities were very much phenomena of pre-war Stalinism. Before he assumed sole power in 1929, Stalin was relatively unknown internationally, and did not receive the largely literary intellectuals he chose to meet in the 1930s. By the end of the decade, the Purges and the Nazi-Soviet Pact had directed Stalin's attention away from the hitherto important priority of influencing Western public opinion. In this light, the 1930s were not only the high point of European and American sympathy for the Soviet experiment, but the heyday of Stalin's attention to Western intellectuals. The most important events of this period were Stalin's reception of Bernard Shaw and Emil Ludwig in 1931, H. G. Wells in 1934, Henri Barbusse on several occasions, Romain Rolland in 1935, and Lion Feuchtwanger in 1937.[61]

Stalin himself reflected and amplified some of the key contradictions of the second revolution vis-à-vis the West. Just as he adopted Western yardsticks in a war against backwardness predicated upon besting enemies in the West, so also he touted the heroic qualities of the Russian people for mobilizational purposes while, for a time, devoting significant effort to winning over Western opinion makers whose views were so respected that they lent crucial support, among other things, for the creation of his cult at home.[62] Despite the lines that were already being drawn between Stalin and the Europeanized Old Bolsheviks, the moustachioed dictator was in his way eminently qualified to be taken for something of an intellectual in power: among foreign literary figures who were not Marxist theoreticians, he assumed authority on Marxist-Leninist theory, and he had a more than decent knowledge of Russian and European literary classics. Stalin also had a "superb memory" and prepared intensively with briefings on the "views, tastes, and preferences" of his famous guests.[63] As he set about crafting his own and the Soviet Union's image abroad, the stage was set for the intellectuals to diverge over whether he was a humble man of the people or a philosopher-king.

With the possible exception of the 1931 meeting with Shaw, the records of which have not been found, the conversations with Stalin in the early part of the decade served raison d'etat and the nascent Stalin cult simultaneously, in the sense that Stalin's own image abroad was closely connected to Western opinion about the Soviet experiment. Stalin's choice of an interview with the writer and journalist Emil Ludwig, whom he received on December 31, 1931, was clearly connected to the international dimensions of the cult: Ludwig had published biographical-fictional works about Bismarck and Napoleon, among other great historical figures.

The didactic and instructional purposes behind the general secretary's foray into international image making are suggested by the uniform structure of Stalin's responses to Ludwig's questions. The standard practice for Soviet publication of such interviews in the 1930s was to first allow both parties to correct them and to include consideration by members of the Politburo before they were edited to eliminate anything deemed unsuitable for a mass audience. In the published version, all of Stalin's comments to Ludwig were directed at denying, correcting, and instructing. For example, Stalin repudiated any comparison between his own modernization program and the Westernization of Peter the Great, denying that power in the USSR was in the hands of one person. The text of the conversation was given a mass domestic audience, as it was published in Soviet newspapers, in an oft-reprinted 1932 brochure, and in the party theoretical journal Bol'shevik on April 30, 1932 (it was also included in Stalin's collected works).[64]

Stalin's attempt to deflect another of Ludwig's queries, by contrast, was strikingly ambivalent: the question of Stalin's knowledge of Europe and the outside world, closely connected to Stalin's history as an underground party worker rather than an émigré party theoretician. Tactfully yet directly, Ludwig asked him to contrast Lenin's long European emigration with his own limited time abroad. Stalin's response was a wonderful reflection of the tensions within the 1930s Soviet order as a whole. On the one hand, he attributed great importance to the study of European economies, technology, labor, and literature, which, he claimed, one could understand just as well from afar; while on the other hand, he took an oft-cited jab at the party intellectuals: "I know many comrades who were abroad for twenty years, lived somewhere in Charlottenburg or in the Latin Quarter, sat for years in cafes and drank beer, and who yet did not manage to acquire a knowledge of Europe and failed to understand it."[65] Ludwig's interview corresponded to a time when key Soviet ideologists and members of Stalin's entourage were intensely vying to write a popular Soviet biography of Stalin, one version for domestic consumption and another for international audiences. Ludwig was one of the earliest candidates considered for the latter option; Gorky became the leading candidate in 1932.[66] The mass promotion of Stalin had international and domestic dimensions, and the two were closely intertwined.

The case of French writer and communist organizer Henri Barbusse, whom Stalin met personally in 1927, 1932, 1933, and 1934, is a prime example of significant internal-external links in the emergence of the Stalin cult. Crucially, both the Stalin cult and its denial were promoted simultaneously after 1929. This was the polar opposite of the cult of Mussolini under Fascism or the *Führerprinzip* enshrined in Nazi ideology, for Marxist materialism and Soviet collectivism appeared incompatible with a personality cult in an age in which right-wing and capitalist leaders were constructing their own. As a result, the very notion of Stalin's personal dictatorship became taboo even as the cult became a central feature of Soviet life. Therefore, an alternative explanation for the glorification of Stalin had to be advanced. The creators of the Stalin cult soon found a solution: to extol Stalin's modesty and grudging acceptance of popular adulation. Behind the scenes, the leader stage-managed his own resistance to acclaim as carefully as the other aspects of the cult around him. Foreigners received by Stalin—Ludwig, Barbusse, and, later, Feuchtwanger—played an important role in propagating the image of his unpretentious modesty.[67] In this context, Barbusse's 1935 biography in French, *Stalin, A New World Seen Through One Man* (published in Russian translation a year later) appears explicitly aimed at demonstrating the authenticity of Soviet popular acclaim for Stalin and the impossibility of his personal dictatorship.[68]

Like Aragon, Barbusse confounded the division between party members and largely non-party fellow-travelers. His status as a Communist allowed him to carry out sensitive missions in the Comintern and Soviet-led front organizations of the 1920s. At the same time, Barbusse was bitterly attacked by cultural militants, especially those based in the Comintern's MORP. Their antagonism, along with the anti-intellectualism of the French Communist Party in this period, prevented him from becoming a fully accepted party insider; at the same time, perhaps as a result, he was still treated not so much as a foreign Communist but in the same category of non-party Western friends by VOKS, which was usually very careful to stay away from public links to international communism.[69]

In line with the goals of Soviet agencies like VOKS (and the Comintern-sponsored Münzenberg) Barbusse wanted to use his journal *Monde* after 1928 to attract a broad coalition of leftist and pro-Soviet, yet non-party intellectuals; like many of the Western friends, he hoped to have an influence on the Soviet order. In 1928, Barbusse even floated a project by which control over Western works translated into Russian would be made by a committee at his journal.[70]

Barbusse formed his allegiance to Stalin before the general secretary's consolidation of sole power at the end of the 1920s and before the first inklings of

Figure 6.3 Henri Barbusse at a Moscow factory, November 28, 1930. The only prominent Western intellectual who met with Stalin in the 1920s as well as the 1930s, Barbusse played a key role in the creation of the Stalin cult. Source: RIA Novosti Photo Library.

the Stalin cult. He was the only intellectual to meet with Stalin in the 1920s as well as in the 1930s. Of great interest is Barbusse's two-and-a-half-hour conversation with Stalin from 1927, for clearly it is not the case, as Medvedev suggests, that Shaw, in 1931, was the first European writer to meet Stalin.[71] In 1927, Barbusse spoke to Stalin on the eve of a visit to Georgia and the South Caucasus. Barbusse approached Stalin with a concrete problem: he needed to distinguish Soviet political violence, including the integration of independent Georgia in 1920, from the fascist violence he was mobilizing intellectuals against in Europe. How should he explain to Europeans the difference between fascist ("white") and Red Terror? Stalin said that after 1918 there was no such thing as Red Terror; the "shootings did not repeat themselves." If it weren't for the ruthlessness and strength of the capitalists, moreover, the Soviet Union might have been able to abolish the death penalty. "Of course," Stalin continued, "the death penalty is an unpleasant thing. Who finds it pleasant to kill people?" Who indeed? At this moment, Barbusse clearly signaled his acceptance: "This is absolutely correct. In current conditions eliminating the death penalty would be suicide for Soviet power."[72] Here was someone upon whom Stalin could rely. Quite unlike the intellectual games of the unpredictable Shaw or the earnest declarations of the didactic Rolland, Barbusse had approached Stalin for his "directive" and conveyed his receipt of the message. The benefits of Soviet travel could work both ways; the goodwill Barbusse built up in Moscow in 1927, including with Stalin, may have allowed him to resist the attacks that ensued with the Comintern's "Left turn" of the late 1920s.[73]

Barbusse's 1928 book on the Caucasus—part travelogue playing on the exotic locale, part semi-fictional interviews with natives, and part political tract—was aimed especially at countering émigré charges of "red imperialism" connected to the end of Menshevik-led independent Georgia in 1920. The work was structured around the canonical "yesterday and today" dichotomy favored in VOKS and Comintern propaganda. It mentioned Stalin only once. Here, in embryonic form, is the modest, simple people's leader of Barbusse's 1935 *Staline*.[74]

The attractiveness of Barbusse to Stalin as a trustworthy biographer must have been heightened by the working relationship they developed over antifascist front organizations in the early 1930s.[75] Stalin's support for Barbusse included his editing of translations of Barbusse's articles for *Pravda,* and when Mekhlis was concerned with the French writer's unorthodox statements on the independence of literature from political movements, Stalin ordered: "It is necessary to publish without changes. The author of the article is responsible for mistakes in the article, for it is a signed piece. Stalin."[76] In the wake of his meeting with Stalin in late 1932, Barbusse, who was in close contact with Willi Münzenberg over the peace movement launched in Amsterdam, announced that he wished to become Stalin's biographer. In December, the chief ideologues at the Central Committee's Kul'tprop, trusted operatives from Stalin's secretariat, and the top experts at the Institute of Marxism-Leninism jumped at the chance and arranged to provide the materials—a chain of reactions unthinkable without Stalin's own assent. The key condition was that Barbusse's entire manuscript would be checked and subject to editorial suggestions. Barbusse's assurances while in Moscow that he would break with the French "Trotskyist elements" whom he had allowed to publish in his journal *Monde* assuaged one significant concern.[77]

Barbusse's meetings with Stalin in 1933 and 1934 occurred at a key moment in the construction of the personality cult, which had been launched during the celebration of the leader's fiftieth birthday in 1929. By mid-1933, according to Plamper, "the cult took off in earnest" and a process of canonizing the depiction of Stalin reached a new level, in part signaled by the increasing centralization of the cult's organization in Stalin's personal secretariat. Although many actors were involved in creating the cult, in part because it could not be labeled as such, Barbusse was put in contact not only with Stalin but also with key Soviet and Comintern players—the head of Stalin's secretariat Poskrebyshev, the head of the Central Committee's Kul'tprop, A. I. Stetskii, and Münzenberg— during the years he was actively preparing the biography and the screenplay for a film about Stalin. The film, for which Barbusse signed a contract with Mezhrabpomfilm, was never made because of Barbusse's death in Moscow in August 1935. By the time he launched his Stalin biography, Barbusse had completely given himself over to the glorification of the leader, referring to him in personal notes as "great comrade." In keeping with the contemporary Soviet debate over which media were suited to portray Stalin, he considered Stalin too great to be portrayed theatrically. The script of his film solved this dilemma by showing a larger-than-life image, the inspiration behind the great historical progression of the class struggle in Russia starting in 1898.[78]

Barbusse's 1935 *Staline*, published in Russian in serial and book form in 1936 after a suitable claimant to the job of domestic biographer failed to emerge, is an example of a foreign friend successfully influencing Soviet affairs—in this case through a major addition to the Stalin cult. One of the book's phrases, which was also its main argument—"Stalin is the Lenin of today"—became one of the cult's most celebrated slogans. According to the recollection of a leading party historian favored by Stalin, Isaak Mints, the *khoziain* (boss) wrote this slogan himself and put it into play at the *Pravda* editorial board via Mekhlis or Gorky, around the same time that it was transmitted to Barbusse by the functionaries who edited his book.[79] Because Barbusse's work was formed and edited with input from Stalin and his chief ideologists, it was not entirely a "foreign" creation. In other ways, its non-Soviet nature assumed great importance.

No matter how committed Barbusse was to the cause of Stalin's glorification, from the point of view of the ideologues of Marxism-Leninism his
work was filled with glaring errors. Stetskii's extensive critique of the manuscript highlighted how Barbusse, an intellectual among Communists, was in
his own way as obsessed with the divide between intellectuals and power as
the Fabians, Rolland, and many other fellow-travelers. The humbleness and
modesty of the proletarian *vozhd'* dictated by the denial of the cult held unexpected repercussions in light of this European intellectual preoccupation. The
French writer initially placed enormous stress on Stalin as an empiricist, an
applied Marxist, and a *praktik* filled with common sense—in other words, a
man of action—rather than, in Stetskii's words, "the greatest theoretician of
Marxism after Lenin." Even after Stetskii's editorial interventions, Stalin in
Barbusse's text was still dubbed a "simple man" and "a man of action." In the
context of leader cults more broadly, there was a longstanding tradition, after
the rise of popular sovereignty, of portraying political leaders as both embody-
ing the masses and standing above them.[80] In the interwar years of mass politics, the balance struck between the two became a key issue in the Stalin cult.
Barbusse's biography became the canonical text, as Coeuré has discussed, for
a specifically French communist image of Stalin as a humble, simple man of
the people, as opposed to the domestic Soviet glorification of the genius theoretician. Indeed, the Soviet censorship impounded a 1935 issue of *Monde* that
contained a review by the communist writer Paul Nizan of the French edition
of Barbusse's biography, because of a well-meaning, yet of course heretical, reference to intellectuals' attraction to Trotsky as a thinker in power as opposed
to Stalin, *l'homme des événements.*[81]

A second, closely related problem that Stetskii worked even harder to alter
was Barbusse's portrayal of Trotsky as a revolutionary of a different "temperament" from Stalin—as opposed to the diabolical incarnation of the opposition's alien social and economic roots. On this point, Barbusse refused to bend,
for the published text—while containing a robust condemnation of Trotsky as
an unreconstructed Menshevik—still focused on the exiled oppositionist as a
different type of leader than Stalin. While the words "theoretician" and "intellectual" were absent in his descriptions of Trotsky, Barbusse did not need to
use them: Barbusse's Trotsky had too much imagination, loved to talk too
much, and was opinionated and verbose, whereas the general secretary was the
"man of the situation" (*l'homme de la situation*) with "practical sense." In sum:
"these are two types of men."[82] In the end, while a number of fellow-travelers
like Shaw and the Webbs were attracted to Stalin as a Marxist-Leninist social
engineer, and hence a kind of intellectual in power, Barbusse's Stalin emerged
as the anti-intellectual as much as the anti-Trotsky, whose understanding of
the true essence of Leninism was virtually instinctual.

While Barbusse manipulated images that had long pedigrees on the European Left, he was also keenly attuned to the role of the intellectual in the communist movement as a result of his own, typical problems operating in the anti-intellectual atmosphere of the French Communist Party. Arriving in Moscow on one of his many visits, Barbusse felt it necessary to apologize for speaking in the name of French workers, advancing the justification that true intelligence consisted in complete unity and merger with the working masses. At one key juncture in his biography, Barbusse treated Stalin not simply as an anti-intellectual man of action but as the incarnation of this ideal merger: "a man with the head of a *savant*, the face of a worker, and the outfit of a simple soldier."[83] This three-headed beast was at once a man of knowledge standing above the masses and a fighter at one with the people. Barbusse could give no higher validation for the role of the *savant* in the communist movement.

It was clearly the biography's utterly non-Soviet style and Barbusse's heightened stature as a European outsider that gave his work its Soviet traction. In 1935, Mikhail Kol'tsov praised *Staline* as Barbusse's greatest accomplishment since *Le Feu*, but he called attention to the author's "typically foreign" definitions and perspectives, "touching in their romanticism, sometimes even naïve for the native ear and eye." Yet Kol'tsov recognized that it was precisely this "foreign aspect" that would make the work appealing to Soviet readers. Especially revealing is how Kol'tsov, the Stalinist Westernizer, called attention to the cultural geography of the book's opening, when the masses chant "Long Live Comrade Stalin!" in Red Square: "He is indeed the center, the heart of everything that radiates with light from Moscow around the entire world." The quotation came from Barbusse, but Kol'tsov had altered it slightly: whereas Barbusse had written about Moscow merely as a "place" (*milieu*), the Soviet mediator made certain to put Stalin at Moscow's "center."[84] Through Stalin, Moscow had become the center of the world rather than the backward periphery, yet it was unable to assume that stature without foreign acclaim.

To the Foreign Commission of the Union of Writers, Kol'tsov spoke more frankly about the Barbusse translation in 1936, revealing that "we could not decide for a long time whether to publish this book in Russian or not." On the one hand, "absolutely everything" in the book was known to Soviet audiences, but the history of the Party was recounted "rather imprecisely." Kol'tsov still thought the decision to translate had been an inspired one: "Nonetheless the book was published and it has had great success, because it has great charm in the sense that it is told by an outsider in another language." This other language was not French, for, after all, the book had been translated; what was attractive was its style not rigidly bound by the formulaic conventions of Soviet ideospeak. One of the cornerstones of the Stalin cult—recognition of Stalin as the Lenin of today— was put in place by this "foreign" contribution.

There was also an ample connection to the burgeoning cult in the decision of Lenin's heir to receive H. G. Wells in the Kremlin on July 23, 1934. For in 1920, the pioneering science fiction writer had famously visited Lenin and hailed the "dreamer in the Kremlin."

Having discussed plans for electrification in Moscow, Wells had, to Lenin's delight, returned home to lobby the British Foreign Office to improve relations with the new Russia. Stalin's proxy, Maiskii, cleverly reminded Wells of Lenin's parting invitation to return a decade later. In 1934, there were immediate tactical reasons to arrange such a meeting with Wells—as, indeed, there appear to have been for several other of Stalin's invitations. In particular, Wells was president of the International PEN club at a time when preparations were being made for the Congress of Soviet Writers; similarly, Rolland was received in 1935 on the heels of the Franco-Soviet mutual assistance treaty. At the same time, Wells had a greater international stature than either Ludwig or Barbusse. He had been invited to the White House by four U.S. presidents, and it is noteworthy that he arrived in Moscow on the heels of the last of those meetings, with Franklin D. Roosevelt. Wells wrote not only science fiction but also

Figure 6.4 Vladimir Lenin conversing with H. G. Wells in his Kremlin study, January 10, 1920. To entice Wells to meet Stalin in 1934, Soviet diplomat Ivan Maiskii reminded him of Lenin's parting invitation to return and see Soviet progress after a decade had passed. Source: RIA Novosti Photo Library.

political works, innovative tracts on futurology, and popular world history. He was a socialist who propounded the idea of a socialist world-state, a former Fabian who, in addition to the friendship with Gorky, moved in the same circles as the Webbs and Shaw. They helped Maiskii to recruit him for the visit.[85]

To the disappointment of Stalin's strategists, however, it turned out that Wells was particularly unsusceptible to the mystique of the philosopher-king, unlike fellow-travelers such as Shaw and Rolland. The technocratic Wells was attracted to the Soviet order for a different reason: he was drawn to the vanguard of the proletariat rather than the notion of revolutionary intellectual leader. A profoundly elitist admirer of those who developed new technology, Wells had long before antagonized the Fabian Society with an outlandish fantasy about turning it into a Samurai-like governing caste. Later, it was Wells' enthusiasm for an administratively advanced order of disciplined organizers that fired him with enthusiasm for Lenin's concept of the Communist Party. His technocratic views meant that he was one of the many interwar critics to think of parliamentary democracy as a relic of the past, even as he disdained the Soviet glorification of the working masses. In his 1934 autobiography, Wells still considered his most successful book to be his 1906 *Modern Utopia*, a treatise that divided citizens into an administrative and creative elite ruling over the untutored proles, whom he dubbed the "dull" and "base" classes. "Particularly the appearance of such successful organizers as the Communist Party and the Italian fascists," he maintained in 1934, "has greatly strengthened my belief in the essential soundness of this conception of the governing order of the future." Like Shaw, Wells was inclined to delude himself about his own links to the founders of Russian communism, for he depicted Lenin as steadily developing "an extraordinarily similar scheme, the reconstructed Communist Party." Wells never quite located the "genetic connection" between Lenin's scheme and his own.[86]

Delusions of grandeur were on full display during Wells' three-hour talk with Stalin, in which Wells tried fruitlessly to convince the inventor of "socialism in one country" that Roosevelt's New Deal and Stalin's Five-Year Plans could be the first steps toward a planned world-state. After reading the transcript, the quick-witted Shaw showed great perception about the nature of the exchange: "Stalin listens attentively and seriously to Wells... always hitting the nail precisely on the head in his reply. Wells does not listen to Stalin: he only waits with suffering patience to begin again when Stalin stops. He thinks he knows better than Stalin all that Stalin knows. He has not come to be instructed by Stalin, but to instruct him."[87] Stalin may not have been converted to Wells' version of world socialism, but he did dispel the Englishman's preconceptions of a power-hungry and fanatical "Georgian highlander whose spirit had never completely emerged from its native mountain glen." In this sense, the meeting was a Stalinist triumph: on return, Wells publicly declared that "I never met a man more candid, fair and honest."[88]

Soviet leaders, however, were not inclined to think in terms of partial success. Wells' critical comments about Stalin in his *Autobiography*, sent by Radek to Stalin in Russian translation on November 9, 1934, inclined top Soviet officials such as Radek and Litvinov to discuss damage control. As Radek wryly remarked to Stalin, this time "we didn't manage to seduce the girl."[89]

Three rounds of high-level Soviet political activity surrounding the Wells visit can be seen as typical for these sorts of visits. First was a round of monitoring, prediction, and jockeying for influence among the officials managing the writer's stay on Soviet soil.[90] Second came the flurry of discussions concerning the publication of the text of Wells' conversation with Stalin. Stalin and Wells both edited the text, which was then reviewed by the high-level diplomat who translated for Stalin, Konstantin Umanskii; by Maiskii, who had played the key role in arranging the visit; and by all the members of the Politburo. Finally, the appearance of Wells' autobiography set off a round of discussion about a Soviet response: Litvinov favored a reply, while Radek was unsure and turned to Stalin for his decision. Radek's advice is revealing. He suggested "mocking" Wells rather than berating or attacking (*rugatiia*). Rather than ad hominem mockery, moreover, Radek advised class analysis of Wells as reflecting the "bourgeois prejudices of the intelligentsia." When Radek discovered Shaw's response to Wells in the *New Statesman and Nation*, however, he found a better solution: to let Shaw do the mockery for him. Shaw's remarks were translated for the Soviet press—minus the maverick playwright's offhand references to Stalin as a nationalist and opportunist.[91]

Stalin's conversation with Wells, as with the meeting with Barbusse, suggests the extent to which Stalin was prompted by a mixture of international and domestic goals in his conversations with Western intellectuals. The predominance of British and French figures among those Stalin met in the 1930s itself speaks to the goal of influencing Western public opinion in countries key to Soviet foreign policy. At the same time, the care that Stalin and his entourage put into editing the conversations with foreigners and the broad dissemination of the talks with Wells and others in Russian suggest that they were deeply preoccupied with the domestic Soviet consumption of the transcripts. The meetings with Ludwig, Wells, and Barbusse were integrally connected to the early stages of the Stalin cult, suggesting how cultivating Stalin's image abroad was a priority in furthering the cult at home.

Romain Rolland—who conversed with Stalin with his bilingual Russian wife, Kudasheva, and his admirer Arosev as translators on June 28, 1935— was the fellow-traveler who was perhaps Soviet cultural diplomacy's most illustrious asset. A Nobel Prize winner who was a writer, dramatist, musicologist, and popular biographer, Rolland came with the authority and reputation of the *grand écrivain*, routinely referred to as *maître* by the Soviet intellectual mediators who addressed him. He was a man of causes: one of the most prominent pacifists in World War I, during which he was vilified for his stance, he was also a prominent spokesman for German-French cultural reconciliation and later a leading champion of anti-fascist culture and East-West dialogue. Very different from the flamboyant Shaw, or, for that matter, the non-conformist Gide, Rolland reminded many observers of a clergyman: thin, frail, earnest, and puritanical, he was a didactic and compulsive correspondent. Rolland's sympathy for Stalinism was neither simple nor fragile; sturdy enough to be battered but not destroyed by purge and pact, it was nourished by a startlingly wide array of sources. Some were ideological and cultural—his longstanding socialism and expertise in the French Revolution, his anti-fascism, his enthusiasm for popular enlightenment. Others were personal: his status as friend; the role of mediators, not least his wife, Kudasheva; his longstanding correspondent, Gorky; and the worriedly attentive Arosev. Perhaps the most striking and the most disturbing factor was the fact that Rolland was an "inveterate hero-worshiper."[92] The year 1935 marked the moment when he transferred his longstanding hero-worship of great historical figures to Stalin.

In the unedited, Russian text of Rolland's talk with Stalin, Rolland hailed Stalin as the first representative and source of the new humanism. In an opening statement, he spoke of how millions in the West looked to the USSR to solve the current economic and moral crisis. One must do more than repeat the words of Beethoven, "*Ô homme, aide-toi toi même!* Rather, one must aid them and give them advice.[93] Beethoven was the life on which Rolland had based his most famous work, the monumental Bildungsroman *Jean-Christophe* (1903–12); Rolland's popular 1903 biography of Beethoven was the prototype for his series of *Lives of Illustrious Men*. In later years, Rolland began his habit of turning East to finding great personalities to mythologize: Tolstoy and Gandhi. They were also role models, however, for Rolland aspired to become the European Tolstoy. In all these works, written for a mass audience in an accessible yet serious style of *haute vulgarisation*, Rolland explored the heroic nature of geniuses who overcame hardship in order to devote themselves to humanity. In his 1920s infatuation with Gandhi, pacifism and pan-European reconciliation were supplanted by anti-imperialism and a grander East-West reconciliation. Rolland kept his doubts about Gandhi's nationalism private, even when the mahatma visited Fascist Italy in 1931, much as he agonized only in private about Stalin and the Soviet Union later in the decade. Since Rolland's pacifism worried the Soviets, Rolland made a point in 1935 of assuring Stalin that as a Soviet sympathizer he would not oppose war in all circumstances.[94]

With this renunciation of his previous views, he cemented his friendship and replaced Gandhi with Stalin as mankind's heroic humanist.

Rolland's earlier heroes had radiated strength, but they were all artists and intellectuals. For Rolland, as for the Fabians, the Bolsheviks represented a potential merger of the intellectual and the man of action. He indicated as much when talking about the "new humanism" to Stalin, referring to Marx and Lenin as founders of *la parti intellectuelle*. This merger was revealed even more clearly in Rolland's 1935 book *Compagnons de route*, in which chapters about his literary "companions" Shakespeare and Goethe were supplemented by a chapter on Lenin as a potential synthesis of the Russian revolutionary tradition with European culture. "Two maxims, which complete each other: 'We must dream,' says the man of action [Lenin]. And the man of the dream [Goethe]: 'We must act!' "[95] At Villaneuve, Arosev found Rolland on the eve of his Soviet journey regretful over his own quiet life and eager to hear stories about Stalin and the revolutionary underground. In a personal letter sent from Moscow during his 1935 visit, Rolland wrote about Hamlet—Arosev's own favorite metaphor for the wavering intellectual—and compared him to Shakespeare's warrior Fortinbras, whose name in French means "strong-in-arm." Rolland talked about how he could not be like Fortinbras—he had too much compassion and too much horror in his heart. "But as opposed to me, Fortinbras is right."[96] After his meeting with Stalin, Arosev crowed to the general secretary, Rolland was so euphoric he was ready to kiss him: Rolland viewed their meeting as the great deed of his life.[97]

At the forefront of Rolland's concerns raised directly with Stalin was the status of "the truest friends of the USSR," by which Rolland, of course, meant himself. All the concrete policy questions Rolland raised—about the exiled Trotsky supporter Victor Serge, who had become a *cause célèbre* in Europe, and about the distinctly non-humanistic Soviet decree of April 7, 1935, establishing criminal responsibility for juveniles over age twelve—were framed in terms of his own desire and ability to help explain Soviet affairs to Europe. "I am completely sure that he [Serge] deserved his punishment...but it was necessary to explain this fact to the mass of friends of the USSR." Rolland called for a "campaign of explanation" for sympathizers, and privileged information for himself, perhaps through the organization of VOKS. Indeed, Rolland had complained to Gorky throughout the early 1930s that he did not have the information to assuage doubts and rebut accusations against the Soviet Union. For his part, Stalin allowed that the Soviets did not sufficiently "inform and arm our friends," but he professed that the reason was simple respect for the autonomy of people living in a completely different place: "To direct these people from Moscow would be from our part too bold."[98] Such passages lend support to the recollection of his wartime translator: "Stalin loved and knew how to throw dust in the eyes of foreigners."[99] The draconian 1935 shift on juvenile delinquency was merely a decree broadcast for pedagogical purposes, Stalin explained, to scare dangerous hooligans and bandits. For obvious reasons, this fact could not be publicized. "This is true, this is true," Rolland answered, and in his diary he reflected on how Westerners forgot about "the old barbarous Russia" Bolshevik leaders were forced to confront.[100] Stalin's explanations may have convinced Rolland, but Soviet audiences might have found them ridiculous. Perhaps this is why the Rolland-Stalin transcript, unlike several others, was never published.

In 1935, Rolland evinced a keen awareness of his status as "friend." In his obligatory parting letter to the *vozhd'* on June 20, 1935, for example, he pledged that as long as he lived he would never retreat from the obligation of defending the heroic construction of the new world. Even after the Purges, he upheld his end of the bargain by not publicly criticizing the Soviets.[101] Stalin did finally decide to give something to Rolland in return. At the January 1935 International Writers' Congress for Defense of Culture in Paris, a number of speakers sympathetic to Trotsky had taken up the cause of the imprisoned Serge. In a gesture that appeared at once the height of reasonableness, or, from another point of view, a magnanimous autocratic amnesty, Stalin announced to Rolland that there was no reason Serge could not be released. Indeed, Soviet leaders were used to such requests from their own intellectuals; Stalin was treating Rolland much like he treated that patron extraordinaire, Gorky. In fact, the Serge affair showed just how crucial Rolland's relationship with Gorky was to his status as friend. After Stalin made his statement, Rolland followed up with Gorky, who wrote his friend Iagoda. Serge soon appeared in Paris.[102]

To the Soviets, however, true friendship meant following the Soviet line, whatever it might be and wherever it might lead, not providing the kind of privileged information Rolland craved on Soviet intentions and policies. Rolland appeared genuinely anguished that European public opinion on the USSR was suffering; but he also presented himself to Stalin as someone who knew Europe and how to handle European debates far better than the Soviets did. If he could have cited insider information, of course, it would have raised his stature among intellectuals and artists preoccupied with the debate over the Soviet Union. But Rolland could not even get an answer on publishing the transcript of his talk with Stalin, or excerpts from it, to use in his European discussions. Numerous petitions to Stalin were of no avail. Rolland even tried to enlist Bukharin, whom he met for the first of three times on June 25, 1935, at a VOKS reception. On the eve of the Purge trials, Bukharin desperately tried to take credit for Rolland's loyalty to the Soviet cause, telling Molotov on December 1, 1936: "I hope that I talked so convincingly that here as well is a drop of my honey, when R[omain] R[olland] does not conduct himself like A[ndré] Gide."[103]

Rolland's marriage made it possible for him to meet with Kudasheva's relatives during his 1935 visit, and in particular her son, Sergei Kudashev, then a student at Moscow University. Sergei met with Rolland in intimate settings to talk about Soviet conditions, ideological conformity, and the terror in Leningrad following the Kirov assassination.[104] Rolland's apologia for Stalinism was not predicated on a complete lack of information.

The decision to uphold his status as loyal friend cannot be explained only by hero worship. There was also a cultural logic that conditioned his uncritical response. Just as German Left intellectuals had experienced a strong synergy with Soviet culture starting in the 1920s, the Popular Front brought to French intellectuals their own houses of culture, Agitprop theater, and workers' universities; popular enlightenment against the fascist danger was one of Rolland's most beloved causes. As early as the turn of the twentieth century, Rolland had been the prime mover in the people's-theater movement, and his writings had influenced the Soviet theorists of mass spectacle. He became enamored, above

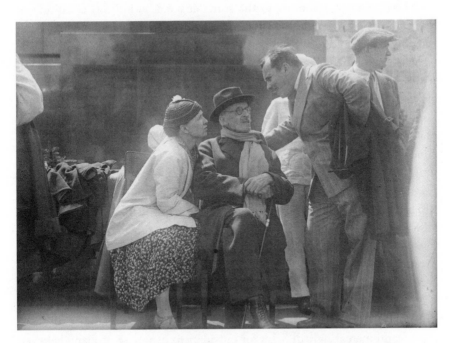

Figure 6.5 Romain Rolland (sitting); Mariia Kudasheva, his wife and translator; and Aleksandr Arosev, the director of VOKS, on the reviewing stand of the Lenin Mausoleum on June 30, 1935. After viewing a physical-culture parade with Stalin, Rolland recorded in his diary: "A festival of the People—magnificent!" Source: *Rossiiskii gosudarstvennyi arkhiv kinofotodokumentov* (RGAKFD).

all, with the notions of a "new man" and the "new world" that would regenerate the ailing West. During his visit, Rolland, like so many others, was inspired by the robust, joyous crowds he saw on Red Square. In his case he sat near Stalin atop the Lenin Mausoleum, reviewing the parade of physical-culture enthusiasts (*fizkul' turniki*) of June 30, 1935. "A festival of the People—magnificent!" he exclaimed.[105]

Rolland, like so many other French intellectuals and scholars, had a strong tendency to view the Russian Revolution through the prism of the French. French views of revolutionary progress in spite of the Terror could lead to "historical" excuses for the Soviets.[106] As this suggests, anti-fascism, and the international anti-fascist cultural movement, had its own valence in different national political cultures.

Finally, the monumentalism of Stalinist culture and of Socialist Realism was not repugnant to Rolland. Some of the components of Rolland's intellectual makeup—notably, Wagner and Nietzsche—were also currents running through Bolshevik culture, from pre-war "godbuilding" to Gorkian "Revolutionary romanticism." Nor did he find the Soviet repudiation of the avant-garde of the mid-late 1930s troubling, as did Gide and Feuchtwanger. For these reasons, a number of the shifts enacted within Soviet culture of the Stalinist 1930s—the logocentric primacy of didactic, mass literature; the popular glorification of enlightenment and the new artistic and scientific establishment; the embrace of nineteenth-century high culture; the values of "culturedness"—appealed to Rolland's outlook. In this light, the grand celebration of Rolland himself in official Stalinist culture was not merely flattery, nor was the ascetic Rolland at all concerned, unlike some others, with Soviet material largesse. He donated Soviet royalties from his collected works to "the educational work of the new Russia."[107] Rather, the Soviet glorification of the writer seemed to confirm his own importance in the creation of that new world toward which anti-fascist culture strove.

For all these reasons, Rolland believed intuitively that he knew and understood Soviet culture, which, as he saw it, was internationalist and universal in its reach.[108] But it was what the French call a *faux ami*—a "false friend," recognized as familiar but in reality not. It was precisely the time when Soviet culture exerted its most universalistic attraction to enthusiasts like Rolland—in the 1930s—when Stalinism, with its ideological codes and Bolshevik language disseminated on a mass scale, its drives for autarky and isolation, was creating a world increasingly difficult for outsiders to penetrate. Rolland believed that both anti-fascist and Soviet culture stood for humanism; yet for most of the early Soviet period, and even in the mid-1930s for the militant cultural Left, *gumanizm* was a bourgeois myth, the opposite of the ruthless logic of Bolshevism. Indeed, in a 1934 Union of Writers' Foreign Commission evaluation of Rolland, "individualistic humanism" was listed alongside pacifism as the weakest part of his ideological credo.[109] Ironically, it was anti-fascist culture that started to legitimize the concept of humanism for domestic Soviet culture. At their talk, Stalin still interpreted Rolland's remarks on humanism entirely in the context of the "internal" Soviet ideological world. He talked of the new person in terms of current notions of labor discipline: "shock-workers are the men and women around whom our new life, our new culture is concentrated." He even added: "In the USSR, we hate lazy do-nothings." Stalin's train of thought, which led him from humanism to hard labor and hatred, was jarring in the context of Rolland's elevated notion of a universalistic world culture. The remarks were eliminated in the "official" text.[110]

The success of Rolland's 1935 visit, from the Soviet point of view, led directly into the massive, all-union celebration of Rolland's seventieth birthday in January 1936. Like the celebration of other foreign friends, the jubilee ostensibly revolved around universalizing Soviet values and depicting the Soviet Union as the standard bearer of the best of progressive world culture.[111] In attempting to emphasize Soviet internationalism, however, the celebration only reinforced its particularism. Rolland shared the spotlight with Stalin; the holiday of culture was openly harnessed to the cult of Stalin, and the cult of the writer reinforced the cult of the leader. The previous year's meeting between Rolland and Stalin made for fresh images of the two together, which were splashed on the front page of *Pravda*. The parallels in the journalistic coverage of the jubilee were less than subtle: Rolland's oeuvre was about geniuses who had changed mankind, like Beethoven, just as he recognized the "greatest genius of mankind," Comrade Stalin; Rolland was a spiritual *vozhd'* just as Stalin was the political one.[112]

When the crowd filed into the celebratory evening (*torzhestvennyi vecher*) in the grand hall of the Moscow conservatory, the epicenter of the jubilee, they found it draped with four portraits: Stalin, Molotov, Kaganovich, and Rolland. The program—which included an exhibition, poems, the screening of a special documentary film of Rolland's 1935 visit, and testimonials from Soviet writers and factory workers—drew on the orchestration of Soviet holidays and festivals but also on the heavy-handed glorification familiar in the Stalin cult. It was not only the Party's leaders and homegrown scientific and cultural icons like the scientist I. P. Pavlov who were celebrated with their own minicults under Stalinism; foreign friends like Rolland got the same kind of adulation. The sheer scale of the Rolland celebration, planned for over a two-month period by Apletin of the Union of Writers' Foreign Commission, was underscored by the allocation of an entire issue of *Literaturnaia gazeta* to the event, reproductions of the celebration by Union of Writers' groups in the capital cities of the union republics, a radio broadcast, and a biography of Rolland mass produced for the occasion.[113] While the Foreign Commission sent Rolland an album of 400 Soviet newspaper clippings, the goal of such an event had to be more than to flatter and impress a single Western intellectual. The core political message that Apletin and his co-organizers conceived of as the organizing principle of the jubilee—"R. Rolland's path to revolution"—was implicitly centered around Soviet uniqueness and superiority.[114] Rolland's life became a teleological progression toward higher consciousness, culminating in its endpoint, his embrace of the Soviet order and of Stalin.

Inevitably less grandiose and more inclusive was the message behind the soirée d'hommage in Paris, held in the main hall of the Palais de la Mutualité and marked by an appearance by Léon Blum, the Socialist Prime Minister of the Popular Front government. Only partly orchestrated by the French Communist Party, this event was structured around a different script; it was a celebration of unity on the Left and of anti-fascism, in which Rolland was lauded as a great humanist and "symbolic grandfather of the Popular Front."[115] Friendship with the USSR had brought Rolland to the height of adulation in Moscow and in Paris, but the different ceremonies marked those very disjunctures between Stalinist and European anti-fascist culture that Rolland himself did not grasp.

Although Stalin's meetings with visiting Western intellectuals were cut off with the onset of the Purge era, they played a notable role in Stalin's own emergence as an international politician. Many of Stalin's guests had yearned for or imagined having an influence over the revolutionary experiment, in what François Hourmant has called a "fantasy of shared power."[116] In one unexpected sense, they succeeded: because of them, Stalin became much better prepared for the barrage of meetings with Western diplomats and heads of state during the grand alliance of World War II.

Explaining the blindness of Western intellectuals when they looked at Stalinism has proven one of the most durable riddles in the history of twentieth-century politics and intellectual life. The patterns of reasoning in the vast literature on fellow-travelers suggest that it has become a special sort of scholarly issue, a way of reckoning with the totalitarian past by holding up a single, underlying explanation that serves as warning and as lesson.[117]

Perhaps the most longstanding master explanation—which can be called the "god that failed" thesis after the famous 1950 book of the same title—came to prominence out of the retrospective analysis of disillusioned ex-communist intellectuals themselves. Portraying their own sympathy for Soviet communism as an ersatz religion—that is, a faith by definition impervious to rational explanation—turned out to be a brilliant means for repentant interwar enthusiasts to explain their own lapses of judgment. Faith, as Arthur Koestler put it in 1950, involved the abandonment of reason: "One does not fall in love with a woman, or enter the womb of a church, as a result of logical persuasion."[118] In recent years, the movement to interpret totalitarianism as a political religion has further eased the tendency to explain Western sympathy for communism as a secular faith.[119] Blaming the god that failed, however, downplays the ways in which intellectuals were able quite rationally to justify the Stalin order and all the concrete benefits and decisions that intellectuals' status as friends of the Soviet Union entailed.

As an explanatory framework, moreover, the secular-faith argument directly collides with another major dimension of Western admiration for communism at the center of David Caute's classic *The Fellow-Travellers*. For Caute, the portrayal of Stalinism as an "experiment" was more than a metaphor; it was emblematic of the intellectuals' championship of the rationality of science and planning and the number of scientists and scholars who sympathized. No ideology presented itself as more scientific, rational, and forward-looking than communism.[120] As Mark Lilla has pointed out, not only do the historians' respective indictments of faith and reason as the cause of philo-Sovietism openly contradict one another; they also suggest the inadequacy of explanations focusing on ideas in isolation.[121]

A third interpretive framework, which might be called the sociological explanation, revolves around the role and nature of intellectuals themselves. Paul Hollander's thesis in *Political Pilgrims* about the roots of "utopia-seeking" in intellectuals' longstanding alienation and estrangement from their own societies is only the best known of a range of indictments of intellectuals that, in general, prompted them toward ideological blindness, utopianism, or even "treason."[122] Since Hollander's cause of causes was the pre-disposition of intellectuals themselves, he was able to flag the important topic of projection—in which aspects of communism are misconstrued in light of observers' critiques of their own societies. As we have already seen, however, negative views among visitors were legion. Recent scholarship has made it increasingly clear that far from all intellectual observers sought or found utopia. Eva Oberloskamp's exhaustive study of fifty French and German "leftist intellectuals" who left travel accounts found numerous critical judgments that challenge the received wisdom. Far from unifying intellectuals as an entity, approaches to the Soviet experiment were highly differentiated and shaped by political orientation, national political cultures, and reactions to numerous specific features of Soviet state, culture, and society. By the same token, far from all foreign admirers of Soviet communism were intellectuals.[123] The temptation exemplified by the sociological explanation to judge all intellectuals (except oneself and like-minded thinkers) is ironically similar to communist "class analysis" of the intelligentsia as a stratum of society.

The most important Anglophone work on French intellectual life in the mid-twentieth century, Tony Judt's *Past Imperfect*, avoids universal claims about intellectuals—who are "no better or no worse than other people" and "not even very different." Instead, Judt, with his focus on the "indigenous anti-liberalism of the French republican intelligentsia," provides a political explanation for intellectual sympathy for communism.[124] While the crisis of liberalism must be taken into account in any discussion of the 1920s and 1930s, committed liberals were also blind to the horrors of Stalinism. The countries with the strongest liberal traditions, Britain and the United States, produced droves of fellow-travelers. We are left contemplating the poverty of explanations that reduce fellow-traveling to a single cause or causes.

Advancing a single master explanation for the blindness of the intellectuals has ended up downplaying the importance of their visits to the Soviet Union and their relationships with the representatives of Soviet culture, for these explanations have all privileged the pre-existing faith, ideas, or nature of the intellectuals themselves. As one historian has expressed this consensus, "Travelers to the Soviet Union in the 1930s tended to confirm their preconceptions, reading into the host countries all their frustrated aspirations for their own."[125] Historicizing the relationship between Western friends and Soviet mediators, however, has suggested that projection is only one part of the story. One reason even short visits could play a crucial role is that they served to cement the role of celebrated foreigners as "friends of the Soviet Union." This was something greatly facilitated by the Bolshevik intellectuals and Soviet diplomats who cultivated and admired them. The major Western intellectual friends became involved in a transaction that fostered illusions of influence and was predicated on their public praise for the USSR. This relationship was significant, ongoing, and clearly important to both sides.

By the mid-1930s, Soviet communism had evolved through so many stages and the internal and externally propagated features of the system held so many possible ways of grabbing observers that no one principle or idea could possibly hold the key to intellectual philocommunism. Just as each and every fellow-traveler had to adapt his or her belief system of a lifetime to fit in with a pro-Soviet stance, each, as well, had to accept, with the often intricate and personal work of Soviet intermediaries, the quasi-formal position of friend of the Soviet Union. The fellow-travelers' historical relationship with the Soviets cannot be explained by some essential feature of intellectuals that pre-determined their journeys to the East. Ideas and experience both had to come together to bind intellectuals to the object of their desire.

7

Going East: Friends and Enemies

For foreign intellectuals, friendship with the Soviets was a status to be upheld and perhaps negotiated. For the Soviets, it was part of a broader communist friend-enemy divide that assumed great importance for their ideology and practices. Much effort has been devoted to understanding the way Bolshevism and Stalinism defined enemies, for this reveals much about the nature of the regime and how it compares to others.[1] It is also crucial in the context of foreign visitors, for the link between internal and external enemies was always live in early Soviet political culture and became a central, even determinative, feature of the Great Terror. But the converse—how the regime determined and treated its friends—has never been perceived as equally revealing. The two deserve to be taken together. Friends as well as enemies provide one of the keys to Soviet history, and they were closely related. Perhaps it is fitting to observe that Carl Schmitt's friend-enemy distinction, the best known political theory in this context, was created by the radical statism and collectivism of a "prophet of extremity" in the same interwar conjuncture.[2]

Even as the Soviets divided the world into black and white, the categories of friend and enemy as applied to foreigners could be strikingly contingent. Friends were almost always treated as potential opponents, but some extreme right-wing and fascist opponents were treated as possible friends. Like the persecution and annihilation of enemies, official friendship assumed monumental proportions. The greatest Western intellectual sympathizers, having been transformed into icons in Soviet culture, were translated, censored, domesticated, and controlled to the point at which, on occasion, they could not interfere with their own legends. The classification of friends and enemies was also an important dimension of the interwar superiority-inferiority calculus, for friends were guided by the Soviets, and a precondition of true friendship was the recognition of the superiority of Soviet socialism. Western friends were embraced with an enthusiasm and even longing that testified to their special place in the Soviet imagination, yet they could be transformed into enemies overnight if they publicly repudiated the idea of Soviet superiority. Much can be learned from how civilizations, like individuals, treat their enemies and friends.

In 1932, a book entitled *Through the Eyes of Foreigners* translated excerpts of foreign writings about the USSR to a mass audience of Soviet readers. The compilation was introduced under a striking title: "Friends and Enemies on the USSR."[3] The division between friend and foe was pictured, unsurprisingly, in black-and-white terms. In the practices of Soviet cultural diplomacy, however, there were in fact many shades of grey. The ambiguities underlying the ostensibly binary Soviet friend-enemy divide assumed great import for visitors traveling east. For one thing, Marxist-Leninist orthodoxy treated the intelligentsia as a stratum wavering between the poles of proletariat and bourgeoisie, so those intellectuals caught in between classes could theoretically gravitate to the side of the working class. Soviet cultural diplomats exploited this ideological opening. In terms of allocating resources or extending invitations, officials judged levels of friendship and enmity with statements and publications about the USSR centrally in mind—and here there were many shades of grey. In Soviet eyes, foreigners' status was mutable: friends, of course, could become enemies, but some enemies could be "neutralized" or even potentially turn into sympathizers. The result was a quintessentially Soviet mixture of flexible and contingent classifications within a radically Manichean worldview.

The Soviet friend-enemy divide applied to foreigners did not completely overlap with another cardinal distinction between *us* and *them* (*svoi/chuzhoi*). Foreigners and non-party intellectuals, even the most ardent of friends, could never be completely "ours." Lunacharskii could hail Henri Barbusse in 1927 as *nash chelovek*, "one of our own"—a brother, friend, and comrade—in part because he was a Communist Party member and in part because he wanted to show his personal support.[4] More common were the words of Fedor Petrov, the head of VOKS, when in 1930 he referred to sympathetic visitors who had indulged in criticisms of the Soviet order: "These kinds of 'friends of the USSR'"—that is to say, false friends—should no longer be invited to enter the country, for they "abused that hospitality that is shown to them here."[5] Famously, when André Gide published a book critical of the regime after his 1936 Soviet tour, one of the most celebrated friends of the decade became a maligned enemy faster than the blink of an eye.

Less well known in the history of Soviet cultural diplomacy are the cases in which those considered enemies—right-wing nationalists, fascist intellectuals, and in rare cases, members of the Nazi Party—were courted and treated as potential friends. The history of sudden or controversial inversions of the Soviet friend-enemy divide assumes great interest in light of the fact that there was a strain of ideological fascination as well as enmity for Bolshevism and Stalinism on the extreme Right of the political spectrum in interwar Europe.

This chapter juxtaposes case studies of these two types of interactions: enemies becoming potential friends and friends becoming enemies. The cases are quite different: the involvement and travel of extreme nationalist and fascist German intellectuals on the eve of the Nazi Revolution is one of the least-known episodes in the history of Soviet cultural diplomacy, while the apostasy of Gide in 1936 and the visit of the anti-fascist émigré writer Lion Feuchtwanger, brought in to provide a response to Gide in the midst of the Purge trials, are among the most famous visits of any European intellectuals in the entire interwar period. The first example was an offshoot of a covert and internally disputed Soviet operation; the second involved receptions so well publicized that they became not merely state visits of the first order but historic events familiar to millions of Soviet citizens. The chapter ends by stepping back to compare the fellow-travelers of communism with those of fascism, considering the differing place of political violence and the emotional identification of foreign intellectuals with the Soviet Union as a socialist homeland. The latter had no analogy in the Nazi racial community, or Volksgemeinschaft, and by the same token was something those revolutionary nationalist figures fascinated by Stalinism and courted by the Soviets could not feel.

Engaging the Radical Right

The fascist movements in Italy and Germany, with their ideological hatred of communism yet simultaneous strain of covert, and sometimes overt, enthrallment with the Bolshevik Revolution, pressed the outer limits of Soviet willingness to pursue influence over the ideologically alien "bourgeois" world, which had formed part of Soviet cultural diplomacy in the Weimar context since the early 1920s. After almost a decade of balancing left-wing German "friends" against influential "bourgeois" nationalists, there emerged a new Soviet effort to infiltrate extreme right-wing nationalist circles on the eve of the Nazi seizure of power. One new potential partner organization, a hybrid Left-Right organization devoted to the study of Soviet planned economics (the *Arbeitsgemeinschaft zum Studium der Sowjetrussichen Planwirtschaft*, or Arplan), was exceptional for including a sizeable contingent of conservative revolutionaries and fascist intellectuals. Historians have long known about Arplan's existence but have possessed little information about it.

This is a topic, however, that deserves a broader debate. Until recently, such interactions were understudied not merely for lack of sources but as a result of self-imposed impediments. Comparative, as opposed to transnational, history has dominated the field of Stalinism and Nazism, both during the heyday of totalitarianism theory and today; whether one approaches this comparative history as a kind of "applied" totalitarianism theory, in order to establish parallels, or reacts by highlighting the divergences between the two regimes, the tangled and often hidden history of exchanges remains slighted. The waters were muddied by the politicized debates (the "historians' conflict" or *Historikerstreit*) over Ernst Nolte's attempt to "establish a 'causal nexus' between the gulag and Auschwitz." In what was arguably the Soviet field's iteration of the Historikerstreit, the debate over the *Black Book of Communism*, tensions flared over which system was more murderous.[6]

In recent years, a new wave of scholarship has begun to recover the range of complex motivations behind Russian-German, Left-Right, and Nazi-Soviet interactions. Even so, Michael Geyer and Sheila Fitzpatrick prominently acknowledged the underdeveloped examination of "entanglements" as opposed to the rather well-explored "image of the other."[7] As it stands, a good deal of the new literature creates a richer picture of the German rather than the Soviet side. Substantial research has emerged on the fascination for and enmity toward Russia and the Bolshevik Revolution by members of the German "conservative revolution" in the 1920s, including important figures within the Nazi Party.[8] On the Soviet side, however, consideration of international motivations has too often revolved around speculation about what Stalin—ever the cipher—may have thought rather than a more systematic investigation of assumptions, practices, or institutions. New Russian archival materials on Arplan offer a fine-grained snapshot of Soviet outreach to the far Right and are revealing about the covert debates and unexpected results of communist-fascist interaction. For both sides, the stakes were high: the groups within the German far Right that were openly attracted to elements of Bolshevism and Stalinism were about to be pushed under the surface with the triumph of Nazism in 1933, but, as this chapter will argue, opening channels of communication with precisely those most pro-Soviet or "National Bolshevik" elements of the fascist Right gave Soviet leaders a disastrously sanguine view about the dangers of the impending fascist triumph in Germany.

In 1932, VOKS and other Soviet diplomats and officials diverged sharply over how much attention and support to give Arplan, as opposed to its long-standing German partner organizations, the German Society of Friends and Otto Hoetzsch's East European studies society. As German politics became ever more sharply polarized in the early 1930s, there emerged a degree of overlap in membership as well as overt rivalry among the two older partners and the new upstart. For example, Hoetzsch's successor at the helm of the East European studies organization from 1931–33 was the young Klaus Mehnert, who had considerably more sympathy for the Soviets than his predecessor because he had come to believe that radical change in Germany was inevitable. Born in Moscow in 1906 and later an influential Sovietologist, Mehnert spoke accent-free Russian, making many contacts in his trips to the USSR in the late 1920s. His tendency in the early 1930s to view the Soviet Union as an experiment-friendly model for Germany brought him into conflict with the Gesellschaft's conservative old guard. In fact, Mehnert for a short time became a radical of the Right: he became an active supporter of the "Left Nazi" Otto Strasser's Black Front, formed in 1930 after Strasser was expelled from the Nazi Party. Although his Soviet experiences and access to Russian culture were unusual, in terms of this political orientation, it was fitting that Mehnert joined Arplan's secretariat. According to one account, he was even responsible for coining the organization's name.[9]

The Arplan right-wing revolutionaries themselves, however, unlike the moderate nationalist Hoetzsch and the vast majority of his group of scholars and policymakers, went beyond the geopolitical calculations of the Eastern orientation—they were propelled into contact with the Soviets out of a specific trajectory of ideological and political interest in Leninism and incipient Stalinism. The violent anti-Occidentalism of Weimar's "conservative revolution" was layered onto a Russophilic strain in the intellectual evolution of German nationalism. This was already evident in the early 1920s, given Oswald Spengler and Moeller van den Bruck's immersion in Dostoevsky as they formulated their landmark "new nationalist" theories of "Prussian socialism" and the "Third Reich."[10] For German revolutionaries of the Right who yearned to reorient the coming revolution from class to nation, the "proletarian revolution" offered instructive lessons, a phenomenon that extended to certain Nazi figures and publications. Others within the conservative revolution went further, openly admiring Bolshevism's revolutionary vanguardism, techniques of political violence, and capacity for mass mobilization.[11] During the Great Depression, German-nationalist interest in the Soviet Union broadened to include planned economics and the Five-Year Plan, which lured the radical Right as a potential model for German economic emancipation from the West.

In each of these cases, certain nationalist and fascist German figures consistently or episodically expressed praise for Bolshevism rather than the usual vitriol. As a result, the term National Bolshevism (*Nationalbolschewismus*), denoting an attempt to harness the experience of Bolshevism to national and volkisch goals, was current in Germany from 1919.[12] This ideological interaction across Left and Right, moreover, was stimulated by a series of precedents to the 1930–33 policies of which the opening to Arplan was a part: Comintern, Soviet, and German communist leaders approved the injection of nationalist slogans into communist propaganda and outreach to nationalism in order to siphon off support from the fascist Right. These strategic openings occurred in the crisis moments of Weimar: its rocky start in 1919, the occupation of the

Ruhr in 1923, and its final crisis in the wake of decisive growth of electoral support for the Nazi Party after 1930.[13]

The single most important liaison between German and Soviet communism during all three of these strategic openings to the nationalist Right was the "revolutionary, diplomat, and intriguer," Karl Radek. Both in 1919 and 1923, Radek was the chief Comintern and Soviet architect of engaging German right-wing nationalists. Fayet, author of the most important biography of Radek, argues that his motivation in publicly entering into a dialogue with fascist intellectuals in 1923 and praising their martyr, the Ruhr Freicorps leader Heinz zu Schlageter, was not Leninist flexibility taken to an extreme, but his "permanent obsession" after 1922 with the danger of fascism. Fayet's evidence suggests that Radek placed his hopes not in converting fascist leaders but rather in winning over some of their troops, just as the Comintern's "united front" was designed to lure workers away from Social Democracy.[14] There was another factor at play: revolutionary optimism. In run-up to the abortive "German October" in 1923 and once again at the start of Weimar's final crisis in 1930, Radek's line was based on expectations of imminent revolutionary victory. As the now ex-Trotskyist Radek capitulated and was readmitted to the party, eagerly promoting himself as Stalin's "servile pen" and international advisor, he calculated that fascist forces would need to be neutralized or enlisted in order to bring down the capitalist state.[15] A new German communist tactic designed to court working-class support from fascist organizations and inject nationalist slogans into communist propaganda began in 1930, and in March 1931, after the high-profile defection of the Nazi army officer Richard Scheringer to the Communist Party, became known as the Scheringer Course.[16] This was the direct successor to the 1923 Schlageter line. In both cases, the communist movement's efforts to woo fascist support yielded only modest results.

Compounding the political implications of outreach to the far Right was the "social fascism" doctrine of the Comintern's "Left turn" after 1928, which branded Social Democrats as the main enemy of communist parties and prevented cooperation against the fascist menace. Comfortable with using the mobilizing power of nationalism through Soviet nationalities policy, Stalin approved the KPD's "national populist" policies, especially through his "man in Berlin," the KPD Politburo member Heinz Neumann, who spoke Russian and visited Stalin's Black Sea dacha at several key moments. The KPD itself, however, pursued nationalism too hotly for the Comintern, and in 1931, the Comintern executive committee tried to reign in the KPD's Scheringer line— before further outreach to the Right was once again sanctioned in 1932.[17]

By 1932, Radek had become Stalin's preeminent German advisor. One sign of this was the Politburo's April 1, 1932, approval of Stalin's initiative to appoint Radek head of the Central Committee's new Bureau of International

Information. This was designed as a center that would provide analytic brief-ings and information on foreign affairs directly to Stalin and his personal apparatus and to the Politburo. Radek's new outfit was also charged with for-mulating strategies for influencing public opinion abroad, the traditional focus of cultural diplomacy.[18] Radek was, thus, a key player in arranging the 1932 opening to the German extreme Right.

Such was the political and ideological context behind the Soviet opening to fascist intellectuals in Arplan and elsewhere in 1932. In the midst of these broad communist hopes to profit from the growing strength of the national revolution stood the chief Soviet handler of Arplan, the VOKS representative in Berlin, Aleksandr Girshfel'd, who simultaneously tried to cultivate far-right figures through covert ties in several other little-known German organizations of intellectuals. Girshfel'd, the former Soviet consul in Königsberg, was intensely interested in pursuing covert Soviet influence in the midst of Germany's right-ward political and ideological drift. He maintained a triple identity: he was also a diplomat with the rank of secretary in the Soviet Embassy in Berlin and had ties to the Soviet secret police. The evidence suggests—and this is a cru-cial point—that he did not act merely on his own initiative. Rather, he worked as a special operative within the broader communist strategy of making over-tures to the German "revolutionaries of the Right." Girshfel'd interpreted his mission as concentrating on ideologists who harbored positive views of the Soviet regime. In October 1932, Girshfel'd explained his understanding of the Soviet "line" on Arplan: "to deeply penetrate various right-radical group-ings of the intelligentsia that have political weight...representing so-called National Bolshevism (Tat, Aufbruch, Vorkämpfer, etc.)."[19] The "ever-deeper and intensive fascist transformation" (*fashizatsii*) of German society required new methods: the Soviets would employ new, "subtle" methods in organiza-tions such as Arplan with a "thoroughly German image." Arplan must not feel Moscow's influence, "which must be deeply and reliably concealed behind the scenes."[20] Girshfel'd made no mention whatsoever of left-wing intellectuals—neither in such institutions as the Society of Friends nor in the left-wing group within Arplan itself.[21]

The way Girshfel'd attempted to achieve this plan, however, was through a tried-and-true Soviet method—operating through a trusted, covert deputy inside the organization. This was the political journalist Arvid von Harnack, who stood next to the leadership of Arplan as the organization's secretary. Significantly, Harnack was a former extreme rightist (a Freicorps member in the early 1920s) who in the early 1930s became an "unofficial," that is to say secret, member of the KPD. The core of Girshfel'd's optimism in cultivating Arplan was his utter certainty that he could control the organization through von Harnack and other well-placed assets.[22] The covert opening to the German far Right in 1932 was not publicized, but it used the same methods developed for pro-Soviet friendship societies and anti-fascist front organizations.

Although Girshfel'd was single-mindedly focused on its right-wing contingent, this represented only about 15 out of Arplan's membership of more than 50.[23] Not only was there a pool of economists, engineers, and other academics interested in studying the Five-Year Plan, but sitting cheek by jowl with their far-right counterparts was a roughly equal-size group of members on the Left. In the fervid days of late Weimar, social mixing and to a certain degree intellectual cross-pollination of the political extremes had become a relatively common phenomenon in Berlin cafes, circles, and salons. Among the six intellectuals making up Arplan's "communist fraction" were the Hungarian philosopher and literary critic György Lukàcs; the China scholar Karl Wittfogel; prominent KPD official German Dunker; and another Hungarian Communist, Alexander Polgar, working in the Soviet trade representation in Berlin. Arplan also included a swathe of non-party Marxist figures. Lukàcs, who joined the Soviet Communist Party during his time in Moscow after 1929 and was directed to Berlin in summer 1931, was in Moscow in exile from 1933–45.

Along with Wittfogel, Lukàcs also played a role in the behind-the-scenes direction of a similar organization, the Bund Geistige Berufe [League of Intellectual Professions], founded in early 1932 as a club for "ideologically influencing" politically rightist professionals (architects, engineers, teachers, and so on). The strategy was to keep communist involvement to a minimum and target figures with an interest in the Soviet Union who were under the sway of the radical Right and "were unreachable by our mass organizations." As with Arplan, Girshfel'd was also the Soviet point man for the Bund Geistige Berufe.[24]

The chairman and initiator of Arplan was Friedrich Lenz of the University of Giessen, a professor of law and economics who was deeply involved in far-right political activity. Lenz, with his background in political economy, converted from a brand of scholarly socialism to ultranationalism during Weimar, but he was realist in his exposition rather than irrationalist and völkisch.[25] Another major Arplan rightist, Ernst Niekisch, like a number of other German national revolutionaries, switched allegiances from the socialist movement; as a revolutionary Social Democrat in 1919 Niekisch had briefly been chairman of the Bavarian Workers', Peasants' and Soldiers' Soviet in Munich. The French and Belgian occupation of the Ruhr in 1923 prompted his conversion by the late 1920s to a fusion of extreme nationalism and workerism that made an alliance with Soviet Russia against the world of Versailles into an *idée fixe*. Niekisch stood first for a hybrid "proletarian nationalism" and then for what he called "Prussian Bolshevism," a concept that glorified a putative line from early modern Prussian military absolutism in Potsdam to the total state in

Moscow, and back again to a future Berlin.[26] By the early 1930s, Niekisch had developed a racial interpretation of Russian and Soviet history. Lenin ("a *Mischling*, half Slav, half Tatar") was a great nationalist politician, and Stalin a virile promoter of total mobilization and terror against the "Western" classes of the population. The carrier of Westernization in the Russian Revolution was "the Jew," epitomized by Trotsky, but this tendency had been decisively replaced by "primordial Russian instincts" (*Urinstinkten*) of enmity toward Western Europe.[27]

In addition to Niekisch, radical rightists in Arplan included Niekisch's friend and political confidante, Ernst Jünger, the icily brilliant loner of the conservative revolution. Famous from his 1920 glorification of total war in *Storms of Steel*, Jünger, who scorned the Nazis as plebeian despite repeated overtures, published a work in 1932 inspired, in part, by the Five-Year Plan. *Der Arbeiter: Herrschaft und Gestalt* [The Worker: Mastery and Form] was "an elaborate vision of a future totalitarian order mobilized for industrial production and destruction," in which the "worker-soldier" would become the "new man."[28] Arplan member Hans Zehrer was the leading figure behind the revival of the journal *Die Tat* [The Deed] in 1929, boosting its circulation from 1,000 to 30,000 and making it into one of the most widely discussed political journals of the day; another member, Hugo Fischer, also belonged to the Tat circle. The group had in common with Niekisch a tendency toward the Eastern orientation and an attempt to transcend Left and Right, although Niekisch and Zehrer had a falling out. The nationalist intellectuals grouped around Zehrer developed the concept of *Zwischeneuropa*, a joint German-Slavic space between East and West, a notion that provided justification for geopolitical partnership with the Soviet Union within the framework of the "conservative revolution."[29] Many of these figures from the new nationalist camp, such as Niekisch and Jünger, were involved in the attempt to combine nationalism and socialism outside the Nazi Party, a group at the time generally termed "national revolutionaries" to distinguish them from the National Socialists. Others were more directly involved in the ideological and political world of Nazism, or can be seen as contributors to the intellectual development of pre-1933 German fascism. This contingent was bolstered by Graf Ernst zu Reventlow, a völkisch social revolutionary who had publicly engaged with Radek in the communist press during the period of the Schlageter line. Reventlow, who joined the Nazi Party in 1927, is counted among the so-called Left Nazis, those who took the socialism in "national socialism" seriously. It should be noted that the membership of Arplan fluctuated after its founding meeting on July 14, 1931. Other documents name as Arplan members the legal philosopher Carl Schmitt, later the court jurist of the Third Reich, and the national-revolutionary publicist Friedrich Hielscher.[30]

On the Soviet side, Girshfel'd briefed VOKS on the unusual new German organization as he helped arrange Arplan's first activities in Berlin. Girshfel'd was able to make himself useful to the German group by arranging lectures, meetings, and teas with Soviet planning and economic officials. At Arplan's opening two-day conference in January 1932, and on later occasions, the communist and nationalist intellectuals of Arplan sparred over the applicability of the Soviet planning model for Germany, the viability of the Soviet economic model, and how to characterize Soviet intentions in Europe.[31]

The VOKS leadership and its German analysts in Moscow were initially unaware that a new German organization was interested in the planned economy. Only in the first half of 1932 did they become acquainted with it, through reports from Girshfel'd. When Shuman, the head of VOKS's Central European Section, first studied the list of Arplan members in early 1932, he appeared confused by the bizarre combination of left-wing and right-wing intellectuals.

> The composition of Arplan itself appears to us as extraordinarily motley. Will the Society be able to work with such a composition? Among the members of "Arplan" there are undoubtedly a range of figures who sincerely sympathize with us...and even some members of the party...but on the other hand the Society has people who are rather alien, such as...Lenz. Some of them even appear to us to have joined with specific intentions of influencing the activity of "Arplan" in ways unprofitable to us—such as, for example, ...Niekisch...Who is this Count Reventlow, the well-known Hitlerite or someone else who has ended up as a member of Arplan?[32]

As this suggests, the VOKS official was thinking in terms of a conventional calculation of friends and enemies and had no idea of a covert operation with the Right that was sanctioned from above. Girshfel'd assured VOKS's Central European sector that von Harnack was "a person completely close to us" and that the composition of Arplan, its activities, and its ties were "being regulated."[33] As VOKS familiarized itself with the nature of Arplan over the course of 1932, this initial bafflement turned into a skepticism that VOKS officials maintained in almost all of their dealings with Girshfel'd. VOKS's German experts consistently touted advantages of Arplan that had nothing to do with its capacities as a vehicle for attracting radical rightists. Instead, they emphasized Arplan's scholarly interest in the planned economy and the attractiveness for Soviet cultural diplomacy of Arplan's connections to German universities and academia (where the presence of the political Left was almost non-existent both before and during Weimar).[34]

After a half-year of skirmishing, tensions came to a head toward the end of 1932. VOKS's E. O. Lerner told Girshfel'd that Arplan and other organizations with rightists could "become an absolutely negative factor in the cause of winning over important layers of the intelligentsia. We all...understand perfectly well what Arplan represents. But we do not share your point of view on its importance for the Embassy." In their resistance to Girshfel'd's "line" on Arplan, mainstream VOKS officials were generally supported by analysts in the Commissariat of Foreign Affairs and by other allies, such as Gosplan, the central state-planning agency. In a crucial concession, however, even Girshfel'd's harshest critics were forced to repeat a standard formula, that the prime task of Soviet cultural work in Germany had become "infiltration of layers of the radical and right-oppositionist intelligentsia."[35] In a revealing piece of evidence, D. T. Shtern, head of Foreign Affairs' Second Western Section, told the deputy head of Gosplan, V. I. Mezhlauk, that hopes placed in Arplan were exaggerated and that he was filled with doubts but "we are obligated to give Arplan aid."[36]

In these clashes with Girshfel'd over Arplan lay a continued commitment to the less covert dimensions of cultural propaganda, as well as a desire to maintain Soviet support for sympathetic friends on the German Left. Those Bolsheviks who would have been the first to insist that culture could never be separated from politics were rendered incapable of discussing directly the political implications of their own cultural policy in Germany. They were forced to express their views through bureaucratic infighting The VOKS leadership succeeded in joining Foreign Affairs and Gosplan officials in blocking significant Soviet financial support for Arplan, however, thus effectively downgrading Arplan's importance for the Soviets.[37]

In sum, VOKS and Foreign Affairs analysts appeared suspicious of the rightist connections and strove not to make it the center of their German policy even when the new line on attracting members of the conservative revolution was openly acknowledged. Girshfel'd, in contrast, placed top priority on infiltration, concealed influence, and the political significance of the rightists in Arplan. This leads us to one more potential motivation in the attempt to cultivate those classified as National Bolsheviks. Lurking behind Girshfel'd's formulation on the importance of seeking new sources of "influence and information" on the Right was another interest not uncommon in the Soviet relationship with Western intellectuals: intelligence and espionage. After 1933, Girshfel'd was involved in recruiting at least one Arplan member and one National Bolshevik figure as Soviet agents.[38]

Some might be tempted to dismiss the importance of Arplan, a short-lived group comprising a relatively small number of intellectuals. There is evidence, however, that Arplan and a broader engagement with German National Bolshevism influenced Soviet views at the highest levels, particularly about potential German stances toward the Soviet Union in the event of a Nazi rise to power. Part of Radek's attempt to establish a direct channel beyond conventional diplomacy between Stalin and the German fascist Right were meetings between top Soviet officials and German "National Bolshevik" intellectuals. For example, in mid-1932, Radek spoke for five to six hours with Arplan member Adolf Grabowsky, a prominent publicist from Berlin's Hochschule für Politik and former member of the Anti-Bolshevik League. Grabowsky also briefed Foreign Affairs analysts on the orientations of various National Bolsheviks and, in particular, focused on the Tat circle, from which a number of Arplan members came.[39] During his time in Moscow as a member of the Arplan delegation, Niekisch also held a "very detailed" political consultation with Radek. Niekisch recalled how impressed he was with Radek's familiarity with the tendencies of the German Right, and Radek's intention to deal with the Nazis even should they come to power.[40]

The back channel opened to the German Right clearly had an influence on the calculations of Soviet leaders. In August 1932, Politburo member Lazar' Kaganovich wrote to Stalin about his readings of transcripts of conversations between Soviet diplomats in Germany and the Nazi Party member Graf Ernst zu Reventlow, another Arplan member, as well as the military agent, adventurer, and professor of military geography Oskar Ritter von Niedermayer, who lived in the USSR for eight years as the Wehrmacht's principal representative in the covert Soviet-German military collaboration. Niedermayer had invited the Soviet embassy in Berlin to contact Nazi leader Hermann Göring and through him build permanent Soviet contacts with the NSDAP. "From the transcripts it is clear," Kaganovich assured Stalin, "that even fascist elements need to trust us, that they are not inclined to disrupt the relations that have grown between us. This, of course, is very important, because, it seems...these elements will remain in power in Germany."[41] Kaganovich's naive reading of the cautious inclinations of German fascism toward communism, soon to be widely branded in the Third Reich as "Judeo-Bolshevism," suggests the dangers for the Soviet leadership of extrapolating from conversations with those figures most willing to engage the Soviets.

Kaganovich's attitude fits the broader picture of how Stalin and his lieutenants at the helm of the Comintern and KPD discounted and gravely underestimated the Nazi danger. In 1932, the year Arplan was formed, Nazi strength was already apparent, but after years of focusing on the "social fascists," that is the Social Democrats, hard information on the Nazis was lacking. Many communist leaders and Soviet diplomats thought they could be easily manipulated. At the same time, as Hoppe has shown, Stalin appears to have thought highly of the potential for pragmatic ties between a pro-Soviet, anti-Western Nazi group that would continue Weimar-Soviet economic and military cooperation.[42]

However utilitarian the interaction between Soviet cultural diplomacy and the German fascist intellectuals was for both sides in 1932, it opened up channels of communication that fed the Soviets a sanguine view of continuing German cooperation with the Soviets in the event of an extreme nationalist triumph in Germany. Of course, it was precisely such "National Bolshevik" and Eastern-oriented strains on the Right, as well as "Left Nazi" forces in the NSDAP, that were curtailed, submerged, or smashed not long after the Nazi seizure of power in 1933. The Soviet external operation to influence German rightists had boomeranged back to affect the Soviets' understanding of German politics in fateful ways.

"The Largest Part Were Fascists": Arplan in Ukraine

In part because Arplan was such an unusual organization, one that had already provoked internal splits on the Soviet side, the Arplan "study delegation" that visited the USSR on VOKS's invitation from August 20 to September 15, 1932, generated revealing discussions that stand out in the large corpus of Soviet archival documentation on foreign intellectual visitors.

The visit of a specialized group of foreign visitors stocked with ideologically distant members during a grim economic downturn presented the Soviet hosts with unusual challenges. All the same, there were a number of features of the trip that can be called typical. The itinerary (Leningrad, Moscow, Khar'kov, Dneprostroi, Odessa, Kiev) was a standard one. Met by VOKS and Gosplan officials and served by Intourist guides, the delegation's itinerary was customized in a manner usually reserved for politically and professionally important guests. A barrage of meetings with planning officials and economic institutes (Gosplan, Jenö Varga's Institute for World Economics and World Politics) was supplemented by museums and cultural institutions, and rounded out by visits to model sites, including Elektrozavod and the Dzerzhinskii Commune. In Khar'kov, some of the far-right nationalists who had vented anti-Semitic sentiments in their publications visited the Jewish milk commune "Red Star." The Arplan report noted only that the buildings and livestock left a "very good impression."[43]

In addition to the Communists and Marxists, including a KPD fraction of six, the twenty-four travelers included academics, engineers, and professionals, as well as the most distinctive and controversial component of Arplan, the right-wing and National Bolshevik contingent. This included Niekisch, Lenz, Grabowsky, and Werner Kreitz, who was close to Jünger and was also Lenz's associate as the publisher of *Vorkämpfer*, sharing the fascination of both these figures for the military-utopian mobilization and national autarky embodied by the Soviet industrialization drive.[44] To a large extent because of the group's strange composition, behind the friendly declarations not everything was going well in the eyes of some key Soviet observers. The first extraordinary document generated by the Arplan visit was written by the head of VOKS's Central European Sector, Timm, who had clashed with Girshfel'd in the lengthy run-up to the delegation's visit. Writing from Moscow to an unknown addressee in German, likely to a Comintern or German Communist involved with Arplan, Timm did not conceal his vitriol. Hosting the right-wing nationalists could not succeed in winning them over, he maintained, because they had revealed themselves as "absolute enemies" of the USSR. Specifically, he argued that their alien ideological convictions made them congenitally impervious to the methods of Soviet hospitality. "The largest part were fascists," he wrote—and not just any fascists, but "the kind who would not be impressed by the visit." Some were using the trip to gather material against the USSR, he noted darkly; as for the influence of von Harnack—the secret Communist in the Arplan leadership, and Girshfel'd's trump card—his influence on the delegation "amounted to ZERO." Timm's denunciation attempted to tar the Arplan delegation with a lethal mix of fascist and "bourgeois" traits, and it ended by openly indicting Girshfel'd.[45] In fact, it is clear from the reports of discussions made by Arplan members that a lively debate continued during the trip between the leftist and rightist blocs within Arplan over the possibility of implementing planned economics under capitalism—or whether Soviet-style nationalization of industry was required.[46]

A second extraordinary document was written by a figure uninvolved in this dispute over Soviet relations with the German conservative revolution: Liubchenko, the head of the Ukrainian VOKS. A report of the delegation's two-day Khar'kov visit, this document represents one of the most detailed inside accounts of Soviet attempts to influence a foreign delegation and assess its outlook. The Ukrainian VOKS had the delicate task of hosting Arplan in a worsening agricultural situation on the eve of massive famine. In 1932–33, foreign correspondents were banned from Ukraine, and starting in winter 1933, Intourist stopped its operations there, canceling bookings for a time.[47] Liubchenko condemned Intourist employees for "interfering in the display," rushing through explanations, and "literally forc[ing] the delegates physically into cars." The delegation's stay in Kiev, which at that time "was completely unsuitable for show (pokaz)," was cut short; the itinerary was changed to avoid Rostov-on-Don when the delegation's guide "received unpleasant information about the situation in the sovkhoz 'Verbliud' and considered it necessary to cancel the visit to Rostov...I contacted the Deputy Head of the Political Subsection of the GPU of the North Caucasus by telephone and confirmed the information...: a showing of 'Verbliud' is undesirable." Instead, "We therefore decided to direct the delegation to Odessa, where they showed them the resorts and had the possibility to swim in the sea, which brought the delegation to ecstasy."[48] Liubchenko boasted about his cleverness in choreographing other aspects of the visit: the German Marxists were "accidentally" paired with a representative of the Communist Academy, while the factory owners were steered toward industrialists from the Commissariat of Heavy Industry.[49]

Liubchenko's detailed records of conversations with the delegation suggested that his on-the-ground activities were animated by a primary strategy: drawing out attitudes and observations about the USSR that would be predictive of what the foreigners would report. For example, it was a matter of great concern that Lenz and Grabowsky visited the German consulate, where there were many well-informed observers of the dire agricultural and economic situation. They reportedly returned with negative views of policies forcing independent farmers into collective farms and the poor harvest. "Finding out about this, I put the question in conversation so as to see whether the agitation of the general consul Walter had made a serious impression on Lenz. Lenz did in fact begin to speak of our difficulties, mentioning the harvest, but nonetheless underscored that we do not hide these difficulties." The hosts' craving for favorable reports was very obvious to the guests; how they adjusted their comments shines through clearly in the report. Grabowsky, for example, explained away his sharp questions on the rights of nationalities in the USSR by claiming he only asked such questions so as to be able to counter anti-Soviet campaigns abroad. Liubchenko, in turn, was aware that Grabowsky knew what he wanted to hear. His verdict: Grabowsky's attitude was one of clear "animosity," and the factory owner Brockhaus was "unquestionably fascist in outlook."[50]

In the weeks that followed, the public statements of the returning Germans were monitored carefully by the Soviet side. In one important matter, the hosts succeeded: an official Arplan report on the trip, while noting that shortages made the situation "very reminiscent of wartime conditions," nonetheless saw a range of positive developments, such as the clear "raising of the cultural level of the wide masses." The healthy faces of the "strong body-builders" in the physical culture parade (in Leningrad) proved that "famine in Russia has no place."[51] Even so, the evidence on whether the trip had succeeded was ambiguous enough so that the pre-existing differences on the Soviet side on the utility of Arplan would continue long after the Germans had returned home.

Lenz, as Arplan's chairman, realized the importance the Soviets placed on press reports and clearly hoped to remain on good terms with Gosplan, VOKS, and other Soviet organizations.[52] After all, Arplan's continued existence depended on keeping up relations with these Soviet partners. Harnack, Arplan's undercover communist secretary, joined Lenz in assuring VOKS that the Arplan members had returned with "very positive impressions."[53]

Yet there were also clear signs, some picked up by the assiduous "foreign information" bulletin of TASS, that Arplan delegates were propagating openly negative and critical impressions from their visit.[54] The head of the Dutch Arplan, Frijda, who according to the Dutch Society of Friends had previously been "delighted" by the Five-Year Plan, spoke publicly after his return of a goods famine, tendentious statistics, and an agricultural crisis threatening to turn collectivization into a catastrophe. Frijda left the Dutch society, and VOKS refused to answer his multiple requests for additional literature on planning.[55] Even Lenz was covered in the German press as speaking in late 1932 to "red student groups" about the "terrible conditions" and "monstrous hardship" (*ungeheure Not*) endured by the Soviet population; any comparison between German conditions and the "monstrous backwardness" of Russia was impossible.[56]

In the case of Arplan, many conventional Soviet methods of cultural diplomacy were deployed as part of a highly unconventional, covert operation. What was unusual was the lengthy behind-the-scenes infighting over policy within the Soviet camp, which revolved around whether Arplan rightists were potential friends or irrevocable enemies. The pre-1933 flirtation between the intellectuals of the German conservative revolution and the agents of Soviet cultural policy in Germany was thus a highly ambiguous attraction in which both sides attempted to use the other for its own purposes. Both were at once attracted and repelled by the other. This was only underscored by the contested 1932 visit of the Arplan delegation. The Nazi Revolution would mark a sea change in the relationship, driving beneath the surface the vestiges of German National Bolshevism and ushering in the era of Soviet-sponsored anti-fascism.

André Gide's Alternative Entourage

Around the time of the Arplan delegation's tour, André Gide was emerging as one of the most prominent and cherished friends of the Soviet Union. Within a few years, quite suddenly, Gide, perhaps the most celebrated friend of the interwar period, was swiftly and publicly transformed into an enemy. This *volte-face* underlines the tenuous position of prominent Soviet intellectual allies who from a communist point of view were still far from ideologically "ours." As David Caute has observed, "In the cases of nine fellow-travelers out of ten the philosophy of a lifetime was merely coaxed and twisted a little to yield a different ideology."[57] This observation was borne out in the lives of those European visitors who conversed with Stalin, for world views formed over decades were decisive in allowing them to believe that the Soviet order had moved toward them, and not the other way around. This holds true even in the case of the best-known fellow-traveler of them all, for Gide's infatuation with Stalinism was relatively short-lived. In this sense, Gide was typical of artists and intellectuals who discovered Soviet socialism not in 1917 or the 1920s, but in the wake of the Depression and the rise of fascism, and who left it with the onset of the Purges. The writer's emergence as a full-fledged friend in 1931–33 was one of the greatest coups in Soviet cultural diplomacy, for Gide was then at the peak of his acclaim in French letters.

Gide's 1936 visit has been written about so often because he ended his Soviet friendship in such a spectacular fashion: within a year, his 1936 *Retour de l'URSS* had been reprinted ten times and translated into fourteen languages. The book took care to leave open the possibility that the Soviet order might yet find the right path, but it was a work more revealing and more critical about Soviet cultural and ideological conformity than anything a celebrated sympathizer had written until that time. The publications sparked a major Soviet and international communist campaign against him, which in turn resulted in his more directly worded 1937 *Retouches à mon Retour de l'URSS*. Yet, despite the fact that there was no long pre-history in Gide's relationship with Marxism, Bolshevism, or the revolution (as with Rolland and the Fabians), the political differences separating him from the Soviets were not intrinsically greater than those of other fellow-travelers. Why, then, did Gide, unlike the other most celebrated friends treated to the most elaborate receptions of the 1930s, decide to end his friendship?

It was not, as much of the literature implies, that Gide's attraction to the Soviet Union was shallower, that he had more doubts or was simply less deluded. It is important to observe that the author of *L'immoraliste* (1902) had rejected bourgeois conformity and injustice his whole life, making him especially sensitive to the deadening strictures of Soviet cultural and political life during his guided tour.[58] This alone does not account for his apostasy, however. Exemplifying the manner in which one issue more than all others animated many intellectuals in their attraction to Soviet communism, Gide's homosexuality and hope that communism would liberate sexuality—a disappointed illusion not uncommon among homosexuals involved in international communism and intellectual observers more broadly—must be at the center of any explanation. Related to this was the ability of Gide, who was cultivated by a host of Soviet emissaries and intermediaries such as Ehrenburg and Kol'tsov, to create a group of alternative "mediators," his entourage of five relatively little-known traveling companions, all younger, all literary figures, all intimate with or loyal to Gide personally, and all professionally in his debt.

Among Gide's alternative entourage were Pierre Herbart and Jef Last, two Communists who knew Soviet life extremely well, and Jacques Schiffrin, a native speaker of Russian. Herbart and Last assume special importance, for they were both homosexual or bisexual, both personally close to Gide, and both informed critics of Stalin's Russia.[59] Both had an important impact on Gide's apostasy, which was shaped by a combination of world view and in-country experience.

To a certain extent, it is accurate to say that Gide was primarily an aesthete who, unlike Rolland, the champion of social art, had little engagement with politics before the 1930s. After all, Gide the writer emerged from the Mallarmé circle of Symbolist poets, and his first fifteen books were published in small quantities at his own expense. Even as he launched what amounted to a second career as a fellow-traveler, producing by his own admission nothing of literary note for four years after 1931, in part because of his pro-Soviet commitments, he worried constantly about his "submission to a dogma." Soviet analysts who monitored Gide and international literary politics were well aware that, even after his prominent pro-Soviet statements in the early 1930s, he openly rejected *partiinost'* (party-mindedness) and remained reluctant to make pronouncements on political and economic issues.[60] However, Gide had a significant history of civic engagements that deeply informed his later relationship with the Soviets. In this sense, his attraction to Soviet communism had deep roots in his biography before he became a fellow-traveler.

Like André Malraux and others, Gide approached communism through the antechamber of anti-colonialism. Long before 1936, Gide had written another book, called *Retour*, establishing himself as a travelogue writer of a very different sort than the pro-Soviet authors. After touring Congo from July 1925 to June 1926, Gide published his *Voyage au Congo* and *Retour de Tchad*. His condemnation of the big rubber companies to a large extent marked his social awakening. As Gide himself recalled in 1937: "As long as I travelled in French Equatorial Africa accompanied by officials, everything seemed to me little short of marvelous. I only began to see things clearly when I left the Governor's car." Conservative defenders of colonial Congo in 1926, like his left-wing critics a decade later, called abuses exceptional, justified the present by comparison to odious conditions before conquest/revolution, and approved everything as a "temporary evil for the sake of greater good."[61] Indeed, the greatest uproar in 1936 was caused by Gide's inclusion of a comparison between the far Right and the far Left: "I doubt whether in any country in the world, even Hitler's Germany, thought be less free, more bowed down, more fearful (terrorized), more vassalized."[62]

If Gide's previous exposé of colonialism figured in his 1936 and 1937 bombshells, an even greater concern coloring his other criticisms of the USSR remained almost completely buried in those works. In a single footnote in *Retour*, Gide deplored the 1936 Soviet law against abortion and the 1934 law criminalizing male homosexuality, for they ensured that "non-conformity" would be "hunted down even in sexual matters."[63]

As early as 1895, Gide started collecting materials in a file labeled *"péder-astsie,"* an effort that came to fruition sixteen years later, when he wrote four Socratic dialogues between a bigoted interviewer and his historically and scientifically enlightened interlocutor, who marshals arguments from a wide array of disciplines about the naturalness of homosexuality. Gide initially produced this volume, *Corydon*, in two tiny, private, and unsigned editions, in 1911 and 1920 before a signed, commercial edition appeared in 1924. According to Alan Sheridan, *Corydon* was the "first serious attempt by a homosexual to defend the practice of homosexuality to the general public."[64] Monique Nemer, author of the most far-reaching exploration of Gide's homosexuality, argues that it was connected to his attraction to communism in two major ways: he associated communism with communion with other people, and he equated the marginality of homosexuals with that of workers. It is logical that Gide's 1936 footnote equated sexual intolerance with political, intellectual, and artistic conformity. His revulsion for the conformity of bourgeois society, and his discovery in the 1920s of the "social question," was rooted in his coming to terms with his own homosexuality. The initial decriminalization of homosexuality after the Bolshevik Revolution raised hopes in Gide and his circle. Starting in the late 1920s, Gide, like a number of Comintern figures and Soviet sympathizers, equated communism with sexual liberation.[65] In 1931, Gide wrote approvingly of the Soviet "suppression of the family," and in a diary entry about the young Soviet Union the same year, he wrote: "A time will come, I imagine, when the manifestations of love will be profoundly modified."[66] During the campaign of adulation during his 1936 visit that preceded the campaign of vilification, the Soviet press openly cheered the condemnation of bourgeois family prejudices in his literary work as the basis of his later opposition to capitalism.[67]

As Gide became a fellow-traveler in the early 1930s, his philosophy of a lifetime was thus merely coaxed and twisted to yield a different ideology. He and his circle were therefore shocked and dismayed by the 1934 law against homosexuality, and in private discussed it extensively. Herbart learned much about the issue during his time in Moscow from November 1935 to June 1936 as editor of the journal *La littérature internationale*—a prestigious post that he likely owed to Gide's status as France's most illustrious fellow-traveler, for Gide had contacted the Soviet embassy on his behalf.[68]

Like Gide, Herbart initially saw in communism the promise of sexual freedom, and in his own literary works sexual and political awakening were intertwined. Then, working for Mikhail Kol'tsov in Moscow, Herbart found himself among "bureaucrats of the pen," and his communist loyalty was shaken but not destroyed by the "grotesque" features of the Stalin cult and heavy-handed censorship. Herbart later worked with Gide to edit his *Retour* in 1936, but, well before the trip, he briefed the older writer extensively about issues such as Soviet living conditions and ordinary workers' salaries. As someone who had sexual relationships with Russian men, he also informed Gide about the "odious" effects of Soviet anti-homosexuality.[69]

The Dutch communist Last, who also accompanied Gide in 1936, had discussed the law against homosexuality with Gide and Herbart in 1934, when he met them at an anti-fascist literary conference. After getting his start a decade earlier as a projectionist and orator screening Soviet films to crowds of Dutch workers, Last had traveled to the USSR three times, starting in 1930. He had been aware of his own homosexual tendencies since adolescence, but "to conform to Dutch society he married and sublimated his homosexuality in, paradoxically, communism." In February 1935, Gide invited Last to travel with him to Morocco, hoping the man twenty-five years his junior would find sexual liberation there the same way Gide had in his North Africa trip of 1895. During their three weeks of travel, Last was indeed liberated.[70]

Gide's experiences inside the USSR were shaped by his ability to gather a loyal group of followers, to whom he was teacher and patron, who effectively replaced those Soviet ambassadors mediating reality to other eminent guests. The native speaker of Russian, Jacques (Yacha) Schiffrin, was a Jew born in Baku who had emigrated in 1914, and during the trip he facilitated unofficial contacts. Gide's status of friend helped him here as well, for he enlisted Louis Aragon to help persuade the Soviets to issue Schiffrin a visa.[71] In fact, the members of his entourage warned Gide about the perils of a guided tour long before they crossed the border. Last had told him about the endless receptions and speeches, monitoring, and tendentious translation to which eminent foreign guests were subjected. "If you go to the USSR on an official visit, as a famous man, you will be used in the stupidest way," he wrote Gide. "You will never see the USSR as it really is."[72] As a number of sources attest, one of Gide's motivations in deciding to travel was to meet Stalin in the misguided belief that Gide could influence Stalin to ameliorate some of the Soviet Union's shortcomings, including the position of homosexuals.[73]

Gide abhorred crowds and felt an especially visceral revulsion for the constraints of a guided tour. From North Africa, he and Last were used to an expedition model of travel that included spontaneity and sexual adventures. Soviet intermediaries knew full well that Gide did not want to be overloaded with official obligations. The Foreign Commission of the Union of Writers, which was in charge of Gide's trip, was aware that the famous writer was, in the words of Apletin, "the kind of person who does not like previously set plans." Kol'tsov's solution had precedents in the history of Soviet cultural diplomacy: they would plan the necessary spontaneity by arranging for leading literary figures such as Sergei Tret'iakov, Boris Pil'niak, and Isaak Babel' to invite Gide to visit their apartments.[74] Despite advance knowledge of Gide's proclivities, by the mid-1930s the Soviet system of receiving eminent "friends" was simply incapable of toning down the pomp and massive scale of the reception. The Foreign Commission produced "an entire system of preparatory activities" a month before Gide's arrival on June 17, 1936, including a campaign to "popularize" Gide's writings in readers' conferences and the media, so that Soviets he met would know his work. Gide was horrified to learn from Herbart that 300,000 postcards with his image had been printed in advance of his arrival: "But everyone will recognize me!" In general, Soviet hosts got great mileage from persuading visitors that their works were honored in Soviet culture. In summer 1934, for example, VOKS arranged for the Museum of Contemporary Western Art in Leningrad to move the works of French artist Albert Marquet from storage to prominent places in its permanent collection during the artist's visit. But to Gide, such flattery was only proof of the political and cultural centralization that so disturbed him. The rounds of sumptuous banquets, receptions, and meetings, especially during the party's time in Moscow, reinforced Gide's conclusions about Soviet conformity and the resurgence of a petty-bourgeois spirit. Herbart made Gide aware of the secret-police apparatus that "followed behind us almost everywhere."[75]

Gide's pronouncements inside the Soviet Union demonstrate that he knew the rules of the game of Soviet friendship. Initially, he did more than make the requisite public statements. For example, in a speech at Gorky's funeral on Red Square, Gide ostentatiously invoked Stalin's formula about writers as engineers of human souls. Gide openly admitted that he, like so many others, contemplated self-censorship: "Deplorable and unsatisfactory as the state of affairs in the Soviet Union is, I would have remained silent if I could have been assured of any faint progress toward something better."[76] His time in Moscow in the middle of the trip turned out to be pivotal; that was when Gide apparently made his decision to abandon his status as friend of the Soviet Union. What changed during Gide's stay in Moscow? Why did this middle part of the journey prove to be the time, to use an expression common later during the Cold War, when the Soviets lost Gide?

Gide's overscheduled visit in the capital city was also the time when Stalin— who was well briefed on the private affairs of his interlocutors and almost certainly knew of Gide's intention to plead with him on the issue of homosexual rights—chose not to receive him in the Kremlin. Ironically, given how Gide wrote about the repulsive nature of the Stalin cult in his book, Stalin's rebuff may have been the straw that broke the camel's back, for Gide would never be able to influence the revolution's retreat on the issue he held most dear. By the time Gide and Herbart met with Boris Pasternak at the writer's colony in

Peredelkino in August 1936, Gide—according to a report sent to the NKVD by an informer in the Writer's Union—was already making plans to write a critical "article" about Soviet lack of "personal freedom" and philistine conformity. In Paris, Ilya Ehrenburg did his best to persuade Gide that it was an inopportune moment to criticize the USSR, but the author of *Corydon* was not inclined to submit to pressure.[77]

In the dangerous blame game that resulted from the failure to seduce Gide, no one, of course, would dare criticize Stalin for not meeting with him. In sharp contrast to the public condemnation of Gide, which identified deep-seated socio-ideological causes for his betrayal, the internal Soviet discussion put the onus on the way he was handled, how the visit was organized, and whom he met. Arosev quickly charged that his rivals on the Union of Writers' Foreign Commission were guilty for allowing Gide close contact with non-party writers, such as Pasternak and Pil'niak.[78] A secret-police informer wrote a denunciation of Gide's special links to Ehrenburg, Babel', and Pasternak.[79] The Gide affair came up again during the Purge era, playing a significant role in NKVD interrogations of Kol'tsov after his arrest in December 1938. After dozens of interrogations and three months of torture by the NKVD in the Lubianka, Kol'tsov signed his first confession. It contained a statement blaming the "bulk of the slanderous writings of A. Gide" on the anti-Soviet conversations Pasternak held with the visitor at his dacha.[80] Behind the scenes, treacherous or incompetent individuals—not ideologies, classes, conditions, or even the visitor himself—were the sole preoccupation of the deadly Soviet search to explain Gide's criticisms of the Soviet order.

The Soviet press campaign launched against Gide at the end of 1936 matched the scale of the previous campaign honoring him, but offered a very different explanation for his apostasy. Harnessing personal vilification of Gide to the ideological condemnation of enemies prevalent on the cusp of the Purge era, Gide's transformation from honored sympathizer to vile foe featured an emphasis on the class enemy hiding behind a friendly mask. The affair was also described in expressly political terms: Gide had always been an agent of the bourgeoisie or even the "Trotskyist-fascist bandits." The personal and the political betrayal were united in scurrilous attacks on Gide's homosexuality. For example, in an article entitled "The Left and the Right Hand of Monsieur Gide," Boris Lavrenev wrote of the writer's "sick and perverted tastes." In case anyone did not get the message, he added that upon departure Gide had "kissed everyone to the left and to the right. These kisses were physically unpleasant, but they had to be endured." On several occasions, Ehrenburg referred to Gide as a "dirty old man."[81] While Gide was one of the Soviet Union's most famous friends, Soviet ideologists had been willing to ignore his personal life and wrote with approval of his hatred of the bourgeois family; once he was declared an enemy, the personal became the very essence of the political.

Trial of an Anti-Fascist: Feuchtwanger in Moscow 1937

In a number of ways, the notorious Moscow visit of Lion Feuchtwanger between December 1, 1936, and February 5, 1937, marked the end of an era. The German-Jewish writer-in-exile was the last in the line of the celebrated fellow-travelers of the interwar period to turn his journey into an "eyewitness" public endorsement of Stalinism; he was the last European intellectual sympathizer to be received on the grand scale of Rolland and Gide, in what was at once a landmark event of Soviet cultural diplomacy and an international cause célèbre. Feuchtwanger, arriving in the era of the great Moscow trials, was the last of the line of prominent foreign literary figures to receive an audience with Stalin. His visit thus marked the beginning of the end of the Popular Front in culture.

Feuchtwanger faced a trial of his own in Moscow: after attending the six-day proceedings of the second great Moscow show trial in January 1937, he was called upon to praise the Stalinist order in the midst of the fantastical confessions of world-famous revolutionaries. For Feuchtwanger, fear and hatred of Nazi Germany crowded out all other motivations, prompting him to remain a "friend of the Soviet Union." Karl Schlögel has convincingly explained that Feuchtwanger's *Moscow 1937* was the product of his powerlessness as an intellectual whose top priority was opposing fascism—and in this, his colossal miscalculation was paradigmatic for those who found it impossible to simultaneously oppose Hitler and criticize Stalin.[82] New archival materials on his time in Moscow, however, also reveal that Feuchtwanger, like so many other Western intellectuals whose public pronouncements later made them appear naïve apologists, delivered his endorsement after deliberately suppressing a series of major reservations and criticisms. His ultimate political subservience was colored by a strong dose of European superiority over Russian culture and life.

Feuchtwanger's political justification of the show trials in *Moscow 1937*, epitomized by his declaration that he witnessed "more light than shadow," became instantly famous. Yet his own trial—that is to say, his own act of self-censorship—has only recently come to light, particularly with the voluminous reports of his VOKS guide-interpreter. Using only published sources, Schlögel was led to conclude that Feuchtwanger's political mistake stemmed from his own disorientation in the unfamiliar contexts of Moscow and the political sphere.[83] On the contrary, Feuchtwanger expressed a certain bewilderment in *Moscow 1937* as a deliberate ploy, to distance himself from the Soviet-provided explanations his own book offered about the confessions of the Bolsheviks on trial. The archival reports suggest that he came to Moscow with firm, outspoken, and skeptical opinions on the show trials and their devastating effects on Western public opinion. Shortly after his arrival, he declared bluntly to his

VOKS guide that in Europe the trial had "deprived the Soviet Union of two thirds of its supporters."[84] Feuchtwanger was also displeased by the scale of the Stalin cult and the anti-formalist campaign against the avant-garde, among other things, but this did not overwhelm his burning desire to continue the fight against fascism.[85] How the conflict between these firmly grounded, yet contradictory, orientations would play themselves out—in other words, how he would sort out his positive and negative views of Moscow and in what form he would express his reservations—would be determined during the course of his stay. In this sense, Feuchtwanger was not so very different from Gide, though from the Soviet point of view they ended up on different sides of the barricades. A prime matter for interpretation, then, involves the extreme itera- tion of an issue that has run throughout this book: the gap between what the Western visitor published for the world upon his departure and the views and interactions recorded on the ground.[86]

The immediate context for Feuchtwanger's visit was Gide's sensational critique in his 1936 travelogue. Gide returned to France in August, and his intent to voice significant criticism was known to the Soviets long before his book was published in December (and rapidly translated for the Soviet leadership). The Politburo, holding Kol'tsov responsible for Gide's visit as head of the Foreign Commission of the Union of Writers, ordered him to issue a book-length rebuttal. By this time, however, Kol'tsov was off playing an outsized role on the front lines of the Spanish Civil War. His response was to organize a visit by Feuchtwanger that would serve the same purpose. Kol'tsov gained approval for a reception on the lavish scale of Gide's, and the Politburo's special commission of "spin doctors" for the January show trial of Radek and Georgii Piatakov steered permissions to attend the trial to two major fellow-travelers, Feuchtwanger and the Danish proletarian writer Martin Andersen Nexø.[87]

The specter of Gide cast its shadow over Feuchtwanger's entire visit. In gam- bling on Feuchtwanger's cooperation, Kol'tsov was playing for high stakes, for it was known that the exiled German writer had been critical of the first Moscow trial. Arosev, for his part, hedged his bets. In a transparent attempt to fix blame for another potential public relations debacle on Kol'tsov, Arosev warned Stalin and Ezhov in forceful language that Feuchtwanger could well become another Gide.[88]

Although Kol'tsov was by nature a risk taker, behind his decision lay an appre- ciation of Feuchtwanger as a figure whose primary concerns were anchored to his Jewish identity and a struggle against National Socialism that predated 1933. The Foreign Commission's biography of the "left-bourgeois writer of the older gen- eration" began with the phrase: "committed anti-fascist," noting accurately that it was anti-fascism (rather than any understanding of communism or Marxism) that prompted him to "stand closer to us than all the German bourgeois writers." Indeed, Feuchtwanger's literary production combined an exploration of Jewish identity in historical novels with anti-fascism. His 1933 *Die Geschwister Oppermann* [The Oppermanns], an explicit rebuttal to Nazism depicting the clash between fascism and humanism, became the first anti-Nazi novel written by a German writer in exile. The international popularity of Feuchtwanger's historical fiction, particularly in England and the United States, increased his value for the Soviets.[89]

Kol'tsov had special grounds to believe that Feuchtwanger stood willing to repudiate Gide. Feuchtwanger was tied to Moscow through the institutions of international anti-fascist culture and the left-wing literary German emigration in Moscow. Particularly significant was his co-editorship of *Das Wort*, the German-language literary journal in Moscow that aspired to lead the anti-fascist diaspora. Kol'tsov's trump card was Feuchtwanger's close relationship with Kol'tsov's common-law wife, the writer and journalist Maria Osten. She was a young German Communist, twenty-nine in 1937, who had helped publish Gorky's works in mass German editions before following Kol'tsov to Moscow in 1932. There, she became deeply involved with the anti-fascist writers' congresses of the mid-1930s. Almost certainly at the advice and instigation of her husband, "Madame Kol'tsov" met Feuchtwanger in 1935 at the Paris Congress for the Defense of Culture, and, as one of the founders of *Das Wort,* she had numerous contacts with him starting in early 1936. In the summer of that year, even before the Gide scandal broke, Osten had sought out Feuchtwanger in the exile of his luxurious villa in Sanary-sur-Mer in the south of France. In order to win him over for a Soviet visit, Kol'tsov's Foreign Commission organized a large-scale celebration of the writer's work in Moscow on June 1, at which Osten also spoke.[90]

The crucial role Osten played as Feuchtwanger's most important mediator is suggested by the archival documentation on his time in Moscow. The core sources are the extensive reports of Dora Karavkina, the conscientious and savvy VOKS guide-translator who later translated works by Hermann Hesse and E. T. A. Hoffmann into Russian.[91] Karavkina's report of December 22, early in the visit, noted that Feuchtwanger had already prepared his article responding to Gide for *Pravda*.[92] Producing an ideologically acceptable publication proved one of the most delicate parts of the journey and a sticking point in co-opting the visiting writer, however. In private, Feuchtwanger was repeatedly willing to use Gide's negative experience as a way of expressing criticism of his hosts. As Karavkina reported on December 16:

> He started a conversation about how "dangerous" it was here to express one's opinions, and look, for example, what happened to André Gide,

that he had been told that in our country they do not like criticisms
here especially from foreigners, etc. On Gide I explained to him *why*
we are indignant: his hypocrisy and that he is now pouring water on
the mill of the fascists. On the last point he completely agreed.[93]

As this passage suggests, Feuchtwanger was aware of all the things Gide
had criticized: censorship, ideological and artistic conformism, and, not least,
a growing Stalinist superiority complex. The key difference was that he was
determined not to let his reservations jeopardize support for the Soviets in the
alliance against fascism. Feuchtwanger said as much in the introduction to
Moscow 1937: "The Soviet Union is engaged in a struggle with many enemies,
and is receiving only half-hearted support from its allies." In the conclusion,
he put the "feebleness and hypocrisy" of the European response to fascism
squarely in terms of the East-West problematic. "The air which one breathes in
the West is stale and foul," he declared. "In the Western civilization there is no
longer clarity and resolution."[94] The resolve he found in Soviet-led anti-fascism
overcame his own lack of clarity when it came to the Soviet domestic order in
the Purge era.

By whom had Feuchtwanger "been told" that the Soviets were especially
sensitive to foreign criticism? As usual for such a visit, the celebrated fellow-
traveler had a heavy schedule of meetings with leading members of the Soviet
intelligentsia, including Il′ia Il′f and Evgenii Petrov, Valentin Kataev, and
Babel′, as well as with German and Hungarian émigrés such as Johannes R.
Becher and György Lukács. Although his handlers, Karavkina and Mikhail
Apletin of the Union of Writers Foreign Commission, strenuously tried to
control access to Feuchtwanger's room at the Metropol hotel, he was besieged
with visitors. Some fed him damaging information—including the fact that
the Russian translation of his own 1925 historical novel *Jud Süss* had been
banned for several years.[95] Even in 1937, foreign visits could not be completely
stage-managed.

Pravda editor Lev Mekhlis returned Feuchtwanger's article on Gide with
the request to change several passages, for the original draft included such
taboo formulations as a reference to the "cult" of Stalin. "I explained to him
the essence of the relations of the Soviet peoples with comrade Stalin…that
it is completely false to call it a 'cult,'" Karavkina reported. Feuchtwanger,
outraged, refused to make any changes. At this juncture, it was Osten who
played the key role in producing the desired result. As Karavkina described it
on December 22, Osten's intervention was crucial: "He was furious for a long
time, saying that he would not change anything, but when Maria Osten arrived
he meekly sat down with her at the desk and corrected what she asked, with the
exception of the sentence about 'tolerance,' which nothing would make him

throw out." Osten's success was clearly only possible because of their close personal relationship. "Feuchtwanger is very close with her and trusts her."[96]

Although Feuchtwanger's public support for the campaign against Gide and the show trials immediately made him appear sycophantic to anti-Stalinists, like so many Western sympathizers Feuchtwanger remained unconsciously arrogant about the superiority of European culture. As the sensitive Karavkina critically monitored his interest in learning about Russian-Soviet achievements, he demonstrated that he was not particularly knowledgeable about Russian culture: "Feuchtwanger said, supposedly quoting the writers whom he met here, that in Russia there was never a tradition of painting and there is none now." Feuchtwanger, like so many European and American visitors before him, also equated the inconveniences of Soviet everyday life with an overall backwardness. "In the morning Feuchtwanger started endless conversations about the inconveniences of life in the Soviet Union and complained about the service in the hotel, inefficient delivery of the mail and a whole range of other defects," Karavkina dutifully recorded. Since, of course, Karavkina defended everything Soviet, he dubbed her a "local patriot." In response, like other guides before her, Karavkina upheld the now-ingrained tradition of enlightening and instructing the visitor, asserting her own superiority: "I objected that I am simply better informed about our conditions and consider it my duty to orient him."[97]

Even as he condemned Western civilization for the appeasement of fascism in *Moscow 1937*, Feuchtwanger's own appeasement of Stalinism smacked of European superiority. Bookended by undiluted statements of allegiance to the Soviet system, Feuchtwanger's work explained various flaws of the Soviet system as the result of its youth and, implicitly or explicitly, its backwardness. "If a community...has risen up from extreme indigence to the beginnings of prosperity, then it inevitably develops certain petit-bourgeois characteristics," Feuchtwanger followed up on Gide's sharp critique of Soviet philistinism. Feuchtwanger must have not intended to express condescension, but rather state the obvious, when he wrote about how easy it was to discover the "material and moral defects" of the Soviet Union, followed by the remark that "it is true that, for a West European, life in Moscow is still by no means comfortable." Such implicit assertions of cultural superiority were evident to the Soviets and were excised in Russian translation. For example, when "The Aesthete in the Soviet Union," Feuchtwanger's *Pravda* article on Gide, was finally published in the "central organ" after a five-day delay, it praised the totally new culture created in the USSR. The German-language text in *Das Wort* more high-handedly referred to a "culture in its infancy."[98] The discrepancies, typical of Soviet translations of Western commentaries, not only made the Russian-language version pro-Soviet politically but also had the effect of describing the Soviet

Union as more advanced than was intended. Soviet intellectuals were very much aware that the celebrated foreign notable issued his praise while looking downward: he reportedly made himself disliked and was indicted in the Union of Writers as a carrier of the "Western disease of skepticism." Feuchtwanger may have retained his status as friend of the Soviet Union, but on the ground he left "few friends behind."[99]

Ironically, in his conversation with Feuchtwanger on January 8, 1937, Stalin himself resorted to Soviet backwardness as an explanation for his own cult of personality. Like Rolland before him, Feuchtwanger made efforts to raise potentially difficult topics but at the same time accepted all of Stalin's answers about the show trials and the intelligentsia's ability to criticize Soviet reality. When it came to the "exaggerated and tasteless" forms of "colossal ecstasy" expressed in praise of Stalin, Feuchtwanger made it clear that the cult was politically and aesthetically offensive to sympathizers abroad. Always ready to emphasize his own modesty, Stalin ascribed the hero worship to primitive behavior, the spontaneous joy of people exploited and oppressed for centuries. When his interlocutor suggested that Stalin might simply order it stopped, the dictator pounced: force could never be used to restrict the "freedom to express opinions." In his book, Feuchtwanger praised Stalin as the "most unpretentious" of "all the men I know who have power."[100]

Feuchtwanger was one of those intellectuals who saw the Soviet domestic order as an expression of reason and progress, and, hence, an extension of the Enlightenment tradition—the opposite of the primitive passions and barbaric anti-Semitism of the Nazi Party. This opposition was made explicit in *Moscow 1937*, in which "reason" was the key indicator of approval of the Soviet social system and fascism was described as "prejudices and passions in the place of reason." This, perhaps, was one reason Feuchtwanger objected so viscerally to the emotional "ecstasy" of the Stalin cult. Feuchtwanger's positive views about the scale of the plan to reconstruct the city of Moscow and the privileged position of writers and artists in Soviet society can both be seen in the context of his conception of rational progress.[101]

Yet, if anything appeared irrational to Feuchtwanger, it was the confessions of revolutionary "spies" and counter-revolutionaries in the show trial he attended and was expected to justify. The guide, Karavkina, had good reason to document every shred of doubt Feuchtwanger expressed in order to illustrate her efforts in the event he became another Gide, but her reports can be independently verified in the case of Feuchtwanger's meetings with Comintern leader Georgi Dimitrov. According to Karavkina, Feuchtwanger was determined to use his meetings with Dimitrov (whom he met, accompanied by Osten, on December 18 and February 2) to complain about the basic incomprehensibility of the show-trial confessions. Dimitrov's diary confirms

Figure 7.1 Lion Feuchtwanger and Iosif Stalin in Moscow, January 8, 1937. When the anti-fascist writer expressed distaste for the Stalin cult, Stalin replied that force could never be used to restrict freedom of expression.

Source: Rossiiskii gosudarstvennyi arkhiv kinofotodokumentov (RGAKFD).

the accuracy of Karavkina's report; as he summarized Feuchtwanger and Osten's visit, he recorded, in part: "1. It is incomprehensible why the accused committed such crimes. 2. It is incomprehensible why all the accused are admitting everything, knowing that it will cost them their lives. 3. It is incomprehensible why, apart from the confessions…no sort of evidence has been produced…The trial is conducted monstrously."[102] In both Karavkina's and Dimitrov's notes, Feuchtwanger took care in his formulations not to categorically deny the possibility that the anti-Soviet conspiracies might be genuine. He expressed his skepticism as forcefully as possible without abandoning his "friendly" position.

In providing to an attentive world his justification of the defendants' unanimous confessions, Feuchtwanger managed to play up the strange incomprehensibility of the trial. A famous example is his passage describing how the condemned Karl Radek, leaving the courtroom, issued a strange and incongruous laugh. Perhaps Feuchtwanger glimpsed some inkling of the fact that Radek, broken after seventy-nine days in the Lubianka, had, in the course of personal meetings with Stalin, become the co-author of the trial's fantastic script. In gingerly touching on this incomprehensibility, however, the only solution the exiled German writer could find was a hoary stereotype, the "whole enormous difference between the Soviet Union and the West." When he was in the

West, "the hysterical confessions of the accused seemed to have been extorted by some mysterious means, and the whole proceedings appeared like a play staged with consummate, strange, and frightful artistry." Only while breathing the Moscow air was he was able to believe in the guilt of the accused. That said, Feuchtwanger termed the confessions of guilt "inexplicable" to "Western minds."[103] The East-West cultural divide he so strongly felt ultimately served a profoundly political purpose.

Feuchtwanger was less naïve and more purposeful in his endorsement of Stalinism and the show trials than commonly understood, but the Karavkina reports also show him to be innocent of crucial knowledge about Soviet cultural politics circa 1937. He trusted his guide-interpreter so openly that her reports often noted the specific writer or intellectual who provided him with information or shaped his opinion, and in the context of 1937, Karavkina's fingerpointing assumed the character of a Purge-era denunciation. As Stern has noted, Karavkina sometimes penciled in the names of the "culprits" on the pages she submitted, which were later underlined and marked up by higher-ups registering politically important or damaging data.[104]

Like others before him, this friend of Stalinism engaged in self-censorship. As Hartmann has shown, in the wake of Kol'tsov's visit to Sanary-sur-Mer in May 1937, Feuchtwanger extensively revised the manuscript of *Moscow 1937*, especially the parts on Trotsky. The Russian translation was published in a print run of 200,000 copies.[105] *Moscow 1937* was already out of date in 1937, however. The work too openly discussed Western critics of the trials, and even its criticisms of Trotsky now too flagrantly broke the Soviet taboo of silence in the rapidly widening vortex of the Great Terror. Within a few months of publication, Feuchtwanger's apology for Stalinism was removed from the bookstores and banned.[106]

Justifications of Violence and the Socialist Homeland

Having juxtaposed European visitors from opposite sides of the political spectrum, we can now stand back to consider the differences between them. For the Arplan rightists, violence was close to the surface in their attraction to militarized mass mobilization; for Gide and Feuchtwanger, it was the subject of wrenching doubts. If philofascist intellectuals and National Bolsheviks were openly entranced by political violence, leftist sympathizers tended to downplay or deny it. At the same time, its justification as historically necessary was, for Soviet friends, an ideological move that held great resonance. Raymond Aron, noting how "violence itself attracts and fascinates more than it repels," wrote that it was precisely because of the violence it spawned that the Russian

Revolution enjoyed the prestige it did among Left intellectuals. "Only revolution...or a revolutionary regime, because it accepts the permanent use of violence, seems capable of attaining the goal of perfection."[107]

The true scale of early Soviet violence was an exceedingly politicized issue, but foreign residents, diplomats, and even sympathizers could be very well informed on the nature and scale of Soviet repressive policies.[108] At issue was not merely acknowledgement but also ideological explanation or justification. When the friends of the Soviet Union justified political violence, Russian history and backwardness loomed large. Just as Soviet socialism when emulated elsewhere would acquire a distinctly more human face, so violence was explainable both in terms of the savage nature of the population and centuries of autocratic rule. After the Webbs had sailed from London to Leningrad on the steamer Smol'nyi for a two-month visit, Beatrice wrote in her notebook that Soviet communism was made out of material "very raw indeed... Owing to this initial backwardness, some features of Soviet Russia will be and remain repulsive to more developed races."[109] David Engerman has shown the prevalence among American Russian experts and observers, many of them far from any affiliation with communism or even pro-Soviet views, of favorable opinions about Soviet modernization and a justification of its costs, fed among those with in-country experience by an often visceral disgust for the beastly peasantry.[110] In August 1936, Beatrice Webb met the first Moscow trial with notes in her diary of torture and lack of judicial due process, but only in the context of British imperial atrocities done with "an easy conscience." Indeed, one of the arguments justifying the brutality of Soviet collectivization in the Webbs' book had been to portray it as historically inevitable when compared to earlier periods of English history, in this case the hardships associated with the enclosure of the English commons in the late eighteenth and early nineteenth centuries. The first Moscow show trial prompted Beatrice to reach back to a much earlier analogy: "The U.S.S.R. is still medieval in its savage pursuit of the heretic."[111]

The irony that apparently escaped Beatrice Webb when she wrote those words was that medieval barbarism had become virtually synonymous with fascism in the anti-fascist culture of the Popular Front. In 1933, the medieval trope had been furthered in the transnational commentary of German émigrés inside the Soviet Union and Europe and was dominant in Soviet commentary as well: "fascist middle ages" was the title of the chronicle of arrests, book burnings, and imprisonments run in the Soviet journal *International Literature* after the Nazi seizure of power.[112] The predominance of this analysis of fascism as an anti-modern phenomenon on the Left not only ignored all modern aspects of fascism but also made National Socialism appear as a throwback to past barbarism rather than an unprecedented novelty. In one of the many commentaries on Nazi policy published in the Soviet Union, militarism was called even less new than "the far from new cult of personality, the idea of the leader (*vozhdia*)." As this suggests, many commentaries on fascist purges, censorship, and terror had to grapple, if only implicitly, with comparisons to Bolshevism. This particular article discussed the fact that Goebbels had studied Eisenstein's *Battleship Potemkin* and had even noted that fascist film was made "according to the 'Bolshevik method,'" but in the end explained rather lamely that Soviet film derived its artistic and political power from its truthful depiction of actual relations. A 1936 article describing the Nuremberg rallies and gigantic construction projects felt it necessary to deny comparisons with the "new life where freedom, labor, and beauty reigns." The real analogy was with the pharaohs.[113] The communist interpretation of fascism as primitive and atavistic fed the dichotomies of barbarism versus civilization, past and future, violence and humanism, lies and truth.

In spite of Soviet and European anti-fascist indictments of Nazi bloodthirstiness and sadism, the older Bolshevik tradition of justifying violence remained available for pro-Soviet Western intellectuals. The 1934 biography of Bertolt Brecht contained in the files of the Union of Writers' Foreign Commission highlighted some key facts: he had innovated a genre of "didactic-publicistic" plays, had worked in close contact with the German Communist Party since 1928, and was connected to the renaissance man of Soviet revolutionary culture, Sergei Tret'iakov. Indeed, Tret'iakov was present in Berlin at the premier of Brecht's didactic 1930 play *Measures Taken* (Die Massnahme), depicting the mercilessness necessary to shoot and kill a comrade who did not obey party directives. Katerina Clark has argued that, in certain ways, this piece was *plus royaliste que le roi* and anticipated certain aspects of Stalinist culture. Brecht's *Measures Taken*—and, by extension, an emphasis on "ruthlessness" (*besposhchadnost'*, a term Brecht had adopted from Lenin) among the avant-garde—was a product of transnational cultural exchange between Berlin and Moscow.[114]

There was another way Western visitors to the Soviet Union could absorb Bolshevik ruthlessness: "going native." The young Arthur Koestler was a Hungarian-Jewish exile attracted by Zionism who joined the Communist Party in Berlin in 1929. Koestler's travels through Ukraine, the Caucasus, and Central Asia starting in the summer of 1932 found him in Khar'kov in the starving winter of 1932–1933, where the marketplace resembled "a scene out of Brueghel or Hieronymous Bosch." There, he strenuously denied the famine and defended the line that only class enemies, the kulaks, were suffering. In Baku, Koestler's affair with a beautiful Russian woman of noble origin ended when he denounced her to the secret police. This was no abstract justification of violence or didactic agitation for the necessity of a purge. It was an example of consequential "measures taken" in his own personal life, and the incident haunted him later in life. Koestler attempted not only to speak Bolshevik but also to go Bolshevik. While on an ensuing five-month trip to Central Asia in 1933, he befriended the American poet Langston Hughes, who recalled Koestler's fascination watching a political trial in Ashkabad. "I guess that was the beginning of *Darkness at Noon,*" wrote Hughes.[115] He might have added *The God that Failed.* The closer a sympathizer was to the Party or the political culture of communism, the more likely he was to attempt to internalize Bolshevik conspiratorial ruthlessness rather than uphold the 1930s taboo on acknowledging political repression that followed Gorky's writings on Solovki.

Upholding Bolshevik ruthlessness, however, was entirely possible without any cultural exchange, proximity to the Party, or going native. Early Soviet political culture may have provided the inspiration in all these cases, but the basic ethical underpinnings on which Bolshevik ideology itself rested—the revolutionary doctrine that the ends justified violent means—was grounded squarely in European social democracy and revolutionary thought, easily accessible by independent political thinkers of many colors. Of the fellow-travelers, Bernard Shaw demonstrates this best. In his unpublished 1932–33 *Rationalization of Russia,* a work that anticipated his justification of violence in his plays of the next several years, Shaw included an entire section on extermination, almost gleefully employing the metaphor of "weeding the garden." Like Beatrice Webb, Shaw normalized Stalinist extermination with reference to the history of Western atrocities: "Cromwell saw that the extermination of the Irish was a logical part of the policy of settling Ireland with English plantation... The red man has been exterminated in North America almost as extensively as the bison." In Shaw's extended justification of mass killing, Fabian social engineering rested on utilitarian social calculation: "Our question is not to kill or not to kill, but how to select the right people to kill." At the same time, Shaw's brief trip to the USSR in 1930 encouraged him to adopt a distinctively Bolshevik inflection to this utilitarian credo. Anyone who opposed the collective must be "liquidated as vermin" and this was "inevitable and irremediable under the stern morality of Communism."[116]

In the introduction to his 1933 play *On the Rocks,* Shaw included an uncharacteristically earnest lecture that developed his thoughts on political violence. Cruelty for its own sake was not right, he avowed, and for a new model, "sooner or later all countries will need to study OGPU." Modern killing must become a "humane science instead of the miserable mixture of piracy, cruelty, vengeance, rare conceit, and superstition it now is."[117] However, in a sequel to *On the Rocks* entitled *The Simpleton of Unexpected Isles,* completed in 1934, Shaw's rational science of killing was transformed into a terrible chorus, as all the characters chant "kill" and repeat the language of extermination with an aestheticized collective unity.[118] Clearly, Shaw was one of those intellectuals attracted to fascism as well as to communism.

The European fellow-travelers of fascism remain far less well-known than their *communisant* cousins. In Britain and France, a small but substantial minority of intellectuals gravitated toward Italian Fascism and German National Socialism, and the factors pushing them are comparable to those attracting others to communism. Just as on the Left, motivations varied widely. The crisis of liberalism, economic collapse, and political malaise pulled intellectuals to the vigor and confidence of the fascist as well as the communist movement. Anti-communism was as significant as anti-fascism in pushing intellectuals to the opposite extreme. As with Soviet sympathy, geopolitics played a distinct role: for example, the Franco-Soviet Pact was of distinct importance to the rise of British sympathy for Germany to its height in 1936.[119] The biographies of left-wing intellectuals converting to the Right have been studied in great depth in these and other national contexts (starting with Mussolini), illuminating how deep-seated personal and ideological concerns that propelled intellectuals to the Left could persist on the other extreme of the political spectrum. One also finds the kind of naïve idealism so often satirized among pro-Soviet intellectuals: Griffiths writes of fellow-travelers of the Right drawn by "a concern for the condition of the working man, a belief in a spiritual lead, or a propensity to see the best in everyone and everything."[120]

There were even the pull factors of travel and cultural diplomacy, and in form Nazi methods bear some resemblance to the Soviet-led effort. For example, foreign minister Joachim von Ribbentrop helped organize the Deutsch-Französische Gesellschaft, and the Comité France-Allegmagne published a journal that became an "excellent vehicle for German propaganda in France." An Anglo-German Fellowship had a counterpart in the Deutsch-Englische Gesellschaft, and free visits of foreigners to Germany were arranged by the Deutsch-Europäische Kulturbund. In addition to Ribbentrop, the Nazi Party formed an Aussenpolitische Amt—the first head of which was Alfred Rosenberg—that became "a kind of foreign information service." Prominent foreigners were received by the top Nazi leadership, and visitors saw youth camps, houses of workers, and, rather than Red Square on May Day, the grandiose regimentation of large-scale Nazi rallies, especially those in Nuremberg.[121] Soviet mediators found their equivalent in Nazi emissaries sent to cultivate elites, such as the Germans whom Isaiah Berlin recalled clumsily equating German territorial demands to British imperial claims in the common room of All Souls, Oxford, in the late 1930s.[122]

Indeed, Soviet cultural officials in various contexts demonstrated an awareness of foreign intellectuals' ability to shift from communism to fascism and vice-versa. In an off-the-mark speculation, Arosev propounded the notion in 1934 that the visiting pro-Soviet publicist Harold Laski's disillusionment with parliaments and the search for "new paths" could well lead him to "a modernized fascism." Italian Fascist cinematographers who praised the achievements of Soviet culture, including one with personal ties to Mussolini, were welcomed in 1932 as potentially genuine friends of the USSR, and in 1936, the Soviet embassy in Paris hoped for a positive response from the Moscow trip of the French anti-Semite and literary admirer of Hitler, Louis-Ferdinand Céline. Céline, however, returned to France declaring that 98 percent of the tourists visiting the USSR were Jews and that "I'd rather have twelve Hitlers than one omnipresent Blum."[123]

Given the parallels and interconnections, the differences between the appeal of fascism and the appeal of communism to the two movements' fellow-travelers are especially revealing. They go beyond the obvious importance of tenets specific to the differing ideologies, such as, of course, nationalism, racism, and anti-Semitism. One of the most important has to do with the nature and relative importance of violence. Céline once said: "Personally I find Hitler, Franco, Mussolini fabulously débonnaire, admirably magnanimous, infinitely to my taste." The aesthetic appeal went beyond the leaders, however: the prominence of aggression and the celebration of violence in Fascism and Nazism was such that it spawned an entire aesthetic in the "literary fascism" of writers such as Robert Brasillach.[124] Ultimately, one of the pillars upon the fascist aesthetic rested on the dark promise of violence; Bolshevik ruthlessness may have had an aesthetic dimension in the image of the leather-jacketed commissar, but it was primarily a mindset resting on the iron logic cultivated by adepts of Marxism-Leninism and felt mostly by those closest to communist political culture. Dominant, rather, were such attractions as the humanism enshrined in anti-fascist culture and the denial of violence in the Gorky-inspired propaganda about humane rehabilitation. Unlike the friends of communism, sympathizers of fascism were inclined to openly embrace violence as a style of rule.

The Soviet Union, moreover, was able to foster an emotional identification among leftist foreigners that extreme nationalism based on an ideology of racial superiority was incapable of developing. The Soviets may have significantly modified their internationalism by the 1930s, presenting Moscow as the world's beacon and the center of all progress, but they continued to actively foster the notion that the USSR was a new homeland for foreign critics of capitalism. For non-Germans, National Socialism allowed only for admiration and emulation, and by definition barred membership in the *Volksgemeinschaft*; for non-Soviets, communism held out the possibility of genuine participation. Even the bourgeoisie was included, for its best part could, like the rehabilitated domestic "bourgeois specialists" in Stalin's 1932 formulation, "come over to the side of the proletariat."[125] Foreigners were encouraged to feel a sense of belonging.

One of the best cases of this kind of emotional identification with the Soviet Union is that of the American Paul Robeson, whom VOKS officials lauded as the "most famous negro singer and actor." By the time of Robeson's first Soviet visit—with his wife, Eslanda Goode, in 1934—hundreds of "black pilgrims" from the United States and the Caribbean, some staying for long visits or permanently, had already forged numerous links in an encounter between "black and red" that included a number of the most influential black intellectuals of the twentieth century.[126] Like his predecessors, Robeson was propelled by the image of a society free of racism. In this sense, Robeson was exemplary; like Gide, he was drawn to Soviet socialism by one issue that colored all the others. For feminists, it was women's liberation. The ways in which concerns fundamental to these observers' identities became paramount factors in their embrace of the revolution were in some ways analogous to the manner in which a wide variety of professionals extrapolated from the professional concerns of greatest importance to their own lives. As Lewis S. Feuer put it in the context of American travelers, "The social worker was ready to see the Soviet Union as a kind of Hull House on a national scale ...; the progressive educator was ready to see the Soviet experiment as a nation-wide Laboratory School."[127]

Unlike Gide, however, Robeson's primary concern was not thwarted by experience and greater knowledge of the country. Rather, his visits made him feel at home. African-American visitors to the early Soviet Union regularly recorded not merely the widespread absence of racism but a warm and enthusiastic welcome fueled by Soviet internationalism. In the 1930s, black visitors were often invited to the front of queues or told not to pay. Robeson famously commented that only visiting the Soviet Union made him "for the first time feel like a full human being."[128]

Robeson's Sovietophilia also involved a strong dose of Russophilia. Robeson learned virtually fluent Russian; in a hotel conversation with his guide, Robeson connected his love of Russian culture with his acceptance among Russians.[129] Many a visiting intellectual's Soviet sympathy had been eased by an immersion in Russian culture. Robeson developed a passion for Pushkin, who became the centerpiece of a monumental Soviet cult shortly after Robeson started visiting the USSR.

Robeson also fell in love with Russian folk culture, and it was his folk aesthetic that gave him fame and enormous popularity among Soviet audiences. Like a number of other black intellectuals, Robeson wished to probe the similarities and solidarities among Russians, as oppressed non-Europeans, and Africans. During his 1935 visit, one of several short trips in the pre-war period

Figure 7.2 Paul Robeson greeting Sergei Eisenstein in Moscow, January 11, 1934. The emotional attachment the American singer and actor felt to the socialist homeland was fueled by cultural Russophilia and the absence of racism he felt during several visits between 1934 and 1938. Source: RIA Novosti Photo Library.

between 1934 and 1938, Robeson impressed VOKS official Isidor Amdur with his view of Russian folk songs as reminiscent of African music. Amdur reported that "of all European languages Russian, in his words, is the closest to the negro language, since it is precisely the Russian language that is closely tied to the East."[130] Robeson developed a theory of the universality of folk music grounded in the pentatonic scale, something Baldwin has referred to as his "own fiction of universality." In other words, Robeson's cultural mission in promoting and performing folk music fit like a glove with his appreciation for Soviet nationalities policy as preserving national cultural traditions while promoting internationalism. VOKS materials on Robeson's visit in 1935 confirm his special interest in Soviet nationalities policy, which, as he euphorically accepted in talks on the achievements of the union republics and meetings with ethnographers, allowed for equality of peoples at the same time as minorities could develop and preserve their own cultures.[131]

Robeson was far from the only foreign visitor to develop this kind of visceral, emotional attachment to the land of victorious socialism. Zdeněk Nejedlý, the Czech professor of musicology and head of the Czechoslovak friendship society, developed such a strong bond to the land of socialism as a model and "teacher" that, after visiting the Bolshevo commune, he tried to convert two Turkish specialists to the view that the Soviet Union was "our best friend." The same summer of Robeson's 1935 visit, Nejedlý linked the nostrum of the revolutionary homeland as new and young to his own personal rejuvenation, announcing that each time he visited he became ten or twenty years younger.[132]

If the wayward foes and wayward friends examined in this chapter—the Arplan rightists, Gide, Feuchtwanger—had anything in common, it was that they all harbored unsettling reservations about Stalin's Soviet Union even as they weighed whether to embrace it. On the other hand, Robeson and Nejedlý, two very different figures in their backgrounds and motivations, personally identified with the notion of an internationalist homeland, or a reconciliation of the national and the international. On the strength of these emotional attachments, they remained loyal to their home away from home, through the Purges and the Pact and for decades to come.

8

Rise of the Stalinist Superiority Complex

Stalin's Depression-era vow to overtake the advanced West, which meshed with Gorky's grandiose goals for Soviet culture, was a promissory note for ever-more-frequent declarations of Soviet superiority. By the time the Five-Year Plan and collectivization justified the mid-1930s declaration that socialism had been successfully built, a sea change had occurred in the official depiction of the Soviet Union's relationship to the rest of the world. Assertions of across-the-board Soviet superiority increasingly disturbed even some of the most sympathetic foreign visitors looking eastward during the heyday of the interwar pilgrimage. André Gide, writing at the height of the Popular Front in 1936, was startled to learn that the Soviet citizen "has been persuaded that everything abroad and in every department is far less prosperous than in the U.S.S.R." When Gide suggested to a group of naval officers that people in France knew more about the Soviet Union than the other way around, "suddenly somebody in a lyrical outburst, stepping out from the group exclaimed: 'In order to describe all the new and splendid and great things that are being done in the Soviet Union, there would not be paper enough in the whole world.'" Gide referred to this set of attitudes as a "superiority complex."[1]

The term "complex" is especially apt, implying not only a group of psychological associations but, as in the military-industrial usage, a range of interlocking practices and institutions. While the promotion of Soviet "achievements" was a central element of Soviet cultural diplomacy of the 1920s, the advent of the Stalinist superiority complex still marks a remarkable turn. By the late 1930s, the party's agitators were instructed to report gushing praise from foreign delegations to underscore the leading place of "the country of victorious socialism" not only in culture and science, but in economics as well. "In machine-building the USSR holds *first place* in Europe and *second place* in the world...In excavation of gold, in production of superphosphate the Soviet Union has *overtaken all the countries of Europe*." As Raisa Orlova recalled: "If one were to do a statistical analysis of newspaper language of these years, phrases like 'the very best [whatever] in the world,' 'for the first time in the history of mankind,' and 'only in our country' would prove to be among the most frequent."[2]

The new willingness to trumpet Soviet superiority over the rest of the world was a far-reaching phenomenon far broader than agitprop. It became engrained in Socialist Realism and popular culture; the fired-up young enthusiasts of the 1930s generation were thirsting for revolutionary achievements of their own. They formed part of what became known as the "first Soviet generation"—itself depicted as "new" and "unprecedented."[3] At the same time, NKVD reports on popular reactions to press coverage and extensive workplace discussions of international affairs noted cynical jokes about the slogan of overtaking the West: "When we catch up, can we stay there?" What is more, observers have noted among the elites a covert and often exaggerated respect for things foreign. This remains true even later, at the apogee of the nativist condemnation of "foreignness" (*inostranshchina*) during the Zhdanov period.[4] When the pendulum had finally swung back again and the Soviet Union during the Thaw once more needed to learn from the advanced West, Ilya Ehrenburg reflected on the dialectical nature of Stalinist aggrandizement: "Unending talk about one's superiority is linked with groveling before things foreign—they are but different aspects of an inferiority complex."[5] In some respects, the two were part of the same ideological worldview: Péteri has referred to "the inevitable oscillation between two diametrically opposite states of mind among the Leninist modernizing elite of a relatively backward country: the hubris of systemic superiority on the one hand, and the admission of the developmental (economic, social, and cultural) inferiority."[6] In the late 1930s and under late Stalinism, that admission for a time became rare, even taboo.

We are faced, therefore, with a paradox, one that to a certain extent confounds any analysis of Stalinism and what it changed after 1928–29. On the one hand, in terms of the reception of foreigners, the "second revolution" in many ways involved merely shifts and modifications of the 1920s system, not radical transformations. In terms of attitudes, representatives of the bourgeois world were already sources of both heightened opportunity and grave suspicion from the first years after the revolution. On the other hand, pre-war Stalinism involved some of the most ostensibly abrupt reversals imaginable toward the outside world: after the height of the carefully cultivated Soviet appeal to Western Europe and the United States during the Popular Front, the international contacts and influence that had brought prestige suddenly became the basis for mass physical annihilation as VOKS and the organs of Soviet cultural diplomacy were decimated during the Great Terror. The antifascism so ingrained in the mid-1930s was first undermined during the Terror, then shockingly reversed with the Nazi-Soviet Pact.

One common way of explaining the shifts and reversals of the 1930s is to simply ascribe all causal change to the dictator and his henchmen, for it was they who started the Purges and signed the Pact. Yet, this begs the question of how the leadership arrived at its decisions and how Stalin responded to pivotal developments in the evolution of the Soviet system. At the same time, the dramatic and rapid changes in the Soviet domestic order and in the international arena in the 1930s had a deep impact on practices and attitudes built up for many years. In the final analysis, Stalin was also a creature of the system that he shaped; his henchmen operated within the system's considerable constraints. Why, then, did such very different phases of the Soviet system occur under his rule?

The Stalin Revolution comprised four substantially different phases: the Great Break of 1928–31, the mid-1930s stabilization of 1932–36, the Great Purges of 1936–39, and the post-Purge period of the Nazi-Soviet Pact of 1939–41. The movement between these very different subperiods is of crucial importance, especially the way these subperiods accompanied radically different stances toward the outside world. For, as in the 1920s, the external and internal dimensions of the Soviet system remained very tightly linked, and each of the four periods had its international counterpart. Most notably, the militant and iconoclastic proletarianization campaigns of the Great Break corresponded with the sectarian stances associated with the "third period" of the Comintern; the post-iconoclastic, mid-1930s stabilization of "socialism achieved" corresponded with the height of Soviet anti-fascism and the flexibility of the Popular Front, in many ways facilitating the heyday of Western attraction to the Soviet order.

Any theory of a simple, anti-internationalist *volte-face* applied to the 1930s glosses over the fact that Stalin-era culture—at least until the Great Terror—remained extensively engaged with the Western world. Stalinism writ large is commonly associated with a repudiation of internationalism and the incorporation or fusion of communist ideology with ethnic Russian nationalism, itself closely associated with Nicholas Timasheff's famous thesis of a "Great Retreat" from revolutionary goals toward a conservative social order. In this context, the promotion of Soviet superiority might be seen as a function of the mid- to late-1930s campaigns for Soviet patriotism, rehabilitation of the tsarist past, and "official Russocentrism." David Brandenberger's study of these campaigns implied as much, noting how "the sense of distinctiveness associated with nationhood often endows constituents with a sense of belonging to a 'superior' or 'elite' group."[7] The Soviet superiority complex represents more than an injection of nationalism into communist ideology, however. Katerina Clark refers to a "great appropriation," rather than a Great Retreat, in which 1930s culture reworked elements from the past and from "world culture" in a bid to turn Moscow into the capital of a world order conceived along various international axes, so that patriotism and cosmopolitanism were not incompatible. Many Soviet intellectuals channeled this endeavor into a pursuit of cultural primacy in their world, Europe, while the party leaders, declaring superiority in all realms, were moved to compete in the cultural sphere as well.[8]

International engagement—the height of which corresponded to the heyday of the Western pilgrimage of the interwar years—thus accompanied the rise of the Stalinist superiority complex in the same period. The key point is that ambitious Soviet international activity, even while drastically different from the anti-foreign spy mania of the Terror, was itself deeply committed to the promotion of Soviet superiority as culture moved to the center of Soviet claims to global pre-eminence. In other words, both the politics of international engagement and the politics of anti-foreign isolationism in the 1930s helped develop a more robust superiority complex, but the ways in which they did so were different. One attempted to promote Soviet hegemony through state-sponsored engagement; the other strove to isolate through vigilance against conflated foreign and domestic foes.

The manner in which forces on each side intersected and clashed is thus key to understanding the Stalinist 1930s and the ultimate, Pyrrhic victory of extreme isolationism and autarky. As this suggests, "Stalinism" itself is best understood as a volatile and often contradictory mix; decisive shifts occurred only when major developments changed the relations among its component strands. Among the competing tendencies of the 1930s, one of the most notable was the sharpening clash of hegemony versus vigilance in the Soviet approach to the outside world.

New Vistas and New Perils: The Popular Front

Several factors combined to make the period from 1934 to 1936 into the height of the interwar "pilgrimage" of Western visitors and the period of greatest success of Soviet cultural diplomacy abroad. The first, of course, was the rise of Nazi Germany in 1933, which polarized the European order into extremes of Right and Left, each with very different claims on global predominance. Soviet-led anti-fascism brought large numbers of previously uninvolved Western intellectuals into front organizations defending civilization and progress against Nazi barbarism. As a result of the politics and ideology of the Popular Front, the Soviets were able to take advantage of the moment. The post-1934 Comintern stance of promoting communist alliances with socialists and other anti-fascist political parties—which contributed to the June 1934 alliance between the French Communist Party and Léon

Blum's Socialists, the short-lived Popular Front government in France after 1936, and the *Frente Popular* in the Second Spanish Republic—was only one of several key developments underpinning this success. For unlike in the days of greatest strain in the "dual policy" of the 1920s, Soviet foreign policy and the Comintern, both controlled by Stalin, operated in greater tandem in this period. After the unusually close diplomatic and cultural relations with Weimar Germany abruptly ended with the Nazi rise to power, Soviet foreign policy and cultural diplomacy turned toward Paris and London and were thus more heavily than ever oriented around points West. The rise of authoritarian right-wing regimes in Central and Eastern Europe throughout this period made Soviet cultural initiatives difficult at best, and analysts frequently noted the fear of intellectuals and professionals in maintaining any Soviet connections at all. In Austria after the Civil War in 1934, for example, the Soviet friendship society was closed, and VOKS found only the slightest opportunities for its activities.[9]

The opposite side of this coin was the greater legitimacy conferred on Soviet-European contacts in those countries where left-coalition politics domestically were supplemented with a foreign-policy alignment with the USSR. Between 1933 and 1934, Intourist scored a 93 percent increase in foreign tourists—a direct result of diplomatic recognition by the United States and warming relations with France. The period of intensive visits by French intellectual and cultural figures to the Soviet Union was initiated by the Franco-Soviet Pact of May 1935, for starting that summer season VOKS's French experts registered a "significant growth in the visits from France of members of the intellectual professions." By the same token, the virtually identical mutual assistance treaty signed with Czechoslovakia produced immediate repercussions. Just two weeks later, VOKS received a report from Prague: "Work in the area of cultural relations has started to develop at great speed." In addition to those traditionally sympathetic groups motivated by political affinity, pan-Slavic solidarity (which Soviet observers labeled "Slavophile moods") and the Depression-fueled desire to work in the USSR played their part. For the first time, even Czechoslovak cultural officials, circles close to the government, and Social Democrats were becoming accessible to the Soviets.[10] In 1935, new opportunities for Soviet initiatives were quickly opening up in Britain, too, including successful visits by Soviet scientists and fruits of the new geopolitically fueled interest in the USSR among members of the political establishment. A congress of peace and friendship in December—which featured the entire gamut of prominent sympathizers, from the Webbs to Margaret Llewelyn Davies, the head of the friendship society, explicitly capitalized on the visit of conservative Foreign Secretary Anthony Eden to Moscow, and the concomitant hope that Anglo-Soviet friendship could prevent war—in order to call attention to Soviet domestic achievements. All in all, VOKS's Amdur gushed that 1935 was the year of a significant "breakthrough."[11]

The heyday of Soviet cultural diplomacy in the mid-1930s was predicated on receptivity to the Soviet message among new groups of potentially sympathetic Western figures and a broader and more flexible Soviet desire to reach them. Popular Front coalition politics legitimized outreach to non-communist leftists abroad, but Popular Front tactics, which began only in 1934, were themselves made possible by the domestic muting of sectarian struggle and the campaign mode after 1931–32. In other words, Comintern policy was itself partially the consequence of the repudiation of the Great Break in domestic cultural politics, and there was a direct link between the two.

Nothing demonstrates the tight interconnection between internal Soviet and external communist cultural politics better than the literary arm of the Comintern, the International Organization of Revolutionary Writers (MORP), which was founded in 1930. The literary figures in Moscow who led MORP—largely Central European émigrés—directly modeled themselves on the Soviet proletarian-writers movement and specifically RAPP, the Russian Association of Proletarian Writers, the most powerful of the Great Break cultural organizations that so deeply imprinted the culture of the Five-Year Plan with infighting and militant proletarianization. MORP upbraided non-communist foreign sympathizers much as RAPP's proletarianizers harshly attacked the non-party intelligentsia within the Soviet Union, and MORP leaders feuded with the Communist Henri Barbusse for his attempts to create a more heterodox coalition. The liquidation of RAPP, a signal event paving the way for a repudiation of Great Break sectarianism and a general shift within Soviet culture in 1931–32, combined with the influx of German émigré writers into MORP to transform it in 1932–34 into an organ of anti-fascism and a professional, extensively organized arm of cultural diplomacy in literature.[12]

A watershed moment in the development of Soviet culture came with the first Congress of the Union of Soviet Writers, the paradigmatic Stalin-era cultural organization that unified the warring factions of the earlier era and set the course for all to rally under the banner of Socialist Realism. At the same time, the 1934 Congress was an international event. Mixing with the 600 Soviet writers and top political figures who were delegates to the Congress were 43 foreigners representing a who's who of leftist literary friends and sympathizers including Louis Aragon, Johannes R. Becher, Jean-Richard Bloch, Oskar Maria Graf, and André Malraux. Their presence cemented the predominance of literary figures as the foreign friend *par excellence*.[13] It was also at the Writers' Congress, as Boris Frezinskii has shown, that a complicated circulation of ideas occurred that planted the seed for the great Soviet-sponsored writers' congresses in Europe. The idea of repeating the Soviet congress of writers abroad was reportedly raised when the foreign writers mixed with Soviet leaders and litterateurs at Gorky's dacha on August 24, 1934. At the congress itself, Karl Radek, perhaps acting on Stalin's wishes, proposed the creation of a united anti-fascist front of writers to Malraux and Bloch, who then shared it with Ehrenburg, likely when he was back in Paris.[14] The European writers' congresses became a centerpiece of anti-fascist culture during the Popular Front.

Completing the circle in this influential chain of interactions begun at the Writers Congress, Ehrenburg seized the initiative, playing a distinct role in inaugurating the Popular Front in culture. From the perspective of this Westernizer who was finding his place in the Stalin order, even MORP's post-1932 moderation in the wake of RAPP's demise was insufficient, for it still displayed short-sighted intolerance toward sympathetic Western intellectuals. A pivotal moment in Ehrenburg's own relations with Stalin came in September 1934—on the heels of the Writers' Congress and Comintern general secretary Georgi Dimitrov's announcements that summer sanctioning anti-fascist alliances among communist and socialist parties. At a clandestine rendezvous in Odessa, Ehrenburg consulted with his old friend Bukharin, veteran party theoretician and ex-Comintern chief who remained prominent in scientific and cultural activities after Stalin defeated him as a "right deviationist" in 1928–29. Bukharin advised Ehrenburg on his detailed and carefully conceived appeal to Stalin for a broad and inclusive coalition of European and American writers, and likely delivered it to Stalin in Moscow. The missive—the first Ehrenburg had ever personally directed to the Soviet leader—shrewdly played up the new potential for anti-fascism to facilitate "active defense of the USSR." Its chief objects of criticism were the émigré writers of the Comintern's MORP. Unimpressed by the group's professionalization after 1932, Ehrenburg described MORP as the creature of "a few Hungarian, Polish, and German writers of the third rank" who remained stuck in the tradition of RAPP. In a revealing criticism, Ehrenburg portrayed them not only as sectarians and hacks but also as people who had—unlike him—"irrevocably separated themselves from life in the West." They were thus blind to the post-1933 opportunities for attracting leading Western intellectuals and constantly on the attack, alienating sympathetic figures such as Barbusse.[15]

Ehrenburg had cannily combined an appeal to internationalize a shift that had already occurred in internal Soviet cultural policy with a recognition of opportunities created by the changed landscape after the Nazi seizure of power. At the same time, Ehrenburg moved against his own nemeses, militants whose attacks he himself had been deflecting for more than a decade. Ehrenburg listed the most famous writers known by their translations into Russian who would be willing "immediately" to follow the Soviet lead—including Rolland, Gide, Malraux, Barbusse, Aragon, Feuchtwanger, Dreiser, Jean-Richard Bloch, Thomas and Heinrich Mann, and John Dos Passos. This played on the Soviet proclivity in cultural diplomacy to seek out figures of influence and responsibility, which mimicked Stalin's strategy in politics: "The West European and American intelligentsia listens to the 'big names.' Therefore the significance of a broad anti-fascist organization led by famous writers will be great indeed."[16]

Stalin was completely convinced. He instructed Politburo member Kaganovich, who during this period often handled questions of ideology: "Read the letter of comrade Ehrenburg. He is right. One must liquidate the RAPP tradition in MORP...This is a big deal. Pay attention to this." Kaganovich was tasked to carry out Ehrenburg's proposal, and the result was MORP self-criticism repudiating "elements of RAPPism" (elementy rappovshchiny) and, in late 1935, the demise of MORP itself. In other words, the Ehrenburg-Bukharin initiative in no small part helped to usher in the resoundingly successful Soviet flexibility of the Popular Front.[17] The more immediate result, although Stalin preferred to work on it himself with Barbusse, his biographer, rather than meet personally with Ehrenburg, was the Congress for the Defense of Culture in Paris, in June 1935, which gathered more than 320 delegates from 35 countries and up to 3,000 spectators a day. Thus did anti-fascist culture come into its own. It was as a hybrid synthesis of international engagements and interactions, involving key concepts differently interpreted in different national and political contexts and the carefully concealed, yet to many observers readily apparent, role of Soviet backing and intellectual agents. The very notion of a writers' congress was previously unknown in France and had been adapted from the 1934 Union of Writers model.[18]

Ironically, MORP had already replaced its discarded model of RAPP with that of the new and dominant Soviet literary organization, the Union of Soviet Writers, paving the way for its own demise. MORP's new leadership before its liquidation included Soviet figures from the Writers Union, such as Sergei Tret'iakov, and incorporated major players with VOKS experience, such as the writer Mikhail Apletin and critic Sergei Dinamov. Having been involved with a transformed MORP in 1934–35, these literary officials and party intellectuals transferred to the Union of Writers itself, specifically to its Foreign Commission, an authoritative new organization that appeared on the scene in 1936. Mikhail Kol'tsov, who had proposed the liquidation of MORP to the Politburo, took charge and was allocated funds to cover travel expenses and Intourist accommodations for ten to twelve visiting foreign writers per year. When Kol'tsov convened his Union of Writers Foreign Commission in 1936, the figures sitting around the table included seasoned veterans with extensive international experience (Apletin, Tret'iakov, and Dinamov) and Soviet poets and writers with international reach such as Boris Pil'niak and Boris Pasternak.[19]

The outset of the Popular Front period in 1934 coincided with the appointment to VOKS of Aleksandr Arosev, who energetically attempted to parlay the new possibilities for Soviet cultural diplomacy into a higher stature for his organization. Arosev's doubts and insecurities were matched by keenly felt political ambitions and a longstanding alliance with the Stalinist wing of the Party dating to the mid-1920s. Arosev repeatedly turned to Stalin to help renovate VOKS, using his old friendships with Molotov, Ezhov, and other party leaders whenever possible. He faced an uphill battle. VOKS, no longer under attack for its focus on the intelligentsia, had nonetheless lost a good deal of prestige since the 1920s and appeared to Arosev a clear demotion from his ambassadorial days. He yearned for a new diplomatic posting in Paris, but this discontent stimulated him all the more to succeed as head of VOKS.

Plagued by his personal doubts about Soviet culture and the West, Arosev in the mid-1930s fired off a barrage of proposals to redeem VOKS's standing: to increase the qualifications of its cadres, to give it a clear-cut stature in the state (in 1936, he proposed subordinating VOKS to Sovnarkom), and to boost its place in the hierarchy through the Central Committee, proposing for the purpose to convene an "authoritative commission on foreign cultural relations." Arosev dreamed that VOKS would be granted a monopoly claim on managing international cultural relations from on high, just as Intourist's monopoly on foreign tourism was solidified in 1936. A newly empowered VOKS, he wrote with bombast to Stalin, would provide "political verification" of all cultural currents flowing in from outside Soviet borders. Arosev used the argument that his agency was neglected to lobby for an increase in his own stature and privileges—for example, in his bid to build a dacha at the writer's colony in Peredel'kino.[20]

Arosev never convinced Stalin or other leaders to upgrade VOKS to a monopoly in the realm of cultural diplomacy. His ambitious flurry of activity, however, set the stage for his agency to take advantage of the great new opportunities of the Popular Front. Like other Soviet cultural institutions involved in the international arena, the organization committed to wooing foreign intellectuals had banner years in 1935 and 1936. Lists of foreign intellectuals from this period who "actively" collaborated with VOKS in cultural relations expanded to include not only the most visible fellow-travelers, like Rolland and Bloch, but also architects, artists, pedagogues, and scientists. A 1936 wish list of foreigners to be invited to visit the USSR reflected the ambitious scope of the new conjuncture; it included the radical American historian Charles Beard and actor Charlie Chaplin, whose 1936 assembly-line film "Modern Times" was hailed as a "great turn to the left."[21]

Arosev's steady stream of proposals to Stalin and the Politburo can also be read for fascinating clues about the embrace by both cultural and political elites of a newly prominent 1930s international cultural agenda. Popular Front-era outreach was fueled by the new Soviet interest in promoting culture as a sign of systemic superiority, for the culture of showcases was now aimed not to point to the bright future of socialism but to turn Moscow into an internationally dominant beacon of socialist culture. This new ethos was apparent in the writings of Arosev, despite his conflicted identity as an Old Bolshevik whose attitudes toward the Europe he had known in his many years abroad frequently bordered on reverence. As he put it, VOKS would not merely, as before, display to foreigners the concrete achievements of Soviet "cultural construction"; it would secure recognition among wide circles of the West European intelligentsia of the historical superiority of the socialist culture created in the USSR. In a 1935 bid to persuade Stalin to put VOKS at the head of the commercially powerful Intourist, Arosev announced that the rival organization discredited the country even as its successes were making it into the "cultural center of the world."[22] The superiority complex had found its expression in cultural diplomacy. Arosev may well have harbored hopes that a program formulated in terms of cultural domination might in fact expose the Soviet side to beneficial exchange with the leftist West European culture that he admired.

Although cultural interaction and intellectual travel between the United States and the USSR picked up noticeably after the United States recognized the Soviet Union diplomatically in 1933, it is noteworthy that America, however important an alternative to Europe as a second site of advanced modernity, was still left out in such formulations by Arosev and other Soviet intellectuals involved in cultural diplomacy. The most influential Soviet text on the United States in this period was Il'f and Petrov's *One-Story America*, a rich, complex, and often sympathetic account of the two satirists' 1935 road trip. But even there, American work efficiency led the list of features praised, while American culture was depicted as decidedly puerile: "There are a lot of annoyingly childish and primitive traits in the people's character. But the most interesting childlike quality, curiosity, is almost absent among Americans." Even some of the most pro-American sentiments expressed by a Soviet politician in the period—the gushing 1936 missive from food supply and trade commissar Anastas Mikoian in the middle of a three-month U.S. visit to Henry Ford and industrial sites—almost ritually invoked a lack of "culturedness" among American experts: "There is much they do not know, they are limited people, but they know their own area, their narrow speciality, wonderfully." Mikoian felt nothing out of place in expressing these sentiments to perhaps the most poorly educated and least literate member of the Soviet leadership, the brutal

Kaganovich. For his part, Arosev deployed a metaphor strikingly similar to that used by Il'f and Petrov in a high-level 1934 party report on VOKS's work in the United States. There, he referred to the inferiority complex of an adolescent American culture, which looked up to Europe because it "lacks its own cultural traditions and customs." Of all European cultures—among which Arosev tellingly included Soviet culture—"our socialist culture" could fill this role and come "to the aid" of the United States.[23]

What is most revealing is the fact that Arosev did not need to provide elaborate justifications for such claims to international cultural-political hegemony. He injected them into his proposals almost as an aside—a politically attractive proclamation that needed no special explanation. This suggests that it was already a preoccupation shared by party intellectuals involved in cultural diplomacy and the political leadership alike.

By definition, these hegemonic ambitions implied some degree of direct engagement, and they thus continued the optimistic Soviet tradition of perceiving vast opportunities in the international arena. In the mid-1930s, however, at the very peak of Soviet international success, the longstanding, countervailing tendency to view foreigners as a pernicious threat was gaining momentum. The most powerful agent for curtailing international contacts as security risks was, as before, the secret police, and starting in 1935, Nikolai Ezhov, chief NKVD implementer of the Terror two years later, began to undermine and eclipse his boss, Iagoda, becoming the de facto "supreme supervisor" of the "organs." Ezhov also replaced Kaganovich, hitherto Stalin's No. 2 man, on a number of Politburo commissions, and acquired control over the direction of the Party's major political campaigns. From the outset, the rise of Ezhov was closely associated with dire denunciations of lack of vigilance and foreign espionage. Starting in early 1935, Ezhov personally directed a campaign against "foreign influences" that targeted resident political émigrés, scholars, and intellectuals in particular, at first with decidedly mixed results. In mid-1935, Ezhov entered the top leadership as the party member charged with overseeing the NKVD, and for a year and a half, he oversaw party purges before himself taking over NKVD operations during the Great Terror.[24]

The intensification of vigilance spearheaded by Ezhov took place in a broader context of policy measures that curtailed the presence of foreigners within the USSR. These included the elimination of the special system of supplies for foreigners (*Insnab*); more restrictions on the mobility; further isolation of foreign press, trade, and diplomatic representatives; and pressure on foreign residents to adopt Soviet citizenship. At the same juncture, a range of "internationalist" academic and literary institutions cultivating or employing foreign Communists and leftists were shuttered, including the Communist Academy and Communist University of the National Minorities of the West in 1936. The effects of the vigilance campaign were felt at Intourist as well, which experienced limitations in issuing visas to foreigners as early as 1935 and a purge of "alien elements" the same year.[25]

At the same time that the internationalist fervor surrounding the Spanish Civil War reached the height of mass popularity in the USSR, party campaigns with Russocentric overtones began rehabilitating prerevolutionary and tsarist heroes. Amid these contradictory signals in 1935–36, even savvy Soviet elites were hard pressed to discern the emerging party line.[26] In the mid-1930s, the divided perception of foreigners also escalated within Soviet cultural output itself, leading to the propagation of diametrically opposed portrayals, as recent students of cinema have suggested. On the one hand was the figure of the sympathetic foreign visitor who is enlightened and converted, culminating in Grigorii Aleksandrov's 1936 *Circus*; on the other hand, far more numerous in the 1930s were depictions of foreigners as evil characters or masked foreign agents. Vigilance against spies was already a live issue not only in popular culture but in cultural diplomacy. As early as March 1935, whether he believed it or not, Arosev cited to Stalin the increased likelihood of foreign spies penetrating Soviet space under a "friendly mask" as an argument for hiring better-qualified VOKS cadres.[27]

Arosev yearned for powerful patrons, but was hemmed in as the cultural politics of the 1930s increasingly centralized decision making on international initiatives in the hands of the Central Committee and the NKVD. The old problem of delays and restrictions resulting from the need to hunt for high-level bureaucratic approval reappeared. In 1936, even relatively minor VOKS events, such as lectures by a British art historian already approved for Soviet entry by Foreign Affairs, required special sanction by the Central Committee. As "the famous and highly influential English economist" John Maynard Keynes prepared to give a talk in Moscow in August 1936, on the recommendation of the Soviet ambassador to Britain, Ivan Maiskii, Arosev needed to secure Central Committee approval even to instruct the audience to treat him with "kid gloves" rather than respond with harsh rebuttals in the question-and-answer session.[28]

The campaign Ezhov launched in 1935 against foreign influences was connected to the cultural politics in the period 1936–38 through the meteoric rise of the figure at the forefront of the anti-formalist campaign, Platon Kerzhentsev. Like Arosev, Kerzhentsev was an Old Bolshevik intellectual with a cosmopolitan European diplomatic past. But if Arosev was a Stalinist Westernizer who wished to join Soviet culture with Europe's, Kerzhentsev allied himself unambiguously with the security interests of the NKVD on the cultural front. Kerzhentsev became chief architect of the anti-formalist campaign, launched with the sensational attack on Dmitrii Shostakovich's opera "Lady Macbeth of Mtsensk" in his unsigned January 28, 1936, *Pravda* article, "Muddle Instead of Music."[29] By so doing, he helped to launch a new period of militant ferment on the cultural front that repelled Western intellectuals who were attracted to the Soviet avant-garde. Kerzhentsev's rapid accumulation of power, partly a function of the anti-formalist campaign, was also, in part, a salvo against the Central Committee's Department of Culture and Enlightenment on behalf of his own new All-Union Committee for Arts Affairs. This agency derived its rising power from the fact that Kerzhentsev was spearheading an effort important to the Stalin cult, the unification of the images of Stalin in non-print media (theater and film). As Leonid Maksimenkov has shown, Kerzhentsev's alliance with the security organs led him to make tactical errors that ultimately led to his downfall. For example, he opposed international travel without appreciating its foreign-policy significance. In one instance of this, he tried to veto Soviet participation in a ballet on the Paris Commune, a performance important to Soviet cultural diplomacy during the Popular Front. He was overruled by Stalin.[30]

During this time, Arosev got caught in the cross-fire over precisely this issue of VOKS's promotion of international travel and cultural exchange. Kerzhentsev lashed out against Arosev on the pretext that he had made irresponsible promises to art figures about Soviet participation in European exhibitions without first clearing them with him, the new power broker. The embattled Arosev sharply defended VOKS's successes in international exhibitions, denying that Kerzhentsev's Arts Committee had any authority to meddle in that arena.[31] As this episode suggests, Kerzhentsev viewed international cultural contacts as a convenient weapon as he tried to ride the crest of the crackdown in the "Stalinist cultural revolution."[32]

In early to mid-1936, the arrest and persecution of former party oppositionists increased dramatically, setting the stage for the first of the great show trials that August. Given the well-worn ideological connections between internal and external enemies, this had the effect of increasing the political and security tensions for those involved in international affairs as well. For VOKS, Central Committee oversight became increasingly difficult to manage. In May 1936, Arosev sent to Ezhov lists of all foreigners invited by VOKS the previous year, as part of a Politburo requirement to review categories of foreigners deemed "dangerous to the USSR." In a separate missive, Arosev appealed to his old Civil War comrade personally: "The entire situation as well as direct party directives on increased vigilance in our cultural ties abroad, as you know, demands from me the *most exact coordination* of almost every VOKS activity with the Central Committee, Foreign Affairs, the NKVD, and other organizations." Confirming that Ezhov was behind the crackdown, he added: "It was precisely from you that a whole range of directives to me originated about increased vigilance and warning against attempts to use VOKS by hostile elements."[33]

Long before the Purges actually hit, Arosev felt a noose of "distrust" tightening around him personally. Love interfered with politics as Arosev's second wife, Gertrude (Gertrud Adol'fovna) Freund, became a liability in the mid-1930s. Arosev had married Gertrude, a Czechoslovak ballerina of Jewish background twenty years his junior, during his time in Prague. She took Soviet citizenship but traveled back to Prague frequently in the mid-1930s to visit her mother. Arosev encountered intensifying suspicions about his intimacy with a "foreign woman" and his fears about his standing in the Party became focused on xenophobic reactions to his marriage. In December 1935, he wrote Ezhov from Paris, asking for permission for Gertrude to travel abroad to meet him with their infant son. She was denied. In April 1936, she was denied again, and Arosev wrote to Stalin as his "only justice," pleading to remove this "undeserved stain." According to Arosev's daughter, Ol'ga Aroseva, suspicions about Gertrude in party circles were raised by the couple's age difference and the fear that she might have come to Moscow for reasons more sinister than amorous devotion to the pudgy intellectual.[34]

By August 4, 1936, two weeks before the opening of the show trial of the "Trotskyist-Zinovievite Center," Arosev's travel requests for Gertrude had again been refused without explanation. Using the lingo of the cult, the Old Bolshevik appealed to "my leader and teacher" Stalin to relieve his "great internal depression." His wife, he maintained, was "to her core one of us, a non-party Bolshevik, but because she is a foreigner it is easier to act poorly toward her." The most difficult thing for him to bear was that he received neither an answer to his pleas nor punishment—increasingly anguished, he appealed repeatedly to Stalin. "What kind of life can come from this at work and in my family?" Arosev ended his plea with an extraordinary statement that almost defiantly affirmed what he himself so often doubted—Soviet supremacy in the face of the traditional Russian-Soviet inferiority complex about the West:

> When certain comrades say, as it were, look, his wife often travels abroad...it has the sound of that servility toward the outside world we are fighting against. Why don't they speak in the same tone of reproach: ah, how often you travel to Kaluga! In fact we, our country is higher and better and cleaner and let Europeans and Americans among themselves grow envious over who travels to the USSR.[35]

Arosev's agony was but one manifestation of the growing fear of foreign penetration of Soviet security during the mid-1930s that, ironically, coincided with the peak of Soviet international success. A key component of the measures taken to promote "vigilance" was a secrecy campaign that quickly impeded everyday administration.[36] In 1935–36, a campaign to purge and restrict foreign publications by the censorship agency Glavlit was connected to the security police, and banned domestic literature linked to vilified party oppositionists, more tightly conflating the internal and external enemy.[37] Combined with the campaign against foreign influences started by Ezhov in 1935, this produced a flurry of activity that changed the atmosphere at VOKS. For example, in July, Arosev charged his subordinates with violating the basic principles of "vigilance" and issued warnings about talking in front of foreigners.[38]

Fear of foreigners created escalating problems for an organization like VOKS that managed a sprawling book exchange, relied heavily on foreign publications for its international work with intellectuals, and received extensive correspondence from abroad. The VOKS book exchange begun by Kameneva continued to be one of its largest operations: in 1934, it brought into the country 163,000 volumes from 84 countries, most of them periodical publications and scientific literature, which were then distributed to well more than 1,500 Soviet institutions.[39] In 1935, Glavlit became deeply involved in tightening procedures for approving the import of literature in foreign languages. Redoubling efforts to prevent violations of the rules for disseminating restricted literature through the VOKS book exchange, it found that banned literature had been improperly received by the Union of Writers, the Anti-Religious Museum, and the Central Medical Library. The VOKS library, moreover, was found to be "tainted" with literature requiring quarantine in the "special collection."[40] In March 1935, the Glavlit crackdown was creating delays of twenty to thirty days in the delivery of foreign newspapers to VOKS analysts.[41]

Correspondence between the VOKS Secrets Department (*Sekretnaia chast'*) in charge of handling restricted publications and the NKVD's Efim Evdokimov over Glavlit's campaign suggests a direct link between the intensifying vigilance campaigns of the censorship and the security organs, both traditionally "hard-line" agencies.[42] In April 1936, the NKVD was briefed on the possibility that secret messages were being conveyed in routine letters from scientists and artists from abroad.[43] All correspondence with foreigners began to be examined, including from those numerous intellectuals and cultural figures who had been drawn to Soviet socialism as a counterweight to the book-burning fascists. Indeed, the watchword for the international movement of anti-fascist culture was the famous line from Heinrich Heine about the Spanish Inquisition: "*Dort, wo man Bücher verbrennt, verbrennt man am Ende auch Menschen*" (Where they burn books, in the end they will also burn people).[44] Little did pro-Soviet intellectuals know that at the height of the Popular Front, the anti-fascist Soviets began to burn the literature that foreign sympathizers themselves had penned.

The Nazi book burnings were public rituals; the Soviet book burnings were secret manifestations of the Party's infallibility, carried out by surreptitiously hauling truckloads of printed materials away to be destroyed. The factory "Kleituk" figures in the documents as the location where literary materials from VOKS were liquidated. Among the English-language books sent to the factory in March 1936 for destruction were issues of the *Left Review*, *The Nation*, *The New Republic*, *The Statesman and Nation*, *The New York Times Book Review*, *The Harvard Lampoon*, and even Soviet publications directed abroad, such as *Soviet Russia Today*. In April, three more truckloads of VOKS-held publications were destroyed. At the same time, access to foreign publications was further restricted among analysts. In 1936, the quantity of materials received and processed by VOKS's own Secrets Department had climbed an estimated 30 to 50 percent over 1934–35. The workload of the department had risen so much that salary increases for its overburdened workers were requested—and a copy of the request sent to the NKVD. A laconic note on one of the lists records that the foreign publications were disposed of "by means of burning."[45] It was no longer enough to quarantine or restrict tainted words and images. In a kind of Stalinist extraterritoriality, diplomats at the Soviet embassy in London also burned material on condemned oppositionists from the library of the supposedly independent cultural friendship society, and foreign newspapers and journals at VOKS continued to be incinerated during the fateful year 1937.[46] As Heine predicted, a year after the Party began to incinerate foreign literature, it turned to the mass destruction of people.

The Great Terror as Great Break

Feuchtwanger returned to France in February 1937. As we saw, his Moscow was caught in the midst of the central show trials and the persecution of former oppositionists, but was still on the cusp of mass purging. Just after his departure, the Central Committee plenum convened between February 22 and March 5. Punctuated with speeches by Stalin, Molotov, and Ezhov about anti-Soviet elements and capitalist encirclement, the plenum escalated the mass terror against "enemies of the people." The February-March plenum became a major turning point in the Great Terror, for in its wake, the net of enemies widened from the previous preoccupation with former oppositionists and inner-party dissent to ubiquitous "wreckers," furthering mass mobilization against them in the workplace throughout the land.[47] The summer of 1937 marked a second intensification of widespread repression with the onset of the "mass operations." By this time, the Great Terror had so decimated the ranks of "Stalinist Westernizers" and altered the conditions in which foreign visitors could be received that Feuchtwanger's visit earlier in the year could scarcely have been repeated.

Natal'ia Semper, the VOKS guide, recalled the day in January 1937 when the analyst Shpindler did not show up for work. Like so many others promoted quickly to replace purged cadres, the twenty-five-year-old Semper agreed to take his place with "joy in my heart." But others quickly followed: "A person disappeared, and his co-workers observed a significant silence and soon forgot him." Semper professed no knowledge in those days about life in the Gulag or what happened after arrest. But she would never forget the "agitation and pain" written on the face of the soon-to-be-purged Arosev after he emerged from the 1937 VOKS general assembly at which he had been "worked over," bombarded by accusations and denunciations in the militant Purge-era style that revived earlier incarnations of revolutionary activism with a deadly, xenophobic twist.[48]

Despite his childhood friendship with Molotov, Arosev was a perfect candidate for purge: a proud member of the soon-to-be decimated Bolshevik "old guard" with a checkered diplomatic past and a foreign wife, not to mention innumerable contacts abroad. At the end of 1936, fearing ominous signs of distrust around him, Arosev had already written in his diary of his own demise: "Life, like a book, suddenly slams itself shut." The *annus horribilus* 1937 began at the foreign-relations society with a January "verification" of all employees, which determined that 22 of 115 staff members had relatives abroad and that some had been employed with recommendations from party members since purged and discredited. The noose continued to tighten around Arosev for half a year. In typical fashion, the Purge-era upheaval at VOKS began by singling out one figure who had been a former oppositionist, but expanded in the spring and summer of 1937 into tangled, vitriolic attacks "from below" against the leadership and any and all ideological, financial, and other workplace irregularities that could serve as ammunition in the frenzy. Around this time, his daughter recalled, Arosev suddenly had a lot of free time. The telephone did not ring, and high-level assignments no longer came down from the party leadership. Shortly before his arrest in July 1937, an agitated Arosev called Molotov on the telephone (his daughter Elena witnessed the call): "Viacha, I ask you to tell me, what should I do?" Two times Molotov hung up the phone; two times Arosev called back. Finally, an answer came: "Make arrangements for the children."[49] Much later, in the early 1970s, Molotov claimed to have no specific knowledge when asked why his "very close comrade" was repressed. "He could have been indicted for only one thing: he could have somewhere thrown around some sort of liberal phrase...He could have gone after some sort of woman (*za baboi kakoi-nibud'*), and she...There was a struggle going on." On February 8, 1938, Arosev was sentenced to death by a troika after having denied all guilt. The sentence was carried out two days later, most likely in the usual way, with a shot to the back of the head.[50]

The era of mass purging that began in 1937 essentially led to the end of Soviet interwar cultural diplomacy and the remarkable era of intensive Western interest in visiting the great experiment. Internally, the show trials and spy mania of the Purge era drastically undercut the position of Soviet cultural diplomacy and outreach to the outside world, which had always been engaged in a delicate balancing act with ideological hostility toward the bourgeois West. Although the Stalin era had begun by heightening the anti-Western element in the late 1920s with a war scare and deepening ideological linkages between international and domestic enemies, the campaigns of the Great Break were formulated in class terms as anti-bourgeois and, therefore, only by extension assumed an anti-foreign and anti-Western cast. The Purge era marked the triumph of Soviet xenophobia, defined by Terry Martin as "the exaggerated Soviet fear of foreign influence and foreign contamination"—in other words, a phenomenon that was in its origins "ideological, not ethnic."[51] This was the point at which the superiority complex, which in the mid-1930s was promoted both by those seeking Soviet cultural hegemony and those intensifying vigilance, was struck by the terror. There was an explicit link between the vilification of Western-oriented revolutionaries such as Radek and Bukharin and crude declarations of across-the-board Soviet superiority. For example, the Presidium of the Union of Writers condemned the two former oppositionists in January 1937 for "capitulationist" cultural conceptions that denigrated the USSR in front of the "West."[52]

The Great Terror is now widely analyzed as a series of distinguishable campaigns that not only bludgeoned political and cultural elites but included the national purges of diaspora populations in borderland regions and mass operations against former kulaks and other "aliens." No matter how disparate these centrally planned operations were, however, they cannot be disaggregated, for they began and ended at the same time. One of the most plausible interpretations that has been advanced is that they were all conceived as a kind of preventative strike that would, once and for all, rid Soviet society of enemies who could not be re-educated, a kind of socially defined final solution that appeared urgent in light of the war that, from 1937 on, Stalin and the leadership firmly expected.[53] In terms of the international-domestic interconnections that this book has traced, it is interesting to note that Oleg Khlevniuk, who has consistently pointed to the eradication of a "fifth column" as the prime motivation behind the Terror, points to Stalin's preoccupation with traitors in the republican camp in Spain as the origin of the "fifth-column factor." As the Purge era began, the Soviet interest in the Spanish struggle paradoxically served simultaneously to highlight Soviet ties to Europe and as a concrete symbol of the coming war.[54]

Ideologically, the various types of purging combined—more than ever before—to conflate two kinds of vilified enemies, internal and external. For example, the so-called national operations against Germans, Finns, Estonians, Latvians, Poles, and others inside the USSR connected domestic populations to hostile bourgeois and fascist states, in this instance in the context of long-standing concerns with unstable border regions. This only reinforced the parallels between foreigners and nationalities classified as dangerous enemies.[55]

The results held drastic implications for cultural relations with the outside world. The Soviet motivations that had kept international outreach to Western intellectuals and public opinion a privileged priority of the Soviet system—whether ideological, economic, scientific, diplomatic, or not least the quest for cultural prestige—were overwhelmed by a tidal wave of spy mania that portrayed domestic enemies as pawns of hostile international forces. This sinister connection, made at the outset of the Terror, was accompanied by a wide variety of policy measures that drastically undercut the position of foreigners visiting and residing in the USSR. Foreign residents and foreign Communists, including many who had not adopted Soviet citizenship, were decimated in the Purges, and the authorities "aimed at not extending the foreign residence permits of foreigners living in the USSR" because of the association with espionage and "wrecking." The repression of Comintern cadres and the German anti-fascist diaspora is best known, but attention has recently focused on the sizeable colony of expatriate United States citizens—many of whom were abandoned to their fate by U.S. diplomats after being seen as sympathetic to communism.[56] Anyone with foreign contacts or even a foreign-sounding name was suspect. Because the most effective figures and offices of the party-state dealing with the outside world were hit hardest by the terror, the cataclysm pulled the rug out from under Soviet cultural diplomacy. Starting in 1937, foreign visitors faced a very different country.

The effects of the Great Terror on international travel to the USSR were felt immediately. The first eight months of 1937, according to one document, saw a decrease of more than 65 percent in the number of foreign tourists from the previous year, while later figures breaking down the numbers by country of origin show further drastic decreases in tourists from the United States, England, France, and Holland between 1937 and 1938. The approach of war was the reason for the drop-off at the end of the decade, of course, but not in 1937. At Intourist, three times as many foreign applications for visas were rejected in 1937 as had been the year before, and so many tours were cancelled that during the Purge era tourism lost its importance to the national economy. Those travelers who did come could not help noticing that few, if any, Soviet citizens would talk to them.[57] Standard warnings about the ubiquity of foreign spies and diversionists, ritualistically citing Stalin's speech against spies and saboteurs at the March 1937 Plenum, not only depicted tourists as undercover spies, but also explicitly stated that previously honored members of the cultural friendship societies and visiting trade-union delegations were likely hidden enemies.[58]

In 1938, the head of counter-espionage at the NKVD was put in charge not only of foreign embassies and national populations of "neighboring bourgeois-fascist states," but also of now equally suspect groups of foreign political émigrés, tourists, and international visitors connected to cultural and economic relations. The Purges went far beyond the destruction of the "old guard" within the Party, but this long-recognized part of the violence was especially significant for foreign intellectual visitors. Physical annihilation wiped out much of the multilingual and multinational generation of cosmopolitan Bolshevik and Comintern elites in Moscow.[59]

In the wake of Arosev's arrest, the purge of VOKS followed a pattern repeated around the country: tense and deadly meetings of the party cell, waves of denunciations, and an ever-widening net of those associated with the condemned enemies of the people. By February 1938, twelve top VOKS officials had been arrested as "alien elements." Like many others who lived through the Great Terror, Semper recalled a chilling silence and tacit agreement not to speak about politics as leading officials disappeared one after the other, including Arosev's two deputies, Kuliabko and Cherniavskii: "No one said a word about what was happening... on politics everyone was as silent as the dead, no one trusted anyone."[60] For organizations whose work was predicated on interactions with foreigners, the spy mania and xenophobia associated with the Purges had particularly devastating consequences. Arosev's temporary replacement, Viktor Fedorovich Smirnov, reported to Molotov in July 1937 that the leadership of VOKS had been "unmasked" and the "apparatus of VOKS was soiled by people who in most cases had ties abroad, had lived abroad, etc."[61] Evidently, he did not see the irony in using "ties abroad" as evidence of guilt in the All-Union Society for Cultural Ties Abroad.

With top posts left unfilled and the organization reeling from accusations of "wrecking," the agency's hard-currency funding was temporarily cut off at the end of 1937—either the outcome of anti-foreign terror, the chaos caused by it, or both. Some funds were restored in 1938, but at less than one-sixth the level of what would be allocated after the era of mass purging came to a close the following year. Many parts of the state, economy, and society experienced severe disruption in these years, but in this case, sheer lack of money led to a virtual standstill in operations. Basic tasks, such as mailing the VOKS bulletin to foreign countries, were not carried out. The rump leadership also had to counter new proposals to liquidate VOKS. These recalled earlier episodes in the late 1920s, but at that time, the importance of cultural diplomacy and its protectors had allowed the institution to weather the upheaval, whereas this time, it abandoned much of its core mission. In 1938, VOKS virtually stopped its activities related to the invitations to and reception of foreigners inside the USSR, focusing only on external operations. A budget document confirms that for the year 1938, expenditures on the reception of foreigners ceased.[62]

What was financially prohibitive and dangerous politically was, inevitably, elevated to the level of ideological principle. In 1938, Smirnov condemned the entire tradition of tours and tailored travel for intelligentsia visitors as an illegitimate and, by implication corrupt, gravy train (*podkarmlivaniia i prikarmlivaniia*) for foreigners.[63] Operations abroad did not fare much better, however, although it was possible for many VOKS activities to continue through the offices of VOKS representatives stationed abroad. In 1939, however, VOKS operations were reportedly reduced to a mere six countries, and, in the words of Smirnov, "the principal connections of VOKS were lost" and "the work of VOKS started to cease." The break in continuity was so severe that the organization that emerged during and after the war can be considered a very different institution. Semper herself, summoned repeatedly to meetings with NKVD agents to discuss VOKS's contacts with foreigners, resigned in 1938. "It became completely boring. VOKS had ceased to be what it once was."[64]

The operations of Soviet cultural diplomacy abroad were considerably hampered, needless to say, by the ideological fallout from the show trials and purges. Arosev's tainted leadership (known as "the time of Arosev," or *Arosevshchina*) and his "wrecking" activities were directly linked to lax control over the cultural friendship societies. While fabricated Trotskyism fueled the purges inside the USSR, foreign leftists and erstwhile Soviet sympathizers did have genuine sympathies for the exiled revolutionary in Mexico—notably New York intellectuals and those associated with the American Committee for the Defense of Leon Trotsky, which began its work under the chairmanship of John Dewey after the first show trial, in late 1936. Unsurprisingly, the presence of "Trotskyists" in New York explicitly figured in the report condemning the legacy of Arosev.[65]

The efforts of the VOKS representative in the United States, Konstantin Umanskii (Oumansky), a high-level diplomat in Washington who became ambassador in 1939, were typical of the challenges encountered by capable and energetic figures active abroad. Umanskii had been a TASS correspondent in Rome and Paris and then a high-level censor of foreign correspondents as chief of the Foreign Affairs press division in the famine years of the early 1930s. After his move to Washington in 1936, he advocated adapting to the international crisis in Europe by shifting the center of gravity in Soviet "cultural-political work" from Europe to the United States—a continuation of the Soviet turn from Berlin to Paris and Western Europe circa 1933. As one historian has recently noted, shortly after Umanskii's arrival in the United States in 1936, "President Roosevelt, via the secretary of state, ordered FBI Director Hoover to investigate potential foreign connections of domestic fascist and Communist groups. The travels of the Soviet counselor, Konstantin Oumansky, were of special concern to the President."[66] Among his destinations was New York, where he traveled on VOKS work.

In a stream of long, incisive reports to Moscow between 1936 and 1938, Umanskii detailed his intricate political and financial maneuverings at the American-Russian Institute in New York in response to the imperative to exclude Dewey and other "Trotskyists." He also faced pressure from the U.S. government through its requirement to register foreign-backed institutions, increasing reluctance on the part of wealthy liberal donors and resistance from an array of non-communist American intellectual sympathizers who found it impossible to exclude or silence colleagues criticizing the show trials. At one point, Umanskii railed in exasperation about being forced to rely upon "little groupings of wavering New York liberal intellectuals." In the era of the show trials, the Soviet modus operandi of acting through a trusted key individual or core group as proxy for the Soviet handler had become elusive. But with potentially real rather than fictitious Trotskyists involved during the fallout from Arosev's purge, Umanskii had to angrily repudiate Smirnov's accusation from Moscow that he himself was "too liberal."[67]

As VOKS declined, some of the slack was taken up by the powerful and well-connected new organization, the Foreign Commission of the Union of Writers. Headed by Kol'tsov, its day-to-day operations were run by its vice chairman, the capable VOKS and MORP veteran Mikhail Apletin. The Foreign Commission kept up the best traditions of information gathering on foreigners, keeping up-to-date biographies and personal evaluations of leading writers with an emphasis on their recent publications and attitudes toward the Soviet Union.[68]

Attitudes toward the show trials and purges became an obligatory new litmus test in the evaluation of foreign intellectuals and tracking markers of their world view, creating considerable complications for Soviet intermediaries. The Foreign Commission's 1937 entry for Bertolt Brecht, for example, noted that "after the trial of the Trotskyists he displayed well-known waverings" and recorded that Brecht and his wife were close friends with a "Trotskyist," the ex-communist Marxist philosopher Karl Korsch. Meeting foreign visitors on the ground, VOKS guides reported that even "friends," including one engineer from Prague, quickly changed the subject and "obviously did not wish to talk about the trial of Trotskyist-Zinovievist terrorists."[69]

A September 1936 letter from the Foreign Commission, perhaps penned by Kol'tsov, directly concerns strategies for presenting the show trials to foreign literary intellectuals. Its recipient was Joshua Kunitz, whom Alan Wald has called one of the "most highly educated" American communist intellectuals and "the Party's undisputed authority on Russian literature." A key figure on the editorial board of the *New Masses*, Kunitz had traveled around the Soviet Union and in 1935 published the ardently pro-Soviet travelogue *cum* history, *Dawn over Samarkand*. This book, dedicated "to the Negro people of the United States," shaped its message around Gorkian/Socialist Realist tropes of "rebirth" and miracles coming true. Although Kunitz received the sensitive and unenviable assignment of justifying the show trials to U.S. leftists, he was, according to Wald, never fully trusted by the U.S. party leadership.[70] In typical fashion, the Foreign Commission letter, addressed to "Dear Jack," began with flattery: "I know that you are a wonderful polemicist." The letter then provided talking points and attempted to influence Kunitz's own reasoning at the same time: deriding the petty-bourgeois intelligentsia for cheering revolutionary events such as 1917 but not understanding the need for the NEP, it called the Purges another episode that demonstrated that intellectuals did not understand the revolution as a whole. Getting down to business, the letter instructed Kunitz to address two issues of great concern to foreign observers: the charges that the trial was fabricated, and that confessions had been extracted by means of torture and mistreatment, including psychological violence. This possibility needed to be tackled delicately: Kunitz should say that foreign witnesses had seen how the defendants "looked excellent and were in complete control of their faculties." In sum, the argument had to be convincing about the psychology of those who confessed while persuading Kunitz's audience that "the confessions were voluntary and legal."[71] The arguments given to Kunitz recall in an uncanny fashion Feuchtwanger's treatment of the January show trial in *Moscow 1937*—notably his insistence, denied by other observers, that the "obvious freshness and vitality of the prisoners" proved they had not been mistreated and his emphasis on explaining the psychology of those who had confessed.[72] Surely Feuchtwanger, most likely orally, was given the same suggestions as Kunitz.

Like Feuchtwanger, Romain Rolland in 1937 remained a Soviet friend and publicly accepted the trials and arrests as genuine conspiracy. In private, he agonized. He sent Stalin a barrage of unanswered letters, hoping to save the arrested Arosev, Bukharin, and others. Rolland was "exceptionally proud" of his Soviet fame—1.3 million copies of his works had been published in the USSR by November 1937—as his position in France weakened after the eclipse of the Popular Front. Remarkably, as late as May 1937 Rolland was still considering a return trip to Moscow. By September, however, after his letters went unanswered and the purges widened, he refused through his wife—whose son remained in Moscow—to continue answering Soviet requests for ritualistic, congratulatory public praise.[73] In an October 1938 letter, Kudasheva warned Apletin about Rolland's new stance. "Telegrams are useless and don't bother calling by telephone...In the West right now one is not up to 'jubilees' and 'congratulations'...It is impossible to keep disturbing him over nonsense...it is even harmful."[74]

At the same time, the Stalinist superiority complex, now inflected with xenophobic dimensions, played a role in Rolland's disillusionment. Rolland criticized Soviet jingoism in a pointed letter he repeatedly attempted to publish in the Soviet press. It was addressed to two Soviet schoolgirls who had written Rolland; Kudasheva translated it into Russian on November 26, 1937:

> It is harmful and dangerous to be overly proud, as it seems to me you are, too self-satisfied...You are incorrect to think that [the USSR] has already overtaken all other countries. (In the USSR, you write, everything is the best. The best scholars, the best writers, the best musicians, athletes, engineers, painters)...You must remember the greatness of the USSR and its internationalism. That is why one must make sure that the sons of the USSR do not reject pan-humanism and fall into nationalism.

National pride, Rolland audaciously concluded, was one of the first phases of fascism. The letter, of course, was never published, but more galling was that the elderly writer, glorified as a giant in Soviet culture, was never given the courtesy of a response to his repeated inquiries. When the Purges began, Rolland was careful not to break with the Soviet Union, although his 1938 play *Robespierre* explored his doubts about the terror. The Nazi-Soviet Pact achieved what the Great Terror could not: in 1939, Rolland quietly resigned his position in the Soviet-French friendship society.[75]

Even as the Purges diminished the ranks of Western intellectual sympathizers willing to assume the mantle of "friend of the Soviet Union," the dramatic late-1930s reordering of Europe—the victory of Franco's nationalists in the Spanish Civil War, Munich in 1938, and the Nazi invasion of Czechoslovakia the following year, and later the fall of Paris and the outbreak of war—gave the Soviets new opportunities for transnational cultural patronage. The cultural bureaucracies were able to provide aid, and sometimes salvation, to beleaguered sympathizers and longstanding committed "friends." For example, the head of the Union of Writers, Aleksandr Fadeev, arranged for aid and in select cases immigration for Spanish writers and responded to appeals from desperate Spanish refugees in France in 1939.[76] After the Munich agreement, the atmosphere in Prague, a major center of Soviet cultural diplomacy for more than a decade, became inhospitable. "People who previously considered it fashionable and even honorable to enter into friendship with the Soviet Union," a diplomatic report noted, "have started to hide in the bushes and have fallen out of our sphere of influence." In Slovakia, all Soviet cultural activities were suddenly halted under the clerico-fascist regime of Father Jozef Tiso in late 1938. After Munich, Zdeněk Nejedlý, the head of the Czechoslovak cultural friendship society in Prague, curtailed its activities after a meeting with the Soviet ambassador in response to a looming ban on the Czechoslovak Communist Party. Nejedlý agreed that the society's main goal should be to refute those blaming Munich on the Soviet Union. In Moscow, the overwhelmed interim head of VOKS, Smirnov, could only brusquely opine that no contacts should be preserved with any fair-weather friends. When Nazi troops entered Bohemia and Moravia on March 15, 1939, Nejedlý evaded arrest by the Gestapo and obtained a Soviet passport from the embassy, after which he fled to the USSR.[77] He returned to Prague after the war to become the Stalinist minister of culture from 1948 to 1953.

The concrete benefits for some Western intellectuals who retained their Soviet contacts after the Purges are perhaps best illustrated by Apletin's late-1930s correspondence with Brecht, who was living in Sweden after April 1939. The letters, of course, observed complete silence about the decimation of the German diaspora and anti-fascist literary émigrés in Moscow, nor did they mention the purge of Brecht's friend Tret'iakov in the summer of 1937 or the arrest of Vsevolod Meyerhold in 1939. The ever-solicitous Apletin was eager to push cooperation with Brecht as far as he was willing to go. He helped Brecht publish in *Literaturnaia gazeta*, wrote with great enthusiasm about the Soviet reception of Brecht's play *Galileo*, tried to gain financial credits for him for a serial publication of his new play *Mother Courage* in 1939, and sent along German translations of Stalin's pronouncements on international affairs. Insight into Brecht's own attitude in this period comes from Walter Benjamin's records of their conversations, in which Brecht told him: "In Russia a dictatorship is in power *over* the proletariat. We must avoid disowning it for as long as this dictatorship still does practical work for the proletariat." When Benjamin mentioned that Brecht had Soviet friends, Brecht replied: "Actually I have no friends there. The Muscovites don't have any, either—like the dead."[78] Still, maintaining Soviet contacts proved useful to the exiled playwright in 1940, when Apletin helped cash in all his extant Soviet honoraria and gain permission to travel across the Soviet Union to Vladivostok.[79] From there he sailed to the United States, arriving in California one day before the start of Operation Barbarossa.

Symbolic Cultural Diplomacy: The Twilight of the Nazi-Soviet Pact

Anti-fascism, one of the most potent weapons remaining in the arsenal of Soviet cultural diplomacy at this time, abruptly vanished with the *volte-face* of the Nazi-Soviet Pact of August 1939. The shock that even well-informed Soviet elites felt with the signing of the Pact came from the extent to which anti-fascism had been built up as a central pillar of Soviet ideology and culture, especially during the Popular Front. After all, Soviet children played not "cowboys and Indians" but "Communists and fascists." In the realm of foreign policy and grand strategy, however, while historians still hotly debate how much Stalin, at the helm, considered realignment before Munich in 1938, it is hard to contest that all options were kept open. The goal of sitting out an armed conflict among the camp of capitalist great powers was more than a well-established orientation—it was a key ideological premise of Marxist-Leninist thought on international relations.[80]

Soviet activities in Germany had been drastically curtailed after the Nazi seizure of power in 1933. By the mid-1930s, cultural diplomacy with Nazi Germany consisted mainly of the VOKS book exchange, focusing on scientific and specialized literature.[81] Instead of contacts, VOKS analysts focused on the "enormous task" of studying the rapidly evolving cultural policy and ideology of Nazi Germany, an effort also undertaken energetically by the "German group" of leftist émigrés in the Soviet Union of Writers after 1934.[82]

With the signing of the Pact in 1939, cultural relations between Nazi Germany and the Soviet Union suddenly assumed great symbolic importance as a means of passing strategically important signals between the two states. There was precedent for this: Fascist Italy, with which the Soviets maintained significant trade and diplomatic relations. Both Fascist Italy and the Soviet Union developed the practice of toning down or ramping up anti-fascist and anti-communist propaganda in the press depending on the fluctuations of their diplomatic relationship.[83] In addition to economic and trade relations, the Soviets and Nazis also became partners in military and secret-police matters related to the partition of Poland; both sides turned to culture (and on the German side, travel) more explicitly in its symbolic and auxiliary function. As the number of foreign visitors to the USSR dropped drastically in the period, the number of German visitors jumped. In 1938, only 5 percent of foreign tourists in the USSR came from Germany; in 1940, they constituted 56 percent. But in contrast to previous clients of Intourist, they were kept away from industrial sites and complained more than ever about being shown only museums and churches, not collective farms and factories.[84]

In the wake of Molotov's attack on "oversimplified anti-fascist agitation," as V. A. Nevezhin has shown, Soviet media ceased criticism of fascism and even avoided use of the word. Anti-fascist literature was removed from sale, and the "Hitlerite fascists" began to be referred to as the National Socialist Workers' Party. Nazi culture was not praised, but Sergei Eisenstein's production of Wagner's *Valkyrie* at the Bol'shoi Theater, which premiered on November 21, 1940, was treated as a state event of great significance. It was also an act of direct, symbolic reciprocity: in late 1939, at the moment when Eisenstein's production was planned, the press attaché in the Soviet embassy was asked for a novel about contemporary Soviet life that could be suitably translated into German and was told that the Berlin Opera Theater would produce Glinka's "Ivan Susanin." The Soviet functionary helpfully provided VOKS with photographs of the opera as it was produced in Moscow.[85]

With the end of mass purging in 1939, VOKS entered a period of relative calm before the storm in 1941. On March 8, 1940, the acting head of VOKS, Smirnov, was replaced by a young and ambitious intellectual, V. S. Kemenov, who had been director of the Tret'iakov Gallery. Kemenov was close to Lukàcs and his group, which by the time of his appointment had become less powerful in literary circles. Raisa Orlova, who worked at VOKS starting that year, recalled Kemenov as rumpled and informal, someone with "unmistakable erudition" rather than a faceless bureaucrat. She described the VOKS staff, mostly young and female, as now friendly and close, in contrast to the recently departed era of denunciations. Figures such as Sergei Eisenstein frequented the VOKS building in order to get the chance to see foreign works. Much of VOKS's activities had been reduced to mailing out albums, books, and articles abroad, however. When Orlova nervously gave a report on theater to distinguished Soviet directors and actors, they were so starved for information that they were grateful for the meager report of an inexperienced twenty-four-year-old.[86] Superiority over the rest of the world and isolation from it were now virtually synonymous. The era of intensive Soviet engagement with Western visitors and the influential interactions of the Western pilgrimage to the Soviet experiment had definitively come to an end.

Epilogue

Toward the Cultural Cold War

Each phase in the history of Soviet cultural diplomacy in the two decades traced in this book was intimately connected to the reception of foreign visitors inside the USSR. In pre-war and wartime Europe, cultural diplomacy had begun as a branch of foreign policy that attempted to harness the realm of culture to newly discovered capabilities of affecting public opinion in foreign countries. In Soviet Russia, by contrast, it was only the first influx of foreign visitors and representatives of the bourgeois West in the early 1920s that prompted the crystallization of a novel and distinctive system to shape the Soviet image abroad and, first and foremost, to put the first socialist society on display. Visits and depictions of the model sites of socialism became the centerpiece of this new type of cultural diplomacy as it was consolidated in the mid- to late 1920s. Stalin's series of meetings with prominent foreign friends and the grandiose celebration of them in Soviet culture, exemplifying a shift to the more choreographed pomp of the 1930s, extended the significance of visiting and showcasing the great experiment. Time spent within the socialist homeland was supposed to work wonders in changing consciousness; it was the touchstone for cementing ties to friendship societies and the most prominent fellow-travelers. Even the drastic reordering of cultural diplomacy during the Great Terror was most immediately manifested in the curtailment of foreign travel.

The reception of foreign visitors was central to the development of Soviet cultural diplomacy for reasons that went well beyond animosity to international communism among the great powers. The Bolsheviks revolutionized a country that had long compared itself against Western models and incorporated this practice into a core component of its national identity; the new regime, in its attempt to leap forward into a more advanced modernity, immediately began to implement its unprecedented aspirations to shape consciousness. As the interwar tour of the Soviet experiment got under way, foreign, and especially Western, audiences became one special target within a novel and extensive enlightenment-propaganda machine. The dictatorship of the proletariat did not feel the need to imitate its European predecessors by carving out a new cultural branch within conventional diplomacy. Rather,

Soviet international cultural missions were pursued in myriad ways by new party-state and communist actors, becoming a prime part of the revolutionary challenge of the Soviet system to the rest of the world. Presenting the new socialist society to foreign eyes became caught up in the systemic competition against capitalism and the bourgeoisie. Thus, VOKS and many related agencies developed their repertoire of programs inside as well as outside the USSR, mobilizing the Soviet intelligentsia for the drive. Insofar as foreign visits were central to the reconfigured contest with the West, the society that received the visitors—and even the ways socialism was constructed with foreign visitors implicitly in mind—were caught up in the effort as well. A regime born in total war quickly innovated a more total form of cultural diplomacy.[1] These interwar innovations anticipated the ideological sweep and systemic clash of the Cultural Cold War.

The grand narratives of Soviet history have been constructed around a largely domestic story about the development of Soviet communism, with diplomacy and external crises thrown into the mix as they affect the making of the Soviet system. Textbook accounts of Soviet history, for example, may mention the powerful attraction felt by Western intellectual sympathizers in discussions of the 1930s, but as this is extraneous to the main storyline, the discussion traditionally returns quickly to internally oriented master themes.[2] The almost exclusively domestic focus of the first two generations of Soviet studies was bolstered by its Cold War exceptionality and driven by the conceptual keys of the successive totalitarian and revisionist schools: in the first instance, the primacy of ideology and political control, and in the second, social forces from below. Partly as a result, the study of Soviet foreign policy and international communism developed as largely segregated subfields; only rarely was international history integrally connected with the formation of Soviet communism at home.[3] As a result, the history of a regime with global aspirations and a frequently obsessive concern with the "cultured" West, set in a multinational communist Mecca and served by cosmopolitan and well-traveled political and intellectual elites, was largely de-internationalized.

This book, using the case of cultural diplomacy and the reception of foreign visitors, has suggested a broader phenomenon: the interaction between the internal and external dimensions of the Soviet system. It is often easiest to perceive how the internal affected the external, or how the crucibles of Soviet politics, culture, and ideology at home deeply affected the conduct and nature of cultural diplomacy abroad. For example, the distinctive Soviet system of cultural diplomacy and receiving foreign visitors emerged from the particular moment of crisis in 1920–22, when the first influx of foreigners after the Civil War arrived in the midst of massive famine after an international appeal to foreign-aid organizations. VOKS and other agencies were part of a set of international agencies with outposts and representatives abroad that spearheaded a range of initiatives in foreign countries, from societies of friends to exhibitions, but they simultaneously had domestic agendas principally relating to the organization of foreign visits and were buffeted by all the pressures and ideological battles of the ongoing cultural revolution at home. Evaluation of foreign visitors became part of an increasingly formal domestic system of surveillance and recordkeeping, and information on the outside world formed part of a highly hierarchical system of censorship and distribution of knowledge.

The external also affected the internal: international agendas and practices boomeranged back to influence internal Soviet affairs. This is not to overestimate the political power of VOKS or any of the other agencies discussed in this book, but rather to point to a more consequential dynamic. More than many have assumed, considerations of what the outside world might see and think—whether explicitly or implicitly, or in ways both subtle and crude—affected the way socialism was constructed, from Lenin to Stalin. These kinds of repercussions are not simple transfers or forms of direct influence, and they are not easy to establish empirically. Yet, this study has suggested the sheer extent of interpenetration between external and internal missions in Soviet history. Students of Soviet communism have weighed many kinds of causes, but have not discussed how crossing borders—on the ground and in the mind—can result in dramatic, unexpected change. How transnational history could become a causal factor in the development of the Soviet system is a prime area for future investigation.

What is almost completely missing from the grand narratives of Soviet history is not international relations per se, but rather the Occident inside the USSR: that is, how the importance of convincing outsiders and the centrality of Western eyes toward self-understandings affected the direction and shape of the Soviet experiment. Once the international dimensions of the Soviet system are treated not as a separate sphere but a central part of Soviet historical development—just as the heyday of Western interest in the Soviet experiment is a crucial piece of twentieth-century history writ large—the making of Soviet communism will no longer appear sui generis, or defined by isolation, even under Stalinism. Rather, every phase of Soviet history was causally shaped by its interactions across borders, even when its reactions were defensive, competitive, hostile, or hidden during extremes of isolationism.

The points of direct contact between European and American visitors and the Soviet Union, organized by the organs of Soviet cultural diplomacy and propaganda, were only one part of this phenomenon of the Occident within, but they help reveal some of its sometimes hidden contours. For example, the naming of a "canonical model" to function as a beacon for all lesser examples of the phenomenon has been called a "defining" tendency in Stalinist culture that was already present in the early 1930s.[4] The history of foreign visitors suggests that this date must be pushed back at least a decade. The promotion of the exceptional miniature—from communes to a vast array of sites and institutions designated as model institutions—took off shortly after 1917 and soon became an important part of early Soviet "cultural show" directed at foreign visitors. It then moved, in ever-more centralized and hierarchical form, to the very center of Stalinist culture, the very building blocks of which were imagined and tangible showcases. The external and internal dimensions of the Soviet system were live wires that contained many conduits.

Perhaps the most significant example of the external-internal nexus in this study has been the methods used to teach foreign observers how to view the positive features of the Soviet system, *kul'tpokaz*, or cultural show. These were among the first methods developed in the 1920s to convey kernels of the great future-in-the-making, as opposed to exceptional showcases amid general squalor. As this book has argued, there were direct and indirect links between cultural show and the rise of Socialist Realism as it became the dominant aesthetic doctrine and a key to culture and ideology under Stalin. This by no means reduces the roots of Stalin-era ideology to *kul'tpokaz*, which itself reflected broader trends. Stalin-era ideology derived from many other sources. Caveats aside, it can be concluded that approaches first innovated for Western visitors affected those later applied on a grand scale to the Soviet population itself.

Finally, there were crucial gaps and disjunctures between the internal and external, or, put another way, cultural diplomacy was always partially insulated from cultural revolution. Soviet international initiatives held a privileged place amid the fierce ideological and political maelstrom of the "cultural front" at home. Foreign bourgeois intellectuals continued to be wooed abroad even as the Russian intelligentsia was most severely persecuted, for example in the early 1930s. Yet, even in this instance, the way "Soviet power" interacted with the intelligentsia and conceptual frameworks about intellectuals cut across the border. Just as foreign observers in this period were sometimes acute in their perceptions but often woefully misled, the history of Soviet analysis of foreigners and foreign countries (in genres from analysts' summaries to the reports of guides and translators) reflected Soviet projections and miscalculations. Even in the heyday of Western sympathy for Stalinism, understanding European and American views solely through the prism of attitudes toward the Soviet Union or attempting to control them from afar produced significant failures of understanding.

The time Europeans and Americans spent inside the Soviet Union—the moment of on-the-ground interaction with the Soviet system—reveals bigger phenomena in interwar politics and intellectual life. Because of the ubiquity of self-censorship among the friends of the Soviet Union, the visits suggest that negative comments and doubts among Western sympathizers, tinged by the long legacy of judgments about Russian inferiority, backwardness, and the East, were more common than is often portrayed even at the heyday of Western sympathy for the Soviet experiment. The attractions of Bolshevism and Stalinism for the radical and fascist Right have often been underestimated or ignored, but the Left-Right exchange this book has documented sometimes resulted in visits that played a role in the entanglements between communism and fascism. Time spent within the Soviet Union played a distinct and influential role in the intellectual and political evolution of the galaxy of prominent thinkers and cultural figures who made the Soviet tour in the 1920s and 1930s. In particular, most of the most celebrated "friends of the Soviet Union" were deeply influenced by Soviet mediators, Soviet officials and intellectuals who brokered their contacts with the Soviet system over time. André Gide, who arrived with his own alternative entourage, was the exception who proves the rule. Visits played a critical role in confirming the status of "friend" for both sides and furthering cross-border Soviet patronage of friendly foreign clients.

The internal-external nexus in Soviet history was from the outset marked by a great and persistent tension in Soviet political culture, traced over the entire course of this book, between the ambitious optimism that revolutionary international engagement would prevail and the pessimistic certainty that it would further ideological contamination and hostile penetration. From the outset, the Bolshevik Revolution ratified a deeply divided view of the outside world. It was at once to be optimistically proselytized and pessimistically quarantined as a mortal threat and contagion to the purity of the revolutionary order. With the consolidation of the Leninist party-state and Stalin's industrialization-era vow to catch up and overtake, this division became reconfigured as a choice between the pursuit of hegemony and an intensification of vigilance.

Stalinism, so uniformly associated with pure isolationism, initially vigorously pursued a far-reaching if rigidly circumscribed engagement that has not been clearly understood. At the height of Soviet international success during the Popular Front, the old dualism came to express itself as a clash between campaigns for international cultural dominance and a hunt to unmask hidden enemies acting from abroad. The two tendencies, always in opposition, openly collided. At the very time when Soviet culture was positioning itself to save the West from itself, extreme xenophobia with one stroke virtually eliminated the linchpin of the Soviet approach to cultural diplomacy—the reception of foreign visitors. This *volte-face*, along with the earlier lurch from the Great Break to Popular Front, and more generally the disparity between Soviet international cultural engagement before and after 1937, suggests that, in crucial respects, Stalinism cannot be conceived as a consistent or unified phenomenon.

Analyzing the world view of communist elites over time, György Péteri has posited an oscillation along two axes: one of inferiority-superiority and one of isolationism-integrationism.[5] Modifying his terms, one can conclude that the balance in the Soviet 1930s shifted between two differing claims on superiority: a hegemonic-integrationist variant that peaked during the Popular Front to the xenophobic-isolationist brand that quickly predominated with the onset of the Great Terror. The consequences of this far-reaching internal clash were the deadly conflation of internal and external enemies and a drastic reordering of relations with foreigners and the outside world.

The superiority complex entrenched by the late 1930s, forged by loud and categorical declarations of Soviet ascendancy over the Western world, was an unstable phenomenon. It was predicated on an extreme isolation during the Great Terror that was quickly punctured, first by the Soviet "revolution from abroad" in the Baltics, western Ukraine, and western Belorussia as a result of the Nazi-Soviet partition of Poland in 1939, and then by the advance of millions of Soviet soldiers west at the end of World War II. "What Red Army conscripts saw in this backwater of provincial Poland, in small villages and towns, not to speak of cities like Lwów and Wilno," in the words of Jan Gross, "were unknown marvels and undreamed of abundance."[6] World War II, alongside the whipped-up hatred and all-out ideological struggle on the Eastern Front, along with pillaging, atrocities, rape, and genocide, was also the era of cultural diplomacy from below. For the first time, soldiers and officers advancing west came into direct contact with bourgeois Europe. "It was not just the striking difference in the material level of life, which dealt a fatal blow to propaganda about the advantages of the Soviet system," Oleg Budnitskii writes. "It may seem paradoxical, but in occupied Germany, as in other European countries not notable for their democratic regimes, Soviet soldiers received a dangerous taste of freedom."[7]

While the Nazi invasion created major disruptions in international cultural contacts already hit hard by the Terror and the Pact, the grand alliance against National Socialism made the war into a period of enormous opportunity for Soviet propaganda and cultural diplomacy. Three days after the invasion, on June 24, 1941, the Sovinformburo was set up to coordinate wartime information and propaganda under the aegis of the Commissariat of Foreign Affairs, but with directions from the Politburo and Central Committee. This powerful organ, with its two most important departments focusing on the wartime allies Britain and the United States, coordinated a massive public relations effort that built directly on the legacy of interwar Soviet cultural diplomacy.

It mobilized and deployed (with a new latitude that was later reversed in post-war campaigns) members of the intelligentsia—including the most popular and talented literary talents and international figures, most famously Ilya Ehrenburg. It supervised international anti-fascist committees for work among Slavs, women, youth, scientists, and as is best known, among Jews in the guise of the Jewish Anti-Fascist Committee (JAC). While pre-war cultural diplomacy had hosted delegations in the USSR, these committees by necessity sent their own delegations abroad. In this limited context, as during the Popular Front, newly flexible forms of direct Soviet cultural diplomacy could harness the force of anti-fascism, now supplemented by alarm among Western Jewry about the Holocaust in the East.[8]

The Jewish Anti-Fascist Committee is by far the best documented of the Sovinformburo organizations, and the range of its activities are a striking confirmation of how the pre-war legacy was renewed and updated in the midst of all-out war. Its goals in developing a "broad anti-fascist campaign" were to operate in a vast array of media, from film, radio, and song to a panoply of literary and journalistic genres. As with the cultural friendship societies, it attempted to create Jewish anti-fascist committees abroad, but it was now also able to raise significant amounts of money. In keeping with pre-war innovations, it aimed to target the most influential individuals in order to influence public opinion. In addition to harnessing the talents of the most Western-oriented Soviet intellectuals, it gathered the information on the Holocaust in the East (in one report euphemistically termed the "situation of the Jews" in occupied territories) that later became the banned Black Book. The highlight of the seven-month mission of Solomon Mikhoels and Itzik Fefer to the United States, Canada, Mexico, and Britain in 1943 was a mass pro-Soviet rally at the Polo Grounds in Manhattan, attended by nearly 50,000 people, during which Paul Robeson sang Russian and Yiddish songs.[9]

The "anti-foreign hysteria" and obsession with secrecy of post-war Stalinism, which was connected to Stalin's decision to reestablish discipline and attain new heights for the official dogma of total superiority, was, underneath the surface, all the more complicated and unstable because it came on the heels of these extraordinary wartime experiences. At the same time, the regime had, in fact, passed the acid test of superiority: it had emerged victorious and found a new lease on legitimacy. Unsurprisingly, though, the new post-war quarantine concealed covert forms of exaggerated admiration and inversions of the official propaganda about the outside world—something that had become noticeable among groups in the Soviet population already in the 1920s.[10] The anti-Western triumphalism of the Zhdanov period hid the continuation, and even growth, of fascination with the illicit or semi-illicit fruits of contact with *kapstrany*, or capitalist countries. This is exemplified by what Stephen Lovell calls "trophy Westernization"—not merely the display of trophy films but the pursuit of every opportunity to acquire Western goods.[11]

At the same time, late Stalinism recapitulated a drastic curtailment of direct cultural diplomacy that recalled the era of the Purges and Pact. Until the mid-1950s, international cultural exchange and the reception of foreign visitors, which had assumed such an important place in early Soviet history, slowed to a trickle. In this respect, the first post-war decade, like the Purge era, marked an exceptional break in the history of Soviet cultural diplomacy. In March 1946, a month after George F. Kennan's famous "Long Telegram," his British counterpart, Frank Roberts, sent his own cable: "Never since the Revolution has the Soviet Union been so cut off from the outside world as today... Cultural contacts are canalised through VOKS, an institution whose purpose is to restrict rather than to encourage exchanges of knowledge and the promotion of real friendship."[12] Between 1947 and 1951, for example, VOKS hosted a mere fifty-seven visitors from the United States, many of them prominent fellow-travelers such as Paul Robeson, who visited in 1949.[13]

The enforced yet brittle isolationism, xenophobia, and official triumphalism of late Stalinism held profound implications for what followed. The cycles of openings and closings to the outside world begun during imperial Russia's Westernization, so intimately connected to the reform and counter-reform of the domestic order, were now recapitulated with special force. The re-engagement with the world that Ehrenburg first dubbed "the Thaw" hit the Soviet Union with bombshell strength. Major increases in travel and cultural traffic between the USSR and Western countries reflected the ambitions of Khrushchev's attempt to enhance Soviet international status through his "peaceful coexistence" strategy and the thoroughgoing, often unwarranted confidence of his cultural diplomacy.[14] This led directly to a series of fateful openings to the West: the sensational and highly charged Picasso exhibit in 1956, the extraordinary and unplanned mass exhilaration of the World Youth Festival in 1957, the remarkable yet vigorously contested attraction of the American National Exhibition at Sokol'niki Park in the summer of 1959.[15] Thaw-era overconfidence was not only a function of the new superpower stature of the Soviet Union or Khrushchev's impulsive personality but in part, ironically, a legacy of the insularity and triumphalism of the Stalinist superiority complex.

At the same time, Soviet cultural diplomacy from the early 1920s to the Popular Front had more in common in certain intriguing respects with the competitive rediscovery of the West during the Thaw than with the extremes of post-1937 Stalinist cultural protectionism. In both the early Soviet experience and the Thaw, the touchstone of cultural diplomacy was the influx of visitors and the reception of foreigners via direct cultural interaction, which were significant for all involved however much they were circumscribed.[16] Both during the drive to build socialism and the search to exorcise the ghosts of Stalinism, engagement with foreign visitors was inextricably linked to far broader issues of the Soviet historical path and the quest to attain an alternative modernity. In both the pre-Purge and post-Stalin order, ambitious optimism about Soviet ability to convince foreign audiences balanced out powerful countervailing fears of capitalist contagion and hostile security breaches. By contrast, late Stalinism displayed an almost unadulterated pessimism about the pernicious effects of contact with the rest of the world.[17] During the periods of the "construction of socialism" and de-Stalinization, a more total form of cultural diplomacy was pursued not only in relatively circumscribed arenas of foreign policy and external propaganda but as key components of dramatic upheavals in the domestic order. Although these restructurings were of differing magnitude, they both made stances toward the leading industrialized countries an overriding issue in domestic politics, culture, and ideology.

The differences between the interwar period and the Cold War, of course, were immense. In the earlier period, the regime launched a massive and wrenching assault on many fronts, whipping up enthusiasm and unleashing unprecedented violence in the service of totalizing aspirations of transformation. Under Khrushchev, the attempt was to shake up and reform an already deeply entrenched, and in certain respects petrified, Stalinist order. In the first instance, overtaking the West was therefore a primary end to be attained by force, whether physical or ideological, whereas in the second it was a function of a superpower rivalry prompting Khrushchev's USSR to compete more intensely in an array of new areas, from the realm of consumption to far-flung outposts in the developing world.

Symptomatically, even within one other crucial similarity between the two periods there lay a decisive difference: after two decades of endless declarations of Soviet superiority, the Thaw-era USSR once again, as in the early 1930s, had to catch up and overtake the West, this time personified by the American consumerist superpower. In the words of Péteri, however much state socialist "discourses of systemic identity had to insist on construing the West as the constitutive other, on mapping it *without*, and on representing it as socialism's past, the Occident was also part of the self; it asserted itself *within*, and appeared to be *ahead* rather than *behind*."[18] Given the birth of a new civic movement in the 1950s, as well as the extreme fascination with the West in the wake of the Stalin era, including among reformist elites, the systemic clash animating Soviet cultural diplomacy had become a far more dangerous game.[19] Connections between interwar and Cold War cultural diplomacy, and the contours of the communist cultural and ideological confrontation with the West, clearly deserve further investigation.

The early Soviet Union's intensive systemic competition with the West—real and imagined, at home and abroad—thus shaped the country that formulated it at least as much as it influenced those outside its borders. The expansive approach to cultural diplomacy innovated in the Soviet Union in the 1920s can be considered more modern—specifically, high modern—in its scope and its statism.[20] In these features, it at once anticipated and paved the way for the great cultural and ideological clash of systems during the Cold War.[21] As David Caute has characterized that later conflict, "Never before had empires felt so compelling a need to prove their virtue, to demonstrate their spiritual superiority, to claim the high ground of 'progress', to win public support and admiration by gaining ascendancy in each and every event of what might be styled the Cultural Olympics."[22]

That the Cultural Cold War was engaged on this scale was a function of the superpower competition in the post-war period, but it got under way in part as a direct result of the precedents set by the Soviets in the inter-war period. To be sure, formative experiences for the United States were its experiments in Latin America and the massive anti-Nazi propaganda effort of World War II.[23] There is ample evidence, however, that the Soviet example and the conviction that it was far ahead in cultural diplomacy set in motion a radical transformation of U.S. state involvement in shaping its image abroad. For example, the 1947 Smith-Mundt act, which finally launched strong U.S. state involvement in cultural diplomacy, came after Congressional committee members had toured Eastern and Western Europe, "being confronted on every hand with the seeming superiority of the Soviet propaganda machine." The legislation's call for a strong "information program" to counter Soviet propaganda anticipated mobilizing all modern media, exhibitions, and exchange programs long before the U.S. cultural offensive broadened in the late 1950s.[24]

Although the United States was the latecomer and continued to rely on a state-private network that appears to have been less lavishly funded than the mature Soviet effort, remarkable similarities quickly emerged between the two superpowers' cultural diplomacy, which formed the "overt, legal, and public part of political or psychological warfare." Both sides minimized access to their own countries, so the key battlegrounds became divided Europe and the developing world. Now the superiority-inferiority complex described in this book assumed its most distilled and confrontational form, as both superpowers tried to persuade European audiences—and themselves—that their "high cultural accomplishments" trumped "Western and Central European claims of cultural superiority." Both Soviet and American efforts to reach Europeans during the Cultural Cold War, at least according to the forthcoming study by Mary Nolan, had limited success.[25]

Despite the perceptions of Soviet strength, affected by the sheer scope of its effort, it appears that for two decades after the devastation of the Great Purges, VOKS became an increasingly sluggish and bureaucratic organ, more geared toward a mechanical cultural-propaganda export as opposed to those areas in which it had proved more nimble and effective, such as the tailoring of programs for visitors or the analysis and adroit cultivation of key foreign sympathizers that had been part of its repertoire starting with Ol'ga Kameneva in the 1920s. Although research on the records of Soviet cultural diplomacy after 1941 remains sparse, it appears that the tone-deaf campaign mode that came to the fore during the Great Break triumphed over Soviet cultural diplomacy's more shrewd and flexible moments, most prominent under Kameneva during NEP and Aleksandr Arosev during the Popular Front. This outcome under late Stalinism appears logical given what the Great Break revealed about VOKS's sensitivity to periods of domestic cultural-ideological crackdown.

Soviet cultural diplomacy in the interwar years had balanced its preoccupation with the West with strong interest in expanding the friendship societies and connections on a more global scale, as well as eagerness from the first to court visitors from revolutionary Mexico and many other parts of the developing world. The bipolar ideological confrontation of the Cold War, combined with the lessening attraction of Soviet communism for European and American intellectuals, gave great impetus to broadening the scope of Soviet post-war involvement with the developing world.[26] At the same time, VOKS found a vast new market for the export of its materials during the Sovietization of the countries of Eastern Europe. In the new friendship societies, which in Poland and East Germany, for example, became mass organizations with millions of members in 1949, VOKS now played a rather inept second fiddle to the national communist parties.[27]

Traditional views of artful communist Machiavellianism in pursuit of international aims, as this book suggests, need to be balanced by an appreciation of exactly how widespread Soviet missteps were. These included misunderstandings of foreign audiences, projections of Soviet assumptions into analysis of the culture and politics of foreign countries, and ineffective, even grotesque, translations of Soviet-speak into other languages. These features of Soviet cultural diplomacy already amply present in the 1920s and 1930s became only more ubiquitous with the heavy-handed ideological bureaucratism and anti-cosmopolitanism of the post-war 1940s—just as the Soviets faced a more vigorous Western pushback in the realm of cultural diplomacy.[28] The mid-1930s Central Committee interference that had hampered Arosev foreshadowed the post-war 1940s, when Andrei Zhdanov, head of both the powerful Central

Committee departments of Agitprop and Foreign Policy, took tight charge over VOKS and other Soviet agencies and "social organizations" with international functions, although the Ministry of Foreign Affairs also struggled for what turned out to be generally ham-handed oversight.[29]

In the 1950s, after longstanding skirmishes for control over VOKS between party organs and Foreign Affairs, VOKS itself—now associated with the Stalinist past—was closed down. As part of the ambitious and optimistic Thaw-era attempt to re-engage the outside world, it was replaced in September 1957 by a new Union of Soviet Societies of Friendship and Cultural Relations with Foreign Countries. At the same time, a new State Committee for Cultural Ties (GKKS) was created to systematize and regularize foreign cultural relations, a move in line with the new willingness to enter into formal agreements on cultural and academic exchange. GKKS was also intended to become a more powerful organization under Central Committee control. A truly authoritative organ to regulate cultural relations with the world never materialized, however, just as VOKS competed with an array of agencies and never managed to consolidate itself as such in the interwar period. In 1967, GKKS was shuttered, and a new Department of Cultural Relations was created under the Ministry of Foreign Affairs.[30] This institutional shift was symbolic, for with it the Soviet Union had finally found its way to putting cultural diplomacy in an institutional home that was fully conventional, in line with what other countries had done since the Great War.

The attempt to "sell" a country's image through culture, travel, and the media has become a ubiquitous part of the modern world. It is, however, a phenomenon of a much different order when that very attempt strikes at the core of the propagandizing country's own sense of self and historical course. Such was the case with the early Soviet Union, but the importance of showcasing the great experiment reaches even beyond that. The manner in which sentiments of superiority and inferiority deeply informed the interactions between those who showcased the Soviet Union and those who visited it in the 1920s and 1930s went on to play a starring role throughout the Cold War—and even to survive the collapse of communism. With its deep roots in early modern European accounts of Eastern backwardness and the strong response during the articulation of Russian national identity in the nineteenth century, this was a phenomenon that predated the Soviet experiment; it was greatly heightened by the challenge of communism, the ubiquitous evaluations of the interwar tour, and the hierarchical Soviet classification of foreign visitors. Long after Stalinism, long after the "Russian moment in world history,"[31] and well after the end of the Soviet Union, exploring interrelated claims of superiority and inferiority on both sides remains one of the most revealing modes for attempting to understand the interactions between "Russia and the West." Communism may be no more, but the perennial problem of backwardness remains along with hierarchical and reflexive comparisons at the core of Russia's love-hate relationship with the Western world. Exploring this issue will remain crucial as long as there persists a set of problems that goes by the name of Russia and the West.

NOTES

Introduction

1. The phrase comes from the classic "pre-archival" work of Sylvia R. Margulies, *The Pilgrimage to Russia: The Soviet Union and the Treatment of Foreigners, 1924–1937* (Madison: University of Wisconsin Press, 1968).

2. A. V. Golubev, et al., *Rossiia i Zapad: Formirovanie vneshnepoliticheskikh stereotipov v soznanii rossiiskogo obshchestva pervoi poloviny XX veka* (Moscow: Institut Istorii RAN, 1998), 146.

3. The literature on intellectuals and communism is analyzed in chap. 6. The best-known work in English has gone through four editions: Paul Hollander, *Political Pilgrims: Western Intellectuals in Search of the Good Society*, 4th ed. (New Brunswick: Transaction Publishers, 1998).

4. Here see also Eva Oberloskamp, *Fremde neue Welten: Reisen deutscher und französischer Linksintellektueller in die Sowjetunion 1917–1939* (Munich: Oldenbourg, 2011); Matthias Heeke, *Reisen zu den Sowjets: Der ausländische Tourismus in Russland 1921–1941* (Münster: Lit Verlag, 2003).

5. Theodore Dreiser, *Dreiser's Russian Diary*, ed. Thomas P. Riggio and James L. W. West III (Philadelphia: University of Pennsylvania Press, 1996), 220; Ruth Epperson Kennell, *Theodore Dreiser and the Soviet Union, 1927–1945: A First-Hand Chronicle* (New York: International Publishers, 1969), 139.

6. Recent years have witnessed a great new interest in Soviet international cultural relations and transnational history. This has led to notable studies focusing on views of Russia and the USSR in individual Western countries: Sophie Coeuré, *La grande lueur à l'Est: Les Français et l'Union soviétique, 1917–1939* (Paris: Seuil, 1999); Heeke, *Reisen zu den Sowjets;* David Engerman, *Modernization from the Other Shore: American Intellectuals and the Romance of Russian Economic Development* (Cambridge, Mass.: Harvard University Press, 2003); and in comparative mode, Donal O'Sullivan, *Furcht und Faszination: Deutsche und britische Russlandbilder 1921–1931* (Cologne, Weimar, Vienna: Böhlau Verlag, 1996). There have also been significant studies of travel and travelogues, including Oberloskamp, *Fremde neue Welten;* Rachel Mazuy, *Croire plutôt que voir? Voyages en Russie soviétique (1919–1939)* (Paris: Odile Jacob, 2002); Christiane Uhlig, *Utopie oder Alptraum? Schweizer Reiseberichte über die Sowjetunion 1917–1941* (Zurich: Verlag Hans Rohr, 1992). Simultaneously, post-Soviet Russian historiography has produced a flowering of works on the history of cultural relations with individual Western countries, including Golubev, et al., *Rossiia i Zapad*. A groundbreaking and complementary contribution to the present study is Katerina Clark's *Moscow, the Fourth Rome: Stalinism, Cosmopolitanism, and the Evolution of Soviet Culture, 1931–1941* (Cambridge, Mass.: Harvard University Press, 2011), which excavates the international dimensions of Soviet culture in the 1930s.

7. This book only became possible to write after the substantial "secret" part of the VOKS archive was declassified in the mid-1990s. Previously almost unknown, VOKS has since figured in a number of studies in the last decade, including, most notably, A. V. Golubev, *"Vzgliad na zemliu obetovannuiu" Iz istorii sovetskoi kul'turnoi diplomatii* 1920–1930-*x godov* (Moscow: Institut istorii RAN, 2004), which has an emphasis on the 1930s and visitors from Britain. See also Ludmila Stern, *Western Intellectuals and the Soviet Union, 1920–1940: From Red Square to the Left Bank* (London: Routledge, 2007); Sheila Fitzpatrick and Carolyn Rasmussen, eds., *Political Tourists: Travellers from Australia to the Soviet Union in the* 1920s–1940s (Melbourne: Melbourne University Press, 2008); Jean-François Fayet, "La VOKS: La société pour les échanges culturels entre l'URSS et l'étranger," *Relations internationales*, 114/115 (Fall 2003): 411–423, and Fayet, "Entre mensonge, engagement et manipulation: Les témoignages d'Occidentaux avant séjournés en URSS," in *Un mensonge déconcertant? La Russie au XXe siècle*, ed. Jean-Philippe Jaccard (Paris: L'Harmattan, 2003), 377–418.

8. Here there is a comparison with the propaganda and cultural diplomacy efforts of East-Central European states after Versailles, which focused above all on influencing Western European and U.S. elites. Andrea Orzoff, *Battle for the Castle: The Myth of Czechoslovakia in Europe, 1914–1948* (New York: Oxford University Press, 2009), introduction, chap. 2.

9. Later, other communist countries would import and adapt this system. For example, the Chinese People's Association for Cultural Relations with Foreign Countries was modeled after VOKS. See Herbert Passin, *China's Cultural Diplomacy* (New York: Praeger, 1962).

10. In this area, some of the most revealing studies treat various kinds of resident foreigners and foreign colonies. See, for example, Sergei Zhuravlev, *"Malen'kie liudi" i "bol'shaia istoriia": Inostrantsy moskovskogo Elektrozavoda v sovetskom obshchestve* 1920-*x* – 1930-*x gg.* (Moscow: ROSSPEN, 2000); Michael Hughes, *Inside the Enigma: British Officials in Russia, 1900–1939* (London: Hamstedon Press, 1997). Less well studied are Soviet personnel and operations abroad, but see Karl Schlögel, *Berlin, Ostbahnhof Europas: Russen und Deutsche in ihrem Jahrhundert* (Berlin: Siedler Verlag, 1998); Oksana Bulgakova, "Proletarskii internatsionalizm na Maslovke, ili eksport 'russkikh' v Berlin," *Kinovedcheskie zapiski*, no. 35 (1997): 37–54; Sabine Dullin, *Des hommes d'influences: Les ambassadeurs de Staline en Europe* 1930–1939 (Paris: Payot, 2001).

11. Leonid Maksimenkov also uses the term *zapadniki* (Westernizers) in "Ocherki nomenklaturnoi istorii sovetskoi literatury: Zapadnye pilgrimy u stalinskogo prestola (Feikhtvanger i dr.), part 2, *Voprosy literatury*, no. 3 (2004): 272–342, quotation 304.

12. Lindsey Hughes, "Attitudes towards Foreigners in Early Modern Russia," in *Russia and the Wider World in Historical Perspective: Essays for Paul Dukes*, ed. Cathryn Brennan and Murray Frame (Houndmills, Bastingstoke, UK: Macmillan, 2000): 1–24; Marshall T. Poe, *"A People Born to Slavery": Russia in Early Modern European Ethnography, 1476–1748* (Ithaca: Cornell University Press, 2000), 47–48, 83–89, 199. On the *nemetskie slobody*, see T. A. Oparina, *Inozemtsy v Rossii XVI–XVII vv.* (Moscow: Progress-Traditsiia, 2007), 15–16.

13. This is the argument in chap. 1 of Eric Lohr's "Russian Citizenship: Empire to Soviet Union," Harvard University Press, forthcoming 2012, drawing on S. P. Orlenko, *Vykhodtsy iz Zapadnoi Evropy v Rossii: Pravovoi status i real'noe polozhenie* (Moscow: Drevlekhranilishche, 2004). On the complex balance of assimilation and isolation of foreigners in late Muscovy, see Oparina, *Inozemtsy*.

14. See Edward L. Keenan, "Muscovite Political Folkways," *Russian Review* 45, 2 (1986): 115–181, and Richard Hellie, "The Structure of Modern Russian History: Toward a Dynamic Model," *Russian History* 4, 1 (1977): 1–22, quotation 22, and the response by Richard Wortman, "Remarks on the Service State Interpretation," ibid., 39–41.

15. Alfred J. Rieber, "Persistent Factors in Russian Foreign Policy: An Interpretive Essay," in *Imperial Russian Foreign Policy*, ed. Hugh Ragsdale (Cambridge: Cambridge University Press, 1993), 315–359, and Rieber, "How Persistent are Persistent Factors?" in *Russian Foreign Policy in the Twenty-First Century and the Shadow of the Past*, ed. Robert Legvold (New York: Columbia University Press, 2007): 205–278.

16. Michael David-Fox, "The Intelligentsia, the Masses, and the West: Particularities of Russian-Soviet Modernity," "Crossing Borders: Modernity, Ideology, and Culture in Soviet Russia" (Pittsburgh: University of Pittsburgh Press, forthcoming).

17. For one example, see A. V. Lunacharskii, *Kul'tura na Zapade i u nas* (Moscow and Leningrad: Gosizdat, 1928).

18. Lohr, "Russian Citizenship," chap. 1.

19. Iver B. Neumann, *Russia and the Idea of Europe: A Study in Identity and International Relations* (London and New York: Routledge, 1996).

20. Catriona Kelly, *Refining Russia: Advice Literature, Polite Culture, and Gender from Catherine to Yeltsin* (Oxford and New York: Oxford University Press, 2001), xviii.

21. Neumann, *Russia and the Idea of Europe*, xiv, 13.

22. Natalie Bayer, "Spreading the Light: European Freemasonry in Russia in the Eighteenth Century" (Ph.D. diss., Rice University, 2007).

23. Catherine Evtuhov, "Guizot in Russia," in *The Cultural Gradient: The Transmission of Ideas in Europe, 1789–1991*, ed. Evtuhov and Stephen Kotkin (Lanham, Md.: Rowman and Littlefield, 2003), 55–72; Andrzej Walicki, *The Slavophile Controversy: History of a Conservative Utopia in Nineteenth Century Russian Thought* (Oxford: Clarendon Press, 1975); Nicholas V. Riazanovsky, *Russia and the West in the Teaching of the Slavophiles: A Study in Romantic Ideology* (Cambridge, Mass.: Harvard University Press, 1952); and, most recently, Susanna Rabow-Edling, *Slavophile Thought and the Politics of Cultural Nationalism* (Albany: SUNY Press, 2006).

24. Neumann, *Russia and the Idea of Europe*, 38–39; Vasilii Shchukin, *Russkoe zapadnichestvo: Genezis – sushchnost' - istoricheskaia rol'* (Łódź: Ibidem, 2001), quotation 36; B. S. Itenberg, *Rossiiskaia intelligentsiia i Zapad: Vek XIX* (Moscow: Nauka, 1999); and the classic study by Martin Malia, *Alexander Herzen and the Birth of Russian Socialism* (Cambridge, Mass.: Harvard University Press, 1961).

25. Lars Lih (in his introduction to *Rediscovered: What Is to Be Done? In Context* [Leiden and Boston: Brill, 2006], 3–40) emphasizes the Europeanness of Russian Social Democracy, whereas Claudio Ingerflom (*Le Citoyen impossible. Les racines russes du léninisme* [Paris: Bibliothèque historique, 1988]), and in "Lenin Rediscovered, or Lenin Redisguised?," *Kritika* 10, 1 [Winter 2009], 139–168) brings out the Russianness in "Russian Marxism" and Leninism.

26. Liah Greenfeld, "The Formation of Russian National Identity: The Role of Status Insecurity and *Ressentiment*," *Comparative Studies in Society and History* 32, 3 (1990): 549–591; the broader argument is in Greenfeld, *Nationalism: Five Roads to Modernity* (Cambridge, Mass.: Harvard University Press, 1992).

27. Here see Boris Grois, "Rossiia kak podsoznanie Zapada," in *Utopiia i obmen* (Moscow: Znak, 1993), 245–259.

28. Gorky, "K inostrannym rabochim," in *Publitsisticheskie stat'i* (Moscow: Gosizdat literatury, 1931), 290–293.

29. For example, see Adam B. Ulam, *The Bolsheviks: The Intellectual and Political History of the Triumph of Communism in Russia* (Cambridge, Mass.: Harvard University Press, 1998), 29.

30. Inter alia, Barbara Walker, *Maximilian Voloshin and the Russian Literary Circle: Culture and Survival in Revolutionary Times* [Bloomington: Indiana University Press, 2005]; Jan Plamper, "The Stalin Cult: A Study in the Alchemy of Power" (New Haven: Yale University Press, forthcoming 2012); Peter Holquist, "Violent Russia, Deadly Marxism? Russia in the Epoch of Violence, 1905–21," *Kritika* 4, 3 (Summer 2003): 627–652; Holquist, *Making War, Forging Revolution: Russia's Continuum of Crisis, 1914–1921* (Cambridge, Mass.: Harvard University Press, 2002).

31. Lohr, "Russian Citizenship," chap. 1, 40. On foreign colonies, residents, and specialists in imperial Russia, see Roger P. Bartlett, *Human Capital: The Settlements of Foreigners in Russia 1762–1804* (Cambridge: Cambridge University Press, 1979); E. V. Alekseeva, *Diffuziia evropeiskikh innovatsii v Rossii (XVII-nachalo XX v.)* (Moscow: ROSSPEN, 2007): 42–62.

32. G. P. Dolzhenko, *Istoriia turizma v dorevoliutsionnoi Rossii i SSSR* (Rostov: Izdatel'stvo Rostovskogo universiteta, 1988), 13.

33. Anton Fedyashin, "Russia's First *Polittekhnolog*: Sergei Witte and the Press," forthcoming article.

34. Paul Gordon Lauren, *"Civilisation* and *Kultur,"* chap. 6 of *Diplomats and Bureaucrats: The First Institutional Responses to Twentieth-Century Diplomacy in France and Germany* (Stanford: Stanford University Press, 1976), 179.

35. Lauren, *Diplomats*, 204. See also Robert J. Young, *Marketing Marianne: French Propaganda in America, 1900–1940* (New Brunswick: Rutgers University Press, 2004); Kurt Düwell and Werner Link, eds., *Deutsche auswärtige Kulturpolitik seit 1871* (Cologne and Vienna: Böhlau Verlag, 1981).

36. Akira Iriye, *Cultural Internationalism and World Order* (Baltimore: Johns Hopkins University Press, 1997), esp. 114.

37. O. D. Kameneva to G. V. Chicherin, no later than 18 June 1925, GARF f. 5283, op. 8, ed. khr. 3, l. 47; F. A. Rotshtein (member of the NKID collegium) to Kameneva, 19 June 1925, ibid., op. 1a, ed. khr. 53, l. 13.

38. Peter Kenez, *The Birth of the Propaganda State: Soviet Methods of Mass Mobilization* (New York: Cambridge University Press, 1985); but for an unflattering comparison between Agitprop and the contemporaneous U.S. science of public relations, see Matthew Lenoe, *Closer to the Masses: Stalinist Culture, Social Revolution, and Soviet Newspapers* (Cambridge, Mass.: Harvard University Press, 2004), 7, 249.

39. On the Creel Committee, see Alan Axelrod, *Selling the Great War: The Making of American Propaganda* (New York: Palgrave Macmillan, 2009).

40. Orzoff, 5.

41. Reinhold Wagnleitner, *Coca-Colonization and the Cold War: The Cultural Mission of the United States in Austria after the Second World War*, trans. Diana M. Wolf (Chapel Hill: University of North Carolina Press, 1994), chap. 2; Frank A. Ninkovich, *The Diplomacy of Ideas: U.S. Foreign Policy and Cultural Relations, 1938–1950* (Cambridge: Cambridge University Press, 1981).

42. Philip M. Taylor, *Munitions of the Mind: A History of Propaganda from the Ancient World to the Present Day* (Manchester: Manchester University Press, 2003), 177–181.

43. The term cultural diplomacy, which has become standard and, for lack of a better alternative, unavoidable in the field, was introduced by Frederick C. Barghoorn, *The Soviet Cultural Offensive: The Role of Cultural Diplomacy in Soviet Foreign Policy* (Princeton: Princeton University Press, 1960); see also Wolfgang Kasack, "Kulturelle Aussenpolitik," in *Kulturpolitik der Sowjetunion*, ed. Oskar Anweiler and Karl-Heinz Ruffmann (Stuttgart: Alfred Kröner Verlag, 1973), 351–354.

44. David Fisher, "Exhibiting Russia at the World's Fairs, 1851–1900" (Ph.D diss., Indiana University, 2003).

45. The case for late-nineteenth-century integration is made, even exaggerated, by Martin Malia, *Russia under Western Eyes: From the Bronze Horseman to the Lenin Mausoleum* (Cambridge, Mass.: Harvard University Press, 1999), chap. 3.

46. Greenfeld, *Nationalism*, 223.

47. Rieber, "Persistent Factors," 344–57. The phrase derives from Adam Olearius, *The Travels of Olearius in Seventeenth-Century Russia*, trans. and ed. Samuel H. Baron (Stanford: Stanford University Press, 1967).

48. See, inter alia, Gabriele Scheidegger, *Perverses Abendland—barbarisches Russland: Begegnungen des 16. und 17. Jahrhunderts im Schatten kultureller Missverständnisse* (Zurich: Chronos, 1993). Poe, bringing the treatment of this topic to a new level, suggested in *"A People Born to Slavery"* that for the most part Muscovy failed to restrict much accurate foreign observation.

49. For examples, see Poe, *"A People Born to Slavery,"* 3–8, 169–174, 200.

50. Larry Wolff, *Inventing Eastern Europe: The Map of Civilization on the Mind of the Enlightenment* (Stanford: Stanford University Press, 1994), 360; Ezequiel Adamovsky, *Euro-Orientalism: Liberal Ideology and the Image of Russia in France (c. 1740–1880)* (Bern: Peter Lang, 2006), 15, 42–45, 62.

51. Michael Adas, *Machines as the Measure of Men: Science, Technology, and Ideologies of Western Dominance* (Ithaca, NY: Cornell University Press, 1990); Jonathan Spence, *The Chan's Great Continent: China in Western Minds* (New York: W. W. Norton, 1998).

52. François Furet, *The Passing of an Illusion: The Idea of Communism in the Twentieth Century*, trans. Deborah Furet (Chicago: University of Chicago Press, 1999), 67.

53. Malia, *Russia under Western Eyes*. Malia's world-historical perch slights actual encounters, as he alternates analysis of the illusion-filled perceptions of the past with his own grand narrative of Russian-Soviet history.

54. Aleksandr Panchenko, "Potemkinskie derevni kak kul'turnyi mif," in *O russkoi istorii i kul'ture* (St. Petersburg: Azbuka, 2000): 411–425, here 416. See also Sara Dickinson, "Russia's First 'Orient': Characterizing the Crimea in 1787," and David Schimmelpenninck van der Oye, "Catherinian Chinoiserie," both in *Orientalism and Empire in Russia*, ed. Michael David-Fox, Peter Holquist, and Alexander Martin (Bloomington, Ind.: Slavica, 2006); O. I. Eliseeva, *Geopoliticheskie proekty G. A. Potemkina* (Moscow: Institut istorii RAN, 2000), chap. 5.

55. Irena Grudzinska Gross, *The Scar of Revolution: Custine, Tocqueville, and the Romantic Imagination* (Berkeley: University of California Press, 1991); Christian Sigrist, *Das Russlandbild des Marquis de Custine: Von der Civilisationskritik zur Russlandfeindlichkeit* (Frankfurt am Main and New York: P. Lang, 1990); Wolff, 364–365; Adamovsky, 103–106.

56. The classic work on theatricality is Iurii M. Lotman, "The Poetics of Everyday Behavior in Eighteenth-Century Russian Culture," in *The Semiotics of Russian Cultural History*, ed. Alexander D. Nakhimovsky and Alice Stone Nakhimovsky (Ithaca: Cornell University Press, 1985, Russian orig. 1977); for a cogent challenge, see Michelle Marrese, "The Poetics of Everyday Behavior Revisited: Lotman, Gender, and the Evolution of Russian Noble Identity," *Kritika* 11, 4 (Fall 2010): 697–700.

57. Bruno Naarden, *Socialist Europe and Revolutionary Russia: Perception and Prejudice 1848–1923* (Cambridge: Cambridge University Press, 1992), 30–31; Iver B. Neumann, *Uses of the Other: The 'East' in European Identity Formation* (Minneapolis: University of Minnesota Press, 1999), 93; Wolff, 362.

58. David C. Fisher, "Russia and the Crystal Palace in 1851," in *Britain, the Empire, and the World at the Great Exhibition of 1851*, ed. Jeffrey A. Auerbach and Peter H. Hoffenberg (Aldershot, UK: Ashgate Publishing, 2008): 123–145.

59. August Freiherr von Haxthausen, *Studies on the Interior of Russia*, ed. S. Frederick Starr, trans. Eleanore L. M. Schmidt (Chicago: University of Chicago Press, 1972, orig. 1846); T. K. Dennison and A. W. Carrus, "The Invention of the Russian Peasant Commune: Haxthausen and the Evidence," *Historical Journal* 46 (2003): 561–582, esp. 567, 569.

60. Daniel L. Schlafly, Jr., "The Great White Bear and the Cradle of Culture: Italian Images of Russia and Russian Images of Italy," *Kritika* 9, 2 (Spring 2008): 389–406, quotations 389, 390.

61. Naarden, *Socialist Europe and Revolutionary Russia*, 27; for counterexamples, see Adamovsky, 134–139.

62. Engerman, *Modernization from the Other Shore*, chap. 2.

63. Steven G. Marks, *How Russia Shaped the Modern World: From Art to Anti-Semitism, Ballet to Bolshevism* (Princeton: Princeton University Press, 2003), chap. 3; Lew Kopelew, ed., *Russen und Russland aus deutscher Sicht*, 5 vols. (Munich: W. Fink, 1985–1990), vol. 4: *19/20. Jahrhundert: Von der Bismarckzeit bis zum Ersten Weltkrieg*; Vol'fram Vette, "Obrazy Rossii u nemtsev v XX v.," in *Rossiia i Germaniia*, ed. B. M. Tupolev, vyp. 1 (Moscow: Nauka, 1998), 225–243.

64. Richard Griffiths, *Fellow Travellers of the Right: British Enthusiasts for Nazi Germany 1933–1939* (London: Constable, 1980); Alastair Hamilton, *The Appeal of Fascism: A Study of Intellectuals and Fascism 1919–1945* (New York: Aron Books, 1971).

65. Peter Wagner, *A Sociology of Modernity: Liberty and Discipline* (London: Routledge, 1994), 66.

66. Wagner, 62–67; Holquist, *Making War*; Mark Mazower, *Dark Continent: Europe's Twentieth Century* (New York: A. A. Knopf, 1999).

67. On persisting images of Russian Asianness and barbarism in literature and film, see Oksana Bulgakowa, "The 'Russian Vogue' in Europe and Hollywood: The Transformation of Russian Stereotypes through the 1920s," *Russian Review* 64 (April 2005): 211–35.

68. Here see David Caute, *The Fellow-Travellers: Intellectual Friends of Communism*, rev. ed. (New Haven: Yale University Press, 1983); Engerman, *Modernization from the Other Shore.*

69. Mary Nolan, *Visions of Modernity: American Business and the Modernization of Germany* (New York: Oxford University Press, 1994). For this division even in Fascist ideology see Pier Giorgio Zunino, "Tra americanismo e bolscevismo," in *L'ideologia del fascismo: Miti, credenze e valore nella stabilizzazione del regime* (Bologna: Il Mulino, 1985), 322–344.

70. Anatolii Lunacharskii, "Mezhdu Vostokom i Zapadom," *Zapad i Vostok: Sbornik VOKS*, book 1–2 (Moscow, 1926), 10–13.

71. Michael Geyer and Sheila Fitzpatrick, "Introduction," in *Beyond Totalitarianism: Stalinism and Nazism Compared*, ed. Geyer and Fitzpatrick (Cambridge: Cambridge University Press, 2009), 37.

72. Here one can make an analogy to the way the emerging culture of Fascism attempted to overcome Italy's traditional inferiority complex vis-à-vis France and Germany. See Ruth Ben-Ghiat, *Fascist Modernities: Italy, 1922–1945* (Berkeley: University of California, 2001).

73. The interpretive framework of control is pursued by G. B. Kulikova, "Pod kontrolem gosudarstva: Prebyvanie v SSSR inostrannykh pisatelei v 1920–1930-x godakh," *Otechestvennaia istoriia*, no. 4 (2003): 43–59; the manipulation framework is reproduced most recently by Stern, *Western Intellectuals and the Soviet Union.*

74. Here see Jochen Hellbeck, *Revolution on My Mind: Writing a Diary under Stalinism* (Cambridge, Mass.: Harvard University Press, 2006).

Chapter 1

1. A. V. Golubev, "...*Vzgliad na zemliu obetovannuiu*": *Iz istorii sovetskoi kul'turnoi diplomatii 1920–1930-x godov* (Moscow: Institut rossiiskoi istorii RAN, 2004), 90; Norman E. Saul, *Friends or Foes? The United States and Russia, 1921–1941* (Lawrence: University of Kansas Press, 2006), 8–18.

2. Gábor T. Rittersporn, "Fremde in einer Gesellschaft der Fremden," in *Fremde und Fremd-Sein in der DDR: Zu historischen Ursachen der Fremdenfeindlichkeit in Ostdeutschland*, ed. Jan C. Behrends, Thomas Lindenberger, and Patrice G. Poutrus (Berlin: Metropol, 2003): 43–55; Golfo Alexopolous, "Soviet Citizenship, More or Less: Rights, Emotions, and States of Civic Belonging," *Kritika* 7, 3 (Summer 2006): 487–528, quotation 492. On the multiple connections between international conflict and revolutionary politics, see Arno J. Mayer, *The Furies: Violence and Terror in the French and Russian Revolutions* (Princeton: Princeton University Press, 2000).

3. James von Geldern, *Bolshevik Festivals, 1917–1920* (Berkeley: University of California Press, 1993), 200–205.

4. Golubev, "...*Vzgliad na zemliu obetovannuiu*," 90–99; N. V. Kiseleva, *Iz istorii bor'by sovetskoi obshchestvennosti za proryv kul'turnoi blokady SSSR (VOKS: seredina 20-x – nachalo 30-x godov* (Rostov na Donu: Izdatel'stvo Rostovskogo Universiteta, 1991), 9–11.

5. "Protokol zasedaniia Redaktsionnoi Komissii pri Biuro Inostrannoi Nauki i Tekhniki, Berlin, 20-go ianvaria 1921 g.," AVP RF f. 0528, op. 1, d. 120, p. 22, l. 70; "Doklad Prezidiuma VSNKh ot Predstavitelia VSNKh v Germanii F. M. Fedorovskogo. 10 fevralia 1921," ibid., l. 87–89; see also ll. 255–256.

6. "Declaration to be Signed by all American Workers that Come to Soviet Russia," 1922, AVP RF f. 0528, op. 1, d. 105, p. 19, l. 52. This *delo* contains correspondence sent to Krasin by foreign workers in various languages.

7. "Spisok knig, otoslannykh v Narkomindel tov. Klyshko s dir. kur'erom Serezhnikovym 18/VIII–1920 goda," AVP RF f. 0528, op. 1, d. 121, p. 22, l. 12.

8. Quoted in Bertrand M. Patenaude, *The Big Show in Bololand: The American Relief Expedition to Soviet Russia in the Famine of* 1921 (Stanford: Stanford University Press, 2002), 27.
9. "Rossiiskomu predstaviteliu v Velikobritanii. Leonidu Borisovichu Krasinu. Paris, 4 August 1921," AVP RF f. 0528, op. 1, d. 125, papka 23, l. 249–253; pamphlet, British "Hands off Russia" Committee, 29 September 1921, ibid., l. 169.
10. Stuart Finkel, *On the Ideological Front: The Russian Intelligentsia and the Making of the Soviet Public Sphere* (New Haven: Yale University Press, 2007), 24–35, quotation 32; Bruno Naarden, *Socialist Europe and Revolutionary Russia: Perception and Prejudice 1848–1923* (Cambridge: Cambridge University Press, 1992), 436–444, here 439.
11. All foreign correspondents would therefore have to submit telegrams for preliminary checking, a practice that became a significant lever of control over foreign press reportage from the USSR. Litvinov to Chicherin, 30 August 1921, AVP RF f. 0528, op. 1, d. 126, p. 23, ll. 144–145.
12. David Engerman, *Modernization from the Other Shore: American Intellectuals and the Romance of Russian Development* (Cambridge, Mass.: Harvard University Press, 2003), chap. 6; Patenaude, 40 and passim; see also Saul, *Friends or Foes*, 44–97.
13. Patenaude, 43, 104–107.
14. Patenaude, 110–12, 346–353.
15. Aleksandr Eiduk, "Narkomindel Tov. Chicherinu," copies Lezhava, Lenin, Tsiuriupa, Litvinov, Kamenev, Molotov. AVP RF f. 0528, op. 1, d. 126, p. 23, l. 85.
16. Saul, *Friends or Foes*, 63, 71–76; Patenaude, 337, 508 and passim.
17. "Itogi deiatel'nosti ARA," *Kommunist*, 24 June 1923, in GARF f. 4283, op. 1a, ed. khr. 6, l. 25.
18. Engerman, *Modernization from the Other Shore*, chap. 6; Saul, *Friends or Foes*, 58.
19. Patenaude, 45, 337, 340, 350–351, 373.
20. Boris Chicherin to Lev Kamenev, 30 July 1921, in *Bol'shevistskoe rukovodstvo: Perepiska. 1912–1927* (Moscow: ROSSPEN, 1996), 208–209.
21. GARF f. 5283, op. 1a, d. 31, ll. 46–47; Patenaude, 84–85, 184–185, 375; Golubev, "…*Vzgliad na zemliu obetovannuiu*," 100.
22. "Opis' sekretnogo dela Komissii Zagranichnoi Pomoshchi pri Prezidiume TsIK SSSR za 1923–24," GARF f. 5283, op. 1a, ed. khr. 7.
23. On the "cultural" functions of KZP, see Kiseleva, *Iz istorii*, 12–28.
24. O. D. Kameneva, "Tov. Moskvinu. TsK VKP(b). Sov. sekretno. 5 ianvaria 1928," GARF f. 5283, op. 1a, d. 118, l. 1–3.
25. O. D. Kameneva, "Narodnomu Komissaru po Inostrannym Delam, tov. G.V. Chicherinu," 8 December 1924, GARF f. 5283, op. 1a, d. 31, ll. 10–12.
26. Posledgol and NKID documents, 1923, GARF f. 5283, op. 1a, d. 3, ll. 7, 63, 66, 101, 137, 143; Kiseleva, *Iz istorii*, quotation 11.
27. GARF f. 5283, op. 8, ed. khr. 3, ll. 108–11; ibid., op. 1a, ed. khr. 37, l. 2–3; Kiseleva, *Iz istorii*, 20.
28. Kameneva to Iagoda, Zam. Pred. OGPU, and Menzhinskii, Zam. Nach. OGPU, 22 February 1924, GARF f. 5283, op. 1a, d. 21, l. 6, 8–9.
29. "Zasedanie politicheskogo i organizatsionnogo biuro ot 10/VII–19 goda," RGASPI f. 17, op. 3, ed. khr. 14, l. 1.
30. Matthias Heeke, *Reisen zu den Sowjets: Der ausländische Tourismus in Russland 1921–1941* (Münster: Lit Verlag, 2003), 25–27.
31. O. D. Kameneva, "K uluchsheniiu byta rabochikh," in Kameneva, ed. *V pomoshch' kul'trabote v rabochem stolovoi* (Moscow-Leningrad: Doloi negramotnost', 1926), 3–6. *Kul'turnost'* has been examined in Soviet history not as a key concept of a decades-long cultural revolution but mainly in the context of the culturedness campaign and so-called "Great Retreat" in the mid- to late 1930s. For example, see Sheila Fitzpatrick, "Becoming Cultured: Socialist Realism and the Representation of Privilege and Taste," in Fitzpatrick, *The Cultural Front: Power and Culture in Revolutionary Russia* (Ithaca: Cornell University Press, 1992), chap. 9, and the discussion in Catriona Kelly and David Shepherd, eds. *Constructing Russian Culture in the Age of Revolution: 1881–1940* (Oxford: Oxford University Press, 1998), 291–313.

32. O. D. Kameneva, "Ot redaktsii," *Zapad i Vostok: Sbornik Vsesoiuznogo Obshchestva kul'turnykh sviazi s zagranitsei* (Moscow, n.p., 1926): 5–6.
33. "Stenogramma poseshcheniia VOKS"a Prezidium i Sektretariatom 2-go Vsesoiuznogo S"ezda nauchnykh rabotnikov, 12/II–27 g.," GARF f. 5283, op. 8, ed. khr. 31, ll. 2–49, here l. 2.
34. GARF f. 5283, op. 6, d. 57, l. 99 ob. (17 July 1927 internal VOKS discussion with Kameneva's successor, F. N. Petrov); Heeke, 25 n. 4. Arrested in the Purges after the execution of Kamenev, she was shot on Stalin's orders in September 1941.
35. Sean McKeekin, *The Red Millionaire: A Political Biography of Willi Münzenberg, Moscow's Secret Propaganda Tsar in the West* (New Haven: Yale University Press, 2003), chap. 2, esp. 47. While presenting new research, McKeekin's book, as its title suggests, is an overheated exposé of Münzenberg's financial mismanagement and lifestyle, not an analysis of his outlook or the content of his propaganda activities.
36. IAH "Antrag," 1 March 1922, AVP RF f. 0528, op. 1, d. 126, p. 23, ll. 40–42; "Biulleten' Mezhdunarodnoi Rabochei Pomoshchi, no. 9 (1 avgusta 1924). Russkoe Izdanie," GARF f. 5451, op. 13a, d. 13b, ll. 17–24.
37. McKeekin, 114–118.
38. Elizabeth Papazian, *Manufacturing Truth: The Documentary Moment in Soviet Culture* (DeKalb: Northern Illinois University Press, 2008); Oksana Bulgakova, "Proletarskii internatsionalizm na Maslovke, ili eksport 'russkikh' v Berlin," *Kinovedcheskie zapiski*, no. 35 (1997): 37–54.
39. "Narkomindel. Otdel Zapada. S. I. Brodovskii," 3 November 1922, AVP RF f. 082, op. 5, d. 50, p. 10, l. 2. See also Golubev, "… *Vzgliad na zemliu obetovannuiu*," 93–94.
40. O. D. Kameneva, "Tezisy k organizatsii Vsesoiuznogo komiteta Mezhdunarodnoi Rabochei Pomoshchi," 3 November 1924, GARF f. 5451, op. 13a, d. 13b, l. 14–15.
41. McKeekin, chap. 7; "Bericht" [IAH], AVP RF f. 0528, op. 1, d. 126, p. 23, ll. 41–42.
42. Münzenberg report on IAH activities, addressed from the Central Committee of IAH to the VTsSPS Mezhrapom Commission, 15 June 1928, GARF f. 5451, op. 13a, d. 214, l. 45–104. According to this document, IAH had its strongest outposts in Germany, Czechoslovakia, France, Holland, and Belgium (and almost no foothold in Great Britain).
43. Helmut Gruber, "Willi Münzenberg's German Communist Propaganda Empire 1921–1933," *Journal of Modern History* 38, 3 (September 1966): 289.
44. "Postanovlenie kollegii NKID ot 8-go dekabria s. g. [1924]," GARF f. 5283, op. 1a, d. 31, l. 3; O. D. Kameneva, "Tov. D.B. Riazanovu. Institut Marksa i Engel'sa," 12 December 1924, GARF f. 5283, op. 1a, d. 31, l. 62.
45. "N. Semashko. RSFSR. Narodnyi komissar Zdravokhraneniia. Predsedateliu komissii zagranichnoi pomoshchi tov. O.D. Kamenevoi," 16 December 1924, GARF f. 5283, op. 1a, d. 31, l. 52.
46. "Ustav Vsesoiuznogo Obshchestva kul'turnoi sviazi s zagranitsei. Moskva. Kreml'," 8 August 1925, GARF f. 5283, op. 1, ed. khr. 1, ll. 1–4; "Spisok uchrezhditelei Vsesoiuznogo Ob-va kul'turnoi Sviazi s za-granitsei," no exact date, 1925, ibid., ed. khr. 4, l. 13. Kameneva personally wrote Ol'denburg on the day of the VOKS charter's ratification to express hope that he would join the governance (*pravleniia*) of VOKS (ibid., ed. khr. 7, l. 30).
47. Kameneva to V. V. Kuibyshev, 18 December 1924, GARF f. 5283, op. 1a, d. 31, l. 75.
48. "Polozhenie ob apparate Vsesoiuznogo Obshchestva kul'turnykh sviazi s zagranitsei," no earlier than 11 August 1925, GARF f. 5283, op. 1, ed. khr. 1, ll. 14–36; "Vypiska iz protokola Orgbiuro, 14/VI–27," GARF f. 5283, op. 1a, d. 97, l. 112; GARF f. 5283, op. 1, d. 76, l. 31; "Spisok Praveleniia VOKS"a (Utverzhden Sektretariatom TsK VKP(b)," 20 September 1927, GARF f. 5283, op. 1a, d. 97, l. 112.
49. These VOKS *referentura* sections were Central Europe, Romance, Anglo-American, and Balkan. An Iberian-American section covering Spain, Portugal, Italy, and Latin America was added, along with the still-not-functioning Eastern section, in late 1926. "Protokol zasedaniia Biuro Referentury ot 26 dekabria 1926 g.," GARF f. 5283, op. 1, ed. khr. 73, l. 1. On the size of VOKS in 1929, see ibid., d. 100, l. 34.

50. This is one of the main topics pursued by Kiseleva, *Iz istorii*; on the purge of social organizations, see Il'ina, 82–95.

51. "F.A. Rotshtein, chlen Kollegii NKID. Po voprosu ob informatsionnom biuro pri Komissii zagranichnoi Pomoshchi," 17 December 1923, GARF f. 5283, op. 1a, ed. khr. 37, l. 54.

52. "O.D. Kamenevu. Tov. Moskvinu. TsK VKP(b). Sov. sekretno," 5 January 1928, GARF f. 5283, op. 1a, d. 118, l. 1ob; "Mezhvedomstvennoe Soveshchanie Organizatsii, vedushchikh zagranitsu rabotu. Soveshchanie," 30 March 1929, GARF f. 5283, op. 1a, ed. khr. 20, l. 10 ob.

53. Kameneva to Kuibyshev, 18 December 1924, GARF f. 5283, op. 1a, d. 31, l. 75; A. Vinokurov (VtsIK) to O. D. Kameneva, 11 December 1924, GARF f. 5283, op. 1a, d. 31, ll. 46–47.

54. "Protokol No. 2 Zasedaniia Praveleniia Vessoiuznogo Obshchestva kul'turnykh Sviazi zagranitsei ot 26 sentiabria [1925]," GARF f. 5283, op. 1, ed. khr. 5, l. 58.

55. GARF f. 5283, op. 1a, ed. khr. 118, l. 50–51.

56. Ludmila Stern, *Western Intellectuals and the Soviet Union, 1920–1940: From Red Square to the Left Bank* (London: Routledge, 2007), 42, 45–46, 48; on the Comintern, see chap. 2.

57. "O postanovke informatsii zagranitsy o SSSR. Prilozhenie k protokolu No. 2 Soveshchaniia pri Inform-otdele TsK RKP(b) po informatsii zagranitsy o SSSR," February or March 1925, GARF f. 5283, op. 1a, ed. khr. 55, ll. 3–5. For 1924 attempts at multi-agency coordination, see "Protokol No. 1 Soveshchnaiia Agitpropa IKKI," 12 October 1924, GARF f. 5283, op. 1a, ed. kihr. 27, l. 22.

58. See, for example, "Plan informatsii kommunisticheskikh partii i trudiashchikhsia mass kap. stran ob SSSR," fall 1924, RGASPI f. 495, op. 30, d. 51, l. 13–21. See also "Protokoll der 1. Sitzung des Kollegiums der Propagandaabteilung [EKKI]," 25 January 1923, ibid., d. 37, ll. 7–8; ibid., l. 21; ibid., d. 51, ll. 1–6, 13–21.

59. "Thesen der Abt. Agitprop des EKKI zur Arbeit des Büros für kulturelle Verbindung mit dem Ausland," 15 June 1926, RGASPI f. 495, op. 30, d. 290, l. 19, also l. 24; O. D. Kameneva, "An Gen. Frumkin. Zum Protokol vom 15/VI 1926," ibid., d. 139, l. 57; Kameneva to A. A. Shtange (VOKS representative in Germany), 24 September 1925, GARF f. 5283, op. 1a, d. 47, ll. 144–145.

60. GARF f. 5283, op. 1a, d. 97, l. 47; "Krestinskii. Tov. Piatnitskomu. Kopiia: O.D. Kamenevoi, 1 Marta 1927," ibid., l. 48.

61. Kameneva, "V sekretariat TsK VKP(b)," no earlier than 2 August 1928, RGASPI f. 495, op. 95, ed. khr. 26, l. 208–10; Christoph Mick, *Sowjetische Propaganda, Fünfjahrplan und deutsche Russlandpolitik 1928–1932* (Stuttgart: Franz Steiner Verlag, 1995): 193–197.

62. A. V. Golubev and V. A. Nevezhin, "VOKS v 1930–1940-e gody," *Minuvshee*, 14 (Moscow and St. Petersburg: Atheneum-Feniks, 1993), 313–364, here 316.

63. For example, "Zasedanie chlenov pravleniia [VOKS]," 26 September 1925, GARF f. 5283, op. 1, ed. khr. 5, ll. 1–22, here l. 2.

64. Report on VOKS sent to Central Committee, 19 March 1927, GARF f. 5283, op. 1a, d. 97, ll. 1–25, here l. 1.

65. "Kameneva, "V Sekretariat TsK VKP(b)," 25 July 1928, GARF f. 5283, op. 1a, ed. khr. 118, ll. 84–85; Golubev, "… *Vzgliad na zemliu obetovannuiu*," 102–106.

66. "O.D. Kameneva. Tov. Smirnovu, otd. pechati TsK VKP(b)," 21 January 1928, GARF f. 5283, op. 1a, ed. khr. 118, l. 13.

67. "O.D. Kamenev. Tov. Smirnovu, otd. pechati TsK VKP(b)," 21 January 1928, l. 20.

68. "Otkrytie kursov gidov pri VOKS"e," 2 January 1927, GARF f. 5283, op. 1, d. 76, ll. 308–324, here l. 308.

69. A view created in no small part by Paul Hollander, *Political Pilgrims: Western Intellectuals in Search of the Good Society*, 4th ed. (New Brunswick: Transaction Publishers, 1998). For a very different view, see Engerman, *Modernization from the Other Shore*; Heeke, *Reisen zu den Sowjets*; and Sheila Fitzpatrick and Carolyn Rasmussen, eds., *Political Tourists: Australian Visitors to the Soviet Union in the 1920s- 1940s* (Melbourne: Melbourne University Press, 2008). State Department diplomats in Riga, Helsinki, and elsewhere collected masses of highly negative impressions from departing U.S. travelers: see Asgar

Asgarov, "Reporting from the Frontlines of the First Cold War: American Diplomatic Despatches about Internal Conditions in the Soviet Union, 1917–1933" (Ph.D. diss., University of Maryland, 2007).

70. The number of foreign visitors VOKS handled expanded rapidly after its founding. In 1925, only 483 foreigners were received, but this jumped to 1,200 in 1926; by 1929 and 1930, this number had increased to approximately 1,500 per year. Numerically, the most visitors came from the United States and Germany, respectively; in a six-month period in 1929, for example, 51 percent of VOKS's visitors came from the United States and 21 percent from Germany. O. D. Kameneva, "Tov. Raivid. Upoln. VOKS v Germanii. Berlin. 8 ianvaria 1927," GARF f. 5283, op. 1, d. 76, l. 3; "Otchet o rabote VOKS. 1 iiulia 1929 - 1 marta 1930 g.," GARF f. 7668, op. 1, d. 215, l. 35. However, large numbers of Americans were uninvited "political tourists"; Germany before 1933 was the most important country in terms of invited and professional travel.

71. "Otchet o prieme inostrantsev O.B.I.," no date, prob. August 1924, GARF f. 5283, op. 8, ed. khr. 3.

72. Kameneva, 1923 circular letter to foreign embassies, no exact date, GARF f. 5283, op. 1a, ed. khr. 37, l. 76; "Kantorovich. Uprav. Delami NKID. Pred. Komissii Zagran. Pomoshchi pri TsIK SSSR tov. O.D. Kamenevoi," 21 August 1924, ibid., l. 49; M. M. Litvinov to O. D. Kameneva, 5 November 1923, ibid., l. 142.

73. "A. Shtraus, Zav. Otd. Priema Inostrantsev," untitled report, GARF f. 5283, op. 8, ed. khr. 73, l. 8; "Dnevnik No. 118. Otdel po priem inostrantsev VOKS. 22.X.27," GARF f. 5283, op. 8, ed. khr. 51, l. 17.

74. E. R. Liberman, "Otchet o rabote s Chekhoslovatskim professorom Needly," GARF f. 5283, op. 1a, d. 298, l. 110; "Otdel po priemu inostrantsev. Otchet No. 98. 29/IX-27 g. Gid-perev. t. Shilenskii," ibid., op. 8, ed. khr. 62, l. 4–5; ibid., op. 1, ed. khr. 334, l. 20, 21.

75. For examples of numerous *ankety* of employees, see GARF f. 5283, op. 1, d. 11, and ibid., op. 8, ed. khr. 41, l. 23; d. 43, l. 5.

76. B. A. Starkov, "Zapad glazami sotrudnikov OGPU," *Rossiia i Zapad: Sbornik statei* (St. Petersburg: Izdatel'stvo S.-Peterburgskogo Universiteta, 1996), 185–208, here 188.

77. On this point see Sheila Fitzpatrick, "Foreigners Observed: Moscow Visitors in the 1930s under the Gaze of their Soviet Guides," *Russian History* 35: 1–2 (2008): 215–234.

78. "Otchet N 54 Gid-Perevoch. t. Trakhterov A. po obsl. 5/IX g. Finch (s plemianitsei)/Amerika/senator sht. Vashington," GARF f. 5283, op. 8, ed. khr. 42, l. 16; "Soobshchenie o rabote. Interpretor Trakhterev Aleksandr L'vovich," no earlier than 8 February 1928, ibid., ed. khr. 62, l. 88. The phrase "personal efficiency" was written in English in the document.

79. "Gid-Perevodchik Gal'perin. Obsluzhival 6–7/X-27. Biberman—Amerika. Otchet," GARF f. 5283, op. 8, ed. khr. 41, l. 17; "Anketa" (Gal'perin), l. 23.

80. "Otchet Gid-perevodchik Trakhterov, A. L. po obslu. 7.IX. Miss Ellen Rid [Reed], Amerika (Zhurnalistka)," GARF f. 5283, op. 8, ed. khr. 42, l. 19.

81. "Otdel po priemu inostrantsev. Otchet No. 84—17/IX-27. Gid-perevodchik Geiman," GARF f. 5283, op. 8, d. 41, l. 13; see also second report, l. 10.

82. Report by A. Shtraus, Zav. Otdelom Priema Inostrantsev, 1929, no exact date, GARF f. 5283, op. 8, ed. khr. 73, l. 8.

83. "Doklad o rabote. M. Pshenitsyna" [on Barbusse], 26 June 1928, GARF f. 5283, op. 8, ed. khr. 62, ll. 155–56 (Lunacharskii and Gorky were present at the Gosizdat talks); "Amerikanskii pisatel' Sinkler Liuis [Sinclair Lewis]. Obsluzhival gid-perevodchik V. Chumak," no earlier than 7 December 1927, GARF f. 5283, op. 8, ed. khr. 62, ll. 69–70; see also other reports, l. 62, l. 65.

84. Leonid Maksimenkov, "Ocherki nomenlaturnoi istorii sovetskoi literatury: Zapadnye pilgrimy u stalinskogo perestola (Feikhtvanger i drugie)," *Voprosy literatury*, no. 2 (2004): 242–291, here 279–280.

85. David Shearer, "Elements Near and Alien: Passportization, Policing, and Identity in the Stalinist State, 1932–1952," *Journal of Modern History* 76 (December 2004): 835–881, quotation 850.

86. On surveillance, see V. S. Izmozik, *Glaza i ushi rezhima: Gosudarstvennyi politicheskii kontrol' za nasleneiem Rossii v 1918–1928 godakh* (St. Petersburg: Izdatel'stvo

Sankt-Peterburgskogo Universiteta Ekonomiki i Finansov, 1995); Peter Holquist, "'Information is the Alpha and Omega of Our Work': Bolshevik Surveillance in its Pan-European Context," *Journal of Modern History* 69 (September 1997): 415–450. For the debate, see Stuart Finkel, "An Intensification of Vigilance: Recent Perspectives on the Institutional History of the Soviet Security Apparatus in the 1920s," *Kritika* 5, 2 (2004): 299–320.

87. Finkel, 314.
88. Finkel, n. 66.
89. Leonid Krasin to I. I. Miroshnikovu (Sovnarkom), 4 November 1925, GARF f. 5283, op. 1a, d. 45, l. 85.
90. Chicherin to Vladimir Lorents, copies to Collegium NKID, 26 September 1927, AVP RF f. 04, op. 13, d. 50314, papka 95, l. 13.
91. "Programma kursov po podgotovke gidov-perevodchikov," GARF f. 5283, op. 1, d. 76, l. 304.
92. "Otkrytie kursov gidov pri VOKS"e," 2 January 1927, GARF f. 5283, op. 1, d. 76, ll. 308–24, here ll. 309, 316.
93. GARF f. 5283, op. 8, ed. khr. 31, l. 9.
94. "Otkrytie kursov gidov." 310, 312.
95. See the 1924 letters selected and translated into German and English by Agitprop IKKI, RGASPI f. 495, op. 30, d. 85, l. 112–113, 164–166, 199–200.
96. *Informatsionnyi biulleten'* [VOKS], 1925–26, with coverage of the Academy of Sciences in 22 August, 10 September, and 17 September issues. The bulletin materials are in GARF f. 5283, op. 1, d. 5a.
97. Herta Wolf, *Glauben machen: Über deutschsprachige Reiseberichte aus der Sowjetunion* (1918–1932) (Vienna: Sonderzafel, 1992), 254; Sheila Fitzpatrick, "Australian Visitors to the Soviet Union in the 1930s: The View from the Soviet Side," in *Australian Visitors to the Soviet Union,* chap. 1.
98. O. D. Kameneva, "Ot redaktsii," and Sergei Ol'denburg, "Vostok i Zapad," in *Zapad i Vostok: Sbornik,* no. 1–2 (Moscow, 1926): 5–7, 14–18, quotations 5–6, 17; on Ol'denburg before and after 1917, see Vera Tolz, "European, National and (Anti-)Imperial: The Formation of Academic Oriental Studies in Late Tsarist and Early Soviet Russia," in *Orientalism and Empire in Russia,* ed. Michael David-Fox, Peter Holquist, and Alexander Martin (Bloomington, Ind.: Slavica Publishers, 2006): 107–134.
99. Kameneva, "Ot redaktsii," 7; "Programma kursov po podgotovke gidov-perevodchikov," l. 308.
100. Kameneva to Chicherin, 12 August 1925, GARF f. 5283, op. 1a, ed. khr. 53, l. 24; "Prof. A. Grebenshchikov. V Prezidium VOKS," 6 August 1925, ibid., l. 20–23.
101. William Richardson, *"To the World of the Future": Mexican Visitors to the USSR, 1920–1940,* Carl Beck Papers, no. 1002 (1993).
102. Vostochnyi otdel VOKS, country reports on China, Japan, and Turkey, no exact dates, 1935, GARF f. 5283, op. 1, d. 278.
103. A. I. Kokurin and N. V. Petrov, *Lubianka: Organy VChK-OGPU-NKVD-NKGB-MGB-MVD-KGB, 1917–1991. Spravochnik* (Moscow: ROSSPEN, 2003): 24, 189, 276, 292.
104. Kokurin and Petrov, *Lubianka,* 24, 439–40; Andrei Artuzov and Oleg Naumov, eds., *Vlast' i khudozhestvennaia intelligentsiia. Dokumenty TsK RKP(b)-VKP(b), VChK-OGPU-NKVD o kul'turnoi politike, 1917–1953* (Moscow: Demokratiia, 1999): 6; G. B. Kulikova, "Pod kontrolem gosudarstva: Prebyvaniie v SSSR inostrannykh pisatelei v 1920–1930-x godakh," *Otechestvennaia istoriia,* no. 4 (2003): 43–59, here 56; Leonid Maksimenkov, "Ocherki nomenklaturnoi istorii sovetskoi literatury: Zapadnye pilgrimy u stalinskogo prestola (Feikhtvanger i drugie)," *Voprosy literatury,* no. 3 (2004): 272–342, here 288, 292.
105. A. Karadi, head of VOKS Secretariat, to Stepanov (OGPU), 22 April 1932, GARF f. 5283, op. 1a, d. 199, l. 9.
106. Golubev, *"...Vzgliad na zemliu obetovannuiu,"* 159.
107. O. D. Kameneva, "Tov. Moskvinu. TsK VKP(b)," 5 January 1928, GARF f. 5283, op. 1a, d. 118, l. 1ob.

108. Theodore Dreiser, *Dreiser's Russian Diary*, ed. Thomas P. Riggio and James L. W. West III (Philadelphia: University of Pennsylvania Press, 1996), entry of 28 November 1927, 147; entry of 3 December 1927, 181.

109. Romain Rolland, *Voyage à Moscou (juin-juillet 1935)*, ed. Bernard Duchatelet (Paris: Albin Michel, 1992), 284.

110. Sidney and Beatrice Webb, *Soviet Communism: A New Civilization?* 2 vols. (London: Longmans, Green and Co., 1935), 2: 586–594.

111. Michael Gelb, "Editor's Introduction," in Zara Witkin, *An American Engineer in Stalin's Russia: The Memoirs of Zara Witkin, 1932–1934* (Berkeley: University of California Press, 1991), 13–14.

112. Nikolai Loboda, Zam. Pred. VOKS, to Trilesser, Nachal'nik INO OGPU, 18 July 1925, GARF f. 5283, op. 1a, d. 42, l. 4.

113. "L. Cherniavskii, BRIO Pred. VOKS. OO. GUGB NKVD tov. Tkachevu," 3 March 1936, GARF f. 5283, op. 1a, d. 307, ll. 51–52.

114. "Beseda O.D. Kamenevy s professorom Al'bertom Dzhonsonom," 6 June 1928, GARF f. 5283, op. 1a, ed. khr. 104, l. 52; A. Ia Arosev to G. G. Iagoda, 21 August 1936, GARF f. 5283, op. 1a, d. 307, l. 148.

115. GARF f. 5283, op. 1a, d. 307 ll. 122–129, 150. The information-gathering function of VOKS has been emphasized by Daniel Kowalsky, *Stalin and the Spanish Civil War*, Gutenberg-e publication, Columbia University Press, 2004, http://www.gutenberg-e. org/kod01/index.html, last accessed August 22, 2011, chap. 6.

Chapter 2

1. Hereafter referred to as the "Gesellschaft."

2. "Vstupitel'noe slovo tov. O.D. Kameneva na vechere sovetsko-germanskogo sblizheniia," 11 October 1926, GARF f. 5283, op. 8, ed. khr. 11, ll. 26-27; invitations, ll. 29-31; on East Prussia, "Levit. Otchet po Germanii za 2-oe polugodie 1929," GARF f. 5283, op. 6, d. 24, ll. 25–28.

3. "Ein Vortrag von Professor Hötzsch [sic] in Moskau," ll. 26–27; "Doklad prof. Getch [Hoetzsch]. Nekotorye soobrazheniia o germanskom vospriiatii istoricheskogo razvitiia Rossii," GARF f. 5283, op. 6, d. 24, ll. 25–28.

4. Gerd Voigt, *Otto Hoetzsch 1876–1946. Wissenschaft und Politik im Leben eines deutschen Historikers* (Berlin [East]: Akademie Verlag, 1978), 178–179; "Hoetzsch an Botschafter Graf Brockdorff-Rantzau. Berlin, 28 Juni 1923," reprinted in ibid., 318–319. See Christiane Scheidemann, *Ulrich Graf Brockdorff-Rantzau (1869–1928): Eine politische Biographie* (Frankfurt am Main: P. Lang, 1998).

5. Kameneva, "Chlenu kollegii NKID V. L. Koppu," 14 October 1923, GARF f. 5283, op. 1a, ed. khr. 37, ll. 2–3; Kameneva, untitled 1924 letter on friends, l. 19. See also Eduard Fuchs to Hugo Marcus, 23.5.25, GARF f. 5283, op. 1a, ed. khr. 53, l. 11; Rolf Elias, *Die Gesellschaft der Freunde des neuen Russland: Mit vollständigen Inhaltsverzeichnis aller Jahrgänge der Zeitschrift "Das neue Russland" 1923 bis 1932* (Cologne: Pahl-Rugenstein Verlag, 1985), 32.

6. See Susan Solomon's critical examination of the German-Soviet "special relationship" in historiography in her introduction to *Doing Medicine Together: Germany and Russia between the Wars*, ed. Solomon (Toronto: University of Toronto Press, 2006). The general literature includes, inter alia, Alexander Nekrich, *Pariahs, Partners, Predators: German-Soviet Relations, 1922–1941* (New York: Columbia University Press, 1997).

7. Sabine Dullin, *Des hommes d'influences: Les ambassadeurs de Staline en Europe, 1930–1939* (Paris: Payot, 2001), 186; "I. Maiskii. Pol. pred. SSSR v Belikobritanii. Brio Pred. VOKS – t. Smirnovu. 9 ianvaria 1938 g.," GARF f. 5283, op. 2a, d. 2, l. 68–72, esp. l. 69.

8. "Proizvodstvennyi plan raboty VOKS v Tsentral'noi Evrope na 1929 god," GARF f. 5283, op. 6, d. 129, l. 135.

9. Carole Fink, "The NEP in Foreign Policy: The Genoa Conference and the Treaty of Rapallo," in *Soviet Foreign Policy 1917–1991: A Retrospective*, ed. Gabriel Gorodetsky (London: Frank Cass, 1994): 13, 18; Jon Jacobson, *When the Soviet Union Entered*

World Politics (Berkeley: University of California Press, 1994) 15–18, 98; Viktor Knoll, "Das Volkskommissariat für Auswärtige Angelegenheiten im Prozess aussenpolitischer Entscheidung in den zwanziger und dreisiger Jahren," in *Zwischen Tradition und Revolution: Dominanten und Strukturen sowjetischer Aussenpolitik 1917–1941*, ed. Knoll and Ludmilla Thomas (Stuttgart: Frank Steiner Verlag, 2000), 9–30.

10. Gabriel Gorodetsky, "The Formation of Soviet Foreign Policy: Ideology and *Realpolitik*," in *Soviet Foreign Policy*, 30–44.

11. The place of Poland in Hoetzsch's thought on Russia has been most forcefully explicated by Friedrich Kuebart, "Otto Hoetzsch — Historiker, Publizist, Politiker. Eine kritische biographische Studie," *Osteuropa*, no. 8–9 (Aug.-Sept. 1975): 603–621. See also Michael Burleigh, *Germany turns Eastward: A Study of Ostforschung in the Third Reich* (Cambridge: Cambridge University Press, 1988), 15–21; Uwe Liszkowski, *Osteuropaforschung und Politik: Ein Beitrag zum historisch-politischen Denken und Wirken von Otto Hoetzsch*, vol. 1 (Berlin: Arno Spitz Verlag, 1988), 229–230.

12. Karl Schlögel, "Von der Vergeblichkeit eines Professorenlebens: Otto Hoetzsch und die deutsche Russlandkunde," *Osteuropa* 55, 12 (December 2005): 5–28, quotations 7.

13. Liszkowski, 1: 230, 204–239.

14. Liszkowski, 2: 494–495.

15. Schlögel, "Von der Vergeblichkeit eines Professorenlebens," 14, 24–28.

16. Burleigh, 14, 25–32; Liszkowski, 2: 485, 488–489.

17. Liszkowski, 2: 490–94, 492 n. 37; Voigt, 320; Christoph Mick, *Sowjetische Propaganda, Fünfjahrplan und deutsche Russlandpolitik 1928–1932* (Stuttgart: Franz Steiner Verlag, 1995): 263–265.

18. Edgar Lersch, *Die auswärtige Kulturpolitik der Sowjetunion in Ihren Auswirkungen auf Deutschland 1921–1929* (Frankfurt am Main: Peter Lang, 1979) 84–91; Voigt, 194–195; A. Shtange to Kameneva, 24 August 1925, GARF f. 5283, op. 1a, d. 47, l. 113.

19. Fritz T. Epstein, "Otto Hoetzsch und sein 'Osteuropa' 1925–1930," *Osteuropa* 25, 8–9 (Aug.-Sept.1975): 541–554, quotation 550; Jutta Unser, "'Osteuropa.' Biographie einer Zeitschrift," *Osteuropa* 25, 8–9 (Aug.-Sept. 1975): 555–602; Mick, *Sowjetische Propaganda*, 20, 51.

20. Kameneva to Sergei Ol'denburg, 30 December 1926, and other correspondence in GARF f. 5283, op. 6, d. 33, l. 1, 2, 8, 9, 16–20.

21. "Shtange. Pol. Pred. SSSR v Germanii. Pred. VOKS tov. O.D. Kamenevoi. 31 iiulia 1925," GARF f. 5283, op. 1a, d. 47, l. 96.

22. Mick, *Sowjetische Propaganda*, 192.

23. A. Shtange to O. D. Kameneva, 24 August 1925. Copies to Fedor Rotshtein (NKID and VOKS pravlenie) and Lorents, Otdel Tsentral'noi Evropy NKID, GARF f. 5283, op. 1a, d. 47, l. 113–115. Lersch, however, points out that *Das neue Russland* contained much material on Soviet culture that seemed new and interesting to the German public. Lersch, *Die auswärtige Kulturpolitik der Sowjetunion*, 83.

24. Shtange. Vo VOKS, tov. O.D. Kameneva," September 1925, copy to Commissariat of Foreign Affair's Central European Section, GARF f. 5283, op 1a, d. 47, l. 127–128.

25. Shtange to Kameneva, 8 Sept. 1925, GARF f. 5283, op. 1a, d. 47, l. 134–135; Kameneva to Shtange, 24 September 1925, ibid., l. 144–46; "Dokladnaia zapiska," no later than 3 Sept. 1925, ibid., l. 48; Kameneva to N. N. Krenstinskii, 2 October 1925, ibid., l. 156–157; Shtange, "Vo VOKS," ibid., l. 126–131. For background on Soviet-German scientific relations after 1925, see Kolchinskii, ed., *Sovetsko-germanskie nauchnye sviazi*, 144–171.

26. GARF f. 5283, op. 6, d. 57, l. 92 ob; *Dukh Rapallo*, 168–70, 113–115; Mick, *Sowjetische Propaganda*, 260–62; *Mezhdunarodnye nauchnye sviazi Akademii nauk SSSR, 1917–1941* (Moscow: Nauka, 1972): 239–246; Kolchinskii, ed., *Sovetsko-germanskie nauchnye sviazi*, 232.

27. O. D. Kameneva to N. P. Gorbunov, 31 October 1925," GARF f. 5283, op. 1a, ed. khr. 45, l. 57–60.

28. Burleigh, 34.

29. See the 1929 NKID correspondence in AVP RF f. 082, op. 12, d. 80, 51, l. 13–14, 21, 24.

30. "Otchet po Germanii za 2-oe polugodie 1929," GARF f. 5283, op. 6, d. 57, l. 88–89; "Levit-Livent, Referent po tsentral'noi Evropy [VOKS]. "Germaniia," 1929, ibid., l. 92 ob; "Doklad referenta [VOKS] po tsentral'noi Evrope – t. Livent-Levit [sic]. 17-go iiulia 1929 g.," ibid., l. 97. The name was written in both ways in the documents.

31. Levit-Livent, "Germaniia," cited in full in previous note, l. 93.

32. "Otchet o rabote VOKS 1 iiulia 1929 - 1 marta 1930 g.," GARF f. 7668, op. 1, d. 215, l. 1–71.

33. Liszkowski, 2: 497, 506–507; Mick, *Sowjetische Propaganda*, 295–97; Voigt, 328–330, 334–335.

34. Unser, "Osteuropa," 590–591; Burleigh, 35–38.

35. Lersch, *Die auswärtige Kulturpolitik der Sowjetunion*.

36. Ann Taylor Allen, "German Radical Feminism and Eugenics, 1900–1908," *German Studies Review* 11, 1 (February 1988): 31–56; Christl Wickert, *Helene Stöcker 1869–1943: Frauenrechtlerin, Sexualreformerin und Pazifistin. Eine Biographie* (Bonn: Dietz, 1991); Amy Hackett, "Helene Stöcker: Left-wing Intellectual and Sex Reformer," in *When Biology Became Destiny: Women in Weimar and Nazi Germany*, ed. Renate Bridenthal, Atina Grossmann, and Marion Kaplan (New York: Monthly Review Press, 1984): 153–174; and Regina Baker, "Helene Stöcker's Pacifism in the Weimar Republic: Between Ideal and Reality," *Journal of Women's History* 13, 3 (2001): 70–97.

37. "O. D. Kameneva. Predsedateliu Leningradskogo OGPU, tov. Messing. 4 iiunia 1925," GARF f. 5283, op. 1a, ed. khr. 37, l. 12.

38. R. S. Veller to O.D. Kameneva, 12 December 1924, GARF f. 5284, op. 6, d. 1, l. 196–202; "Polozhenie v Germanii," prob. 1925, GARF f. 5283, op. 1a, d. 47, l. 5; "Otchet o rabote VOKS 1 iiulia 1929 - 1 marta 1930," GARF f. 7668, op. 1, d. 215, l. 155; "Doklad referenta po Tsentral'noi Evrope—t. Livent-Levit [sic]," 17 July 1929, GARF f. 5283, op. 6, d. 57, l. 98.

39. "Kameneva. Chlenu kollegii NKID V. L. Koppu. 14 oktiabria 1923," GARF f. 5283, op. 1a, ed. khr. 37, l. 5; "V otdel Dal'nego Vostoka NKID tov. Baranovskomu," ibid., l. 16; Kameneva, untitled letter on Society of Friends, May 1924, ibid., l. 19.

40. GARF f. 5283, op. 1a, d. 24, l. 22–24; Erich Baron to Kameneva, no date, 1928, ibid., ed. khr. 118, l. 168–169. The Society organized medical, technological, legal, and pedagogical sections, the largest of which was the pedagogical. "Polozhenie v Germanii," l. 5.

41. Baron to Kameneva, ibid., l. 169 ob.

42. Quoted in Herta Wolf, *Glauben machen: Über deutschsprachige Reiseberichte aus der Sowjetunion (1918–1932)* (Vienna: Sonderzafel, 1992), 202, 209.

43. The 1924 Kameneva-Baron correspondence is in GARF f. 5284, op. 6, d. 1.

44. "Polnomochnoe Predstavitel'stvo SSSR v Germanii. Dmitriev. Tov. O.D. Kamenevoi. Berlin, 14 Iiulia 1924," GARF f. 5283, op. 1a, ed. khr. 17, l. 33; Iu. Gol'dshtein to O. D. Kameneva, 27 June 1924, ibid., d. 21, l. 36.

45. Kameneva to A. A. Shtange, 24 September 1925, GARF f. 5283, op. 1a, d. 47, l. 146; Kameneva to N. N. Krestinskii, 2 October 1925, ibid., 156–157.

46. "Zam. pred. VOKS"a. E. O. Lerner. Upolnomochennomu VOKS v Germanii t. Girshfel'du," 2 January 1933, AVP RF f. 082, op. 15, d. 28, p. 71, l. 11. On other occasions, Baron did display familiarity with several regional affiliates that in fact were active.

47. R. S. Veller to Kameneva, Berlin, 12 December 1924, GARF f. 5283, op. 6, d. 1, l. 197.

48. "Levit. Otchet po Germanii za 2-oe polugodie 1929," GARF f. 5283, op. 6, d. 57, l. 86–87; "Doklad referenta po tsentral'noi Evrope—t. Livent-Levit," 17 July 1929, ibid., l. 96–193; Mick, *Sowjetische Propaganda*, 218.

49. "Ob"edinennoe Biuro Informatsii Komissii zagranichnoi pomoshchi," GARF f. 5283, op. 8, ed. khr. 3, l. 108.

50. Kameneva to A. A. Shtange, 24 September 1925, GARF f. 5283, op. 1a, d. 47, l. 46; Kameneva, "An Gen. Frumkin. Zum Protokol [Agitprop EKKI] vom 15/VI 1926," RGASPI f. 495, op. 30, d. 139, l. 157; on the KPD, Protokoll über die Sitzung von 10. Februar 1932, betr. Gesellschaft der Freunde des Neuen Russlands," AVP RF f. 082, op. 15, papka 71, ll. 70–75, quotation 74.

51. Veller to Kameneva, 12 December 1924, cited above, l. 197.

52. Shtange to Kameneva, 8 September 1925, GARF f. 5283, op. 1a, d. 47, l. 134–135; Kameneva to Shtange, 24 September 1925, ibid., l. 144–46; "Dokladnaia zapiska," no later than 3 September 1925, ibid., l. 48.

53. Kameneva to Smirnov (Otdel pechati TsK), 21 January 1928, and "V TsK VKP(b)," no date, 1928, in GARF f. 5283, op. 1a, d. 118, l. 9–20, 115, respectively.

54. A. V. Lunacharskii, "Druz'ia Rossii," no exact date, RGASPI f. 142, op. 1, d. 148, l. 3–4. The figures Lunacharskii mentioned were the Futurist artist Ardengo Soffici, the Futurist leader and avant-garde literary figure Giovanni Papini (who in 1921 turned to Roman Catholicism and in the 1930s to Fascism), and the journalist and writer Giuseppe Prezzolini.

55. "O.D. Kameneva, Pred. Komissii. Upolnomochennomu Komissii Zagranichnoi Pomoshchi v Avstrii. Tov. Bogomolovu," no earlier than 7 January 1924, GARF f. 5283, op. 1a, d. 24, l. 5.

56. "Zarubezhnaia set' VOKS v ee dinamike," no later than 1 April 1931, GARF f. 5283, op. 1, d. 157, l. 2.

57. Donal O'Sullivan, *Furcht und Faszination: Deutsche und britische Russlandbilder* 1921–1933 (Cologne: Böhlau, 1996), 322.

58. D. Bogomolov (VOKS representative in Vienna) to KZP, 7 January 1924, GARF f. 5283, op. 1a, d. 24, l. 1; V. Kh. Aussem (VOKS representative in Vienna) to Ol'ga Kameneva, 12 June 1924, ibid., l. 19; Bogomolov to Roman Veller, otvetstvennyi sekretar' KZP, ibid., l. 20–21. The society was much smaller than in Germany, and in 1931 had 200 dues-paying members ("Plan raboty VOKS," no date, 1931, GARF f. 5283, op. 1, d. 158, l. 58).

59. Bogomolov to Kamaneva, 7 January 1924; Kameneva to Bogomolov, no date, GARF f. 5283, op. 1a, d. 24, l. 1, 5; Klyshko (Narkomvneshtorg) to KZP, 2 February 1924, ibid., l. 7.

60. "M. [Mikhail] Apletin. Upolnomochennomu VOKS v Avstrii tov. Nekunde," 17 March 1934, AVP RF f. 066, op. 17, p. 116, d. 270, l. 11; "Vypiska iz pis'ma t. Nikunde [sic]," 3 March 1934, GARF f. 5283, op. 1a, d. 196, ll. 36–37.

61. "Plan raboty VOKS," for 1931, GARF f. 5283, op. 1, d. 158, l. 55, 59, which logically counted interwar Czechoslovakia as part of Western Europe.

62. Erich Baron to Ol'ga Kameneva, 24 November 1924, GARF f. 5284, op. 6, d. 1, l. 184–189.

63. Bradley F. Abrams, *The Struggle for the Soul of the Nation: Czech Culture and the Rise of Communism* (Lanham, MD: Rowman & Littlefield, 2004): 41–44.

64. "Vypiska iz otcheta Konsul'skogo Otele Polpredstva SSSR v Chekhoslovakii. Za Aprel. mesiats 1927 g.," GARF f. 5283, op. 6, d. 563, l. 85.

65. "Arosev, Aleksandr Iakovlevich," RGASPI f. 124, op. 1, ed. khr. 80, l. 13–14.

66. Ibid., l. 4–14; Ol'ga Aleksandrovna Aroseva and Vera Maksimova, *Bez grima* (Moscow: Tsentrpoligraf, 1999), 28–30, 32–33, 86; Natal'ia Aroseva, *Sled na zemle*, 146–165; Nikolai Trachenko, "Sled na zemle," introduction to Arosev, *Belaia lestnitsa: Roman, povesti, rasskazy* (Moscow: Sovremennik, 1989), 4–9.

67. On his literary activities, see Michael David-Fox, "Stalinist Westernizer? Aleksandr Arosev's Literary and Political Depictions of Europe," *Slavic Review*, 62, no. 4 (Winter 2003): 733–759.

68. Aroseva and Maksimova, 15, 20; Natal'ia Aroseva, *Sled na zemle: Dokumental'naia povest' ob ottse* (Moscow: Izdatel'stvo politicheskoi literatury, 1987), 206, 227. On December 10, 1932, the Politburo approved his resignation as ambassador and put him at the disposal of the Central Committee, but to his anguish he received no posting until his appointment as head of VOKS in 1934. "Protokol No. 125 zasedaniia Politbiuro TsK VKP(b) ot 10 dekabria 1932 g.," RGASPI f. 17, op. 3, ed. khr. 910 (53/47).

69. Aroseva and Maksimova, 47. Diary entry from 7 November 1932; David-Fox, "Stalinist Westernizer."

70. Arosev to Stalin, 3 December 1929, RGASPI f. 558, op. 11, ed. khr. 695, l. 2–4.

71. Arosev to Stalin, no date, prob. 1929, RGASPI f. 558, op. 11, ed. khr. 695, ll. 5–15. In 1931, Arosev finally received a short reply to one of his letters from Stalin, prompting two more effusive, rambling responses in which he requested a "responsible post" in Paris. Arosev to Stalin, 23 May and 31 July 1931, ibid., ll. 56–57, ll. 59–60.

72. E. M. Iaroslavskii to G. K. Ordzhonikidze, 1 February 1929, in *Sovetskoe rukovodstvo. Perepiska. 1928–1941*, ed. A. V. Krashonkin, et al. (Moscow: ROSSPEN, 1999): 62–65, here 63.

73. "Dnevnik po Chekhoslovakii ianvar'-fevral' 1931 goda," GARF f. 5283, op. 6, d. 563, ll. 33–34; also, l. 38, l. 39; "Sviazi VOKS"a s otdel'nymi vazhneishimi deiateliami Chekhoslovakii," ibid., d. 658, l. 12; E. Cherniak, "Pred. VOKS – tov. A. Ia. Arosevu. Dokladnaia zapiska o rabote t. Lingardta [Linhardt] – Sekretaria Chekhoslovatskogo Obshchestva kul'tsviazi," GARF f. 5283, op. 1a, d. 319, l. 16.

74. On improved diplomatic relations, see G.E.O. Knight, "Anglo-Russian Relations: An Appeal" and correspondence, GARF f. 5283, op. 1a, ed. khr. 37, ll. 152–154; on initiative of Soviet *aktiv*, ibid., d. 158, l. 67. A physician, Polovtsevaia was also the Soviet representative of the Russian Red Cross and the Bureau of Foreign Information of the Commissariat of Health.

75. "Proof (confidential)," 1924 organizing brochure, GARF f. 5283, op. 1a, ed. khr. 16, ll. 1–2; A. V. Golubev, "Intelligentsiia Velikobritanii i 'novaia tsivilizatsiia' (Iz istorii sovetskoi kul'turnoi diplomatii 1930-x gg.), in *Rosiia i vneshnii mir: Dialog kul'tur*, ed. Iu. S. Borisov, et al. (Moscow: Institut istorii RAN, 1997): 261–262.

76. V. N. Polovtsevaia to O. D. Kameneva, 4 January 1924; Kameneva to M. N. Pokrovskii, no earlier than 4 January 1924, GARF f. 5283, op. 1a, d. 16, l. 3, ll. 19–21. In 1925, Soviet embassy personnel were delegated for membership in the London Society for Cultural Relations with the sanction of the party cell of the embassy. In 1936, two representatives of the "Soviet colony" were elected to the executive committee of the Society, with 450 votes cast (GARF f. 5283, op. 1a, ed. khr. 55, ll. 12–13; ibid., d. 296, l. 6).

77. Margaret Llewelyn Davies, introduction to *Life as We have Known It*, ed. Llewelyn Davies (London: Hogart Press, 1931), ix.

78. Polovtsevaia to Kameneva, 2 October 1925, GARF f. 5283, op. 1a, ed. khr. 43, l. 59; ibid., l. 68.

79. Margaret Llewelyn Davies to Polovtsevaia, 30 September 1925, GARF f. 5283, op. 1a, ed. khr. 43, ll. 61–63; Golubev, "Intelligentsiia Velikobritanii," 263.

80. Kameneva to A. Rozengol'ts, 5 December 1925, GARF f. 5283, op. 1a, ed. khr. 43, l. 87.

81. Michael Hughes, *Inside the Enigma: British Officials in Russia, 1900–1939* (London: Hambledon Press, 1997), 211–221; Jacobson, *When the Soviet Union Entered World Politics*, 216–22; O'Sullivan, *Furcht und Faszination*, 261. A main conclusion of O'Sullivan's comparative study is that British views of the Soviet Union shifted with the foreign policy situation (23–26).

82. Helen Crawford, "Memorandum on the Society for Promoting Cultural Relations Between Russia and Great Britain known as SCR," GARF f. 5283, op. 1a, d. 125, l. 71, 74.

83. Kameneva to comrade Gurevich ("Direktor Tsentrosoiuz v Anglii"), 13 April 1928, GARF f. 5283, op. 1a, ed. khr. 104, l. 119; also ibid., l. 142; "Plan raboty VOKS," 1931, GARF f. 5283, op. 1, d. 158, ll. 67–68; "Society of Cultural Relations. Special Meeting of Executive Committee," 2 July 1936, ibid., d. 296, ll. 52–53 (see also l. 45); ibid., op. 3, ed. khr. 325, l. 3. For a rather different account of Crawford's report, citing the Russian translation, see Ludmila Stern, *Western Intellectuals and the Soviet Union: From Red Square to the Left Bank* (London: Routledge, 2007), 101–102.

84. For the impact of the vociferously anti-communist Right in France on Franco-Soviet relations, see Michael Jabara Carley, "Episodes from the Early Cold War: Franco-Soviet Relations, 1917–1927," *Europe-Asia Studies* 52, 7 (2000): 1275–1305.

85. Stern, *Western Intellectuals*, 97–105, and Stern, "The All-Union Society for Cultural Relations with Foreign Countries and French Intellectuals, 1925–29," *Australian Journal of Politics and History* 45, 1 (1999): 99–109.

86. "Deviatin, Polnomochnoe Predstavitel'stvo SSSR vo Frantsii. Predsedateliu VOKS tov. O.D. Kamenevoi," 7 December 1925, GARF f. 5283, op. 1a, d. 45, l. 132; N. P. Gorbunov to Paul Langevin, ibid., ll. 45–51.

87. Stern, *Western Intellectuals*, 103–4; Stern, "Iz predistorii sozdaniia frantsuzskogo obshchestva kul'turnogo sblizheniia *Novaia Rossiia* (po ranee neopublikovannym materialam VOKSa)," *Australian Slavonic and East European Studies* 11, 1–2 (1997): 143–159, here 143, 145, 155.

88. Leonid Krasin to I. I. Miroshnikov, 4 November 1925, GARF f. 5283, op. 1a, d. 45, ll. 84–86, also ll. 4, 7–8, 9, 14–16, 38, 93–98, 120–122; Ia. Deviatin [VOKS representative

in France] to O. D. Kameneva, 7 December 1925, ibid., l. 132; O. D. Kameneva to Kh. G. Rakovskii, 18 April 1924, GARF f. 5283, op. 1a, ed. khr. 17, ll. 6–7; "Soobrazheniia po vorposu o vozmozhnostiakh deiatel'nosti Obshchestva Druzei Novoi Rossii vo Frantsii," 18 April 1924, ibid., ll. 12–13. Of course, influence and loyal ideological sympathy were not infrequently combined, as in the case of the well-known physicist and fellow-traveler Paul Langevin.

89. "B. Barkov. III-i otdel Zapada tov. Rubininu," 5 March 1931, AVP RF f. 010, op. 2, papka 13a, d. 249, l. 5

90. "V. Dovgalevskii. Parizh. Narkomindel tov. M. M. Litvinovu," AVP RF f. 010, op. 2, papka 13a, d. 249, l. 6; see also l. 8.

91. Norman E. Saul, *Friends or Foes? The United States and Russia, 1921–1941* (Lawrence: University Press of Kansas, 2006), 193.

92. R. S. Veller, untitled report, no earlier than 29 January 1925, GARF f. 5283, op. 3, ed. khr. 5, ll. 3–14; Saul, 151–152, 277.

93. Bertrand M. Patenaude, *The Big Show in Bololand: The American Relief Expedition to Soviet Russia in the Famine of 1921* (Stanford: Stanford University Press, 2002): 373–375.

94. "Plan raboty VOKS," 1931, GARF f. 5283, op. 1a, d. 158, l. 67; "Otchet o rabote VOKS 1 iiulia 1929–1 marta 1930 g.," GARF f. 7668, op. 1, d. 215, ll. 1–71, here l. 14.

95. Quotation from Saul, 157; J. D. Parks, *Culture, Conflict and Coexistence: American-Soviet Cultural Relations, 1917–1958* (Jefferson, NC: McFarland, 1983), 22–23; RGASPI f. 142, op. 1, d. 780, l. 14.

96. On Dewey's evolving attitudes toward the Soviet Union, see David C. Engerman, "John Dewey and the Soviet Union: Pragmatism Meets Revolution," *Modern Intellectual History* 3, 1 (2006): 33–63.

97. "D-r Kaunts o Sovetskom Soiuze," GARF f. 5283, op. 3, ed. khr. 125, ll. 46–49; ibid., d. 127, l. 37. Counts was one of those figures who combined admiration for Soviet models with cultural prejudice. As he was becoming the foremost American expert on Soviet education, he "worked hard to apply the lessons from the 'sociological laboratory' he observed in Russia," at the same time as he saw the collectivization-era peasantry as "natural and instinctual, not civilized and rational." David C. Engerman, *Modernization from the Other Shore: American Intellectuals and the Romance of Russian Development* (Cambridge, Mass.: Harvard University Press, 2003), 176, 178.

98. Boas' theoretical orientation differed from the paradigms of national character dominant among American experts on Russia before World War II, as described by Engerman, *Modernization*, 274 (on Boas).

99. Svirksii quoted in Saul, 157; I. Umanskii. Polpredstvo SSSR v SShA. Tov. Cherniavskomu. VOKS," 1 December 1936, GARF f. 5283, op. 1a, d. 296, ll. 32–34.

100. "Mezhvedomstvennoe soveshchanie organizatsii, vedushchikh zagranitsu rabotu. Soveshchanie – 30.III.29 g.," GARF f. 5283, op. 1a, ed. khr. 20, l. 9; "O.D. Kameneva. V Sekretariat TsK VKP(b)," no earlier than 25 July 1928, GARF f. 5283, op. 1a, ed. khr. 118, l. 84–85; "O.D. Kameneva. Tov. Moskvinu. TsK VKP(b)," 5 January 1928, ibid., l. 1–3.

101. "O.D. Kameneva. Tov. Smirnovu, otd. pechati TsK VKP(b)," 21 January 1928, GARF f. 5283, op. 1a, d. 118, ll. 9–20, quotation l. 20; Kameneva, "Sekretariat TsK VKP(b)," copy to Agitprop, 2 August 1928, ibid., ll. 117–126, here 119; "Plan raboty VOKS," 1931, ibid., op. 1, d. 158, l. 47; "Zarubezhnaia set' VOKS v ee dinamike," no later than 1 April 1931, ibid., d. 157, l. 2.

102. GARF f. 5283, op. 1a, ed. khr. 43, l. 68.

103. To give only one example, academician Vladimir Steklov, a mathematician and physicist whom Kameneva asked to speak in London in 1925, also held the position of vice president of the Society for Cultural Relations. Kameneva, telegram to V. A. Steklov, 2 November 1925, GARF f. 5283, op. 1a, d. 47, l. 186.

104. "O.D. Kameneva. Tov. Trilesser. Nach. INO OGPU," no date, May or June 1925, GARF f. 5283, op. 1a, ed. khr. 55, l. 39; Kameneva to S. Chlenovu (VOKS representative in Paris), 27 June 1925, GARF f. 5283, op. 1a, ed. khr. 45, l. 4. Kameneva also used Narkompros and other sources for lists of travelers in the 1920s (ibid., ed. khr. 55, l. 9; d. 95, l. 1–42).

105. Otto Hoetzsch, letter to Soviet embassy, April 1923; Soviet embassy (Raznoboi) to Maksim Litvinov, 17 April 1923, AVP RF f. 04, op. 13, d. 49988, p. 80, ll. 6, 8.

106. For example, Elizabeth W. Clark, Executive Secretary, American Russian Institute (New York), to Anatolii Lunacharskii, 6 January 1931, and additional correspondence from Daniil Novomirskii, VOKS head of Anglo-American sector, GARF f. 5283, op. 3, d. 139, ll. 37, 41–44; Armand Hammer to O. D. Kameneva, 25 August 1928, ibid., op. 1, ed. khr. 91, l. 7.

107. Such was the case with the German physician Heinz Zeiss (letter to VOKS, 26 April 1929, GARF f. 5283, op. 1, d. 115, l. 31). On Zeiss as German-Soviet scientific broker, traveler, and lobbyist, see Susan Solomon, ed., *Doing Medicine Together: Germany and Russia between the Wars* (Toronto: University of Toronto Press, 2006), chaps. 4–7.

108. "Plan raboty VOKS," 1931, GARF f. 5283, op. 1, d. 158, l. 49.

109. S. Vinogradov to Zam. Pred. VOKS Cherniavskii, 9 May 1936, ibid., op. 1a, d. 296, l. 45; Ivan Maiskii to Aleksandr Arosev, 24 July 1936, ibid., ll. 57–58; Arosev to Maiskii, 4 August 1936, ibid., l. 59. On the broader financial and political crisis in the British society to which this incident contributed, see "Society for Cultural Relations. Special Meeting of Executive Committee, 2 July 1936," ibid., ll. 52–53, and also l. 6, l. 47; "Split in Anglo-Soviet Society," *Daily Mail*, 1 July 1936.

110. "L. Cherniavskii. Biuro pred. VOKS. TsK VKP(b) tov. Angarov," 5 July 1936, GARF f. 5283, op. 1a, d. 308, l. 75.

111. O. D. Kameneva to M. N. Pokrovskii (head of State Scholarly Council, GUS), 13 May 1925, GARF f. 5283, op. 1a, ed. khr. 55, l. 9; Kameneva, "V Valiutnoe Upravlenie NKF SSSR," 10 May 1927, ibid., d. 93, l. 38; ibid., l. 105, l. 254.

112. GARF f. 5283, op. 1, d. 115, l, 97, 100, 123.

113. Robert Aron to VOKS, 28 June 1929 GARF f. 5283, op. 1, d. 115, l. 139.

114. GARF f. 5286, op. 1, d. 115, l. 70.

115. On Marr, see inter alia Vera Tolz, *Russian Academicians and Revolution: Combining Professionalism and Politics* (Houndmills, Basingstoke and New York: Macmillan, 1997); Yuri Slezkine, "N. Ia. Marr and the National Origins of Soviet Ethnogenetics," *Slavic Review* 55, 4 (1996): 826–862.

116. "Zasedanie Predstavitelei sekstii nauchnykh rabotnikov VOKS. 7 dekabria 1928," GARF f. R-5283, op. 1, d. 91, l. 100.

117. "Memorandum zur Frage der internationalen Massenaktion zur Schutz der Sowjet-Union," 10 July 1925, RGASPI f. 495, op. 30, d. 139, ll. 7–11; "Otchet po kampanii VOKS protiv interventsii za period s 20 noiabria po 20 ianvaria s.g.," GARF f. 5283, op. 1, ed. khr. 139, l. 110; I. N. Il'ina, *Obshchestvennye organizatsii Rossii v 1920-e gody* (Moscow: Institut istorii RAN, 2000), 140.

118. Unsigned denunciation sent to Kameneva "with communist greetings," prob. 1929, GARF f. 5283, op. 1a, d. 136, l. 19; see also "Zasedanie Predstavitelei sekstii nauchnykh rabotnikov VOKS. 7 dekabria 1928," ibid., d. 91, l. 99–100.

119. Prof. A. A. Sidorov (*Uchenyi sekretar'* GAKhN) to O. D. Kameneva, 16 April 1929, GARF f. 5283, op. 1, d. 115, l. 7.

120. Katerina Clark, "The Avant-Gardes of Russia and Germany (1917–1933): A Transnational Entity?" paper presented at the conference "Fascination and Enmity: Russian-German Encounters in the Twentieth Century and the Idea of a Non-Western Historical Path," Berlin, June 2007; Clark, "Tretiakov, Benjamin and Brecht in Pre-Nazi Berlin: A Case of Cross-Cultural Dialogue," paper presented at the "Workshop on New Approaches to Russian and Soviet History," University of Maryland, May 2003.

121. "Zapiska pred. VChK F. E. Dzerzhhinskogo v TsK RKP(b)," 19 April 1921, in *Vlast' i khudozhestvennaia intelligentsiia. Dokumenty TsK RKP(b)-VKP(b), VChK-OGPU-NKVD o kul'turnoi politike, 1917–1935*, ed. Andrei Artuzov and Oleg Naumov (Moscow: Demokratiia, 1999): 15, see also 17, 19, 22, 24, 25, 28–29. The materials of the Central Committee commission on foreign travel are contained in several *dela* in RGASPI f. 17, op. 85. On travel destinations, see d. 666, 1–20; on rejection rates and reasons, d. 665, ll. 8–22, d. 652, ll. 1–233; on political and bureaucratic strife around campaigns to reduce travelers in 1927 and secret-police involvement, d. 655, ll. 37–43.

122. N. V. Kiseleva, *Iz istorii bor'by sovetskoi obshchestvennosti za proryv kul'turnoi blokady SSSR (VOKS: seredina 20-x – nachalo 30-x godov)* (Rostov-na-Donu: Izdatel'stvo Rostovskogo Universiteta, 1991), 26–27. For Kameneva's endorsement of Boianus, see GARF f. 5283, op. 1, ed. khr. 104, l. 128; he was turned down on the level of Narkompros on 21 February 1930 (ibid., op. 8, ed. khr. 79, l. 204). On Griuner, see Kameneva letter, 10 December 1927, ibid., d. 81, l. 141. On Bunak, see ibid., op. 8, ed. khr. 79, ll. 171, 172.

123. "Protokol Zasedaniia Komissii Sovetskogo Otdela na mezhdunarodnoi Vystavke Kinometografii v Gollandii…23 marta 1928"; "Zam. Pred. Sovnarkom A.M. Lezhava. Uchraspred TsK VKP(b). Sekretno. Kopiia – tov. Ol'khovomu, Kino-Setskiia Agitpropa TsK VKP(b)," RGASPI f. 17, op. 85, d. 663, l. 133, ll. 134–136.

124. Kameneva, "V Sekretariat TsK," no exact date, summer 1927, GARF f. 5283, op. 1a, d. 97, l. 70; Radek to Stalin, 1 May 1932, RGASPI f. 558, op. 11, d. 789, l. 48, also ll. 54, 55, 58.

125. See Sheila Fitzpatrick, "Introduction," in *Stalinism: New Directions*, ed. Fitzpatrick (London and New York: Routledge, 2000), 11; Fitzpatrick, *Everyday Stalinism: Ordinary Life in Extraordinary Times. Soviet Russia in the 1930s* (Oxford: Oxford University Press, 1999), 109–114, quotation 114; Fitzpatrick, "Intelligentsia and Power: Client-Patron Relations in Stalin's Russia," in *Stalinismus vor dem zweiten Weltkrieg: Neue Wege der Forschung*, ed. Manfred Hildermeier (Munich: R. Oldenbourg Verlag, 1998), 35–53.

126. See, for example, Professor Iulii Shkal'skii to A. Ia. Arosev, 22 July 1936, GARF f. R-5283, op. 1a, d. 308, l. 80. On the underestimation of institutions and the remarkable "institutional stubbornness" of the Soviet state, see Stephen Kotkin, "Mongol Commonwealth? Exchange and Governance across the Post-Mongol Space," *Kritika* 8,3 (Summer 2007): 487–531, quotation 526. For a discussion of a "hybrid mode" of personalistic and modern, bureaucratic administration in the context of late Stalinism, see Yoram Gorlizki, "Ordinary Stalinism: The Council of Ministers and the Soviet Neopatrimonial State, 1946–1953," *Journal of Modern History* 74 (December 2002): 699–736.

127. Ian (Jan) Plamper, *Alkhimiia vlasti: Kul't Stalina v izobrazitel'nom iskusstve* (Moscow: NLO, 2010), 253.

Chapter 3

1. "Plan raboty s inostrannymi spetsialistami," Dzerzhinskii Club for foreign specialists and workers in Moscow, for which VOKS arranged excursions, prob. June 1931, GARF f. 5283, op. 8, d. 86, ll. 8–9.

2. A. G. Man'kov, *Dnevniki 30-x godov* (St. Petersburg: Evropeiskii dom, 2001): 93. On Herriot's tour as part of a Soviet countercampaign to deny reports of famine by émigré Ukrainian groups in Poland, see Iaroslav Papuha, *Zakhidna Ukraïna i holodomor 1932–1933 rokiv* (Lviv: Astroliabiia, 2008), 56.

3. See Vladimir Solonari, *Purifying the Nation: Population Exchange and Ethnic Cleansing in Nazi-Allied Romania* (Baltimore: Johns Hopkins University Press, 2009), Part II, chap. 2; and Solonari, "'Model Province': Explaining the Holocaust of Bessarabian and Bukovinian Jewry," *Nationalities Papers* 34, 4 (Sept. 2006): 471–494.

4. "Biuro po Delam Inostrannoi Kooperatsii (illeg.)" to Georgii Chicherin, 18 May 1926, AVP RF f. 69, op. 14, d. 60, p. 47, l. 1; "Professional'no dvizhenie. Rabochaia delegatsiia v Rossii," no date, 1925 or 1926, GARF f. 5451, op. 13a, d. 68, ll. 5–6; "O nedochetakh obsluzhivaniia delegatov," Agitprop IKKI report on 1927 Congress of Friends, RGASPI f. 495, op. 95, ed. khr. 21, ll. 148–162, here l. 152.

5. "Otchet o rabote s g. Bekker po Germanii perev. Liberman," no earlier than 29 May 1932, GARF f. 5283, op. 8, d. 112, l. 54; on the ubiquity and changing use of the term among travelers from Germany, where press reports on "Potemkin villages" were most widespread, see Matthias Heeke, *Reisen zu den Sowjets: Der ausländische Tourismus in Russland 1921–1941* (Münster: Lit, 2004), 485–494.

6. Michael Gelb, ed., *An American Engineer in Stalin's Russia: The Memoirs of Zara Witkin, 1932–1934* (Berkeley: University of California Press, 1991), 43.

7. Heeke, *Reisen zu den Sowjets,* esp. 167.

8. Correspondence on the English Trade-Union Delegation to the Sixth All-Union Congress of Trade Unions, Prezidium VTsSPS, 1924, GARF f. 5451, op. 13, d. 10, ll. 59–65.

9. "Zasedanie komissii po vneshnym snosheniiam," 28 October 1925, GARF f. 5451, op. 13, d. 10, l. 133; "Spravka o rabote Komissii Vneshnikh Snoshenii VTsSPS za vremia s aprelia 1925 po dekabr' 1926, " ibid., ed. khr. 21, l. 1–3, here l. 1.

10. "Otchet o poezdke finliandskoi rabochei delegatsii po SSSR po 11/IX po 14/X-1929 goda," GARF f. 5451, op. 13a, d. 268, ll. 91–92; Rachel Mazuy, *Croire plutôt que voir? Voyages en Russie soviétique (1919–1939)* (Paris: Odile Jacob, 2002), 216–220; "O nedochetakh obluzhivaniia delegatov," ll. 159–161.

11. "O posylke delegatsii v SSSR," RGASPI f. 495, op. 99, d. 22, ll. 34–39, here l. 34, l. 39. Later, especially after 1951, the practice of connecting delegations to immediate foreign-policy considerations—along with visits to model sites such as reform-through-labor camps, guiding travel through accompanying personnel, tailored and differentiated itineraries, and direct analogues to VOKS and Intourist—were adopted in the People's Republic of China. See Herbert Passin, *China's Cutural Diplomacy* (New York: Praeger, 1962).

12. Mazuy, 28–29, 74–75, 209, 245; on the scope and cover-up of the 1932–33 famine see, most recently, Timothy Snyder, *Bloodlands: Europe between Hitler and Stalin* (New York: Basic Books, 2010), chap. 1. On labor delegations see also Heeke, *Reisen zu den Sowjets*, 83–88; Sylvia R. Margulies, *The Pilgrimage to Russia: The Soviet Union and the Treatment of Foreigners, 1927–1937* (Madison: University of Wisconsin Press, 1968): 36–54; on their place in "political tourism," A. A. Kriuchkov, *Istoriia mezhdunarodnogo i otechestvennogo turizma* (Moscow: Luch, 1999), 61–67. Procedures in the smaller U.S. Communist Party were more haphazard; see Albert Inkpin, International Committee of the Friends of the Soviet Union, Berlin, to G. G. [sic] Ballam, New York, 1 April 1931, GARF f. 5451, op. 13a, d. 329, ll. 121–122; Inkpin to J. J. Ballam, 23 July 1931, ibid., ll. 21–22; also ibid., l. 23; ibid., d. 327, ll. 38–39, 40–45, 46, 53.

13. Quotations from the two letters from Inkpin to Ballam cited in the previous note.

14. "Spisok plakatov, fotografii i fotoserii, zakazannykh dlia delegatov k 15 godovshchina oktiabria," GARF. f. 5451, op. 13a, d. 423, l. 94.

15. Tamara Solonevich, *Zapiski sovetskoi perevodchitsy* (Sofia: Izdatel'stvo "Golos Rossii," 1937), here 75, 127–130, a firsthand account published outside the reach of Soviet censorship, was written as an anti-communist exposé for the Russian emigration. It included anti-Semitic statements (see 173). For an example, see "Statement of British Workers Delegation," no earlier than 1 May 1933, GARF f. 5451, op. 13a, ed. khr. 513, ll. 12–13; d. 433 contains declarations with strong generic similarities in various languages.

16. Margulies, *Pilgrimage to Russia*; Paul Hollander, *Political Pilgrims: Western Intellectuals in Search of the Good Society*, 4th ed. (New Brunswick: Transaction Publishers, 1998), chap. 3.

17. Solonevich, *Zapiski*, 66, 79, 82, quotation 55.

18. "Réponses aux questions de la Delegation Français," GARF f. 5451, op. 13a, ed. khr. 187, ll. 898–904; for other examples, see ibid. ll. 888–897, and "Protokol zasedanii komissii germanskoi rabochei delegatsii sovmestno s predstaviteliami zavkoma zavoda 'Krasnyi Putilovets,'" 17 July 1925, ibid., d. 64, ll. 10–14.

19. "Otchet Upolnomochennogo Skandinavskoi delegatsii 2-oi gruppy Timofeev Luka Petrovicha," 14 November 1929, GARF f. 5451, op. 13a, d. 268, l. 94.

20. Mazuy, 9–10, 135, 171.

21. For examples, see GARF f. 5451, op. 13a, d. 268, l. 93; ibid., l. 94; Solonevich, 59. Mazuy points out that quasi-religious terminology on the part of some foreign workers was discouraged by Communists in favor of this positivistic language of "truth" (Mazuy, 205–6).

22. E. Dobkin, Zav. Otdelom po priemu inostrantsev, "Predsedateliu VOKS—tov. Petrovu. Dokladnaia zapiska," 18 October 1930, GARF f. 5283, op. 1, d. 158, l. 109.

23. "Doklad tov. Smirnova ob itogakh obsluzhivaniia inostrannykh turistov v 1936 g.," GARF f. 9612, op. 1, d. 36, ll. 234–60, quotation l. 242; "Predlozheniia po upravleniiu obsluzhivaniia," 9 December 1936, ibid., l. 201.

24. E. Dobkin, "Plan raboty Otdela po priemu inostrantsev za period s noiabria 1930 po oktiabr' 1931 g.," GARF f. 5283, op. 1, d. 158, ll. 162–64; ibid., d. 87, ll. 1–107; Heeke, *Reisen zu den Sowjets*, 486–88; G. V. Kulikova, "Pod kontrolem gosudarstva: Prebyvanie inostrannykh pisatelei v 1920–1930-x godakh," *Otechestvennaia istoriia*, no. 4 (2003): 43–59, here 47–48.

25. *Politbiuro TsK RKP(b)-VKP(b) i Komintern*, 1919–1943. *Dokumenty* (Moscow: ROSSPEN, 2004): 316–317; "Spisok predpriiatii dlia osmotra nemetskoi delegatsiei v gorode Moskva," July 1925, GARF f. 5451, op. 13a, d. 65, l. 24; "Spisok zavodov i pred-priiatii dlia poseshcheniia inodelegatsiiami. Moskovskaia oblast'," 1932, ibid., d. 423, l. 71; "Spisok rekomendovannykh ob"ektov dlia poseshcheniia zavodov i kul'tuchrezhdenii ino. rabochikh delegatsiei, priezzhaiushchei k 15-letiiu oktiabr'skoi revoliutsii—gor. Khar'kov," ibid., l. 74.

26. B. E. Bagasarian, et al., *Sovetskoe zazerkal'e: Inostrannyi turizm v SSSR v 1930–1980-e gody* (Moscow: Forum, 2007), 29.

27. "Doklad tov. Smirnova ob itogakh obsluzhivaniia inostrannykh turistov v 1936 g.," GARF f. 9612, op. 1, d. 36, ll. 234–260, here l. 242, l. 245; "Predlozheniia po upravleniiu obslu-zhivaniia," Intourist, 9 December 1936, ibid., ll. 199–208, here l. 202; "Otchet o priezde grupp inostrannykh turistov v Sovetskii Soiuz za 1936 g.," ibid., d. 40, ll. 1–8, here l. 6.

28. Hollander, *Political Pilgrims*, quotations 21, 87, 137. Two meticulous recent studies have revealed far more skepticism and negative impressions among travelers and intellectuals alike: Heeke, *Reisen zu den Sowjets*, and Eva Oberloskamp, *Fremde neue Welten: Reisen deutscher und französischer Linksintellektueller in die Sowjetunion 1917–1939* (Munich: Oldenbourg, 2011).

29. See Uhlig, *Utopie oder Alptraum*, 23; Elizabeth Papazian, *Manufacturing Truth: The Documentary Moment in Soviet Culture* (DeKalb: Northern Illinois University Press, 2008); Herta Wolf, *Glauben machen: Über deutschsprachige Reiseberichte aus der Sowjetunion (1918–1932)* (Vienna: Sonderzahl, 1992).

30. Oberloskamp, *Fremde neue Welten*, conclusion.

31. Natal'ia Evgen'evna Semper (Sokolova), "Portrety i peizazhi: Chastnye vospominaniia o XX veke," *Druzhba narodov*, no. 2 (1997): 73–115, here 109, 111.

32. "Sotsialisticheskoe pereustroistvo sel'skogo khoziaistva. Kolkhozy," sent to VOKS by Moscow oblast' Kolkhoz Center (Mosoblkolkhozsoiuz), no date, early 1930s, GARF f. 5283, op. 8, d. 168, l. 5; "Protokol zasedaniia otvetstevennykh rabotikov VOKS po voprosu o rabote Otdela Priema Inostrantsev," 28 May 1931, ibid., op. 1, d. 163, l. 2 ob; "Programmy zagorodnykh poseshchenii dlia inospetsialistov," no later than 1 June 1931, ibid., op. 8, d. 86, l. 5; P. Nekunde (First Secretary, Soviet Embassy in Austria) to Timm (VOKS), 6 January 1934, AVP RF f. 066, op. 17, p. 116, d. 270, l. 7.

33. Valentin Berezhkov, *Kak ia stal perevodchikom Stalina* (Moscow: Dem, 1993), 179.

34. Deborah Fitzgerald, *Every Farm a Factory: The Industrial Ideal in American Agriculture* (New Haven: Yale University Press, 2003), chap. 6, quotation 181.

35. "M. Liubchenko. Pred. Vseukrainskogo Obshchestva kul'tsviazi. Tov. Lerneru. Zam. Pred. VOKS. 8 avgusta 1932 (Kharkiv)," AVP RF f. 082, op. 15, d. 28, p. 27, l. 187.

36. Witkin, *American Engineer*, 57–59.

37. Economist quoted in "Pred. VOKS A. Arosev. Sekretariu TsIK SSSR tov. Akulovu I.A.," 5 November 1936, GARF f. 5283, op. 1a, d. 311, l. 7; "Stenogramma soveshchanie pravleniia kolkhoztsentra s predstaviteliami inostrannykh rabochikh delegatsii," 8 avgusta 1930 g., GARF f. 5451, op. 13, ed. khr. 290, ll. 1–18; "Beseda predsedatelia Kolkhoztsentra tov. Kaminskogo s inostrannymi predstaviteliami," 21 November 1929, ibid., ed. khr. 264, ll. 2–33.

38. Marcello Flores, *L'immagine dell'URSS: L'Occidente e la Russia di Stalin (1927–1956)* (Milan: Il Saggiatore, 1990): 112; S. O. Pidhainy, *The Black Deeds of the Kremlin: A White Book*, vol. 1: *Book of Testimonies* (Toronto: Ukrainian Association of Victims of Russian Communist Terror, 1953); Ewald Ammende, *Human Life in Russia* (London, 1936), 230–231; Robert Conquest, *Harvest of Sorrow: Soviet Collectivization and the Terror-Famine* (New York: Oxford University Press, 1986), 313–315.

39. Michael Jabara Carley, "A Soviet Eye on France from the Rue de Grenelle in Paris, 1924–1940," *Diplomacy and Statecraft* 17 (2006): 298–299, 315, quotation 314; Ludmila

Stern, "Iz predistorii sozdaniia frantsuzskogo obshchestva kul'turnogo sblizheniia *Novaia Rossiia,*" *Australian Slavonic and East European Studies* 11, 1–2 (1997): 146.

40. "Beseda. Sharl' Faiet Tailor—SshA—professor aviostroeniia," 17 August 1937, GARF f. 5283, op. 3, d. 1003, l. 23 (for other guide reports of positive impressions of kolkhozy, see, for example, ibid., op. 1, d. 298, l. 93); "Poseshchenie kolkhoza Litovskoi gruppoi professorov," 22 June 1935, GARF f. 5283, op. 1, d. 298, l. 93.

41. Sheila Fitzpatrick, "Foreigners Observed: Moscow Visitors in the 1930s under the Gaze of their Soviet Guides," *Russian History* 35, 1–2 (2008): 215–234.

42. As discussed by Nikolai Krementsov, *A Martian Stranded on Earth: Alexander Bogdanov, Blood Transfusions, and Proletarian Science* (Chicago: University of Chicago Press, 2011), chaps. 1–2.

43. "Otchet o rabote s chlenom Turetskoi Delegatsii General'nym Direktorom Departamenta Ministerstva Prosveshcheniia Ikhan-Bei," no earlier than 4 May 1932, GARF f. 5283, op. 8, d. 112, ll. 50–51.

44. Larry E. Holmes, *Stalin's School: Moscow's Model School No. 25, 1931–1937* (Pittsburgh: University of Pittsburgh Press, 1999).

45. Götz Hillig [Getts Khillig], *Poltavskaia trudovaia koloniia im M. Gor'kogo: Polemika, dokumenty, portrety (1920–1926 gg.)* (Marburg: Institut für Erziehungswissenschaft, 2003), 13; René Bosewitz, *Waifdom in the Soviet Union: Features of the Sub-Culture and Re-Education* (Frankfurt am Main: Peter Lang, 1988), esp. 103–131; Alan M. Ball, *And Now My Soul is Hardened: Abandoned Children in Soviet Russia, 1918–1930* (Berkeley: University of California, 1994), chap. 7.

46. Solonevich, 156; "Delegatsiia MOPR"a," 1927, RGASPI f. 495, op. 99, ed. khr. 21, l. 14.

47. RGASPI f. 495, op. 99, ed. khr. 21, ll. 86–96.

48. "Politprosvetrabota v mestakh zakliucheniia g. Moskvy, po dannym obsledovaniia komissii Gubpolitprosveta," 13 April 1925, RGASPI f. 495, op. 30, d. 193, ll. 149–154; Heeke, *Reisen zu den Sowjets,* 216.

49. Report on VOKS and Mezhrabpom delegations, 1927, RGASPI f. 495, op. 99, ed. khr. 21, l. 94–96; Hollander, *Political Pilgrims,* 142; Heeke, *Reisen zu den Sowjets,* 215–216; Solonevich, 150 (she was incorrect to write that the Lefortovo isolator was the only prison foreigners were shown). See also Hollander, "Socialist Prisons and Imprisoned Minds," *National Interest* 10 (Winter 1987): 69–78.

50. "O nedochetakh obsluzhivaniia delegatov," l. 155; "Stennogramma besedy 2-i bel'giiskoi rabochei delegatsii s predsedatelem GPU Gruzii tov. BERIIA," Tbilisi, 1 November 1927, GARF f. 5451, op. 13, ed. khr. 187, ll. 591–597; Heeke, *Reisen zu den Sowjets,* 216.

51. Uhlig, 23 and passim.

52. Walter Benjamin, *Moscow Diary,* ed. Gary Smith, trans. Richard Sieburth (Cambridge, Mass.: Harvard University Press, 1986), quotations 44, 114.

53. See esp. Harald Bodenschatz and Christiane Post, eds., *Städtbau im Schattens Stalins: Die internationale Suche nach der sozialistischen Stadt in der Sowjetunion 1929–1935* (Berlin: Verlagshaus Braun, 2003).

54. "Doklad tov. Smirnova ob itogakh obluzhivaniia," l. 237.

55. Andrei Bubnov's 1932 letter to the Council of People's Commissars outlining the proposal for the construction of a new Moscow University, GARF f. A2307, op. 17, ed. khr. 169, l. 21–26.

56. Timothy Colton, *Moscow: Governing the Socialist Metropolis* (Cambridge: Harvard University Press, 1995), 253, 280 (for explicit evidence that foreign visitors influenced Stalin's plans for post-war reconstruction of Moscow, 329); Karl Schlögel, *Terror und Traum: Moskau 1937* (Munich: Carl Hanser Verlag, 2008): 60–85, esp. 78; Katerina Clark, "Socialist Realism and the Sacralizing of Space," in *The Landscape of Stalinism: The Art and Ideology of Soviet Space,* ed. Clark and Evgeny Dobrenko (Seattle: University of Washington Press, 2003): 3–18; and Mikhail Ryklin, "'The Best in the World': The Discourse of the Moscow Metro in the 1930s," in ibid., 261–276.

57. David Shearer, "Elements Near and Alien: Passportization, Policing, and Identity in the Stalinist State, 1932–1952," *Journal of Modern History* 76 (December 2004): 835–881, quotation 855.

58. Schlögel, *Terror und Traum*, 592–602; Jan C. Behrends, *Die erfundene Freundschaft: Propaganda für die Sowjetunion in Polen und in der DDR* (Cologne: Böhlau Verlag, 2006): 57–64; Ann E. Gorsuch, "'There's No Place Like Home': Soviet Tourism in Late Stalinism," *Slavic Review* 62, 4 (2003): 771–775; Gorsuch and Diane P. Koenker, "Introduction," in *Turizm: The Russian and East European Tourist Under Capitalism and Socialism*, ed. Gorsuch and Koenker (Ithaca: Cornell University Press, 2006): 9.

59. "Doklad tov. Smirnova ob itogakh obsluzhivaniia inostrannykh turistov v 1936 g.," l. 242.

60. Semper, 108.

61. "Otdel po priemu inostrantsev. Gid-perevodchik G. M. Rabinovich. Gr. Leven— Shvedtsiia," 18 November 1927, GARF f. 5283, op. 8, ed. khr. 44, l. 27.

62. VOKS circular letter to commissariats, 8 January 1932, GARF f. 5283, op. 1, d. 177, l. 69; "Stenogramma vystupleniia t. Kurts na soveshchanii ot 9-go febralia 1936 g. po voprosu o povyshenii kvalifikatsii gidov," GARF f. 9682, op. 1, d. 36, l. 27; "Otchet o prebyvanii i obsluzhivanii po Moskve i o politicheskikh nastroeniiakh inostrannykh rabochikh delegatsii, priezzhavshikh k 15-i godovshchine oktiabria (oktiabr' 1932 g.)," published in A.V. Golubev, *"Vzgliad na zemliu obetovannuiu": Iz istorii sovetskoi kul'turnoi diplomatii 1920– 1930-x godov* (Moscow: Institut istorii RAN, 2004), 200–215, here 202; "Organizatsiia i metodika kul'tpokaza," Intourist, 9 December 1936, ibid., l. 201.

63. Witkin, *American Engineer*, 46; "Doklad tov. Smirnova," l. 243–244.

64. "O nedochetakh obsluzhivaniia delegatov," 1927, l. 151.

65. "Brio Pred. VOKS (N. Kuliabko). Narkompros tov. Bubnovu," 7 October 1935, GARF f. 5283, op. 1a, d. 283, l. 23; "O nedochetakh obsluzhivaniia delegatov," 1927, ll. 148–55; Witkin, *American Engineer*, 43–44, 178.

66. Heeke, *Reisen zu den Sowjets*, 436–440, 476.

67. Semper, 85–90.

68. "Ot redaktsii," *Na sushe i na more*, no. 1 (January 1929), 1; "O mestnom turizme," *Na sushe i na more*, no. 16 (1931): 2–3, quotation 3.

69. G. P. Dolzhenko, *Istoriia turizma v dorevoliutsionnoi Rossii i SSSR* (Rostov: Izdatel'stvo Rostovskogo Universiteta, 1988): 76–86; on the proletarian-tourist movement, Diane P. Koenker, "The Proletarian Tourist in the 1930s: Between Mass Excursion and Mass Escape," in *Turizm*, 119–140. Visits to industrial sites are mentioned on 128.

70. VOKS to VTsSPS on the guidebook *Ves' SSSR*, no date, 1929 or 1930, GARF f. 5451, op. 13a, d. 239, l. 13.

71. "Proletarskii turizm sluzhit delu rabochego klassa: Moskovskie rabochie turisty na frontakh piatiletki," *Na sushe i na more*, no. 12 (1931): 8–9; K. Grigor'ev, "Voennyi turizm na zapade," ibid., no. 4 (1931): 18–20.

72. V. A. Emel'ianchenko and G. N. Pan'shin, *Puteshestvuete po Moskovskoi oblasti* (Moscow: MOSTEU VTsSPS, 1940).

73. Untitled reports on delegations, 1927, RGASPI f. 495, op. 99, ed. khr. 21, ll. 64–68, l. 91; "O nedochetakh obsluzhivaniia delegatov," ibid., l. 149.

74. Numerous Agitprop IKKI documents include "O posylke delegatsii v SSSR," 21 May 1927, RGASPI f. 495, op. 99, d. 22, l. 37 (also ll. 76, 134); ibid., ed. khr. 21, l. 67, l. 92; "Gegen die Lügenmeldungen der sowjetfeindlichen Presse. Für die Wahrheit über Sowjetrussland," resolution of German workers' delegation, 13 October 1927, ibid., ed. khr. 9, l. 91.

75. "O nedochetakh obsluzhivaniia delegatov."

76. "Vystupleniia delegatov za rubezhom," RGASPI f. 495, op. 95, ed. khr. 21, ll. 123–62, here l. 144, 150.

77. Quotation from "Shugar," in "O nedochetakh obsluzhivaniia delegatov," 1927, RGASPI f. 495, op. 95, ed. khr. 21, ll. 148–162, here l. 49.

78. Rykov speech to Congress of Friends first session, 10 November 1927, RGASPI f. 495, op. 99, ed. khr. 1, l. 27; on coordinating the message of achievements, "Vystupleniia delegatov za rubezhom," l. 144.

79. "Congress of Friends, Second Session" (in English and German), 11 November 1927, RGASPI f. 495, op. 99, ed. khr. 3, l. 6–7, 28–30, l. 62.

80. Ibid., l. 6; also, stenographic report of delegate meeting with Valerian Kuibyshev, chairman of VSNKh (in English), GARF f. 5451, op. 13, ed. khr. 187, ll. 96–113, here l. 112.

81. "Otzyvy delegatov," l. 184 ob.

82. Untitled transcript of first session of Congress of Friends of the USSR, RGASPI f. 495, op. 99, ed. khr. 1, l. 3; "Veranstellung der WOKS," 4 November 1927, ibid., ed. khr. 23, l. 189. In terms of citizenship the delegates included 173 Germans, 146 French, 127 English, 74 Czechoslovak, 47 Austrian, 34 American, 22 Chinese, and small numbers of delegates from 28 other countries.

83. "V. Miuntsenberg. Pervoe predlozhenie dlia organizatsii v 1927 g. bol'shoi mezhdunarodnoi volnoi simpatii k Sovetskoi Rossii," 26 November 1926, RGASPI f. 495, op. 99, d. 25, l. 4–10, here l. 4.

84. A. I. Rykov, "Zamechaniia k proektu Rezoliutsii," no date, ibid., d. 12, ll. 15–16.

85. "O nedochetakh obsluzhivaniia delegatov," RGASPI f. 495, op. 95, ed. khr. 21, ll. 148–62; untitled report on VOKS delegation, RGASPI f. 495, op. 99, ed. khr. 21, ll. 86–96.

86. "O nedochetakh obsluzhivaniia delegatov," RGASPI f. 495, op. 95, ed. khr. 21, ll. 148–162.

87. "Rezoliutsiia vynesennaia obshcheevropeiskoi konferentsiei oktiabr'skikh gostei-chlenov Obshchestv sblizhenie s SSSR," RGASPI f. 495, op. 99, d. 22, l. 113–115.

88. "O posylke delegatsii v SSSR," l. 34.

89. "Foreign Delegation's Interview with Stalin," in English, 5 November 1927, GARF f. 5451, op. 13, ed. khr. 187, ll. 69–95. Fischer and Maslow were German Left oppositionists who allied with the United Opposition in the USSR.

90. Theodore Dreiser, *Dreiser's Russian Diary*, ed. Thomas P. Riggio and James L. W. West III (Philadelphia: University of Pennsylvania Press, 1996), 28–29.

91. Ruth Epperson Kennell, *That Boy Nikolka and Other Tales of Soviet Children* (New York: Russian War Relief, 1945). On Kennell's later career, see Julia L. Mickenberg, *Learning from the Left: Children's Literature, the Cold War, and Radical Politics in the United States* (New York: Oxford University Press, 2005).

92. Ruth Epperson Kennell, *Theodore Dreiser and the Soviet Union, 1927–1945. A First-Hand Chronicle* (New York: International Publishers, 1969), 32–33. The translator here mistranslates: it should be "not completely a Soviet woman." In archival documents, including a letter from a provincial informant on Dreiser (GARF f. 5283, op. 1, d. 142, l. 89), this guide is identified as S. P. Trivas, *referent* in the VOKS Anglo-American section.

93. Kennell, *Theodore Dreiser*, 119, 200.

94. R. N. Mookerjee, *Theodore Dreiser: His Thought and Social Criticism* (Delhi: National Publishing House, 1974); Riggio, "Introduction," *Russian Diary*, 15.

95. Dinamov to Dreiser, 10 December 1926, and Dreiser to Dinamov, 5 January 1927, Dreiser Collection, University of Pennsylvania Rare Book Division, cited by Mookerjee, 96.

96. O. D. Kameneva, "Tov. I. V. Stalinu. Ts.K. VKP(b). 25 noiabria 1927," GARF f. R-5283, op. 1a, d. 97, l. 43; Kennell, *Theodore Dreiser*, 88, 94.

97. *Dreiser's Russian Diary*, entry of 30 November 1927, 162.

98. See diary excerpts given to Iaroshevskii, the head of VOKS's Anglo-American sector at the time, in GARF f. 5283, op. 1, d. 142, l. 96–108.

99. *Dreiser's Russian Diary*, entry of 24 Nov. 1927, 137. This is in keeping with the editorial practice of the published edition.

100. Kennell, *Theodore Dreiser*, 87–88, citing her own diary from 1927.

101. Ibid., entry of 5 Dec. 1927, 186, 188, 270. The whole interview with Bukharin is recorded on 183–192.

102. *Dreiser's Russian Diary*, entry of 29 Nov. 1927, 157, and also 102, 108, 129, 136, 173–174 and passim. For his defense of the genius of American "financial giants" Vanderbilt, Rockerfeller, Carnegie, and Pullman, see 158.

103. Riggio, "Introduction," 12; Kennell, *Theodore Dreiser*, 216–217.

104. Ibid., entry of 18 November 1927, 108; Kennell, *Theodore Dreiser*, 200.

105. *Dreiser's Russian Diary*, entry of 28 October 1927, 46.

106. Ibid., entry of 3 November 1927, 54, 56.

107. Ibid., entry of 8 November 1927, 72.

108. Theodore Dreiser, *Dreiser Looks at Russia* (New York: Horace Liveright, 1928), 20, 21; *Dreiser's Russian Diary*, entry of 31 December 1927, 259.

109. Ibid., entry of 4 November 1927, 59.

110. Kennell, *Theodore Dreiser*, 81.

111. The quotations are from David C. Engerman, "Modernization from the Other Shore: American Observers and the Costs of Soviet Economic Development," *American Historical Review* 105: 2 (April 2000), 382–416, here 382, 383.

112. *Dreiser's Russian Diary*, entry of 4 December 1927, 182.

113. *Dreiser Looks at Russia*, 50–67.

114. Ibid., entry of 4 January 1928, 264.

115. Kennell, *Theodore Dreiser*, 206.

116. James Farson, *Black Bread and Red Coffins* (1930), quoted and discussed in Donal O'Sullivan, *Furcht und Faszination: Deutsche und britische Russlandbilder 1921–1931* (Cologne, Weimar, and Vienna: Böhlau Verlag, 1996): 249.

117. *Dreiser's Russian Diary*, entries of 10 and 13 January 1928, 272, 276.

118. Sergei Dinamov to Kameneva, GARF f. 5283, op. 1, d. 142, l. 9. The text follows, l. 10–15; reprinted in *Dreiser's Russian Diary*, 287–291.

119. Theodore Dreiser, untitled letter from Odessa, 13 January 1928. GARF f. 5283, op. 1, d. 142, l. 10–15.

120. O. D. Kameneva to Stalin; Kameneva to Bukharin, 25 November 1927, GARF f. 5283, op. 1a, d. 97, l. 147. On the Sovietization of the old intelligentsia ethos of self-evaluation, see Jochen Hellbeck, *Revolution on My Mind: Writing a Diary under Stalinism* (Cambridge, Mass.: Harvard University Press, 2006), esp. 351–356.

121. "O prebyvanii Dreizera v SSSR," 28 January 1928, GARF f. 5283, op. 1, d. 142, l. 62–64.

122. Eric Naiman and Christina Kaier, eds., *Everyday Life in Early Soviet Russia: Taking the Revolution Inside* (Bloomington: Indiana University Press, 2005).

123. A particularly striking example of a guide attributing the criticisms of a sympathetic "friend" (a female French pacifist) to the absence of bourgeois comfort can be found in GARF f. 5283, op. 8, d. 112, ll. 24–25.

124. "O prebyvanii Dreizera v SSSR."

125. *Dreiser Looks at Russia*, 90, 115–116, 121, 123. The last quotation was the title of chap. 3.

126. Quoted in Kennell, *Theodore Dreiser*, 213, 216.

127. Kennell, *Theodore Dreiser*, 212–213.

128. Kennell, *Theodore Dreiser*, 211–316; Mookerjee, 113–227.

129. "O prebyvanii Dreizera v SSSR."

Chapter 4

1. M. Gor'kii, "Po Souzu sovetov," *Nashi dostizheniia*, no. 1 (1929), 11–43, here 38.

2. M. A. Babicheva, "Tragicheskie stranitsy istorii Solovkov" in *"V Belom more krasnyi SLON": Vospominaniia uznikov Solovetskogo lageria osobogo naznacheniia i literatura o nem*, ed. Babicheva (Moscow: Pashkov Dom, 2006): 6–35, esp. 6, 8, 13, 17, 21 (see also the bibliography, 418–426); Oleg V. Khlevniuk, *The History of the Gulag: From Collectivization to the Great Terror*, trans. Vadim Staklo (New Haven: Yale University Press, 2005), 28–29.

3. In the first category, see Mikhail Geller, "Gor'kii i lozh'," *Cahiers du monde russe et soviétique* 29, 1 (1988): 5–12, and, more recently, Dariusz Tolczyk, *See No Evil: Literary Cover-Ups and Discoveries of the Soviet Camp Experience* (New Haven: Yale University Press, 1999): 94–183; in the second, for example, V. N. Chernukhina, "Poezdka M. Gor'kogo na Solovki (Svidetel'stva ochevidtsev)," in *Neizvestnyi Gor'kii, vyp. 4, M. Gor'kii i ego epokha: Materialy i issledovaniia* (Moscow: Nasledie, 1995): 124–135.

4. Elizabeth Papazian, chap. 3 of *Manufacturing Truth: The Documentary Moment in Early Soviet Culture, 1921–1934* (DeKalb: Northern Illinois University Press, 2009), quotations 127, 129.

5. Mary Louise Loe, "Maksim Gor'kii and the *Sreda* Circle: 1899–1905," *Slavic Review* 44, 1 (Spring 1985): 49–66, quotation 52. See also Andrew Barratt and Barry P. Scherr,

"Introduction," in *Maksim Gorky: Selected Letters*, ed. Barrat and Scherr (Oxford: Clarendon Press, 1997): xxv–xxvi.

6. In 1921, Lenin and Zinoviev's relations with Gorky became strained, and Lenin insisted that Gorky leave the country, ostensibly for rest (Viacheslav Ivanov, "Why Did Stalin Kill Gorky?" *Russian Studies in Literature* 30, 4 (1994): 5–40, here 9; L. A. Spiridonova, *M. Gor'kii: Novyi vzgliad* [Moscow: IMLI RAN, 2004]: 106). In the same year, the Politburo formally prohibited Gorky from publishing in Comintern journals (Andrei Artuzov and Oleg Naumov, eds., *Vlast' i khudozhestvennaia intelligentsiia. Dokumenty TsK RKP(b)-VKP(b), VChK-OGPU-NKVD o kul'turnoi politike, 1917–1953* [Moscow: Demokratiia, 1999], 14–15). By the mid-1920s, Gorky was drawn more and more into Soviet literary affairs (Natal'ia Nikolaevna Primochkina, *Pisatel' i vlast': M. Gor'kii v literaturnom dvizhenii 20-x godov*, 2nd ed. [Moscow: ROSSPEN, 1998]).

7. Evgeny Dobrenko, *The Making of the State Writer: Social and Aesthetic Origins of Soviet Literary Culture*, trans. Jessica M. Savage (Stanford: Stanford University Press, 2001), 361.

8. Tolczyk, *See No Evil*, 122.

9. Papazian, 130–154.

10. The correspondence is contained in RGASPI f. 558, op. 11.

11. Spiridonova, 124–135, quotation 146; S. V. Zaika, et al., eds., *M. Gor'kii: Neizdannaia perepiska s Bogdanovym, Leninym, Stalinym, Zinov'evym, Kamenevym, Korolenko* (Moscow: Nasledie, 1998): 275–309.

12. See, for example, the exchange of 25 and 28 January 1928 in *M. Gor'kii i R. Rollan* (Moscow: Nasledie, 1996): 144–151; and Stuart Finkel, *On the Ideological Front: The Russian Intelligentsia and the Making of the Soviet Public Sphere* (New Haven: Yale University Press, 2007), 161.

13. Gorky to Iagoda, 6 February 1930, and Gorky to Iagoda, 2 November 1930, both in "Perepiska M. Gor'kogo s G. G. Iagodoi," *Neizvestnyi Gor'kii (k 125-letiiu so dnia rozhdeniia)*, ed. V. S. Barakhov et al. (Moscow: Nasledia, 1994): 162–206, here 172–174.

14. M. Gor'kii, "Rabsel'koram," *Sobranie sochinenii*, 30 vols., vol. 24: *Stat'i, rechi, privetstviia 1907–1928* (Moscow: Gosizdat khudozhestvennoi literatury, 1953): 304–307, quotation 306; see also 299, 301–303, 313–315 (orig. 1928). On the mass journalism of NEP as a key site for the emergence of Socialist Realism's focus on the adventurous hero, see Matthew A. Lenoe, *Closer to the Masses: Stalinist Culture, Social Revolution, and Soviet Newspapers* (Cambridge: Harvard University Press, 2004).

15. Erika Wolf, "*USSR in Construction*: From Avant-Garde to Socialist Realist Practice" (Ph.D. diss., University of Michigan, 1999): 16–34.

16. Tovah Yidlin, *Maxim Gorky: A Political Biography* (Westport: Praeger, 1999): 150.

17. Gor'kii, "Desiat' let," in *Publitsisticheskie stat'i* (Moscow: Gosizdat literatury, 1931), orig. *Pravda*, 6–7 November 1927.

18. Ibid., 9, 11–12.

19. Hans Günther, "The Heroic Myth in Socialist Realism," in *Traumfabrik Kommunismus: Die visuelle Kultur der Stalinzeit / Dream Factory Communism: The Visual Culture of the Stalin Era*, ed. Boris Groys and Max Hollein (Frankfurt: Schirn Kunsthalle, 20003), 106–123, here 108–111.

20. Mishel' Nike, "Revoliutsionnyi romantizm," in *Sotsrealisticheskii kanon*, ed. Gans Giunter [Hans Günther] and Evgenii Dobrenko (St. Petersburg: Akademicheskii proekt, 2000): 473–480, esp. 475.

21. Gorky to Stalin, 8 January 1930, in *Vlast' i khudozhestvennaia intelligentsiia*, 124–125.

22. Timo Vikhavainen, *Vnutrennyi vrag: Bor'ba s meshchanstvom kak moral'naia missiia russkoi intelligentsii* (St. Petersburg: Kolo, 2004): 209–214.

23. Stalin to Gorky, no later than 15 December 1930, in *Vlast' i khudozhestvennaia intelligentsiia*, 138.

24. Ivanov, "Why Did Stalin Kill Gorky?" 12. This article is unusual in that it combines interesting observations from the author's research with what he learned from his father, the writer Vsevolod Ivanov, who was under Gorky's patronage in the 1930s; it also contains unfounded speculation.

25. "Protokol zasedaniia Politbiuro TsK VKP(b) ot 17-go maia 1928 goda," RGASPI f. 17, op. 3, ed. khr. 687, l. 1; Politburo resolution from 15 December 1929, in *Vlast' i khudoz-hestvennaia intelligentsiia*, 123–124; Vikhavainen, 209; Kaganovich to Stalin (on Gorky), 23 June 1932, in Oleg Khlevniuk, et al., eds., *Stalin i Kaganovich: Perepiska, 1931–1936 gg.* (Moscow: ROSSPEN, 2001): 198; Ivanov, "Why Did Stalin Kill Gorky?" 33; and, for an example of Gorky's proposals to Stalin on "cultural construction" forwarded to the Politburo, see 25 May 1932, RGASPI f. 558, op. 11, d. 719, ll. 50–54. Despite the falling out and Gorky's virtual house arrest at the end of his life, Stalin continued to approve Gorky's proposals in 1936 (ibid., d. 720, ll. 110–112, 116). For one take on the ambiguities of Gorky's relationship with Stalin over time, see Lidiia Spiridonova, "Gorky and Stalin (According to New Materials from A. M. Gorky's Archive)," *Russian Review* 54, 3 (July 1995): 413–424.

26. Telegram from Kriuchkov to Poskrebyshev and related correspondence, March 1932, RGASPI f. 558, op. 11, d. 719, ll. 46–48.

27. "Art. Khalatov. Zav. 'OGIZ.' Predsedateliu Soveta Narodnykh Komissarov tov. Molotovu, V.M.," 29 March 1932; "Zav. OGIZ Art. Khalatov. Valiutnoi komissii pri SNK SSSR," 21 March 1932, both in RGASPI f. 558, op. 11, d. 719, ll. 45, 46.

28. Ivanov, "Why Did Stalin Kill Gorky?" 6 (relying on the recollections of V. M. Khodasevich, who was present).

29. A. S. Smykalin, *Kolonii i tiur'my v sovetskoi Rossii* (Ekateriinburg: Izdatel'stvo Ural'skoi gosudarstvennoi akademii, 1997): 59, 235–246.

30. Iurii Brodskii, *Solovki: Dvatsat' let Osobogo naznacheniia* (Moscow: ROSSPEN, 2002), 13; Michael Jakobson, *Origins of the Gulag: The Soviet Prison System, 1917–1934* (Lexington, KY: University Press of Kentucky, 1993): 112–114; Khlevniuk, 9; G. M. Ivanova, *Istoriia GULAGa 1918–1958: Sotsial'no-ekonomicheskii i politiko-pravovoi aspekty* (Moscow: Nauka, 2006): 161, 165; Roy R. Robson, *Solovki: The Story of Russia Told Through Its Most Remarkable Islands* (New Haven: Yale University Press, 2004): 205, 221. Among the 700 photographs in Brodskii's extraordinary book is one of Gorky in a worker's cap surrounded by leather-jacketed *Chekisty* on the Solovki camp boat and one of the writer standing in front of workers' barracks (325).

31. Ivanova, 149.

32. On the NEPman N. A. Frenkel', see Babicheva, "Tragicheskie stranitsy," 6.

33. Khlevniuk, 39–40, quotation 39; Brodskii, 15; Robson, 243.

34. On this film, see Cristina Vatulescu, *Police Aesthetics: Literature, Film, and the Secret Police in Soviet Times* (Stanford: Stanford University Press, 2010), 124–135.

35. Brodskii, 58, 258–259, 326, 525 n. 95.

36. M. Gor'kii, "Po soiuzu sovetov," *Nashi dostizheniia*, no. 6 (1929): 3–22, quotation 21. On *inoskazanie* (hidden meanings) in the text—such as Gorky's long discussions of nature, his avoidance of central topics such as food, labor, and political prisoners, the replacement of the very word "prisoner" in favor of euphemisms—as evidence of Gorky's "moral dilemma" in writing what he did, see Papazian, 152–154. In a letter of 22 January 1930, Gorky felt it necessary to apologize to Iagoda, apparently because the roundabout essay did not provide everything the secret police had wished (Chernukhina, 124).

37. Papazian, chap. 3.

38. M. Gor'kii, "Po Soiuzu sovetov," *Nashi dostizheniia*, no. 1 (1929), 11–43; ibid., no. 4 (1929): 3–10.

39. Ibid., no. 3 (1929): 5; no. 4 (1929): 7.

40. "Protokol No. 1 Soveshchaniia Agitpropa IKKI 12-go oktiabria 1924 goda," GARF f. 5283, op. 1a, ed. khr. 27, l. 22; "Vypiska iz protokola No. 1 Soveshchaniia pri Informotdele TsK RKP(b) po informatsii zagranitsy o SSSR," 17 February 1925, RGASPI f. 495, op. 30, d. 139, l. 1; Tsirkuliar o presse v sviazi s II Internatsionalom," 4 May 1925, ibid., ll. 2–4; "O postanovke informatsii zagranitsy o SSSR," February 1925, GARF f. 5283, op. 1a, ed. khr. 55, ll. 3–5; "An alle Sektionen der K.I.," RGASPI f. 495, op. 30, d. 139, l. 14; "Dokladnaia zapiska ob organizatsii informatsii ob SSSR Zagran. kompartii," 26 May 1926, ibid., d. 272, ll. 3–12.

41. Ibid., no. 6 (1929): 21–22.

42. Gor'kii, "K inostrannym rabochim," in *Publitsisticheskie stat'i*, 290–93, orig. *Pravda*, 14 July 1931. For Gorky's earlier attacks on European intellectuals who failed to appreciate unprecedented Soviet successes, see Gor'kii, "Anoninam i psevdonimam," ibid., 13–15, orig. *Izvestiia TsIK SSSR*, 25 December 1927.

43. "Ot redaktsii. O 'malen'kikh' liudiakh i o velikoi ikh rabote," *Nashi dostizheniia*, no. 1 (1929): 5–10.

44. M. Gor'kii, "Po Soiuzu sovetov," *Nashi dostizheniia*, no. 4 (1929): 7, 10; Tolczyk, *See No Evil*, 127.

45. M. Gor'kii, "Po Soiuzu sovetov," *Nashi dostizheniia*, no. 6 (1929): 5.

46. Ibid., no. 1 (1929): 22; see also no. 5 (1929): 33–34.

47. Aleksandr Solzhenitsyn, *Arkhipelag GULag, 1918–1956: Opyt khudozhestvennogo issledovaniia*, 3 vols. (Paris: YMCA Press, 1973–1975).

48. The relevant passages of six such prisoners are reproduced in Brodskii, who unfortunately does little to identify the memoirists beyond giving their names; but biographical details are given by Chernukhina, who discusses two additional sources.

49. Yedlin, 185; Brodskii, 325–28; Chernukhina, 129–132.

50. N. Zhilov, cited in Brodskii, 207, 326.

51. D. S. Likhachev, "Iz knigi Vospominaniia," in *"V Belom more krasnyi SLON,"* ed. Babicheva, 264–296, quotation 170.

52. Khlevniuk, 47–53.

53. Karl Schlögel, *Terror und Traum: Moskau 1937* (Munich: Carl Hanswer Verlag, 2008), 361–385, quotation 382.

54. Stephen Barnes, "Researching Daily Life in the Gulag," *Kritika* 1, 2 (Spring 2000): 377–390. It is important to note that shortly after Gorky's visit to Solovki, the sharply deteriorating conditions helped prompt the curtailment of the camp press and the removal of the theater troupe in December 1929 (Robson, 245). For a remarkable analysis of a prisoner using the camp publications and cultural-enlightenment activities to become winner of the Stalin prize for literature, see Thomas Lahusen, *How Life Writes the Book: Real Socialism and Socialist Realism in Stalin's Russia* (Ithaca: Cornell University Press, 1997).

55. Lynne Viola, "The Aesthetic of Stalinist Planning and the World of the Special Villages," *Kritika* 4, 1 (Winter 2003): 101–128.

56. Eikhmans and Iagoda are discussed in Kate Brown, "Out of Solitary Confinement: History of the Gulag," in *Kritika* 8, 1 (2007): 84–86, citing documents from N. I. Vladimirtsev and N. V. Petrov, eds., *Istoriia staliniskogo Gulaga*, vol. 2: *Karatel'nye sistema. Struktura i kadry* (Moscow: ROSSPEN, 2004); on Likhachev, see Brodskii, 189. On the large literature on special settlements, see Oxana Klimkova, "Special Settlements in Soviet Russia," *Kritika* 8, 1 (2007): 105–140.

57. Brodskii, 117.

58. Tolczyk, *See No Evil*, 100; Evgeny Dobrenko, "Nadzirat'—Nakazyvat'—Nadzirat': Sotsrealizm kak pribavochnyi produkt nasiliia," *Revue des études slaves* 73, 4 (2001): 667–712.

59. Lennard Gerson, *The Secret Police in Lenin's Russia* (Philadelphia: Temple University Press, 1976), 127.

60. Douglas Weiner, "Dzerzhinskii and the Gerd Case: The Politics of Intercession and the Evolution of 'Iron Felix' in NEP Russia," *Kritika* 7, 4 (Fall 2006): 759–791, quotations 770, 788.

61. Gerson, 128.

62. Jakobson, *Origins of the Gulag*, 53, 59.

63. N. M. Pogrebinskii, "O moem ottse," in *Bolshevo: Literaturnyi istoriko-kraevedcheskii al'manakh*, vyp. 3 (Bolshevo: Pisatel', 1994): 14–15, special issue on Bolshevskaia trudovaia kommuna OGPU, cited hereafter as *"Bolshevo"*; on Melikhov, see Getz Khillig [Götz Hillig], ""Bolshevskaia kommuna—'starshii brat' makarenkovskoi 'dzerzhinki,'" *Besprizornik*, no. 1 (2006): 19–37, here 20, 28; for various documents on Melikhov's Luxemburg Commune, see Svetlana Gladysh, *Deti bol'shoi bedy* (Moscow: Zvonitsa, 2004): 297–321.

64. William Reswick, "An Experiment in Freedom," *The Nation*, 11 November 1925; Marian Tyler, Extension Division, *The Nation*, to Boris Svirskii, 23 November 1925, GARF f. 5283, op. 3, ed. khr. 5, l. 153; Svirskii to Ol'ga Kameneva, 27 November 1925, ibid., l. 54; Letter from Ts. Rabinovich, Biuro Sviazi. to "St. Bolyshevo, Sev. zh.d. Sovkhoz 'Kost'kino,'" no date, l. 156.

65. R. Pozamantir, "Predislovie," *Bolshevo*, 3.

66. Gladysh, 102, 104.

67. Catriona Kelly, *Children's World: Growing up in Russia, 1890–1991* (New Haven: Yale University Press, 2007): 184–185.

68. Reswick, "An Experiment in Freedom."

69. On conditions and their disparity both with propaganda and policy statements, see Kelly, *Children's World*, 198–203, 215–219.

70. Pozamantir, "Predislovie"; Ia. G. Rezinovskii, "Govoriat dokumenty"; S. P. Bogoslovskii, "Bolshevskaia 'Pedagogicheskaia Poema'"; A. G. Dreirin, "Iskusstvo v kommune"; all in *Bolshevo*, 3–4, 6, 19–20; 91–104. Most communards were boys accepted at the age of fifteen or sixteen, but some as early as thirteen; the first group of females was accepted in 1927 (ibid., 19). On the FED, see Oskar Fricke, "The Dzerzhinskii Commune: Birth of the Soviet 35mm Camera Industry," *History of Photography* 3, 2 (April 1979), available at: http://www.fedka.com/Useful_info/Commune_by_Fricke/commune_A.htm, last accessed August 28, 2011.

71. Zara Witkin, *An American Engineer in Stalin's Russia: The Memoirs of Zara Witkin, 1932–1934*, ed. Michael Gelb (Berkeley: University of California, 1991), 55.

72. Kelly, *Children's World*, 72.

73. *Bolshevo*, cited in full in n. 63. What little analysis is contained in this rich collection of sources largely corresponds to the "lacquered" versions of the commune's success propagated in the interwar period. More recently, journalist Svetlana Gladysh was given access to KGB archival documents for her 2004 book centered on Bolshevo, *Deti bol'shoi bedy*; despite this work's sometimes heavy-handed efforts to uncover a tradition of *Chekist* humanism, it contains many document publications and is an invaluable source.

74. Oleg Kharkhardin, *The Collective and the Individual in Russia: A Study of Practices* (Berkeley: University of California Press, 1999), chap. 3, quotation 75, on Makarenko, 90–97.

75. Gladysh, 66–67; Hillig, "Bolshevskaia kommuna," 22–27.

76. See the recollections of S. P. Bogoslovskii, who worked in the commune from 1924, in GARF f. 7952, op. 3, d. 4, ll. 53–81, 82–134, reprinted in *Bolshevo*, 15–21; L. D. Vul', "Prestupnyi mir i besprizornost'," ibid., 9–11; M. S. Pogrebinskii, *Trudovaia kommuna OGPU* (Moscow: Gosizdat, 1928), 46; Hillig, "Bolshevskaia kommuna," 25.

77. See the documents in Gladysh, 141–153.

78. Pogrebinskii, *Trudovaia kommuna OGPU*, 18.

79. Vincent N. Lunetta, "A Comparative Study: The Gorky Youth Colony and Boys Town," *Educational Theory* 11, 2 (1961): 93–98.

80. For an example, see A. N. Pogodin, "V kommune ia budto rodilsia vtoroi raz," and M. F. Sokolov-Ovchinnikov, "Segodnia, zavtra, vsegda," in *Bolshevo*, 34–39, 39–41.

81. Götz Hillig, "Anton Semenovič Makarenko – ein Nicht-Kommunist im Dienst der sowjetischen Sicherheitsorgane," *Jahrbuch für Forschungen zur Geschichte der Arbeiterbewegung* 4, 3 (2005): 48–63, here 53. On the broader dynamic, see Jochen Hellbeck, *Revolution on my Mind: Writing a Diary under Stalin* (Cambridge: Harvard University Press, 2006).

82. Bogoslovskii, in *Bolshevo*, quotation 20; on von Körber, ibid., 135–142; see also von Körber, *Sowjetrussland kämpft gegen das Verbrechen* (Berlin: Rowohlt, 1933).

83. G. G. Iagoda to A. S. Enukidze, 20 August 1925, in *Bolshevo*, 26; Iagoda *prikaz* of 10 June 1936, cited in Gladysh, 322.

84. "Daten zu Leben und Werk A. Makarenkos," in Anton Makarenko, *Gesammelte Werke: Marburger Ausgabe*, vol. 1: *Veröffentlikchungen 1923–1931*, ed. Siegried Weitz and Götz Hillig (Ravensburg: Otto Maier Verlag, 1976): 141–152; Götz Hillig and Svetlana Nevskaja, eds., *Perepiska A.S. Makarenko s M. Gor'kim: Akademicheskoe izdanie / Makarenkos Briefwechsel mit Gor'kij: Kritische Ausgabe* (Marburg: Makarenko-Referat, 1990).

85. Hillig, "Anton Semenovič Makarenko," 48–63, quotation 60.

86. *Perepiska A. S. Makarenko s M. Gor'kim*, 6–65.

87. Götz Hillig [Getts Khillig], *Poltavskaia trudovaia koloniia im M. Gor'kogo: Polemika, dokumenty, portrety (1920-1926 gg.)* (Marburg: Institut für Erziehungswissenschaft, 2003), 13; Hillig, "Bolshevskaia kommuna"; "Daten zu Leben und Werk A. Makarenkos," 150–58 (Gorky and Makarenko also had extensive contacts in 1934–36; see ibid., 159–74; Krupskaia's article in *Komsolmol'skaia pravda*, no. 113, 1928, 2, is cited on 152). On Makarenko's pedagogy, see also René Bosewitz, *Waifdom in the Soviet Union: Features of the Sub-Culture and Re-Education* (Frankfurt am Main: Peter Lang, 1988), esp. 103–131; Alan M. Ball, *And Now My Soul is Hardened: Abandoned Children in Soviet Russia, 1918–1930* (Berkeley: University of California, 1994), chap. 7

88. Pogrebinskii, *Trudovaia kommuna OGPU*, quotation 10, with introduction by Gorky, 5–10; Pogrebinskii, *Fabrika liudei* (Moscow: Ogonek, 1929), quotations 17, 35.

89. See the 1931 original of *Putevka v zhizn'* (an edited version was re-released in 1957). The above also draws on M. I. Isimetov, *Iyvan Kyrlia: Ocherki zhizni i tvorchestva*, 2nd ed. (Ioshkar-Ola: Mariiskoe knizhnoe izdatel'stvo, 2003): 8, 10, 13–14, 17, 25, 28; for an example of the militants' criticism, see "Putevka v zhizn'," *Proletarskoe kino*, no. 5–6 (1931): 25–31. For an extended interpretation, see Vatulescu, *Police Aesthetics*, 135–147.

90. On Bolshevo as a standard destination, see "Otchet po priemu Inostrantsev s noiabria 1929 po okt. 1930 g.," GARF f. 5283, op. 1, d. 158, l. 105; "Programmy zagorodnykh poseshchenii dlia inospetsialistov. A. Bruk. Zav. Nauchno-Tekhnicheskim Sektorom [VOKS]," no later than 1 June 1931, ibid., op. 8, d. 86, l. 5; on Duchêne, see Rachel Mazuy, *Croire plutôt que voir? Voyages en Russie soviétique, 1919–1939* (Paris: Odile Jacob, 2002): 139–40; Bernard Shaw, *The Rationalization of Russia*, ed. Harry M. Geduld (Bloomington: Indiana University Press, 1964): 89–93; André Gide, *Return from the USSR*, trans. Dorothy Bussy (New York: Alfred A. Knopf, 1937), 116. See also Romain Rolland, *Voyage à Moscou (juin-juillet 1935)*, ed. Bernard Duchatelet (Paris: Albin Michel, 1992), 287.

91. "Poseshchenie trudkommuny (Bolshevo)," 20 June 1935, GARF f. 5283, op. 3, ed. khr. 655, l. 271.

92. "Zam. Zav. III Zapadnym Otdelom [NKID] (Veinberg). Vtoromu sekretariu Polpredstva SSSR v SShA tov. Gokhmanu," 29 October 1935, AVP RF f. 129, op. 19, d. 32, p. 19, l. 19.

93. The phrase is from David Shearer, *Policing Stalin's Socialism: Repression and Social Order in the Soviet Union, 1924–1953* (New Haven: Yale University Press, 2009); see also Paul Hagenloh, *Stalin's Police: Public Order and Mass Repression in the USSR, 1926–1941* (Baltimore: Johns Hopkins University Press, 2009), esp. 103–114.

94. Hagenloh, 113 (quotation), 182–194; Kelly, *Children's World*, 230.

95. For example, see A. Antonomov, "Bolshevskaia kommuna OGPU," *Nashi dostizheniia*, no. 7 (1930): 35–42.

96. Likhachev, in *"V Belom more krasnyi SLON,"* ed. Babicheva, 169, 178.

97. Gor'kii, "Po soiuzu sovetov," *Nashi dostizheniia*, no. 6 (1929): 21, 22; Bogoslovskii, in *Bolshevo*, 20; Chernukhina, 124, 127; "Perepiska M. Gor'kogo s G. G. Iagodoi," 199 n. 1. Pogrebinskii accompanied the writer not only on four visits to Bolshevo, in 1928 and 1931–32, but also to the sovkhoz "Gigant" and a children's colony near Stalingrad; the *Chekist* was a frequent guest at Gorky's house and dacha (Hillig, "Bolshevskaia kommuna," 29).

98. Daniel Beer, *Renovating Russia: The Human Sciences and the Fate of Liberal Modernity, 1880–1930* (Ithaca: Cornell University Press, 2008): 200, 72 n. 41.

99. M. Gor'kii, "Trudovaia kommuna OGPU," in *Publitsisticheskie stat'i*, orig. *Izvestiia TsIK SSSR*, 18 July 1928 (see also Gor'kii, "O trudkoloniiakh OGPU," ibid., 293–303, orig. *Pravda*, 14 July 1931; Gor'kii, "Predislovie," in *Bolshevtsy: Ocherki istorii Bolshevskoi imeni G. G. Iagody trudkommuny NKVD*, ed. Gor'kii, et al. [Moscow: OGIZ, 1936], 10).

100. M. Gor'kii, "Po Soiuzu Sovetov," *Nashi dostizheniia*, no. 2 (1929): 14–38, quotations 29. In this piece Gorky praises Makarenko (27).

101. Papazian, 159; according to Room's *Pravda* article of 6 July 1976, Gorky stopped working on the screenplay of *Prestupniki* because he was very busy and sick. But the Room expert Irina Nikolaevna Grashchenkova, to whom I am grateful for sharing her view,

gives another explanation for why the film was never made. Room, like Gorky a friend of Iagoda, planned to make it in a documentary manner, but the advisability of this was thrown into doubt by the "mythological" mode of Nikolai Ekk's 1931 *Putevka v zhizn'*.

102. Solonevich was the son of Tamara Solonevich, author of *Zapiski sovetskoi perevodchitsy*, discussed in Chapter 3.

103. Iurii Solonevich, *Povest' o 22-x neschast'iakh* (Sofia: Golos Rossii, 1938): 50–51, 142–183, quotations 173; on Dewey, see Gladysh, 106.

104. See documents published by Gladysh, 252–54, 260, 277–289; see also Hagenloh, 182–194 (statistic of 85,000 from 189); Kelly, *Children's World*, 231, 235; Smykalin, 105–107.

105. Hillig, "Anton Semenovič Makarenko," 58; Gladysh, 249.

106. On the end of Bolshevo in the Purges, see G. V. Filaretov to Molotov, 9 December 1938, and P. P. Poletaev, "Malen'kaia respublika," both in *Bolshevo*, 8, 80, respectively; Gladysh, 168–172; Hillig, "Bolshevskaia kommuna," 33–36.

107. Robson, 245.

Chapter 5

1. For a discussion of these restrictions with a secret-police component to the correspondence, see: Litvinov to Stalin and Politburo members, 20 October 1928, GARF f. 5283, op. 1a, ed. khr. 104, ll. 98–99; Kameneva to Central Committee and Stalin's Secretariat, 31 December 1928, ibid., l. 152; Kameneva to Central Committee Secretariat, 15 March 1929, ibid., d. 125, l. 36; Kameneva to Litvinov, 25 May 1929, ibid., l. 30; Iu. V. Mal'tsev (acting director of VOKS) to Meer Abramovich Trilesser (Zam. Pred. OGPU), 8 August 1929, ibid., d. 125, l. 57; Mal'tsev to Stalin, 13 August 1929, ibid., l. 53; Litvinov to Molotov, 9 October 1929, ibid., ll. 60–61. Trilesser was also head of the secret police's foreign section, INO OGPU.

2. One example: of the approximately 10,000 engineers in the Soviet Union, several thousand, about 30 percent, were arrested during the Great Break. See Loren R. Graham, *The Ghost of the Executed Engineer: Technology and the Fall of the Soviet Union* (Cambridge, Mass.: Harvard University Press, 1993), 45.

3. On the early history of Intourist, see V. E. Bagdasarian, et al., *Sovetskoe zazerkal'e: Inostrannyi turizm v SSSR v 1930–1980-e gody* (Moscow: Forum, 2007).

4. Ivan Maiskii to O. D. Kameneva, 9 November 1926, GARF f. 5283, op. 1a, d. 79, ll. 1–2; Kameneva to Knorin, Zav. Agitpropom TsK VKP(b), 15 December 1926, ibid., l. 27.

5. "N. M. Epshtein. Sekretariu TsK VKP(b) tov. Shverniku," no later than December 1926, GARF f. 5283, op. 1a, d. 97, ll. 26–35.

6. "Protokol mezhduvedomstvennogo soveshchaniia pri VOKS"e po voprosu o turizme," 3 December 1926, GARF f. 5283, op. 1a, d. 79, ll. 34; "Zasedanie Kommissii po Turizmu pri VOKS"e ot 18-go dekabria 1926 g," ibid., ll. 30–31; Chicherin to Krestinskii, 27 July 1928, citing views of the OGPU's Trilesser, AVP RF f. 04, op. 13, d. 50396, p. 98, l. 7.

7. "Vypiska iz protokola Zasedaniia Orgbiuro TsK VKP(b)," 4 March 1927, GARF f. 5283, op. 1a, d. 97, l. 52; "Protokol uchrezhditel'skogo sobraniia Gosudarstvennogo aktsionernogo obshchestva po inostrannomu turizmu v Soiuze SSSR /"Inturist"/," GARF f. 9612, op. 1, d. 1, ll. 1–3. On Sovtorgflot and the origins of Intourist, see Matthias Heeke, *Reisen zu den Sowjets: Der ausländische Tourismus in Russland 1921–1941* (Münster: Lit Verlag, 2004), 31–37; "Ustav Gos. Akts. Obshchestva po ino. turizmu v Soiuze SSSR (Inturist)," ibid., l. 2.

8. Shawn Salmon, "Marketing Socialism: Inturist in the Late 1950s and Early 1960s," in *Turizm: The Russian and East European Tourist under Capitalism and Socialism*, ed. Anne E. Gorsuch and Diane P. Koenker (Ithaca: Cornell University Press, 2006), 186–204, quotation 188; Salmon, "To the Land of the Future: A History of Intourist and Travel to the Soviet Union, 1929–1991" (Ph.D. diss., University of California at Berkeley, 2008), 40, and more generally Part I on the early history of Intourist.

9. For example, "Zakliuchenie Revizionnoi komissii po otchetu za 1929 g. i Balansu na 1/1 1930 goda Gos. Akts. Obshchestva 'Inturist,'" GARF f. 9612, op. 1, d. 1, ll. 13, 14, 16; "Opisatel'nyi otchet," 1931, ibid., d. 9, ll. 1–4.

10. "Doklad tov. Smirnova ob itogakh obsluzhivaniia inostrannykh turistov v 1936 g. i podgotovke obsluzhivaniia v 1937 g.," GARF f. 9612, op. 1, d. 36, ll. 234–260, here 234; Heeke, *Reisen zu den Sowjets*, 39; on Intourist's monopoly and 1936, see Bagdasarian, et al., *Sovetskoe zazerkal'e*, 14.

11. "Upolnomochennomu VOKS v Leningrade t. Pokrovskomu," 26 December 1932, no author indicated, GARF f. 5283, op. 1, d. 177, l. 5

12. *General'naia instruktsiia po obluzhivaniiu inostrannykh turistov v SSSR* (Moscow: Inturist, 1936), 38–39; Aleksandr Arosev to Stalin, 7 June 1935, ibid., d. 276, ll. 134–138; Arosev to Ivan Akulov, TsIK secretary, ibid., op. 1a, d. 311, ll. 7–9; RGASPI f. 495, op. 95, d. 39, ll. 40–42. On the conflict between VOKS and Intourist in the early 1930s, see also Salmon, "To the Land of the Future," 53–56.

13. Salmon, "To the Land of the Future," 43.

14. "Kon"iunkturnyi obzor Evropeiskogo rynka turizma," "O mirovom rynke turizma i o znachenii inturizma v platezhnom balanse strane," and "Avtomobil'nyi turizm," lectures delivered in Oct. and Nov. 1931 by Marshevskii (Zampredsedatel' pravleniia Gos. AO "Inturist"), GARF f. 9682, op. 1, d. 8, ll. 10–20, ll. 21–35, ll. 51–59. On the rhetoric of "cultured trade," see esp. Julie Hessler, "Cultured Trade: The Stalinist Turn Toward Consumerism," in *Stalinism: New Directions*, ed. Sheila Fitzpatrick (London: Routledge, 2000): 182–209; Hessler, *A Social History of Soviet Trade: Trade Policy, Retail Practices, and Consumption* (Princeton: Princeton University Press, 2004), chap. 5, which links it to a new 1930s model of Soviet-type consumerism.

15. *"Inturizm." Vnutrennyi informatsionnyi biulleten'*, Jan. 1931, and *Vnutrenii Informatsionnyi biulleten'*, Aug. 1931, GARF f. 9682, op. 1, d. 8, ll. 60–91, 110–131.

16. "Doklad tov. Smirnova," l. 238–242; "Predlozheniia po upravleniiu obsluzhivaniia," 9 December 1936, GARF f. 9612, op. 1, d. 36, l. 203.

17. Hermann H. Field, addressee unknown, 9 November 1934, GARF f. 5283, op. 3, ed. khr. 655, ll. 201–206; "Tourist Travel in the Soviet Union," unidentified American author, 28 February 1934, AVP RF f. 69, op. 23, d. 5, p. 76, ll. 212–14; B. Jenkins to V. A. Kurtz, Chairman of Intourist, 21 July 1935, ibid., ll. 178–192.

18. James Harris, "Encircled by Enemies: Stalin's Perceptions of the Capitalist World, 1918–1941," *Journal of Strategic Studies* 30, 3 (2007): 515–521, quotations 543; David R. Stone, *Hammer and Rifle: The Militarization of the Soviet Union, 1926–1933* (Lawrence: University Press of Kansas, 2000), chap. 2. See also Jon Jacobson, *When the Soviet Union Entered World Politics* (Berkeley: University of California Press, 1994), 206–232.

19. Anthony C. Sutton, *Western Technology and Soviet Economic Development 1917 to 1930* (Stanford: Hoover Institution on War, Revolution and Peace, 1968), vol. 2: 325–326.

20. Stone, chap. 3.

21. The above is drawn from chap. 7 of Eric Lohr, "Russian Citizenship: Empire to Soviet Union," Harvard University Press, forthcoming 2012.

22. A. V. Golubev, *"... Vzgliad na zemliu obetovannuiu ..." Iz istorii sovetskoi kul'turnoi diplomatii 1920–1930-x godov* (Moscow: Institut istorii RAN, 2004), 49; S. V. Zhuravlev and V. S. Tiazhel'nikova, "Inostrannaia koloniia v Sovetskoi Rossii v 1920–1930 gody (Postanovka problem i metody issledovaniia)," *Otechestvennaia istoriia*, no. 1 (1994): 179–189.

23. Anatole Kopp, "Foreign Architects in the Soviet Union During the First Two Five-Year Plans," in *Reshaping Russian Architecture: Western Technology, Utopian Dreams*, ed. William C, Brumfield (New York: Cambridge University Press and Woodrow Wilson Center, 1990), 176–214, quotation 178; see Witkin's recollections on May's disillusionments and bureaucratic misadventures in Michael Gelb, ed., *An American Engineer in Stalin's Russia: The Memoirs of Zara Witkin, 1932–1934* (Berkeley: University of California Press, 1991), esp. 232–235, 240, 245.

24. Aleksandr Etkind, *Tolkovanie puteshestvii: Rossiia i Amerika v travelogakh i intertekstakh* (Moscow: NLO, 2001), chap. 5.

25. Harald Bodenschatz and Christiane Post, eds., *Städtbau im Schattens Stalins: Die internationale Suche nach der sozialistischen Stadt in der Sowjetunion 1929–1935* (Berlin: Verlagshaus Braun, 2003), 9, 125–28; Sergei Zhuravlev, *"Malen'kie liudi" i "bol'shaia*

istoriia": Inostrantsy moskovskogo Elektrozavoda v sovetskom obshchestve 1920-x – 1930-x gg. (Moscow: ROSSPEN, 2000), Sutton, *Western Technology*, 2: 316–324. At the same time, as Yves Cohen has pointed out, "Germanism" remained more important than "Americanism" in terms of the most influential models of economic organization during the Five-Year Plan. See Cohen, "Circulatory Localities: The Example of Stalinism in the 1930s," *Kritika* 11, 1 (Winter 2010): 11–45.

26. "Spravki o khode vypolneniia postanovleniia TsK VKP(b) i VTsSPS po rabote sredi inostrannykh rabochikh i spetsialistov," 23 October 1931, GARF f. 5451, op. 13a, d. 342, l. 78–91.

27. On falsified qualifications, Sylvia R. Margulies, *The Pilgrimage to Russia: The Soviet Union and the Treatment of Foreigners, 1924–1937* (Madison: University of Wisconsin Press, 1968), 87. For opposition to foreigner specialists and workers from the plant level on up, see Sutton, *Western Technology*, 2: 306–308.

28. "Plan politicheskogo i kul'turnogo obsluzhivaniia udarnikov inorabochikh i spetsialistov vo vremia Eksursii po Volge," 1933, prob. August, GARF f. 5451, op. 39, d. 70, ll. 13–15; Zhuravlev and Tiazhel'nikova, "Inostrannaia koloniia," 182–183. As in the case of important foreign delegations, special editions of local newspapers were published to greet the foreign shockworkers (GARF f. 5451, op. 39, d. 70, l. 26).

29. "Soglashenie mezhdu [VOKS] i Sektorom proizvodstvenno-tekhnicheskoi propagandy Narkomata tiazheloi promyshlennosti," no exact date, GARF f. 5283, op. 1, d. 173, l. 30; "I-ia konferentsiia inostrannykh spetsialistov," evening session, 29 July 1932, GARF f. 5451, op. 13a, d. 302, ll. 18, 19; Zhuravlev and Tiazhel'nikova, "Inostrannaia koloniia," 179–189.

30. GARF f. 5451, op. 13a, d. 302, l. 305; Elena Osokina, *Our Daily Bread: Socialist Distribution and the Art of Survival in Stalin's Russia*, trans. Kate Transchel and Greta Bucher (London: M.E. Sharpe, 2001), 76, 121–29; E. A. Osokina, *Zoloto dlia industrializatsii: Torgsin* (Moscow: ROSSPEN, 2009).

31. "Spravka ob inostrannykh rabochikh i spetsialistov rabotaiushchikh na predpriiatiiakh Sovetskogo Soiuza," no exact date, 1933, GARF f. 5451, op. 13a, d. 456, ll. 89–91.

32. Zhuravlev, *Malen'kie liudi*, 282–93; Osokina, *Our Daily Bread*, 76.

33. Untitled plan for VOKS work, November 1929, GARF f. 5283, op. 1, ed. khr. 124, l. 18; for similar formulations from Kameneva, see her letter to Smirnov, Otdel pechati TsK VKP(b), 21 January 1928, ibid., op. 1a, d. 118, ll. 9–20.

34. N. V. Kiseleva, *Iz istorii bor'by sovetskoi obshchestvennosti za proryv kul'turnoi blokady SSSR (VOKS: seredina 20-x B nachalo 30-x godov)* (Rostov-na-Donu: Izdatel'stvo Rostovskogo Universiteta, 1991), 142; "Zapiski o polozhenii i rabote [VOKS]," 1931, GARF f. 5283, op. 1, d. 158, l. 98ob.

35. Petrov in "Doklad referenta," l.102ob; "Protokol obshchego sobraniia sotrudnikov VOKS," 7 January 1930, ibid., op. 1, ed. khr. 131, ll. 44–46.

36. "Tseli i zadachi VOKS"a (Proekt utverzhdenyi kollegiei NKID v zasedanii ot 23 marta 1931 goda," GARF f. 5283, op. 1a, ed. khr. 189, l. 39–42.

37. Kameneva, "V Sekretariat TsK VKP(b)," 2 August 1928, GARF f. 5283, op. 1a, d. 118, ll. 117–126, quotation l. 123. In fact, the bulletin had its origins before 1925 in a dry *khronika*, or calendar of events.

38. GARF f. 5283, op. 1, d. 254 (materials on the commissioning of publications).

39. Here, see Michael David-Fox, "Science, Political Enlightenment and Agitprop: On the Typology of Social Knowledge in the Early Soviet Period," *Minerva* 34, 4 (Winter 1996): 347–366.

40. Harris, "Encircled by Enemies," 524–525, 529.

41. "Protokol No. 2 Komissii po rabote VOKS v sviazi s protsessom 'Prompartii' ot 20.XI.30," GARF f. 5283, op. 1, ed. khr. 139, ll. 3–4; "Protokol soveshchaniia otvetstvennykh rabotnikov VOKS o rabote VOKS v sviazi s nadvigaiushcheisia voennoi opasnost'iu ot 19 noiabria 1930," ibid., ll. 1–2.

42. "Plan provedeniia kampanii v sviazi s protsessom 'Prompartii,'" 1931, GARF f. 5283, op. 1, ed. khr. 139, ll. 54–61.

43. GARF f. 5283, op. 1, ed. khr. 139, l. 4ob.

44. "Svedeniia po VOKS s 1.VII-30 g. po 1-IX-31 g.," ibid., d. 157, l. 34.

45. On the economic situation and its foreign observers, see, inter alia, Osokina, *Our Daily Bread*, 3–58, esp. 47; 100.
46. "To All Former Workers' Delegates to the Soviet Union" (in English), VTsSPS Otdel vneshnikh snoshenii, 28 February 1931, GARF f. 5451, op. 13a, d. 325, ll. 30–34, quotation l. 31; Amy Randall, *The Soviet Dream World of Retail Trade and Consumption in the 1930s* (London: Palgrave Macmillan, 2008).
47. Erika Maria Wolf, "*USSR in Construction*: From Avant-Garde to Socialist Realist Practice" (Ph.D. diss., University of Michigan, 1999): 80–123.
48. Bagdasarian, et al., *Sovetskoe zazerkal'e*, 21.
49. See the conclusion of this book.
50. For more on this shift, see Michael David-Fox, "From Illusory 'Society' to Intellectual 'Public': VOKS, International Travel, and Party-Intelligentsia Relations in the Interwar Period," *Contemporary European History* 11, 1 (February 2002): 7–32.
51. "Poiasnenie povestki dnia dlia mitinga, sozyvaemogo VOKSom 23 noiabria 1930 g. v TsEKUBU," GARF f. 5283, op. 1, ed. khr. 139, l. 16, 29).
52. "Zapiski o polozhenii i rabote [VOKS]," not signed, 1931, GARF f. 5283, op. 1, d. 158, ll. 100–101; "V. Pokrovskii, Upolnomochennyi VOKS v Leningrade. Predsedateliu VOKS t. Petrovu," 8 February 1931, ibid., op. 1a, d. 189, l. 23; "Protokol udarnoi komissii ot 26.XI [1931]," ibid., op. 1, ed. khr. 139, ll. 33–35.
53. See GARF f. 5283, op. 1, d. 158, l. 100; ibid., d. 100, l. 119.
54. See Katerina Clark, "The Travelling Mode and the Horizon of Identity," chap. 4 of *Moscow, the Fourth Rome: Stalinism, Cosmopolitanism, and the Evolution of Soviet Culture, 1931–1941* (Cambridge, Mass.: Harvard University Press, 2011).
55. "Doklad referenta po tsentral'noi Evrope – t. Livit-Levent [sic], 17 iiulia 1929 g.," GARF f. 5283, op. 6, d. 57, ll. 96–103, here l. 99ob. In a number of documents, Levent-Livit's name was written as Livit-Levent.
56. Needless to say, Piscator, who lived in the Soviet Union from 1931–36, did not see himself as a mere asset; he hoped his Soviet and Comintern engagements would influence the Soviet Union in a "reciprocal process." See Lynn Mally, "Erwin Piscator and Soviet Cultural Politics," *Jahrbücher für Geschichte Osteuropas* 51, 2 (2003): 236–253, quotation 237.
57. "Zasedanie Predstavitelei sektsii nauchnykh rabotnikov v VOKS 7 dekabria 1928," GARF f. 5283, op. 1a, d. 91, l. 92; untitled plan for VOKS work, Biuro referentury, November 1929, ibid., op. 1, ed. khr. 124, ll. 18–19, quotation l. 19ob; "Proizvodstevennyi plan raboty VOK v Tsentral'noi Evrope na 1929 god," ibid., op. 6, d. 129, ll. 135–138, quotation l. 135ob.
58. Katerina Clark, "The Author as Producer: Cultural Revolution in Berlin and Moscow (1930–1931)," chap. 1 of *Moscow, the Fourth Rome*.
59. Indeed, the attempt to place Soviet articles abroad originated with "providing service" for friendship societies' journals. Counter-propaganda remained a consistent motivation over the years, GARF f. 5283, op. 1., d. 47, l. 91, 96, 113–115; "Otchet po kampanii VOKS protiv interventsii za period s 20 noiabria po 20 ianvaria s. g. [1930]," ibid., ed. khr. 139, l. 109; "Otchet o rabote VOKS 1 iiulia 1929–1 marta 1930 g.," GARF f. 7668, op. 1, d. 215, ll. 1–71, here l. 33; Kiseleva, 59–61. In her examination of VOKS materials in France in the late 1920s, Stern showed that outlets included a range of scholarly and cultural periodicals and specialist journals, as well as publishing houses and the communist *l'Humanité*. Ludmila Stern, *Western Intellectuals and the Soviet Union, 1920–1940: From Red Square to the Left Bank* (London: Routledge, 2007), 94–97.
60. The above is based on Herta Wolf, *Glauben machen: Über deutschsprachige Reiseberichte aus der Sowjetunion (1918–1932)* (Vienna: Sonderzahl, 1992), 225–256, quotation 230.
61. Wolf, "*USSR in Construction*," chap. 2, esp. 80–82.
62. "Protokol Sekretariata VOKS," 18 May 1926, GARF f. 5283, op. 1, d. 62, ll. 3–6.
63. O. D. Kameneva, "V Otdel Pechati TsK VKP(b)," 22 March 1928, ibid., op. 1a, ed. khr. 118, ll. 42–43.
64. Shubin (NKID Otdel pechati i informatsii) to O. D. Kameneva, no date, 1928, GARF f. 5283, op. 1, ed. khr. 63, l. 90; E. Levin (first secretary of Soviet embassy in Rome) to F. N. Petrov, 10 July 1930, ibid., op. 1a, d. 145, l. 49.

65. J. Calvitt Clark III, *Russia and Italy Against Hitler: The Bolshevik-Fascist Rapprochement Against Hitler* (New York: Greenwood Press, 1991); Pier Giorgio Zunino, *L'ideologia del fascismo: Miti, credenze e valore nella stabilizzazione del regime* (Bologna: Il Mulino, 1985), 322–44; I. A. Khorman, "Dogovor o druzhbe, nenapadenii i neitralitete SSSR i Italii 2 sentriabria 1933," in *Rossiia i Italiia: XX vek*, vyp. 3, ed. N. P. Komolova, et al. (Moscow: Nauka, 1998), 71–96.

66. On various Italo-Soviet cultural contacts in 1930, see GARF f. 5283, op. 1a, d. 145, l. 23, l. 26, l. 38, l. 41, l. 41, l. 51. In 1933, the VOKS representative in Italy was TASS correspondent Viktor Kin, who resigned after VOKS repeatedly was late for or backed out of agreements and did not reimburse him for expenses. See Kin's letter from 5 September 1933 and his resignation letter, ibid., d. 210, l. 12, l. 24.

67. Ralph A. Reynolds, "Social Hygiene in Soviet Russia," *Journal of Social Hygiene* 16, 8 (November 1930): 465–482, here 478–479; Isidor Amdur (head of Anglo-American Sector of VOKS) to Dr. Ralph Reynolds, 1 October 1931, GARF f. 5283, op. 3, d. 187, l. 122. Reynolds also kept VOKS informed about his similar 24 September 1930 *Nation* article on the "Doctor in Soviet Russia."

68. O. A. Merritt-Hawkes to Amdur, 18 August 1932, GARF f. 5283, op. 3, ed. khr. 325, l. 3; Louis Anderson Fenn to Amdur, 28 September 1932, ibid., ll. 5–7; Amdur to Fenn, 9 October 1932, ibid., l. 4; Amdur to "Mrs. Mernitt-Hawkes" [sic], no date, ibid., l. 2.

69. Niels Erik Rosenfeldt, *The "Special" World: Stalin's Power Apparatus and the Soviet System's Secret Structures of Communication*, 2 vols. (Copenhagen: Museum Tusculanum Press, 2009), 1: esp. 192–223.

70. "Polozhenie o referenture V.O.K.S. fevral' 1929," GARF f. 5283, op. 1, ed. khr. 123, l. 1; "Protokol zasedaniia Biuro Pravleniia sovmestno s Biuro OVS [Otdel vneshnykh sviazi]," 28 December 1930, ibid., d. 193, l. 2.

71. For example, "Dvukhnedel'nyi otchet No. 2 Sektora Tsentral'noi Evropy s 16-go po 31 dekabria 1932 g.," GARF f. 5283, op. 1, ed. khr. 219, ll. 15–23; "Dvukhnedel'nyi otchet No. 3 Sektora Tsentral'noi Evropy s 15-go po 31 ianvaria 1933 g.," ibid., ll. 8–15.

72. I. Korinets (Acting Director of VOKS) to V. M. Molotov, 13 May 1927, GARF f. 5283, op. 1a, d. 97, l. 68; Leonid Krasin and Kameneva letters to the Politburo, no exact date, early 1926, ibid., d. 42, ll. 17–22, 32–34; Kameneva, "V komissiiu Vneshnykh Otnoshenii TsK VKP," 2 June 1926, RGASPI f. 17, op. 85, d. 38, l. 3. The Orgburo approved VOKS organization of the Frankfurt musical exhibition on 20 May 1927 (GARF f. 5283, op. 1a, d. 97, l. 70). For high-level concern in 1922 that traveling Soviet artists would fall under the influence of émigrés, see the correspondence among Lunacharskii, the NKID, and INO OGPU in AVP RF f. 082, op. 5, d. 50, p. 10, ll. 1–5.

73. Wolf, "*USSR in Construction*," 24.

74. Karl Schlögel, "Moskau in Paris," chap. 12 of *Terror und Traum: Moskau 1937* (Munich: Carl Hanser Verlag, 2008), 267–79, quotation 271; Ivan Maiskii, *Dnevnik diplomata: London 1934–1943*, 2 vols. (Moscow: Nauka, 2006), 1:180. For another major case, see Anthony Swift, "The Soviet World of Tomorrow of the New York World's Fair, 1939," *Russian Review* 57 (July 1998): 364–379.

75. O. D. Kameneva, "V APO TsK VKP(b)," 17 January 1928 (on 10th anniversary of October exhibitions), GARF f. 5283, op. 1a, d. 118, ll. 5–7; I. I. Ionov, "Vystavka v S.A.S.Sh.," sent to VOKS and the Central Committee, 18 January 1928, ibid., ed. khr. 104, ll. 2–11; Zam. Pred. VOKS L. Cherniavskii, "V Komissiiu sovetskogo kontrolia tov. Shneersonu," 7 January 1937 (on small exhibitions and political control); "Plan sovetskogo otdela Mezhdunarodnogo vystavki knigopechatanii dlia slepykh," ibid., d. 276, l. 28.

76. V. N. Polovtsevaia to O. D. Kameneva, GARF f. 5283, op. 1a, ed. khr. 43, ll. 26–29; "Russian Posters. Appeals to People to be Clean," *Westminster Gazette*, 18 May 1925 (ibid., l. 30). For clippings of press reviews of a German Society of Friends exhibition in 1928, see GARF f. 5451, op. 13a, d. 239, ll. 33–34.

77. I. I. Ionov, "Vystavka v S.A.S.Sh.," ll. 2–11 (cited above).

78. F. N. Petrov, "Tov. Ugarovu. OGPU," 30 May 1930, GARF f. 5283, op. 1a, d. 145, l. 22; Petrov, "Inostr. Otdel. AOMS," 19 May 1930, ibid., l. 21; Petrov to comrade Kristi (director of Tret'iakov Gallery), 29 April 1930, ibid., l. 13 (see also ibid., l. 12, l. 18).

79. GARF f. 5283, op. 1, d. 158, ll. 47–75; ibid., op. 1a, d. 145, l. 2; ibid., l. 21.

80. "Otdel SSSR Na Trekhgodichnoi Vystavke v Montse," translated into Russian from *Il Popolo di Roma*, 16 September 1930, AVP RF f. 010, op. 1, p. 1, d. 20, ll. 2–3.

81. Iosif Stalin, "O zadachakh khoziaistvennikov," *Sochineniia*, vol. 13 (Moscow: Politizdat, 1953), 38–39.

82. On this strategy, see Harris, "Encircled by Enemies," 529.

83. The term comes from Ian Buruma and Avishai Margalit, *Occidentalism: The West in the Eyes of Its Enemies* (New York: Penguin Press, 2004).

Chapter 6

1. David Caute, *The Fellow-Travellers: Intellectual Friends of Communism*, rev. ed. (New Haven: Yale University Press, 1988), 154.

2. Lev Trotskii, "Literaturnye poputchiki revoliutsii," in *Literatura i revoliutsiia* (Moscow: Izdatel'stvo 'Krasnaia nov', 1923), 40–83.

3. For just one example, see GARF f. 5283, op. 1a, ed. khr. 118, l. 46.

4. T. F. Evans, "Introduction: The Political Shaw," and "Shaw as a Political Thinker, or the Dogs that Did Not Bark," in *Shaw and Politics*, ed. Evans (University Park: Penn State University Press, 1991), 1–21, 21–26, quotations 21, 22.

5. George Bernard Shaw, *Shaw: An Autobiography 1856–1898*, ed. Stanley Weintraub (Toronto: Max Reinhardt, 1969), 115, 129, 132; Paul A. Hummert, *Bernard Shaw's Marxian Romance* (Lincoln: Max Reinhardt, 1969), 14.

6. Quoted in Evans, "Shaw as a Political Thinker," 26–28; see also Shaw, *The Intelligent Woman's Guide to Socialism and Capitalism* (New Brunswick: Transaction Books, 1984), 373–374, 380, 441.

7. Beatrice Webb, "GBS and Mussolini," in A. M. Gibbs, ed. *Shaw: Interviews and Recollections* (Iowa City: University Press of Iowa, 1990), 354; Shaw, "Preface, On the Rocks: A Political Comedy. 1933," in *Too True to Be Good, Village Wooing, and On the Rocks: Three Plays* (New York: Dodd, Mead and Col, 1934), 180; H. M. Geduld, "Bernard Shaw and Adolf Hitler," *The Shaw Review* 4, 1 (January 1961): 11–20.

8. Hummert, 164.

9. Hummert, xii, 40, 199–200.

10. Geduld, "Bernard Shaw and Adolf Hitler," 11.

11. T. F. Evans, "Myopia or Utopia? Shaw in Russia," in *Shaw Abroad*, ed. Rodelle Weintraub (University Park: Penn State University Press, 1985), 128; F. N. Petrov (Pred. VOKS), circular letter, 16 March 1930, GARF f. 5283, op. 3, ed. khr. 325, l. 1.

12. The most detailed reconstruction is in Harry M. Geduld's introduction to Shaw, *The Rationalization of Russia*, ed. Geduld (Bloomington: Indiana University Press, 1964), 9–32.

13. J. P. Wearing, ed. *Bernard Shaw and Nancy Astor* (Toronto: University of Toronto Press, 2005), xvi, xxi, 29–31.

14. H.W.L. Dana, "Shaw in Moscow," *The American Mercury* 25, 99 (March 1932): 343–352, here 344.

15. Untitled speech by Bernard Shaw, 26 July 1931, GARF f. 5283, op. 12, d. 328, ll. 8–9.

16. "Vecher v kolonnom zale doma Soiuzov v chest' Bernarda Shou v den' ego semidesiatip-iatiletiia. 26 iiulia 1931 goda," GARF f. 5283, op. 12, d. 328, ll. 2–7; Lunacharskii, "K priezdu Bernardu Shou," RGASPI f. 142, op. 1, d. 152, ll. 9–10.

17. Arosev to Stalin, 31 July 1931, RGASPI f. 558, op. 11, ed. khr. 695, l. 60; Arosev returned to the topic after Shaw's ardently pro-Soviet U.S. radio address on 11 October 1931, Arosev to Stalin, 21 October 1931, ibid., l. 90. Shaw's *Times* articles from 13 and 20 August are in Bernard Shaw, *Agitations: Letters to the Press 1875–1950*, ed. Dan H. Laurence and James Rambeau (New York: Frederick Unger Publishing Co., 1985), 267–277; on Potemkin villages and famine, 287; on forced labor, Evans, 133; Hummert, 159.

18. Sergei Dinamov, "Bernard Shou posle poseshcheniia SSSR," in Bernard Shou [Shaw], *Izbrannye proizvedeniia*, trans. Mikhail Levidov (Moscow-Leningrad: Gosizdat khudo-zhestvennoi literatury, 1933): 3–5; Aleksandr Deich, "Bernard Shou," in Shou [Shaw],

Mysli i fragmenty (Moscow: Zhurnal'no-Gazetnoe Ob"edinenie, 1933): 7–9; see also S. Krzhizhanovskii, "Bernard Shou, ego obrazy, mysli i obraz mysli," *Internatsional'naia literatura*, no. 9 (1935): 112–122.

19. "Spravka o S. Vebbe," GARF f. 5283, op. 2, d. 311, l. 49; Samuel H. Beer, "Introduction to this Edition," in Sidney and Beatrice Webb, *A Constitution for the Socialist Commonwealth of Great Britain* (Cambridge: Cambridge University Press, 1975), x, xxxi–xxxii; Norman and Jeanne MacKenzie, "Editors' Introduction to Part III," *The Diary of Beatrice Webb*, vol. 4: 1924–1943."*The Wheel of Life*" (Cambridge, Mass.: Harvard University Press, 1985), 269. On cooperation, see Sidney and Beatrice Webb, *Soviet Communism: A New Civilization?* 2 vols. (London: Longmans, Green and Co., 1935), 1: chap. 4, 2: chap. 8, and conclusion, 1123–1125.

20. For a recent investigation of the intellectual influences on Sidney Webb (noting their similarity to those on Beatrice), see Mark Bevir, "Sidney Webb: Utilitarianism, Positivism, and Social Democracy," *Journal of Modern History* 74, 2 (2002): 217–252. See also Gertrude Himmelfarb, "The Intellectual in Politics: The Case of the Webbs," *Journal of Contemporary History* 6, 3 (1971): 3–11.

21. *The Diary of Beatrice Webb*, 4: 302, 304, 356; see also 444.

22. Ibid., 365.

23. I. M. Maiskii, *Vospominaniia sovetskogo diplomata 1925–1945 gg.* (Moscow: Nauka, 1971), 193; *The Diary of Beatrice Webb*, 4: 315.

24. *The Diary of Beatrice Webb*, 4: 300; see also Malcolm Muggeridge, *Winter in Moscow* (Boston: Little, Brown, 1934), with its blasts at "Fabian Fairyland" and "imbecilic foreign admirers" of the Soviets (vi, viii).

25. *The Diary of Beatrice Webb*, 4: 275–276 ("Editor's Introduction to Part III"), citing surviving, unpublished entries from Beatrice's 1932 "Russian Tour" notebook.

26. "Otchet o poseshchenii S. Vebba," 19 September 1934, reprinted in A. V. Golubev, *"Vzgliad na zemliu obetovanuiu…" Iz istorii sovetskoi kul'turnoi diplomatii 1920–1930-x godov* (Moscow: Institut istorii RAN, 2004), 228.

27. Webbs, *Soviet Communism*, 1: 258–272, quotation 260.

28. A. Ia. Arosev to Lazar' Kaganovich, 17 September 1934, GARF f. 5283, op. 1a, d. 255, ll. 205–206; "Otchet o poseshchenii S. Vebba," reprinted in Golubev, 227–228. Beatrice Webb solicited published State Bank documents from VOKS and Foreign Affairs in order to avoid "mistakes and misinterpretations of the statistics supplied by other sources," 28 November 1933, GARF f. 5283, op. 3, ed. khr. 347, l. 5.

29. Arosev to Kaganovich, l. 105.

30. Webbs, *Soviet Communism*, 1: 415; 2: 550–552; 554, 557, 573, 600.

31. RGASPI f. 17, op. 163, d. 1109, ll. 120–21, discussed in G. B. Kulikova, "Pod kontrolem gosudarstva: Prebyvanie v SSSR inostrannykh pisatelei v 1920–1930-x godakh," *Otechestvennaia istoriia*, no. 4 (2003), 49; Maksimenkov, "Ocherki nomenklaturnoi istorii sovetskoi literatury: Zapadnye pilgrimy u stalinskogo prestola (Feikhtvanger i drugie)," *Voprosy literatury*, no. 2 (2004): 322–327.

32. *The Diary of Beatrice Webb*, vol. 4, 375–385 (on the Purges), 438–441 (on the Pact).

33. Paul Preston, *We Saw Spain Die: Foreign Correspondents in the Spanish Civil War* (New York: Skyhorse Publishing, 2009), chap. 6.

34. Kol'tsov is a major figure in Katerina Clark, *Moscow, the Fourth Rome: Stalinism, Cosmopolitanism, and the Evolution of Soviet Culture, 1931–1941* (Cambridge, Mass.: Harvard University Press, 2011); the above is informed by this and by Clark, "Germanophone Intellectuals in Stalin's Russia: Diaspora and Cultural Identity in the 1930s," *Kritika* 2, 3 (Summer 2001), 535; Boris Frezinskii, *Pisateli i sovetskie vozhdi* (Moscow: Ellis Lak, 2008), 278–279; Sophie Coeuré, " 'Comme ils disent SSSR': Louis Aragon et L'Union soviétique dans l'années 1930," in *Les Engagements d'Aragon*, ed. Bernard Bonnier and Jacques Girault (Paris: L'Harmattan, 1997), 63–64. His collection of his writings was entitled "us and them": E. M. Kol'tsov, *Chuzhie i svoi* (Moscow-Leningrad: Gosekonomizdat, 1932); for works in praise of the OGPU and of military top brass, see Kol'tsov, *Zelenye petlitsy* (Moscow: Zhurnal'no-gazetno Ob"edinenie, 1932), and Kol'tsov, *Komandiry* (Moscow: Zhurnal'no-gazetno Ob"edinenie, 1936).

35. "Zasedanie Inostrannoi komissii SSP SSSR 29-go maia 1936 g.," RGALI f. 631, op. 14, d. 5, ll. 2–34.

36. Elizabeth Papazian, chap. 1 of *Manufacturing Truth: The Documentary Moment in Early Soviet Culture, 1921–1934* (DeKalb: Northern Illinois University Press, 2009); Maria Gough, "Radical Tourism: Sergei Tret'iakov at the Communist Lighthouse," *October*, no. 118 (Fall 2006): 159–178; Clark, "Germanophone," 535, and Clark, *Moscow, the Fourth Rome*.

37. B. Ia. Frezinskii, "Kniga vremeni i zhizni," in *Il'ia Erenburg, Pis'ma 1908–1967*, 2 vols., ed. Frezinskii, vol. 2: *Na tsokole istoriii...Pis'ma 1931–1967* (Moscow: Argaf, 2004), 5, 8. The best biography of Ehrenburg remains Joshua Rubenstein, *Tangled Loyalties: The Life and Times of Ilya Ehrenburg* (Tuscaloosa: University of Alabama Press, 1999, orig. 1996).

38. "Rech' na pervom vsesoiuznom s"ezde sovetskikh pisatelei," in Il'ia Erenburg, *Sobranie sochinenii v vos'mi tomakh*, vol. 4: *Ocherki, Reportazhi, Esse 1922–1939* (Moscow: Khudozhestvennaia literatura, 1991), 567–578, quotation 570.

39. Coeuré, "Comme ils disent SSSR," 63, 64, 67; on Ehrenburg and Kol'tsov as antagonists and mutual denunciations and complaints among the Westernizers, see Maksimenkov, "Ocherki," 330.

40. Karl Schlögel, *Berlin, Ostbahnhof Europas: Russen und Deutsche in ihrem Jahrhundert* (Berlin: Siedler Verlag, 1998), chap. 5, quotations 112, 123.

41. Sabine Dullin, *Hommes d'influences: Les ambassadeurs de Staline en Europe 1930–1939* (Paris: Payot, 2001), 182–204, esp. 185; Dullin,"Les ambassades soviétiques en Europe dans les années 1930," *Communisme*, no. 49–50 (1997): 17–28.

42. "Arosev, Alekandr Iakovlevich," 1931 autobiography for Society of Old Bolsheviks, RGASPI f. 124, op. 1, ed. khr. 80, ll. 4–14; Ol'ga Aroseva and V. A. Maksimova, *Bez grima* (Moscow: Izdatel'stvo Tsentrpoligraf, 1999), 12.; A. Chernobaev, *V vikhre veka* (Moscow: Moskovskii rabochii, 1987), 166.

43. Having survived the Purges, like Ehrenburg, Maiskii also pushed de-Stalinization forward during the Thaw. Robert D. English, *Russia and the Idea of the West: Gorbachev, Intellectuals, and the End of the Cold War* (New York: Columbia University Press, 2000), 91, 283 n. 192.

44. A. O. Chubar'ian, "Predislovie," in Ivan Mikhailovich Maiskii, *Dnevnik diplomata: London 1934–1943*, 2 vols. (Moscow: Nauka, 2006), 1: 6.

45. Neal Wood, *Communism and British Intellectuals* (London: Victor Gollancz, 1959), 31, 43–47.

46. Maiskii, *Dnevnik*, 1: 410–411.

47. *The Diary of Beatrice Webb*, 4: 301, 349, 363.

48. Maiskii, *Vospominaniia*, 194.

49. Maiskii, *Dnevnik*, 1: 93, 202–203, 410.

50. Arosev, diary entry of 4 June 1935, in Aroseva and Maksimova, *Bez grima*; for more on Arosev, see Michael David-Fox, "Stalinist Westernizer? Aleksandr Arosev's Literary and Political Depictions of Europe," *Slavic Review* 62, 4 (Winter 2003): 733–759.

51. Application to Society of Old Bolsheviks, prob. 1931, RGASPI f. 124, op. 1, ed. khr. 80, ll. 6, 14; Nikolai Trachenko, "Sled na zemle," introduction to Arosev, *Belaia lestnitsa: Roman, povesti, rasskazy* (Moscow: Sovremennik, 1989), 8.

52. Arosev, diary entry of 6 March 1935, in Aroseva and Maksimova, *Bez grima*, 73.

53. Arosev, diary entries of 6 August 1933, 24 October 1933, 9 December 1933, December 1935 (no day), in Aroseva and Maksimova, *Bez grima*, 48, 61, 72; on Stalin as *aziat*, 37.

54. Arosev to Stalin, 12 March 1929, RGASPI f. 558, op. 11, ed. khr. 695, ll. 2–4 (the italicized phrase is in capital letters in the orig.); Arosev to Stalin, 3 March 1934, ibid., ll. 107–108; Arosev to Stalin, 23 May 1931, ibid., ll. 56–57.

55. Aroseva and Maksimova, *Bez grima*, 84.

56. Arosev, diary entry of 7 January 1935, in Aroseva and Maksimova, *Bez grima*, 68. For similar sentiments toward Shaw and other British intellectuals after a London meeting, see entry from 18 June 1935, 70.

57. "Stenogramma doklada A. Ia. Aroseva, 'O vstrechakh i besedakh s vidneishimi predstaveiteliami zapadno-evropeiskoi intelligentsii," 4 May 1935, RGALI f. 631, op. 14, ed.

khr. 3, ll. 1-24, quotations l. 17, l. 21. Arosev was a member of the *pravlenie* (administration) of the Foreign Section.

58. "Stenogramma doklada A. Ia. Aroseva," quotations l. 16, l. 22; Arosev, entries of 24 September 1934 and 18 June 1935, in Aroseva and Maksimova, *Bez grima*, 65, 70.

59. Arosev, diary entry of 26 September 1934, in Aroseva and Maksimova, *Bez grima*, 65.

60. Arosev, *Besedy i vstrechy s nashimi druz'iami v Evrope* (Moscow, 1935), 13, 31-32, and passim (quotation 38).

61. The last of these meetings was with the anti-fascist writers from Republican Spain, Rafael Alberti and Maria Teresa León, in March 1937 (Maksimenkov, "Ocherki," 279. For a full list of Stalin's visitors, see "Alfavitnyi ukazatel' posetitelei kremlevskogo kabineta I.V. Stalina," *Istoricheskii arkhiv*, no. 4 (1998): 16-203.

62. On these points, see Erik van Ree, "Heroes and Merchants: Stalin's Understanding of National Character," *Kritika* 8, 1 (2007): 41-65; Roy Medvedev, "European Writers on their Meetings with Stalin," *Russian Politics and Law* 42, 5 (Sept.-Oct. 2004): 78-92.

63. Medvedev, "European Writers," 91.

64. "Beseda s nemetskim pisatelem Emilem Liudvigom, 13 dekabria 1931 g.," in Stalin, *Sochineniia*, vol. 13 (Moscow: Gospolitizdat, 1951), 104-123.

65. Ibid. 121.

66. David Brandenberger, "Stalin as Symbol: A Case Study of the Personality Cult and its Construction," in *Stalin: A New History*, ed. Sarah Davies and James Harris (Cambridge: Cambridge University Press, 2005): 257-259; G. B. Kulikova, "Iz istorii formirovaniia kul'ta lichnosti Stalina (A. Barbius i sozdanie biografii 'otsa narodov' v nachale 1930-x gg.," *Otechestvennaia istoriia*, no. 6 ((2006), 98-99.

67. Ian [Jan] Plamper, *Alkhimiia vlasti: Kul't Stalina v izobrazitel'nom iskusstve* (Moscow: NLO, 2010), sections on "Stalin's Modesty," 185-208; the above remarks also draw on Yves Cohen, "The Cult of Number One in an Age of Leaders," *Kritika* 8, 3 (Summer 2007): 597-634. See also Balász Apor, et al., eds. *The Leader Cult in Communist Dictatorships: Stalin and the Eastern Bloc* (New York: Palgrave Macmillan, 2004), and Klaus Heller and Jan Plamper, eds., *Personality Cults in Stalinism / Personenkulte im Stalinismus* (Göttingen: V&R unipress, 2004).

68. Henri Barbusse, *Staline: Un monde nouveau vu à travers un homme* (Paris: Flammarion, 1935); Cohen, 603-604. Unwanted yet democratic adulation by a still backward people became the standard explanation given to foreigners and anti-fascists, such as Lion Feuchtwanger in 1937, who were troubled by the all-pervasive Soviet celebration of the leader.

69. On the ratification of plans for Barbusse's 1927 reception, "Otdel po priemu inostrantsev VOKS"a. Otchet o priezde i prebyvanii v Moskve Anri Barbiussa v techenii 10 i 11 sentiabria 1927 g.," RGASPI f. 495, op. 95, d. 22, ll. 152-156; see also VOKS report on Barbusse, 26 June 1928, GARF f. 5283, op. 8, ed. khr. 62, l. 155-156; Henri Barbusse to O. D. Kameneva, GARF f. 5283, op. 1a, ed. khr. 118, l. 175. On the feud between Barbusse and MORP, see Stern, chap. 3, esp. 56-65; on good relations between Barbusse and VOKS, 149-153. MORP attacks peaked in early to mid-1932; see, e.g., "Zadachi Soiuza revoliutsionnykh pisatelei Frantsii," *Literatura mirovoi revoliutsii*, no. 2 (1932): 59-65; Bruno-Iasenskii, "Monde. Directeur: Henri Barbusse," in ibid., 66-67.

70. A. Barbius, "K voprosu o perevodakh," *Vestnik inostrannoi literatury*, no. 8 (August 1928): 131-132.

71. Medvedev, "European Writers," 78

72. "Kratkoe izlozhenie Besedy s tov. Barbiussom ot 16.IX.27," RGASPI f. 558, op. 11, ed. khr. 699, ll. 2-10, quotations l. 6.

73. Barbusse to Stalin, 20 November 1929, RGASPI f. 558, op. 11, ed. khr. 699, l. 21-22.

74. Henri Barbusse, *Voici ce qu'on a fait de la Géorgie* (Paris: Flammarion, 1929), 127-128.

75. "Svidanie tov. Stalina s Anri Barbiussom," 5 October 1932, RGASPI f. 558, op. 11, ed. khr. 699, ll. 35-41.

76. Lev Mekhlis to Stalin, 4 November 1932, RGASPI f. 558, op. 11, ed. khr. 699, l. 60 (Stalin's response is handwritten on the letter); see also Mekhlis to Stalin, 6 May 1932, ibid., ll. 27-28.

77. Barbusse to Münzenberg (in French and Russian translation), RGASPI f. 558, op. 11, ed. khr. 699, l. 63, 64; Kul'tprop TsK to Sekretariat t. Stalina, 8 December 1932, ibid., l. 61; additional correspondence on Barbusse's meeting with and biography of Stalin, l. 55, ll. 71–72, ll. 84–85. Barbusse had defended the *Monde* publications of articles by Victor Serge and Madeleine Paz in May 1932 (Stern, 62). For his correspondence with Münzenberg, see Kulikova, "Iz istorii," 102.

78. "Nabrosok stsenariia" for Barbusse film with the possible titles: Creators, Builders, Saviors, New People (Tvortsy, Stroiteli, Spasiteli, Novye Liudi), RGASPI f. 558, op. 11, ed. khr. 700, ll. 8–17; Kulikova, "Iz istorii," 102–103.

79. V. S. Lel'chuk, "Beseda I.V. Stalina s angliiskim pisatelem G. Uellsom (dokumenty, interpretatsiia, razmyshleniia)," in *Istoricheskaia nauka na rubezhe vekov*, ed. A. A. Fursenko (Moscow: Nauka, 2001): 345, citing transcript of interview with Mints in the author's personal archive.

80. Plamper, *Alkhimiia vlasti*, chap. 1.

81. A. I. Stetskii to Henri Barbusse, 29 September 1934, RGASPI f. 558, op. 11, ed. khr. 699, ll. 124–125; Barbusse, *Staline*, quotations 21, 36; Sophie Coeuré, *La grande lueur a l'Est: Les français et l'Union soviètique 1917–1939* (Paris: Éditions du Seuil, 1999), 233–35. For the Glavlit prohibition on the import of the 13 June 1935 issue of *Monde*, see RGASPI f. 558, op. 11, ed. khr. 700, l. 123.

82. Stetskii to Barbusse, ll. 124–125; Barbusse, *Staline*, 43, 189, 192, 201.

83. VOKS report on Barbusse by Iu. Mazel', Sept. 1927, RGASPI f. 495, op. 95, d. 22, ll. 152–156, quotation l. 153; Barbusse, *Staline*, 87, cited in Coeuré, *La grande lueur*, 235; Stetskii, "Predislovie," in Anri Barbius, *Stalin: Chelovek, cherez kotorogo raskryvaetsia novyi mir*, ed. and trans. Stetskii (Moscow: n.p., 1936), ix, x.

84. Mikhail Kol'tsov, "Barbius o Staline," in Anri Barbius, *Iunost' Stalina (Otryvok iz knigi "Stalin")* (Moscow: Molodoi kommunar, 1935), reprinted from *Pravda*, 5, 7; Barbusse, *Staline*, 6.

85. Lel'chuk, 336, 339, 344, 346; Leonid Maksimenkov, "Ocherki nomenklaturnoi istorii sovetskoi literatury: Zapadnye pilgrimy u stalinskogo prestola (Feikhtvanger i drugie). Chast' II," *Voprosy literatury*, no. 3 (2004): 303–304.

86. H. G. Wells, *Experiment in Autobiography: Discourses and Conclusions of a Very Ordinary Brain* (Since 1866) (New York: Macmillan, 1934), 626, 562, 563; Wells, *After Democracy* (London: Watts, 1932).

87. "Stalin and Wells: A Comment by Bernard Shaw," *New Statesman and Nation*, 3 November 1934, 613; for confirmation of Shaw's judgment, see Wells, *Experiment in Autobiography*, 689. The text of the conversation is in I. V. Stalin, *Beseda s angliiskim pisatelem G. D. Uellsom* (Moscow: Partizdat TsK VKP(b), 1935), and in English in *New Statesman and Nation*, 27 October 1934.

88. Wells, *Experiment in Autobiography*, 684, 689.

89. "Glava iz knigi g. Uel'sa 'Opyt avtobiografii' posveshchennaia ego poslednei poezdke v SSSR," RGASPI f. 558, op. 11, d. 792, ll. 122–46; Radek to Stalin, 9 November 1934, ibid., l. 121.

90. Arosev to Stalin, 30 July 1934, GARF f. 5283, op. 1a, d. 255, l. 70; Lel'chuk, 350.

91. Kaganovich to Stalin, 24 September 1934, in Oleg Khelvniuk, et al., eds., *Stalin i Kaganovich: Perepiska 1931–1936 gg.* (Moscow: ROSSPEN, 2001), 495, 496 n. 5; Radek to Stalin, 9 November 1934, l. 121; Lel'chuk, 351.

92. Fisher, 27–29.

93. The unedited version, which has never been published, is: "Beseda t. Stalina s Romen Rollanom. Perevodil razgovor t. A. Arosev. 28.VI.sg [1935]," with handwritten addition: "ne dlia pechati," RGASPI f. 558, op. 11, ed. khr. 775, l. 1–16, here l. 13; for Rolland's opening statement, see Rolland, *Voyage à Moscou (juin–juillet 1935)*, ed. Bernard Duchatelet (Paris: Albin Michel, 1992), 127. An appendix to *Voyage* contains an "official" transcript of the discussion with Stalin, which was edited by Stalin personally and then sent to Rolland when he was visiting with Gorky; Rolland made a few more changes. Historians in the past have referred only to the sanitized variants in French and Russian. I have argued elsewhere that while the variations of the text need to be compared, the

unedited version is the most revealing, and it is here that Rolland appears most worshipful of Stalin. See Michael David-Fox, "The 'Heroic Life' of a Friend of Stalinism: Romain Rolland and Soviet Culture," *Slavonica* 11, 1 (2005): 3–29.

94. Romain Rolland to Maxim Gorky, 10 August 1931, in *Correspondance entre Romain Rolland et Maxime Gorki* (Paris: Éditions Albin Michel, 1991), 243; "Beseda t. Stalina s Romen Rollanom," l. 4; *Romain Rolland and Gandhi Correspondence (Letters, Diary Extracts, Articles, Etc.)* (New Delhi: Publications Division, Ministry of Information and Broadcasting, 1976), 163–230; Fisher, 29–31.

95. Rolland, *Voyage*, 133; quotation in Fisher, 255. Goethe was the key icon in the Germanophone anti-fascist culture of the period.

96. Arosev, diary entry of 7 January 1935, in Aroseva and Maksimova, 67–69; 1935 letter from Rolland to J.-P. Samson cited in Duchatelet, *Romain Rolland*, 321–322.

97. Arosev to Stalin, 29 June 1935, GARF f. 5283, op. 1, d. 276, ll. 71–72.

98. "Beseda t. Stalina s Romen Rollanom," ll. 2, 3, 4.

99. Valentin Berezhkov, *Kak ia stal perevodchikom Stalina* (Moscow: Dem, 1993), 177.

100. "Beseda t. Stalina s Romen Rollanom," l. 8; Rolland to Gorky, 28 March 1931, in *Correspondance*, 225; Gorky to Rolland, 1–2 August 1933, in *M. Gor'kii i R. Rollan. Perepiska (1916–1936)* (Moscow: Nasledie, 1995), 273.

101. "Pis'mo Romen Rollana tovarishchu Stalinu," 20 June 1935, RGALI f. 631, op. 11, d. 283, l. 13. See also, for example, Rolland to Platon Kerzhentsev, 4 April 1936, RGASPI f. 631, op. 14, ed. khr. 729, l. 19.

102. "Beseda t. Stalina s Romen Rollanom," l. 3, 13; Gorky to Rolland, 29 August 1935 and 12 September 1935, in *M. Gor'kii i R. Rollan*, 313–315; Duchatelet, *Romain Rolland*, 315; Liudmilla Stern, *Western Intellectuals*, 27–28.

103. Rolland to Stalin, 1 October 1935, RGASPI f. 558, op. 11, ed. khr. 775, l. 120; Rolland to Stalin 27 December 1935, ibid., ll. 125–130; Gor'kii to Stalin, 8 July and 29 August 1935, ibid., ed. khr. 720, l. 80, 82–83; Bukharin quoted in G. B. Kulikova, "Pod kontrolem gosudarstva: Prebyvanie v SSSR inostrannykh pisatelei v 1920–1930-x godakh," *Otechestvennaia istoriia*, no. 4 (2003), 52. On Bukharin's interrupted meeting with Gide, see Caute, 105.

104. Rolland, *Voyage*, 142–43, 161, 182, 199, 284; Fisher, 248–249; Duchatelet, 317–325.

105. Rolland, *Voyage*, 137–139; Fisher, 236; Duchatelet, 322.

106. RGALI f. 631, op. 14, d. 74, l. 91; Coeuré, *La grande lueur*, 26; Michel Vovelle, "1789–1917: The Game of Analogies," in *The Terror*, vol. 4 of *The French Revolution and the Creation of Modern Political Culture*, ed. Keith Michael Baker (Tarrytown, N.Y.: Pergamon, 1994), 349–378; Eva Oberloskamp, *Fremde neue Welten: Reisen deutscher und französischer Linksintellektueller in die Sowjetunion 1917–1939* (Munich: Oldenbourg, 2011), chap. 5, section B.

107. Rolland to Mariia Kudasheva, 18 September 1929, GARF f. 5283, op. 1a, d. 129, l. 120–121.

108. See Rolland to Gorky, 20 July 1933, in *Correspondance*, 312.

109. "Inostrannaia komissiia. Frantsiia. Biograficheskie svedeniia o frantszuskikh pisateliakh," RGALI f. 631, op. 14, ed. khr. 716.

110. "Beseda t. Stalina s. Romen Rollanom," l. 15; Rolland, *Voyage*, 133, 246.

111. As noted by Jeffrey Brooks, *Thank You, Comrade Stalin! Soviet Public Culture from Revolution to Cold War* (Princeton: Princeton University Press, 2000), 149.

112. "Stat'i sovetskoi pechati o prazdnovanii 70-letiia so dnia rozhdeniia R. Rollana," RGALI f. 631, op. 14, ed. khr. 735. Arosev's article "Romen Rollan (k 70-letiiu so dnia rozhdeniia)" was published in *Pravda Vostoka* and many other newspapers on 29 and 30 January 1936.

113. "70 let Romen Rollanu. Torzhestvennyi vecher v bol'shom zale konservatorii," *Komsomolskaia Pravda*, 30 January 1936, in RGALI f. 631, op. 14, ed. khr. 735, l. 17; "V Bol'shom zale konservatorii," program of 29 January 1936, ibid., op. 11, d. 283, l. 63.

114. Mikhail Apletin to Mikhail Kol'tsov, 8 December 1935, RGALI f. 631, op. 11, d. 283, l. 76, see also l. 75; on the album, ibid., op. 14, ed. khr. 729, ll. 55–56.

115. Fisher, 256–257, quotation 257; Duchatelet, 324.

116. François Hourmant, *Au pays de l'avenir radieux: Voyages des intellectuels français en URSS, à Cuba et en Chine populaire* (Paris: Aubier, 2000), 166.

117. With his view of communism as the great myth of the twentieth century, François Furet bucked this tendency by suggesting its flexible ability to appeal to vastly different figures. Furet, *The Passing of an Illusion: The Idea of Communism in the Twentieth Century*, trans. Deborah Furet (Chicago: Chicago University Press, 1999).

118. Arthur Koestler, untitled essay in *The God that Failed*, ed. Richard Crossman (New York: Columbia University Press, 2001, orig. 1949), 15.

119. For example, see Lee Congdon, *Seeing Red: Hungarian Intellectuals in Exile and the Challenge of Communism* (DeKalb: Northern Illinois University Press, 2001), 3.

120. Caute, 264–284.

121. Mark Lilla, *The Reckless Mind: Intellectuals and Politics* (New York: NYRB, 2001), 200–202. Having pointed out the failures of other all-encompassing theories of intellectuals and communism, Lilla then provides one of his own, which might be called the psychological explanation: intellectuals are by nature inclined to abandon moderate self-control and embrace tyranny, thus giving in to "a drive that could become a reckless passion" (214).

122. See Paul Hollander, *Political Pilgrims: Travels of Western Intellectuals to the Soviet Union, China, and Cuba, 1928–1978*, 4th ed. (New York: Oxford University Press, 1981); Robert Conquest, "The Great Error: Soviet Myths and Western Minds," in Conquest, *Reflections on a Ravaged Century* (New York: Norton, 2001), 115–149; Stéphane Courtois, introduction to Courtois, et al., *Le livre noir du communisme. Crimes, terreur, répression* (Paris: Robert Laffont, 1997). For the charge of treason, see Stephen Schwartz, *Intellectuals and Assassins: Writings at the End of Soviet Communism* (London: Anthem Press, 2000), 9–17, 80, 139.

123. Oberloskamp, *Fremde neue Welten*; David C. Engerman, *Modernization from the Other Shore: American Intellectuals and the Romance of Russian Development* (Cambridge, Mass.: Harvard University Press, 2003); Sheila Fitzpatrick and Carolyn Rasmussen, eds., *Political Tourists: Travellers from Australia to the Soviet Union in the 1920s–1940s* (Carlton, Vic.: Melbourne University Press, 2008).

124. Tony Judt, *Past Imperfect: French Intellectuals, 1944–1956* (Berkeley: University of California Press, 1992), 149, 205–226; by contrast, Oberloskamp, *Fremde neue Welten*, found a notable commitment to universal Enlightenment ideals among French Left intellectual commentators of the interwar period.

125. Daniel Soyer, "Back to the Future: American Jews Visit the Soviet Union in the 1920s and 1930s," *Jewish Social Studies* 6, 3 (2000): 124–59, quotation 129; see also Lewis S. Feuer, "American Travelers to the Soviet Union 1917–32: The Formation of a Component of New Deal Ideology," *American Quarterly* 42, 2, part 1 (Summer 1962): 119–49, on this point 121.

Chapter 7

1. See, most recently, Michael Geyer and Sheila Fitzpatrick, eds., *Beyond Totalitarianism: Stalinism and Nazism Compared* (Cambridge: Cambridge University Press, 2009); A. V. Golubev, *"Esli mir obrushitsia na nashu Respubliku": Sovetskoe obshchestvo i vneshnaia ugroza* (Moscow: Kuchkova pole, 2008).

2. The phrases come from Alan Megill, *Prophets of Extremity: Nietzsche, Heiddegger, Foucault, Derrida* (Berkeley: University of California Press, 1985), and Stephen Kotkin, "Modern Times: The Soviet Union and the Interwar Conjuncture," *Kritika* 2, 1 (2001): 111–164. In Schmitt's key passage on the friend-enemy distinction—"the high points of politics are simultaneously the moments in which the enemy is, in concrete clarity, recognized as the enemy"—he approvingly points to Lenin's attacks against "bourgeois and western capitalism." Carl Schmitt, *The Concept of the Political*, trans. George Schwab (Chicago: University of Chicago Press, 2007), 67. Interestingly, Schmitt's concept of friend, much like the Bolsheviks', was generated out of his idea of enemy (Tracy B. Strong, "Foreword: Dimensions of the New Debate around Carl Schmitt," in ibid., xxiv).

3. M. Zhivov, "Druz'ia i vragi o SSSR (ot sostavitelia)," in *Glazami inostrantsev 1917–1932*, ed. L. Gasviani (Moscow: Gosizdat khudozhestvennoi literatury, 1932), xiii–xxxi.

4. A. V. Lunacharskii, "Dlia 'Vechernei Moskvy," RGASPI f. 142, op. 1, d. 152, l. 7–8; "Privetstevennoe slovo t. A. V. Lunacharskii Anri Barbiuss. 18 sentiabria 1927 g.," l. 5.

5. F. N. Petrov to M. M. Litvinov, copy Zam. Pred. OGPU Messing, 3 January 1930, GARF f. 5283, op. 1a, ed. khr. 160, l. 24.

6. Ernst Nolte, "From the Gulag to Auschwitz," in François Furet and Ernst Nolte, *Fascism and Communism*, trans. Katherine Golsan (Lincoln: University of Nebraska Press, 1998): 23–30, here 27; *Historikerstreit: Die Dokumentation der Kontroverse um die Einzigartigkeit der nationalsozialistischen Judenvernichtung* (Munich: R. Piper, 1987); Ernst Nolte, *Der kausale Nexus: Über Revisionen und Revisionismen in der Geschichtswissenschaft. Studien, Artikel und Vorträge, 1990–2000* (Munich: Herbig, 2002).

7. Michael Geyer and Sheila Fitzpatrick, "Introduction," in *Beyond Totalitarianism: Stalinism and Nazism Compared*, 35; but for one such investigation, see "Fascination and Enmity: Russia and Germany as Entangled Histories, 1914–1945," special issue of *Kritika* 10, 3 (Summer 2009).

8. See, for example, Gerd Koenen, *Der Russland-Komplex: Die Deutschen und der Osten 1900–1945* (Munich: C. H. Beck, 2005); Michael Kellogg, *The Russian Roots of Nazism: White Émigrés and the Making of National Socialism, 1917–1945* (Cambridge: Cambridge University Press, 2005).

9. Michael Kohlstruck, "'Salonbolschewist' und Pioner der Sozialforschung: Klaus Mehnert und die Deutsche Gesellschaft zum Studium Osteuropas 1931–1934," *Osteuropa* 55, 12 (December 2005): 29–47; on Mehnert and the Arplan name, see Louis Dupeux, *"National-bolchevisme": Stratégie communiste et dynamique conservatrice. Essai sur les différent sens de L'Expression en Allegmagne, sous la Republique de Weimar (1919–1933)*, doctoral thesis, University of Paris I, 1974 (Lille: Atelier reproduction des theses, 1976), 458 n. 3. On Mehnert's position in Arplan, see "Otchet Obshchestva po izucheniiu sovetskogo planovogo khoziaistva," in *Dukh Rapallo: Sovetsko-germanskie otnosheniia 1925–1933*, ed. G. N. Sevostianov (Ekaterinburg: Nauchno-prosvetitel'skii tsentr "Universitet," 1997): 247–249.

10. In 1924, the Soviet embassy in Berlin was told that OBI and the Commissariat of Enlightenment considered it "highly desirable" that Spengler visit the USSR. "O.D. Kameneva. Pred. Komissii zagranichnoi pomoshchi Prezidiuma TsIK. Sovetniku Polpredstva v Germanii S. I. Brodovskomu," 30 September 1924, AVP RF f. 082, op. 7, d. 52, p. 18, l. 14. The condition was that Spengler "not use the trip for political or propagandistic activity."

11. On the conservative revolution, see, inter alia, Armin Mohler and Karlheinz Weissmann, *Die Konservative Revolution in Deutschland 1918–1932: Ein Handbuch*, 6th ed. (Graz: Ares, 2005); the classic Fritz Stern, *The Politics of Cultural Despair: A Study in the Rise of the Germanic Ideology* (Berkeley: University of California Press, 1961); Louis Dupeux, ed., *La "Révolution conservatrice" dans l'Allemagne de Weimar* (Paris: Éditions Kimé, 1992).

12. See esp. Otto-Ernst Schüddenkopf, *National-bolschewismus in Deutschland 1918–1933*, rev. ed. (Frankfurt: Verlag Ullstein, 1972, orig. 1960), and Dupeux, *"National-bolchevisme."* Following Dupeux, Erik van Ree argues for a restrictive definition of National Bolshevism, applying it only to the handful of "diehards" who subscribed to the original mix of nationalism and a communist economic program, not to "all those who hoped to unify rightist and leftist extremism on a nationalist platform." Van Ree, "The Concept of 'National Bolshevism': An Interpretative Essay," *Journal of Political Ideologies* 6, 3 (2001): 289–307. If one is attempting not to define but to recover the history of the concept, however, it reveals the breadth of German nationalist fascination for the Soviet project.

13. Schüddekopf, 7, 55–56, 61–62, 70–86, 111–25, 175, 287. The hardest evidence on German and Soviet communism in this period can be found in Bert Hoppe, *In Stalins Gefolgschaft: Moskau und die KPD 1928–1933* (Munich: R. Oldenbourg Verlag, 2007).

14. Jean-François Fayet, *Karl Radek: Biographie politique* (Bern: Peter Lang, 2004): 289–311, 445–467, 661–682; see also Warren Lerner, *Karl Radek: The Last Internationalist* (Stanford: Stanford University Press, 1970), 120–121.

15. Hoppe, 178, 221; cf. Fayet, *Karl Radek*, 452–460, 661–682 (quotations 453, chap. 5 title); *Politbiuro TsK RKP(b) i Komintern, 1919–1943: Dokumenty* (Moscow: ROSSPEN, 2004): 647–652.

16. For an important recent work centering on Scheringer, see Timothy S. Brown, *Weimar Radicals: Nazis and Communists between Authenticity and Performance* (New York: Berghan Books, 2009).

17. Hoppe, 88 and chaps. 5 and 8, esp. 184–188, 291–297, 311, 263.

18. Rosenfeldt, *The "Special" World: Stalin's Power Apparatus and the Soviet System's Secret Structures of Communication*, 2 vols., trans. Sally Laird and John Kendal (Copenhagen: Museum Tusculanums Forlag, 2009), 1: 205–216; see also E. A. Gnedin, *Iz istorii otnoshenii mezhdu SSSR i fashistskoi Germaniei* (New York: Khronika, 1977): 23–28.

19. "Girshfel'd. Berlin, 27 oktiabria 1932. NKID 2-i Zapadnyi Otdel – t. Sheininu," copies to Krestinskii and VOKS, GARF f. 5283, op. 1a, d. 196, ll. 193–195.

20. "Ibid., l. 193, 193 ob.

21. Ibid., l. 193.

22. Girshfel'd to F. N. Petrov, 5 February 1932, GARF f. 5283, op. 1a, d. 196, ll. 156–158; Girshfel'd to Lerner (VOKS), 18 November 1932, AVP RF f. 082, op. 15, d. 28, p. 27, l. 204. On Harnack's KPD affiliation, see B. Lange and A. N. Dmitriev, "Rabochee ob"edinenie po izucheniiu sovetskogo planovogo khoziastva (Arplan)," in *Sovetsko-germanskie nauchnye sviazi vremeni Veimarskoi Respubliki*, ed. E. I. Kolchinskii (St. Petersburg: Nauka, 2001): 197–206, here 205.

23. My discussion of Arplan membership below is based on the "Mitgliederliste" sent by Friedrich Lenz to VOKS in summer 1932: GARF f. 5283, op. 6, d. 172, l. 190. This document represents the first fully reliable confirmation of the organization's members.

24. Lukàcs, "An die Kaderabteilung der Komintern," 1941, RTsKhIDNI f. 495, op. 199, d. 181, ll. 49, 49a, published by Reinhard Müller in *Mitelweg* 5, 5 [no. 36] (1996): 66–70; see also Lange and Dmitriev, "Rabochee ob"edinenie," 205; A. N. Dmitriev, "K istorii sovetsko-germanskikh nauchnykh i politicheskikh sviazei nachala 1930-x gg.: Arplan (nemetskoe obshchestvo po izucheniiu sovetskogo planovogo khoziaistva)," in *Nemsty v Rossii: Problemy nauchnykh i kul'turnkykh sviazei* (St. Petersburg: Dmitrii Bulanin, 2000), 258, 263, 265.

25. Dupeux, "*National-bolchevisme*," 428–463.

26. For a full-length treatment of Niekisch's ideological evolution, see Michael David-Fox, "A 'Prussian Bolshevik' in Stalin's Russia: Ernst Niekisch at the Crossroads between Communism and National Socialism," in David-Fox, "Crossing Borders: Modernity, Ideology, and Culture in Soviet Russia," forthcoming book, Pittsburgh University Press. The principal studies of Niekisch are Uwe Sauermann, *Ernst Niekisch und der Revolutionäre Nationalismus* (Munich: Bibliothekdienst Angerer, 1985); Sauermann, *Ernst Niekisch zwischen allen Fronten* (Munich: Herbig Aktuell, 1980); Birgit Rätsch-Langejürgen, *Das Prinzip Widerstand: Leben und Wirken von Ernst Niekisch* (Bonn: Bouvier Verlag, 1997); and Michael Pittwald, *Ernst Niekisch: Völkische Sozialismus, nationale Revolution, deutsche Endimperium* (Cologne: PapyRossa Verlag, 2002). Niekisch also figures prominently in the major studies of German National Bolshevism: Schüddenkopf, *National-bolschewismus*; Dupeux, "*National-bolchevisme*"; Dupeux, ed., *La "Révolution conservatrice*," and he is analyzed comparatively in Stefan Breuer, *Anatomie der konservativen Revolution* (Darmstadt: Wissenschaftliche Buchgesellschaft, 1982).

27. Quotations are from Ernst Niekisch, "Der Fünfjarhplan," *Widerstand*, no. 6 (1930): 197, 199. See also Sylvia Taschka, *Das Russlandbild von Ernst Niekisch* (Erlangen and Jena: Palme & Enke, 1999).

28. Jeffrey Herf, *Reactionary Modernism: Technology, Culture and Politics in Weimar and the Third Reich* (Cambridge: Cambridge University Press, 1984), 72.

29. Koenen, 342–343; Rätsch-Langejürgen, *Das Prinzip Widerstand*, 173–80. Two members of Arplan from Heidelberg, Giselhert Wirsing and Ernst Wilhelm Eschmann, were also politically on the far Right, the first close to *Die Tat* and the second to the Nazis.

30. "Spravka o deiatel'nosti Arbplana [sic] i Soiuza rabotnikov umstvennogo truda v Germanii, podgotovlennnaia D. Lukachem dlia otdela kadrov IKKI," in *Besedy na Lubianke: Sledstvennoe delo Dërda Lukacha. Materialy k biografii*, ed. Reinhard Müller and Ia. G. Rokitianskii, 2nd rev. ed. (Moscow: Institut slavianovedeniia RAN, 2001): 118–120; Klaus Mehnert, "Memorandum über die 'Arbeitsgemeinschaft zum Studium

der sowjet russischen Planwirtschaft,' 8 January 1932," in Gerd Voigt, *Russland in der deutschen Geschichtsschreibung* 1843–1945 (Berlin: Akademie-Verlag, 1994): 381–382.

31. "Dnevnik t. Girshfel'da. Berlin, 30-go aprelia 1932," GARF f. 5283, op. 1a, d. 196, l. 182–83; Girshfel'd to Petrov, 25 April 1932, AVP RF f. 082, op. 15, d. 28, p. 71, ll. 95–98.

32. "Shuman. Zav. Otdelom Tsentral'noi Evropy [VOKS]. Tov. Girshfel'du. Upolnomochennomu VOKS v Germanii," 19 March 1932, AVP RF f. 082, op. 15, d. 28, p. 71, l. 37. See ll. 10, 22.

33. Girshfel'd, "V sektor tsentral'noi Evropy VOKS," 29 February 1932, AVP RF f. 082, op. 15, d. 28, p. 71, l. 32.

34. For example, see "Linde. Upolnomochnoe predstavitel'stvo v Germanii. Pred. VOKS tov. Petrovu. Berlin," 1 July 1932, GARF f. 5283, op. 1a, d. 196, l. 125.

35. E. O. Lerner (Zam. Pred. VOKS) to Girshfel'd, 16 December 1932, AVPR RF f. 082, op. 15, d. 28, p. 71, ll. 214–215; "Zav. 2-m Zapadnym otdelom (Shtern). Referent (Sheinan). V kollegiiu NKID," 16 November 1932, ibid., ll. 207–208; Shtern and Stroianker to Girshfel'd, 27 April 1932, ibid., l. 68.

36. D. T. Shtern, "Zam. Pred. Gos. Planovoi Komissii—tov. Mezhlauku," AVP RF f. 082, op. 16, d. 33, p. 76, ll. 1–2.

37. "G. Timm. Zav. Sektorom Tsentral'noi Evropy [VOKS]. NKID Zav. Vtorym Zap. Otdelom t. Shtern," 3 January 1932, GARF f. 5283, op. 6, d. 172, l. 23; F. N. Petrov to Girshfel'd, 17 May 1932, AVP RF f. 082, op. 15, d. 28, p. 71, l. 89; V. I. Mezhlauk to Petrov, 11 May 1932, ibid., l. 88.

38. Girshfel'd to Sheinin, 27 October 1932, GARF f. 5283, op. 1a, d. 196, ll. 193–195; Lange and Dmitriev, 204–6; Dmitriev, "K istorii," 262–266.

39. "Otdel pechati NKID. Zav. (Umanskii). Otvet. referent (Muronov). Tov. Vinogradovu, Berlin," 3 September 1932, AVP RF f. 082, op. 15, d. 28, p. 71, l. 173; O.V. Klevniuk, et al., eds., *Stalin i Kaganovich: Perepiska, 1931–1936 gg.* (Moscow: ROSSPEN, 2001), 196 n. 9.

40. Ernst Niekisch, *Erinnerungen eines deutschen Revolutionärs*, vol. 1 (Cologne: Verlag Wissenschaft und Politik, 1974): 217.

41. Kaganovich to Stalin, 3 August 1932, in *Stalin i Kaganovich*, ed. Khlevniuk, et al., 259, 304. The editors note that Hitler's growing power did not elicit significant commentary from Stalin, who was preoccupied with internal Soviet upheavals and wished to avoid an open breach with Germany. See also *Politbiuro TsK RKP(b) i Komintern*, 666–667. On Niedermayer, see Hans-Ulrich Seidt, *Berlin, Kabul, Moskau: Oskar Ritter von Niedermayer und Deutschlands Geopolitik* (Munich: Universitas Verlag, 2002). The Soviet embassy in Berlin was highly interested in Reventlow in 1932 and pursued contacts with him (Hoppe, 315, 315 n. 131).

42. Hoppe, 311–315.

43. Arplan, *Protokolle der Studienreise nach der Sowjet-Union vom 20. August bis 12. September* 1932 (Berlin: n.p., 1932), sec. 2, no pagination.

44. "Anmeldungen zur Reise nach der UdSSR," 14 July 1932, GARF f. 5283, op. 6, d. 172, l. 209; ibid., l. 171–172. A Dutch branch of Arplan opened in Amsterdam, which had more than thirty largely scholarly members and was represented in the delegation by its founder, the economist H. Frijda.

45. H. Timm, untitled report in German, GARF f. 5283, op. 6, d. 172, l. 171–176; see also "Otchet po delegatsii Arplana, pribyshei v Leningrad 23/VIII i vyekhavshei v Moskvu 26/VIII," signed V. Pokrovskii, GARF f. 5283, op. 6, d. 172, l. 143.

46. Arplan, *Protokolle*, sections 3 and 4.

47. Matthias Heeke, *Reisen zu den Sowjets: Der ausländische Tourismus in Russland* 1921–1941 (Münster: Lit Verlag, 2003), 240.

48. "M. Liubchenko. Pred. Vseukrainskogo Obshchestva kul'tsviazi. Tov. Lerneru. Zam. Pred. VOKS. 8 avgusta 1932 (Kharkiv)," AVP RF f. 082, op. 15, d. 28, p. 27, l. 187. As noted in Chapter 3, Witkin visited the sovkhoz Verbliud a few months earlier, in May 1932, with disastrous impressions.

49. Ibid., l. 187 ob.

50. Ibid., l. 187 ob, ll. 186–187.

51. "Bericht der 'Arplan'-Delegation über die Reise in der Sowjet-Union vom 23 August bis 12. September 1932," written by Dr. ing. Kelen, Privatdozent an der Technischen Hochschule, Berlin, GARF f. 5283, op. 6, d. 172, l. 66–121, here l. 74, 119–120. See also "Priem delegatsii 'Arplana' v VOKS," *Pravda*, 6 September 1932; Untitled Arplan declaration, signed by Friedrich Lenz, AVP RF f. 082, op. 15, d. 28, p. 17, l. 185.

52. Friedrich Lenz to H. Timm, 10 November 1932, GARF f. 5283, op. 6, d. 172, l. 52–54.

53. Lenz and Harnack to Lerner (VOKS), 2 October 1932, GARF f. 5283, op. 6, d. 172, l. 63.

54. "Biulleten' ne dlia pechati No. 39 Inostrannoi informatsii Tass, 9/11–33. List No. 15. 'Antisovetskii doklad fon-Gofmanstal','" Berlin, 2 November 1932, ibid., l. 11.

55. "Perevod s gollandskogo stat'i iz tsentral'nogo organa Gollandskoi sotsialisticheskoi-demokraticheskoi partii "Khet Folk," late 1932, AVP RF f. 082, op. 15, d. 28, p. 71, l. 217–26; H. Frijda, "Vier Jaren Sovjet-Economie," *De Telegraaf* (Holland), 3 November 1932, GARF f. 5283, op. 5, d. 203, l. 6; letters from Dutch Society of Friends and Frijda, November 1932, ibid. l. 30–35.

56. "Wir sind alle krank und hungern…," *Sport Zeitung*, 28 December 1932, GARF f. 5283, op. 6, d. 172, l. 11.

57. David Caute, *The Fellow-Travellers: Intellectual Friends of Communism*, rev. ed. (New Haven: Yale University Press, 1983), 137.

58. Caute, 101–106; Rachel Mazuy, *Croire plutôt que coire? Voyages en Russie soviétique (1919–1939)* (Paris: Odile Jacob, 2002), 159; Alan Sheridan, *André Gide: A Life in the Present* (Cambridge, Mass.: Harvard University Press, 1999), xv–xvi; Frederick John Harris, *André Gide and Romain Rolland: Two Men Divided* (New Brunswick: Rutgers University Press, 1973), 132.

59. The best work on Gide's entourage is, regrettably, unpublished: Florence Louisa Talks, "André Gide's Companions on his Journey to the Soviet Union in 1936: Jacques Schiffrin, Eugène Dabit, Louis Guilloux, Jef Last and Pierre Herbart" (Ph.D. diss., University of Warwick, 1987).

60. Sheridan, xii, 473, 477; "Romanskaia komissiia MORP (svodka No. 3). Frantsuzskaia komissiia. Sotsial-fashizm pytaetsia umalit' znachenie zaiavlenii Andre Zhida," 14 February 1933, RGALI f. 631, op. 14, d. 714, ll. 3–4.

61. André Gide, *Afterthoughts: A Sequel to Back from the U.S.S.R*, 2nd ed., trans. Dorothy Bussy (London: Martin Secker and Warburg, Ltd, 1937), 9, 11.

62. André Gide, *Return from the USSR*, trans. Dorothy Bussy (New York: Alfred A. Knopf, 1937), 42.

63. Ibid., 38 n. 1.

64. Sheridan, 375–379, 626.

65. On intellectuals' reactions to Soviet treatment of homosexuality, in the context of European approaches, see Eva Oberloskamp, *Fremde neue Welten: Reisen deutscher under französischer Linksintellektueller in die Sowjetunion 1917–1939* (Munich: Oldenbourg, 2011): chap. 3, sec. B. For the counter-example of Benjamin's attraction not to the notion of sexual liberation but liberation from sexuality, see Evgenii Bernshtein, "'The Withering of Private Life': Walter Benjamin in Moscow," in *Everyday Life in Early Soviet Russia: Taking the Revolution Inside*, ed. Christina Kiaer and Eric Naiman (Bloomington: Indiana University Press, 2006): 217–229.

66. Monique Nemer, *Corydon Citoyen: Essai sur André Gide et l'homosexualité* (Paris: Gallimard, 2006): 266–283, quoting diary entry of 21 June, 1931 (267). See also Caute, 101–102.

67. Evg. Gal'perina, "Put' Andre Zhida," in "Ino. Komissiia. Frantsiia. Stat'i sovetskoi pechati o prebyvanii v SSSR Andre Zhida. Vyrezki iz gazet. 11 iiulia 1936–1937," RGALI f. 631, op. 14, d. 734, ll. 1–4.

68. Talks, 59–60, 431; Sheridan, 445, 484, 505.

69. Pierre Herbart, *En U.R.S.S.* (Paris: Gallimard, 1937), 22, 27–28; Talks, 441.

70. Talks, 330 (quotation), 347, 517–518, 366–367; C. J. Greschoft, ed., *André Gide. Jef Last. Correspondance, 1934–1950* (Lyon: Presses Universitaires de Lyon, 1985). Much later, Last published *Mijn Vriend André Gide* (Amsterdam: Van Ditmar, 1966), which discussed their sexual encounters in Morocco and the USSR.

71. On Schiffrin, see Talks, chap. 2.

72. Quoted in Sheridan, 483. The other two companions, Dabit and Guilloux, were both independent-minded writers involved in the French proletarian-literature movement (Talks, chaps. 3 and 4).

73. Sheridan, 498; Talks, 520–521.

74. "Zasedanie Inostrannoi Komissii SSP SSR 29-go maia 1936 g.," RGALI f. 631, op. 14, ed. khr. 5, ll. 19–20.

75. Zasedanie Inostrannoi Komissii SSP SSR 29-go maia 1936 g.," l. 19; on the postcards, Sheridan, 498; Herbart, *En U.R.S.S.*, 85; Gide, *Afterthoughts*, 59. On Marquet, see Ludmila Stern, *Western Intellectuals and the Soviet Union, 1920–1940: From Red Square to the Left Bank* (London: Routledge, 2007): 146–149.

76. Gide, *Return*, 67; RGALI f. 631, op. 14, d. 734, ll. 4, 24; "André Gide," in *The God that Failed*, ed. Richard H. Crossman (New York: Columbia University Press, 2001), quotation 195.

77. Leonid Maximenkov and Christopher Barnes, "Boris Pasternak in August 1936—An NKVD Memorandum," *Toronto Slavic Quarterly*, no. 6 (Fall 2003), http://www.utoronto. ca/tsq/06/pasternak06.shtml, last accessed 31 August 2011; Sheridan, 506; Mazuy, 161. On Ehrenburg, see Nemer, 280–281.

78. Arosev to Stalin, copies to Molotov, Ezhov, and Andreev, 13 December 1936, GARF f. 5283, op. 1a, d. 308, ll. 133–137.

79. Andrei Artuzov and Oleg Naumov, eds., *Vlast' i khudozhestvennaia intelligentsiia. Dokumenty TsK RKP(b)-VKP(b), VChK-OGPU-NKVD o kul'turnoi politike 1917–1953 gg.* (Moscow: Demokratiia, 1999), 317, 325–326, 348; "B. Pasternak o svoikh vstrechakh s A. Zhidom," informant's report published in Maximenkov and Barnes; G. B. Kulikova, "Pod kontrolem gosudarstva: Prebyvanie v SSSR inostrannykh pisatelei v 1920–1930-x godakh," *Otechestvennaia istoriia*, no. 4 (2003), 56–57.

80. "Lichnye pokazaniia Kol'tsova Mikhaila Efimovicha ot 9 aprelia 1939 goda," in Viktor Fradkin, *Delo Kol'tsova* (Moscow: Vagrius, 2002), 91; see also 210–218.

81. "Chudesnye prevrashcheniia Andre Zhida," *Kommunist* [Erevan], 17 December 1936; Boris Lavrenev, "Pravaia i levaia ruka gospodina Zhida," *Literaturnyi Leningrad*, 10 December 1936, and other press clippings, RGALI f. 631, op. 14, d. 734, l. 35, l. 88, and throughout the *delo*; Il'ia Erenburg, "Velikodushie i malodushie," *Izvestiia*, 28 December 1937, and Sheridan, 510.

82. Schlögel, *Terror und Traum*, 126.

83. Schlögel, *Terror und Traum*, 129; Lion Feuchtwanger, *Moscow 1937: My Visit Described for My Friends*, trans. Irene Josephy (London: Victor Gallancz, 1937), quotation 12.

84. Feuchtwanger, *Moscow 1937*, 152–153; "Lion Feikhtvanger, Germaniia. 2-i Zapadnyi otdel [VOKS]," report by D. Karavkina, 17 December 1936, GARF f. 5283, op. 1, ed. khr. 334, l. 8.

85. For Feuchtwanger's openly critical remark about the anti-formalism campaign in the introduction to the Soviet edition of his collected works, see Lion Feikhtvanger, "K moim sovetskim chitateliam," *Polnoe sobranie sochinenii*, vol. 1 (Moscow: Gosizdat khudozhest-vennoi literatury, 1939), viii.

86. This disjuncture is discussed by two other scholars who have used the documents: Anne Hartmann, "Abgründige Vernunft: Lion Feuchtwangers *Moskau 1937*," in *Neulektüren - New Readings: Festschrift für Gerd Labroisse zum 80. Geburtstag*, ed. Norbert Otto Eke und Gerhard P. Knapp (Amsterdam: Rodopi, 2009): 149–177, and Ludmila Stern, "*Moscow 1937*: The Interpreter's Story," *Australian Slavonic and East European Studies* 21, 1–2 (2007): 73–95.

87. Maximenkov and Barnes, "Boris Pasternak"; Leonid Maksimenkov, "Ocherki nomenkla-turnoi istorii sovetskoi literatury: Zapadnye pilgrimy u stalinskogo prestola (Feichtvanger i drugie)," *Voprosy literatury*, no. 3 (2004): 296, 327.

88. Arosev to Stalin, copies to Molotov, Ezhov, and Andreev, 13 December 1936, GARF f. 5283, op. 1a, d. 308, ll. 133–137.

89. Karl Kröhnke, *Lion Feuchtwanger—Der Ästhet in der Sowjetunion. Ein Buch nicht nur für seine Freunde* (Stuttgart: J. B. Metzler, 1991); Joseph Pischel, "Nachwort," in Feuchtwanger, *Moskau 1937: Eine Reisebericht für meine Freunde* (Berlin: Aufbau, 993): 113–136; Katerina

Clark, *Moscow, the Fourth Rome: Stalinism, Cosmopolitanism, and the Evolution of Soviet Culture, 1931–1941* (Cambridge, Mass.: Harvard University Press, 2011), chap. 4.

90. Reinhard Müller, "Exil im 'Wunderland' Sowjetunion - Maria Osten (1908–1942)," *Exil: Forschung, Erkenntnisse, Ergebnisse* 27, 2 (2007): 73–95; Müller, "Erschossen im Wunderland: Maria Osten (1908–1942). Exil in der Sowjetunion, in Spanien und Frankreich," chap. 1 of his from his forthcoming book "Stalinismus und Exil: Biographien im Kontext des Terrors." On the German-language publications in Moscow, see Katerina Clark, "Germanophone Intellectuals in Stalin's Russia: Diaspora and Cultural Identity in the 1930s," *Kritika* 2, 3 (2001): 529–551.

91. Some were published in *Sovetskie arkhivy*, no. 4 (1989): 55–63; the others are contained in GARF f. 5283, op. 1, d. 334; op. 5, d. 745; op. 8, dd. 290, 292.

92. "2-i Zapadnyi Otdel [VOKS]. LION FEIKHTVANGER. Pisatel'. Germaniia," 22 December 1936, GARF f. 5283, op. 1, ed. khr. 334, l. 6.

93. "2-i Zapadnyi otdel. Lion Feikhtvanger—pisatel', Germaniia," 16 December 1936, GARF f. 5283, op. 1, ed. khr. 334, l. 9.

94. Feuchtwanger, *Moscow 1937*, introduction and conclusion.

95. "Lion Feikhtvanger—pisatel'. Germanii. II-i Zapadnyi Otdel," report by Karavkina, 29 December 1936, GARF f. 5283, op. 1, d. 334, l. 1; Karavkina report of 15 December 1936, GARF f. 5283, op. 8, d. 290, l. 11; Hartmann, "Abgründige Vernunft," 157; Stern, "*Moscow 1937*," 83; Pischel, 115–116.

96. Karavkina reports on Feuchtwanger, 22 December 1936, GARF f. 5283, op. 1, ed. khr. 334, l. 6; 24 December 1936, ibid., l. 5; 27 December 1936, ibid., l. 3.

97. Karavkina report of 29 December 1936, l. 1. For more of Feuchtwanger's complaints and disparaging comments on Soviet living standards, as quoted by Karavkina, see Stern, "*Moscow 1937*," 80–81.

98. Feuchtwanger, *Moscow 1937*, 171, 172; idem, "Estet o Sovetskom Soiuze," *Pravda* 30 December 1936; "Der Ästhet in der Sowjetunion," *Das Wort*, no. 2 (1937): 86–88; the discrepancies are discussed by Hartmann, "Abgründige Vernunft," 163 n. 68.

99. Hartmann, "Abgründige Vernunft," 164–165, citing diary of Austrian émigré Hugo Huppert, who reported on a Union of Writers speech by Vsevolod Vishnevskii on 30 January 1936.

100. "Zapis' besedy tovarishcha Stalina s Germanskim pisatelem Lionom Feikhtvangerom," 8 January 1937, RGASPI f. 558, op. 11, d. 820, ll. 3–22, here ll. 10–11; Feuchtwanger, *Moscow 1937*, 93. The text of Feuchtwanger's interview with Stalin (published in full in Maksimenkov, "Ocherki," 249–270) is likely an edited and partial version circulated among Soviet leaders in preparation for possible publication, which was never authorized. See Anne Hartmann, "Lost in Translation: Lion Feuchtwanger bei Stalin 1937," *Exil: Forschung, Erkentnisse, Ergebnisse* 28, 2 (2008): 5–18.

101. Feuchtwanger, *Moscow 1937*, 8, 108; Karavkina report of 28 December 1936, GARF f. 5283, op. 1, ed. khr. 334, l. 2; Lion Feikhtvanger, "Schast'e byt' sovetskim uchitelem," *International'naia literatura*, no. 2 (1937): 252–253.

102. "2-i Zapadnyi otdel. LION FEIKHTVANGER. Pisatel'. Germaniia," report by Karavkina of 19 December 1936, GARF f. 5283, op. 1, ed. khr. 334, l. 7; *The Diary of Georgi Dimitrov 1933–1949*, ed. Ivo Banac (New Haven: Yale University Press, 2003), 44, 51.

103. Feuchtwanger, *Moscow 1937*, 134–135, 152–153; on Radek, see B. Ia. Frezinskii, *Pisateli i sovetskie vozhdi: Izbrannye siuzhety 1919–1960 godov* (Moscow: Ellis Lak, 2008), 148, 150.

104. Stern, "*Moscow 1937*," 92, 94–95.

105. Anne Hartmann, "Lion Feuchtwanger, zurück aus Sowjetrussland: Selbstzensur eines Reiseberichts," *Exil* 29, 1 (2009): 16–40; "Ot izdatel'stva," in Lion Feikhtvanger, *Moskva 1937: Otchet o poezdke dlia moikh druzei* (Moscow: Gosizdat khudozhestvennoi literatury, 1937).

106. Maximenkov and Barnes, n. 8.

107. Raymond Aron, *The Opium of the Intellectuals* (New Brunswick: Transaction Publishers, 2001), 65.

108. For one example that deserves to be better known, see the book on Czechoslovak diplomat Josef Girsa by V. A. Shishkin, *Rossiia v gody 'Velikogo pereloma' v vospriiatii inostrannogo diplomata (1925–1931 gg.)* (St. Petersburg: Dmitrii Bulanin, 1999).

109. Norman and Jeanne Mackenzie, "Editor's Introduction to Part III," in *The Diary of Beatrice Webb*, vol. 4, 1924–1943: *The Wheel of Life*, citing surviving, unpublished entries from Beatrice's 1932 "Russian Tour" notebook, 275.

110. David Engerman, *Modernization from the Other Shore: American Intellectuals and the Romance of Russian Development* (Cambridge: Harvard University Press, 2003).

111. *The Diary of Beatrice Webb*, vol. 4, 374–375, 380; Webbs, *Soviet Communism*, 2: 567–571.

112. "Fashistskoe srednevekov'e," *Internatsional'naia literatura*, no. 3 (1933): 140–141.

113. Trude Rikhter, "Kul'turnaia politika natsional-sotsializma," *Internatsional'naia literatura*, no. 3 (1933): 109–117, quotations 109, 115; Ernst Otval't, "Fashistskaia kul'tura," in ibid., no. 2 (1936): 140–143. On the Soviet Image of Nazi Germany, see Katerina Clark and Karl Schlögel, "Mutual Perceptions and Projections: Stalin's Russia in Nazi Germany – Nazi Germany in the Soviet Union," in *Beyond Totalitarianism*, 422–438.

114. "Bert Brekht," in RGALI f. 631, op. 14, ed. khr. 399, l. 5; Katerina Clark, "The Author as Producer: Cultural Revolution in Berlin and Moscow," unpublished paper presented at the Workshop on New Approaches to Russian and Soviet History," University of Maryland, May 2003.

115. Michael Scammel, *Koestler: The Literary and Political Odyssey of a Twentieth-Century Skeptic* (New York: Random House, 2009), 88–98, quotation 97; Sandra Goldstein, "Red Days: Intellectuals and the Failing Gods," *Tel Aviver Jahrbuch für deutsche Geschichte* 24 (1995): 157–178; Lee Congdon, *Seeing Red: Hungarian Intellectuals in Exile and the Challenge of Communism* (DeKalb: Northern Illinois University Press, 2001), 8–10.

116. Shaw, *The Rationalization of Russia*, 76–77, 111–112.

117. Shaw, "On the Rocks: A Political Comedy. 1933," in *Too True to be Good, Village Wooing and On the Rocks: Three Plays* (New York: Dodd, Mead and Co, 1934), 177.

118. Quoted in Paul A. Hummert, *Bernard Shaw's Marxian Romance* (Lincoln: University of Nebraska Press, 1973), 178; on Shaw's treatment of violence in this period, 175–178.

119. Richard Griffiths, *Fellow-Travellers of the Right: British Enthusiasts for Nazi Germany* (London: Constable, 1980), esp. 4, 153, 157, 167, 204; Alastair Hamilton, *The Appeal of Fascism: A Study of Intellectuals and Fascism 1919–1945* (New York: Aron Books, 1971).

120. Griffiths, 3. For a penetrating analysis of a left-right conversion, see Michael B. Loughlin, "Gustav Hervé's Transition from Socialism to National Socialism," *Journal of Contemporary History* 36,1 (2001): 5–39.

121. On Britain, Griffiths, esp. 110–113, 124, 227, 273, 377; on France, Hamilton, esp. 240–244.

122. Michael Ignatieff, *Isaiah Berlin: A Life* (New York: Henry Holt and Co., 1988): 75.

123. "A. Ia. Arosev. Sekretariu TsK VKP(b) – tov. Zhdanovu. Kul'tprop TsK VKP(b) – t. Stetskomu," 21 June 1934, GARF f. 5283, op. 1a, d. 255, ll. 43–44; report on visits of Italian Fascist cinematographers, 27 June 1932, ibid., op. 8, d. 112, ll. 43–44; on Céline, see Hamilton, 232–234.

124. David Carroll, "Literary Fascism or the Aestheticizing of Politics: The Case of Robert Brasillach," *New Literary History* 23, 3 (1992): 691–726; Céline quoted in Hamilton, 234.

125. Karl Radek, "Intelligentsiia i oktiabr' (predislovie)," in *Glazami inostrantsev*, xi, echoing Stalin's phrase rehabilitating the "bourgeois specialists" in the context of foreign intellectuals. On the Soviet bid to replace the United States and Palestine as an "ideological *vaterland*" among American Jews, see Daniel Soyer, "Back to the Future: American Jews Visit the Soviet Union in the 1920s and 1930s," *Jewish Social Studies* 6, 3 (2000): 124–159.

126. Kate A. Baldwin, *Beyond the Color Line and the Iron Curtain: Reading Encounters between Black and Red, 1922–1963* (Durham, NC: Duke University Press, 2002); Allison Blakely, *Russia and the Negro: Blacks in Russian History and Thought* (Washington, D.C.: Howard University Press, 1986), chap. 7; Joy Gleason Carew, *Blacks, Reds, and Russians: Sojourners in Search of the Soviet Promise* (New Brunswick: Rutgers University Press, 2008), chap. 9.

127. Lewis S. Feuer, "American Travelers to the Soviet Union 1917–32: The Formation of a Component of New Deal Ideology," *American Quarterly* 42, 2, part 1 (Summer 1962): 119–149, quotation 121.

128. Blakely, 84, 98, 100–101; Baldwin, 207.

129. Untitled report, 26 July 1935, GARF f. 5283, op. 3, ed. khr. 655, l. 4.

130. "Pol' Robson i zhena. I. A. Amdur," 23 July 1935, GARF f. 5283, op. 3, ed. khr. 65., l. 5. Robeson was consistently praised as a great and loyal Soviet friend by VOKS, the Soviet embassy in Washington, and the London Society of Friends, in which he was active: see "Beseda s Pol' Robson," 23 May 1937, GARF f. 5283, op. 1a, d. 371, l. 51; D. Chubakhin, first secretary of Soviet embassy in USA, to head of VOKS Anglo-American Sector Kislova, 15 March 1940, in ibid., op. 2a, d. 4, l. 102.

131. Robeson met with ethnographers in Leningrad in January 1935: GARF f. 5283, op. 3, ed. khr. 655, ll. 7, 8, 15; on the particular appeal of Soviet nationalities policy for Robeson, see Baldwin, 210–211.

132. "E. P. Liberman, 'Otchet o rabote s Chekhoslovatskim prof. Needly,'" no earlier than 13 June 1935, GARF f. 5283, op. 1, d. 298, l. 110.

Chapter 8

1. André Gide, *Return from the U.S.S.R*, trans. Dorothy Bussy (New York: Alfred A. Knopf, 1937), 31–33.

2. "SSSR—moguchaia industrial'naia derzhava," "Pod znamenem internatsional'noi solidarnosti," and "Nasha rodina," in *Sputnik agitatora*, no. 19 (October 1938): 38–39, 45–47, and no. 13 (July 1938): 13, respectively; Raisa Orlova, *Memoirs*, trans. Samueli Cioran (New York: Random House, 1983), 81.

3. See Anna Krylova, *Soviet Women in Combat: A History of Violence on the Eastern Front* (Cambridge: Cambridge University Press, 2010), chap. 1.

4. Sheila Fitzpatrick, *Everyday Stalinism: Ordinary Life in Extraordinary times. Soviet Russia in the 1930s* (Oxford: Oxford University Press, 1999),184; Catriona Kelly, *Refining Russia: Advice Literature, Polite Culture, and Gender from Catherine to Yeltsin* (Oxford: Oxford University Press, 2001), 232.

5. Ilya Ehrenburg, *Memoirs: 1921--1941*, trans. Tatiana Shebunina (New York: Grosset and Dunlap, 1966), 26.

6. György Péteri, "Nylon Curtain: Transnational and Transsystemic Tendencies in the Cultural Life of State-Socialist Russia and East-Central Europe," *Slavonica* 10, 2 (2004): 113–123, quotation 119.

7. David Brandenberger, *National Bolshevism: Stalinist Mass Culture and the Formation of Modern Russian National Identity, 1931–1956* (Cambridge, Mass.: Harvard University Press, 2002), 5. Brandenberger, however, also noted the contradictory and multiple tendencies of the mid-1930s.

8. Katerina Clark, *Moscow, the Fourth Rome: Stalinism, Cosmopolitanism, and the Evolution of Soviet Culture, 1931–1941* (Cambridge, Mass.: Harvard University Press, 2011), esp. introduction, chaps. 1 and 5; Clark developed the term "great appropriation" in "From Production Sketches to 'World Literature': The Search for a Grander Narrative," paper presented at the Wissenschaftskolleg zu Berlin, June 2010.

9. See, for example, the numerous country reports in GARF f. 5283, op. 1a, d. 278; on Austria, l. 32.

10. Isidor Amdur, "Memorandum," no exact date, 1935, GARF f. 5283, op. 1a, d. 278, ll. 66–67; "Osnovnye meropriiatiia po Chekhoslovakii," 1935, no exact date, ibid., l. 25. On Intourist, see B. E. Bagdasarian, et al., *Sovetskoe zazerkal'e: Inostrannyi turizm v SSSR v 1930–1980-e gody* (Moscow: Forum, 2007), 47.

11. "Rabota Anglo-Amerikanskogo otdela," GARF f. 5283, op. 1, d. 278, ll. 71–75; Josephine Smith to VOKS, 18 October 1935, AVP RF f. 69, op. 23, d. 5, papka 76, l. 74; "Peace and Friendship with the USSR. National Week and Congress, December 7 and 8" (brochure), ibid., ll. 75–77.

12. On MORP, see esp. chaps. 3 and 4 of Ludmila Stern, *Western Intellectuals and the Soviet Union, 1920–1940: From Red Square to the Left Bank* (London: Routledge, 2007); for examples of its extensive monitoring of foreign-language press and cultural periodicals after 1932 as a sign of professionalization, see RGALI f. 631, op. 14, ed. khr. 715; ibid., op. 14, ed, khr. 1; ibid., op. 11, d. 1, ll. 2–18, 19–23.

13. On these points, see Anne Hartmann, "Literarische Staatsbesuche: Prominente Autoren des Westens zu Gast in Stalins Sowjetunion (1931–1937)," in *Die Ost-West-Problematik in den europäischen Kulturen und Literaturen*, ed. Helena Ulbrechtova and Siegfried Ulbrecht (Dresden: Niesse Verlag, 2008), 229–275, here 237–239.

14. Boris Frezinskii, *Pisateli i sovetskie vozhdi: Izbrannye siuzhety 1919–1960 godov* (Moscow: Ellis Lak, 2008), 280–282.

15. Ehrenburg to Stalin, 13 September 1934, *Il'ia Erenburg, Pis'ma* 1908–1967, 2: 134–139; Boris Frezinskii, "Il'ia Erenburg i Nikolai Bukharin," *Pisateli*, 156–216, esp. 176–178, 282–283; Joshua Rubenstein, *Tangled Loyalties: The Life and Times of Ilya Ehrenburg* (Tuscaloosa: University of Alabama Press, 1996), 134–136. On the Comintern, see Jonathan Haslam, "The Comintern and the Origins of the Popular Front, 1934–1935," *Historical Journal* 22, 3 (1979): 673–91, and Haslam, "Comintern and Soviet Foreign Policy, 1919–1941," in *The Cambridge History of Russia*, vol. 3: *The Twentieth Century*, ed. Ronald Grigor Suny (Cambridge: Cambridge University Press, 2006), 650–651.

16. Ehrenburg to Stalin, 13 September 1934. For the manner in which Ehrenburg linked his foreign communist critics with the discredited approach of domestic cultural militants, see "Otvet F. Fernadesu Armesto," *International'naia literatura*, no. 1 (1933): 121–122.

17. Ehrenburg to Stalin, 13 September 1934; Kaganovich to Stalin, 28 September 1934; Kaganovich to Stalin, 3 October 1934, in *Stalin i Kaganovich: Perepiska. 1931–1936 gg.*, ed. O. V. Khlevniuk, et al. (Moscow: ROSSPEN, 2001), 718–719, 502–503, 509; Rubenstein, 134–136.

18. Pascal Ory, *La belle illusion: Culture et politique sous le signe du Front populaire* 1935–1938 (Paris: Plon, 1994), 184–195; Frezinskii, "Mezhdunarodnoe antifashistskoe pisatel'skoe predstavlenie v 3-x aktakh (prodiuser I. Stalin)," *Pisateli*, 273–475 (a second International Writers Congress was held in Valencia and Madrid in 1937).

19. Politburo resolution in Andrei Artizov and Oleg Naumov, eds., *Vlast' i khudozhestvennaia intelligentsiia. Dokumenty TsK RKP(b) - VKP(b) - VChK-OGPU-NKVD o kul'turnoi politike. 1917–1953 gg* (Moscow: Demokratiia, 1999), 279; Zasedanie Inostrannoi Komissii SSP SSSR 29-go maia 1936 g.," RGALI f. 631, op. 14, ed. khr. 23, ll. 2–34; Stern, *Western Intellectuals*, 8, 82.

20. Arosev, "Sekretariu TsK VKP(b) tovarishchu Stalinu. Dokladnaia zapiska. O propagande sovetskoi kul'ture zagranitsei i razvitie raboty VOKS," 3 May 1935, GARF f. 5283, op. 1a, d. 276, ll. 72–83; "Ukreplenie i rasshirenie sviazei VOKS"a," 1935, no exact date, ibid., ll. 57–70; "Proekt dokladnoi zapiski v Politbiuro o VOKS"e," 11 June 1936, ibid., d. 308, ll. 59–64; on the dacha in Peredel'kino, ibid., ll. 132–133.

21. "Spisok deiatelei, aktivno rabotaiushchikh v oblasti kul'turnogo sblizheniia s SSSR," late 1935, no exact date, GARF f. 5283, op. 1, d. 278, l. 10–11; "Spisok inostrantsev dlia priglasheniia v SSSR," 20 August 1936, ibid., op. 1a, d. 308, ll. 103–10. A professional breakdown of foreigners for whom VOKS "provided service" in ten months in 1935 shows the largest group (205) to be artists and writers, followed by pedagogues (117), scholars (108), and physicians (102). By contrast, there were, for example, far fewer engineers (31), economists (14), or architects (6). Ibid., op. 1, d. 278, l. 12.

22. Arosev to A. A. Andreev, 11 June 1936, GARF f. 5283. op. 1a, d. 308, l. 58; Arosev, "Proekt dokladnoi zapiski v Politbiuro TsK VKP(b) o VOKS"e," ibid., ll. 59–64, quotation l. 59; Arosev to Stalin, 7 June 1935, ibid., d. 276, ll. 134–38, quotation l. 37. On portrayals of Soviet culture in this period as the culmination of the great European tradition and Moscow as capital of world civilization, see Clark, *Moscow, the Fourth Rome*, chap. 5.

23. Erika Wolf, ed., *Ilf and Petrov's American Road Trip: The 1935 Travelogue of Two Soviet Writers Ilya Ilf and Evgeny Petrov* (New York: Princeton Architectural Press and Cabinet Books, 2007), 26; A. I. Mikoian to L. M. Kaganovich, no later than 17 September 1936, in *Sovetskoe rukovodstvo: Perepiska 1928–1941 gg.* (Moscow: ROSSPEN, 1999), 346–349, quotation 346; A. Ia. Arosev to Stetskii, Dinamov, and Zhdanov in the Central Committee's Kul'tprop, 25 May 1934, GARF f. 5283, op. 1a, d. 255, ll. 27–29, quotations l. 27. On the broader Russian-American cross-cultural context, often conditioned by fascination from afar, see, inter alia, Aleksandr Etkind, *Tolkovanie puteshestvii: Rossiia i Amerika v travelogakh i intertekstakh* (Moscow: NLO, 2001).

24. Oleg V. Khlevniuk, *Master of the House: Stalin and His Inner Circle*, trans. Nora Seligman Favorov (New Haven: Yale University Press, 2009), 139–142; Marc Jansen and Nikita Petrov, *Stalin's Loyal Executioner: People's Commissar Nikolai Ezhov, 1895–1940* (Stanford: Hoover Institution Press, 2002), 24–25, 28, 32–34, 40–41. In 1935 Ezhov's efforts in this campaign were successfully rebuffed by Jenö Varga, head of the Institute of World Economics and World Politics (38–39). On "Yagoda's eclipse within his own bailiwick by Yezhov," see J. Arch Getty and Oleg Naumov, *The Road to Terror: Stalin and the Self-Destruction of the Bolsheviks, 1932–1939* (New Haven: Yale University Press, 1999), 275, and on "growing tensions" in 1935, chap. 4.

25. This is the argument in Carola Tischler, *Flucht in die Verfolgung: Deutsche Emigranten im sowjetischen Exil 1933 bis 1945* (Münster: LIT, 1996): 87–91; on Intourist, see Bagdasarian, et al., *Sovetskoe zazerkal'e*, 67; Shawn Salmon, "To the Land of the Future: A History of Intourist and Travel to the Soviet Union, 1929–1991" (Ph.D. diss., University of California at Berkeley, 2008), 108.

26. Brandenberger, *National Bolshevism*, 49.

27. Julian Graffy, "The Foreigner's Journey to Consciousness in Early Soviet Cinema: The Case of Protozanov's *Tommi*," in *Insiders and Outsiders in Russian Cinema*, ed. Stephen M. Norris and Zara M. Torlone (Bloomington: Indiana University Press, 2008), 1–22; Josephine Woll, "Under the Big Top: America Goes to the Circus," in ibid., 68–80; GARF f. 5283, op. 1a, d. 276, l. 82.

28. A. Arosev, "Sekretariu TsK VKP(b) tov. Ezhovu," 5 May 1936, GARF f. 5283, op. 1a, d. 308, l. 42; on Keynes, A. Ia. Arosev, "Zam. Zav. Otdela Kul'turno-Prosvetitel'noi Raboty. TsK VKP(b) t. A. I. Angarovu," 11 August 1936, GARF f. 5283, op. 1a, d. 308, l. 85.

29. Leonid Maksimenkov, *Sumbur vmesto muzyki: Stalinskaia kul'turnaia revoliutsiia 1936–1938* (Moscow: Iuridicheskaia kniga, 1997), 60–66, 83, and passim.

30. Maksimenkov, *Sumbur*, 88–112, 158, 160–162.

31. Platon Kerzhentsev to V. M. Molotov, "O VOKSe," 2 March 1937, GARF f. 5283, op. 1a, d. 342, l. 22; Arosev to N. K. Antipov, Zam. Pred. Sovnarkoma, 10 March 1937, ibid., ll. 23–25.

32. The phrase comes from the subtitle of Maksimenkov's *Sumbur vmesto muzyki*.

33. Arosev to Ezhov, no exact date, prob. May 1936, GARF f. 5283, op. 1a, d. 308, l. 47. On the Central Committee as the main "instance" controlling cultural diplomacy during its heyday in the 1930s, see A. V. Golubev, "… *Vzgliad na zemliu obetovannuiu*": *Iz istorii sovetskoi kul'turnoi diplomatii 1920–1930-x godov* (Moscow: Institut istorii RAN, 2004), 127.

34. Arosev to Ezhov, December 1935 (no day, from Paris), GARF f. 5283, op. 1a, d. 324, l. 31; Arosev to Stalin (from Paris), RGASPI f. 558, op. 11, ed. khr. 695, l. 161; interview with Ol'ga Aroseva, Moscow, 16 October 2003.

35. Arosev to Stalin, 4 August 1936, RGASPI f. 558, op. 11, ed. khr. 655, ll. 162–166.

36. Similarly, as the Cold War and Zhdanov periods began in 1947, a campaign to tighten secrecy wreaked havoc on routine administration (Yoram Gorlizki, "Ordinary Stalinism: The Council of Ministers and the Soviet Neopatrimonial State, 1946–1953," *Journal of Modern History* 74 [December 2002]: 721–722).

37. In 1935, Glavlit approved nineteen VOKS officials to use "banned" foreign literature, but it prevented VOKS from expanding its activities in producing restricted reports (*svodki*) on Western cultural life. "Proekt organizatsii ezhednevnykh informsvodok VOKS"a," 2 December 1934, GARF f. 5283, op. 1, d. 277, ll. 28–29; Zam. Pred. VOKS N. Kuliabko to V. M. Volin, Glavlit, ibid, op. 1a, d. 283, l. 5; Glavlit to VOKS, 23 September 1935, ibid., l. 22; "Spisok sotrudnikov VOKS"a, imeiushchikh pravo pol'zovat'sia zapreshchennoi ino-literaturoi," 1935, no exact date, ibid., l. 35.

38. Arosev, "Rasporiazhenie po VOKS," 4 July 1935, GARF f. 5283, op. 1, d. 277, l. 2.

39. "Otchet Otdela Mezhdunarodnogo knigoobmena," GARF f. 5283, op. 1a, d. 91, ll. 62–73.

40. "Dokladnaia zapiska o kontrole nad inostrannoi literaturoi, postupaiushchei v VOKS. Nachal'niku Glavlita Ingulovu S.E. ot Nachal'niko Ino. Sektora Glavlita Barshchevskogo," 16 December 1935, GARF f. 5283, op. 1a, d. 283, ll. 36–42.

41. Zam. Pred. VOKS N. Kuliabko to V. M. Volin, Glavlit, GARF f. 5283, op. 1a, d. 283, l. 5; "Prikaz No. 40," (Glavlit), ibid., d. 292, l. 11. Disruptions in VOKS's work due to Glavlit continued in 1936: GARF f. 5283, op. 1a, d. 307, l. 28.

42. "Zav. Sekretnoi Chast'iu VOKS Kuresar. V Spetsotdel GUGB NKVD. Tov. Evdokimovu," 8 January 1936, GARF f. 5283, op. 1a, d. 307, ll. 3–4.

43. "BRIO Pred. VOKS L. Cherniavskii. V Spetsotdel GUGB NKVD t. Sharikovu," 9 April 1936, ibid., l. 86; see also "Zav. Sekretnoi Chast'iu VOKS Kuresar. V Spetsotdel GUGB NKVD. Tov. Evdokimovu," 28 January 1936, GARF f. 5283, op. 1a, d. 307, l. 19.

44. On Nazi book-burnings as an originary moment for pan-European anti-fascist culture, see Clark, *Moscow, the Fourth Rome,* chap. 4.

45. "Akt" (Glavlit), 29 March 1936, GARF f. 5283, op. 1a, d. 321, l. 8; ibid., l. 51; "Zav. Sektr. Chast'iu VOKS A. Kuresar. BRIO Pred VOKS tov. Cherniavskii. Kop. Spetsotdel GUGB NKVD t. Sharikovu," 19 April 1936, ibid., d. 307, l. 112. At Leningrad Communist University, book-burning operations began somewhat later than those of the foreign materials at VOKS—after a late May 1936 operation to purge "Trotskyist-Zinovievist" literature (Igal Halfin, *Stalinist Confessions: Messianism and Terror at the Leningrad Communist University* [Pittsburgh: University of Pittsburgh Press, 2009], 204–208).

46. GARF f. 5283, op. 1a, d. 350, ll. 6–17; on the London book burning, see VOKS representative Grinev to Smirnov, 24 April 1938, GARF f. 5283, op. 2a, d. 2, l. 91.

47. David Priestland, *Stalinism and the Politics of Mobilization: Ideas, Power, and Terror in Inter-war Russia* (Oxford: Oxford University Press, 2007), 352–388; Wendy Z. Goldman, *Terror and Democracy in the Age of Stalin: The Social Dynamics of Repression* (Cambridge: Cambridge University Press, 2007), chap. 3.

48. Natal'ia Semper (Sokolova), "Portrety i peizazhi: Chastnye vospominaniia o XX veke," *Druzhba narodov,* no. 2 (1997): 115.

49. On the 1937 *proverka* (verification) of VOKS employees with relatives and ties abroad, GARF f. 5283, op. 1a, d. 350, ll. 18–19; Arosev to Nikita Khrushchev, secretary of the Moscow party organization, 22 March 1937, GARF f. 5283, op. 1a, d. 342, ll. 41–48; see also l. 128, l. 133; Arosev, diary entry of 15 November 1936, in Ol'ga Aroseva and V. A. Maksimova, *Bez grima* (Moscow: Izdatel'stvo Tsentrpoligraf, 1999), 85.

50. Aroseva and Maksimova, *Bez grima,* 86–90; Feliks Chuev, *Sto sorok besed s Molotovym: Iz dnevnika F. Chueva* (Moscow: Terra, 1991), 420–23, quotations 420, 423.

51. Terry Martin, "The Origins of Soviet Ethnic Cleansing," *Journal of Modern History* 70 (December 1998): 813–861, here 829.

52. Frezinskii, *Pisateli,* 148.

53. Jansen and Petrov, 108.

54. Khlevniuk, *Master of the House,* 173; Karl Schlögel, *Terror und Traum: Moskau 1937* (Munich: Carl Hanswer Verlag, 2008), 150.

55. Here see Jörg Baberowski and Anselm Doering-Manteuffel, "The Quest for Order and the Pursuit of Terror: Nationalist Socialist Germany and the Stalinist Soviet Union as Multiethnic Empires," in *Beyond Totalitarianism: Stalinism and Nazism Compared,* ed. Michael Geyer and Sheila Fitzpatrick (Cambridge: Cambridge University Press, 2009), 180–230, esp. 210–11.

56. Jansen and Petrov, 93; Sergei Zhuravlev, "American Victims of the Stalin Purges, 1930s," in *Stalinistiche Subjekte / Sujets staliniens / Stalinist Subjects,* ed. Birgitte Studer and Heiko Haumann (Zurich: Chronos Verlag, 2006), 397–414; Tim Tzouliadis, *The Foresaken: An American Tragedy in Stalin's Russia* (New York: Penguin Books, 2008), esp. 105–107.

57. "Otchet o priezde grupp inostrannykh turistov v SSSR za I-e polugodie 37 g.," 2 September 1938, GARF f. 9612, op. 1, d. 40, l. 83; "Spravka o kolichestve inostrannykh turistov iz Ameriki i Evropy, posetivshikh Sov. Soiuz po godam," no earler than 1941, ibid., d. 71, l. 2; Salmon, "To the Land of the Future," 108–110.

58. "Ispol'zovanie inostrannogo turizma v kapitalisticheskikh stranakh v tseliakh razvedki, shpionazh i podryvnoi raboty," no exact date, GARF f. 9612, op. 1, d. 63, ll. 238–259, esp. 257–258.

59. Maksimenkov, "Ocherki nomenklaturnoi istorii sovetskoi literatury: Zapadnye pilgrimy u staliniskogo prestola (Feikhtvanger i drugie)," *Voprosy literatury*, no. 3 (2004): 275, 287–288.

60. "Zav. Sekretnoi Chast'iu VOKS (Kuresar). 9-i Otdel GUGB NKVD t. Poliakovu," 23 July 1937, GARF f. 5283, op. 1a, d. 335, l. 41; Semper, 115.

61. "V. Smirnov (BRIO Pred. VOKS). Predsedateliu SNK SSSR tov. Molotovu, V.M.," 16 September 1937, GARF f. 5283, op. 1a, d. 334, l. 62.

62. GARF f. 5283, op. 2a, d. 1, l. 22; "V. Smirnov (BRIO Pred. VOKS). V TsK VKP(b). Otdel kul'tury i prosveshcheniia. Tov. Shablonskomu," 3 October 1937, GARF f. 5283, op. 1a, d. 322, l. 56.

63. GARF f. 5283, op. 1a, d. 322, l. 56.

64. Smirnov, "Otdel Propaganda i Agitatsii TsK VKP(b). Tov. Aleksandrovu," 13 February 1937 GARF f. 5283, op. 2a, d. 3, ll. 70–72 (on finances); Smirnov, "Dokladnaia zapiska," sent to M. M. Litvinov (Narkomindel), 1938, no exact date, ibid., op. 2a, d. 1, ll. 19–25; Smirnov to P. A. Bulganinu, zam. Pred. Sovnarkom, 31 January 1939, ibid., op. 2a, d. 3, ll. 1–3; Pred. Praveleniia VOKS V. Kemenov to V. M. Molotov, Zam. Pred. Soveta Ministrov SSSR, 5 February 1947, RGASPI f. 56, op. 1, d. 1013, l. 8; Semper, 115.

65. "V. Smirnov, BRIO Pred. VOKS. Sekretariu TsK VKP(b) tov. Andreevu, A. A.," 22 March 1938, GARF f. 5283, op. 2a, d. 1, ll. 1–5, here l. 3; on Dewey, see David Engerman, "John Dewey and the Soviet Union: Pragmatism Meets Revolution," *Modern Intellectual History* 3, 1 (2006): 33–63, and, more broadly on the U.S. anti-Stalinist Left and the Moscow trials, Alan M. Wald, *The New York Intellectuals: The Rise and Decline of the Anti-Stalinist Left from the 1930s to the 1980s* (Chapel Hill: The University of North Carolina Press, 1987), chap. 5.

66. John J. Fox, Jr., "What the Spiders Did: U.S. and Soviet Counterintelligence before the Cold War," *Journal of Cold War Studies* 11, 3 (Summer 2009): 210.

67. The first report is from Umanskii to deputy VOKS director Cherniavskii from 1 December 1936 (GARF f. 5283, op. 1a, d. 296, ll. 32–34); next see Umanskii to Smirnov, 12 April 1938, ibid., op. 2a, d. 2, ll. 24–25 (also l. 4, ll. 8–12, l. 29, l. 41, 42–43, 44–45); Umanskii to Smirnov, no earlier than 28 October 1938, ibid. l. 61 (and ibid., d. 3, ll. 162–163; ibid., op. 3, d. 1003, l. 18); Umanskii to Smirnov, 19 April 1940, ibid., op. 2a, d. 4, ll. 109–116.

68. For just one example, Apletin's correspondence with Upton Sinclair from 1936–39 is in RGALI f. 631, op. 11, d. 78. On Apletin's methods, see Stern, *Western Intellectuals*, 174–201.

69. "Inostrannaia Komissiia SSP. Sekretariat. V TsK VKP(b) tov. Andreevu A.A.," no exact date, 1937, RGALI f. 631, op. 14, ed. khr. 8, l. 12; "Sekretno. R. Zel'dt. Inzhiner L. Lingardt, sek. Obshchestva Kul'tsviazi v Prage," no exact date, GARF f. 5283, op. 1a, d. 319, l. 14. Information on how European and American writers reacted to the trials in 1937 is in RGALI f. 631, op. 14, d. 1050, ll. 1, 3.

70. Joshua Kunitz, *Dawn over Samarkand: The Rebirth of Central Asia* (New York: Van Rees Press, 1935); Alan M. Wald, *Exiles from a Future Time: The Forging of the Mid-Twentieth-Century Literary Left* (Chapel Hill: University of North Carolina Press, 2002), 121; on the *New Masses*, see chap. 4.

71. Inostrannaia komissia SSP. N'iu Messis. Dzhoshua K'iunits, korrespondent 'N'iu Messis' chlen KP SShA," 4 September 1936, RGALI f. 631, op. 14, ed. khr. 1046, ll. 3–6. Kunitz later published a two-part article, "The Moscow Trial," *New Masses*, 15 and 22 March 1938.

72. Feuchtwanger, *Moscow 1937*, chap. 7, quotation 143. Piatakov, who had been tortured for thirty-three days, according to one report resembled "not Piatakov but his shadow, a skeleton with his teeth knocked out" (Tzouliadis, 114).

73. Rolland to Stalin, 18 March 1937; 4 August 1937; 20 August 1937; 16 September 1937; 29 December 1937, RGASPI f. 558, op. 11, ed. khr. 775, ll. 140–141, 145, 146, 149–150, 154–155; Mariia Rollan [Kudasheva] to Mikhail Apletin, 4 September 1937, RGALI f. 631, op. 14, d. 741, ll. 70–71; on the topic of a return trip to Moscow, Rolland to Apletin, 2 May 1937, ibid., ll. 42–43; David James Fisher, *Romain Rolland and the Politics of Intellectual Engagement* (Berkeley: University of California, 1988), 274–278, quotation 278. As Stalin

and Politburo members were informed from the contents of Kudasheva's letters, Rolland in the wake of his first visit in 1935 had been considering a return in 1937 (RGASPI f. 558, op. 11, ed. khr. 775, l. 123).

74. M. P. Rollan (Kudasheva) to Mikhail Apletin, 26 October 1938, RGALI f. 631, op. 14, d. 754, l. 40.

75. Romain Rolland to Galya and Natasha Isaevaia (Novgorod), 26 November 1937; Mariia Rollan [Kudasheva] to Mikhail Apletin, 27 November 1937 and 29 December 1937, RGALI f. 631, op. 14, d. 74, ll. 98–99, 97, 104. On Rolland's *Robespierre* see Bernard Duchatelet, *Romain Rolland tel qu'en lui-même* (Paris: Albin Michel, 2002).

76. RGALI f. 631, op. 14, d. 22, l. 8, 13, 17.

77. "V. Iakovlev, 2-i sekretar' Polpredstva SSSR v Chekhoslovakii. 2-oi Zapadnyi Otdel NKID tov. Vainshteinu. Pred. VOKS—tov. Smirnovu," Prague, 19 October 1938, GARF f. 5283, op. 2a, d. 2, ll. 154–162; Smirnov to Iakovlev, 10 March 1938, ibid., l. 24; on Nejedlý, V. F. Smirnov to V. M. Molotov, 14 May 1939, ibid., d. 3, l. 4 (see also l. 66).

78. Walter Benjamin, "Conversations with Brecht," in *Reflections: Essays, Aphorisms, Autobiographical Writings*, ed. Peter Demetz, trans. Edmund Jephcott (New York: Schocken Books, 1978), 217, 218–219.

79. Bertolt Brecht to Mikhail Apletin no later than 5 February 1939, RGALI f. 631, op. 11, d. 412, l. 4; Apletin to Brecht, 5 February 1939, 20 May 1939, 10 June 1939, 29 July 1939, 23 August 1939 (ibid., l. 5, 6, 9, 13, 15, see also l. 17); Brecht to Apletin, 4 July 1940, ibid., l. 20; Apletin to Brecht, 27 July 1940, ibid., l. 22.

80. For a recent intervention, see Sergej Slutsch, "Stalin und Hitler 1933–1941: Kalküle und Fehlkalkulationen des Kreml," in *Stalin und die Deutschen: Neue Beiträge der Forschung*, ed. Jürgen Zarusky (Munich: R. Oldenbourg, 2006): 59–88. On shock expressed by Soviet intellectuals, see A. V. Golubev, et al., *Rossiia i Zapad: Formirovanie vneshnepolit-icheskikh stereotipov v soznanii rossiiskogo obshchestva pervoi poloviny XX veka* (Moscow: Institut rossiiskoi istorii RAN, 1998), 199–234. For the most recent scholarship on the Pact, see "Der Hitler-Stalin-Pakt," special issue of *Osteuropa*, no. 7–8 (2009).

81. By far the largest number of books was received from the United States, but Germany still came in second place in 1935 (more than 10,000 books received in the first half of that year). "Dokladnaia zapiska o kontrole nad inostrannoi literaturoi," 16 December 1935, GARF f. 5283, op. 1a, d. 283, ll. 36–42. For an example of the sporadic contacts, see "Zapis' besedy s predstavitelem 'Doitche Gezel'shaft tsum studium osteuropas' doktorom Shiule," 10 June 1935, ibid. op. 6, d. 510, l. 2; see also l. 129, l. 133, l. 135, l. 145.

82. N. Pozdniakov (Berlin) to Cherniavskii (BRIO pred. VOKS), 11 March 1936, GARF f. 5283, op. 1a, d. 300, l. 3; "Rabota nemetskoi gruppy SSP," 1934, RGALI f. 631, op. 12, ed. khr. 2, ll. 16–28. For a compilation of newly declassified documents on Nazi-Soviet relations, see Sergei Kudriashov, ed., *SSSR-Germaniia: 1933–1941* (Moscow: Vestnik Arkhiv Prezidenta Rossiiskoi Federatsii, 2009).

83. J. Calvitt Clark III, *Russia and Italy against Hitler: The Bolshevik-Fascist Rapprochement against Hitler* (New York: Greenwood Press, 1991); on the economic dimension to Soviet-German relations, see Edward E. Ericson III, *Feeding the German Eagle: Soviet Economic Aid to Nazi Germany, 1933–1941* (Westport, Conn.: Praeger, 1999).

84. For example, see "Otzyv o rabote Inturista v SSSR," 1940, GARF f. 9612, op. 1, d. 62, ll. 36–37; Bagdasarian, et al., *Sovetskoe zazerkal'e*, 21.

85. V. A. Nevezhin, "Sovetskaia politika i kul'turnye sviazi s Germaniei (1939–1941 gg.)," *Otechestvennaia istoriia*, no. 1 (1993): 18–34; "Dnevnik Press-Atashe Polpredstva SSSR v Germanii," 2 December 1939, GARF f. 5283, op. 21, d. 3, l. 220.

86. Orlova, *Memoirs*, 109.

Epilogue

1. For a similar metaphor in the later context of "public information" programs in wartime and postwar United States, see Daniel L. Lykins, *From Total War to Total Diplomacy: The Advertising Council and the Construction of the Cold War Consensus* (Westport, Conn.: Greenwood Publishers, 2003).

2. For just one example, see Ronald Grigor Suny, *The Soviet Experiment: Russia, The USSR, and the Successor States* (New York: Oxford University Press, 1997). A major new documentary history of Soviet culture contains no international headings among its 24 chapters and only a handful of documents with any sort of international dimension in its more than 500 pages: Katerina Clark and Evgeny Dobrenko, eds., *Soviet Culture and Power: A History in Documents, 1917–1953*, compiled by Andrei Artizov and Oleg Naumov, trans. Marian Schwartz (New Haven: Yale University Press, 2007).

3. An important exception is Jon Jacobson, *When the Soviet Union Entered World Politics* (Berkeley: University of California, 1994).

4. Katerina Clark, "Socialist Realism and the Sacralizing of Space," in *The Landscape of Stalinism: The Art and Ideology of Soviet Space*, ed. Clark and Evgeny Dobrenko (Seattle: University of Washington Press, 2003), 3–18, here 6.

5. György Péteri, "Nylon Curtain: Transnational and Transsystemic Tendencies in the Cultural Life of State-Socialist Russia and East-Central Europe," *Slavonica* 10, 2 (2004): 113–123, esp. 117–120.

6. Jan Gross, *Revolution from Abroad: the Soviet Conquest of Poland's Western Ukraine and Western Belorussia* (Princeton: Princeton University Press, 1988), 45–50, quotation 46.

7. Oleg Budnitskii, "The Intelligentsia Meets the Enemy: Educated Soviet Officers in Defeated Germany, 1945," *Kritika* 10, 3 (Summer 2009): 629–682, quotations 679–670.

8. On the Sovinformburo, see Shimon Redlich's introduction to *War, Holocaust and Stalinism: A Documented Study of the Jewish Anti-Fascist Committee in the USSR*, ed. Redlich, comp. Ilia Altman, et al. (Luxembourg: Harwood Academic, 1995); see also Katerina Clark, "Ehrenburg and Grossman: Two Cosmopolitan Jewish Writers Reflect on Nazi Germany at War," *Kritika* 10, 3 (Summer 2009): 607–628.

9. "Outline of Jewish Anti-Fascist Committee Goals February 5, 1942," in Redlich, ed., 196–197; see also 75; Jeffrey Veidlinger, *The Moscow State Yiddish Theater: Jewish Culture on the Soviet Stage* (Bloomington: Indiana University Press, 2000), chap. 7. On the tangled publication history of the Black Book, see Harvey Asher, "The Soviet Union, the Holocaust, and Auschwitz," *Kritika* 4, 4 (Fall 2003): 886–912.

10. Yoram Gorlizki and Oleg Khlevniuk, *Cold Peace: Stalin and the Soviet Ruling Circle, 1945–1953* (Oxford: Oxford University Press, 2004), 18; A. V. Golubev, et al., *Rossiia i Zapad: Formirovanie vneshnepoliticheskikh stereotipov v soznanii rossiiskogo obshchestva pervoi poloviny XX veka* (Moscow: Institut Istorii RAN, 1998), 136–144.

11. Stephen Lovell, "From Isolationism to Globalization," chap. 9 of *The Shadow of War: The Soviet Union and Russia, 1941 to the Present* (Oxford: Wiley-Blackwell, 2010). For a view of Andrei Zhdanov as Stalin's "factotum" in pursuing an "ideological war with the West" and the anti-intelligentsia campaigns in 1946–47, see Gorlizki and Khlevniuk, 32–43.

12. "The Roberts Cables," in *Origins of the Cold War: The Novikov, Kennan, and Roberts "Long Telegrams" of 1946*, ed. Kenneth M. Jenson, rev. ed. (Washington, D.C.: United States Institute of Peace Press, 1993), 59–60.

13. Rósa Magnúsdóttir, "Keeping up Appearances: How the Soviets Failed to Control Popular Attitudes toward the United States of America" (Ph.D. diss., University of North Carolina at Chapel Hill, 2006), 134, 254 and passim.

14. Vladislav Zubok, *Zhivago's Children: The Last Russian Intelligentsia* (Cambridge: Harvard University Press, 2009), chap. 3; Magnúsdóttir, chaps. 5–6.

15. Eleanory Gilburd, "Picasso in Thaw Culture," *Cahiers du monde russe* 47, 1–2 (2006): 65–108; Pia Koivunen, "The 1957 Moscow Youth Festival: Propagating a New, Peaceful Image of the Soviet Union," in *Soviet State and Society under Nikita Khrushchev*, ed. Melanie Ilič and Jeremy Smith (London: Routledge, 2009), 45–65; Susan E. Reid, "Who Will Beat Whom? Soviet Popular Reception of the American Exhibition in Moscow, 1959," *Kritika:* 9, 4 (Fall 2008): 855–904. On 23 July 2009, on the fiftieth anniversary of the Sokol'niki exhibition, I attended the commemorative conference at George Washington University, "Face-off to Facebook: From the Nixon-Khrushchev Kitchen Debate to Public Diplomacy in the 21st Century," whose participants included dozens of former exhibit guides and staff.

16. Lovell, chap. 9; Yale Richmond, *Cultural Exchange and the Cold War: Raising the Iron Curtain* (University Park, Pa.: Pennsylvania State University Press, 2003).

17. For this point I draw on Miriam Dobson, *Khrushchev's Cold Summer: Gulag Returnees, Crime, and the Fate of Reform after Stalin* (Ithaca: Cornell University Press, 2009); and Anne E. Gorsuch, "From Iron Curtain to Silver Screen: Imagining the West in the Khrushchev Era," *Imagining the West in Eastern Europe and the Soviet Union*, ed. György Péteri (Pittsburgh: Pittsburgh University Press, 2010): 153–171.

18. György Péteri, "The Oblique Coordinate Systems of Modern Identity," in *Imagining the West*, 1–12, quotation 11.

19. On reformist elites, see Robert D. English, *Russia and the Idea of the West: Gorbachev, Intellectuals and the End of the Cold War* (New York: Columbia University Press, 2000); on the birth of a new civic consciousness, see Zubok, *Zhivago's Children*.

20. James Scott, "Authoritarian High Modernism," chap. 3 of *Seeing Like a State: How Certain Schemes to Improve the Human Condition Have Failed* (New Haven: Yale University Press, 1998).

21. The unprecedented etatism of the Soviet new regime made this anticipation possible, just as in Stephen Kotkin's argument the absence of private property allowed the rapid adoption of Fordist mass production on an unprecedented scale (Kotkin, "Modern Times: The Soviet Union and the Interwar Conjuncture," *Kritika* 2, 1 [Winter 2001]: 111–164). On how the import was adapted and modified to become something distinctively new, see Yves Cohen, "Circulatory Localities: The Example of Stalinism in the 1930s," *Kritika* 11, 1 (Winter 2010): 11–45.

22. David Caute, *The Dancer Defects: The Struggle for Cultural Supremacy during the Cold War* (Oxford: Oxford University Press, 2003), quotation 3.

23. Reinhold Wagnleitner, *Coca-Colonization and the Cold War: The Cultural Mission of the United States in Austria after the Second World War*, trans. Diana M. Wolf (Chapel Hill: University of North Carolina Press, 1994), 46–53.

24. Wagnleitner, 55; Zubok, *Zhivago's Children*, 114; Magnúsdóttir, 105. For other postwar U.S. reactions to Soviet cultural diplomacy, see Frank A. Ninkovich, *The Diplomacy of Ideas: U.S. Foreign Policy and Cultural Relations, 1938–1950* (Cambridge: Cambridge University Press, 1981), 108, 143. More broadly on the strategies and limitations of the U.S. effort in the Cultural Cold War, see Laura A. Belmonte, *Selling the American Way: U.S. Propaganda and the Cold War* (Philadelphia: University of Pennsylvania Press, 2008).

25. Mary Nolan, "Europe and America in the Twentieth Century" (Cambridge: Cambridge University Press, forthcoming), chap. on cultural diplomacy.

26. David Engerman, "The Second World's Third World," *Kritika* 12, 1 (2011): 183–211; Stephen G. Marks, *How Russia Changed the Modern World* (Princeton: Princeton University Press, 2004): chaps. 8–9.

27. Jan C. Behrends, *Die erfundene Freundschaft: Propaganda für die Sowjetunion in Polen und in der DDR* (Cologne: Böhlau, 2006): 160–161, 241–254; Norman M. Naimark, *The Russians in Germany: A History of the Soviet Zone of Occupation, 1945–1949* (Cambridge, Mass.: Harvard University Press, 1995), 411–418.

28. Vladimir Pechatnov, "Exercise in Frustration: Soviet Foreign Propaganda in the Early Cold War, 1945–47," *Cold War History* 11, 2 (January 2001): 1–27.

29. Pechatnov, 7; Magnúsdóttir, 127 n. 63; on shifts brought about by anti-cosmopolitanism see Ethan Pollock, *Stalin and the Soviet Science Wars* (Princeton: Princeton University Press, 2006).

30. Nigel Gould-Davies, "The Logic of Soviet Cultural Diplomacy," *Diplomatic History* 27, 2 (April 2003): 193–214.

31. The phrase comes from Marshall T. Poe, *The Russian Moment in World History* (Princeton: Princeton University Press, 2003).

BIBLIOGRAPHY OF ARCHIVAL
COLLECTIONS

I. Gosudarstvennyi arkhiv Rossiiskoi Federatsii (GARF). State Archive of the Russian Federation

f. 3385. Komissiia zagranichnoi pomoshchi pri Prezidiume TsIK [Commission on Foreign Aid of the Presidium of the Central Executive Committee].

f. 5283. Vsesoiuznoe obshchesvto kul'turnykh sviazi s zagranitsei [All-Union Society for Cultural Ties Abroad, or VOKS].

f. 5451. Vsesoiuznyi tsentral'nyi sovet professional'nykh soiuzov (VTsSPS) Komissiia po vneshnym snosheniiam [All-Union Central Council of Trade Unions Commission on External Relations]

f. 7668. Uchenyi komitet pri TsIK SSSR [Scholarly Committee of the Central Executive Committee of the USSR]

f. 9612. Vsesoiuznoe aktsionernoe obshchestvo po inostrannomu turizmu v SSSR (VAO "Inturist") [All-Union Joint-Stock Society on Foreign Tourism in the USSR, or Intourist]

II. Rossiiskii gosudarstvennyi arkhiv sotsial'no-politicheskoi istorii (RGASPI). Russian State Archive of Socio-Political History

f. 17. Fondy dokumentov KPSS [Collections of Documents of the Communist Party of the Soviet Union]. Includes Politburo, Orgburo, Department of Agitation and Propaganda, Commission on Foreign Travel

f. 82. Lichnyi fond V. M. Molotova [Personal collection of V. M. Molotov]

f. 124. Obshchestvo starykh bol'shevikov [Society of Old Bolsheviks]

f. 142. Lichnyi fond A. V. Lunacharskogo [Personal collection of A. V. Lunacharskii]

f. 495. Otdel agitatsii i propagandy IKKI [Department of Agitation and Propaganda of the Executive Committee of the Communist International, or the Comintern's Agitprop].

f. 558. Lichnyi fond I.V. Stalina [Personal Collection of I.V. Stalin]

III. Rossiiskii gosudarstvennyi arkhiv literatury i iskusstva (RGALI). Russian State Archive of Literature and Art

f. 631. Inostrannaia komissiia Soiuza sovetskikh pisatelei [Foreign Commission of the Union of Soviet Writers]

IV. Arkhiv vneshnei politiki Rossiiskoi Federatsii (AVP RF). Archive of the Foreign Policy of the Russian Federation

f. 04 Fond G. V. Chicherina [Collection of G. V. Chicherin]

f. 010. Sekretariat N. N. Krestinskogo [Secretariat of N. N. Krestinskii]

f. 066. 2-i Zapadnyi otdel NKID [Second Western Department of the Commissariat of Foreign Affairs]

f. 082. 2-i Zapadnyi otdel NKID [Second Western Department of the Commissariat of Foreign Affairs]

f. 0528. Arkhiv L. B. Krasina [Archive of L. B. Krasin]

f. 69. Referentura po Anglii NKID [Analysis Unit for England of the Commissariat of Foreign Affairs]

f. 129 Referentura po SShA NKID [Analysis Unit for the USA of the Commissariat of Foreign Affairs]

INDEX

Note: Page numbers in *italics* indicate photographs.